THE
ENGLISH PARNASSUS

AN ANTHOLOGY CHIEFLY OF LONGER POEMS

WITH INTRODUCTION AND NOTES

BY

W. MACNEILE DIXON

PROFESSOR OF ENGLISH LITERATURE IN THE UNIVERSITY
OF GLASGOW

AND

H. J. C. GRIERSON

PROFESSOR OF RHETORIC AND ENGLISH LITERATURE IN THE
UNIVERSITY OF EDINBURGH

OXFORD
AT THE CLARENDON PRESS

OXFORD UNIVERSITY PRESS
AMEN HOUSE, E.C. 4
LONDON EDINBURGH GLASGOW
LEIPZIG NEW YORK TORONTO
MELBOURNE CAPETOWN BOMBAY
CALCUTTA MADRAS SHANGHAI
HUMPHREY MILFORD
PUBLISHER TO THE
UNIVERSITY

First published 1909
Reprinted 1911, 1913, 1916,
1917, 1919, 1921, 1922, 1925,
1928, 1933

PRINTED IN GREAT BRITAIN

PREFACE

THE intention of the editors, which was to avoid selections, and to include in this Anthology only complete poems, exactly as they were given to the world by their authors, will appear in three instances to be violated. The first sestiad of *Hero and Leander* is here printed but not the second, the third and fourth cantos of *Childe Harold* without those that preceded them, and several passages from Wordsworth which are to be found in the *Prelude*. In Marlowe's case, since the author himself left his poem uncompleted, the editors have ventured to omit that portion which is perhaps not so well suited to modern taste ; the third and fourth cantos of *Childe Harold* are included since they compose a poem wholly distinct from the first and second, written after an interval of years, and in a high degree characteristic of Byron in the maturity of his genius. The passages from Wordsworth were printed by the poet himself as separate poems before they were incorporated into his longer philosophical work.

Though a glossary has been provided for the use of the general reader no explanatory notes have been added to the texts. It was not the intention of the editors to supersede the work of the teacher, nor to supply such easily obtained information as is generally to be found in the annotated editions of single poems. Their purpose in this volume was rather to afford both teachers and students the opportunity for the comparative study of poetry belonging to different periods and different types. The condensed, somewhat informal, historical and critical notes are naturally far from exhaustive. They suggest merely some problems of literary interest, raise in the case of each author a few points for consideration or discussion, and attempt briefly to indicate the position of a poet or poem in the historical development of English literature. The texts are printed from the most authoritative versions available, and with as little alteration of spelling and punctuation as was possible. For the text of Chaucer the editors are indebted, and desire to express their gratitude, to Professor Skeat. In printing Burns, the poet's own spelling and italics, with which considerable liberties have often been taken, are restored. Burns's spelling, when phonetic, is a clue to his pronunciation, and his italics were frequently intended to indicate emphasis.

In the case of Tennyson, Browning, Arnold, and Fitzgerald, considerations of copyright have excluded the use of some later emendations. The editors especially regret that they are unable to print the fuller and more finished version of *Omar Khayyám*. But the present text is that of the poem which so delighted and stimulated Rossetti and Swinburne, and first became famous.

The editors desire to acknowledge with warm thanks the encouragement and assistance they have received from their friends, Professors Bradley, Dowden, Raleigh, Saintsbury, and Mr. J. C. Smith. Mr. R. S. Wallace, M.A., lecturer in English Language at the University of Aberdeen, and Miss Augusta Rudmose-Brown, M.A., University Assistant, Aberdeen, have rendered valuable assistance in the preparation of the glossary, which owes much to the labours of editors of Chaucer from Tyrwhitt to Morris and Skeat, Mr. A. W. Pollard and Miss Bentinck-Smith. The editors are also indebted to the Clarendon Press for unfailing courtesy and help while the book was passing through the press.

1909.

*** In response to many requests the editors have, in this issue, enlarged the index of proper names and allusions. While necessarily studying compression they have endeavoured to supply all that is essential to the right understanding of the text ; and, at the same time, to supply such references, especially to the poet's own sources, classical and other, as will interest a reader who cares to turn to them. Such a curious reader, if not already a classical student, will quickly realize how much a knowledge of classical mythology and literature enriches his appreciation of the best English poetry, how subtly the very words and cadences of Latin and Greek poetry are echoed in the lines of Spenser and Milton, Gray and Tennyson. The classics of Greece and Rome, the literature of the Old and New Testament, the romantic tradition of the Middle Ages constitute the variegated background of English poetry, the body of story and thought and literature to which an English poet might allude with the confidence that his readers would understand, and not only under-

stand but gather from the allusion a shade of emotion,
a subtle flavour that nothing else could communicate :

Not that fair field
Of Enna, where Proserpin gathering flowers,
Herself a fairer flower, by gloomy Dis
Was gather'd, which cost Ceres all that pain
To seek her through the world.

So Lycidas sunk low, but mounted high,
Through the dear might of Him that walk'd the waves ;
Where, other groves and other streams along,
With nectar pure his oozy locks he laves,
And hears the unexpressive nuptial song,
In the blest kingdoms meek of joy and love.

When Charlemain with all his peerage fell
By Fontarabia.

No reader who is ignorant of classical, biblical, romantic
literature can quite savour such lines. No notes will supply
the want of an early familiarity with the Bible and the
classics, but references to the original sources may lead
a good student farther.

For assistance in this enlargement, and for some additions
to and corrections in the Glossary, we are indebted to
Mr. Bruce Dickins, Lecturer on the English Language in
the University of Edinburgh.

INTRODUCTION

THE Editors of this collection have endeavoured within the compass of a single volume to bring together those English poems, neither epical in scope nor yet wholly lyrical in quality, which have attained a high measure of critical approbation. There will be found here poems of very varied type—narrative, didactic, satirical, elegiac, eulogistic, and reflective verses. Some odes have also been included, which though properly classed as lyrical are separated by their elaborate structure from song or ballad.

The choice of the editors has been guided by principles more easily indicated in a general fashion than precisely defined. Their aim was to select, in the first instance, all those poems which had as it were been chosen for them—had received, that is, the approval of successive generations of readers, and so in some sense and measure become classic. It was not their aim to begin with the poets usually reckoned the greatest in our literature and to give examples of their work, but rather to begin with the poems, by whomsoever written ; a method which may lead to unexpected results, the exclusion, for example, of so great a poet as Scott from the present collection.

The book was thus planned to contain in the first instance those longer English pieces which were familiar to many readers never numbered among professional students, and probably not acquainted with the less popular works by the same authors. The question soon emerged, What is the cause of this comparative popularity and what is its worth as a critical test ? Understanding by the word ' popular ' simply favour or preference among readers of poetry, one naturally asks, How far is such favour or preference to be taken as conferring classic rank upon a poem, and without it is that rank attainable ? Consider

Gray's *Elegy*, for example. Is it, as some eminent critics have declared, a second-rate performance, a much over-rated poem, or is it indeed a classic, a composition the authorship of which is an exploit more enviable, as Wolfe thought it, than to capture the heights of Abraham and win a province for the empire ? Or consider Donne's *Second Anniversary* or Shelley's *Alastor* and *Epipsychidion*. Are these classic in the same sense as the more famous *Elegy* ? They are certainly not as popular. The wide divergence, indeed, between the general and the critical estimate has provoked at times the angry protest of the specialist. 'That Chance is the ruler of the world,' said Swinburne, 'I should be sorry to believe and reluctant to affirm ; but it would be difficult for any competent and careful student to maintain that Chance is not the ruler of the world of letters. Gray's *Odes* are still, I suppose, familiar to thousands who know nothing of Donne's *Anniversaries*, and Bacon's *Essays* are conventionally, if not actually, familiar to thousands who know nothing of Ben Jonson's *Discoveries*. And yet it is certain that in fervour of inspiration, in depth and force and glow of thought and emotion and expression, Donne's verses are as far above Gray's as Jonson's notes or observations on men and morals, on principles and on facts, are superior to Bacon's in truth of insight, in breadth of view, in vigour of reflection and in concision of eloquence.' This is the verdict of the enthusiast and poet, stated with entire conviction and eloquence. But the philosopher, always loath to accept the intervention of chance in any sphere, disposed to regard the cutting of the knot by the sword of chance as a mere method of despair, will prefer to dispute the particular instances upon which the induction is based than to accept the conclusion. 'You have indicated,' he might urge, 'with unerring precision the great qualities of Donne's poems in which Gray's are relatively wanting, but you have omitted the other side of the account. You have said nothing of the ' gross and revolting hyperboles', the fantastic strain of argument, the frigid and far-fetched conceits which for some readers so obscure the splendours of Donne's poetry, that they turn with relief to the rhetorical felicities and finish, the liquid trillings and studied sonorities, the romantic colouring of Gray's Odes.' He may cite against Swinburne's, the dictum upon Donne and his school of a critic, Dr. Johnson, not less eminent : ' Nature and Art are ransacked for illustrations, comparisons and allusions ; their learning instructs and their subtlety surprises, but the reader commonly thinks his improvement dearly bought, and though he sometimes admires is seldom pleased.' Pondering with some interest and curiosity such divergences of opinion, the philosopher may seek a middle way. He may ask, Is it not probable that Donne's *Anniversary* and Shelley's *Alastor* and Gray's *Odes* and even the *Elegy* are all classical, are all in a high, though doubtless a varying degree, excellent as poems ? He may ask, Is it not probable that enduring popularity in a poem argues some kind of poetical merit, above and beyond mere interest of theme or sentiment, and yet that theme and sentiment will necessarily and naturally count for much with the simply human, uncritical, and unsophisticated reader ? He may even venture to follow Dr. Johnson when he says of Gray : ' In the character of his *Elegy* I rejoice to concur with the common reader, for by the common sense of readers uncorrupted with literary prejudice, after all the refinements of subtlety and the dogmatism of learning, must be finally decided all claim to poetical honours. The *Churchyard* abounds with images which find a mirror in every mind, and with sentiments to which every bosom returns an echo.' Yet while admitting that the qualities which give a poem the power to find an echo in every bosom are certainly great qualities, *Haud facile communia dicere*, he will remind himself that in poetry, as in science and philosophy, common sense is a useful though neither a far-reaching nor an unerring guide. Even within her own sphere her judgements must be endorsed by the critic, by subtlety and learning, for subtlety is not necessarily sophistry, nor learning pedantry. Left to itself 'the common sense of readers uncorrupted with literary prejudice' might assign to *The May Queen* or *The Psalm of Life* equal rank with the *Elegy*. Nor is it well to forget that there are spheres where common sense ceases to be a guide. Poetry has its Newtons,

Voyaging through strange seas of thought alone

but returning from these far journeys to enrich the sum of human experience.

My song, I fear that thou wilt find but few
Who fitly shall conceive thy reasoning—

The *Vita Nuova*, nay, even the *Divina Commedia*, could never be popular in the same way as the *Elegy in a Country Churchyard*. Their position among the world's classics is none the less high and secure. It seems indisputable that there are classic poems which can never in any true sense be popular, by reason it may be of the very purity of their poetic interest, because they are 'poet's poetry', or by reason of the remoteness of their themes from the sphere of ordinary human occupations, or because blended with their undeniable beauties are equally undeniable faults of form or feeling due to individual idiosyncrasy or the passing fashions of a day. Yet the worth even of poems in the last of these classes may be, for some readers at least, profound and perennial.

In the attempt, therefore, to place in the hands of the student or general reader a book of superlative poems, the editor must follow a perilous and precipitous path where danger lies both to left and right. If he inclines to the belief that *Securus iudicat orbis terrarum*, he will be quickly reminded that in literary, as in ecclesiastical history, truth has often been on the side of *Athanasius contra mundum* : if, on the other hand, he leans towards the acceptance of authority, he will find the Fathers at variance, the Church without a head, the kingdom of letters divided against itself. Yet he need not accept despair as his portion. For reflection reveals the fact that it is not in the region of literature alone that counsels are divided, that here indeed there is greater unanimity than in most fields of intellectual activity. It reveals the fact that moral philosophy has not yet provided us with an undisputed definition of ' the good ', nor aesthetic of ' the beautiful ', that in science there are fundamental problems still unsolved. The advance of science has witnessed a continuous warfare between common sense and the individual thinker, for the former has never found it easy to discriminate immediately between truth and paradox, a Copernicus and a Paracelsus. To ask more from criticism than from philosophy or from science, to ask it for some magic touchstone whereby the best may infallibly and at all times be known, is to overlook the true nature of the problem presented, the character of our own selves and the constitution of the world itself. The best for one is not the best for all of us ; the best to-day and for the child, is not the best to-morrow and for the man. My needs are my criterion, not yours nor yet another's. And if we narrow the issue, as narrow it we must, it cannot be to apply even to a given body of poetry a recognized canon, for no recognized canon exists or can ever exist. We are here employed, as every critic, as every reader of poetry is continually employed, not in the application of ascertained principles, but rather with the judgements which go to their making, with estimates, placed one by one, as builders place stone after stone, in a building which no generation can call its own. Errors in judgement, too, may have their use, and a good anthology might prove bad by its very excellence. For, containing nothing that any one dislikes, it might well produce a taste unfriendly to new or varied types of excellence, and

One good custom should corrupt the world.

A taste formed on the best art of the British Academy

failed to appreciate either the pure and passionate sincerity of the Pre-Raphaelites or the brilliant impressionism of Whistler. The correct and refined taste of the editor of the *Golden Treasury* refused admittance to a single lyric by Donne or Rochester, while making room for more than one by Campbell and Moore. It might indeed be argued that a good anthology must contain some poems which certain readers will frankly dislike, while omitting others which seem to them worth all the rest. The badness of an anthology will be in proportion to the number of poems it contains about which lovers of poetry feel indifferent. Poetry is an ecstasy; the success of a poem is tested by the degree to which it transports us out of the world of our waking experience into another of the poet's own creation. Success here will depend in the first place on ourselves, and again not so much on the character of that world, as on the degree to which the poet himself has realized it, and can communicate his own mood by the magic and music of his style. The *Dolores* may transport us as completely as the *Ode to Duty*. But it will depend on the largeness of the world revealed, the completeness with which it satisfies the craving for beauty which is also truth whether we are willing to remain there or to return thither again and again for high companionship and spiritual refreshment.

CONTENTS

xvi CONTENTS

GEOFFREY CHAUCER

THE CANTERBURY TALES

THE PROLOGUE

WHAN that Aprille with his shoures sote
The droghte of Marche hath perced to the rote,
And bathed every veyne in swich licour,
Of which vertu engendred is the flour ;
Whan Zephirus eek with his swete breeth
Inspired hath in every holt and heeth
The tendre croppes, and the yonge sonne
Hath in the Ram his halfe cours y-ronne,
And smale fowles maken melodye,
That slepen al the night with open yë,   10
(So priketh hem nature in hir corages) :
Than longen folk to goon on pilgrimages
(And palmers for to seken straunge strondes)
To ferne halwes, couthe in sondry londes ;
And specially, from every shires ende
Of Engelond, to Caunterbury they wende,
The holy blisful martir for to seke,
That hem hath holpen, whan that they were seke.
    Bifel that, in that seson on a day,
In Southwerk at the Tabard as I lay   20
Redy to wenden on my pilgrimage
To Caunterbury with ful devout corage,
At night was come in-to that hostelrye
Wel nyne and twenty in a companye,
Of sondry folk, by aventure y-falle
In felawshipe, and pilgrims were they alle,
That toward Caunterbury wolden ryde ;
The chambres and the stables weren wyde,
And wel we weren esed atte beste.
And shortly, whan the sonne was to reste,   30
So hadde I spoken with hem everichon,
That I was of hir felawshipe anon,
And made forward erly for to ryse,
To take our wey, ther as I yow devyse.
    But natheles, whyl I have tyme and space,
Er that I ferther in this tale pace,
Me thinketh it acordaunt to resoun,
To telle yow al the condicioun

Of ech of hem, so as it semed me,
And whiche they weren, and of what degree;   40
And eek in what array that they were inne:
And at a knight than wol I first biginne.
   A KNIGHT ther was, and that a worthy man,   KNIGHT.
That fro the tyme that he first bigan
To ryden out, he loved chivalrye,
Trouthe and honour, fredom and curteisye.
Ful worthy was he in his lordes werre,
And therto hadde he riden (no man ferre)
As wel in Cristendom as hethenesse,
And ever honoured for his worthinesse.   50
At Alisaundre he was, whan it was wonne;
Ful ofte tyme he hadde the bord bigonne
Aboven alle naciouns in Pruce.
In Lettow hadde he reysed and in Ruce,
No Cristen man so ofte of his degree.
In Gernade at the sege eek hadde he be
Of Algezir, and riden in Belmarye.
At Lyeys was he, and at Satalye,
Whan they were wonne; and in the Grete See
At many a noble aryve hadde he be.   60
At mortal batailles hadde he been fiftene,
And foughten for our feith at Tramissene
In listes thryes, and ay slayn his foo.
This ilke worthy knight had been also
Somtyme with the lord of Palatye,
Ageyn another hethen in Turkye:
And evermore he hadde a sovereyn prys.
And though that he were worthy, he was wys,
And of his port as meke as is a mayde.
He never yet no vileinye ne sayde   70
In al his lyf, un-to no maner wight.
He was a verray parfit gentil knight.
But for to tellen yow of his array,
His hors were gode, but he was nat gay.
Of fustian he wered a gipoun
Al bismotered with his habergeoun;
For he was late y-come from his viage,
And wente for to doon his pilgrimage.
   With him ther was his sone, a yong SQUYER,   SQUYER.
A lovyere, and a lusty bacheler,   80
With lokkes crulle, as they were leyd in presse.
Of twenty yeer of age he was, I gesse.
Of his stature he was of evene lengthe,
And wonderly deliver, and greet of strengthe.
And he had been somtyme in chivachye,
In Flaundres, in Artoys, and Picardye,
And born him wel, as of so litel space,
In hope to stonden in his lady grace.

Embrouded was he, as it were a mede
Al ful of fresshe floures, whyte and rede.   90
Singinge he was, or floytinge, al the day ;
He was as fresh as is the month of May.
Short was his goune, with sleves longe and wyde.
Wel coude he sitte on hors, and faire ryde.
He coude songes make and wel endyte,
Juste and eek daunce, and wel purtreye and wryte.
So hote he lovede, that by nightertale
He sleep namore than dooth a nightingale.
Curteys he was, lowly, and servisable,
And carf biforn his fader at the table.   100

    A YEMAN hadde he, and servaunts namo   YEMAN.
At that tyme, for him liste ryde so ;
And he was clad in cote and hood of grene ;
A sheef of pecok-arwes brighte and kene
Under his belt he bar ful thriftily ;
(Wel coude he dresse his takel yemanly :
His arwes drouped noght with fetheres lowe),
And in his hand he bar a mighty bowe.
A not-heed hadde he, with a broun visage.
Of wode-craft wel coude he al the usage.   110
Upon his arm he bar a gay bracer,
And by his syde a swerd and a bokeler,
And on that other syde a gay daggere,
Harneised wel, and sharp as point of spere ;
A Cristofre on his brest of silver shene.
An horn he bar, the bawdrik was of grene ;
A forster was he, soothly, as I gesse.

   There was also a Nonne, a PRIORESSE,   PRIORESSE.
That of hir smyling was ful simple and coy ;
Hir gretteste ooth was but by sëynt Loy ;   120
And she was cleped madame Eglentyne.
Ful wel she song the service divyne,
Entuned in hir nose ful semely ;
And Frensh she spak ful faire and fetisly,
After the scole of Stratford atte Bowe,
For Frensh of Paris was to hir unknowe.
At mete wel y-taught was she with-alle ;
She leet no morsel from hir lippes falle,
Ne wette hir fingres in hir sauce depe.
Wel coude she carie a morsel, and wel kepe,   130
That no drope ne fille up-on hir brest.
In curteisye was set ful muche hir lest.
Hir over lippe wyped she so clene,
That in hir coppe was no ferthing sene
Of grece, whan she dronken hadde hir draughte.
Ful semely after hir mete she raughte,
And sikerly she was of greet disport,
And ful plesaunt, and amiable of port,

And peyned hir to countrefete chere
Of court, and been estatlich of manere,   140
And to ben holden digne of reverence.
But, for to speken of hir conscience,
She was so charitable and so pitous,
She wolde wepe, if that she sawe a mous
Caught in a trappe, if it were deed or bledde.
Of smale houndes had she, that she fedde
With rosted flesh, or milk and wastel-breed.
But sore weep she if oon of hem were deed,
Or if men smoot it with a yerde smerte :
And al was conscience and tendre herte.   150
Ful semely hir wimpel pinched was ;
Hir nose tretys ; hir eyen greye as glas ;
Hir mouth ful smal, and ther-to softe and reed ;
But sikerly she hadde a fair forheed ;
It was almost a spanne brood, I trowe ;
For, hardily, she was nat undergrowe.
Ful fetis was hir cloke, as I was war.
Of smal coral aboute hir arm she bar
A peire of bedes, gauded al with grene ;
And ther-on heng a broche of gold ful shene,   160
On which ther was first write a crowned A,
And after, *Amor vincit omnia.*
    Another NONNE with hir hadde she,   NONNE.
That was hir chapeleyne, and PREESTES three. 3 PREESTES.
    A MONK ther was, a fair for the maistrye,   MONK.
An out-rydere, that lovede venerye ;
A manly man, to been an abbot able.
Ful many a deyntee hors hadde he in stable :
And, whan he rood, men mighte his brydel here
Ginglen in a whistling wind as clere,   170
And eek as loude as dooth the chapel-belle,
Ther as this lord was keper of the celle.
The reule of seint Maure or of seint Beneit,
By-cause that it was old and some-del streit,
This ilke monk leet olde thinges pace,
And held after the newe world the space.
He yaf nat of that text a pulled hen,
That seith, that hunters been nat holy men ;
Ne that a monk, whan he is cloisterlees,
Is lykned til a fish that is waterlees ;   180
This is to seyn, a monk out of his cloistre.
But thilke text held he nat worth an oistre ;
And I seyde, his opinioun was good.
What sholde he studie, and make him-selven wood,
Upon a book in cloistre alwey to poure,
Or swinken with his handes, and laboure,
As Austin bit ? How shal the world be served ?
Lat Austin have his swink to him reserved.

Therfore he was a pricasour aright;
Grehoundes he hadde, as swifte as fowel in flight;   19C
Of priking and of hunting for the hare
Was al his lust, for no cost wolde he spare.
I seigh his sleves purfiled at the hond
With grys, and that the fyneste of a lond;
And, for to festne his hood under his chin,
He hadde of gold y-wroght a curious pin:
A love-knotte in the gretter ende ther was.
His heed was balled, that shoon as any glas,
And eek his face, as he had been anoint.
He was a lord ful fat and in good point;   200
His eyen stepe, and rollinge in his heed,
That stemed as a forneys of a leed;
His botes souple, his hors in greet estat.
Now certeinly he was a fair prelat;
He was nat pale as a for-pyned goost.
A fat swan loved he best of any roost.
His palfrey was as broun as is a berye.
  A FRERE ther was, a wantown and a merye,   FRERE.
A limitour, a ful solempne man. *a beggat important*
In alle the ordres foure is noon that can   210
So muche of daliaunce and fair langage.
He hadde maad ful many a mariage
Of yonge wommen, at his owne cost.
Un-to his ordre he was a noble post.
Ful wel biloved and famulier was he
With frankeleyns over-al in his contree,
And eek with worthy wommen of the toun:
For he had power of confessioun,
As seyde him-self, more than a curat,
For of his ordre he was licentiat.   220
Ful swetely herde he confessioun,
And plesaunt was his absolucioun;
He was an esy man to yeve penaunce
Ther as he wiste to han a good pitaunce;
For unto a povre ordre for to yive
Is signe that a man is wel y-shrive.
For if he yaf, he dorste make avaunt,
He wiste that a man was repentaunt.
For many a man so hard is of his herte,
He may nat wepe al-thogh him sore smerte.   230
Therfore, in stede of weping and preyeres,
Men moot yeve silver to the povre freres.
His tipet was ay farsed ful of knyves
And pinnes, for to yeven faire wyves.
And certeinly he hadde a mery note;
Wel coude he singe and pleyen on a rote.
Of yeddinges he bar utterly the prys.
His nekke whyt was as the flour-de-lys;

Ther-to he strong was as a champioun.
He knew the tavernes wel in every toun,   240
And everich hostiler and tappestere
Bet than a lazar or a beggestere ;
For un-to swich a worthy man as he
Acorded nat, as by his facultee,
To have with seke lazars aqueyntaunce.
It is nat honest, it may nat avaunce
For to delen with no swich poraille,
But al with riche and sellers of vitaille.
And over-al, ther as profit sholde aryse,
Curteys he was, and lowly of servyse.   250
Ther nas no man no-wher so vertuous.
He was the beste beggere in his hous ;
[And yaf a certeyn ferme for the graunt ;
Noon of his bretheren cam ther in his haunt ;]
For thogh a widwe hadde noght a sho,
So plesaunt was his ' In principio,'
Yet wolde he have a ferthing, er he wente.
His purchas was wel bettre than his rente.
And rage he coude, as it were right a whelpe.
In love-dayes ther coude he muchel helpe.   260
For there he was nat lyk a cloisterer,
With a thredbar cope, as is a povre scoler,
But he was lyk a maister or a pope.
Of double worsted was his semi-cope,
That rounded as a belle out of the presse.
Somwhat he lipsed, for his wantownesse,
To make his English swete up-on his tonge ;
And in his harping, whan that he had songe,
His eyen twinkled in his heed aright,
As doon the sterres in the frosty night.   276
This worthy limitour was cleped Huberd.

A MARCHANT was ther with a forked berd,   MARCHANT.
In mottelee, and hye on horse he sat,
Up-on his heed a Flaundrish bever hat ;
His botes clasped faire and fetisly.
His resons he spak ful solempnely,
Souninge alway thencrees of his winning.
He wolde the see were kept for any thing
Bitwixe Middelburgh and Orewelle.
Wel coude he in eschaunge sheeldes selle.   280
This worthy man ful wel his wit bisette ;
Ther wiste no wight that he was in dette,
So estatly was he of his governaunce,
With his bargaynes, and with his chevisaunce.
For sothe he was a worthy man with-alle,
But sooth to seyn, I noot how men him calle.

A CLERK ther was of Oxenford also,   CLERK.
That un-to logik hadde longe y-go.

As lene was his hors as is a rake,
And he nas nat right fat, I undertake ; 290
But loked holwe, and ther-to soberly.
Ful thredbar was his overest courtepy ;
For he had geten him yet no benefyce,
Ne was so worldly for to have offyce.
For him was lever have at his beddes heed
Twenty bokes, clad in blak or reed,
Of Aristotle and his philosophye,
Than robes riche, or fithele, or gay sautrye.
But al be that he was a philosophre,
Yet hadde he but litel gold in cofre ; 300
But al that he mighte of his freendes hente,
On bokes and on lerninge he it spent,
And bisily gan for the soules preye
Of hem that yaf him wher-with to scoleye.
Of studie took he most cure and most hede.
Noght o word spak he more than was nede,
And that was seyd in forme and reverence,
And short and quik, and ful of hy sentence.
Souninge in moral vertu was his speche,
And gladly wolde he lerne, and gladly teche. 310
   A SERGEANT OF THE LAWE, war and wys, MAN OF LAWE.
That often hadde been at the parvys,
Ther was also, ful riche of excellence.
Discreet he was, and of greet reverence :
He semed swich, his wordes weren so wyse.
Justyce he was ful often in assyse,
By patente, and by pleyn commissioun ;
For his science, and for his heigh renoun
Of fees and robes hadde he many oon.
So greet a purchasour was no-wher noon. 320
Al was fee simple to him in effect,
His purchasing mighte nat been infect.
No-wher so bisy a man as he ther nas,
And yet he semed bisier than he was.
In termes hadde he caas and domes alle,
That from the tyme of king William were falle.
Therto he coude endyte, and make a thing,
Ther coude no wight pinche at his wryting ;
And every statut coude he pleyn by rote.
He rood but hoomly in a medlee cote 330
Girt with a ceint of silk, with barres smale ;
Of his array telle I no lenger tale.
   A FRANKELEYN was in his companye ;   FRANKELEYN.
Whyt was his berd, as is the dayesye.
Of his complexioun he was sangwyn.
Wel loved he by the morwe a sop in wyn.
To liven in delyt was ever his wone,
For he was Epicurus owne sone,

That heeld opinioun, that pleyn delyt
Was verraily felicitee parfyt.   340
An housholdere, and that a greet, was he ;
Seint Julian he was in his contree.
His breed, his ale, was alwey after oon ;
A bettre envyned man was no-wher noon.
With-oute bake mete was never his hous,
Of fish and flesh, and that so plentevous,
It snewed in his hous of mete and drinke,
Of alle deyntees that men coude thinke.
After the sondry sesons of the yeer,
So chaunged he his mete and his soper.   350
Ful many a fat partrich hadde he in mewe,
And many a breem and many a luce in stewe.
Wo was his cook, but-if his sauce were
Poynaunt and sharp, and redy al his gere.
His table dormant in his halle alway
Stood redy covered al the longe day.
At sessiouns ther was he lord and sire ;
Ful ofte tyme he was knight of the shire.
An anlas and a gipser al of silk
Heng at his girdel, whyt as morne milk.   360
A shirreve hadde he been, and a countour ;
Was no-wher such a worthy vavasour.

    An HABERDASSHER and a CARPENTER,   HABER-
A WEBBE, a DYERE, and a TAPICER,—   DASSHER.
Were with us eek, clothed in o liveree,   CARPENTER.
Of a solempne and greet fraternitee.   WEBBE.
Ful fresh and newe hir gere apyked was ;   DYERE.
Hir knyves were y-chaped noght with bras,   TAPICER.
But al with silver, wroght ful clene and weel,
Hir girdles and hir pouches every-deel.   370
Wel semed ech of hem a fair burgeys,
To sitten in a yeldhalle on a deys.
Everich, for the wisdom that he can,
Was shaply for to been an alderman.
For catel hadde they y-nogh and rente,
And eek hir wyves wolde it wel assente ;
And elles certein were they to blame.
It is ful fair to been y-clept ' *ma dame*,'
And goon to vigilyës al bifore,
And have a mantel royalliche y-bore.   380

    A COOK they hadde with hem for the nones,   COOK.
To boille the chiknes with the mary-bones,
And poudre-marchant tart, and galingale.
Wel coude he knowe a draughte of London ale.
He coude roste, and sethe, and broille, and frye,
Maken mortreux, and wel bake a pye.
But greet harm was it, as it thoughte me,
That on his shine a mormal hadde he ;

For blankmanger, that made he with the beste.   389
   A SHIPMAN was ther, woning fer by weste :   SHIPMAN.
For aught I woot, he was of Dertemouthe. *Dartmouth*
He rood up-on a rouncy, as he couthe, *hackney*
In a gowne of falding to the knee. *coarse cloth*
A daggere hanging on a laas hadde he
Aboute his nekke under his arm adoun.
The hote somer had maad his hewe al broun ; *face*
And, certeinly, he was a good felawe.
Ful many a draughte of wyn had he y-drawe
From Burdeux-ward, whyl that the chapman sleep. *merchant*
Of nyce conscience took he no keep.   400
If that he faught, and hadde the hyer hond,
By water he sente hem hoom to every lond.
But of his craft to rekene wel his tydes,
His stremes and his daungers him bisydes,
His herberwe and his mone, his lodemenage, *compass*
Ther nas noon swich from Hulle to Cartage.
Hardy he was, and wys to undertake ;
With many a tempest hadde his berd been shake.
He knew wel alle the havenes, as they were,
From Gootlond to the cape of Finistere,   410
And every cryke in Britayne and in Spayne ;
His barge y-cleped was the Maudelayne.
   With us ther was a DOCTOUR OF PHISYK,   DOCTOUR.
In al this world ne was ther noon him lyk
To speke of phisik and of surgerye ;
For he was grounded in astronomye.
He kepte his pacient a ful greet del
In houres, by his magik naturel. *astronomical hours*
Wel coude he fortunen the ascendent
Of his images for his pacient.   420
He knew the cause of everich maladye,
Were it of hoot or cold, or moiste, or drye,
And where engendred, and of what humour ;
He was a verrey parfit practisour.
The cause y-knowe, and of his harm the rote,
Anon he yaf the seke man his bote.
Ful redy hadde he his apothecaries,
To sende him drogges and his letuaries,
For ech of hem made other for to winne ;
Hir frendschipe nas nat newe to biginne.   430
Wel knew he the olde Esculapius,
And Deiscorides, and eek Rufus,
Old Ypocras, Haly, and Galien ;
Serapion, Razis, and Avicen ;
Averrois, Damascien, and Constantyn ;
Bernard, and Gatesden, and Gilbertyn.
Of his diete mesurable was he,
For it was of no superfluitee,

But of greet norissing and digestible.
His studie was but litel on the Bible.   440
In sangwin and in pers he clad was al,
Lyned with taffata and with sendal;
And yet he was but esy of dispence;
He kepte that he wan in pestilence.
For gold in phisik is a cordial,
Therfore he lovede gold in special.

A good Wyf was ther of bisyde Bathe,   Wyf of Bathe.
But she was som-del deef, and that was scathe.
Of clooth-making she hadde swiche an haunt,
She passed hem of Ypres and óf Gaunt.   450
In al the parisshe wyf ne was ther noon
That to the offring bifore hir sholde goon;
And if ther dide, certeyn, so wrooth was she,
That she was out of alle charitee.
Hir coverchiefs ful fyne were of ground;
I dorste swere they weyeden ten pound
That on a Sonday were upon hir heed.
Hir hosen weren of fyn scarlet reed,
Ful streite y-teyd, and shoos ful moiste and newe.
Bold was hir face, and fair, and reed of hewe.   460
She was a worthy womman al hir lyve,
Housbondes at chirche-dore she hadde fyve,
Withouten other companye in youthe;
But therof nedeth nat to speke as nouthe.
And thryes hadde she been at Jerusalem;
She hadde passed many a straunge streem;
At Rome she hadde been, and at Boloigne,
In Galice at seint Jame, and at Cologne.
She coude muche of wandring by the weye.
Gat-tothed was she, soothly for to seye.   470
Up-on an amblere esily she sat,
Y-wimpled wel, and on hir heed an hat
As brood as is a bokeler or a targe;
A foot-mantel aboute hir hipes large,
And on hir feet a paire of spores sharpe.
In felawschip wel coude she laughe and carpe.
Of remedyes of love she knew per-chaunce,
For she coude of that art the olde daunce.

A good man was ther of religioun,   Persoun.
And was a povre Persoun of a toun;   480
But riche he was of holy thoght and werk.
He was also a lerned man, a clerk,
That Cristes gospel trewely wolde preche;
His parisshens devoutly wolde he teche.
Benigne he was, and wonder diligent,
And in adversitee ful pacient;
And swich he was y-preved ofte sythes.
Ful looth were him to cursen for his tythes,

But rather wolde he yeven, out of doute,
Un-to his povre parisshens aboute   490
Of his offring, and eek of his substaunce.
He coude in litel thing han suffisaunce.
Wyd was his parisshe, and houses fer a-sonder,
But he ne lafte nat, for reyn ne thonder,
In siknes nor in meschief, to visyte
The ferreste in his parisshe, muche and lyte,
Up-on his feet, and in his hand a staf.
This noble ensample to his sheep he yaf,
That first he wroghte, and afterward he taughte;
Out of the gospel he tho wordes caughte;   500
And this figure he added eek ther-to,
That if gold ruste, what shal iren do ?
For if a preest be foul, on whom we truste,
No wonder is a lewed man to ruste;
And shame it is, if a preest take keep,
A shiten shepherde and a clene sheep.
Wel oghte a preest ensample for to yive,
By his clennesse, how that his sheep shold live.
He sette nat his benefice to hyre,
And leet his sheep encombred in the myre,   510
And ran to London, un-to sëynt Poules,
To seken him a chaunterie for soules,
Or with a bretherhed to been withholde;
But dwelte at hoom, and kepte wel his folde,
So that the wolf ne made it nat miscarie;
He was a shepherde and no mercenarie.
And though he holy were, and vertuous,
He was to sinful man nat despitous,
Ne of his speche daungerous ne digne,
But in his teching discreet and benigne.   520
To drawen folk to heven by fairnesse
By good ensample, was his bisinesse:
But it were any persone obstinat,
What-so he were, of heigh or lowe estat,
Him wolde he snibben sharply for the nones.
A bettre preest, I trowe that nowher noon is.
He wayted after no pompe and reverence,
Ne maked him a spyced conscience,
But Cristes lore, and his apostles twelve,
He taughte, and first he folwed it him-selve.   530
   With him ther was a PLOWMAN, was his brother,
That hadde y-lad of dong ful many a fother, PLOWMAN.
A trewe swinker and a good was he,
Livinge in pees and parfit charitee.
God loved he best with al his hole herte
At alle tymes, thogh him gamed or smerte,
And thanne his neighebour right as him-selve.
He wolde thresshe, and ther-to dyke and delve,

For Cristes sake, for every povre wight,
Withouten hyre, if it lay in his might.   540
His tythes payed he ful faire and wel,
Bothe of his propre swink and his catel.
In a tabard he rood upon a mere.
   There was also a Reve and a Millere,
A Somnour and a Pardoner also,
A Maunciple, and my-self ; ther were namo. *for the time being*
   The MILLER was a stout carl, for the nones,   MILLER.
Ful big he was of braun, and eek of bones ;
That proved wel, for over-al ther he cam,
At wrastling he wolde have alwey the ram.   550
He was short-sholdred, brood, a thikke knarre,
Ther nas no dore that he nolde heve of harre,
Or breke it, at a renning, with his heed.
His berd as any sowe or fox was reed,
And ther-to brood, as though it were a spade.
Up-on the cop right of his nose he hade *of anything*
A werte, and ther-on stood a tuft of heres,
Reed as the bristles of a sowes eres ;
His nose-thirles blake were and wyde.
A swerd and bokeler bar he by his syde ;   560
His mouth as greet was as a greet forneys.
He was a janglere and a goliardeys,
And that was most of sinne and harlotryes.
Wel coude he stelen corn, and tollen thryes ;
And yet he hadde a thombe of gold, pardee.
A whyt cote and a blew hood wered he.
A baggepype wel coude he blowe and sowne,
And ther-with-al he broghte us out of towne.
   A gentil MAUNCIPLE was ther of a temple, MAUNCIPLE.
Of which achatours mighte take exemple   570
For to be wyse in bying of vitaille.
For whether that he payde, or took by taille, *credit*
Algate he wayted so in his achat, *business*
That he was ay biforn and in good stat.
Now is nat that of God a ful fair grace,
That swich a lewed mannes wit shal pace
The wisdom of an heep of lerned men ?
Of maistres hadde he mo than thryes ten,
That were of lawe expert and curious ;
Of which ther were a doseyn in that hous,   580
Worthy to been stiwardes of rente and lond
Of any lord that is in Engelond,
To make him live by his propre good,
In honour dettelees, but he were wood,
Or live as scarsly as him list desire ;
And able for to helpen al a shire
In any cas that mighte falle or happe ;
And yit this maunciple sette hir aller cappe. *not the late of them*

The REVE was a sclendre colerik man, *quick temper* REVE *factor*
His berd was shave as ny as ever he can.   590
His heer was by his eres round y-shorn.
His top was dokked lyk a preest biforn.
Ful longe were his legges, and ful lene,
Y-lyk a staf, ther was no calf y-sene.
Wel coude he kepe a gerner and a binne; *garner, bin-chest*
Ther was noon auditour coude on him winne.
Wel wiste he, by the droghte, and by the reyn,
The yelding of his seed, and of his greyn.
His lordes sheep, his neet, his dayerye, *cattle:*
His swyn, his hors, his stoor, and his pultrye, *stock* 600
Was hoolly in this reves governing,
And by his covenaunt yaf the rekening,
Sin that his lord was twenty yeer of age;
Ther coude no man bringe him in arrerage. *arrears*
Ther nas baillif, ne herde, ne other hyne,
That he ne knew his sleighte and his covyne; *deceit*
They were adrad of him, as of the deeth.
His woning was ful fair up-on an heeth,
With grene treës shadwed was his place.
He coude bettre than his lord purchace.   610
Ful riche he was astored prively,
His lord wel coude he plesen subtilly,
To yeve and lene him of his owne good,
And have a thank, and yet a cote and hood.
In youthe he lerned hadde a good mister; *trade*
He was a wel good wrighte, a carpenter.
This reve sat up-on a ful good stot, *horse*
That was al pomely grey, and highte Scot.
A long surcote of pers up-on he hade,
And by his syde he bar a rusty blade.   620
Of Northfolk was this reve, of which I telle,
Bisyde a toun men clepen Baldeswelle.
Tukked he was, as is a frere, aboute,
And ever he rood the hindreste of our route.
    A SOMNOUR was ther with us in that place, SOMNOUR. *summoner*
That hadde a fyr-reed cherubinnes face,
For sawcefleem he was, with eyen narwe.
As hoot he was, and lecherous, as a sparwe;
With scalled browes blake, and piled berd;
Of his visage children were aferd.   630
Ther nas quik-silver, litarge, ne brimstoon,
Boras, ceruce, ne oille of tartre noon,
Ne oynement that wolde clense and byte,
That him mighte helpen of his whelkes whyte,
Nor of the knobbes sittinge on his chekes.
Wel loved he garleek, oynons, and eek lekes,
And for to drinken strong wyn, reed as blood.
Thanne wolde he speke, and crye as he were wood.

And whan that he wel dronken hadde the wyn,
Than wolde he speke no word but Latyn.   640
A fewe termes hadde he, two or three,
That he had lerned out of som decree ;
No wonder is, he herde it al the day ;
And eek ye knowen wel, how that a jay
Can clepen ' Watte,' as well as can the pope.
But who-so coude in other thing him grope,
Thanne hadde he spent al his philosophye ;
Ay ' *Questio quid iuris* ' wolde he crye.
He was a gentil harlot and a kinde ;
A bettre felawe sholde men noght finde.   650
He wolde suffre, for a quart of wyn,
A good felawe to have his concubyn
A twelf-month, and excuse him atte fulle :
Ful prively a finch eek coude he pulle.
And if he fond o-wher a good felawe,
He wolde techen him to have non awe,
In swich cas, of the erchedeknes curs,
But-if a mannes soule were in his purs ;
For in his purs he sholde y-punisshed be.
' Purs is the erchedeknes helle,' seyde he.   660
But wel I woot he lyed right in dede ;
Of cursing oghte ech gilty man him drede—
For curs wol slee, right as assoilling saveth—
And also war him of a *significavit*.
In daunger hadde he at his owne gyse
The yonge girles of the diocyse,
And knew hir counseil, and was al hir reed.
A gerland hadde he set up-on his heed,
As greet as it were for an ale-stake ;
A bokeler hadde he maad him of a cake.   670
  With him ther rood a gentil PARDONER   PARDONER.
Of Rouncival, his freend and his compeer,
That streight was comen fro the court of Rome.
Ful loude he song, ' Com hider, love, to me.'
This somnour bar to him a stif burdoun,
Was never trompe of half so greet a soun.
This pardoner hadde heer as yelow as wex,
But smothe it heng, as dooth a strike of flex ;
By ounces henge his lokkes that he hadde,
And ther-with he his shuldres overspradde ;   680
But thinne it lay, by colpons oon and oon ;
But hood, for jolitee, ne wered he noon,
For it was trussed up in his walet.
Him thoughte, he rood al of the newe jet ;
Dischevele, save his cappe, he rood al bare.
Swiche glaringe eyen hadde he as an hare.
A vernicle hadde he sowed on his cappe.
His walet lay biforn him in his lappe,

Bret-ful of pardoun come from Rome al hoot.
A voys he hadde as smal as hath a goot.   690
No berd hadde he, ne never sholde have,
As smothe it was as it were late y-shave ;
I trowe he were a gelding or a mare.
But of his craft, fro Berwik into Ware,
Ne was ther swich another pardoner.
For in his male he hadde a pilwe-beer,
Which that, he seyde, was our lady veyl:
He seyde, he hadde a gobet of the seyl
That sëynt Peter hadde, whan that he wente
Up-on the see, til Jesu Crist him hente.   700
He hadde a croys of latoun, ful of stones,
And in a glas he hadde pigges bones.
But with thise relikes, whan that he fond
A povre person dwelling up-on lond,
Up-on a day he gat him more moneye
Than that the person gat in monthes tweye.
And thus, with feyned flaterye and japes,
He made the person and the peple his apes.
But trewely to tellen, atte laste,
He was in chirche a noble ecclesiaste.   710
Wel coude he rede a lessoun or a storie,
But alderbest he song an offertorie ;
For wel he wiste, whan that song was songe,
He moste preche, and wel affyle his tonge,
To winne silver, as he ful wel coude ;
Therefore he song so meriely and loude.
    Now have I told you shortly, in a clause,
Thestat, tharray, the nombre, and eek the cause
Why that assembled was this companye
In Southwerk, at this gentil hostelrye,   720
That highte the Tabard, faste by the Belle.
But now is tyme to yow for to telle
How that we baren us that ilke night,
Whan we were in that hostelrye alight.
And after wol I telle of our viage,
And al the remenaunt of our pilgrimage.
But first I pray yow, of your curteisye,
That ye narette it nat my vileinye,
Thogh that I pleynly speke in this matere,
To telle yow hir wordes and hir chere ;   730
Ne thogh I speke hir wordes properly.
For this ye knowen al-so wel as I,
Who-so shal telle a tale after a man,
He moot reherce, as ny as ever he can,
Everich a word, if it be in his charge,
Al speke he never so rudeliche and large ;
Or elles he moot telle his tale untrewe,
Or feyne thing, or finde wordes newe.

He may nat spare, al-thogh he were his brother;
He moot as wel seye o word as another. 740
Crist spak him-self ful brode in holy writ,
And wel ye woot, no vileinye is it.
Eek Plato seith, who-so that can him rede,
The wordes mote be cosin to the dede.
Also I prey yow to foryeve it me,
Al have I nat set folk in hir degree
Here in this tale, as that they sholde stonde;
My wit is short, ye may wel understonde.

Greet chere made our hoste us everichon,
And to the soper sette he us anon; 750
And served us with vitaille at the beste.
Strong was the wyn, and wel to drinke us leste.
A semely man our hoste was with-alle
For to han been a marshal in an halle;
A large man he was with eyen stepe,
A fairer burgeys is ther noon in Chepe:
Bold of his speche, and wys, and wel y-taught,
And of manhod him lakkede right naught.
Eek therto he was right a mery man,
And after soper pleyen he bigan, 760
And spak of mirthe amonges othere thinges,
Whan that we hadde maad our rekeninges;
And seyde thus: 'Now, lordinges, trewely,
Ye been to me right welcome hertely:
For by my trouthe, if that I shal nat lye,
I ne saugh this yeer so mery a companye
At ones in this herberwe as is now.
Fayn wolde I doon yow mirthe, wiste I how.
And of a mirthe I am right now bithoght,
To doon yow ese, and it shal coste noght. 770

Ye goon to Caunterbury; God yow spede,
The blisful martir quyte yow your mede.
And wel I woot, as ye goon by the weye,
Ye shapen yow to talen and to pleye;
For trewely, confort ne mirthe is noon
To ryde by the weye doumb as a stoon;
And therfore wol I maken yow disport,
As I seyde erst, and doon yow som confort.
And if yow lyketh alle, by oon assent,
Now for to stonden at my jugement, 780
And for to werken as I shal yow seye,
To-morwe, whan ye ryden by the weye,
Now, by my fader soule, that is deed,
But ye be merye, I wol yeve yow myn heed.
Hold up your hond, withouten more speche.'

Our counseil was nat longe for to seche;
Us thoughte it was noght worth to make it wys,
And graunted him withouten more avys,

And bad him seye his verdit, as him leste.
  'Lordinges,' quod he, ' now herkneth for the beste ; 790
But tak it not, I prey yow, in desdeyn ;
This is the poynt, to speken short and pleyn,
That ech of yow, to shorte with your weye,
In this viage, shal telle tales tweye,
To Caunterbury-ward, I mene it so,
And hom-ward he shal tellen othere two,
Of aventures that whylom han bifalle.
And which of yow that bereth him best of alle,
That is to seyn, that telleth in this cas
Tales of best sentence and most solas,   800
Shal have a soper at our aller cost
Here in this place, sitting by this post,
Whan that we come agayn fro Caunterbury.
And for to make yow the more mery,
I wol my-selven gladly with yow ryde,
Right at myn owne cost, and be your gyde.
And who-so wol my jugement withseye
Shal paye al that we spenden by the weye.
And if ye vouche-sauf that it be so,
Tel me anon, with-outen wordes mo,   810
And I wol erly shape me therfore.'
  This thing was graunted, and our othes swore
With ful glad herte, and preyden him also
That he wold vouche-sauf for to do so,
And that he wolde been our governour,
And of our tales juge and reportour,
And sette a soper at a certeyn prys ;
And we wold reuled been at his devys,
In heigh and lowe ; and thus, by oon assent,
We been acorded to his jugement.   820
And ther-up-on the wyn was fet anon ;
We dronken, and to reste wente echon,
With-outen any lenger taryinge.
  A-morwe, whan that day bigan to springe,
Up roos our host, and was our aller cok,
And gadrede us togidre, alle in a flok,
And forth we riden, a litel more than pas,
Un-to the watering of seint Thomas.
And there our host bigan his hors areste,
And seyde ; ' Lordinges, herkneth, if yow leste.   830
Ye woot your forward, and I it yow recorde.
If even-song and morwe-song acorde,
Lat se now who shal telle the firste tale.
As ever mote I drinke wyn or ale,
Who-so be rebel to my jugement
Shal paye for al that by the weye is spent.
Now draweth cut, er that we ferrer twinne ;
He which that hath the shortest shal biginne.

Sire knight,' quod he, ' my maister and my lord,
Now draweth cut, for that is myn acord. 840
Cometh neer,' quod he, ' my lady prioresse ;
And ye, sir clerk, lat be your shamfastnesse,
Ne studieth noght ; ley hond to, every man.'
 Anon to drawen every wight bigan,
And shortly for to tellen, as it was,
Were it by aventure, or sort, or cas,
The sothe is this, the cut fil to the knight,
Of which ful blythe and glad was every wight;
And telle he moste his tale, as was resoun,
By forward and by composicioun, 850
As ye han herd ; what nedeth wordes mo ?
And whan this gode man saugh it was so,
As he that wys was and obedient
To kepe his forward by his free assent,
He seyde : ' Sin I shal biginne the game,
What, welcome be the cut, a Goddes name !
Now lat us ryde, and herkneth what I seye.'
 And with that word we riden forth our weye ;
And he bigan with right a mery chere
His tale anon, and seyde in this manere. 860

THE KNIGHTES TALE

Iamque domos patrias, Scithice post aspera gentis
Prelia laurigero, &c. [Statius, *Theb.* xii. 519.]

WHYLOM, as olde stories tellen us,
Ther was a duk that highte Theseus ;
Of Athenes he was lord and governour,
And in his tyme swich a conquerour,
That gretter was ther noon under the sonne.
Ful many a riche contree hadde he wonne ;
What with his wisdom and his chivalrye,
He conquered al the regne of Femenye,
That whylom was y-cleped Scithia ;
And weddede the quene Ipolita, 10
And broghte hir hoom with him in his contree
With muchel glorie and greet solempnitee,
And eek hir yonge suster Emelye.
And thus with victorie and with melodye
Lete I this noble duk to Athenes ryde,
And al his hoost, in armes, him bisyde.
 And certes, if it nere to long to here,
I wolde han told yow fully the manere,

How wonnen was the regne of Femenye
By Theseus, and by his chivalrye ; 20
And of the grete bataille for the nones
Bitwixen Athenës and Amazones ;
And how asseged was Ipolita,
The faire hardy quene of Scithia ;
And of the feste that was at hir weddinge,
And of the tempest at hir hoom-cominge ;
But al that thing I moot as now forbere.
I have, God woot, a large feeld to ere,
And wayke been the oxen in my plough.
The remenant of the tale is long y-nough. 30
I wol nat letten eek noon of this route ;
Lat every felawe telle his tale aboute,
And lat see now who shal the soper winne ;
And ther I lefte, I wol ageyn biginne.

This duk, of whom I make mencioun,
When he was come almost unto the toun,
In al his wele and in his moste pryde,
He was war, as he caste his eye asyde,
Wher that ther kneled in the hye weye
A companye of ladies, tweye and tweye, 40
Ech after other, clad in clothes blake ;
But swich a cry and swich a wo they make,
That in this world nis creature livinge,
That herde swich another weymentinge ;
And of this cry they nolde never stenten,
Til they the reynes of his brydel henten.

'What folk ben ye, that at myn hoom-cominge
Perturben so my feste with cryinge ? '
Quod Theseus, 'have ye so greet envye
Of myn honour, that thus compleyne and crye ? 50
Or who hath yow misboden, or offended ?
And telleth me if it may been amended ;
And why that ye ben clothed thus in blak ? '

The eldest lady of hem alle spak,
When she hadde swowned with a deedly chere,
That it was routhe for to seen and here,
And seyde : 'Lord, to whom Fortune hath yiven
Victorie, and as a conquerour to liven,
Noght greveth us your glorie and your honour ;
But we biseken mercy and socour. 60
Have mercy on our wo and our distresse.
Som drope of pitee, thurgh thy gentillesse,
Up-on us wrecched wommen lat thou falle.
For certes, lord, ther nis noon of us alle,
That she nath been a duchesse or a quene ;
Now be we caitifs, as it is wel sene :
Thanked be Fortune, and hir false wheel,
That noon estat assureth to be weel.

And certes, lord, to abyden your presence,
Here in the temple of the goddesse Clemence   70
We han ben waytinge al this fourtenight;
Now help us, lord, sith it is in thy might.
  I wrecche, which that wepe and waille thus,
Was whylom wyf to king Capaneus,
That starf at Thebes, cursed be that day!
And alle we, that been in this array,
And maken al this lamentacioun,
We losten alle our housbondes at that toun,
Whyl that the sege ther-aboute lay.
And yet now the olde Creon, weylaway!   80
That lord is now of Thebes the citee,
Fulfild of ire and of iniquitee,
He, for despyt, and for his tirannye,
To do the dede bodyes vileinye,
Of alle our lordes, whiche that ben slawe,
Hath alle the bodyes on an heep y-drawe,
And wol nat suffren hem, by noon assent,
Neither to been y-buried nor y-brent,
But maketh houndes ete hem in despyt.'
And with that word, with-outen more respyt,   90
They fillen gruf, and cryden pitously,
' Have on us wrecched wommen som mercy,
And lat our sorwe sinken in thyn herte.'
  This gentil duk doun from his courser sterte
With herte pitous, whan he herde hem speke.
Him thoughte that his herte wolde breke,
Whan he saugh hem so pitous and so mat,
That whylom weren of so greet estat.
And in his armes he hem alle up hente,
And hem conforteth in ful good entente;   100
And swoor his ooth, as he was trewe knight,
He wolde doon so ferforthly his might
Up-on the tyraunt Creon hem to wreke,
That al the peple of Grece sholde speke
How Creon was of Theseus y-served,
As he that hadde his deeth ful wel deserved.
And right anoon, with-outen more abood,
His baner he desplayeth, and forth rood
To Thebes-ward, and al his host bisyde;
No neer Athenës wolde he go ne ryde,   110
Ne take his ese fully half a day,
But onward on his wey that night he lay;
And sente anoon Ipolita the quene,
And Emelye hir yonge suster shene,
Un-to the toun of Athenës to dwelle;
And forth he rit; ther nis namore to telle.
  The rede statue of Mars, with spere and targe,
So shyneth in his whyte baner large,

That alle the feeldes gliteren up and doun;
And by his baner born is his penoun 120
Of gold ful riche, in which ther was y-bete
The Minotaur, which that he slough in Crete.
Thus rit this duk, thus rit this conquerour,
And in his host of chivalrye the flour,
Til that he cam to Thebes, and alighte
Faire in a feeld, ther as he thoghte fighte.
But shortly for to speken of this thing,
With Creon, which that was of Thebes king,
He faught, and slough him manly as a knight
In pleyn bataille, and putte the folk to flight; 130
And by assaut he wan the citee after,
And rente adoun bothe wal, and sparre, and rafter;
And to the ladyes he restored agayn
The bones of hir housbondes that were slayn,
To doon obsequies, as was tho the gyse.
But it were al to long for to devyse
The grete clamour and the waymentinge
That the ladyes made at the brenninge
Of the bodyes, and the grete honour
That Theseus, the noble conquerour, 140
Doth to the ladyes, whan they from him wente;
But shortly for to telle is myn entente.
Whan that this worthy duk, this Theseus,
Hath Creon slayn, and wonne Thebes thus,
Stille in that feeld he took al night his reste,
And dide with al the contree as him leste.

To ransake in the tas of bodyes dede,
Hem for to strepe of harneys and of wede,
The pilours diden bisinesse and cure,
After the bataille and disconfiture. 150
And so bifel, that in the tas they founde,
Thurgh-girt with many a grevous blody wounde,
Two yonge knightes ligging by and by,
Bothe in oon armes, wroght ful richely,
Of whiche two, Arcita hight that oon,
And that other knight hight Palamon.
Nat fully quike, ne fully dede they were,
But by hir cote-armures, and by hir gere,
The heraudes knewe hem best in special,
As they that weren of the blood royal 160
Of Thebes, and of sustren two y-born.
Out of the tas the pilours han hem torn,
And han hem caried softe un-to the tente
Of Theseus, and he ful sone hem sente
To Athenës, to dwellen in prisoun
Perpetuelly, he nolde no raunsoun.
And whan this worthy duk hath thus y-don,
He took his host, and hoom he rood anon

With laurer crowned as a conquerour;
And there he liveth, in joye and in honour,   170
Terme of his lyf; what nedeth wordes mo?
And in a tour, in angwish and in wo,
Dwellen this Palamoun and eek Arcite,
For evermore, ther may no gold hem quyte.
    This passeth yeer by yeer, and day by day,
Til it fil ones, in a morwe of May,
That Emelye, that fairer was to sene
Than is the lilie upon his stalke grene,
And fressher than the May with floures newe—
For with the rose colour stroof hir hewe,   180
I noot which was the fairer of hem two—
Er it were day, as was hir wone to do,
She was arisen, and al redy dight;
For May wol have no slogardye a-night.
The sesoun priketh every gentil herte,
And maketh him out of his sleep to sterte,
And seith, 'Arys, and do thyn observaunce.'
This maked Emelye have remembraunce
To doon honour to May, and for to ryse.
Y-clothed was she fresh, for to devyse;   190
Hir yelow heer was broyded in a tresse,
Bihinde hir bak, a yerde long, I gesse.
And in the gardin, at the sonne up-riste,
She walketh up and doun, and as hir liste
She gadereth floures, party whyte and rede,
To make a sotil gerland for hir hede,
And as an aungel hevenly she song.
The grete tour, that was so thikke and strong,
Which of the castel was the chief dongeoun,
(Ther-as the knightes weren in prisoun,   200
Of whiche I tolde yow, and tellen shal)
Was evene joynant to the gardin-wal,
Ther as this Emelye hadde hir pleyinge.
Bright was the sonne, and cleer that morweninge,
And Palamon, this woful prisoner,
As was his wone, by leve of his gayler,
Was risen, and romed in a chambre on heigh,
In which he al the noble citee seigh,
And eek the gardin, ful of braunches grene,
Ther-as this fresshe Emelye the shene   210
Was in hir walk, and romed up and doun.
This sorweful prisoner, this Palamoun,
Goth in the chambre, roming to and fro,
And to him-self compleyning of his wo;
That he was born, ful ofte he seyde, 'alas!'
And so bifel, by aventure or cas,
That thurgh a window, thikke of many a barre
Of yren greet, and square as any sparre,

He caste his eye upon Emelya,
And ther-with-al he bleynte, and cryde 'a!'　　　220
As though he stongen were un-to the herte.
And with that cry Arcite anon up-sterte,
And seyde, 'Cosin myn, what eyleth thee,
That art so pale and deedly on to see?
Why crydestow? who hath thee doon offence?
For Goddes love, tak al in pacience
Our prisoun, for it may non other be;
Fortune hath yeven us this adversitee.
Som wikke aspect or disposicioun
Of Saturne, by sum constellacioun,　　　230
Hath yeven us this, al-though we hadde it sworn;
So stood the heven whan that we were born;
We moste endure it: this is the short and pleyn.'
　This Palamon answerde, and seyde ageyn,
'Cosyn, for sothe, of this opinioun
Thou hast a veyn imaginacioun.
This prison caused me nat for to crye.
But I was hurt right now thurgh-out myn yë
In-to myn herte, that wol my bane be.
The fairnesse of that lady that I see　　　240
Yond in the gardin romen to and fro,
Is cause of al my crying and my wo.
I noot wher she be womman or goddesse;
But Venus is it, soothly, as I gesse.'
And ther-with-al on kneës doun he fil,
And seyde: 'Venus, if it be thy wil
Yow in this gardin thus to transfigure
Bifore me, sorweful wrecche creature,
Out of this prisoun help that we may scapen.
And if so be my destinee be shapen　　　250
By eterne word to dyen in prisoun,
Of our linage have som compassioun,
That is so lowe y-broght by tirannye.'
And with that word Arcite gan espye
Wher-as this lady romed to and fro.
And with that sighte hir beautee hurte him so,
That, if that Palamon was wounded sore,
Arcite is hurt as muche as he, or more.
And with a sigh he seyde pitously:
'The fresshe beautee sleeth me sodeynly　　　260
Of hir that rometh in the yonder place;
And, but I have hir mercy and hir grace,
That I may seen hir atte leeste weye,
I nam but deed; ther nis namore to seye.'
　This Palamon, whan he tho wordes herde,
Dispitously he loked, and answerde:
'Whether seistow this in ernest or in pley?'
　'Nay,' quod Arcite, 'in ernest, by my fey!

God help me so, me list ful yvele pleye.'
  This Palamon gan knitte his browes tweye :   270
' It nere,' quod he, ' to thee no greet honour
For to be fals, ne for to be traytour
To me, that am thy cosin and thy brother
Y-sworn ful depe, and ech of us til other,
That never, for to dyen in the peyne,
Til that the deeth departe shal us tweyne,
Neither of us in love to hindren other,
Ne in non other cas, my leve brother ;
But that thou sholdest trewely forthren me
In every cas, and I shal forthren thee.   280
This was thyn ooth, and myn also, certeyn ;
I wot right wel, thou darst it nat withseyn.
Thus artow of my counseil, out of doute.
And now thou woldest falsly been aboute
To love my lady, whom I love and serve,
And ever shal, til that myn herte sterve.
Now certes, fals Arcite, thou shalt nat so.
I loved hir first, and tolde thee my wo
As to my counseil, and my brother sworn
To forthre me, as I have told biforn.   290
For which thou art y-bounden as a knight
To helpen me, if it lay in thy might,
Or elles artow fals, I dar wel seyn.'
  This Arcitë ful proudly spak ageyn,
' Thou shalt,' quod he, ' be rather fals than I ;
But thou art fals, I telle thee, utterly ;
For *par amour* I loved hir first er thow.
What wiltow seyn ? thou wistest nat yet now
Whether she be a womman or goddesse !
Thyn is affeccioun of holinesse,   300
And myn is love, as to a creature ;
For which I tolde thee myn aventure
As to my cosin, and my brother sworn.
I pose, that thou lovedest hir biforn ;
Wostow nat wel the olde clerkes sawe,
That " who shal yeve a lover any lawe ? "
Love is a gretter lawe, by my pan,
Than may be yeve to any erthly man.
And therefore positif lawe and swich decree
Is broke al-day for love, in ech degree.   310
A man moot nedes love, maugree his heed.
He may nat fleen it, thogh he sholde be deed,
Al be she mayde, or widwe, or elles wyf.
And eek it is nat lykly, al thy lyf,
To stonden in hir grace ; namore shal I ;
For wel thou woost thy-selven, verraily,
That thou and I be dampned to prisoun
Perpetuelly ; us gayneth no raunsoun.

We stryve as dide the houndes for the boon,
They foughte al day, and yet hir part was noon ;   320
Ther cam a kyte, whyl that they were wrothe,
And bar awey the boon bitwixe hem bothe.
And therfore, at the kinges court, my brother,
Ech man for him-self, ther is non other.
Love if thee list ; for I love and ay shal ;
And soothly, leve brother, this is al.
Here in this prisoun mote we endure,
And everich of us take his aventure.'
  Greet was the stryf and long bitwixe hem tweye,
If that I hadde leyser for to seye ;   330
But to theffect. It happed on a day,
(To telle it yow as shortly as I may)
A worthy duk that highte Perotheus,
That felawe was un-to duk Theseus
Sin thilke day that they were children lyte,
Was come to Athenes, his felawe to visyte,
And for to pleye, as he was wont to do,
For in this world he loved no man so :
And he loved him as tendrely ageyn.
So wel they loved, as olde bokes seyn,   340
That whan that oon was deed, sothly to telle,
His felawe wente and soghte him doun in helle ;
But of that story list me nat to wryte.
Duk Perotheus loved wel Arcite,
And hadde him knowe at Thebes yeer by yere ;
And fynally, at requeste and preyere
Of Perotheus, with-oute any raunsoun,
Duk Theseus him leet out of prisoun,
Freely to goon, wher that him liste over-al,
In swich a gyse, as I you tellen shal.   350
  This was the forward, pleynly for tendyte,
Bitwixen Theseus and him Arcite :
That if so were, that Arcite were y-founde
Ever in his lyf, by day or night or stounde
In any contree of this Theseus,
And he were caught, it was acorded thus,
That with a swerd he sholde lese his heed ;
Ther nas non other remedye ne reed,
But taketh his leve, and homward he him spedde ;
Let him be war, his nekke lyth to wedde !   360
  How greet a sorwe suffreth now Arcite !
The deeth he feleth thurgh his herte smyte ;
He wepeth, wayleth, cryeth pitously ;
To sleen him-self he wayteth prively.
He seyde, ' Allas that day that I was born !
Now is my prison worse than biforn ;
Now is me shape eternally to dwelle
Noght in purgatorie, but in helle.

Allas! that ever knew I Perotheus!
For elles hadde I dwelled with Theseus   370
Y-fetered in his prisoun ever-mo.
Than hadde I been in blisse, and nat in wo.
Only the sighte of hir, whom that I serve,
Though that I never hir grace may deserve,
Wolde han suffised right y-nough for me.
O dere cosin Palamon,' quod he,
' Thyn is the victorie of this aventure,
Ful blisfully in prison maistow dure;
In prison? certes nay, but in paradys!
Wel hath fortune y-turned thee the dys,   380
That hast the sighte of hir, and I thabsence.
For possible is, sin thou hast hir presence,
And art a knight, a worthy and an able,
That by som cas, sin fortune is chaungeable,
Thou mayst to thy desyr som-tyme atteyne.
But I, that am exyled, and bareyne
Of alle grace, and in so greet despeir,
That ther nis erthe, water, fyr, ne eir,
Ne creature, that of hem maked is,
That may me helpe or doon confort in this.   390
Wel oughte I sterve in wanhope and distresse;
Farwel my lyf, my lust, and my gladnesse!
    Allas, why pleynen folk so in commune
Of purveyaunce of God, or of fortune,
That yeveth hem ful ofte in many a gyse
Wel bettre than they can hem-self devyse?
Som man desyreth for to han richesse,
That cause is of his mordre or greet siknesse.
And som man wolde out of his prison fayn,
That in his hous is of his meynee slayn.   400
Infinite harmes been in this matere;
We witen nat what thing we preyen here.
We faren as he that dronke is as a mous;
A dronke man wot wel he hath an hous,
But he noot which the righte wey is thider;
And to a dronke man the wey is slider.
And certes, in this world so faren we;
We seken faste after felicitee,
But we goon wrong ful often, trewely.
Thus may we seyen alle, and namely I,   410
That wende and hadde a greet opinioun,
That, if I mighte escapen from prisoun,
Than hadde I been in joye and perfit hele,
Ther now I am exyled fro my wele.
Sin that I may nat seen yow, Emelye,
I nam but deed; ther nis no remedye.'
    Up-on that other syde Palamon,
Whan that he wiste Arcite was agon,

Swich sorwe he maketh, that the grete tour
Resouneth of his youling and clamour. 420
The pure fettres on his shines grete
Weren of his bittre salte teres wete.
' Allas ! ' quod he, ' Arcita, cosin myn,
Of al our stryf, God woot, the fruyt is thyn.
Thow walkest now in Thebes at thy large,
And of my wo thou yevest litel charge.
Thou mayst, sin thou hast wisdom and manhede,
Assemblen alle the folk of our kinrede,
And make a werre so sharp on this citee,
That by som aventure, or som tretee, 430
Thou mayst have hir to lady and to wyf,
For whom that I mot nedes lese my lyf.
For, as by wey of possibilitee,
Sith thou art at thy large, of prison free,
And art a lord, greet is thyn avauntage,
More than is myn, that sterve here in a cage.
For I mot wepe and wayle, whyl I live,
With al the wo that prison may me yive,
And eek with peyne that love me yiveth also,
That doubleth al my torment and my wo.' 440
Ther-with the fyr of jelousye up-sterte
With-inne his brest, and hente him by the herte
So woodly, that he lyk was to biholde
The box-tree, or the asshen dede and colde.
Tho seyde he ; ' O cruel goddes, that governe
This world with binding of your word eterne,
And wryten in the table of athamaunt
Your parlement, and your eterne graunt,
What is mankinde more un-to yow holde
Than is the sheep, that rouketh in the folde ? 450
For slayn is man right as another beste,
And dwelleth eek in prison and areste,
And hath siknesse, and greet adversitee,
And ofte tymes giltelees, pardee !
  What governaunce is in this prescience,
That giltelees tormenteth innocence ?
And yet encreseth this al my penaunce,
That man is bounden to his observaunce,
For Goddes sake, to letten of his wille,
Ther as a beest may al his lust fulfille. 460
And whan a beest is deed, he hath no peyne :
But man after his deeth moot wepe and pleyne,
Though in this world he have care and wo :
With-outen doute it may stonden so.
The answere of this I lete to divynis,
But wel I woot, that in this world gret pyne is.
Allas ! I see a serpent or a theef,
That many a trewe man hath doon mescheef,

Goon at his large, and wher him list may turne.
But I mot been in prison thurgh Saturne,   470
And eek thurgh Juno, jalous and eek wood,
That hath destroyed wel ny al the blood
Of Thebes, with his waste walles wyde.
And Venus sleeth me on that other syde
For jelousye, and fere of him Arcite.'
    Now wol I stinte of Palamon a lyte,
And lete him in his prison stille dwelle,
And of Arcita forth I wol yow telle.
    The somer passeth, and the nightes longe
Encresen double wyse the peynes stronge   480
Bothe of the lovere and the prisoner.
I noot which hath the wofullere mester.
For shortly for to seyn, this Palamoun
Perpetuelly is dampned to prisoun,
In cheynes and in fettres to ben deed ;
And Arcite is exyled upon his heed
For ever-mo as out of that contree,
Ne never-mo he shal his lady see.
    Yow loveres axe I now this questioun,
Who hath the worse, Arcite or Palamoun ?   490
That oon may seen his lady day by day,
But in prison he moot dwelle alway.
That other wher him list may ryde or go,
But seen his lady shal he never-mo.
Now demeth as yow liste, ye that can,
For I wol telle forth as I bigan.

    EXPLICIT PRIMA PARS.   SEQUITUR PARS SECUNDA.

    Whan that Arcite to Thebes comen was,
Ful ofte a day he swelte and seyde ' allas,'
For seen his lady shal he never-mo.
And shortly to concluden al his wo,   500
So muche sorwe had never creature
That is, or shal, whyl that the world may dure.
His sleep, his mete, his drink is him biraft,
That lene he wex, and drye as is a shaft.
His eyen holwe, and grisly to biholde ;
His hewe falwe, and pale as asshen colde,
And solitarie he was, and ever allone,
And wailling al the night, making his mone.
And if he herde song or instrument,
Then wolde he wepe, he mighte nat be stent ;   510
So feble eek were his spirits, and so lowe,
And chaunged so, that no man coude knowe
His speche nor his vois, though men it herde.
And in his gere, for al the world he ferde
Nat oonly lyk the loveres maladye
Of Hereos, but rather lyk manye

Engendred of humour malencolyk,
Biforen, in his celle fantastyk.
And shortly, turned was al up-so-doun
Bothe habit and eek disposicioun   520
Of him, this woful lovere daun Arcite.
  What sholde I al-day of his wo endyte ?
Whan he endured hadde a yeer or two
This cruel torment, and this peyne and wo,
At Thebes, in his contree, as I seyde,
Up-on a night, in sleep as he him leyde,
Him thoughte how that the winged god Mercurie
Biforn him stood, and bad him to be murye.
His slepy yerde in hond he bar uprighte ;
An hat he werede up-on his heres brighte.   530
Arrayed was this god (as he took keep)
As he was whan that Argus took his sleep ;
And seyde him thus : ' To Athenes shaltou wende ;
Ther is thee shapen of thy wo an ende.'
And with that word Arcite wook and sterte.
' Now trewely, how sore that me smerte,'
Quod he, ' to Athenes right now wol I fare ;
Ne for the drede of deeth shal I nat spare
To see my lady, that I love and serve ;
In hir presence I recche nat to sterve.'   540
  And with that word he caughte a greet mirour,
And saugh that chaunged was al his colour,
And saugh his visage al in another kinde.
And right anoon it ran him in his minde,
That, sith his face was so disfigured
Of maladye, the which he hadde endured,
He mighte wel, if that he bar him lowe,
Live in Athenes ever-more unknowe,
And seen his lady wel ny day by day.
And right anon he chaunged his array,   550
And cladde him as a povre laborer,
And al allone, save oonly a squyer,
That knew his privetee and al his cas,
Which was disgysed povrely, as he was,
To Athenes is he goon the nexte way.
And to the court he wente up-on a day,
And at the gate he profreth his servyse,
To drugge and drawe, what so men wol devyse.
And shortly of this matere for to seyn,
He fil in office with a chamberleyn,   560
The which that dwelling was with Emelye.
For he was wys, and coude soon aspye
Of every servaunt, which that serveth here.
Wel coude he hewen wode, and water bere,
For he was yong and mighty for the nones,
And ther-to he was strong and big of bones

To doon that any wight can him devyse.
A yeer or two he was in this servyse,
Page of the chambre of Emelye the brighte;
And 'Philostrate' he seide that he highte.   570
But half so wel biloved a man as he
Ne was ther never in court, of his degree;
He was so gentil of condicioun,
That thurghout al the court was his renoun.
They seyden, that it were a charitee
That Theseus wolde enhauncen his degree,
And putten him in worshipful servyse,
Ther as he mighte his vertu excercyse.
And thus, with-inne a whyle, his name is spronge
Bothe of his dedes, and his goode tonge,   580
That Theseus hath taken him so neer
That of his chambre he made him a squyer,
And yaf him gold to mayntene his degree;
And eek men broghte him out of his contree
From yeer to yeer, ful prively, his rente;
But honestly and slyly he it spente,
That no man wondred how that he it hadde.
And three yeer in this wyse his lyf he ladde,
And bar him so in pees and eek in werre,
Ther nas no man that Theseus hath derre.   590
And in this blisse lete I now Arcite,
And speke I wol of Palamon a lyte.

   In derknesse and horrible and strong prisoun
This seven yeer hath seten Palamoun,
Forpyned, what for wo and for distresse;
Who feleth double soor and hevinesse
But Palamon? that love destreyneth so,
That wood out of his wit he gooth for wo;
And eek therto he is a prisoner
Perpetuelly, noght oonly for a yeer.   600
Who coude ryme in English proprely
His martirdom? for sothe, it am nat I;
Therefore I passe as lightly as I may.

   It fel that in the seventhe yeer, in May,
The thridde night, (as olde bokes seyn,
That al this storie tellen more pleyn,)
Were it by aventure or destinee,
(As, whan a thing is shapen, it shal be,)
That, sone after the midnight, Palamoun,
By helping of a freend, brak his prisoun,   610
And fleeth the citee, faste as he may go;
For he had yive his gayler drinke so
Of a clarree, maad of a certeyn wyn,
With nercotikes and opie of Thebes fyn,
That al that night, thogh that men wolde him shake,
The gayler sleep, he mighte nat awake;

And thus he fleeth as faste as ever he may.
The night was short, and faste by the day,
That nedes-cost he moste him-selven hyde,
And til a grove, faste ther besyde,⁣   620
With dredful foot than stalketh Palamoun.
For shortly, this was his opinioun,
That in that grove he wolde him hyde al day,
And in the night than wolde he take his way
To Thebes-ward, his freendes for to preye
On Theseus to helpe him to werreye ;
And shortly, outher he wolde lese his lyf,
Or winnen Emelye un-to his wyf ;
This is theffect and his entente pleyn.
   Now wol I torne un-to Arcite ageyn,   630
That litel wiste how ny that was his care,
Til that fortune had broght him in the snare.
   The bisy larke, messager of day,
Saluëth in hir song the morwe gray ;
And fyry Phebus ryseth up so brighte,
That al the orient laugheth of the lighte,
And with his stremes dryeth in the greves
The silver dropes, hanging on the leves.
And Arcite, that is in the court royal
With Theseus, his squyer principal,   640
Is risen, and loketh on the myrie day.
And, for to doon his observaunce to May,
Remembring on the poynt of his desyr,
He on a courser, sterting as the fyr,
Is riden in-to the feeldes, him to pleye,
Out of the court, were it a myle or tweye ;
And to the grove, of which that I yow tolde,
By aventure, his wey he gan to holde,
To maken him a gerland of the greves,
Were it of wodebinde or hawethorn-leves,   650
And loude he song ageyn the sonne shene :
'May, with alle thy floures and thy grene,
Wel-come be thou, faire fresshe May,
I hope that I som grene gete may.'
And from his courser, with a lusty herte,
In-to the grove ful hastily he sterte,
And in a path he rometh up and doun,
Ther-as, by aventure, this Palamoun
Was in a bush, that no man mighte him see,
For sore afered of his deeth was he.   660
No-thing ne knew he that it was Arcite :
God wot he wolde have trowed it ful lyte.
But sooth is seyd, gon sithen many yeres,
That ' feeld hath eyen, and the wode hath eres.'
It is ful fair a man to bere him evene,
For al-day meteth men at unset stevene.

Ful litel woot Arcite of his felawe,
That was so ny to herknen al his sawe,
For in the bush he sitteth now ful stille.
  Whan that Arcite had romed al his fille,   670
And songen al the roundel lustily,
In-to a studie he fil sodeynly,
As doon thise loveres in hir queynte geres,
Now in the croppe, now doun in the breres,
Now up, now doun, as boket in a welle.
Right as the Friday, soothly for to telle,
Now it shyneth, now it reyneth faste,
Right so can gery Venus overcaste
The hertes of hir folk ; right as hir day
Is gerful, right so chaungeth she array.   680
Selde is the Friday al the wyke y-lyke.
  Whan that Arcite had songe, he gan to syke,
And sette him doun with-outen any more :
' Alas ! ' quod he, ' that day that I was bore !
How longe, Juno, thurgh thy crueltee,
Woltow werreyen Thebes the citee ?
Allas ! y-broght is to confusioun
The blood royal of Cadme and Amphioun ;
Of Cadmus, which that was the firste man
That Thebes bulte, or first the toun bigan,   690
And of the citee first was crouned king,
Of his linage am I, and his of-spring
By verray ligne, as of the stok royal :
And now I am so caitif and so thral,
That he, that is my mortal enemy,
I serve him as his squyer povrely.
And yet doth Juno me wel more shame,
For I dar noght biknowe myn owne name ;
But ther-as I was wont to highte Arcite,
Now highte I Philostrate, noght worth a myte.   700
Allas ! thou felle Mars, allas ! Juno,
Thus hath your ire our kinrede al fordo,
Save only me, and wrecched Palamoun,
That Theseus martyreth in prisoun.
And over al this, to sleen me utterly,
Love hath his fyry dart so brenningly
Y-stiked thurgh my trewe careful herte,
That shapen was my deeth erst than my sherte.
Ye sleen me with your eyen, Emelye ;
Ye been the cause wherfor that I dye.   710
Of al the remenant of myn other care
Ne sette I nat the mountaunce of a tare,
So that I coude don aught to your plesaunce ! '
And with that word he fil doun in a traunce
A longe tyme ; and after he up-sterte.
  This Palamoun, that thoughte that thurgh his herte

He felte a cold swerd sodeynliche glyde,
For ire he quook, no lenger wolde he byde.
And whan that he had herd Arcites tale,
As he were wood, with face deed and pale,   720
He sterte him up out of the buskes thikke,
And seyde : ' Arcite, false traitour wikke,
Now artow hent, that lovest my lady so,
For whom that I have al this peyne and wo,
And art my blood, and to my counseil sworn,
As I ful ofte have told thee heer-biforn,
And hast by-japed here duk Theseus,
And falsly chaunged hast thy name thus ;
I wol be deed, or elles thou shalt dye.
Thou shalt nat love my lady Emelye,   730
But I wol love hir only, and namo ;
For I am Palamoun, thy mortal fo.
And though that I no wepne have in this place,
But out of prison am astert by grace,
I drede noght that outher thou shalt dye,
Or thou ne shalt nat loven Emelye.
Chees which thou wilt, for thou shalt nat asterte.'
   This Arcitë, with ful despitous herte,
Whan he him knew, and hadde his tale herd,
As fiers as leoun, pulled out a swerd,   740
And seyde thus : ' by God that sit above,
Nere it that thou art sik, and wood for love,
And eek that thou no wepne hast in this place,
Thou sholdest never out of this grove pace,
That thou ne sholdest dyen of myn hond.
For I defye the seurtee and the bond
Which that thou seyst that I have maad to thee.
What, verray fool, think wel that love is free,
And I wol love hir, maugre al thy might !
But, for as muche thou art a worthy knight,   750
And wilnest to darreyne hir by batayle,
Have heer my trouthe, to-morwe I wol nat fayle,
With-outen witing of any other wight,
That here I wol be founden as a knight,
And bringen harneys right y-nough for thee ;
And chees the beste, and leve the worste for me.
And mete and drinke this night wol I bringe
Y-nough for thee, and clothes for thy beddinge.
And, if so be that thou my lady winne,
And slee me in this wode ther I am inne,   760
Thou mayst wel have thy lady, as for me.'
This Palamon answerde : ' I graunte it thee.'
And thus they been departed til a-morwe,
When ech of hem had leyd his feith to borwe.
  O Cupide, out of alle charitee !
O regne, that wolt no felawe have with thee !

Ful sooth is seyd, that love ne lordshipe
Wol noght, his thankes, have no felaweshipe ;
Wel finden that Arcite and Palamoun.
Arcite is riden anon un-to the toun,   770
And on the morwe, er it were dayes light,
Ful prively two harneys hath he dight,
Bothe suffisaunt and mete to darreyne
The bataille in the feeld bitwix hem tweyne.
And on his hors, allone as he was born,
He carieth al this harneys him biforn ;
And in the grove, at tyme and place y-set,
This Arcite and this Palamon ben met.
Tho chaungen gan the colour in hir face ;
Right as the hunter in the regne of Trace,   780
That stondeth at the gappe with a spere,
Whan hunted is the leoun or the bere,
And hereth him come russhing in the greves,
And breketh bothe bowes and the leves,
And thinketh, ' heer cometh my mortel enemy,
With-oute faile, he moot be deed, or I ;
For outher I mot sleen him at the gappe,
Or he mot sleen me, if that me mishappe : '
So ferden they, in chaunging of hir hewe,
As fer as everich of hem other knewe.   790
Ther nas no good day, ne no saluing ;
But streight, with-outen word or rehersing,
Everich of hem halp for to armen other,
As freendly as he were his owne brother ;
And after that, with sharpe speres stronge
They foynen ech at other wonder longe.
Thou mightest wene that this Palamoun
In his fighting were a wood leoun,
And as a cruel tygre was Arcite :
As wilde bores gonne they to smyte,   800
That frothen whyte as foom for ire wood.
Up to the ancle foghte they in hir blood.
And in this wyse I lete hem fighting dwelle ;
And forth I wol of Theseus yow telle.
    The destinee, ministre general,
That executeth in the world over-al
The purveyaunce, that God hath seyn biforn,
So strong it is, that, though the world had sworn
The contrarie of a thing, by ye or nay,
Yet somtyme it shal fallen on a day   810
That falleth nat eft with-inne a thousand yere.
For certeinly, our appetytes here,
Be it of werre, or pees, or hate, or love,
Al is this reuled by the sighte above.
This mene I now by mighty Theseus,
That for to honten is so desirous,

And namely at the grete hert in May,
That in his bed ther daweth him no day,
That he nis clad, and redy for to ryde
With hunte and horn, and houndes him bisyde.   820
For in his hunting hath he swich delyt,
That it is al his joye and appetyt
To been him-self the grete hertes bane ;
For after Mars he serveth now Diane.
  Cleer was the day, as I have told er this,
And Theseus, with alle joye and blis,
With his Ipolita, the fayre quene,
And Emelye, clothed al in grene,
On hunting be they riden royally.
And to the grove, that stood ful faste by,   830
In which ther was an hert, as men him tolde,
Duk Theseus the streighte wey hath holde.
And to the launde he rydeth him ful right,
For thider was the hert wont have his flight,
And over a brook, and so forth on his weye.
This duk wol han a cours at him, or tweye,
With houndes, swiche as that him list comaunde.
  And whan this duk was come un-to the launde,
Under the sonne he loketh, and anon
He was war of Arcite and Palamon,   840
That foughten breme, as it were bores two ;
The brighte swerdes wenten to and fro
So hidously, that with the leeste strook
It seemed as it wolde felle an ook ;
But what they were, no-thing he ne woot.
This duk his courser with his spores smoot,
And at a stert he was bitwix hem two,
And pulled out a swerd and cryed, ' ho !
Namore, up peyne of lesing of your heed.
By mighty Mars, he shal anon be deed,   850
That smyteth any strook, that I may seen !
But telleth me what mister men ye been,
That been so hardy for to fighten here
With-outen juge or other officere,
As it were in a listes royally ? '
  This Palamon answerde hastily,
And seyde : ' sire, what nedeth wordes mo ?
We have the deeth deserved bothe two.
Two woful wrecches been we, two caytyves,
That been encombred of our owne lyves ;   860
And as thou art a rightful lord and juge
Ne yeve us neither mercy ne refuge,
But slee me first, for seynte charitee ;
But slee my felawe eek as wel as me.
Or slee him first ; for, though thou knowe it lyte,
This is thy mortal fo, this is Arcite,

That fro thy lond is banished on his heed.
For which he hath deserved to be deed.
For this is he that cam un-to thy gate,
And seyde, that he highte Philostrate.   870
Thus hath he japed thee ful many a yeer,
And thou has maked him thy chief squyer;
And this is he that loveth Emelye.
For sith the day is come that I shal dye,
I make pleynly my confessioun,
That I am thilke woful Palamoun,
That hath thy prison broken wikkedly.
I am thy mortal fo, and it am I
That loveth so hote Emelye the brighte,
That I wol dye present in hir sighte.   880
Therfore I axe deeth and my juwyse;
But slee my felawe in the same wyse,
For bothe han we deserved to be slayn.'
    This worthy duk answerde anon agayn,
And seyde, 'This is a short conclusioun:
Youre owne mouth, by your confessioun,
Hath dampned you, and I wol it recorde,
It nedeth noght to pyne yow with the corde.
Ye shul be deed, by mighty Mars the rede!'
    The quene anon, for verray wommanhede,   890
Gan for to wepe, and so dide Emelye,
And alle the ladies in the companye.
Gret pitee was it, as it thoughte hem alle,
That ever swich a chaunce sholde falle;
For gentil men they were, of greet estat,
And no-thing but for love was this debat;
And sawe hir blody woundes wyde and sore;
And alle cryden, bothe lasse and more,
'Have mercy, lord, up-on us wommen alle!'
And on hir bare knees adoun they falle,   900
And wolde have kist his feet ther-as he stood,
Til at the laste aslaked was his mood;
For pitee renneth sone in gentil herte.
And though he first for ire quook and sterte,
He hath considered shortly, in a clause,
The trespas of hem bothe, and eek the cause:
And al-though that his ire hir gilt accused,
Yet in his reson he hem bothe excused;
As thus: he thoghte wel, that every man
Wol helpe him-self in love, if that he can,   910
And eek delivere him-self out of prisoun;
And eek his herte had compassioun
Of wommen, for they wepen ever in oon;
And in his gentil herte he thoghte anoon,
And softe un-to himself he seyde: 'fy
Up-on a lord that wol have no mercy,

But been a leoun, bothe in word and dede,
To hem that been in repentaunce and drede
As wel as to a proud despitous man
That wol maynteyne that he first bigan!   920
That lord hath litel of discrecioun,
That in swich cas can no divisioun,
But weyeth pryde and humblesse after oon.'
And shortly, whan his ire is thus agoon,
He gan to loken up with eyen lighte,
And spak thise same wordes al on highte :—
' The god of love, a! *benedicite,*
How mighty and how greet a lord is he!
Ayeins his might ther gayneth none obstacles,
He may be cleped a god for his miracles ;   930
For he can maken at his owne gyse
Of everich herte, as that him list devyse.
Lo heer, this Arcite and this Palamoun,
That quitly weren out of my prisoun,
And mighte han lived in Thebes royally,
And witen I am hir mortal enemy,
And that hir deeth lyth in my might also,
And yet hath love, maugree hir eyen two,
Y-broght hem hider bothe for to dye!
Now loketh, is nat that an heigh folye ?   940
Who may been a fool, but-if he love ?
Bihold, for Goddes sake that sit above,
Se how they blede! be they noght wel arrayed ?
Thus hath hir lord, the god of love, y-payed
Hir wages and hir fees for hir servyse!
And yet they wenen for to been ful wyse
That serven love, for aught that may bifalle!
But this is yet the beste game of alle,
That she, for whom they han this jolitee,
Can hem ther-for as muche thank as me ;   950
She woot namore of al this hote fare,
By God, than woot a cokkow or an hare!
But al mot been assayed, hoot and cold ;
A man mot been a fool, or yong or old ;
I woot it by my-self ful yore agoon :
For in my tyme a servant was I oon.
And therfore, sin I knowe of loves peyne,
And woot how sore it can a man distreyne,
As he that hath ben caught ofte in his las,
I yow foryeve al hoolly this trespas,   960
At requeste of the quene that kneleth here,
And eek of Emelye, my suster dere.
And ye shul bothe anon un-to me swere,
That never-mo ye shul my contree dere,
Ne make werre up-on me night ne day,
But been my freendes in al that ye may ;

I yow foryeve this trespas every del.'
And they him swore his axing fayre and wel,
And him of lordshipe and of mercy preyde,
And he hem graunteth grace, and thus he seyde: 970
  'To speke of royal linage and richesse,
Though that she were a quene or a princesse,
Ech of yow bothe is worthy, doutelees,
To wedden whan tyme is, but nathelees
(I speke as for my suster Emelye,
For whom ye have this stryf and jelousye)
Ye woot your-self, she may not wedden two
At ones, though ye fighten ever-mo:
That oon of yow, al be him looth or leef,
He moot go pypen in an ivy-leef;   980
This is to seyn, she may nat now han bothe,
Al be ye never so jelous, ne so wrothe.
And for-thy I yow putte in this degree,
That ech of yow shal have his destinee
As him is shape; and herkneth in what wyse;
Lo, heer your ende of that I shal devyse.
  My wil is this, for plat conclusioun,
With-outen any replicacioun,
If that yow lyketh, tak it for the beste,
That everich of yow shal gon wher him leste   990
Frely, with-outen raunson or daunger;
And this day fifty wykes, fer ne ner,
Everich of yow shal bringe an hundred knightes,
Armed for listes up at alle rightes,
Al redy to darreyne hir by bataille.
And this bihote I yow, with-outen faille,
Up-on my trouthe, and as I am a knight,
That whether of yow bothe that hath might,
This is to seyn, that whether he or thou
May with his hundred, as I spak of now,   1000
Sleen his contrarie, or out of listes dryve,
Him shal I yeve Emelya to wyve,
To whom that fortune yeveth so fair a grace.
The listes shal I maken in this place,
And God so wisly on my soule rewe,
As I shal even juge been and trewe.
Ye shul non other ende with me maken,
That oon of yow ne shal be deed or taken.
And if yow thinketh this is wel y-sayd,
Seyeth your avys, and holdeth yow apayd.   1010
This is your ende and your conclusioun.'
  Who loketh lightly now but Palamoun?
Who springeth up for joye but Arcite?
Who couthe telle, or who couthe it endyte,
The joye that is maked in the place
Whan Theseus hath doon so fair a grace?

But doun on knees wente every maner wight,
And thanked him with al her herte and might,
And namely the Thebans ofte sythe.
And thus with good hope and with herte blythe   1020
They take hir leve, and hom-ward gonne they ryde
To Thebes, with his olde walles wyde.

EXPLICIT SECUNDA PARS.   SEQUITUR PARS TERCIA.

I trowe men wolde deme it necligence,
If I foryete to tellen the dispence
Of Theseus, that goth so bisily
To maken up the listes royally ;
That swich a noble theatre as it was,
I dar wel seyn that in this world ther nas.
The circuit a myle was aboute,
Walled of stoon, and diched al with-oute.   1030
Round was the shap, in maner of compas,
Ful of degrees, the heighte of sixty pas,
That, whan a man was set on o degree,
He letted nat his felawe for to see.
Est-ward ther stood a gate of marbel whyt,
West-ward, right swich another in the opposit.
And shortly to concluden, swich a place
Was noon in erthe, as in so litel space ;
For in the lond ther nas no crafty man,
That geometrie or ars-metrik can,   1040
Ne purtreyour, ne kerver of images,
That Theseus ne yaf him mete and wages
The theatre for to maken and devyse.
And for to doon his ryte and sacrifyse,
He est-ward hath, up-on the gate above,
In worship of Venus, goddesse of love,
Don make an auter and an oratorie ;
And west-ward, in the minde and in memorie
Of Mars, he maked hath right swich another,
That coste largely of gold a fother.   1050
And north-ward, in a touret on the wal,
Of alabastre whyt and reed coral
An oratorie riche for to see,
In worship of Dyane of chastitee,
Hath Theseus don wroght in noble wyse.
But yet hadde I foryeten to devyse
The noble kerving, and the portreitures,
The shap, the countenaunce, and the figures,
That weren in thise oratories three.
First in the temple of Venus maystow see   1060
Wroght on the wal, ful pitous to biholde,
The broken slepes, and the sykes colde ;
The sacred teres, and the waymenting ;
The fyry strokes of the desiring,

That loves servaunts in this lyf enduren;
The othes, that hir covenants assuren;
Plesaunce and hope, desyr, fool-hardinesse,
Beautee and youthe, bauderie, richesse,
Charmes and force, lesinges, flaterye,
Dispense, bisynesse, and jelousye, 1070
That wered of yelwe goldes a gerland,
And a cokkow sitting on hir hand;
Festes, instruments, caroles, daunces,
Lust and array, and alle the circumstaunces
Of love, whiche that I rekne and rekne shal,
By ordre weren peynted on the wal,
And mo than I can make of mencioun.
For soothly, al the mount of Citheroun,
Ther Venus hath hir principal dwelling,
Was shewed on the wal in portreying, 1080
With al the gardin, and the lustinesse.
Nat was foryeten the porter Ydelnesse,
Ne Narcisus the faire of yore agon,
Ne yet the folye of king Salamon,
Ne yet the grete strengthe of Hercules—
Thenchauntements of Medea and Circes—
Ne of Turnus, with the hardy fiers corage,
The riche Cresus, caytif in servage.
Thus may ye seen that wisdom ne richesse,
Beautee ne sleighte, strengthe, ne hardinesse, 1090
Ne may with Venus holde champartye;
For as hir list the world than may she gye.
Lo, alle thise folk so caught were in hir las,
Til they for wo ful ofte seyde ' allas!'
Suffyceth heer ensamples oon or two,
And though I coude rekne a thousand mo.
 The statue of Venus, glorious for to see,
Was naked fleting in the large see,
And fro the navele doun all covered was
With wawes grene, and brighte as any glas. 1100
A citole in hir right hand hadde she,
And on hir heed, ful semely for to see,
A rose gerland, fresh and wel smellinge;
Above hir heed hir dowves flikeringe.
Biforn hir stood hir sone Cupido,
Up-on his shuldres winges hadde he two;
And blind he was, as it is ofte sene;
A bowe he bar and arwes brighte and kene.
 Why sholde I noght as wel eek telle yow al
The portreiture, that was up-on the wal 1110
With-inne the temple of mighty Mars the rede?
Al peynted was the wal, in lengthe and brede,
Lyk to the estres of the grisly place,
That highte the grete temple of Mars in Trace,

In thilke colde frosty regioun,
Ther-as Mars hath his sovereyn mansioun.
  First on the wal was peynted a foreste,
In which ther dwelleth neither man ne beste,
With knotty knarry bareyn treës olde
Of stubbes sharpe and hidous to biholde ;   1120
In which ther ran a rumbel and a swough,
As though a storm sholde bresten every bough :
And downward from an hille, under a bente,
Ther stood the temple of Mars armipotente,
Wroght al of burned steel, of which thentree
Was long and streit, and gastly for to see.
And ther-out cam a rage and such a vese,
That it made al the gates for to rese.
The northren light in at the dores shoon,
For windowe on the wal ne was ther noon,   1130
Thurgh which men mighten any light discerne.
The dores were alle of adamant eterne,
Y-clenched overthwart and endelong
With iren tough ; and, for to make it strong,
Every piler, the temple to sustene,
Was tonne-greet, of iren bright and shene.
  Ther saugh I first the derke imagining
Of felonye, and al the compassing ;
The cruel ire, reed as any glede ;
The pykepurs, and eek the pale drede ;   1140
The smyler with the knyf under the cloke ;
The shepne brenning with the blake smoke ;
The treson of the mordring in the bedde ;
The open werre, with woundes al bi-bledde ;
Contek, with blody knyf and sharp manace ;
Al ful of chirking was that sory place.
The sleere of him-self yet saugh I ther,
His herte-blood hath bathed al his heer ;
The nayl y-driven in the shode a-night ;
The colde deeth, with mouth gaping up-right.   1150
Amiddes of the temple sat meschaunce,
With disconfort and sory contenaunce.
Yet saugh I woodnesse laughing in his rage ;
Armed compleint, out-hees, and fiers outrage.
The careyne in the bush, with throte y-corve :
A thousand slayn, and nat of qualm y-storve ;
The tiraunt, with the prey by force y-raft ;
The toun destroyed, ther was no-thing laft.
Yet saugh I brent the shippes hoppesteres ;
The hunte strangled with the wilde beres :   1160
The sowe freten the child right in the cradel ;
The cook y-scalded, for al his longe ladel.
Noght was foryeten by the infortune of Marte ;
The carter over-riden with his carte,

Under the wheel ful lowe he lay adoun.
Ther were also, of Martes divisioun,
The barbour, and the bocher, and the smith
That forgeth sharpe swerdes on his stith.
And al above, depeynted in a tour,
Saw I conquest sittinge in greet honour,   1170
With the sharpe swerde over his heed
Hanginge by a sotil twynes threed.
Depeynted was the slaughtre of Julius,
Of grete Nero, and of Antonius ;
Al be that thilke tyme they were unborn,
Yet was hir deeth depeynted ther-biforn,
By manasinge of Mars, right by figure ;
So was it shewed in that portreiture
As is depeynted in the sterres above,
Who shal be slayn or elles deed for love.   1180
Suffyceth oon ensample in stories olde,
I may not rekne hem alle, thogh I wolde.
    The statue of Mars up-on a carte stood,
Armed, and loked grim as he were wood ;
And over his heed ther shynen two figures
Of sterres, that been cleped in scriptures,
That oon Puella, that other Rubeus.
This god of armes was arrayed thus :—
A wolf ther stood biforn him at his feet
With eyen rede, and of a man he eet ;   1190
With sotil pencel was depeynt this storie,
In redoutinge of Mars and of his glorie.
    Now to the temple of Diane the chaste
As shortly as I can I wol me haste,
To telle yow al the descripcioun.
Depeynted been the walles up and doun
Of hunting and of shamfast chastitee.
Ther saugh I how woful Calistopee,
Whan that Diane agreved was with here,
Was turned from a womman til a bere,   1200
And after was she maad the lode-sterre ;
Thus was it peynt, I can say yow no ferre ;
Hir sone is eek a sterre, as men may see.
Ther saugh I Dane, y-turned til a tree,
I mene nat the goddesse Diane,
But Penneus doughter, which that highte Dane.
Ther saugh I Attheon an hert y-maked,
For vengeaunce that he saugh Diane al naked ;
I saugh how that his houndes have him caught,
And freten him, for that they knewe him naught.   1210
Yet peynted was a litel forther-moor,
How Atthalante hunted the wilde boor,
And Meleagre, and many another mo,
For which Diane wroghte him care and wo.

Ther saugh I many another wonder storie,
The whiche me list nat drawen to memorie.
This goddesse on an hert ful hye seet,
With smale houndes al aboute hir feet ;
And undernethe hir feet she hadde a mone,
Wexing it was, and sholde wanie sone.   1220
In gaude grene hir statue clothed was,
With bowe in honde, and arwes in a cas.
Hir eyen caste she ful lowe adoun,
Ther Pluto hath his derke regioun.
A womman travailinge was hir biforn,
But, for hir child so longe was unborn,
Ful pitously Lucyna gan she calle,
And seyde, ' help, for thou mayst best of alle.'
Wel couthe he peynten lyfly that it wroghte,
With many a florin he the hewes boghte.   1230

Now been thise listes maad, and Theseus,
That at his grete cost arrayed thus
The temples and the theatre every del,
Whan it was doon, him lyked wonder wel.
But stinte I wol of Theseus a lyte,
And speke of Palamon and of Arcite.

The day approcheth of hir retourninge,
That everich sholde an hundred knightes bringe,
The bataille to darreyne, as I yow tolde ;
And til Athenes, hir covenant for to holde,   1240
Hath everich of hem broght an hundred knightes
Wel armed for the werre at alle rightes.
And sikerly, ther trowed many a man
That never, sithen that the world bigan,
As for to speke of knighthod of hir hond,
As fer as God hath maked see or lond,
Nas, of so fewe, so noble a companye.
For every wight that lovede chivalrye,
And wolde, his thankes, han a passant name,
Hath preyed that he mighte ben of that game ;   1250
And wel was him, that ther-to chosen was.
For if ther fille to-morwe swich a cas,
Ye knowen wel, that every lusty knight,
That loveth paramours, and hath his might,
Were it in Engelond, or elles-where,
They wolde, hir thankes, wilnen to be there.
To fighte for a lady, *benedicite !*
It were a lusty sighte for to see.

And right so ferden they with Palamon.
With him ther wenten knightes many oon ;   1260
Som wol ben armed in an habergeoun,
In a brest-plat and in a light gipoun ;
And somme woln have a peyre plates large ;
And somme woln have a Pruce sheld, or a targe ;

Somme woln ben armed on hir legges weel,
And have an ax, and somme a mace of steel.
Ther nis no newe gyse, that it nas old.
Armed were they, as I have you told,
Everich after his opinioun.
Ther maistow seen coming with Palamoun   1270
Ligurge him-self, the grete king of Trace;
Blak was his berd, and manly was his face.
The cercles of his eyen in his heed,
They gloweden bitwixe yelow and reed;
And lyk a griffon loked he aboute,
With kempe heres on his browes stoute;
His limes grete, his braunes harde and stronge,
His shuldres brode, his armes rounde and longe.
And as the gyse was in his contree,
Ful hye up-on a char of gold stood he,   1280
With foure whyte boles in the trays.
In-stede of cote-armure over his harnays,
With nayles yelwe and brighte as any gold,
He hadde a beres skin, col-blak, for-old.
His longe heer was kembd bihinde his bak,
As any ravenes fether it shoon for-blak:
A wrethe of gold arm-greet, of huge wighte,
Upon his heed, set ful of stones brighte,
Of fyne rubies and of dyamaunts.
Aboute his char ther wenten whyte alaunts,   1290
Twenty and mo, as grete as any steer,
To hunten at the leoun or the deer,
And folwed him, with mosel faste y-bounde,
Colers of gold, and torets fyled rounde.
An hundred lordes hadde he in his route
Armed ful wel, with hertes sterne and stoute.
    With Arcita, in stories as men finde,
The grete Emetreus, the king of Inde,
Up-on a stede bay, trapped in steel,
Covered in cloth of gold diapred weel,   1300
Cam ryding lyk the god of armes, Mars.
His cote-armure was of cloth of Tars,
Couched with perles whyte and rounde and grete.
His sadel was of brend gold newe y-bete;
A mantelet upon his shuldre hanginge
Bret-ful of rubies rede, as fyr sparklinge.
His crispe heer lyk ringes was y-ronne,
And that was yelow, and glitered as the sonne.
His nose was heigh, his eyen bright citryn,
His lippes rounde, his colour was sangwyn,   1310
A fewe fraknes in his face y-spreynd,
Betwixen yelow and somdel blak y-meynd,
And as a leoun he his loking caste.
Of fyve and twenty yeer his age I caste.

His berd was wel bigonne for to springe;
His voys was as a trompe thunderinge.
Up-on his heed he wered of laurer grene
A gerland fresh and lusty for to sene.
Up-on his hand he bar, for his deduyt,
An egle tame, as eny lilie whyt.   1320
An hundred lordes hadde he with him there,
Al armed, sauf hir heddes, in al hir gere,
Ful richely in alle maner thinges.
For trusteth wel, that dukes, erles, kinges,
Were gadered in this noble companye,
For love and for encrees of chivalrye.
Aboute this king ther ran on every part
Ful many a tame leoun and lepart.
And in this wyse thise lordes, alle and some,
Ben on the Sonday to the citee come   1330
Aboute pryme, and in the toun alight.
    This Theseus, this duk, this worthy knight,
Whan he had broght hem in-to his citee,
And inned hem, everich in his degree,
He festeth hem, and dooth so greet labour
To esen hem, and doon hem al honour,
That yet men weneth that no mannes wit
Of noon estat ne coude amenden it.
The minstralcye, the service at the feste,
The grete yiftes to the moste and leste,   1340
The riche array of Theseus paleys,
Ne who sat first ne last up-on the deys,
What ladies fairest been or best daunsinge,
Or which of hem can dauncen best and singe,
Ne who most felingly speketh of love:
What haukes sitten on the perche above,
What houndes liggen on the floor adoun:
Of al this make I now no mencioun;
But al theffect, that thinketh me the beste;
Now comth the poynt, and herkneth if yow leste.   1350
    The Sonday night, er day bigan to springe,
When Palamon the larke herde singe,
Although it nere nat day by houres two,
Yet song the larke, and Palamon also.
With holy herte, and with an heigh corage
He roos, to wenden on his pilgrimage
Un-to the blisful Citherea benigne,
I mene Venus, honurable and digne.
And in hir houre he walketh forth a pas
Un-to the listes, ther hir temple was,   1360
And doun he kneleth, and with humble chere
And herte soor, he seyde as ye shul here.
    'Faireste of faire, o lady myn, Venus,
Doughter to Jove and spouse of Vulcanus,

Thou glader of the mount of Citheroun,
For thilke love thou haddest to Adoun,
Have pitee of my bittre teres smerte,
And tak myn humble preyer at thyn herte.
Allas! I ne have no langage to telle
Theffectes ne the torments of myn helle ;   1370
Myn herte may myne harmes nat biwreye ;
I am so confus, that I can noght seye.
But mercy, lady bright, that knowest weel
My thought, and seest what harmes that I feel,
Considere al this, and rewe up-on my sore,
As wisly as I shal for evermore,
Emforth my might, thy trewe servant be,
And holden werre alwey with chastitee ;
That make I myn avow, so ye me helpe.
I kepe noght of armes for to yelpe,   1380
Ne I ne axe nat to-morwe to have victorie,
Ne renoun in this cas, ne veyne glorie
Of pris of armes blowen up and doun,
But I wolde have fully possessioun
Of Emelye, and dye in thy servyse ;
Find thou the maner how, and in what wyse.
I recche nat, but it may bettre be,
To have victorie of hem, or they of me,
So that I have my lady in myne armes.
For though so be that Mars is god of armes,   1390
Your vertu is so greet in hevene above,
That, if yow list, I shal wel have my love.
Thy temple wol I worshipe evermo,
And on thyn auter, wher I ryde or go,
I wol don sacrifice, and fyres bete.
And if ye wol nat so, my lady swete,
Than preye I thee, to-morwe with a spere
That Arcita me thurgh the herte bere.
Thanne rekke I noght, whan I have lost my lyf,
Though that Arcita winne hir to his wyf.   1400
This is theffect and ende of my preyere,
Yif me my love, thou blisful lady dere.'
   Whan thorisoun was doon of Palamon,
His sacrifice he dide, and that anon
Ful pitously, with alle circumstaunces,
Al telle I noght as now his observaunces.
But atte laste the statue of Venus shook,
And made a signe, wher-by that he took
That his preyere accepted was that day.
For thogh the signe shewed a delay,   1410
Yet wiste he wel that graunted was his bone ;
And with glad herte he wente him hoom ful sone.
   The thridde houre inequal that Palamon
Bigan to Venus temple for to goon,

Up roos the sonne, and up roos Emelye,
And to the temple of Diane gan hye.
Hir maydens, that she thider with hir ladde,
Ful redily with hem the fyr they hadde,
Thencens, the clothes, and the remenant al
That to the sacrifyce longen shal;　　　　　　1420
The hornes fulle of meth, as was the gyse;
Ther lakked noght to doon hir sacrifyse.
Smoking the temple, ful of clothes faire,
This Emelye, with herte debonaire,
Hir body wessh with water of a welle;
But how she dide hir ryte I dar nat telle,
But it be any thing in general;
And yet it were a game to heren al;
To him that meneth wel, it were no charge.
But it is good a man ben at his large.　　　　　1430
Hir brighte heer was kempt, untressed al;
A coroune of a grene ook cerial
Up-on hir heed was set ful fair and mete.
Two fyres on the auter gan she bete,
And dide hir thinges, as men may biholde
In Stace of Thebes, and thise bokes olde.
Whan kindled was the fyr, with pitous chere
Un-to Diane she spak, as ye may here.
'O chaste goddesse of the wodes grene,
To whom bothe hevene and erthe and see is sene,　1440
Quene of the regne of Pluto derk and lowe,
Goddesse of maydens, that myn herte hast knowe
Ful many a yeer, and woost what I desire,
As keep me fro thy vengeaunce and thyn ire,
That Attheon aboughte cruelly.
Chaste goddesse, wel wostow that I
Desire to been a mayden al my lyf,
Ne never wol I be no love ne wyf.
I am, thou woost, yet of thy companye,
A mayde, and love hunting and venerye,　　　　1450
And for to walken in the wodes wilde,
And noght to been a wyf, and be with childe.
Noght wol I knowe companye of man.
Now help me, lady, sith ye may and can,
For tho thre formes that thou hast in thee.
And Palamon, that hath swich love to me,
And eek Arcite, that loveth me so sore,
This grace I preye thee with-oute more,
As sende love and pees bitwixe hem two;
And fro me turne awey hir hertes so,　　　　　1460
That al hir hote love, and hir desyr,
And al hir bisy torment, and hir fyr
Be queynt, or turned in another place;
And if so be thou wolt not do me grace,

Or if my destinee be shapen so,
That I shal nedes have oon of hem two,
As sende me him that most desireth me.
Bihold, goddesse of clene chastitee,
The bittre teres that on my chekes falle.
Sin thou are mayde, and keper of us alle, 1470
My maydenhede thou kepe and wel conserve,
And whyl I live a mayde, I wol thee serve.'
  The fyres brenne up-on the auter clere,
Whyl Emelye was thus in hir preyere ;
But sodeinly she saugh a sighte queynte,
For right anon oon of the fyres queynte,
And quiked agayn, and after that anon
That other fyr was queynt, and al agon ;
And as it queynte, it made a whistelinge,
As doon thise wete brondes in hir brenninge, 1480
And at the brondes ende out-ran anoon
As it were blody dropes many oon ;
For which so sore agast was Emelye,
That she was wel ny mad, and gan to crye,
For she ne wiste what it signifyed ;
But only for the fere thus hath she cryed,
And weep, that it was pitee for to here.
And ther-with-al Diane gan appere,
With bowe in hond, right as an hunteresse,
And seyde : ' Doghter, stint thyn hevinesse. 1490
Among the goddes hye it is affermed,
And by eterne word write and confermed,
Thou shalt ben wedded un-to oon of tho
That han for thee so muchel care and wo ;
But un-to which of hem I may nat telle.
Farwel, for I ne may no lenger dwelle.
The fyres which that on myn auter brenne
Shul thee declaren, er that thou go henne,
Thyn aventure of love, as in this cas.'
And with that word, the arwes in the cas 1500
Of the goddesse clateren faste and ringe,
And forth she wente, and made a vanisshinge ;
For which this Emelye astoned was,
And seyde, ' What amounteth this, allas !
I putte me in thy proteccioun,
Diane, and in thy disposicioun.'
And hoom she gooth anon the nexte weye.
This is theffect, ther is namore to seye.
  The nexte houre of Mars folwinge this,
Arcite un-to the temple walked is 1510
Of fierse Mars, to doon his sacrifyse,
With alle the rytes of his payen wyse.
With pitous herte and heigh devocioun,
Right thus to Mars he seyde his orisoun :

'O stronge god, that in the regnes colde
Of Trace honoured art, and lord y-holde,
And hast in every regne and every lond
Of armes al the brydel in thyn hond,
And hem fortunest as thee list devyse,
Accept of me my pitous sacrifyse.   1520
If so be that my youthe may deserve,
And that my might be worthy for to serve
Thy godhede, that I may been oon of thyne,
Than preye I thee to rewe up-on my pyne.
For thilke peyne, and thilke hote fyr,
In which thou whylom brendest for desyr,
Whan that thou usedest the grete beautee
Of fayre yonge fresshe Venus free,
And haddest hir in armes at thy wille,
Al-though thee ones on a tyme misfille   1530
Whan Vulcanus had caught thee in his las,
And fond thee ligging by his wyf, allas!
For thilke sorwe that was in thyn herte,
Have routhe as wel up-on my peynes smerte.
I am yong and unkonning, as thou wost,
And, as I trowe, with love offended most,
That ever was any lyves creature;
For she, that dooth me al this wo endure,
Ne reccheth never wher I sinke or flete.
And wel I woot, er she me mercy hete,   1540
I moot with strengthe winne hir in the place;
And wel I woot, withouten help or grace
Of thee, ne may my strengthe noght availle.
Than help me, lord, to-morwe in my bataille,
For thilke fyr that whylom brente thee,
As wel as thilke fyr now brenneth me;
And do that I to-morwe have victorie.
Myn be the travaille, and thyn be the glorie!
Thy soverein temple wol I most honouren
Of any place, and alwey most labouren   1550
In thy plesaunce and in thy craftes stronge,
And in thy temple I wol my baner honge,
And alle the armes of my companye;
And evere-mo, un-to that day I dye,
Eterne fyr I wol biforn thee finde.
And eek to this avow I wol me binde:
My berd, myn heer that hongeth long adoun,
That never yet ne felte offensioun
Of rasour nor of shere, I wol thee yive,
And ben thy trewe servant whyl I live.   1560
Now lord, have routhe up-on my sorwes sore,
Yif me victorie, I aske thee namore.'
   The preyere stinte of Arcita the stronge,
The ringes on the temple-dore that honge,

And eek the dores, clatereden ful faste,
Of which Arcita som-what him agaste.
The fyres brende up-on the auter brighte,
That it gan al the temple for to lighte ;
And swete smel the ground anon up-yaf,
And Arcita anon his hand up-haf,   1570
And more encens in-to the fyr he caste,
With othere rytes mo ; and atte laste
The statue of Mars bigan his hauberk ringe.
And with that soun he herde a murmuringe
Ful lowe and dim, that sayde thus, ' Victorie :'
For which he yaf to Mars honour and glorie.
And thus with joye, and hope wel to fare,
Arcite anon un-to his inne is fare,
As fayn as fowel is of the brighte sonne.
    And right anon swich stryf ther is bigonne   1580
For thilke graunting, in the hevene above,
Bitwixe Venus, the goddesse of love,
And Mars, the sterne god armipotente,
That Jupiter was bisy it to stente ;
Til that the pale Saturnus the colde,
That knew so manye of aventures olde,
Fond in his olde experience an art,
That he ful sone hath plesed every part.
As sooth is sayd, elde hath greet avantage ;
In elde is bothe wisdom and usage ;   1590
Men may the olde at-renne, and noght at-rede.
Saturne anon, to stinten stryf and drede,
Al be it that it is agayn his kynde,
Of al this stryf he gan remedie fynde.
  ' My dere doghter Venus,' quod Saturne,
' My cours, that hath so wyde for to turne,
Hath more power than wot any man.
Myn is the drenching in the see so wan ;
Myn is the prison in the derke cote ;
Myn is the strangling and hanging by the throte ;   1600
The murmure, and the cherles rebelling,
The groyning, and the pryvee empoysoning :
I do vengeance and pleyn correccioun
Whyl I dwelle in the signe of the leoun.
Myn is the ruine of the hye halles,
The falling of the toures and of the walles
Up-on the mynour or the carpenter.
I slow Sampsoun in shaking the piler ;
And myne be the maladyes colde,
The derke tresons, and the castes olde ;   1610
My loking is the fader of pestilence.
Now weep namore, I shal doon diligence
That Palamon, that is thyn owne knight,
Shal have his lady, as thou hast him hight.

Though Mars shal helpe his knight, yet nathelees
Bitwixe yow ther moot be som tyme pees,
Al be ye noght of o complexioun,
That causeth al day swich divisioun.
I am thin ayel, redy at thy wille;
Weep thou namore, I wol thy lust fulfille.'   1620
  Now wol I stinten of the goddes above,
Of Mars, and of Venus, goddesse of love,
And telle yow, as pleynly as I can,
The grete effect, for which that I bigan.

  EXPLICIT TERCIA PARS. SEQUITUR PARS QUARTA.

  Greet was the feste in Athenes that day,
And eek the lusty seson of that May
Made every wight to been in swich plesaunce,
That al that Monday justen they and daunce,
And spenden it in Venus heigh servyse.
But by the cause that they sholde ryse   1630
Erly, for to seen the grete fight,
Unto hir reste wente they at night.
And on the morwe, whan that day gan springe,
Of hors and harneys noyse and clateringe
Ther was in hostelryes al aboute;
And to the paleys rood ther many a route
Of lordes, up-on stedes and palfreys.
Ther maystow seen devysing of herneys
So uncouth and so riche, and wroght so weel
Of goldsmithrie, of browding, and of steel;   1640
The sheeldes brighte, testers, and trappures;
Gold-hewen helmes, hauberks, cote-armures;
Lordes in paraments on hir courseres,
Knightes of retenue, and eek squyeres
Nailinge the speres, and helmes bokelinge,
Gigginge of sheeldes, with layneres lacinge;
Ther as need is, they weren no-thing ydel;
The fomy stedes on the golden brydel
Gnawinge, and faste the armurers also
With fyle and hamer prikinge to and fro;   1650
Yemen on fote, and communes many oon
With shorte staves, thikke as they may goon;
Pypes, trompes, nakers, clariounes,
That in the bataille blowen blody sounes;
The paleys ful of peples up and doun,
Heer three, ther ten, holding hir questioun,
Divyninge of thise Thebane knightes two.
Somme seyden thus, somme seyde it shal be so;
Somme helden with him with the blake berd,
Somme with the balled, somme with the thikke-herd; 1660
Somme sayde, he loked grim and he wolde fighte;
He hath a sparth of twenty pound of wighte.

Thus was the halle ful of divyninge,
Longe after that the sonne gan to springe.
   The grete Theseus, that of his sleep awaked
With minstralcye and noyse that was maked,
Held yet the chambre of his paleys riche,
Til that the Thebane knightes, bothe y-liche
Honoured, were into the paleys fet.
Duk Theseus was at a window set,   1670
Arrayed right as he were a god in trone.
The peple preesseth thider-ward ful sone
Him for to seen, and doon heigh reverence,
And eek to herkne his hest and his sentence.
   An heraud on a scaffold made an ho,
Til al the noyse of the peple was y-do ;
And whan he saugh the peple of noyse al stille,
Tho showed he the mighty dukes wille.
   ' The lord hath of his heigh discrecioun
Considered, that it were destruccioun   1680
To gentil blood, to fighten in the gyse
Of mortal bataille now in this empryse ;
Wherfore, to shapen that they shul not dye,
He wol his firste purpos modifye.
No man therfor, up peyne of los of lyf,
No maner shot, ne pollax, ne short knyf
Into the listes sende, or thider bringe ;
Ne short swerd for to stoke, with poynt bytinge,
No man ne drawe, ne bere it by his syde.
Ne no man shal un-to his felawe ryde   1690
But o cours, with a sharp y-grounde spere ;
Foyne, if him list, on fote, him-self to were.
And he that is at meschief, shal be take,
And noght slayn, but be broght un-to the stake
That shal ben ordeyned on either syde ;
But thider he shal by force, and ther abyde.
And if so falle, the chieftayn be take
On either syde, or elles slee his make,
No lenger shal the turneyinge laste.
God spede yow ; goth forth, and ley on faste.   1700
With long swerd and with maces fight your fille.
Goth now your wey ; this is the lordes wille.'
   The voys of peple touchede the hevene,
So loude cryden they with mery stevene :
' God save swich a lord, that is so good,
He wilneth no destruccioun of blood ! '
Up goon the trompes and the melodye.
And to the listes rit the companye
By ordinaunce, thurgh-out the citee large,
Hanged with cloth of gold, and nat with sarge.   1710
Ful lyk a lord this noble duk gan ryde,
Thise two Thebanes up-on either syde ;

And after rood the quene, and Emelye,
And after that another companye
Of oon and other, after hir degree.
And thus they passen thurgh-out the citee,
And to the listes come they by tyme.
It nas not of the day yet fully pryme,
Whan set was Theseus ful riche and hye,
Ipolita the quene and Emelye,   1720
And other ladies in degrees aboute.
Un-to the seetes preesseth al the route.
And west-ward, thurgh the gates under Marte,
Arcite, and eek the hundred of his parte,
With baner reed is entred right anon;
And in that selve moment Palamon
Is under Venus, est-ward in the place,
With baner whyt, and hardy chere and face.
In al the world, to seken up and doun,
So even with-outen variacioun,   1730
Ther nere swiche companyes tweye.
For ther nas noon so wys that coude seye,
That any hadde of other avauntage
Of worthinesse, ne of estaat, ne age,
So even were they chosen, for to gesse.
And in two renges faire they hem dresse.
Whan that hir names rad were everichoon,
That in hir nombre gyle were ther noon,
Tho were the gates shet, and cryed was loude:
'Do now your devoir, yonge knightes proude!'   1740
  The heraudes lefte hir priking up and doun;
Now ringen trompes loude and clarioun;
Ther is namore to seyn, but west and est
In goon the speres ful sadly in arest;
In goth the sharpe spore in-to the syde.
Ther seen men who can juste, and who can ryde;
Ther shiveren shaftes up-on sheeldes thikke;
He feleth thurgh the herte-spoon the prikke.
Up springen speres twenty foot on highte;
Out goon the swerdes as the silver brighte.   1750
The helmes they to-hewen and to-shrede;
Out brest the blood, with sterne stremes rede.
With mighty maces the bones they to-breste.
He thurgh the thikkeste of the throng gan threste.
Ther stomblen stedes stronge, and doun goth al.
He rolleth under foot as dooth a bal.
He foyneth on his feet with his tronchoun,
And he him hurtleth with his hors adoun.
He thurgh the body is hurt, and sithen y-take,
Maugree his heed, and broght un-to the stake,   1760
As forward was, right ther he moste abyde;
Another lad is on that other syde.

And som tyme dooth hem Theseus to reste,
Hem to refresshe, and drinken if hem leste.
Ful ofte a-day han thise Thebanes two
Togidre y-met, and wroght his felawe wo ;
Unhorsed hath ech other of hem tweye.
Ther nas no tygre in the vale of Galgopheye,
Whan that hir whelp is stole, whan it is lyte,
So cruel on the hunte, as is Arcite   1770
For jelous herte upon this Palamoun :
Ne in Belmarye ther nis so fel leoun,
That hunted is, or for his hunger wood,
Ne of his praye desireth so the blood,
As Palamon to sleen his fo Arcite.
The jelous strokes on hir helmes byte ;
Out renneth blood on bothe hir sydes rede.
  Som tyme an ende ther is of every dede ;
For er the sonne un-to the reste wente,
The stronge king Emetreus gan hente   1780
This Palamon, as he faught with Arcite,
And made his swerd depe in his flesh to byte :
And by the force of twenty is he take
Unyolden, and y-drawe unto the stake.
And in the rescous of this Palamoun
The stronge king Ligurge is born adoun ;
And king Emetreus, for al his strengthe,
Is born out of his sadel a swerdes lengthe,
So hitte him Palamon er he were take ;
But al for noght, he was broght to the stake.   1790
His hardy herte mighte him helpe naught ;
He moste abyde, whan that he was caught
By force, and eek by composicioun.
  Who sorweth now but woful Palamoun,
That moot namore goon agayn to fighte ?
And whan that Theseus had seyn this sighte,
Un-to the folk that foghten thus echoon
He cryde, ' Ho ! namore, for it is doon !
I wol be trewe juge, and no partye.
Arcite of Thebes shal have Emelye,   1800
That by his fortune hath hir faire y-wonne.'
Anon ther is a noyse of peple bigonne
For joye of this, so loude and heigh with-alle,
It semed that the listes sholde falle.
  What can now faire Venus doon above ?
What seith she now ? what dooth this quene of love ?
But wepeth so, for wanting of hir wille,
Til that hir teres in the listes fille ;
She seyde : ' I am ashamed, doutelees.'
Saturnus seyde : ' Doghter, hold thy pees.   1810
Mars hath his wille, his knight hath al his bone,
And, by myn heed, thou shalt ben esed sone.'

The trompes, with the loude minstralcye,
The heraudes, that ful loude yolle and crye,
Been in hir wele for joye of daun Arcite.
But herkneth me, and stinteth now a lyte,
Which a miracle ther bifel anon.

This fierse Arcite hath of his helm y-don,
And on a courser, for to shewe his face,
He priketh endelong the large place,   1820
Loking upward up-on this Emelye ;
And she agayn him caste a freendlich yë,
(For wommen, as to speken in comune,
They folwen al the favour of fortune),
And she was al his chere, as in his herte.
Out of the ground a furie infernal sterte,
From Pluto sent, at requeste of Saturne,
For which his hors for fere gan to turne,
And leep asyde, and foundred as he leep ;
And, er that Arcite may taken keep,   1830
He pighte him on the pomel of his heed,
That in the place he lay as he were deed,
His brest to-brosten with his sadel-bowe.
As blak he lay as any cole or crowe,
So was the blood y-ronnen in his face.
Anon he was y-born out of the place
With herte soor, to Theseus paleys.
Tho was he corven out of his harneys,
And in a bed y-brought ful faire and blyve,
For he was yet in memorie and alyve,   1840
And alway crying after Emelye.

Duk Theseus, with al his companye,
Is comen hoom to Athenes his citee,
With alle blisse and greet solempnitee.
Al be it that this aventure was falle,
He nolde noght disconforten hem alle.
Men seyde eek, that Arcite shal nat dye ;
He shal ben heled of his maladye.
And of another thing they were as fayn,
That of hem alle was ther noon y-slayn,   1850
Al were they sore y-hurt, and namely oon,
That with a spere was thirled his brest-boon.
To othere woundes, and to broken armes,
Some hadden salves, and some hadden charmes ;
Fermacies of herbes, and eek save
They dronken, for they wolde hir limes have.
For which this noble duk, as he wel can,
Conforteth and honoureth every man,
And made revel al the longe night,
Un-to the straunge lordes, as was right.   1860
Ne ther was holden no disconfitinge,
But as a justes or a turneyinge ;

For soothly ther was no disconfiture,
For falling nis nat but an aventure ;
Ne to be lad with fors un-to the stake
Unyolden, and with twenty knightes take,
O persone allone, with-outen mo,
And haried forth by arme, foot, and to,
And eek his stede driven forth with staves,
With footmen, bothe yemen and eek knaves,　　1870
It nas aretted him no vileinye,
Ther may no man clepen it cowardye.
　For which anon duk Theseus leet crye,
To stinten alle rancour and envye,
The gree as wel of o syde as of other,
And either syde y-lyk, as otheres brother ;
And yaf hem yiftes after hir degree,
And fully heeld a feste dayes three ;
And conveyed the kinges worthily
Out of his toun a journee largely.　　1880
And hoom wente every man the righte way.
Ther was namore, but ' far wel, have good day!'
Of this bataille I wol namore endyte,
But speke of Palamon and of Arcite.
　Swelleth the brest of Arcite, and the sore
Encreesseth at his herte more and more.
The clothered blood, for any lechecraft,
Corrupteth, and is in his bouk y-laft,
That neither veyne-blood, ne ventusinge,
Ne drinke of herbes may ben his helpinge.　　1890
The vertu expulsif, or animal,
Fro thilke vertu cleped natural
Ne may the venim voyden, ne expelle.
The pypes of his longes gonne to swelle,
And every lacerte in his brest adoun
Is shent with venim and corrupcioun.
Him gayneth neither, for to gete his lyf,
Vomyt upward, ne dounward laxatif ;
Al is to-brosten thilke regioun,
Nature hath now no dominacioun.　　1900
And certeinly, ther nature wol nat wirche,
Far-wel, phisyk ! go ber the man to chirche !
This al and som, that Arcita mot dye,
For which he sendeth after Emelye,
And Palamon, that was his cosin dere ;
Than seyde he thus, as ye shul after here.
　' Naught may the woful spirit in myn herte
Declare o poynt of alle my sorwes smerte
To yow, my lady, that I love most ;
But I biquethe the service of my gost　　1910
To yow aboven every creature,
Sin that my lyf may no lenger dure.

Allas, the wo! allas, the peynes stronge,
That I for yow have suffred, and so longe!
Allas, the deeth! allas, myn Emelye!
Allas, departing of our companye!
Allas, myn hertes quene! allas, my wyf!
Myn hertes lady, endere of my lyf!
What is this world? what asketh men to have?
Now with his love, now in his colde grave   1920
Allone, with-outen any companye.
Far-wel, my swete fo! myn Emelye!
And softe tak me in your armes tweye,
For love of God, and herkneth what I seye.
    I have heer with my cosin Palamon
Had stryf and rancour, many a day a-gon,
For love of yow, and for my jelousye.
And Jupiter so wis my soule gye,
To speken of a servant proprely,
With alle circumstaunces trewely,   1930
That is to seyn, trouthe, honour, and knighthede,
Wisdom, humblesse, estaat, and heigh kinrede,
Fredom, and al that longeth to that art,
So Jupiter have of my soule part,
As in this world right now ne knowe I non
So worthy to ben loved as Palamon,
That serveth yow, and wol don al his lyf.
And if that ever ye shul been a wyf,
Foryet nat Palamon, the gentil man.'
And with that word his speche faille gan,   1940
For from his feet up to his brest was come
The cold of deeth, that hadde him overcome.
And yet more-over, in his armes two
The vital strengthe is lost, and al ago.
Only the intellect, with-outen more,
That dwelled in his herte syk and sore,
Gan faillen, when the herte felte deeth,
Dusked his eyen two, and failled breeth.
But on his lady yet caste he his yë;
His laste word was, ' mercy, Emelye! '   1950
His spirit chaunged hous, and wente ther,
As I cam never, I can nat tellen wher.
Therfor I stinte, I nam no divinistre;
Of soules finde I nat in this registre,
Ne me ne list thilke opiniouns to telle
Of hem, though that they wryten wher they dwelle.
Arcite is cold, ther Mars his soule gye;
Now wol I speken forth of Emelye.
    Shrighte Emelye, and howleth Palamon,
And Theseus his suster took anon   1960
Swowninge, and bar hir fro the corps away.
What helpeth it to tarien forth the day,

To tellen how she weep, bothe eve and morwe?
For in swich cas wommen have swich sorwe,
Whan that hir housbonds been from hem ago,
That for the more part they sorwen so,
Or elles fallen in swich maladye,
That at the laste certeinly they dye.
Infinite been the sorwes and the teres
Of olde folk, and folk of tendre yeres,   1970
In al the toun, for deeth of this Theban;
For him ther wepeth bothe child and man;
So greet a weping was ther noon, certayn,
Whan Ector was y-broght, al fresh y-slayn,
To Troye; allas! the pitee that was ther,
Cracching of chekes, rending eek of heer.
'Why woldestow be deed,' thise wommen crye,
'And haddest gold y-nough, and Emelye?'
No man mighte gladen Theseus,
Savinge his olde fader Egeus,   1980
That knew this worldes transmutacioun,
As he had seyn it chaungen up and doun,
Joye after wo, and wo after gladnesse:
And shewed hem ensamples and lyknesse.
'Right as ther deyed never man,' quod he,
'That he ne livede in erthe in som degree,
Right so ther livede never man,' he seyde,
'In al this world, that som tyme he ne deyde.
This world nis but a thurghfare ful of wo,
And we ben pilgrimes, passinge to and fro;   1990
Deeth is an ende of every worldly sore.'
And over al this yet seyde he muchel more
To this effect, ful wysly to enhorte
The peple, that they sholde hem reconforte.
Duk Theseus, with al his bisy cure,
Caste now wher that the sepulture
Of good Arcite may best y-maked be,
And eek most honurable in his degree.
And at the laste he took conclusioun,
That ther as first Arcite and Palamoun   2000
Hadden for love the bataille hem bitwene,
That in that selve grove, swote and grene,
Ther as he hadde his amorous desires,
His compleynt, and for love his hote fires,
He wolde make a fyr, in which thoffice
Funeral he mighte al accomplice;
And leet comaunde anon to hakke and hewe
The okes olde, and leye hem on a rewe
In colpons wel arrayed for to brenne;
His officers with swifte feet they renne   2010
And ryde anon at his comaundement.
And after this, Theseus hath y-sent

After a bere, and it al over-spradde
With cloth of gold, the richest that he hadde.
And of the same suyte he cladde Arcite;
Upon his hondes hadde he gloves whyte;
Eek on his heed a croune of laurer grene,
And in his hond a swerd ful bright and kene.
He leyde him, bare the visage, on the bere,
Therwith he weep that pitee was to here.   2020
And for the peple sholde seen him alle,
Whan it was day, he broghte him to the halle,
That roreth of the crying and the soun.
    Tho cam this woful Theban Palamoun,
With flotery berd, and ruggy asshy heres,
In clothes blake, y-dropped al with teres;
And, passing othere of weping, Emelye,
The rewfulleste of al the companye.
In as muche as the service sholde be
The more noble and riche in his degree,   2030
Duk Theseus leet forth three stedes bringe,
That trapped were in steel al gliteringe,
And covered with the armes of daun Arcite.
Up-on thise stedes, that weren grete and whyte,
Ther seten folk, of which oon bar his sheeld,
Another his spere up in his hondes heeld;
The thridde bar with him his bowe Turkeys,
Of brend gold was the cas, and eek the harneys;
And riden forth a pas with sorweful chere
Toward the grove, as ye shul after here.   2040
The nobleste of the Grekes that ther were
Upon hir shuldres carieden the bere,
With slakke pas, and eyen rede and wete,
Thurgh-out the citee, by the maister-strete,
That sprad was al with blak, and wonder hye
Right of the same is al the strete y-wrye.
Up-on the right hond wente old Egeus,
And on that other syde duk Theseus,
With vessels in hir hand of gold ful fyn,
Al ful of hony, milk, and blood, and wyn;   2050
Eek Palamon, with ful greet companye;
And after that cam woful Emelye,
With fyr in honde, as was that tyme the gyse,
To do thoffice of funeral servyse.
    Heigh labour, and ful greet apparaillinge
Was at the service and the fyr-makinge,
That with his grene top the heven raughte,
And twenty fadme of brede the armes straughte;
This is to seyn, the bowes were so brode.
Of stree first ther was leyd ful many a lode.   2060
But how the fyr was maked up on highte,
And eek the names how the treës highte,

As ook, firre, birch, asp, alder, holm, popler,
Wilow, elm, plane, ash, box, chasteyn, lind, laurer,
Mapul, thorn, beech, hasel, ew, whippeltree,
How they weren feld, shal nat be told for me ;
Ne how the goddes ronnen up and doun,
Disherited of hir habitacioun,
In which they woneden in reste and pees,
Nymphes, Faunes, and Amadrides ;   2070
Ne how the bestes and the briddes alle
Fledden for fere, whan the wode was falle ;
Ne how the ground agast was of the light,
That was nat wont to seen the sonne bright ;
Ne how the fyr was couched first with stree,
And than with drye stokkes cloven a three,
And than with grene wode and spycerye,
And than with cloth of gold and with perrye,
And gerlandes hanging with ful many a flour,
The mirre, thencens, with al so greet odour ;   2080
Ne how Arcite lay among al this,
Ne what richesse aboute his body is ;
Ne how that Emelye, as was the gyse,
Putte in the fyr of funeral servyse ;
Ne how she swowned whan men made the fyr,
Ne what she spak, ne what was hir desyr ;
Ne what jeweles men in the fyr tho caste,
Whan that the fyr was greet and brente faste ;
Ne how som caste hir sheeld, and som hir spere,
And of hir vestiments, whiche that they were,   2090
And cuppes ful of wyn, and milk, and blood,
Into the fyr, that brente as it were wood ;
Ne how the Grekes with an huge route
Thryës riden al the fyr aboute
Up-on the left hand, with a loud shoutinge,
And thryës with hir speres clateringe ;
And thryës how the ladies gonne crye ;
Ne how that lad was hom-ward Emelye ;
Ne how Arcite is brent to asshen colde ;
Ne how that liche-wake was y-holde   2100
Al thilke night, ne how the Grekes pleye
The wake-pleyes, ne kepe I nat to seye ;
Who wrastleth best naked, with oille enoynt,
Ne who that bar him best, in no disioynt.
I wol nat tellen eek how that they goon
Hoom til Athenes, whan the pley is doon ;
But shortly to the poynt than wol I wende,
And maken of my longe tale an ende.
   By processe and by lengthe of certeyn yeres
Al stinted is the moorning and the teres   2110
Of Grekes, by oon general assent.
Than semed me ther was a parlement

At Athenes, up-on certeyn poynts and cas ;
Among the whiche poynts y-spoken was
To have with certeyn contrees alliaunce,
And have fully of Thebans obeisaunce.
For which this noble Theseus anon
Leet senden after gentil Palamon,
Unwist of him what was the cause and why ;
But in his blake clothes sorwefully   2120
He cam at his comaundement in hye.
Tho sente Theseus for Emelye.
Whan they were set, and hust was al the place,
And Theseus abiden hadde a space
Er any word cam from his wyse brest,
His eyen sette he ther as was his lest,
And with a sad visage he syked stille,
And after that right thus he seyde his wille.
' The firste moevere of the cause above,
Whan he first made the faire cheyne of love,   2130
Greet was theffect, and heigh was his entente ;
Wel wiste he why, and what ther-of he mente ;
For with that faire cheyne of love he bond
The fyr, the eyr, the water, and the lond
In certeyn boundes, that they may nat flee ;
That same prince and that moevere,' quod he,
' Hath stablissed, in this wrecched world adoun,
Certeyne dayes and duracioun
To al that is engendred in this place,
Over the whiche day they may nat pace,   2140
Al mowe they yet tho dayes wel abregge ;
Ther needeth non auctoritee allegge,
For it is preved by experience,
But that me list declaren my sentence.
Than may men by this ordre wel discerne,
That thilke moevere stable is and eterne.
Wel may men knowe, but it be a fool,
That every part deryveth from his hool.
For nature hath nat take his beginning
Of no partye ne cantel of a thing,   2150
But of a thing that parfit is and stable,
Descending so, til it be corrumpable.
And therfore, of his wyse purveyaunce,
He hath so wel biset his ordinaunce,
That speces of thinges and progressiouns
Shullen enduren by successiouns,
And nat eterne be, with-oute lye :
This maistow understonde and seen at eye.
  Lo the ook, that hath so long a norisshinge
From tyme that it first biginneth springe,   2160
And hath so long a lyf, as we may see,
Yet at the laste wasted is the tree.

Considereth eek, how that the harde stoon
Under our feet, on which we trede and goon,
Yit wasteth it, as it lyth by the weye.
The brode river somtyme wexeth dreye.
The grete tounes see we wane and wende.
Than may ye see that al this thing hath ende.
  Of man and womman seen we wel also,
That nedeth, in oon of thise termes two,   2170
This is to seyn, in youthe or elles age,
He moot ben deed, the king as shal a page;
Som in his bed, som in the depe see,
Som in the large feeld, as men may se;
Ther helpeth noght, al goth that ilke weye.
Thanne may I seyn that al this thing moot deye.
What maketh this but Jupiter the king?
The which is prince and cause of alle thing,
Converting al un-to his propre welle,
From which it is deryved, sooth to telle.   2180
And here-agayns no creature on lyve
Of no degree availleth for to stryve.
  Thanne is it wisdom, as it thinketh me,
To maken vertu of necessitee,
And take it wel, that we may nat eschue,
And namely that to us alle is due.
And who-so gruccheth ought, he dooth folye,
And rebel is to him that al may gye.
And certeinly a man hath most honour
To dyen in his excellence and flour,   2190
Whan he is siker of his gode name;
Than hath he doon his freend, ne him, no shame.
And gladder oghte his freend ben of his deeth,
Whan with honour up-yolden is his breeth,
Than whan his name apalled is for age;
For al forgeten is his vasselage.
Than is it best, as for a worthy fame,
To dyen whan that he is best of name.
The contrarie of al this is wilfulnesse.
Why grucchen we? why have we hevinesse,   2200
That good Arcite, of chivalrye flour
Departed is, with duetee and honour,
Out of this foule prison of this lyf?
Why grucchen heer his cosin and his wyf
Of his wel-fare that loved hem so weel?
Can he hem thank? nay, God wot, never a deel,
That bothe his soule and eek hem-self offende,
And yet they mowe hir lustes nat amende.
  What may I conclude of this longe serie,
But, after wo, I rede us to be merie,   2210
And thanken Jupiter of al his grace?
And, er that we departen from this place,

I rede that we make, of sorwes two,
O parfyt joye, lasting ever-mo ;
And loketh now, wher most sorwe is her-inne,
Ther wol we first amenden and biginne.
    Suster,' quod he, ' this is my fulle assent,
With al thavys heer of my parlement,
That gentil Palamon, your owne knight,
That serveth yow with wille, herte, and might,   2220
And ever hath doon, sin that ye first him knewe,
That ye shul, of your grace, up-on him rewe,
And taken him for housbonde and for lord :
Leen me your hond, for this is our acord.
Lat see now of your wommanly pitee.
He is a kinges brother sone, pardee ;
And, though he were a povre bacheler,
Sin he hath served yow so many a yeer,
And had for yow so greet adversitee,
It moste been considered, leveth me ;   2230
For gentil mercy oghte to passen right.'
    Than seyde he thus to Palamon ful right ;
' I trowe ther nedeth litel sermoning
To make yow assente to this thing.
Com neer, and tak your lady by the hond.'
Bitwixen hem was maad anon the bond,
That highte matrimoine or mariage,
By al the counseil and the baronage.
And thus with alle blisse and melodye
Hath Palamon y-wedded Emelye.   2240
And God, that al this wyde world hath wroght,
Sende him his love, that hath it dere a-boght.
For now is Palamon in alle wele,
Living in blisse, in richesse, and in hele ;
And Emelye him loveth so tendrely,
And he hir serveth al-so gentilly,
That never was ther no word hem bitwene
Of jelousye, or any other tene.
Thus endeth Palamon and Emelye ;
And God save al this faire companye !—Amen.   2250

THE NONNE PREESTES TALE

OF THE COK AND HEN, CHAUNTECLEER AND PERTELOTE.

A POVRE widwe, somdel stope in age,
Was whylom dwelling in a narwe cotage,
Bisyde a grove, stonding in a dale.
This widwe, of which I telle yow my tale,
Sin thilke day that she was last a wyf,
In pacience ladde a ful simple lyf,
For litel was hir catel and hir rente ;
By housbondrye, of such as God hir sente,
She fond hir-self, and eek hir doghtren two.
Three large sowes hadde she, and namo,   10
Three kyn, and eek a sheep that highte Malle.
Ful sooty was hir bour, and eek hir halle,
In which she eet ful many a sclendre meel.
Of poynaunt sauce hir neded never a deel.
No deyntee morsel passed thurgh hir throte ;
Hir dyete was accordant to hir cote.
Repleccioun ne made hir never syk ;
Attempree dyete was al hir phisyk,
And exercyse, and hertes suffisaunce.
The goute lette hir no-thing for to daunce,   20
Napoplexye shente nat hir heed ;
No wyn ne drank she, neither whyt ne reed ;
Hir bord was served most with whyt and blak,
Milk and broun breed, in which she fond no lak,
Seynd bacoun, and somtyme an ey or tweye,
For she was as it were a maner deye.
A yerd she hadde, enclosed al aboute
With stikkes, and a drye dich with-oute,
In which she hadde a cok, hight Chauntecleer,
In al the land of crowing nas his peer.   30
His vois was merier than the mery orgon
On messe-dayes that in the chirche gon ;
Wel sikerer was his crowing in his logge,
Than is a clokke, or an abbey orlogge.
By nature knew he ech ascencioun
Of equinoxial in thilke toun ;
For whan degrees fiftene were ascended,
Thanne crew he, that it mighte nat ben amended.
His comb was redder than the fyn coral,
And batailed, as it were a castel-wal.   40
His bile was blak, and as the jeet it shoon ;
Lyk asur were his legges, and his toon ;

His nayles whytter than the lilie flour,
And lyk the burned gold was his colour.
This gentil cok hadde in his governaunce
Sevene hennes, for to doon al his plesaunce,
Whiche were his sustres and his paramours,
And wonder lyk to him, as of colours.
Of whiche the faireste hewed on hir throte
Was cleped faire damoysele Pertelote.   50
Curteys she was, discreet, and debonaire,
And compaignable, and bar hir-self so faire,
Sin thilke day that she was seven night old,
That trewely she hath the herte in hold
Of Chauntecleer loken in every lith ;
He loved hir so, that wel was him therwith.
But such a joye was it to here hem singe,
Whan that the brighte sonne gan to springe,
In swete accord, ' my lief is faren in londe.'
For thilke tyme, as I have understonde,   60
Bestes and briddes coude speke and singe.

And so bifel, that in a daweninge,
As Chauntecleer among his wyves alle
Sat on his perche, that was in the halle,
And next him sat this faire Pertelote,
This Chauntecleer gan gronen in his throte,
As man that in his dreem is drecched sore.
And whan that Pertelote thus herde him rore,
She was agast, and seyde, ' O herte dere,
What eyleth yow, to grone in this manere ?   70
Ye been a verray sleper, fy for shame ! '
And he answerde and seyde thus, ' madame,
I pray yow, that ye take it nat a-grief :
By god, me mette I was in swich meschief
Right now, that yet myn herte is sore afright.
Now god,' quod he, ' my swevene recche aright,
And keep my body out of foul prisoun !
Me mette, how that I romed up and doun
Withinne our yerde, wher-as I saugh a beste,
Was lyk an hound, and wolde han maad areste   80
Upon my body, and wolde han had me deed.
His colour was bitwixe yelwe and reed ;
And tipped was his tail, and bothe his eres,
With blak, unlyk the remenant of his heres ;
His snowte smal, with glowinge eyen tweye.
Yet of his look for fere almost I deye ;
This caused me my groning, doutelees.'
  ' Avoy !' quod she, ' fy on yow, hertelees !
Allas !' quod she, ' for, by that god above,
Now han ye lost myn herte and al my love ;   90
I can nat love a coward, by my feith.
For certes, what so any womman seith,

We alle desyren, if it mighte be,
To han housbondes hardy, wyse, and free,
And secree, and no nigard, ne no fool,
Ne him that is agast of every tool,
Ne noon avauntour, by that god above!
How dorste ye seyn for shame unto your love,
That any thing mighte make yow aferd ?
Have ye no mannes herte, and han a berd ?   100
Allas! and conne ye been agast of swevenis ?
No-thing, god wot, but vanitee, in sweven is.
Swevenes engendren of replecciouns,
And ofte of fume, and of complecciouns,
Whan humours been to habundant in a wight.
Certes this dreem, which ye han met to-night,
Cometh of the grete superfluitee
Of youre rede *colera*, pardee,
Which causeth folk to dreden in here dremes
Of arwes, and of fyr with rede lemes,   110
Of grete bestes, that they wol hem byte,
Of contek, and of whelpes grete and lyte ;
Right as the humour of malencolye
Causeth ful many a man, in sleep, to crye,
For fere of blake beres, or boles blake,
Or elles, blake develes wole hem take.
Of othere humours coude I telle also,
That werken many a man in sleep ful wo ;
But I wol passe as lightly as I can.
   Lo Catoun, which that was so wys a man,   120
Seyde he nat thus, ne do no fors of dremes ?
Now, sire,' quod she, ' whan we flee fro the bemes,
For Goddes love, as tak som laxatyf ;
Up peril of my soule, and of my lyf,
I counseille yow the beste, I wol nat lye,
That bothe of colere and of malencolye
Ye purge yow ; and for ye shul nat tarie,
Though in this toun is noon apotecarie,
I shal my-self to herbes techen yow,
That shul ben for your hele, and for your prow ;   130
And in our yerd tho herbes shal I finde,
The whiche han of hir propretee, by kinde,
To purgen yow binethe, and eek above.
Forget not this, for goddes owene love !
Ye been ful colerik of compleccioun.
Ware the sonne in his ascencioun
Ne fynde yow nat repleet of humours hote ;
And if it do, I dar wel leye a grote,
That ye shul have a fevere terciane,
Or an agu, that may be youre bane.   140
A day or two ye shul have digestyves
Of wormes, er ye take your laxatyves,

Of lauriol, centaure, and fumetere,
Or elles of ellebor, that groweth there,
Of catapuce, or of gaytres beryis,
Of erbe yve, growing in our yerd, that mery is :
Pekke hem up right as they growe, and ete hem in.
Be mery, housbond, for your fader kin !
Dredeth no dreem ; I can say yow na-more.'
  'Madame,' quod he, ' *graunt mercy* of your lore. 150
But nathelees, as touching daun Catoun,
That hath of wisdom such a greet renoun,
Though that he bad no dremes for to drede,
By god, men may in olde bokes rede
Of many a man, more of auctoritee
Than ever Catoun was, so mote I thee,
Than al the revers seyn of his sentence,
And han wel founden by experience,
That dremes ben significaciouns,
As wel of joye as tribulaciouns   160
That folk enduren in this lyf present.
Ther nedeth make of this noon argument ;
The verray preve sheweth it in dede.
  Oon of the gretteste auctours that men rede
Seith thus, that whylom two felawes wente
On pilgrimage, in a ful good entente ;
And happed so, thay come into a toun,
Wher-as ther was swich congregacioun
Of peple, and eek so streit of herbergage,
That they ne founde as muche as o cotage,   170
In which they bothe mighte y-logged be.
Wherfor thay mosten, of necessitee,
As for that night, departen compaignye ;
And ech of hem goth to his hostelrye,
And took his logging as it wolde falle.
That oon of hem was logged in a stalle,
Fer in a yerd, with oxen of the plough ;
That other man was logged wel y-nough,
As was his aventure, or his fortune,
That us governeth alle as in commune.   180
  And so bifel, that, longe er it were day,
This man mette in his bed, ther-as he lay,
How that his felawe gan up-on him calle,
And seyde, "allas ! for in an oxes stalle
This night I shal be mordred ther I lye.
Now help me, dere brother, er I dye ;
In alle haste com to me," he sayde.
This man out of his sleep for fere abrayde ;
But whan that he was wakned of his sleep,
He turned him, and took of this no keep ;   190
Him thoughte his dreem nas but a vanitee.
Thus twyës in his sleping dremed he.

And atte thridde tyme yet his felawe
Cam, as him thoughte, and seide, " I am now slawe ;
Bihold my blody woundes, depe and wyde !
Arys up erly in the morwe-tyde,
And at the west gate of the toun," quod he,
" A carte ful of donge ther shaltow see,
In which my body is hid ful prively ;
Do thilke carte aresten boldely.   200
My gold caused my mordre, sooth to sayn ; "
And tolde him every poynt how he was slayn,
With a ful pitous face, pale of hewe.
And truste wel, his dreem he fond ful trewe ;
For on the morwe, as sone as it was day,
To his felawes in he took the way ;
And whan that he cam to this oxes stalle,
After his felawe he bigan to calle.
    The hostiler answered him anon,
And seyde, " sire, your felawe is agon,   210
As sone as day he wente out of the toun."
This man gan fallen in suspecioun,
Remembring on his dremes that he mette,
And forth he goth, no lenger wolde he lette,
Unto the west gate of the toun, and fond
A dong-carte, as it were to donge lond,
That was arrayed in the same wyse
As ye han herd the dede man devyse ;
And with an hardy herte he gan to crye
Vengeaunce and justice of this felonye :—   220
" My felawe mordred is this same night,
And in this carte he lyth gapinge upright.
I crye out on the ministres," quod he,
" That sholden kepe and reulen this citee ;
Harrow ! allas ! her lyth my felawe slayn ! "
What sholde I more un-to this tale sayn ?
The peple out-sterte, and caste the cart to grounde,
And in the middel of the dong they founde
The dede man, that mordred was al newe.
    O blisful god, that art so just and trewe !   230
Lo, how that thou biwreyest mordre alway !
Mordre wol out, that see we day by day.
Mordre is so wlatsom and abhominable
To god, that is so just and resonable,
That he ne wol nat suffre it heled be ;
Though it abyde a yeer, or two, or three,
Mordre wol out, this my conclusioun.
And right anoon, ministres of that toun
Han hent the carter, and so sore him pyned,
And eek the hostiler so sore engyned,   240
That thay biknewe hir wikkednesse anoon,
And were an-hanged by the nekke-boon.

Here may men seen that dremes been to drede.
And certes, in the same book I rede,
Right in the nexte chapitre after this,
(I gabbe nat, so have I joye or blis,)
Two men that wolde han passed over see,
For certeyn cause, in-to a fer contree,
If that the wind ne hadde been contrarie,
That made hem in a citee for to tarie,   250
That stood ful mery upon an haven-syde.
But on a day, agayn the even-tyde,
The wind gan chaunge, and blew right as hem leste.
Jolif and glad they wente un-to hir reste,
And casten hem ful erly for to saille;
But to that oo man fil a greet mervaille.
That oon of hem, in sleping as he lay,
Him mette a wonder dreem, agayn the day;
Him thoughte a man stood by his beddes syde,
And him comaunded, that he sholde abyde,   260
And seyde him thus, "if thou to-morwe wende,
Thou shalt be dreynt; my tale is at an ende."
He wook, and tolde his felawe what he mette,
And preyde him his viage for to lette;
As for that day, he preyde him to abyde.
His felawe, that lay by his beddes syde,
Gan for to laughe, and scorned him ful faste.
"No dreem," quod he, "may so myn herte agaste,
That I wol lette for to do my thinges.
I sette not a straw by thy dreminges,   270
For swevenes been but vanitees and japes.
Men dreme al-day of owles or of apes,
And eke of many a mase therwithal;
Men dreme of thing that nevere was ne shal.
But sith I see that thou wolt heer abyde,
And thus for-sleuthen wilfully thy tyde,
God wot it reweth me; and have good day.'
And thus he took his leve, and wente his way.
But er that he hadde halfe his cours y-seyled,
Noot I nat why, ne what mischaunce it eyled,   280
But casuelly the shippes botme rente,
And ship and man under the water wente
In sighte of othere shippes it byside,
That with hem seyled at the same tyde.
And therfor, faire Pertelote so dere,
By swiche ensamples olde maistow lere,
That no man sholde been to recchelees
Of dremes, for I sey thee, doutelees,
That many a dreem ful sore is for to drede.
Lo, in the lyf of seint Kenelm, I rede,   290
That was Kenulphus sone, the noble king
Of Mercenrike, how Kenelm mette a thing;

A lyte er he was mordred, on a day
His mordre in his avisioun he say.
His norice him expouned every del
His sweven, and bad him for to kepe him wel
For traisoun ; but he nas but seven yeer old,
And therfore litel tale hath he told
Of any dreem, so holy was his herte.
By god, I hadde lever than my sherte   300
That ye had rad his legende, as have I.
Dame Pertelote, I sey yow trewely,
Macrobeus, that writ the avisioun
In Affrike of the worthy Cipioun,
Affermeth dremes, and seith that they been
Warning of thinges that men after seen.
    And forther-more, I pray yow loketh wel
In the olde testament, of Daniel,
If he held dremes any vanitee.
Reed eek of Joseph, and ther shul ye see   310
Wher dremes ben somtyme (I sey nat alle)
Warning of thinges that shul after falle.
Loke of Egipt the king, daun Pharao,
His bakere and his boteler also,
Wher they ne felte noon effect in dremes.
Who-so wol seken actes of sondry remes,
May rede of dremes many a wonder thing.
    Lo Cresus, which that was of Lyde king,
Mette he nat that he sat upon a tree,
Which signified he sholde anhanged be ?   320
Lo heer Andromacha, Ectores wyf,
That day that Ector sholde lese his lyf,
She dremed on the same night biforn,
How that the lyf of Ector sholde be lorn,
If thilke day he wente in-to bataille ;
She warned him, but it mighte nat availle ;
He wente for to fighte nathelees.
But he was slayn anoon of Achilles.
But thilke tale is al to long to telle,
And eek it is ny day, I may nat dwelle.   330
Shortly I seye, as for conclusioun,
That I shal han of this avisioun
Adversitee ; and I seye forther-more,
That I ne telle of laxatyves no store,
For they ben venimous, I woot it wel ;
I hem defye, I love hem never a del.
    Now let us speke of mirthe, and stinte al this ;
Madame Pertelote, so have I blis,
Of o thing god hath sent me large grace ;
For whan I see the beautee of your face,   340
Ye ben so scarlet-reed about your yën,
It maketh al my drede for to dyen ;

For, also siker as *In principio,*
Mulier est hominis confusio ;
Madame, the sentence of this Latin is—
Womman is mannes joye and al his blis.
For whan I fele a-night your softe syde,
Al-be-it that I may nat on you ryde,
For that our perche is maad so narwe, alas !
I am so ful of joye and of solas   350
That I defye bothe sweven and dreem.'
And with that word he fley doun fro the beem,
For it was day, and eek his hennes alle ;
And with a chuk he gan hem for to calle,
For he had founde a corn, lay in the yerd.
Royal he was, he was namore aferd ;
He fethered Pertelote twenty tyme,
And trad as ofte, er that it was pryme.
He loketh as it were a grim leoun ;
And on his toos he rometh up and doun,   360
Him deyned not to sette his foot to grounde.
He chukketh, whan he hath a corn y-founde,
And to him rennen thanne his wyves alle.
Thus royal, as a prince is in his halle,
Leve I this Chauntecleer in his pasture ;
And after wol I telle his aventure.
    Whan that the month in which the world bigan,
That highte March, whan god first maked man,
Was complet, and [y]-passed were also,
Sin March bigan, thritty dayes and two   370
Bifel that Chauntecleer, in al his pryde,
His seven wyves walking by his syde,
Caste up his eyen to the brighte sonne,
That in the signe of Taurus hadde y-ronne
Twenty degrees and oon, and somwhat more ;
And knew by kynde, and by noon other lore,
That it was pryme, and crew with blisful stevene.
' The sonne,' he sayde, ' is clomben up on hevene
Fourty degrees and oon, and more, y-wis.
Madame Pertelote, my worldes blis,   380
Herkneth thise blisful briddes how they singe,
And see the fresshe floures how they springe ;
Ful is myn herte of revel and solas.'
But sodeinly him fil a sorweful cas ;
For ever the latter ende of joye is wo.
God woot that worldly joye is sone ago ;
And if a rethor coude faire endyte,
He in a cronique saufly mighte it wryte,
As for a sovereyn notabilitee.
Now every wys man, lat him herkne me ;   390
This storie is al-so trewe, I undertake,
As is the book of Launcelot de Lake,

That wommen holde in ful gret reverence.
Now wol I torne agayn to my sentence.
　A col-fox, ful of sly iniquitee,
That in the grove hadde woned yeres three,
By heigh imaginacioun forn-cast,
The same night thurgh-out the hegges brast
Into the yerd, ther Chauntecleer the faire
Was wont, and eek his wyves, to repaire;　　　　400
And in a bed of wortes stille he lay,
Til it was passed undern of the day,
Wayting his tyme on Chauntecleer to falle,
As gladly doon thise homicydes alle,
That in awayt liggen to mordre men.
O false mordrer, lurking in thy den!
O newe Scariot, newe Genilon!
False dissimilour, O Greek Sinon,
That broghtest Troye al outrely to sorwe!
O Chauntecleer, acursed be that morwe,　　　　410
That thou into that yerd flough fro the bemes!
Thou were ful wel y-warned by thy dremes,
That thilke day was perilous to thee.
But what that god forwoot mot nedes be,
After the opinioun of certeyn clerkis.
Witnesse on him, that any perfit clerk is,
That in scole is gret altercacioun
In this matere, and greet disputisoun,
And hath ben of an hundred thousand men.
But I ne can not bulte it to the bren,　　　　420
As can the holy doctour Augustyn,
Or Boece, or the bishop Bradwardyn,
Whether that goddes worthy forwiting
Streyneth me nedely for to doon a thing,
(Nedely clepe I simple necessitee);
Or elles, if free choys be graunted me
To do that same thing, or do it noght,
Though god forwoot it, er that it was wroght;
Or if his witing streyneth nevere a del
But by necessitee condicionel.　　　　430
I wol not han to do of swich matere;
My tale is of a cok, as ye may here,
That took his counseil of his wyf, with sorwe,
To walken in the yerd upon that morwe
That he had met the dreem, that I yow tolde.
Wommennes counseils been ful ofte colde;
Wommannes counseil broghte us first to wo,
And made Adam fro paradys to go,
Ther-as he was ful mery, and wel at ese.
But for I noot, to whom it mighte displese,　　　　440
If I counseil of wommen wolde blame,
Passe over, for I seyde it in my game.

Rede auctours, wher they trete of swich matere,
And what thay seyn of wommen ye may here.
Thise been the cokkes wordes, and nat myne;
I can noon harm of no womman divyne.
　　Faire in the sond, to bathe hir merily,
Lyth Pertelote, and alle hir sustres by,
Agayn the sonne; and Chauntecleer so free
Song merier than the mermayde in the see;　　　　450
For Phisiologus seith sikerly,
How that they singen wel and merily.
And so bifel that, as he caste his yë,
Among the wortes, on a boterflye,
He was war of this fox that lay ful lowe.
No-thing ne liste him thanne for to crowe,
But cryde anon, 'cok, cok,' and up he sterte,
As man that was affrayed in his herte.
For naturelly a beest desyreth flee
Fro his contrarie, if he may it see,　　　　　　　460
Though he never erst had seyn it with his yë.
　　This Chauntecleer, whan he gan him espye,
He wolde han fled, but that the fox anon
Seyde, 'Gentil sire, allas! wher wol ye gon?
Be ye affrayed of me that am your freend?
Now certes, I were worse than a feend,
If I to yow wolde harm or vileinye.
I am nat come your counseil for tespye;
But trewely, the cause of my cominge
Was only for to herkne how that ye singe.　　　 470
For trewely ye have as mery a stevene
As eny aungel hath, that is in hevene;
Therwith ye han in musik more felinge
Than hadde Boece, or any that can singe.
My lord your fader (god his soule blesse!)
And eek your moder, of hir gentilesse,
Han in myn hous y-been, to my gret ese;
And certes, sire, ful fayn wolde I yow plese.
But for men speke of singing, I wol saye,
So mote I brouke wel myn eyen tweye,　　　　　480
Save yow, I herde never man so singe,
As dide your fader in the morweninge;
Certes, it was of herte, al that he song.
And for to make his voys the more strong
He wolde so peyne him, that with bothe his yën
He moste winke, so loude he wolde cryen,
And stonden on his tiptoon ther-with-al,
And strecche forth his nekke long and smal.
And eek he was of swich discrecioun,
That ther nas no man in no regioun　　　　　　 490
That him in song or wisdom mighte passe
I have wel rad in daun Burnel the Asse,

Among his vers, how that ther was a cok,
For that a preestes sone yaf him a knok
Upon his leg, whyl he was yong and nyce,
He made him for to lese his benefyce.
But certeyn, ther nis no comparisoun
Bitwix the wisdom and discrecioun
Of youre fader, and of his subtiltee.
Now singeth, sire, for seinte charitee,　　　　　　　　500
Let see, conne ye your fader countrefete ? '
This Chauntecleer his winges gan to bete,
As man that coude his tresoun nat espye,
So was he ravisshed with his flaterye.
　　Allas ! ye lordes, many a fals flatour
Is in your courtes, and many a losengeour,
That plesen yow wel more, by my feith,
Than he that soothfastnesse unto yow seith.
Redeth Ecclesiaste of flaterye ;
Beth war, ye lordes, of hir trecherye.　　　　　　　　510
　　This Chauntecleer stood hye up-on his toos,
Strecching his nekke, and heeld his eyen cloos,
And gan to crowe loude for the nones ;
And daun Russel the fox sterte up at ones,
And by the gargat hente Chauntecleer,
And on his bak toward the wode him beer,
For yet ne was ther no man that him sewed.
O destinee, that mayst nat been eschewed !
Allas, that Chauntecleer fleigh fro the bemes !
Allas, his wyf ne roghte nat of dremes !　　　　　　　520
And on a Friday fil al this meschaunce.
O Venus, that art goddesse of plesaunce,
Sin that thy servant was this Chauntecleer,
And in thy service dide al his poweer,
More for delyt, than world to multiplye,
Why woldestow suffre him on thy day to dye ?
O Gaufred, dere mayster soverayn,
That, whan thy worthy king Richard was slayn
With shot, compleynedest his deth so sore,
Why ne hadde I now thy sentence and thy lore,　　530
The Friday for to chide, as diden ye ?
(For on a Friday soothly slayn was he.)
Than wolde I shewe yow how that I coude pleyne
For Chauntecleres drede, and for his peyne.
　　Certes, swich cry ne lamentacioun
Was never of ladies maad, whan Ilioun
Was wonne, and Pirrus with his streite swerd,
Whan he hadde hent king Priam by the berd,
And slayn him (as saith us *Eneydos*),
As maden alle the hennes in the clos,　　　　　　　　540
Whan they had seyn of Chauntecleer the sighte.
But sovereynly dame Pertelote shrighte,

Ful louder than dide Hasdrubales wyf,
Whan that hir housbond hadde lost his lyf,
And that the Romayns hadde brend Cartage;
She was so ful of torment and of rage,
That wilfully into the fyr she sterte,
And brende hir-selven with a stedfast herte.
O woful hennes, right so cryden ye,
As, whan that Nero brende the citee   550
Of Rome, cryden senatoures wyves,
For that hir housbondes losten alle hir lyves;
Withouten gilt this Nero hath hem slayn.
Now wol I torne to my tale agayn :—
  This sely widwe, and eek hir doghtres two,
Herden thise hennes crye and maken wo,
And out at dores sterten they anoon,
And syen the fox toward the grove goon,
And bar upon his bak the cok away;
And cryden, 'Out! harrow! and weylaway!   560
Ha, ha, the fox!' and after him they ran,
And eek with staves many another man;
Ran Colle our dogge, and Talbot, and Gerland,
And Malkin, with a distaf in hir hand;
Ran cow and calf, and eek the verray hogges
So were they fered for berking of the dogges
And shouting of the men and wimmen eke,
They ronne so, hem thoughte hir herte breke.
They yelleden as feendes doon in helle;
The dokes cryden as men wolde hem quelle;   570
The gees for fere flowen over the trees;
Out of the hyve cam the swarm of bees;
So hidous was the noyse, a! *benedicite!*
Certes, he Jakke Straw, and his meynee,
Ne made never shoutes half so shrille,
Whan that they wolden any Fleming kille,
As thilke day was maad upon the fox.
Of bras thay broghten bemes, and of box,
Of horn, of boon, in whiche they blewe and pouped,
And therwithal thay shryked and they houped;   580
It semed as that heven sholde falle.
Now, gode men, I pray yow herkneth alle!
  Lo, how fortune turneth sodeinly
The hope and pryde eek of hir enemy!
This cok, that lay upon the foxes bak,
In al his drede, un-to the fox he spak,
And seyde, 'sire, if that I were as ye,
Yet sholde I seyn (as wis god helpe me),
Turneth agayn, ye proude cherles alle!
A verray pestilence up-on yow falle!   590
Now am I come un-to this wodes syde,
Maugree your heed, the cok shal heer abyde;

I wol him ete in feith, and that anon.'—
The fox answerde, ' in feith, it shal be don,'—
And as he spak that word, al sodeinly
This cok brak from his mouth deliverly,
And heighe up-on a tree he fleigh anon.
And whan the fox saugh that he was y-gon,
' Allas ! ' quod he, ' O Chauntecleer, allas !
I have to yow,' quod he, ' y-doon trespas,   600
In-as-muche as I maked yow aferd,
Whan I yow hente, and broghte out of the yerd ;
But, sire, I dide it in no wikke entente ;
Com doun, and I shal telle yow what I mente.
I shal seye sooth to yow, god help me so.'
' Nay than,' quod he, ' I shrewe us bothe two,
And first I shrewe my-self, bothe blood and bones,
If thou bigyle me ofter than ones.
Thou shalt na-more, thurgh thy flaterye,
Do me to singe and winke with myn yë.   610
For he that winketh, whan he sholde see,
Al wilfully, god lat him never thee ! '
' Nay,' quod the fox, ' but god yeve him meschaunce,
That is so undiscreet of governaunce,
That jangleth whan he sholde holde his pees.'
    Lo, swich it is for to be recchelees,
And necligent, and truste on flaterye.
But ye that holden this tale a folye,
As of a fox, or of a cok and hen,
Taketh the moralitee, good men.   620
For seint Paul seith, that al that writen is,
To our doctryne it is y-write, y-wis.
Taketh the fruyt, and lat the chaf be stille.
    Now, gode god, if that it be thy wille,
As seith my lord, so make us alle good men :
And bringe us to his heighe blisse. Amen.

THOMAS SACKVILLE

A MIROUR FOR MAGISTRATES

THE INDUCTION

THE wrathful winter prochinge on a pace,
With blustring blasts had al ybarde the treen,
And olde Saturnus with his frosty face
With chilling colde had pearst the tender green:
The mantels rent, wherein enwrapped been
The gladsom groves that nowe laye overthrowen,
The tapets torne, and every blome downe blowen.

The soyle that earst so seemely was to seen,
Was all despoyled of her beauties hew:
And soot freshe flowers (wherewith the sommers queen   10
Had clad the earth) now Boreas blastes downe blewe:
And small fowles flocking, in theyr song did rewe
The winters wrath, wherwith eche thing defaste
In woful wise bewayld the sommer past.

Hawthorne had lost his motley lyverye,
The naked twigges were shivering all for colde:
And, dropping downe the teares abundantly,
Eche thing (me thought) with weping eye me tolde
The cruell season, bidding me withholde
My selfe within; for I was gotten out   20
Into the feldes whereas I walkte about.

When lo the nighte with mistie mantels spred
Gan darke the daye, and dim the azure skyes,
And Venus in her message Hermes sped
To bluddy Mars, to wyl him not to ryse,
While she her selfe approcht in speedy wise;
And Virgo hiding her disdaineful brest
With Thetis nowe had layd her downe to rest.

Whiles Scorpio dreading Sagittarius dart,
Whose bowe prest bent in fight, the string had slypt,   30
Downe slyd into the Ocean flud aparte,
The Beare that in the Iryshe seas had dipt
His griesly feete, with spede from thence he whypt:
For Thetis hasting from the Virgines bed,
Pursued the Bear, that ear she came was fled.

And Phaeton nowe neare reaching to his race
With glistering beames, gold-streamynge where they bent,
Was prest to enter in his resting-place.
Erythius that in the cart fyrste went
Had even nowe attaynde his journeyes stent.   40
And fast declining hid away his head,
While Titan coucht him in his purple bed.

And pale Cinthea with her borowed light
Beginning to supply her brothers place,
Was past the Noonesteede syxe degrees in sight
When sparklyng starres amyd the heavens face
With twinkling light shoen on the earth apace,
That whyle they brought about the nightes chare,
The darke had dimmed the daye eare I was ware.

And sorowing I to see the sommer flowers,   50
The lively greene, the lusty leas forlorne,
The sturdy trees so shattered with the showers,
The fieldes so fade that floorisht so beforne,
It taught me wel all earthly thinges be borne
To dye the death, for nought long time may last.
The sommers beauty yeeldes to winters blast.

Then looking upward to the heavens leames
With nightes starres thicke powdred every where,
Which erst so glistened with the golden streames
That chearefull Phebus spred downe from his sphere,   60
Beholding darke oppressing day so neare :
The sodayne sight reduced to my minde,
The sundry chaunges that in earth we fynde.

That musing on this worldly wealth in thought,
Which comes and goes more faster than we see
The flyckering flame that with the fyer is wrought,
My busie minde presented unto me
Such fall of pieres as in this realme had be :
That ofte I wisht some would their woes descryve,
To warne the rest whom fortune left alive.   70

And strayt forth stalking with redoubled pace
For that I sawe the night drewe on so fast,
In blacke all clad, there fell before my face
A piteous wight, whom woe had al forwaste,
Furth from her iyen the cristall teares outbrast,
And syghing sore her handes she wrong and folde,
Tare al her heare, that ruth was to beholde.

Her body small, forwithered and forespent,
As is the stalke that sommers drought opprest,
Her wealked face with woful teares besprent,   80
Her colour pale, and (as it seemd her best)
In woe and playnt reposed was her rest.
And as the stone that droppes of water weares,
So dented were her cheekes with fall of teares.

Her iyes swollen with flowing streames aflote,
Wherewith her lookes throwen up full piteouslye,
Her forceles handes together ofte she smote,
With dolefull shrikes, that eckoed in the skye:
Whose playnt such sighes dyd strayt accompany,
That in my doome was never man did see   90
A wight but half so woe begon as she.

I stoode agast beholding all her plight,
Tweene dread and dolour so distreynd in hart
That while my heares upstarted with the sight,
The teares out streamde for sorowe of her smart:
But when I sawe no ende that could aparte
The deadly dewle, which she so sore dyd make,
With dolefull voice then thus to her I spake.

Unwrap thy woes what ever wight thou be
And stint betime to spill thy self with playnt,   100
Tell what thou art, and whence, for well I see
Thou canst not dure wyth sorowe thus attaynt.
And with that worde of sorowe all forfaynt
She looked up, and prostrate as she laye
With piteous sounde lo thus she gan to saye.

Alas, I wretche whom thus thou seest distreyned
With wasting woes that never shall aslake,
Sorrow I am, in endeles tormentes payned,
Among the furies in the infernall lake:
Where Pluto god of Hel so griesly blacke   110
Doth holde his throne, and *Letheus* deadly taste
Doth rieve remembraunce of eche thing forepast.

Whence come I am, the drery destinie
And luckeles lot for to bemone of those,
Whom Fortune in this maze of miserie
Of wretched chaunce most wofull myrours chose,
That when thou seest how lightly they did lose
Theyr pompe, theyr power, and that they thought most sure,
Thou mayest soone deeme no earthly joye may dure.

Whose rufull voyce no sooner had out brayed   120
Those wofull wordes, where with she sorrowed so,
But out alas she shryght and never stayed,
Fell downe, and all to dasht her selfe for woe.
The colde pale dread my lyms gan overgo,
And I so sorrowed at her sorrowes eft,
That what with griefe and feare my wittes were reft.

I stretcht my self, and strayt my hart revives,
That dread and dolour erst did so appale,
Lyke him that with the fervent fever stryves
When sickenes seekes his castell health to skale: 130
With gathered spirites so forst I fear to avale.
And rearing her with anguishe all fordone,
My spirits returnd, and then I thus begonne.

O Sorrowe, alas, sith Sorrowe is thy name,
And that to thee this drere doth well pertayne,
In vayne it were to seeke to ceas the same:
But as a man hymselfe with sorrowe slayne,
So I alas do comfort thee in payne,
That here in sorrowe art forsonke so depe
That at thy sight I can but sigh and wepe.   140

I had no sooner spoken of a sike
But that the storme so rumbled in her brest,
As Eolus could never roare the like,
And showers downe rayned from her iyen so fast,
That all bedreynt the place, till at the last
Well eased they the dolour of her minde,
As rage of rayne doth swage the stormy wynde.

For furth she paced in her fearfull tale:
Cum, cum, (quod she) and see what I shall shewe,
Cum heare the playning, and the bytter bale   150
Of worthy men, by Fortune overthrowe.
Cum thou and see them rowing all in rowe.
They were but shades that erst in minde thou rolde:
Cum, cum with me, thine eyes shall them beholde.

What could these wordes but make me more agast:
To heare her tell whereon I musde while eare?
So was I mazed therewyth, tyll at the last,
Musing upon her wurdes, and what they were,
All sodaynly well lessoned was my feare:
For to my minde returned howe she telde   160
Both what she was, and where her wun she helde.

Whereby I knewe that she a Goddesse was,
And therewithall resorted to my minde
My thought, that late presented me the glas
Of brittle state, of cares that here we finde,
Of thousand woes to silly men assynde:
And howe she nowe byd me come and beholde,
To see with iye that erst in thought I rolde.

Flat downe I fell, and with al reverence
Adored her, perceyving nowe that she   170
A Goddesse sent by godly providence,
In earthly shape thus showed her selfe to me,
To wayle and rue this worldes uncertayntye:
And while I honourd thus her godheds might,
With playning voyce these wurdes to me she shryght.

I shal the guyde first to the griesly lake,
And thence unto the blisfull place of rest.
Where thou shalt see and heare the playnt they make,
That whilom here bare swinge among the best.
This shalt thou see, but great is the unrest   180
That thou must byde before thou canst attayne
Unto the dreadfull place where these remayne.

And with these wurds as I upraysed stood,
And gan to folowe her that strayght furth paced,
Eare I was ware, into a desert wood
We nowe were cum : where hand in hand imbraced,
She led the way, and through the thicke so traced,
As but I had bene guyded by her might,
It was no waye for any mortall wight.

But loe, while thus amid the desert darke,   190
We passed on with steppes and pace unmete :
A rumbling roar confusde with howle and barke
Of Dogs, shoke all the ground under our feete,
And stroke the din within our eares so deepe,
As halfe distraught unto the ground I fell,
Besought retourne, and not to visite hell.

But she forthwith uplifting me apace
Removed my dread, and with a stedfast minde
Bad me come on, for here was now the place,
The place where we our travayle ende should finde.   200
Wherwith I arose, and to the place assynde
Astoynde I stalke, when strayht we approched nere
The dredfull place, that you wil dread to here.

An hydeous hole al vaste, withouten shape,
Of endles depth, orewhelmde with ragged stone,
Wyth ougly mouth, and grisly jawes doth gape,
And to our sight confounds it selfe in one.
Here entred we, and yeding forth, anone
An horrible lothly lake we might discerne
As blacke as pitche, that cleped is Averne.   210

A deadly gulfe where nought but rubbishe growes,
With fowle blacke swelth in thickned lumpes that lyes,
Which up in the ayer such stinking vapors throwes
That over there, may flye no fowle but dyes,
Choakt with the pestilent savours that aryse.
Hither we cum, whence forth we still dyd pace,
In dreadful feare amid the dreadfull place.

And first within the portche and jawes of Hell
Sate diepe Remorse of conscience, al besprent
With teares : and to her selfe oft would she tell   220
Her wretchednes, and cursing never stent
To sob and sigh : but ever thus lament,
With thoughtful care, as she that all in vayne
Would weare and waste continually in payne.

Her iyes unstedfast rolling here and there,
Whurld on eche place, as place that vengeauns brought,
So was her minde continually in feare,
Tossed and tormented with the tedious thought
Of those detested crymes which she had wrought :
With dreadful cheare and lookes throwen to the skye,   230
Wyshyng for death, and yet she could not dye.

Next sawe we Dread al trembling how he shooke,
With foote uncertayne profered here and there:
Benumde of speache, and with a gastly looke
Searcht every place al pale and dead for feare,
His cap borne up with staring of his heare,
Stoynde and amazde at his owne shade for dreed,
And fearing greater daungers than was nede.

And next within the entry of this lake
Sate fell Revenge gnashing her teeth for yre,   240
Devising meanes howe she may vengeaunce take,
Never in rest tyll she have her desire:
But frets within so farforth with the fyer
Of wreaking flames, that nowe determines she,
To dye by death, or vengde by death to be.

When fell Revenge with bloudy foule pretence
Had showed her selfe as next in order set,
With trembling limmes we softly parted thence,
Tyll in our iyes another sight we met:
When fro my hart a sigh forthwith I fet   250
Rewing alas upon the wofull plight
Of Miserie, that next appered in sight.

His face was leane, and sumdeale pyned away,
And eke his handes consumed to the bone,
But what his body was I can not say,
For on his carkas, rayment had he none
Save cloutes and patches pieced one by one.
With staffe in hand, and skrip on shoulders cast,
His chiefe defence agaynst the winters blast.

His foode for most, was wylde fruytes of the tree,   260
Unles sumtime sum crummes fell to his share:
Which in his wallet, long God wot kept he,
As on the which full dayntlye would he fare.
His drinke the running streame, his cup the bare
Of his palme closed, his bed the hard colde grounde:
To this poore life was Miserie ybound.

Whose wretched state when we had well behelde,
With tender ruth on him and on his feres,
In thoughtful cares, furth then our pace we helde.
And by and by, an other shape apperes   270
Of Greedy care, stil brushing up the breres,
His knuckles knobd, his fleshe deepe dented in,
With tawed handes, and hard ytanned skyn.

The morrowe graye no sooner hath begunne
To spreade his light even peping in our iyes.
When he is up and to his worke yrunne,
But let the nightes blacke mistye mantels rise,
And with fowle darke never so much disguyse
The fayre bright day, yet ceaseth he no whyle,
But hath his candels to prolong his toyle.   280

By him lay Heavy slepe the cosin of death
Flat on the ground, and stil as any stone,
A very corps, save yelding forth a breath.
Small kepe tooke he whom Fortune frowned on,
Or whom she lifted up into the throne
Of high renowne, but as a living death,
So dead alyve, of lyf he drewe the breath.

The bodyes rest, the quyete of the hart,
The travayles ease, the still nightes feer was he:
And of our life in earth the better parte;   290
Rever of sight, and yet in whom we see
Thinges oft that tide, and ofte that never bee;
Without respect esteming equally
King Cresus pompe, and Irus povertie.

And next in order sad Olde age we found,
His beard all hoare, his iyes hollow and blynde,
With drouping chere still poring on the ground,
As on the place where nature him assinde
To rest, when that the sisters had untwynde
His vitall threde, and ended with theyr knyfe   300
The fleting course of fast declining life.

There heard we him with broken and hollow playnt
Rewe with him selfe his ende approching fast,
And all for nought his wretched minde torment,
With swete remembraunce of his pleasures past,
And freshe delites of lusty youth forwaste.
Recounting which, how would he sob and shrike?
And to be yong againe of Jove beseke.

But and the cruell fates so fixed be
That time forepast can not retourne agayne,   310
This one request of Jove yet prayed he:
That in such withered plight, and wretched paine,
As eld (accompanied withe his lothsom trayne)
Had brought on him, all were it woe and griefe,
He myght a while yet linger forth his lief,

And not so soone descend into the pit:
Where death, when he the mortall corps hath slayne,
With retchles hande in grave doth cover it,
Thereafter never to enjoye agayne
The gladsome light, but in the ground ylayne,   320
In depth of darkenes waste and weare to nought,
As he had never into the world been brought.

But who had seene him sobbing, howe he stoode
Unto him selfe, and howe he would bemone
His youth forepast, as though it wrought hym good
To talke of youth, al wer his youth foregone,
He would have musde, and mervayl'd much whereon
This wretched age should life desyre so faine,
And knowes ful wel life doth but length his payne.

Crookebackt he was, toothshaken, and blere iyed,   330
Went on three feete, and sometime crept on fower,
With olde lame bones, that ratled by his syde,
His skalpe all pilde, and he with elde forlore:
His withered fist stil knocking at deathes dore:
Fumbling and driveling as he drawes his breth:
For briefe: the shape and messenger of death.

And fast by him pale Maladie was plaste,
Sore sicke in bed, her colour al forgone,
Bereft of stomake, savor, and of taste,
Ne could she brooke no meat but brothes alone: 340
Her breath corrupt, her kepers every one
Abhorring her, her sickenes past recure,
Detesting phisicke, and all phisickes cure.

But oh the doleful sight that then we see,
We turnde our looke and on the other side
A griesly shape of Famine mought we see,
With greedy lookes, and gaping mouth that cryed,
And roard for meat as she should there have dyed,
Her body thin and bare as any bone,
Wherto was left nought but the case alone.   350

And that alas was knawen on every where,
All full of holes, that I ne mought refrayne
From teares, to se how she her armes could teare
And with her teeth gnashe on the bones in vayne:
When all for nought she fayne would so sustayne
Her starven corps, that rather seemde a shade,
Then any substaunce of a creature made.

Great was her force whom stone wall could not stay,
Her tearyng nayles snatching at all she sawe:
With gaping jawes that by no meanes ymay   360
Be satisfyed from hunger of her mawe,
But eates her selfe as she that hath no lawe:
Gnawyng alas her carkas all in vayne,
Where you may count eche sinow, bone, and vayne.

On her while we thus firmely fixt our iyes,
That bled for ruth of such a drery sight,
Loe sodaynelye she shryght in so huge wyse,
As made hell gates to shyver with the myght,
Wherewith a darte we sawe howe it did lyght
Ryght on her brest, and therewithal pale death   370
Enthryllyng it to reve her of her breath.

And by and by a dum dead corps we sawe,
Heavy and colde, the shape of death aryght,
That dauntes all earthly creatures to his lawe:
Agaynst whose force in vayne it is to fyght.
Ne piers, ne princes, nor no mortall wyght,
Ne townes, ne realmes, cities, ne strongest tower,
But al perforce must yeeld unto his power.

His Dart anon out of the corps he tooke,
And in his hand (a dreadfull sight to see)   380
With great tryumph eftsones the same he shooke,
That most of all my feares affrayed me:
His bodie dight with nought but bones perdye,
The naked shape of man there sawe I playne,
All save the fleshe, the synowe, and the vayne.

Lastly stood Warre in glitteryng armes yclad,
With visage grym, sterne lookes, and blackely hewed:
In his right hand a naked sworde he had,
That to the hiltes was al with blud embrewed:
And in his left (that kinges and kingdomes rewed)   390
Famine and fyer he held, and there wythall
He razed townes, and threwe downe towers and all.

Cities he sakt, and realmes that whilom flowred
In honor, glory, and rule above the best,
He overwhelmde, and all theyr fame devowred,
Consumde, destroyde, wasted, and never ceast,
Tyll he theyr wealth, theyr name, and all opprest.
His face forhewed with woundes, and by his side
There hunge his targe, with gashes depe and wyde.

In mids of which, depaynted there we founde   400
Deadly debate, all ful of snaky heare,
That with a bloudddy fillet was ybound,
Outbrething nought but discord every where.
And round about were portrayd here and there
The hugie hostes, Darius and his power,
His kinges, prynces, his pieres, and all his flower.

Whom great Macedo vanquisht there in fight,
With diepe slaughter, dispoylyng all his pryde,
Pearst through his realmes, and daunted all his might.
Duke Hanniball beheld I there beside,   410
In Cannas field, victor howe he did ride,
And woful Romaynes that in vayne withstoode,
And Consull Paulus covered all in blood.

Yet sawe I more the fight at Trasimene,
And Trebery field, and eke when Hanniball
And worthy Scipio last in armes were seene
Before Carthago gate, to trye for all
The worldes empyre, to whom it should befal:
There sawe I Pompeye, and Cesar clad in armes,
Theyr hostes alyed and al theyr civil harmes: 420

With conquerours hands forbathde in their owne blood,
And Cesar weping over Pompeyes head.
Yet sawe I Scilla and Marius where they stoode,
Theyr great crueltie, and the diepe bludshed
Of frendes: Cyrus I sawe and his host dead,
And howe the Queene with great despyte hath flonge
His head in bloud of them she overcome.

Xerxes the Percian kyng yet sawe I there
With his huge host that dranke the rivers drye,
Dismounted hilles, and made the vales uprere,   430
His hoste and all yet sawe I slayne perdye.
Thebes I sawe all razde howe it dyd lye
In heapes of stones, and Tyrus put to spoyle,
With walles and towers flat evened with the soyle.

But Troy alas (me thought) above them all,
It made myne eyes in very teares consume:
When I beheld the wofull werd befall,
That by the wrathfull wyl of Gods was come:
And Joves unmooved sentence and foredoome
On Priam kyng, and on his towne so bent.   440
I could not lyn, but I must there lament.

And that the more sith destinie was so sterne
As force perforce, there might no force avayle,
But she must fall: and by her fall we learne,
That cities, towres, wealth, world, and al shall quayle.
No manhoode, might, nor nothing mought prevayle,
Al were there prest ful many a prynce and piere
And many a knight that solde his death full deere.

Not worthy Hector wurthyest of them all,
Her hope, her joye, his force is nowe for nought.   450
O Troy, Troy, there is no boote but bale,
The hugie horse within thy walles is brought:
Thy turrets fall, thy knightes that whilom fought
In armes amyd the fyeld, are slayne in bed,
Thy Gods defylde, and all thy honour dead.

The flames upspring, and cruelly they crepe
From wall to roofe, til all to cindres waste,
Some fyer the houses where the wretches slepe,
Sum rushe in here, sum run in there as fast.
In every where or sworde or fyer they taste.   460
The walles are torne, the towers whurld to the ground,
There is no mischiefe but may there be found.

Cassandra yet there sawe I howe they haled
From Pallas house, with spercled tresse undone,
Her wristes fast bound, and with Greeks rout empaled:
And Priam eke in vayne howe he did runne
To armes, whom Pyrrhus with despite hath done
To cruel death, and bathed him in the bayne
Of his sonnes blud before the altare slayne.

But howe can I descryve the doleful sight,   470
That in the shylde so livelike fayer did shyne?
Sith in this world I thinke was never wyght
Could have set furth the halfe, not halfe so fyne.
I can no more but tell howe there is seene
Fayre Ilium fal in burning red gledes downe,
And from the soyle great Troy Neptunus towne.

Herefrom when scarce I could mine iyes withdrawe
That fylde with teares as doeth the spryngyng well,
We passed on so far furth tyl we sawe
Rude Acheron, a lothsome lake to tell 480
That boyles and bubs up swelth as blacke as hell,
Where grisly Charon at theyr fixed tide
Still ferries ghostes unto the farder side.

The aged God no sooner Sorowe spyed,
But hasting strayt unto the banke apace
With hollow call unto the rout he cryed,
To swarve apart, and geve the Goddesse place.
Strayt it was done, when to the shoar we pace,
Where hand in hand as we then linked fast,
Within the boate we are together plaste. 490

And furth we launch ful fraughted to the brinke,
Whan with the unwonted weyght, the rustye keele
Began to cracke as if the same should sinke.
We hoyse up mast and sayle, that in a whyle
We fet the shore, where scarcely we had while
For to arryve, but that we heard anone
A thre sound barke confounded al in one.

We had not long furth past, but that we sawe,
Blacke Cerberus the hydeous hound of hell,
With bristles reard, and with a thre mouthed jawe, 500
Foredinning the ayer with his horrible yel.
Out of the diepe darke cave where he did dwell,
The Goddesse strayt he knewe, and by and by
He peaste and couched, while that we passed by.

Thence cum we to the horrour and the hel,
The large greate kyngdomes, and the dreadful raygne
Of Pluto in his trone where he dyd dwell,
The wyde waste places, and the hugye playne:
The waylinges, shrykes, and sundry sortes of payne,
The syghes, the sobbes, the diepe and deadly groane, 510
Earth, ayer, and all resounding playnt and moane.

Here pewled the babes, and here the maydes unwed,
With folded handes theyr sory chaunce bewayled.
Here wept the gyltles slayne, and lovers dead,
That slewe them selves when nothyng els avayled:
A thousand sortes of sorrowes here that wayled
With sighes and teares, sobs, shrykes, and all yfere,
That (oh alas) it was a hel to heare.

We stayed us strayt, and wyth a ruful feare,
Beheld this heavy sight, while from mine eyes 520
The vapored teares downstilled here and there,
And Sorrow eke in far more woful wyse
Tooke on with playnt, up heaving to the skies
Her wretched handes, that with her crye the rout
Gan all in heapes to swarme us round about.

Lo here (quod Sorowe) Prynces of renowne,
That whilom sat on top of Fortunes wheele
Nowe layed ful lowe, like wretches whurled downe,
Even with one frowne, that stayed but with a smyle,
And nowe behold the thing that thou erewhile,   530
Saw only in thought, and what thou now shalt heare,
Recompt the same to Kesar, King, and Peer.

Then first came Henry duke of Buckingham,
His cloke of blacke all pilde and quite forworne,
Wringing his handes, and Fortune ofte doth blame,
Which of a duke hath made him nowe her skorne.
With gastly lookes as one in maner lorne,
Oft spred his armes, stretcht handes he joynes as fast,
With ruful chere, and vapored eyes upcast.

His cloke he rent, his manly breast he beat,   540
His heare al torne about the place it laye,
My hart so molte to see his griefe so great,
As felingly me thought it dropt awaye:
His iyes they whurled about withouten staye,
With stormy syghes the place dyd so complayne,
As if his hart at eche, had burst in twayne.

Thryse he began to tell his doleful tale,
And thrise the sighes did swalowe up his voyce,
At eche of which he shryked so wythal
As though the heavens rived with the noyse: 550
Tyll at the last recovering his voyce,
Supping the teares that all his brest beraynde,
On cruel Fortune weping thus he playnde.

EDMUND SPENSER

EPITHALAMION

Ye learned sisters which have oftentimes
Beene to me ayding, others to adorne:
Whom ye thought worthy of your gracefull rymes,
That even the greatest did not greatly scorne
To heare theyr names sung in your simple layes,
But joyed in theyr praise;
And when ye list your owne mishaps to mourne,
Which death, or love, or fortunes wreck did rayse,
Your string could soone to sadder tenor turne,
And teach the woods and waters to lament   10
Your dolefull dreriment:
Now lay those sorrowfull complaints aside,
And having all your heads with girlands crownd,
Helpe me mine owne loves prayses to resound,
Ne let the same of any be envide:
So Orpheus did for his owne bride,
So I unto my selfe alone will sing;
The woods shall to me answer and my Eccho ring.

Early before the worlds light-giving lampe,
His golden beame upon the hils doth spred,   20
Having disperst the nights unchearefull dampe,
Doe ye awake, and with fresh lusty-hed,
Go to the bowre of my beloved love,
My truest turtle dove,
Bid her awake; for Hymen is awake,
And long since ready forth his maske to move,
With his bright Tead that flames with many a flake,
And many a bachelor to waite on him,
In theyr fresh garments trim.
Bid her awake therefore and soone her dight,   30
For lo the wished day is come at last,
That shall for al the paynes and sorrowes past,
Pay to her usury of long delight;
And whylest she doth her dight,
Doe ye to her of joy and solace sing,
That all the woods may answer and your eccho ring.

Bring with you all the Nymphes that you can heare
Both of the rivers and the forrests greene:
And of the sea that neighbours to her neare
Al with gay girlands goodly wel beseene.   40

And let them also with them bring in hand,
Another gay girland,
For my fayre love, of lillyes and of roses,
Bound truelove wize with a blew silke riband.
And let them make great store of bridale poses,
And let them eeke bring store of other flowers
To deck the bridale bowers.
And let the ground whereas her foot shall tread,
For feare the stones her tender foot should wrong,
Be strewed with fragrant flowers all along,   50
And diapred lyke the discolored mead.
Which done, doe at her chamber dore awayt,
For she will waken strayt,
The whiles doe ye this song unto her sing,
The woods shall to you answer and your Eccho ring.

Ye Nymphes of Mulla, which with carefull heed
The silver scaly trouts doe tend full well,
And greedy pikes which use therein to feed,
(Those trouts and pikes all others doo excell)
And ye likewise which keepe the rushy lake,   60
Where none doo fishes take,
Bynd up the locks the which hang scatterd light,
And in his waters which your mirror make,
Behold your faces as the christall bright,
That when you come whereas my love doth lie,
No blemish she may spie.
And eke ye lightfoot mayds which keepe the deere,
That on the hoary mountayne use to towre,
And the wylde wolves which seeke them to devoure,
With your steele darts doo chace from comming neer 70
Be also present heere,
To helpe to decke her and to help to sing,
That all the woods may answer and your eccho ring.

Wake now my love, awake; for it is time,
The Rosy Morne long since left Tithones bed,
All ready to her silver coche to clyme,
And Phoebus gins to shew his glorious hed.
Hark how the cheerefull birds do chaunt theyr laies
And carroll of loves praise.
The merry Larke hir mattins sings aloft,   80
The thrush replyes, the Mavis descant playes,
The Ouzell shrills, the Ruddock warbles soft,
So goodly all agree with sweet consent,
To this dayes merriment.
Ah my deere love why doe ye sleepe thus long,
When meeter were that ye should now awake,
T'awayt the comming of your joyous make,
And hearken to the birds lovelearned song,
The deawy leaves among:

For they of joy and pleasance to you sing,   90
That all the woods them answer and theyr eccho ring.

My love is now awake out of her dreame,
And her fayre eyes like stars that dimmed were
With darksome cloud, now shew theyr goodly beams
More bright then Hesperus his head doth rere.
Come now ye damzels, daughters of delight,
Helpe quickly her to dight,
But first come ye fayre houres which were begot
In Joves sweet paradice, of Day and Night,
Which doe the seasons of the yeare allot,   100
And al that ever in this world is fayre
Doe make and still repayre.
And ye three handmayds of the Cyprian Queene,
The which doe still adorne her beauties pride,
Helpe to addorne my beautifullest bride ;
And as ye her array, still throw betweene
Some graces to be seene :
And as ye use to Venus, to her sing,
The whiles the woods shal answer and your eccho ring.

Now is my love all ready forth to come,   110
Let all the virgins therefore well awayt,
And ye fresh boyes that tend upon her groome
Prepare your selves, for he is comming strayt.
Set all your things in seemely good aray
Fit for so joyfull day,
The joyfulst day that ever sunne did see.
Faire Sun, shew forth thy favourable ray,
And let thy life-full heat not fervent be
For feare of burning her sunshyny face,
Her beauty to disgrace.   120
O fayrest Phoebus, father of the Muse,
If ever I did honour thee aright,
Or sing the thing, that mote thy mind delight,
Doe not thy servants simple boone refuse,
But let this day, let this one day be myne,
Let all the rest be thine.
Then I thy soverayne prayses loud wil sing,
That all the woods shal answer and theyr eccho ring.

Harke how the Minstrils gin to shrill aloud
Their merry Musick that resounds from far,   130
The pipe, the tabor, and the trembling Croud,
That well agree withouten breach or jar.
But most of all the Damzels doe delite,
When they their tymbrels smyte,
And thereunto doe daunce and carrol sweet,
That all the sences they doe ravish quite,
The whyles the boyes run up and downe the street,

Crying aloud with strong confused noyce,
As if it were one voyce.
Hymen io Hymen, Hymen they do shout,   140
That even to the heavens theyr shouting shrill
Doth reach, and all the firmament doth fill;
To which the people standing all about,
As in approvance doe thereto applaud
And loud advaunce her laud,
And evermore they Hymen Hymen sing,
That al the woods them answer and theyr eccho ring.

Loe where she comes along with portly pace,
Lyke Phoebe from her chamber of the East,
Arysing forth to run her mighty race,   150
Clad all in white, that seemes a virgin best.
So well it her beseemes that ye would weene
Some angel she had beene.
Her long loose yellow locks lyke golden wyre,
Sprinckled with perle, and perling flowres atweene,
Doe lyke a golden mantle her attyre,
And being crowned with a girland greene,
Seeme lyke some mayden Queene.
Her modest eyes abashed to behold
So many gazers, as on her do stare,   160
Upon the lowly ground affixed are.
Ne dare lift up her countenance too bold,
But blush to heare her prayses sung so loud,
So farre from being proud.
Nathlesse doe ye still loud her prayses sing,
That all the woods may answer and your eccho ring.

Tell me ye merchants daughters, did ye see
So fayre a creature in your towne before?
So sweet, so lovely, and so mild as she,
Adornd with beautyes grace and vertues store,   170
Her goodly eyes lyke Saphyres shining bright,
Her forehead yvory white,
Her cheekes lyke apples which the sun hath rudded,
Her lips lyke cherryes charming men to byte,
Her brest like to a bowle of creame uncrudded,
Her paps lyke lyllies budded,
Her snowie necke lyke to a marble towre,
And all her body like a pallace fayre,
Ascending uppe with many a stately stayre,
To honors seat and chastities sweet bowre.   180
Why stand ye still ye virgins in amaze,
Upon her so to gaze,
Whiles ye forget your former lay to sing,
To which the woods did answer and your eccho ring?

But if ye saw that which no eyes can see,
The inward beauty of her lively spright,

Garnisht with heavenly guifts of high degree,
Much more then would ye wonder at that sight,
And stand astonisht lyke to those which red
Medusaes mazeful hed.   190
There dwels sweet love and constant chastity,
Unspotted fayth and comely womanhood,
Regard of honour and mild modesty,
There vertue raynes as Queene in royal throne,
And giveth lawes alone,
The which the base affections doe obay,
And yeeld theyr services unto her will,
Ne thought of thing uncomely ever may
Thereto approch to tempt her mind to ill.
Had ye once seene these her celestial threasures,   200
And unrevealed pleasures,
Then would ye wonder and her prayses sing,
That al the woods should answer and your echo ring.

Open the temple gates unto my love,
Open them wide that she may enter in,
And all the postes adorne as doth behove,
And all the pillours deck with girlands trim,
For to recyve this Saynt with honour dew,
That commeth in to you.
With trembling steps and humble reverence,   210
She commeth in, before th'almighties vew,
Of her ye virgins learne obedience,
When so ye come into those holy places,
To humble your proud faces:
Bring her up to th'high altar, that she may
The sacred ceremonies there partake,
The which do endlesse matrimony make,
And let the roring Organs loudly play,
The praises of the Lord in lively notes,
The whiles with hollow throates   220
The Choristers the joyous Antheme sing,
That al the woods may answere and their eccho ring.

Behold whiles she before the altar stands
Hearing the holy priest that to her speakes
And blesseth her with his two happy hands,
How the red roses flush up in her cheekes,
And the pure snow with goodly vermill stayne,
Like crimsin dyde in grayne,
That even th'Angels which continually,
About the sacred Altare doe remaine,   230
Forget their service and about her fly,
Ofte peeping in her face that seemes more fayre,
The more they on it stare.
But her sad eyes still fastened on the ground,
Are governed with goodly modesty.

That suffers not one looke to glaunce awry,
Which may let in a little thought unsownd.
Why blush ye Love to give to me your hand,
The pledge of all our band?
Sing ye sweet Angels, Alleluya sing,   240
That all the woods may answere and your eccho ring.

Now al is done; bring home the bride againe,
Bring home the triumph of our victory,
Bring home with you the glory of her gaine,
With joyance bring her and with jollity.
Never had man more joyfull day then this,
Whom heaven would heape with blis.
Make feast therefore now all this live long day,
This day for ever to me holy is,
Poure out the wine without restraint or stay,   250
Poure not by cups, but by the belly full,
Poure out to all that wull,
And sprinkle all the postes and wals with wine,
That they may sweat, and drunken be withall.
Crowne ye God Bacchus with a coronall,
And Hymen also crowne with wreathes of vine,
And let the Graces daunce unto the rest;
For they can doo it best:
The whiles the maydens doe theyr carroll sing,
To which the woods shall answer and theyr eccho ring. 260

Ring ye the bels, ye yong men of the towne,
And leave your wonted labors for this day:
This day is holy; doe ye write it downe,
That ye for ever it remember may.
This day the sunne is in his chiefest hight,
With Barnaby the bright,
From whence declining daily by degrees,
He somewhat loseth of his heat and light,
When once the Crab behind his back he sees.
But for this time it ill ordained was,   270
To chose the longest day in all the yeare,
And shortest night, when longest fitter weare:
Yet never day so long, but late would passe.
Ring ye the bels, to make it weare away,
And bonefiers make all day,
And daunce about them, and about them sing:
That all the woods may answer, and your eccho ring.

Ah! when will this long weary day have end,
And lende me leave to come unto my love?
How slowly do the houres theyr numbers spend?   280
How slowly does sad Time his feathers move?
Hast thee O fayrest Planet to thy home
Within the Westerne fome:
Thy tyred steedes long since have need of rest.
Long though it be, at last I see it gloome,

And the bright evening star with golden creast
Appeare out of the East.
Fayre childe of beauty, glorious lampe of love,
That all the host of heaven in rankes doost lead,
And guydest lovers through the nights sad dread,   290
How chearefully thou lookest from above,
And seemst to laugh atweene thy twinkling light
As joying in the sight
Of these glad many which for joy doe sing,
That all the woods them answer and their echo ring.

Now ceasse ye damsels your delights forepast;
Enough is it, that all the day was youres:
Now day is doen, and night is nighing fast:
Now bring the Bryde into the brydall boures.
The night is come, now soon her disaray   300
And in her bed her lay;
Lay her in lillies and in violets,
And silken courteins over her display,
And odourd sheetes, and Arras coverlets.
Behold how goodly my faire love does ly
In proud humility;
Like unto Maia, when as Jove her tooke,
In Tempe, lying on the flowry gras,
Twixt sleepe and wake, after she weary was,
With bathing in the Acidalian brooke.   310
Now it is night, ye damsels may be gon,
And leave my Love alone,
And leave likewise your former lay to sing:
The woods no more shall answere, nor your echo ring.

Now welcome night, thou night so long expected,
That long daies labour doest at last defray,
And all my cares, which cruell love collected,
Hast sumd in one, and cancelled for aye:
Spread thy broad wing over my Love and me,
That no man may us see,   320
And in thy sable mantle us enwrap,
From feare of perrill and foule horror free.
Let no false treason seeke us to entrap,
Nor any dread disquiet once annoy
The safety of our joy:
But let the night be calme and quietsome,
Without tempestuous storms or sad afray:
Lyke as when Jove with fayre Alcmena lay,
When he begot the great Tirynthian groome:
Or lyke as when he with thy selfe did lie,   330
And begot Majesty.
And let the mayds and yongmen cease to sing:
Ne let the woods them answer, nor theyr eccho ring.

Let no lamenting cryes, nor dolefull teares,
Be heard all night within nor yet without:
Ne let false whispers, breeding hidden feares,
Breake gentle sleepe with misconceived dout.
Let no deluding dreames, nor dreadful sights
Make sudden sad affrights ;
Ne let house fyres, nor lightnings helpelesse harmes,   340
Ne let the Pouke, nor other evill sprights,
Ne let mischivous witches with theyr charmes,
Ne let Hob-Goblins, names whose sence we see not,
Fray us with things that be not.
Let not the shriech Oule, nor the Storke be heard:
Nor the night Raven that still deadly yels,
Nor damned ghosts cald up with mighty spels,
Nor griesly vultures make us once affeard :
Ne let th'unpleasant Quyre of Frogs still croking
Make us to wish theyr choking.   350
Let none of these theyr drery accents sing ;
Ne let the woods them answer, nor theyr eccho ring.

But let stil Silence trew night watches keepe,
That sacred peace may in assurance rayne,
And tymely sleep, when it is tyme to sleepe,
May poure his limbs forth on your pleasant playne,
The whiles an hundred little winged loves,
Like divers fethered doves,
Shall fly and flutter round about your bed,
And in the secret darke, that none reproves,   360
Their prety stealthes shal worke, and snares shal spread,
To filch away sweet snatches of delight,
Conceald through covert night.
Ye sonnes of Venus, play your sports at will,
For greedy pleasure, carelesse of your toyes,
Thinks more upon her paradise of joyes,
Then what ye do, albe it good or ill.
All night therefore attend your merry play,
For it will soone be day :
Now none doth hinder you, that say or sing,   370
Ne will the woods now answer, nor your Eccho ring.

Who is the same, which at my window peepes ?
Or whose is that faire face which shines so bright,
Is it not Cinthia, she that never sleepes,
But walkes about high heaven al the night ?
O fayrest goddesse, do thou not envy
My love with me to spy :
For thou likewise didst love, though now unthought,
And for a fleece of wooll, which privily,
The Latmian shephard once unto thee brought,   380
His pleasures with thee wrought.
Therefore to us be favorable now ;
And sith of wemens labours thou hast charge,

And generation goodly dost enlarge,
Encline thy will t'effect our wishfull vow,
And the chast wombe informe with timely seed,
That may our comfort breed :
Till which we cease our hopefull hap to sing,
Ne let the woods us answere, nor our Eccho ring.

And thou great Juno, which with awful might   390
The lawes of wedlock still dost patronize,
And the religion of the faith first plight
With sacred rites hast taught to solemnize :
And eeke for comfort often called art
Of women in their smart,
Eternally bind thou this lovely band,
And all thy blessings unto us impart.
And thou glad Genius, in whose gentle hand,
The bridale bowre and geniall bed remaine,
Without blemish or staine,   400
And the sweet pleasures of theyr loves delight
With secret ayde doest succour and supply,
Till they bring forth the fruitfull progeny,
Send us the timely fruit of this same night.
And thou fayre Hebe, and thou Hymen free,
Grant that it may so be.
Til which we cease your further prayse to sing,
Ne any woods shal answer, nor your Eccho ring.

And ye high heavens, the temple of the gods,
In which a thousand torches flaming bright   410
Doe burne, that to us wretched earthly clods,
In dreadful darknesse lend desired light ;
And all ye powers which in the same remayne,
More then we men can fayne,
Poure out your blessing on us plentiously,
And happy influence upon us raine,
That we may raise a large posterity,
Which from the earth, which they may long possesse,
With lasting happinesse,
Up to your haughty pallaces may mount,   420
And for the guerdon of theyr glorious merit
May heavenly tabernacles there inherit,
Of blessed Saints for to increase the count.
So let us rest, sweet love, in hope of this,
And cease till then our tymely joyes to sing,
The woods no more us answer, nor our eccho ring.

Song made in lieu of many ornaments,
With which my love should duly have been dect,
Which cutting off through hasty accidents,
Ye would not stay your dew time to expect,   430
But promist both to recompens,
Be unto her a goodly ornament,
And for short time an endlesse moniment.

PROTHALAMION

OR

A SPOUSALL VERSE MADE BY

EDM. SPENSER

IN HONOUR OF THE DOUBLE MARIAGE OF THE TWO HONORABLE
AND VERTUOUS LADIES, THE LADIE ELIZABETH AND THE
LADIE KATHERINE SOMERSET, DAUGHTERS TO THE
RIGHT HONOURABLE THE EARLE OF WORCESTER,
AND ESPOUSED TO THE TWO WORTHIE
GENTLEMEN M. HENRY GILFORD, AND
M. WILLIAM PETER, ESQUYERS.

CALME was the day, and through the trembling ayre,
Sweete breathing *Zephyrus* did softly play
A gentle spirit, that lightly did delay
Hot *Titans* beames, which then did glyster fayre:
When I whom sullein care,
Through discontent of my long fruitlesse stay
In Princes Court, and expectation vayne
Of idle hopes, which still doe fly away,
Like empty shaddowes, did afflict my brayne,
Walkt forth to ease my payne   10
Along the shoare of silver streaming *Themmes*;
Whose rutty Bancke, the which his River hemmes,
Was paynted all with variable flowers,
And all the meades adornd with daintie gemmes,
Fit to decke maydens bowres,
And crowne their Paramours,
Against the Brydale day, which is not long:
  Sweet *Themmes* runne softly, till I end my Song.

There, in a Meadow, by the Rivers side,
A Flocke of *Nymphes* I chaunced to espy,   20
All lovely Daughters of the Flood thereby,
With goodly greenish locks all loose untyde,
As each had bene a Bryde,
And each one had a little wicker basket,
Made of fine twigs entrayled curiously,
In which they gathered flowers to fill their flasket:
And with fine Fingers, cropt full feateously
The tender stalkes on hye.
Of every sort, which in that Meadow grew,
They gathered some, the Violet pallid blew,   30
The little Dazie, that at evening closes,
The virgin Lillie, and the Primrose trew,

With store of vermeil Roses,
To decke their Bridegromes posies,
Against the Brydale day, which was not long:
   Sweete *Themmes* runne softly, till I end my Song.

With that I saw two Swannes of goodly hewe,
Come softly swimming downe along the Lee;
Two fairer Birds I yet did never see:
The snow which doth the top of *Pindus* strew,   40
Did never whiter shew,
Nor *Jove* himselfe when he a Swan would be
For love of *Leda*, whiter did appeare:
Yet *Leda* was they say as white as he,
Yet not so white as these, nor nothing neare;
So purely white they were,
That even the gentle streame, the which them bare,
Seem'd foule to them, and bad his billowes spare
To wet their silken feathers, least they might
Soyle their fayre plumes with water not so fayre,   50
And marre their beauties bright,
That shone as heavens light,
Against their Brydale day, which was not long:
   Sweete *Themmes* runne softly, till I end my Song.

Eftsoones the *Nymphes*, which now had Flowers their fill,
Ran all in haste, to see that silver brood,
As they came floating on the Christal Flood,
Whom when they sawe, they stood amazed still,
Their wondring eyes to fill,
Them seem'd they never saw a sight so fayre,   60
Of Fowles so lovely, that they sure did deeme
Them heavenly borne, or to be that same payre
Which through the Skie draw Venus silver Teeme,
For sure they did not seeme
To be begot of any earthly Seede,
But rather Angels or of Angels breede:
Yet were they bred of Somers-heat they say,
In sweetest Season, when each Flower and weede
The earth did fresh aray,
So fresh they seem'd as day,   70
Even as their Brydale day, which was not long:
   Sweete *Themmes* runne softly till I end my Song.

Then forth they all out of their baskets drew,
Great store of Flowers, the honour of the field,
That to the sense did fragrant odours yeild,
All which upon those goodly Birds they threw,
And all the Waves did strew,
That like old *Peneus* Waters they did seeme,
When downe along by pleasant *Tempes* shore
Scattred with Flowres, through Thessaly they streeme,   80

That they appear through Lillies plenteous store,
Like a Brydes Chamber flore:
Two of those *Nymphes*, meane while, two Garlands bound,
Of freshest Flowres which in that Mead they found,
The which presenting all in trim Array,
Their snowie Foreheads therewithall they crownd,
Whil'st one did sing this Lay,
Prepar'd against that Day,
Against their Brydale day, which was not long:
  Sweete *Themmes* runne softly till I end my Song.   90

Ye gentle Birdes, the worlds faire ornament,
And heavens glorie, whom this happie hower
Doth leade unto your lovers blisfull bower,
Joy may you have and gentle hearts content
Of your loves couplement:
And let faire *Venus*, that is Queene of love,
With her heart-quelling Sonne upon you smile,
Whose smile they say, hath vertue to remove
All Loves dislike, and friendships faultie guile
For ever to assoile.   100
Let endlesse Peace your steadfast hearts accord,
And blessed Plentie wait upon your bord,
And let your bed with pleasures chast abound,
That fruitful issue may to you afford,
Which may your foes confound,
And make your joyes redound,
Upon your Brydale day, which is not long:
  Sweete *Themmes* runne softlie, till I end my Song.

So ended she; and all the rest around
To her redoubled that her undersong,   110
Which said, their bridale daye should not be long.
And gentle Eccho from the neighbour ground,
Their accents did resound.
So forth, those joyous Birdes did passe along,
Adowne the Lee, that to them murmurde low,
As he would speake, but that he lackt a tong
Yet did by signes his glad affection show,
Making his streame run slow.
And all the foule which in his flood did dwell
Gan flock about these twaine, that did excell   120
The rest, so far, as *Cynthia* doth shend
The lesser starres. So they enranged well,
Did on those two attend,
And their best service lend,
Against their wedding day, which was not long:
  Sweete *Themmes* run softly, till I end my song.

At length they all to mery *London* came,
To mery London, my most kyndly Nurse,
That to me gave this Lifes first native sourse:

Though from another place I take my name,   130
An house of auncient fame.
There when they came, whereas those bricky towres,
The which on *Themmes* brode aged backe doe ryde,
Where now the studious Lawyers have their bowers,
There whylome wont the Templer Knights to byde,
Till they decayd through pride :
Next whereunto there standes a stately place,
Where oft I gayned giftes and goodly grace
Of that great Lord, which therein wont to dwell,
Whose want too well now feeles my freendles case :   140
But Ah here fits not well
Olde woes, but joyes, to tell
Against the bridale daye, which is not long :
   Sweete Themmes ! runne softly, till I end my Song.

Yet therein now doth lodge a noble Peer,
Great *Englands* glory and the Worlds wide wonder,
Whose dreadfull name, late through all *Spaine* did thunder,
And *Hercules* two pillors standing neere,
Did make to quake and feare :
Faire branch of Honor, flower of Chevalrie,   150
That fillest *England* with thy triumphes fame
Joy have thou of thy noble victorie,
And endlesse happinesse of thine owne name
That promiseth the same :
That through thy prowesse and victorious armes,
Thy country may be freed from forraine harmes :
And great *Elisaes* glorious name may ring
Through al the world, fil'd with thy wide Alarmes,
Which some brave muse may sing
To ages following,   160
Upon the Brydale day, which is not long :
   Sweete *Themmes* runne softly till I end my Song.

From those high Towers this noble Lord issuing,
Like Radiant *Hesper* when his golden hayre
In th' *Ocean* billowes he hath bathed fayre,
Descended to the Rivers open vewing,
With a great traine ensuing.
Above the rest were goodly to bee seene
Two gentle Knights of lovely face and feature
Beseeming well the bower of anie Queene,   170
With gifts of wit and ornaments of nature,
Fit for so goodly stature :
That like the twins of *Jove* they seem'd in sight,
Which decke the Bauldricke of the Heavens bright.
They two forth pacing to the Rivers side,
Received those two faire Brides, their Loves delight,
Which at th' appointed tyde,
Each one did make his Bryde,
Against their Brydale day, which is not long :
   Sweete *Themmes* runne softly, till I end my Song.   180

CHRISTOPHER MARLOWE

HERO AND LEANDER

TO THE RIGHT WORSHIPFULL, SIR THOMAS WALSINGHAM, KNIGHT.

Sir, wee thinke not our selves discharged of the dutie wee owe to our friend, when wee have brought the breathlesse bodie to the earth : for albeit the eye there taketh his ever farwell of that beloved object, yet the impression of the man, that hath beene deare unto us, living an after life in our memory, there putteth us in mind of farther obsequies due unto the deceased. And namely of the performance of whatsoever we may judge shal make to his living credit, and to the effecting of his determinations prevented by the stroke of death. By these meditations (as by an intellectuall will) I suppose my selfe executor to the unhappily deceased author of this Poem, upon whom knowing that in his life time you bestowed many kind favors, entertaining the parts of reckoning and woorth which you found in him, with good countenance and liberall affection : I cannot but see so far into the will of him dead, that whatsoever issue of his brain should chance to come abroad, that the first breath it should take might be the gentle aire of your liking : for since his selfe had been accustomed therunto, it would proove more agreeable and thriving to his right children, than any other foster countenance whatsoever. At this time seeing that this unfinished Tragedy happens under my hands to be imprinted ; of a double duty, the one to your selfe, the other to the deceased, I present the same to your most favourable allowance, offring my utmost selfe now and ever to bee readie, At your Worships disposing :

EDWARD BLUNT.

THE ARGUMENT OF THE FIRST SESTYAD

Heros *description and her Loves,*
The Phane of Venus ; *where he moves*
His worthie Love-suite, and attaines ;
Whose blisse the wrath of Fates restraines,
For Cupids *grace to* Mercurie,
Which tale the Author doth implie.

ON *Hellespont* guiltie of True loves blood,
In view and opposit two citties stood,
Seaborderers, disjoin'd by *Neptunes* might :
The one *Abydos*, the other *Sestos* hight.
At *Sestos, Hero* dwelt ; *Hero* the faire,
Whom young *Apollo* courted for her haire,
And offred as a dower his burning throne,
Where she should sit for men to gaze upon.
The outside of her garments were of lawne,
The lining, purple silke, with guilt starres drawne,   10

Her wide sleeves greene, and bordered with a grove,
Where *Venus* in her naked glory strove,
To please the carelesse and disdainfull eies,
Of proud *Adonis* that before her lies.
Her kirtle blew, whereon was many a staine,
Made with the blood of wretched Lovers slaine.
Upon her head she ware a myrtle wreath,
From whence her vaile reacht to the ground beneath.
Her vaile was artificiall flowers and leaves,
Whose workmanship both man and beast deceaves.　　20
Many would praise the sweet smell as she past,
When t'was the odour which her breath foorth cast,
And there for honie, bees have sought in vaine,
And beat from thence, have lighted there againe.
About her necke hung chaines of peble stone,
Which lightned by her necke, like Diamonds shone.
She ware no gloves, for neither sunne nor wind
Would burne or parch her hands, but to her mind
Or warme or coole them, for they tooke delite
To play upon those hands, they were so white.　　30
Buskins of shels all silvered, used she,
And brancht with blushing corall to the knee ;
Where sparrowes pearcht, of hollow pearle and gold,
Such as the world would woonder to behold :
Those with sweet water oft her handmaid fils,
Which as shee went would cherupe through the bils.
Some say, for her the fairest *Cupid* pyn'd,
And looking in her face, was strooken blind.
But this is true, so like was one the other,
As he imagyn'd *Hero* was his mother ;　　40
And oftentimes into her bosome flew,
About her naked necke his bare armes threw ;
And laid his childish head upon her brest,
And with still panting rockt, there tooke his rest.
So lovely faire was *Hero*, *Venus* Nun,
As nature wept, thinking she was undone ;
Because she tooke more from her than she left,
And of such wondrous beautie her bereft :
Therefore in signe her treasure suffred wracke,
Since *Heroes* time, hath halfe the world beene blacke.　　50
　Amorous *Leander*, beautifull and yoong,
(Whose tragedie divine *Musaeus* soong)
Dwelt at *Abydos* ; since him, dwelt there none,
For whom succeeding times make greater mone.
His dangling tresses that were never shorne,
Had they beene cut, and unto *Colchos* borne,
Would have allur'd the vent'rous youth of *Greece*,
To hazard more, than for the golden Fleece.
Faire *Cynthia* wisht, his armes might be her spheare,
Greefe makes her pale, because she mooves not there.　　60

His bodie was as straight as *Circes* wand,
Jove might have sipt out *Nectar* from his hand.
Even as delicious meat is to the tast,
So was his necke in touching, and surpast
The white of *Pelops* shoulder, I could tell ye,
How smooth his brest was, and how white his bellie,
And whose immortall fingars did imprint,
That heavenly path, with many a curious dint,
That runs along his backe, but my rude pen,
Can hardly blazon foorth the loves of men,   70
Much lesse of powerfull gods, let it suffise,
That my slacke muse, sings of *Leanders* eies.
Those orient cheekes and lippes, exceeding his
That leapt into the water for a kis
Of his owne shadow, and despising many,
Died ere he could enjoy the love of any.
Had wilde *Hippolytus Leander* seene,
Enamoured of his beautie had he beene,
His presence made the rudest paisant melt,
That in the vast uplandish countrie dwelt,   80
The barbarous *Thracian* soldier moov'd with nought,
Was moov'd with him, and for his favour sought.
Some swore he was a maid in mans attire,
For in his lookes were all that men desire,
A pleasant smiling cheeke, a speaking eye,
A brow for love to banquet roiallye,
And such as knew he was a man would say,
Leander, thou art made for amorous play :
Why art thou not in love, and lov'd of all ?
Though thou be faire, yet be not thine owne thrall.   90
    The men of wealthie *Sestos*, everie yeare,
(For his sake whom their goddesse held so deare,
Rose-cheekt *Adonis*) kept a solemne feast,
Thither resorted many a wandring guest,
To meet their loves ; such as had none at all,
Came lovers home from this great festivall.
For everie street like to a Firmament
Glistered with breathing stars, who where they went,
Frighted the melancholie earth, which deem'd,
Eternall heaven to burne, for so it seem'd,   100
As if another *Phaethon* had got
The guidance of the sunnes rich chariot.
But far above the loveliest, *Hero* shin'd,
And stole away th'inchaunted gazers mind,
For like Sea-nimphs inveigling harmony,
So was her beautie to the standers by.
Nor that night-wandring pale and watrie starre,
(When yawning dragons draw her thirling carre,
From *Latmus* mount up to the glomie skie,
Where crown'd with blazing light and majestie,   110

She proudly sits) more over-rules the flood,
Than she the hearts of those that neere her stood.
Even as, when gawdie Nymphs pursue the chace,
Wretched *Ixions* shaggie footed race,
Incenst with savage heat, gallop amaine,
From steepe Pine-bearing mountains to the plaine:
So ran the people foorth to gaze upon her,
And all that view'd her, were enamour'd on her.
And as in furie of a dreadfull fight,
Their fellowes being slaine or put to flight, 120
Poore soldiers stand with fear of death dead strooken,
So at her presence all surpris'd and tooken,
Await the sentence of her scornefull eies :
He whom she favours lives, the other dies.
There might you see one sigh, another rage,
And some (their violent passions to asswage)
Compile sharpe satyrs, but alas too late,
For faithfull love will never turne to hate.
And many seeing great princes were denied,
Pyn'd as they went, and thinking on her died. 130
On this feast day, (O cursed day and hower,)
Went *Hero* thorow *Sestos*, from her tower
To *Venus* temple, where unhappilye,
As after chaunc'd, they did each other spye.
So faire a church as this, had *Venus* none,
The wals were of discoloured *Jasper* stone,
Wherein was *Proteus* carved, and o'rehead
A livelie vine of greene sea agget spread ;
Where by one hand, light headed *Bacchus* hoong,
And with the other, wine from grapes out wroong. 140
Of Christall shining faire, the pavement was,
The towne of *Sestos*, cal'd it *Venus* glasse,
There might you see the gods in sundrie shapes,
Committing headdie ryots, incest, rapes :
Blood-quaffing *Mars*, heaving the yron net,
Which limping *Vulcan* and his *Cyclops* set :
Love kindling fire, to burne such townes as *Troy*,
Sylvanus weeping for the lovely boy
That now is turn'd into a *Cypres* tree,
Under whose shade the Wood-gods love to bee. 150
And in the midst a silver altar stood,
There *Hero* sacrificing turtles blood,
Vaild to the ground, vailing her eie-lids close,
And modestly they opened as she rose :
Thence flew Loves arrow with the golden head,
And thus *Leander* was enamoured.
Stone still he stood, and evermore he gazed,
Till with the fire that from his count'nance blazed,
Relenting *Heroes* gentle heart was strooke,
Such force and vertue hath an amorous looke. 160

It lies not in our power to love, or hate,
For will in us is over-rul'd by fate.
When two are stript, long ere the course begin
We wish that one should loose, the other win.
And one especiallie doe we affect,
Of two gold Ingots like in each respect ;
The reason no man knowes, let it suffise,
What we behold is censur'd by our eies.
Where both deliberat, the love is slight,
Who ever lov'd, that lov'd not at first sight ?   170
    He kneel'd, but unto her devoutly praid ;
Chast *Hero* to her selfe thus softly said :
Were I the saint hee worships, I would heare him,
And as shee spake those words, came somewhat nere him.
He started up, she blusht as one asham'd ;
Wherewith *Leander* much more was inflam'd.
He toucht her hand, in touching it she trembled,
Love deepely grounded, hardly is dissembled,
These lovers parled by the touch of hands,
True love is mute, and oft amazed stands.   180
Thus while dum signs their yeelding harts entangled,
The aire with sparkes of living fire was spangled,
And night deepe drencht in mystie *Acheron*,
Heav'd up her head, and halfe the world upon
Breath'd darkenesse forth (darke night is *Cupids* day):
And now begins *Leander* to display
Loves holy fire, with words, with sighs and teares,
Which like sweet musicke entred *Heroes* eares,
And yet at everie word shee turn'd aside,
And alwaies cut him off as he replide,   190
At last, like to a bold sharpe Sophister,
With chearefull hope thus he accosted her.
    Faire creature, let me speake without offence,
I would my rude words had the influence,
To lead thy thoughts, as thy faire lookes doe mine,
Then shouldst thou bee his prisoner who is thine,
Be not unkind and faire, mishapen stuffe
Are of behaviour boisterous and ruffe.
O shun me not, but heare me ere you goe,
God knowes I cannot force love, as you doe.   200
My words shall be as spotlesse as my youth,
Full of simplicitie and naked truth.
This sacrifice (whose sweet perfume descending,
From *Venus* altar to your footsteps bending)
Doth testifie that you exceed her farre,
To whom you offer, and whose Nunne you are.
Why should you worship her ? her you surpasse,
As much as sparkling Diamonds flaring glasse.
A Diamond set in lead his worth retaines,
A heavenly Nimph, belov'd of humane swaines,   210

Receives no blemish, but oft-times more grace ;
Which makes me hope, although I am but base,
Base in respect of thee, divine and pure,
Dutifull service may thy love procure,
And I in dutie will excell all other,
As thou in beautie doest exceed Loves mother.
Nor heaven, nor thou, were made to gaze upon :
As heaven preserves all things, so save thou one.
A stately builded ship, well rig'd and tall,
The Ocean maketh more majesticall :   220
Why vowest thou then to live in *Sestos* here,
Who on Loves seas more glorious wouldst appeare ?
Like untun'd golden strings all women are,
Which long time lie untoucht, will harshly jarre.
Vessels of Brasse oft handled, brightly shine,
What difference betwixt the richest mine
And basest mold, but use ? for both not us'de,
Are of like worth. Then treasure is abus'de,
When misers keepe it ; being put to lone,
In time it will returne us two for one.   230
Rich robes, themselves and others do adorne,
Neither themselves nor others, if not worne.
Who builds a palace and rams up the gate,
Shall see it ruinous and desolate.
Ah simple *Hero*, learne thy selfe to cherish,
Lone women like to emptie houses perish.
Lesse sinnes the poore rich man that starves himselfe,
In heaping up a masse of drossie pelfe,
Than such as you : his golden earth remains,
Which after his disceasse, some other gains.   240
But this faire jem, sweet, in the losse alone,
When you fleet hence, can be bequeath'd to none.
Or if it could, downe from th'enameld skie,
All heaven would come to claime this legacie,
And with intestine broiles the world destroy,
And quite confound natures sweet harmony.
Well therefore by the gods decreed it is,
We humane creatures should enjoy that blisse.
One is no number, mayds are nothing then,
Without the sweet societie of men.   250
Wilt thou live single still ? one shalt thou bee,
Though never-singling *Hymen* couple thee.
Wild savages, that drinke of running springs,
Thinke water farre excels all earthly things :
But they that dayly tast neat wine, despise it.
Virginitie, albeit some highly prise it,
Compar'd with marriage, had you tried them both,
Differs as much, as wine and water doth.
This idoll which you terme *Virginitie*,
Is neither essence subject to the eie,   260

No, nor to any one exterior sence,
Nor hath it any place of residence,
Nor is't of earth or mold celestiall,
Or capable of any forme at all.
Of that which hath no being, doe not boast,
Things that are not at all, are never lost.
Men foolishly doe call it vertuous,
What vertue is it, that is borne with us ?
Much lesse can honour bee ascrib'd thereto,
Honour is purchac'd by the deedes wee do.   270
Beleeve me *Hero*, honour is not wone,
Untill some honourable deed be done.
Seeke you for chastitie, immortall fame,
And know that some have wrong'd *Dianas* name ?
Whose name is it, if she be false or not,
So she be faire, but some vile toongs will blot ?
But you are faire (aye me) so wondrous faire,
So yoong, so gentle, and so debonaire,
As *Greece* will thinke, if thus you live alone,
Some one or other keepes you as his owne.   280
Then *Hero* hate me not, nor from me flie,
To follow swiftly blasting infamie.
Perhaps, thy sacred Priesthood makes thee loath,
Tell me, to whom mad'st thou that heedlesse oath ?
    To *Venus*, answered shee, and as shee spake,
Foorth from those two tralucent cesternes brake,
A streame of liquid pearle, which downe her face
Made milk-white paths, wheron the gods might trace
To *Joves* high court. Hee thus replide : The rites
In which Loves beauteous Empresse most delites,   290
Are banquets, Dorick musicke, midnight-revell,
Plaies, maskes, and all that stern age counteth evill.
Thee as a holy Idiot doth she scorne,
For thou in vowing chastitie, hast sworne
To rob her name and honour, and thereby
Commit'st a sinne far worse than perjurie.
Even sacrilege against her Dietie,
Through regular and formall puritie.
To expiat which sinne, kisse and shake hands,
Such sacrifice as this, *Venus* demands.   300
    Thereat she smild, and did denie him so,
As put thereby, yet might he hope for mo.
Which makes him quickly re-enforce his speech,
And her in humble manner thus beseech.
    Though neither gods nor men may thee deserve,
Yet for her sake whom you have vow'd to serve,
Abandon fruitlesse cold Virginitie,
The gentle queene of Loves sole enemie.
Then shall you most resemble *Venus* Nun,
When *Venus* sweet rites are perform'd and done,   310

Flint-brested *Pallas* joies in single life,
But *Pallas* and your mistresse are at strife.
Love *Hero* then, and be not tirannous,
But heale the heart, that thou hast wounded thus,
Nor staine thy youthfull years with avarice,
Faire fooles delight, to be accounted nice.
The richest corne dies, if it be not reapt,
Beautie alone is lost, too warily kept.
These arguments he us'de, and many more,
Wherewith she yeelded, that was woon before,   320
Heroes lookes yeelded, but her words made warre,
Women are woon when they begin to jarre.
Thus having swallow'd *Cupids* golden hooke,
The more she striv'd, the deeper was she strooke.
Yet evilly faining anger, strove she still,
And would be thought to graunt against her will.
So having paus'd a while, at last shee said:
Who taught thee Rhethoricke to deceive a maid?
Aye me, such words as these should I abhor,
And yet I like them for the Orator.   330
  With that *Leander* stoopt, to have imbrac'd her,
But from his spreading armes away she cast her,
And thus bespake him: Gentle youth forbeare
To touch the sacred garments which I weare.
  Upon a rocke, and underneath a hill,
Far from the towne (where all is whist and still,
Save that the sea playing on yellow sand,
Sends foorth a ratling murmure to the land,
Whose sound allures the golden *Morpheus*,
In silence of the night to visite us)   340
My turret stands, and there God knowes I play
With *Venus* swannes and sparrowes all the day,
A dwarfish beldame beares me companie,
That hops about the chamber where I lie,
And spends the night (that might be better spent)
In vaine discourse, and apish merriment.
Come thither; As she spake this, her toong tript,
For unawares (*Come thither*) from her slipt,
And sodainly her former colour chang'd,
And here and there her eies through anger rang'd.   350
And like a planet, mooving severall waies,
At one selfe instant, she poore soule assaies,
Loving, not to love at all, and everie part,
Strove to resist the motions of her hart.
And hands so pure, so innocent, nay such,
As might have made heaven stoope to have a touch,
Did she uphold to *Venus*, and againe,
Vow'd spotlesse chastitie, but all in vaine,
Cupid beats downe her praiers with his wings,
Her vowes above the emptie aire he flings: 360

All deepe enrag'd, his sinowie bow he bent,
And shot a shaft that burning from him went,
Wherewith she strooken, look'd so dolefully,
As made Love sigh, to see his tirannie.
And as she wept, her teares to pearle he turn'd,
And wound them on his arme, and for her mourn'd.
Then towards the pallace of the destinies,
Laden with languishment and griefe he flies.
And to those sterne nymphs humblie made request,
Both might enjoy ech other, and be blest.   370
But with a ghastly dreadfull countenaunce,
Threatning a thousand deaths at everie glaunce,
They answered Love, nor would vouchsafe so much
As one poore word, their hate to him was such:
Harken a while, and I will tell you why.
Heavens winged herrald, *Jove-borne Mercury*,
The selfe-same day that he asleepe had layd
Inchaunted Argus, spied a countrie mayd,
Whose carelesse haire, in stead of pearle t'adorne it,
Glist'red with deaw, as one that seem'd to skorne it: 380
Her breath as fragrant as the morning rose,
Her mind pure, and her toong untaught to glose.
Yet prowd she was, (for loftie pride that dwels
In tow'red courts, is oft in sheapheards cels)
And too too well the faire vermilion knew,
And silver tincture of her cheekes, that drew
The love of everie swaine: On her, this god
Enamoured was, and with his snakie rod,
Did charme her nimble feet, and made her stay,
The while upon a hillocke downe he lay,   390
And sweetly on his pipe began to play,
And with smooth speech, her fancie to assay,
Till in his twining armes he lockt her fast.
Maids are not woon by brutish force and might,
But speeches full of pleasure and delight.
And knowing *Hermes* courted her, was glad
That she such lovelinesse and beautie had
As could provoke his liking, yet was mute,
And neither would denie, nor graunt his sute.
Still vowd he love, she wanting no excuse   400
To feed him with delaies, as women use,
Or thirsting after immortalitie,
(All women are ambitious naturallie,)
Impos'd upon her lover such a taske,
As he ought not performe, nor yet she aske.
A draught of flowing *Nectar*, she requested,
Wherewith the king of Gods and men is feasted.
He readie to accomplish what she wil'd,
Stole some from *Hebe* (*Hebe*, *Joves* cup fil'd,)
And gave it to his simple rustike love,   410

Which being knowne (as what is hid from *Jove*)
He inly storm'd, and waxt more furious,
Than for the fire filcht by *Prometheus*
And thrusts him down from heaven. He wandring here,
In mournfull tearmes, with sad and heavie cheare
Complaind to *Cupid*, *Cupid* for his sake,
To be reveng'd on Jove, did undertake ;
And those on whom heaven, earth, and hell relies,
I mean the Adamantine Destinies,
He wounds with love, and forst them equallie,   420
To dote upon deceitfull *Mercurie*.
They offred him the deadly fatall knife,
That sheares the slender threads of humane life,
At his faire feathered feet, the engins layd,
Which th'earth from ougly *Chaos* den up-wayd :
These he regarded not, but did intreat,
That Jove, usurper of his fathers seat,
Might presently be banisht into hell,
And aged *Saturne* in *Olympus* dwell.
They granted what he crav'd, and once againe,   430
Saturne and *Ops*, began their golden raigne.
Murder, rape, warre, lust and trecherie,
Were with *Jove* clos'd in *Stigian* Emprie.
But long this blessed time continued not ;
As soone as he his wished purpose got,
He recklesse of his promise did despise
The love of th'everlasting Destinies.
They seeing it, both Love and him abhor'd,
And *Jupiter* unto his place restor'd.
And but that Learning, in despight of Fate,   440
Will mount aloft, and enter heaven gate,
And to the seat of *Jove* it selfe aduaunce,
Hermes had slept in hell with Ignoraunce.
Yet as a punishment they added this,
That he and *Povertie* should alwaies kis.
And to this day is everie scholler poore,
Grosse gold, from them runs headlong to the boore.
Likewise the angrie sisters thus deluded,
To venge themselves on *Hermes*, have concluded
That *Midas* brood shall sit in Honors chaire,   450
To which the *Muses* sonnes are only heire :
And fruitfull wits that in aspiring are,
Shall discontent, run into regions farre ;
And few great lords in vertuous deeds shall joy,
But be surpris'd with every garish toy,
And still inrich the loftie servile clowne,
Who with incroching guile, keepes learning downe.
Then muse not, *Cupids* sute no better sped,
Seeing in their loves the Fates were injured.

The end of the first Sestyad.

BEN JONSON

TO THE MEMORY OF MY BELOVED, THE AUTHOR
MR. WILLIAM SHAKESPEARE
AND WHAT HE HATH LEFT US

To draw no envy (*Shakespeare*) on thy name,
  Am I thus ample to thy Booke, and Fame:
While I confesse thy writings to be such,
  As neither *Man*, nor *Muse*, can praise too much.
'Tis true, and all mens suffrage. But these wayes
  Were not the paths I meant unto thy praise:
For seeliest Ignorance on these may light,
  Which, when it sounds at best, but eccho's right;
Or blinde Affection, which doth ne're advance
  The truth, but gropes, and urgeth all by chance;   10
Or crafty Malice, might pretend this praise,
  And thinke to ruine, where it seem'd to raise.
These are, as some infamous Baud, or Whore,
  Should praise a Matron. What could hurt her more?
But thou art proofe against them, and indeed
  Above th'ill fortune of them, or the need.
I, therefore will begin. Soule of the Age!
  The applause! delight! the wonder of our Stage!
My *Shakespeare*, rise; I will not lodge thee by
  Chaucer, or *Spenser*, or bid *Beaumont* lye   20
A little further, to make thee a roome:
  Thou art a Moniment, without a tombe,
And art alive still, while thy Booke doth live,
  And we have wits to read, and praise to give.
That I not mixe thee so, my braine excuses;
  I meane with great, but disproportion'd *Muses*:
For, if I thought my judgement were of yeeres,
  I should commit thee surely with thy peeres,
And tell, how farre thou didst our *Lily* out-shine,
  Or sporting *Kid*, or *Marlowes* mighty line.   30
And though thou hadst small *Latine*, and lesse *Greeke*,
  From thence to honour thee, I would not seeke
For names; but call forth thund'ring *Æschilus*,
  Euripides, and *Sophocles* to us,
Paccuvius, *Accius*, him of *Cordova* dead,
  To life againe, to heare thy Buskin tread,
And shake a Stage: Or, when thy Sockes were on,
  Leave thee alone, for the comparison

Of all, that insolent *Greece*, or haughtie *Rome*
  Sent forth, or since did from their ashes come.   40
Triúmph, my *Britaine*, thou hast one to showe,
  To whom all Scenes of *Europe* homage owe.
He was not of an age, but for all time!
  And all the *Muses* still were in their prime,
When like *Apollo* he came forth to warme
  Our eares, or like a *Mercury* to charme!
Nature her selfe was proud of his designes,
  And joy'd to weare the dressing of his lines!
Which were so richly spun, and woven so fit,
  As, since, she will vouchsafe no other Wit.   50
The merry *Greeke*, tart *Aristophanes*,
  Neat *Terence*, witty *Plautus*, now not please;
But antiquated, and deserted lye
  As they were not of Natures family.
Yet must I not give Nature all: Thy Art,
  My gentle *Shakespeare*, must enjoy a part.
For though the *Poets* matter, Nature be,
  His Art doth give the fashion. And, that he,
Who casts to write a living line, must sweat,
  (Such as thine are) and strike the second heat   60
Upon the *Muses* anvile: turne the same,
  (And himselfe with it) that he thinkes to frame;
Or for the lawrell, he may gaine a scorne,
  For a good *Poet's* made, as well as borne.
And such wert thou. Looke how the fathers face
  Lives in his issue, even so, the race
Of *Shakespeares* minde, and manners brightly shines
  In his well torned, and true-filed lines:
In each of which, he seemes to shake a Lance,
  As brandish't at the eyes of Ignorance.   70
Sweet Swan of *Avon*! what a sight it were
  To see thee in our waters yet appeare,
And make those flights upon the bankes of *Thames*,
  That so did take *Eliza*, and our *James*!
But stay, I see thee in the *Hemisphere*
  Advanc'd, and made a Constellation there!
Shine forth, thou Starre of *Poets*, and with rage,
  Or influence, chide, or cheere the drooping Stage;
Which, since thy flight from hence, hath mourn'd like night,
  And despaires day, but for thy Volumes light.   80

JOHN DONNE

OF THE PROGRESSE OF THE SOULE

WHEREIN BY OCCASION OF THE UNTIMELY DEATH OF
MISTRIS ELIZABETH DRURY, THE FRAILTY AND
THE DECAY OF THE WHOLE WORLD
IS REPRESENTED

THE SECOND ANNIVERSARY

NOTHING could make me sooner to confesse
That this world had an everlastingnesse,
Then to consider, that a yeare is runne,
Since both this lower world's, and the Sunnes Sunne,
The Lustre, and the vigor of this all,
Did set; 'twere blasphemie to say, did fall.
But as a ship which hath strooke saile, doth runne
By force of that force which before it wonne:
Or as sometimes in a beheaded man,
Though at those two Red seas, which freely ranne,   10
One from the Trunke, another from the Head,
His soule be sail'd, to her eternall bed,
His eyes will twinckle, and his tongue will roll,
As though he beckned, and cal'd backe his soule,
He graspes his hands, and he pulls up his feet,
And seemes to reach, and to step forth to meet
His soule; when all these motions which we saw,
Are but as Ice, which crackles at a thaw:
Or as a Lute, which in moist weather rings
Her knell alone, by cracking of her strings.   20
So struggles this dead world, now shee is gone;
For there is motion in corruption.
As some daies are at the Creation nam'd,
Before the Sunne, the which fram'd daies, was fram'd,
So after this Sunne's set, some shew appeares,
And orderly vicissitude of yeares.
Yet a new deluge, and of *Lethe* flood,
Hath drown'd us all, All have forgot all good,
Forgetting her, the maine reserve of all.
Yet in this deluge, grosse and generall,   30
Thou seest me strive for life; my life shall bee,
To be hereafter prais'd, for praysing thee;
Immortall maid, who though thou would'st refuse
The name of Mother, be unto my Muse

A Father, since her chast Ambition is
Yearely to bring forth such a child as this.
These Hymnes may worke on future wits, and so
May great-grand-children of thy prayses grow ;
And so, though not revive, embalme and spice
The world, which else would putrifie with vice.   40
For thus, Man may extend thy progeny,
Untill man doe but vanish, and not die.
These Hymnes thy issue, may encrease so long,
As till Gods great *Venite* change the song.
Thirst for that time, O my insatiate soule,   *A just*
And serve thy thirst, with Gods safe-sealing Bowle. *esti-*
Be thirstie still, and drinke still till thou goe   *mation*
To th'only Health, to be Hydroptique so.   *of this*
Forget this rotten world ; And unto thee   *world.*
Let thine owne times as an old storie bee.   50
Be not concern'd : studie not why nor when ;
Doe not so much as not beleeve a man.
For though to erre be worst, to try truths forth,
Is far more businesse, then this world is worth.
The world is but a carkasse ; thou art fed
By it, but as a worme that carkasse bred ;
And why should'st thou, poor worme, consider more
When this world will grow better then before,
Then those thy fellow wormes doe thinke upon
That carkasses last resurrection ?   60
Forget this world, and scarce think of it so,
As of old clothes, cast off a yeare agoe.
To be thus stupid is Alacritie ;
Men thus Lethargique have best Memory.
Look upward ; that's towards her, whose happy state
We now lament not, but congratulate.
Shee, to whom all this world 'twas but a stage,
Where all sat harkning how her youthfull age
Should be emploi'd, because in all she did
Some Figure of the Golden times was hid ;   70
Who could not lacke, what e'er this world could give,
Because shee was the forme, that made it live ;
Nor could complaine, that this world was unfit
To be staid in, then when shee was in it ;
Shee, that first tried indifferent desires
By vertue, and vertue by religious fires ;
Shee to whose person Paradise adher'd,
As Courts to Princes ; shee whose eyes ensphear'd
Star-light enough, t'have made the South controule,
(Had shee beene there) the Star-full Northerne Pole,   80
Shee, she is gone ; she is gone ; when thou knowest this,
What fragmentary rubbidge this world is
Thou knowest, and that it is not worth a thought ;
He honors it too much that thinkes it nought.

Thinke then, my soule, that death is but a Groome, *Contem-*
Which brings a Taper to the outward roome,   *plation of*
Whence thou spiest first a little glimmering light,   *our state*
And after brings it nearer to thy sight :   *in our*
For such approaches doth heaven make in death.   *death-bed.*
Think thy selfe labouring now with broken breath,   90
And thinke those broken and soft Notes to bee
Division, and thy happyest Harmonie.
Thinke thee laid on thy death-bed, loose and slacke ;
And thinke that, but unbinding of a packe,
To take one precious thing, thy soule from thence.
Thinke thy selfe parch'd with fevers violence ;
Anger thine ague more, by calling it
Thy Physicke ; chide the slacknesse of the fit.
Thinke that thou hear'st thy knell and think no more,
But that, as Bels cal'd thee to Church before,   100
So this, to the Triumphant Church, calls thee.
Thinke Satans Sergeants round about thee bee,
And thinke that but for Legacies they thrust ;
Give one thy Pride, to'another give thy Lust :
Give them those sinnes which they gave thee before,
And trust th'immaculate blood to wash thy score.
Thinke thy friends weeping round, and thinke that they
Weepe but because they goe not yet thy way.
Thinke that they close thine eyes, and thinke in this,
That they confesse much in the world amisse,   110
Who dare not trust a dead mans eye with that,
Which they from God, and Angels cover not.
Thinke that they shroud thee up, and think from thence
They reinvest thee in white innocence.
Thinke that thy body rots, and (if so low,
Thy soule exalted so, thy thoughts can goe,)
Think thee a Prince, who of themselves create
Wormes which insensibly devoure their State.
Thinke that they bury thee, and thinke that right
Laies thee to sleepe but a Saint Lucies night.   120
Thinke these things cheerefully : and if thou bee
Drowsie or slacke, remember then that shee,
Shee whose complexion was so even made,
That which of her ingredients should invade
The other three, no Feare, no Art could guesse ;
So far were all remov'd from more or lesse.
But as in Mithridate, or just perfumes,
Where all good things being met, no one presumes
To governe, or to triumph on the rest,
Only because all were, no part was best ;   130
And as, though all doe know, that quantities
Are made of lines, and lines from Points arise,
None can these lines or quantities unjoynt,
And say this is a line, or this a point :

So though the Elements and Humors were
In her, one could not say, this governes there,
Whose even constitution might have woon
Any disease to venter on the Sunne,
Rather then her : and make a spirit feare,
That hee to disuniting subject were :   140
To whose proportions if we would compare
Cubes, th'are unstable ; Circles, Angular ;
She who was such a chaine as Fate employes
To bring mankinde all Fortunes it enjoyes ;
So fast, so even wrought, as one would thinke,
No accident could threaten any linke ;
Shee, shee embrac'd a sicknesse, gave it meat,
The purest blood, and breath, that e'r it eate ;
And hath taught us, that though a good man hath
Title to heaven, and plead it by his Faith,   150
And though he may pretend a conquest, since
Heaven was content to suffer violence,
Yea though hee plead a long possession too,
(For they're in heaven on earth who heavens workes do)
Though hee had right and power and place, before,
Yet death must usher, and unlocke the door.
Thinke further on thy selfe, my Soule, and thinke *Incom-*
How thou at first wast made but in a sinke ;   *modities*
Thinke that it argued some infirmitie,   *of the*
That those two soules, which then thou foundst in me, *soule*
Thou fedst upon, and drewst into thee both   *in the*
My second soule of sense, and first of growth.   *bodie.*
                                                        162
Thinke but how poore thou wast, how obnoxious ;
Whom a small lumpe of flesh could poyson thus.
This curded milke, this poore unlittered whelpe
My body, could, beyond escape or helpe,
Infect thee with Originall sinne, and thou
Couldst neither then refuse, nor leave it now.
Thinke that no stubborne sullen Anchorit,
Which fixt to a pillar, or a grave, doth sit   170
Bedded, and bath'd in all his ordures, dwels
So fowly as our Soules in their first built Cels.
Thinke in how poore a prison thou didst lie
After, enabled but to suck, and crie.
Thinke, when 'twas growne to most, 'twas a poore Inne,
A Province pack'd up in two yards of skinne,
And that usurp'd or threatned with a rage
Of sicknesses, or their true mother, Age.
But thinke that death hath now enfranchis'd thee,   *Her liberty*
Thou hast thy'expansion now, and libertie ;   *by death.*
Thinke that a rustie Peece discharg'd is flowne   181
In peeces, and the bullet is his owne,
And freely flies : this to thy Soule allow,
Thinke thy shell broke, thinke thy Soule hatch'd but now.

And think this slow-pac'd soule which late did cleave
To'a body, and went but by the bodies leave,
Twenty perchance or thirty mile a day,
Dispatches in a minute all the way
Twixt heaven, and earth ; she stayes not in the ayre,
To looke what Meteors there themselves prepare ;   190
She carries no desire to know, nor sense,
Whether th'ayres middle region be intense ;
For th'Element of fire, she doth not know,
Whether she past by such a place or no ;
She baits not at the Moone, nor cares to trie
Whether in that new world, men live, and die ;
Venus retards her not, to'enquire, how shee
Can (being one starre) *Hesper*, and *Vesper* bee ;
Hee that charm'd *Argus* eyes, sweet *Mercury*,
Workes not on her, who now is growne all eye ;   200
Who if she meet the body of the Sunne,
Goes through, not staying till his course be runne ;
Who findes in *Mars* his Campe no corps of Guard ;
Nor is by *Jove*, nor by his father barr'd ;
But ere she can consider how she went,
At once is at, and through the Firmament.
And as these starres were but so many beads
Strung on one string, speed undistinguish'd leads
Her through those Spheares, as through the beads a string,
Whose quick succession makes it still one thing :   210
As doth the pith, which, lest our bodies slacke,
Strings fast the little bones of necke, and backe ;
So by the Soule doth death string Heaven and Earth ;
For when our Soule enjoyes this her third birth,
(Creation gave her one, a second, grace,)
Heaven is as neare, and present to her face,
As colours are, and objects, in a roome
Where darknesse was before, when tapers come.
This must, my Soule, thy long-short Progresse bee,
To'advance these thoughts ; Remember then that she, 220
She, whose faire body no such prison was,
But that a soule might well be pleas'd to passe
An age in her ; she whose rich beauty lent
Mintage to other beauties, for they went
But for so much as they were like to her ;
Shee, in whose body (if we dare preferre
This low world, to so high a marke as shee,)
The Westerne treasure, Easterne spicerie,
Europe, and Afrique, and the unknowne rest
Were easily found, or what in them was best ;   230
And when w'have made this large discoverie
Of all, in her some one part then will bee
Twenty such parts, whose plenty and riches is
Enough to make twenty such worlds as this ;

Shee, whom had they knowne who did first betroth
The Tutelar Angels, and assigned one, both
To Nations, Cities, and to Companies,
To Functions, Offices, and dignities,
And to each severall man, to him, and him,
They would have given her one for every limbe ;   240
She, of whose soule, if wee may say, 'twas gold,
Her body was th'Electrum, and did hold
Many degrees of that ; wee understood
Her by her sight ; her pure, and eloquent blood
Spoke in her cheekes, and so distinctly wrought,
That one might almost say, her body thought ;
Shee, shee, thus richly and largely hous'd, is gone ;
And chides us slow-pac'd snailes who crawle upon
Our prisons prison, earth, nor thinke us well,
Longer then whil'st wee beare our brittle shell.   250
But 'twere but little to have chang'd our roome,   *Her ig-*
If, as we were in this our living Tombe   *norance*
Oppress'd with ignorance, wee still were so.   *in this*
Poore soule, in this thy flesh what dost thou know ?   *life and*
Thou know'st thy selfe so little, as thou know'st not,   *know-*
How thou didst die, nor how thou wast begot.   *ledge in*
Thou neither know'st, how thou at first cam'st in,   *the next.*
Nor how thou took'st the poyson of mans sinne.
Nor dost thou, (though thou know'st, that thou art so)
By what way thou art made immortall, know.   260
Thou art too narrow, wretch, to comprehend
Even thy selfe : yea though thou wouldst but bend
To know thy body. Have not all soules thought
For many ages, that our body'is wrought
Of aire, and fire, and other Elements ?
And now they thinke of new ingredients :
And one Soule thinkes one, and another way
Another thinkes, and 'tis an even lay.
Know'st thou but how the stone doth enter in
The bladders cave, and never brake the skinne ?   270
Know'st thou how blood, which to the heart doth flow,
Doth from one ventricle to th'other goe ?
And for the putrid stuffe, which thou dost spit,
Know'st thou how thy lungs have attracted it ?
There are no passages, so that there is
(For aught thou know'st) piercing of substances.
And of those many opinions which men raise
Of Nailes and Haires, dost thou know which to praise ?
What hope have wee to know our selves, when wee
Know not the least things, which for our use be ?   280
Wee see in Authors, too stiffe to recant,
A hundred controversies of an Ant ;
And yet one watches, starves, freeses, and sweats,
To know but Catechismes and Alphabets

Of unconcerning things, matters of fact;
How others on our stage their parts did Act;
What *Cæsar* did, yea, and what *Cicero* said.
Why grasse is greene, or why our blood is red,
Are mysteries which none have reach'd unto.
In this low forme, poore soule, what wilt thou doe ?   290
When wilt thou shake off this Pedantery,
Of being taught by sense, and Fantasie ?
Thou look'st through spectacles ; small things seeme great
Below ; But up unto the watch-towre get,
And see all things despoyl'd of fallacies :
Thou shalt not peepe through lattices of eyes,
Nor heare through Labyrinths of eares, nor learne
By circuit, or collections to discerne.
In heaven thou straight know'st all, concerning it,
And what concernes it not, shalt straight forget.   300
There thou (but in no other schoole) maist bee
Perchance, as learned, and as full, as shee,
Shee who all libraries had throughly read
At home in her owne thoughts, and practised
So much good as would make as many more :
Shee whose example they must all implore,
Who would or doe, or thinke well, and confesse
That all the vertuous Actions they expresse,
Are but a new, and worse edition
Of her some one thought, or one action :   310
She who in th'art of knowing Heaven, was growne
Here upon earth, to such perfection,
That she hath, ever since to Heaven she came,
(In a far fairer print,) but read the same :
Shee, shee not satisfied with all this waight,
(For so much knowledge, as would over-fraight
Another, did but ballast her) is gone
As well t'enjoy, as get perfection.
And cals us after her, in that shee tooke,
(Taking her selfe) our best, and worthiest booke.   320
Returne not, my Soule, from this extasie,   *Of our com-*
And meditation of what thou shalt bee,   *pany in this*
To earthly thoughts, till it to thee appeare,   *life and in the*
With whom thy conversation must be there.   *next.*
With whom wilt thou converse ? what station
Canst thou chose out, free from infection,
That will not give thee theirs, nor drinke in thine ?
Shalt thou not finde a spungie slacke Divine,
Drinke and sucke in th'instructions of great men,
And for the word of God, vent them agen ?   330
Are there not some Courts (and then, no things bee
So like as Courts) which in this let us see,
That wits, and tongues of Libellers are weake,
Because they do more ill, then these can speake ?

The poyson's gone through all: poysons affect
Chiefly the chiefest parts, but some, effect
In nailes, and haires, yea excrements, will show ;
So lyes the poyson of sinne in the most low.
Up, up, my drowsie Soule, where thy new care
Shall in the Angels songs no discord heare ;   340
Where thou shalt see the blessed Mother-maid
Joy in not being that which men have said :
Where she is exalted more for being good,
Then for her interest of Mother-hood.
Up to those Patriarchs, which did longer sit
Expecting Christ, then they'have enjoy'd him yet.
Up to those Prophets, which now gladly see
Their Prophesies growne to be Historie.
Up to th'Apostles, who did bravely runne
All the Suns course, with more light then the sunne. 350
Up to those Martyrs, who did calmly bleed
Oyle to th'Apostles Lamps, dew to their seed.
Up to those Virgins, who thought, that almost
They made joyntenants with the Holy Ghost,
If they to any should his Temple give.
Up, up, for in that squadron there doth live
She, who hath carried thither new degrees
(As to their number) to their dignities.
Shee, who being to her selfe a State, injoy'd
All royalties which any State employ'd ;   360
For shee made warres, and triumph'd ; reason still
Did not o'erthrow, but rectifie her will :
And she made peace, for no peace is like this,
That beauty, and chastitie together kisse :
She did high justice, for she crucified
Every first motion of rebellious pride :
And she gave pardons, and was liberall,
For, onely her selfe except, she pardon'd all :
She coy'nd in this, that her impression gave
To all our actions all the worth they have :   370
She gave protections ; the thoughts of her brest
Satans rude Officers could ne'er arrest.
As these prerogatives being met in one,
Made her a sovereigne State, religion
Made her a Church ; and these two made her all.
She who was all this All, and could not fall
To worse by company, (for she was still
More Antidote, then all the world was ill,)
Shee, shee doth leave it, and by Death, survive
All this, in Heaven ; whither who doth not strive   380
The more, because shees there, he doth not know
That accidentall joyes in Heaven doe grow.
But pause, my soule ; And study ere thou fall *Of essentiall*
On accidentall joyes, th'essentiall.   *joy in this*

Still before Accessories doe abide   *life, and in*
A triall, must the principall be tride.   *the next.*
And what essentiall joy can'st thou expect
Here upon earth ? what permanent effect
Of transitory causes ?   Dost thou love
Beauty ? (And beauty worthy'st is to move)   390
Poore cousened cousenor, *that* she, and *that* thou,
Which did begin to love, are neither now ;
You are both fluid, chang'd since yesterday ;
Next day repaires but ill last dayes decay.
Nor are, (although the river keepe the name)
Yesterdaies waters and to-daies the same :
So flowes her face, and thine eyes.   Neither now
That Saint nor Pilgrime, which your loving vow
Concern'd, remaines ; but whil'st you thinke you bee
Constant, you'are hourely in inconstancie.   400
Honour may have pretence unto our love,
Because that God did live so long above
Without this Honour, and then lov'd it so,
That he at last made creatures to bestow
Honour on him ; not that he needed it,
But that, to his hands, man might grow more fit.
But since all Honours from inferiours flow,
(For they doe give it ; Princes doe but shew
Whom they would have so honor'd) and that this
On such opinions, and capacities   410
Is built, as rise and fall, to more and lesse :
Alas, 'tis but a casuall happinesse.
Hath ever any man to'himselfe assign'd
This or that happinesse to'arrest his minde,
But that another man which takes a worse,
Thinks him a foole for having ta'en that course ?
They who did labour Babels tower to'erect,
Might have considered, that for that effect
All this whole solid Earth could not allow
Nor furnish forth materialls enough ;   420
And that his Center, to raise such a place,
Was farre too little to have beene the Base ;
No more affords this world foundation
To erect true joy, were all the meanes in one.
But as the Heathen made them severall gods,
Of all Gods benefits, and all his rods,
(For as the Wine, and Corne, and Onions are
Gods unto them, so Agues bee, and warre)
And as by changing that whole precious Gold
To such small Copper coyns, they lost the old,   430
And lost their only God, who ever must
Be sought alone, and not in such a thrust :
So much mankinde true happinesse mistakes ;
No joy enjoyes that man, that many makes.

Then, Soule, to thy first pitch worke up againe ;
Know that all lines which circles doe containe,
For once that they the Center touch, doe touch
Twice the circumference ; and be thou such ;
Double on heaven thy thoughts on earth emploid.
All will not serve ; Only who have enjoy'd   440
The sight of God, in fulnesse can thinke it.
For it is both the object, and the wit.
This is essentiall joy, where neither hee
Can suffer diminution, nor wee ;
'Tis such a full, and such a filling good ;
Had th'Angels once look'd on him, they had stood.
To fill the place of one of them, or more,
Shee whom wee celebrate, is gone before.
She, who had here so much essentiall joy,
As no chance could distract, much lesse destroy ;   450
Who with Gods presence was acquainted so,
(Hearing, and speaking to him) as to know
His face in any naturall Stone or Tree,
Better then when in Images they bee :
Who kept by diligent devotion,
Gods Image, in such reparation,
Within her heart, that what decay was growne,
Was her first Parents fault, and not her owne :
Who being solicited to any act,
Still heard God pleading his safe precontract ;   460
Who by a faithfull confidence, was here
Betroth'd to God, and now is married there ;
Whose twilights were more cleare, then our mid-day ;
Who dreamt devoutlier, then most use to pray ;
Who being here fil'd with grace, yet strove to bee,
Both where more grace, and more capacitie
At once is given : she to Heaven is gone,
Who made this world in some proportion
A heaven, and here, became unto us all,
Joy, (as our joyes admit) essentiall.   470
But could this low world joyes essentiall touch,   *Of acci-*
Heavens accidentall joyes would passe them much.   *dentall*
How poore and lame, must then our casuall bee ?   *joyes in*
If thy Prince will his subjects to call thee   *both*
My Lord, and this doe swell thee, thou art than,   *places.*
By being greater, growne to be lesse Man.
When no Physitian of redresse can speake,
A joyfull casuall violence may breake
A dangerous Apostem in thy breast ;
And whil'st thou joyest in this, the dangerous rest,   480
The bag, may rise up, and so strangle thee.
What e'er was casuall may ever bee.
What should the nature change ? Or make the same
Certaine, which was but casuall when it came ?

All casuall joy doth loud and plainly say,
Only by comming, that it can away.
Only in Heaven joyes strength is never spent;
And accidentall things are permanent.
Joy of a soules arrivall ne'r decayes;
For that soule ever joyes and ever stayes.   490
Joy that their last great Consummation
Approaches in the resurrection;
When earthly bodies more celestiall
Shall be, then Angels were, for they could fall;
This kinde of joy doth every day admit
Degrees of growth, but none of losing it.
In this fresh joy 'tis no small part, that shee,
Shee, in whose goodnesse he that names degree,
Doth injure her ('Tis losse to be cal'd best,
There where the stuffe is not such as the rest)   500
Shee, who left such a bodie, as even shee
Only in Heaven could learne, how it can bee
Made better, for shee rather was two soules;
Or like to full on both sides written Rols,
Where eyes might reade upon the outward skin
As strong Records for God, as mindes within.
Shee, who by making full perfection grow
Peeces a Circle, and still keepes it so,
Long'd for, and longing for it, to heaven is gone,
Where shee receives, and gives addition.   510
Here in a place, where mis-devotion frames   *Conclusion.*
A thousand Prayers to Saints, whose very names
The ancient Church knew not, Heaven knows not yet:
And where, what lawes of Poetry admit,
Lawes of Religion have at least the same:
Immortall Maide, I might invoke thy name.
Could any Saint provoke that appetite,
Thou here should'st make me a French convertite.
But thou would'st not; nor would'st thou be content,
To take this for my second yeares true Rent,   520
Did this Coine beare any other stampe, then his,
That gave thee power to doe, me, to say this.
Since his will is, that to posteritie,
Thou should'st for life, and death, a patterne bee,
And that the world should notice have of this,
The purpose, and th'authoritie is his:
Thou art the Proclamation; and I am
The Trumpet, at whose voyce the people came.

JOHN MILTON

ON THE MORNING OF CHRIST'S NATIVITY

I

This is the Month, and this the happy morn
Wherin the Son of Heav'ns eternal King,
Of wedded Maid, and Virgin Mother born,
Our great redemption from above did bring
For so the holy sages once did sing,
   That he our deadly forfeit should release,
And with his Father work us a perpetual peace.

II

That glorious Form, that Light unsufferable,
And that far-beaming blaze of Majesty,
Wherwith he wont at Heav'ns high Councel-Table,   10
To sit the midst of Trinal Unity,
He laid aside; and here with us to be,
   Forsook the Courts of everlasting Day,
And chose with us a darksom House of mortal Clay.

III

Say Heav'nly Muse, shall not thy sacred vein
Afford a present to the Infant God ?
Hast thou no vers, no hymn, or solemn strein,
To welcom him to this his new abode,
Now while the Heav'n by the Suns team untrod,
   Hath took no print of the approching light,   20
And all the spangled host keep watch in squadrons bright ?

IV

See how from far upon the Eastern rode
The Star-led Wisards haste with odours sweet,
O run, prevent them with thy humble ode,
And lay it lowly at his blessed feet ;
Have thou the honour first, thy Lord to greet,
   And joyn thy voice unto the Angel Quire,
From out his secret Altar toucht with hallow'd fire.

THE HYMN.

I

I⊤ was the Winter wilde,
While the Heav'n-born-childe,   **30**
  All meanly wrapt in the rude manger lies;
Nature in aw to him
Had doff't her gawdy trim,
  With her great Master so to sympathize:
It was no season then for her
To wanton with the Sun her lusty Paramour.

II

Only with speeches fair
She woo's the gentle Air
  To hide her guilty front with innocent Snow,
And on her naked shame,   **40**
Pollute with sinfull blame,
  The Saintly Vail of Maiden white to throw,
Confounded, that her Makers eyes
Should look so neer upon her foul deformities.

III

But he her fears to cease,
Sent down the meek-eyd Peace,
  She crown'd with Olive green, came softly sliding
Down through the turning sphear
His ready Harbinger,
  With Turtle wing the amorous clouds dividing.   **50**
And waving wide her mirtle wand,
She strikes a universall Peace through Sea and Land.

IV

No War, or Battails sound
Was heard the World around,
  The idle spear and shield were high up hung;
The hooked Chariot stood
Unstain'd with hostile blood,
  The Trumpet spake not to the armed throng,
And Kings sate still with awfull eye,
As if they surely knew their sovran Lord was by.   **60**

V

But peacefull was the night
Wherin the Prince of light
  His raign of peace upon the earth began:
The Windes with wonder whist,
Smoothly the waters kist,
  Whispering new joyes to the milde Ocean,
Who now hath quite forgot to rave,
While Birds of Calm sit brooding on the charmed wave.

VI

The Stars with deep amaze
Stand fixt in stedfast gaze,   70
   Bending one way their pretious influence,
And will not take their flight,
For all the morning light,
   Or *Lucifer* that often warn'd them thence ;
But in their glimmering Orbs did glow,
Untill their Lord himself bespake, and bid them go.

VII

And though the shady gloom
Had given day her room,
   The Sun himself with-held his wonted speed,
And hid his head for shame,   80
As his inferiour flame,
   The new enlightn'd world no more should need ;
He saw a greater Sun appear
Then his bright Throne, or burning Axletree could bear.

VIII

The Shepherds on the Lawn,
Or ere the point of dawn,
   Sate simply chatting in a rustick row ;
Full little thought they than,
That the mighty *Pan*
   Was kindly com to live with them below ;   90
Perhaps their loves, or els their sheep,
Was all that did their silly thoughts so busie keep.

IX

When such musick sweet
Their hearts and ears did greet,
   As never was by mortall finger strook,
Divinely-warbled voice
Answering the stringed noise,
   As all their souls in blisfull rapture took :
The Air such pleasure loth to lose,
With thousand echo's still prolongs each heav'nly close.

X

Nature that heard such sound   101
Beneath the hollow round
   Of *Cynthia's* seat, the Airy region thrilling,
Now was almost won
To think her part was don,
   And that her raign had here its last fulfilling ;
She knew such harmony alone
Could hold all Heav'n and Earth in happier union.

XI

At last surrounds their sight
A Globe of circular light,   110
    That with long beams the shame-fac't night array'd,
The helmed Cherubim
And sworded Seraphim,
    Are seen in glittering ranks with wings displaid,
Harping in loud and solemn quire,
With unexpressive notes to Heav'ns new-born Heir.

XII

Such Musick (as 'tis said)
Before was never made,
    But when of old the sons of morning sung,
While the Creator Great   120
His constellations set,
    And the well-ballanc't world on hinges hung,
And cast the dark foundations deep,
And bid the weltring waves their oozy channel keep.

XIII

Ring out ye Crystall sphears,
Once bless our human ears,
    (If ye have power to touch our senses so)
And let your silver chime
Move in melodious time;
    And let the Base of Heav'ns deep Organ blow,   130
And with your ninefold harmony
Make up full consort to th'Angelike symphony.

XIV

For if such holy Song
Enwrap our fancy long,
    Time will run back, and fetch the age of gold,
And speckl'd vanity
Will sicken soon and die,
    And leprous sin will melt from earthly mould.
And Hell it self will pass away,
And leave her dolorous mansions to the peering day.   140

XV

Yea Truth, and Justice then
Will down return to men,
    Orb'd in a Rain-bow; and like glories wearing
Mercy will sit between,
Thron'd in Celestiall sheen,
    With radiant feet the tissued clouds down stearing,
And Heav'n as at som festivall,
Will open wide the Gates of her high Palace Hall.

XVI

But wisest Fate sayes no,
This must not yet be so, 150
   The Babe lies yet in smiling Infancy,
That on the bitter cross
Must redeem our loss;
   So both himself and us to glorifie:
Yet first to those ychain'd in sleep,
The wakefull trump of doom must thunder through the deep.

XVII

With such a horrid clang
As on mount *Sinai* rang
   While the red fire, and smouldring clouds out brake:
The aged Earth agast 160
With terrour of that blast,
   Shall from the surface to the center shake;
When at the worlds last session,
The dreadfull Judge in middle Air shall spread his throne.

XVIII

And then at last our bliss
Full and perfect is,
   But now begins; for from this happy day
Th'old Dragon under ground
In straiter limits bound,
   Not half so far casts his usurped sway, 170
And wrath to see his Kingdom fail,
Swindges the scaly Horrour of his foulded tail.

XIX

The Oracles are dumm,
No voice or hideous humm
   Runs through the arched roof in words deceiving.
Apollo from his shrine
Can no more divine,
   With hollow shreik the steep of *Delphos* leaving.
No nightly trance, or breathed spell,
Inspire's the pale-ey'd Priest from the prophetic cell. 180

XX

The lonely mountains o're,
And the resounding shore,
   A voice of weeping heard, and loud lament;
From haunted spring, and dale
Edg'd with poplar pale,
   The parting Genius is with sighing sent,
With flowre-inwov'n tresses torn
The Nimphs in twilight shade of tangled thickets mourn.

XXI

In consecrated Earth,
And on the holy Hearth,　　　　　　　　　　　190
　　The *Lars*, and *Lemures* moan with midnight plaint,
In Urns, and Altars round,
A drear, and dying sound
　　Affrights the *Flamins* at their service quaint;
And the chill Marble seems to sweat,
While each peculiar power forgoes his wonted seat.

XXII

Peor, and *Baalim*
Forsake their Temples dim,
　　With that twise-batter'd god of *Palestine*,
And mooned *Ashtaroth*,　　　　　　　　　　　200
Heav'ns Queen and Mother both,
　　Now sits not girt with Tapers holy shine,
The Libyc *Hammon* shrinks his horn,
In vain the *Tyrian* Maids their wounded *Thamuz* mourn.

XXIII

And sullen *Moloch* fled,
Hath left in shadows dred,
　　His burning Idol all of blackest hue,
In vain with Cymbals ring,
They call the grisly king,
　　In dismall dance about the furnace blue;　　　210
The brutish gods of *Nile* as fast,
Isis and *Orus*, and the Dog *Anubis* hast.

XXIV

Nor is *Osiris* seen
In *Memphian* Grove, or Green,
　　Trampling the unshowr'd Grasse with lowings loud;
Nor can he be at rest
Within his sacred chest,
　　Naught but profoundest Hell can be his shroud,
In vain with Timbrel'd Anthems dark
The sable-stoled Sorcerers bear his worshipt Ark.　　220

XXV

He feels from *Juda's* Land
The dredded Infants hand,
　　The rayes of *Bethlehem* blind his dusky eyn;
Nor all the gods beside,
Longer dare abide,
　　Not *Typhon* huge ending in snaky twine:
Our Babe to shew his Godhead true,
Can in his swadling bands controul the damned crew.

XXVI

So when the Sun in bed,
Curtain'd with cloudy red,   230
   Pillows his chin upon an Orient wave,
The flocking shadows pale,
Troop to th'infernall jail,
   Each fetter'd Ghost slips to his severall grave,
And the yellow-skirted *Fayes*,
Fly after the Night-steeds, leaving their Moon-lov'd maze.

XXVII

But see the Virgin blest,
Hath laid her Babe to rest,
   Time is our tedious Song should here have ending:
Heav'ns youngest teemed Star,   240
Hath fixt her polisht Car,
   Her sleeping Lord with Handmaid Lamp attending:
And all about the Courtly Stable,
Bright-harnest Angels sit in order serviceable.

AT A SOLEMN MUSICK

BLEST pair of *Sirens*, pledges of Heav'ns joy,
Sphear-born harmonious Sisters, Voice, and Vers,
Wed your divine sounds, and mixt power employ
Dead things with inbreath'd sense able to pierce,
And to our high-rais'd phantasie present,
That undisturbed Song of pure concent,
Ay sung before the saphire-colour'd throne
To him that sits theron
With Saintly shout, and solemn Jubily,
Where the bright Seraphim in burning row   10
Their loud up-lifted Angel trumpets blow,
And the Cherubick host in thousand quires
Touch their immortal Harps of golden wires,
With those just Spirits that wear victorious Palms,
Hymns devout and holy Psalms
Singing everlastingly;
That we on Earth with undiscording voice
May rightly answer that melodious noise;
As once we did, till disproportion'd sin
Jarr'd against natures chime, and with harsh din   20
Broke the fair musick that all creatures made
To their great Lord, whose love their motion sway'd
In perfect Diapason, whilst they stood
In first obedience, and their state of good.
O may we soon again renew that Song
And keep in tune with Heav'n, till God ere long
To his celestial consort us unite,
To live with him, and sing in endles morn of light.

LYCIDAS

In this Monody the Author bewails a learned Friend, unfortunately
drown'd in his Passage from *Chester* on the *Irish* Seas, 1637.
And by occasion foretels the ruine of our corrupted
Clergy then in their height.

YET once more, O ye Laurels, and once more
Ye Myrtles brown, with Ivy never-sear,
I com to pluck your Berries harsh and crude,
And with forc'd fingers rude,
Shatter your leaves before the mellowing year.
Bitter constraint, and sad occasion dear,
Compels me to disturb your season due :
For *Lycidas* is dead, dead ere his prime
Young *Lycidas*, and hath not left his peer :
Who would not sing for *Lycidas* ? he knew   10
Himself to sing, and build the lofty rhyme.
He must not flote upon his watry bear
Unwept, and welter to the parching wind,
Without the meed of som melodious tear.
  Begin then, Sisters of the sacred well,
That from beneath the seat of *Jove* doth spring,
Begin, and somwhat loudly sweep the string.
Hence with denial vain, and coy excuse,
So may som gentle Muse
With lucky words favour my destin'd Urn,   20
And as he passes turn,
And bid fair peace be to my sable shroud.
For we were nurst upon the self-same hill,
Fed the same flock, by fountain, shade, and rill.
Together both, ere the high Lawns appear'd
Under the opening eye-lids of the morn,
We drove a field, and both together heard
What time the Gray-fly winds her sultry horn,
Batt'ning our flocks with the fresh dews of night,
Oft till the Star that rose, at Ev'ning, bright   30
Toward Heav'ns descent had slop'd his westering wheel.
Mean while the Rural ditties were not mute,
Temper'd to th'Oaten Flute ;
Rough *Satyrs* danc'd, and *Fauns* with clov'n heel,
From the glad sound would not be absent long,
And old *Damaetas* lov'd to hear our song.
  But O the heavy change, now thou art gon,
Now thou art gon, and never must return !
Thee Shepherd, thee the Woods, and desert Caves,
With wilde Thyme and the gadding Vine o'regrown,   40
And all their echoes mourn.
The Willows, and the Hazle Copses green,
Shall now no more be seen,

Fanning their joyous Leaves to thy soft layes.
As killing as the Canker to the Rose,
Or Taint-worm to the weanling Herds that graze,
Or Frost to Flowers, that their gay wardrop wear, *clothes*
When first the White thorn blows;
Such, *Lycidas*, thy loss to Shepherds ear.
    Where were ye Nymphs when the remorseless deep 50
Clos'd o're the head of your lov'd *Lycidas?*
For neither were ye playing on the steep,
Where your old *Bards*, the famous *Druids* ly,
Nor on the shaggy top of *Mona* high, *Anglesey*
Nor yet where *Deva* spreads her wisard stream: *Dee (Cheshire)*
Ay me, I fondly dream!
Had ye bin there—for what could that have don?
What could the Muse her self that *Orpheus* bore, *Calliope (mother)*
The Muse her self, for her inchanting son
Whom Universal nature did lament,   60
When by the rout that made the hideous roar,
His goary visage down the stream was sent,
Down the swift *Hebrus* to the *Lesbian* shore.
    Alas! What boots it with uncessant care
To tend the homely slighted Shepherds trade,
And strictly meditate the thankles Muse,
Were it not better don as others use,
To sport with *Amaryllis* in the shade,
Or with the tangles of *Neaera's* hair?
Fame is the spur that the clear spirit doth raise   70
(That last infirmity of Noble mind)
To scorn delights, and live laborious dayes;
But the fair Guerdon when we hope to find,
And think to burst out into sudden blaze,
Comes the blind *Fury* with th'abhorred shears,
And slits the thin spun life. But not the praise, *old superstition*
Phoebus repli'd, and touch'd my trembling ears; *Fame (real)*
Fame is no plant that grows on mortal soil,
Nor in the glistering foil
Set off to th'world, nor in broad rumour lies,   80
But lives and spreds aloft by those pure eyes,
And perfet witnes of all judging *Jove*;
As he pronounces lastly on each deed,
Of so much fame in Heav'n expect thy meed.
    O Fountain *Arethuse*, and thou honour'd floud,
Smooth-sliding *Mincius*, crown'd with vocall reeds,
That strain I heard was of a higher mood:
But now my Oate proceeds,
And listens to the Herald of the Sea *Triton*
That came in *Neptune's* plea,   90
He ask'd the Waves, and ask'd the Fellon winds,
What hard mishap hath doom'd this gentle swain?
And question'd every gust of rugged wings
That blows from off each beaked Promontory,

They knew not of his story,
And sage *Hippotades* their answer brings, *wise ruler of the wind*
That not a blast was from his dungeon stray'd,
The Ayr was calm, and on the level brine,
Sleek *Panope* with all her sisters play'd. *cause of death*
It was that fatall and perfidious Bark   100
Built in th'eclipse, and rigg'd with curses dark,
That sunk so low that sacred head of thine.
    Next *Camus*, reverend Sire, went footing slow, *spirit / River*
His Mantle hairy, and his Bonnet sedge, *banks of river*
Inwrought with figures dim, and on the edge
Like to that sanguine flower inscrib'd with woe. *hyacinth*
Ah ; Who hath reft (quoth he) my dearest pledge ?
Last came, and last did go, *Peter*
The Pilot of the *Galilean* lake,
Two massy Keyes he bore of metals twain,   110
(The Golden opes, the Iron shuts amain) *with force*
He shook his Miter'd locks, and stern bespake,
How well could I have spar'd for thee, young swain,
Anow of such as for their bellies sake,
Creep and intrude, and climb into the fold ?
Of other care they little reck'ning make,
Then how to scramble at the shearers feast,
And shove away the worthy bidden guest.
Blind mouthes ! that scarce themselves know how to hold
A Sheep-hook, or have learn'd ought els the least   120
That to the faithfull Herdmans art belongs ! *get what*
What recks it them ? What need they ? They are sped *want*
And when they list, their lean and flashy songs
Grate on their scrannel Pipes of wretched straw,
The hungry Sheep look up, and are not fed,
But swoln with wind, and the rank mist they draw,
Rot inwardly, and foul contagion spread :
Besides what the grim Woolf with privy paw *R C Church*
Daily devours apace, and nothing sed,
But that two-handed engine at the door,   130
Stands ready to smite once, and smite no more. *Reformation is at*
    Return *Alpheus*, the dread voice is past, *St Peters power*
That shrunk thy streams ; Return *Sicilian* Muse,
And call the Vales, and bid them hither cast
Their Bels, and Flourets of a thousand hues.
Ye valleys low where the milde whispers use,
Of shades and wanton winds, and gushing brooks,
On whose fresh lap the swart Star sparely looks,
Throw hither all your quaint enameld eyes,
That on the green terf suck the honied showres,   140
And purple all the ground with vernal flowres.
Bring the rathe Primrose that forsaken dies. *early*
The tufted Crow-toe, and pale Gessamine,
The white Pink, and the Pansie freakt with jeat,
The glowing Violet,

again tears
Pilot of the ship

NB.

The Musk-rose, and the well attir'd Woodbine,
With Cowslips wan that hang the pensive hed,
And every flower that sad embroidery wears:
Bid *Amaranthus* all his beauty shed,
And Daffadillies fill their cups with tears,　　　　150
To strew the Laureat Herse where *Lycid* lies.
For so to interpose a little ease,
Let our frail thoughts dally with false surmise.
Ay me! Whilst thee the shores, and sounding Seas
Wash far away, where ere thy bones are hurld,
Whether beyond the stormy *Hebrides*,
Where thou perhaps under the whelming tide
Visit'st the bottom of the monstrous world;
Or whether thou to our moist vows deny'd,
Sleep'st by the fable of *Bellerus* old,　　　　160
Where the great vision of the guarded Mount
Looks toward *Namancos* and *Bayona's* hold;
Look homeward Angel now, and melt with ruth.
And, O ye *Dolphins*, waft the haples youth.
　Weep no more, woful Shepherds weep no more,
For *Lycidas* your sorrow is not dead,
Sunk though he be beneath the watry floar,
So sinks the day-star in the Ocean bed,
And yet anon repairs his drooping head,
And tricks his beams, and with new spangled Ore,　　170
Flames in the forehead of the morning sky:
So *Lycidas* sunk low, but mounted high,
Through the dear might of him that walk'd the waves,
Where other groves, and other streams along,
With *Nectar* pure his oozy Lock's he laves,
And hears the unexpressive nuptiall Song,
In the blest Kingdoms meek of joy and love.
There entertain him all the Saints above,
In solemn troops, and sweet Societies
That sing, and singing in their glory move,　　　　180
And wipe the tears for ever from his eyes.
Now *Lycidas* the Shepherds weep no more;
Hence forth thou art the Genius of the shore,
In thy large recompense, and shalt be good
To all that wander in that perilous flood.
　Thus sang the uncouth Swain to th'Okes and rills,
While the still morn went out with Sandals gray,
He touch'd the tender stops of various Quills,
With eager thought warbling his *Dorick* lay:
And now the Sun had stretch'd out all the hills,　　190
And now was dropt into the Western bay;
At last he rose, and twitch'd his Mantle blew:
To morrow to fresh Woods, and Pastures new.

L'ALLEGRO

HENCE loathed Melancholy,
  Of *Cerberus* and blackest midnight born,
In *Stygian* Cave forlorn
  'Mongst horrid shapes, and shreiks, and sights unholy,
Find out som uncouth cell,
  Where brooding darknes spreads his jealous wings,
And the night-Raven sings ;
  There under *Ebon* shades, and low-brow'd Rocks,
As ragged as thy Locks,
  In dark *Cimmerian* desert ever dwell.   10
But com thou Goddes fair and free,
In Heav'n ycleap'd *Euphrosyne*,
And by men, heart-easing Mirth,
Whom lovely *Venus* at a birth
With two sister Graces more
To Ivy-crowned *Bacchus* bore ;
Or whether (as som sager sing)
The frolick Wind that breathes the Spring,
Zephir with *Aurora* playing,
As he met her once a Maying,   20
There on Beds of Violets blew,
And fresh-blown Roses washt in dew,
Fill'd her with thee a daughter fair,
So bucksom, blith, and debonair.
Haste thee nymph, and bring with thee
Jest and youthful Jollity,
Quips and Cranks, and wanton Wiles,
Nods and Becks, and Wreathed Smiles,
Such as hang on *Hebe's* cheek,
And love to live in dimple sleek ;   30
Sport that wrincled Care derides,
And Laughter holding both his sides.
Com, and trip it as ye go
On the light fantastick toe,
And in thy right hand lead with thee,
The Mountain Nymph, sweet Liberty ;
And if I give thee honour due,
Mirth, admit me of thy crue
To live with her, and live with thee,
In unreproved pleasures free ;   40
To hear the Lark begin his flight,
And singing startle the dull night,
From his watch-towre in the skies,
Till the dappled dawn doth rise ;

Then to com in spight of sorrow,
And at my window bid good morrow,
Through the Sweet-Briar, or the Vine,
Or the twisted Eglantine:
While the Cock with lively din,
Scatters the rear of darknes thin,   50
And to the stack, or the Barn dore,
Stoutly struts his Dames before:
Oft list'ning how the Hounds and horn
Chearly rouse the slumbring morn,
From the side of som Hoar Hill,
Through the high wood echoing shrill.
Som time walking not unseen
By Hedge-row Elms, on Hillocks green,
Right against the Eastern gate,
Wher the great Sun begins his state,   60
Rob'd in flames, and Amber light,
The clouds in thousand Liveries dight.
While the Plowman neer at hand,
Whistles ore the Furrow'd Land,
And the Milkmaid singeth blithe,
And the Mower whets his sithe,
And every Shepherd tells his tale
Under the Hawthorn in the dale.
Streit mine eye hath caught new pleasures
Whilst the Lantskip round it measures,   70
Russet Lawns, and Fallows Gray,
Where the nibling flocks do stray,
Mountains on whose barren brest
The labouring clouds do often rest:
Meadows trim with Daisies pide,
Shallow Brooks, and Rivers wide.
Towers, and Battlements it sees
Boosom'd high in tufted Trees,
Wher perhaps som beauty lies,
The Cynosure of neighbouring eyes.   80
Hard by, a Cottage chimney smokes,
From betwixt two aged Okes,
Where *Corydon* and *Thyrsis* met,
Are at their savory dinner set
Of Hearbs, and other Country Messes,
Which the neat-handed *Phillis* dresses;
And then in haste her Bowre she leaves,
With *Thestylis* to bind the Sheaves;
Or if the earlier season lead
To the tann'd Haycock in the Mead,   90
Som times with secure delight
The up-land Hamlets will invite,
When the merry Bells ring round
And the jocond rebecks sound

To many a youth, and many a maid,
Dancing in the Chequer'd shade;
And young and old com forth to play
On a Sunshine Holyday,
Till the live-long day-light fail,
Then to the Spicy Nut-Brown Ale,   100
With stories told of many a feat,
How *Faery Mab* the junkets eat,
She was pincht, and pull'd she sed,
And he by Friars Lanthorn led;
Tells how the drudging *Goblin* swet,
To ern his Cream-bowle duly set,
When in one night, ere glimps of morn,
His shadowy Flale hath thresh'd the Corn
That ten day-labourers could not end;
Then lies him down the Lubbar Fend,   110
And stretch'd out all the Chimney's length,
Basks at the fire his hairy strength;
And Crop-full out of dores he flings,
Ere the first Cock his Mattin rings.
Thus don the Tales, to bed they creep,
By whispering Windes soon lull'd asleep.
Towred Cities please us then,
And the busie humm of men,
Where throngs of Knights and Barons bold,
In weeds of Peace high triumphs hold,   120
With store of Ladies, whose bright eies
Rain influence, and judge the prise
Of Wit, or Arms, while both contend
To win her Grace, whom all commend.
There let *Hymen* oft appear
In Saffron robe, with Taper clear,
And pomp, and feast, and revelry,
With mask, and antique Pageantry,
Such sights as youthfull Poets dream
On Summer eeves by haunted stream.   130
Then to the well-trod stage anon,
If *Jonsons* learned Sock be on,
Or sweetest *Shakespear* fancies childe,
Warble his native Wood-notes wilde,
And ever against eating Cares,
Lap me in soft *Lydian* Aires,
Married to immortal verse
Such as the meeting soul may pierce
In notes, with many a winding bout
Of lincked sweetnes long drawn out,   140
With wanton heed, and giddy cunning,
The melting voice through mazes running;
Untwisting all the chains that ty
The hidden soul of harmony;

That *Orpheus* self may heave his head
From golden slumber on a bed
Of heapt *Elysian* flowres, and hear
Such streins as would have won the ear
Of *Pluto*, to have quite set free
His half regain'd *Eurydice*.   150
These delights, if thou canst give,
Mirth with thee, I mean to live.

IL PENSEROSO

HENCE vain deluding joyes,
  The brood of folly without father bred,
How little you bested,
  Or fill the fixed mind with all your toyes ;
Dwell in som idle brain,
  And fancies fond with gaudy shapes possess,
As thick and numberless
  As the gay motes that people the Sun Beams,
Or likest hovering dreams
  The fickle Pensioners of *Morpheus* train.   10
But hail thou Goddes, sage and holy,
Hail divinest Melancholy,
Whose Saintly visage is too bright
To hit the Sense of human sight ;
And therfore to our weaker view,
Ore laid with black staid Wisdoms hue.
Black, but such as in esteem,
Prince *Memnons* sister might beseem,
Or that Starr'd *Ethiope* Queen that strove
To set her beauties praise above   20
The Sea Nymphs, and their powers offended.
Yet thou art higher far descended,
Thee bright-hair'd *Vesta* long of yore,
To solitary *Saturn* bore ;`
His daughter she (in *Saturns* raign,
Such mixture was not held a stain)
Oft in glimmering Bowres, and glades
He met her, and in secret shades
Of woody *Ida's* inmost grove,
While yet there was no fear of *Jove*.   30
Com pensive Nun, devout and pure,
Sober, stedfast, and demure,
All in a robe of darkest grain,
Flowing with majestick train.

And sable stole of *Cipres* Lawn,
Over thy decent shoulders drawn.
Com, but keep thy wonted state,
With eev'n step, and musing gate,
And looks commercing with the skies,
Thy rapt soul sitting in thine eyes :　　　　　40
There held in holy passion still,
Forget thy self to Marble, till
With a sad Leaden downward cast,
Thou fix them on the earth as fast.
And joyn with thee calm Peace, and Quiet,
Spare Fast, that oft with gods doth diet,
And hears the Muses in a ring,
Ay round about *Joves* Altar sing.
And adde to these retired Leasure,
That in trim Gardens takes his pleasure ;　　　　50
But first, and chiefest, with thee bring,
Him that yon soars on golden wing,
Guiding the fiery-wheeled throne,
The Cherub Contemplation,
And the mute Silence hist along,
'Less *Philomel* will daign a Song,
In her sweetest, saddest plight,
Smoothing the rugged brow of night,
While *Cynthia* checks her Dragon yoke,
Gently o're th'accustom'd Oke ;　　　　　60
Sweet Bird that shunn'st the noise of folly,
Most musicall, most melancholy !
Thee Chauntress oft the Woods among,
I woo to hear thy eeven-Song ;
And missing thee, I walk unseen
On the dry smooth-shaven Green,
To behold the wandring Moon,
Riding neer her highest noon,
Like one that had bin led astray
Through the Heav'ns wide pathles way ;　　　　70
And oft, as if her head she bow'd,
Stooping through a fleecy cloud.
Oft on a Plat of rising ground,
I hear the far-off *Curfeu* sound,
Over som wide-water'd shoar,
Swinging slow with sullen roar ;
Or if the Ayr will not permit,
Som still removed place will fit,
Where glowing Embers through the room
Teach light to counterfeit a gloom,　　　　80
Far from all resort of mirth,
Save the Cricket on the hearth,
Or the Belmans drousie charm,
To bless the dores from nightly harm :

Or let my Lamp at midnight hour,
Be seen in som high lonely Towr,
Where I may oft out-watch the *Bear*,
With thrice great *Hermes*, or unsphear
The spirit of *Plato* to unfold
What Worlds, or what vast Regions hold   90
The immortal mind that hath forsook
Her mansion in this fleshly nook :
And of those *Daemons* that are found
In fire, air, flood, or under ground,
Whose power hath a true consent
With Planet, or with Element.
Som time let Gorgeous Tragedy
In Scepter'd Pall com sweeping by,
Presenting *Thebs*, or *Pelops* line,
Or the tale of *Troy* divine,   100
Or what (though rare) of later age,
Ennobled hath the Buskind stage.
But, O sad Virgin, that thy power
Might raise *Musaeus* from his bower,
Or bid the soul of *Orpheus* sing
Such notes as warbled to the string,
Drew Iron tears down *Pluto's* cheek,
And made Hell grant what Love did seek.
Or call up him that left half told
The story of *Cambuscan* bold,   110
Of *Camball*, and of *Algarsife*,
And who had *Canace* to wife,
That own'd the vertuous Ring and Glass,
And of the wondrous Hors of Brass,
On which the *Tartar* King did ride ;
And if ought els, great *Bards* beside,
In sage and solemn tunes have sung,
Of Turneys and of Trophies hung ;
Of Forests, and inchantments drear,
Where more is meant then meets the ear.   120
Thus night oft see me in thy pale career,
Till civil-suited Morn appeer,
Not trickt and frounc't as she was wont,
With the Attick Boy to hunt,
But Kerchef't in a comly Cloud,
While rocking Winds are Piping loud,
Or usher'd with a shower still,
When the gust hath blown his fill,
Ending on the russling Leaves,
With minute drops from off the Eaves :   130
And when the Sun begins to fling
His flaring beams, me Goddes bring
To arched walks of twilight groves,
And shadows brown that *Sylvan* loves

Of Pine, or monumental Oake,
Where the rude Ax with heaved stroke,
Was never heard the Nymphs to daunt,
Or fright them from their hallow'd haunt.
There in close covert by som Brook,
Where no profaner eye may look,   140
Hide me from Day's garish eie,
While the Bee with Honied thie,
That at her flowry work doth sing,
And the Waters murmuring
With such consort as they keep,
Entice the dewy-feather'd Sleep ;
And let som strange mysterious dream,
Wave at his Wings in Airy stream,
Of lively portrature display'd,
Softly on my eye-lids laid.   150
And as I wake, sweet musick breath
Above, about, or underneath,
Sent by som spirit to mortals good,
Or th'unseen Genius of the Wood.
But let my due feet never fail,
To walk the studious Cloysters pale,
And love the high embowed Roof,
With antick Pillars massy proof,
And storied Windows richly dight,
Casting a dimm religious light.   160
There let the pealing Organ blow,
To the full voic'd Quire below,
In Service high, and Anthems cleer,
As may with sweetnes, through mine ear,
Dissolve me into extasies,
And bring all Heav'n before mine eyes.
And may at last my weary age
Find out the peacefull hermitage,
The Hairy Gown and Mossy Cell,
Where I may sit and rightly spell   170
Of every Star that Heav'n doth shew,
And every Herb that sips the dew ;
Till old experience do attain
To somthing like Prophetic strain.
These pleasures *Melancholy* give,
And I with thee will choose to live.

AN EPITAPH ON THE ADMIRABLE DRAMATIC POET, W. SHAKESPEARE

WHAT needs my *Shakespear* for his honour'd Bones,
The labour of an age in piled Stones,
Or that his hallow'd reliques should be hid
Under a Star-ypointing *Pyramid?*
Dear son of memory, great heir of Fame,
What need'st thou such weak witnes of thy name?
Thou in our wonder and astonishment
Hast built thy self a live-long Monument.
For whilst to th'shame of slow-endeavouring art,
Thy easie numbers flow, and that each heart　　　10
Hath from the leaves of thy unvalu'd Book,
Those Delphick lines with deep impression took,
Then thou our fancy of it self bereaving,
Dost make us Marble with too much conceaving;
And so Sepulcher'd in such pomp dost lie,
That Kings for such a Tomb would wish to die.

ANDREW MARVELL

AN HORATIAN ODE UPON CROMWELL'S RETURN FROM IRELAND

THE forward youth that would appeare,
Must now forsake his muses deare,
    Nor in the shadows sing
    His numbers languishing:
'Tis time to leave the books in dust,
And oyle th'unused armour's rust;
    Removing from the wall
    The corselett of the hall.
So restlesse Cromwell could not cease
In the inglorious arts of peace,   10
    But through adventurous warre
    Urged his active starre;
And like the three-forked lightning first,
Breaking the clouds where it was nurst,
    Did thorough his own side
    His fiery way divide.
(For 'tis all one to courage high,
The emulous, or enemy;
    And with such to enclose,
    Is more than to oppose.)   20
Then burning through the aire he went,
And palaces and temples rent;
    And Caesar's head at last
    Did through his laurels blast.
'Tis madness to resist or blame
The face of angry heaven's flame;
    And if we would speak true,
    Much to the man is due:
Who from his private gardens, where
He lived reserved, and austere,   30
    As if his highest plott
    To plant the bergamott:
Could by industrious valour clime
To ruine the great work of time,
    And cast the kingdoms old,
    Into another mold,
Though justice against fate complaine,
And plead the antient rights in vaine;
    But those do hold or breake,
    As men are strong or weake.   40

Nature, that hateth emptinesse,
Allows of penetration lesse ;
  And therefore must make roome
  Where greater spirits come.
What field of all the civil warre,
Where his were not the deepest scarre ?
  And Hampton shows what part
  He had of wiser art :
Where twining subtile fears with hope,
He wove a net of such a scope,   50
  That Charles himself might chase
  To Caresbrook's narrow case.
That thence the royal actor borne,
The tragic scaffold might adorne,
  While round the armed bands,
  Did clap their bloudy hands :
He nothing common did, or mean,
Upon that memorable scene ;
  But with his keener eye
  The axe's edge did trye.   60
Nor call'd the gods with vulgar spight
To vindicate his helplesse right :
  But bow'd his comely head
  Downe, as upon a bed.
This was that memorable houre,
Which first assured the forced power ;
  So when they did designe
  The capitol's first line,
A bleeding head where they begun,
Did fright the architects to run ;   70
  And yet in that the state
  Foresaw its happy fate.
And now the Irish are asham'd
To see themselves in one year tam'd ;
  So much one man can doe,
  That does both act and know.
They can affirme his praises best,
And have, though overcome, confest
  How good he is, how just,
  And fit for highest trust.   80
Nor yet grown stiffer with command,
But still in the republick's hand,
  How fit he is to sway,
  That can so well obey !
He to the commons feet presents
A kingdom for his first year's rents :
  And what he may forbears
  His fame, to make it theirs ;
And has his sword and spoyls ungirt,
To lay them at the publick's skirt.   90

So when the falcon high,
Falls heavy from the skigh,
She having kill'd, no more doth search,
But on the next green bough to perch ;
Where, when he first does lure,
The faulkner has her sure.
What may not then our isle presume,
While victory his crest does plume ?
What may not others feare,
If thus he crowns each yeare ?　　　　　100
As Caesar, he, ere long to Gaul,
To Italy an Hannibal,
And to all states not free,
Shall clymacterick be.
The Pict no shelter now shall find
Within his party-colour'd mind,
But, from this valour, sad,
Shrink underneath the plad ;
Happy, if in the tufted brake,
The English hunter him mistake ;　　　　　110
Nor lay his hounds in neere
The Caledonian deer.
But thou, the warr's and fortune's sonne,
March indefatigably on,
And for the last effect,
Still keep the sword erect :
Besides the force it has to fright
The spirits of the shady night,
The same arts that did gain
A pow'r, must it maintain.　　　　　120

ROBERT HERRICK

UPON MASTER FLETCHERS
INCOMPARABLE PLAYES

APOLLO sings, his harpe resounds ; give roome,
For now behold the golden Pompe is come,
The Pompe of Playes which thousands come to see,
With admiration both of them and thee.
O Volume worthy leafe, by leafe and cover
To be with juice of Cedar washt all over ;
Here words with lines, and lines with Scenes consent,
To raise an Act to full astonishment ;
Here melting numbers, words of power to move
Young men to swoone, and Maides to dye for love.   10
Loves lyes a bleeding here, *Evadne* there
Swells with brave rage, yet comely every where,
Here's a mad lover, there that high designe
Of *King and no King* (and the rare Plot thine):
So that wher'ere wee circumvolve our Eyes,
Such rich, such fresh, such sweet varietyes,
Ravish our spirits, that entranc't we see
None writes lov's passion in the world, like Thee.

JOHN DRYDEN

ABSALOM AND ACHITOPHEL

In pious times, ere priestcraft did begin,
Before polygamy was made a sin,
When man on many multiplied his kind,
Ere one to one was cursedly confined,
When nature prompted and no law denied,
Promiscuous use of concubine and bride,
Then Israel's monarch after Heaven's own heart
His vigorous warmth did variously impart
To wives and slaves, and, wide as his command,
Scattered his Maker's image through the land.   10
Michal, of royal blood, the crown did wear,
A soil ungrateful to the tiller's care:
Not so the rest; for several mothers bore
To god-like David several sons before.
But since like slaves his bed they did ascend,
No true succession could their seed attend.
Of all this numerous progeny was none
So beautiful, so brave, as Absalon:
Whether, inspired by some diviner lust,
His father got him with a greater gust,   20
Or that his conscious destiny made way
By manly beauty to imperial sway.
Early in foreign fields he won renown
With kings and states allied to Israel's crown;
In peace the thoughts of war he could remove
And seemed as he were only born for love.
Whate'er he did was done with so much ease,
In him alone 'twas natural to please;
His motions all accompanied with grace,
And Paradise was opened in his face.   30
With secret joy indulgent David viewed
His youthful image in his son renewed;
To all his wishes nothing he denied
And made the charming Annabel his bride.
What faults he had (for who from faults is free?)
His father could not or he would not see.
Some warm excesses, which the law forbore,
Were construed youth that purged by boiling o'er;
And Amnon's murder by a specious name
Was called a just revenge for injured fame.   40

Thus praised and loved, the noble youth remained,
While David undisturbed in Sion reigned.
But life can never be sincerely blest;
Heaven punishes the bad, and proves the best.
The Jews, a headstrong, moody, murmuring race
As ever tried the extent and stretch of grace;
God's pampered people, whom, debauched with ease,
No king could govern nor no God could please;
Gods they had tried of every shape and size
That godsmiths could produce or priests devise; 50
These Adam-wits, too fortunately free,
Began to dream they wanted liberty;
And when no rule, no precedent was found
Of men by laws less circumscribed and bound,
They led their wild desires to woods and caves
And thought that all but savages were slaves.
They who, when Saul was dead, without a blow
Made foolish Ishbosheth the crown forego;
Who banished David did from Hebron bring,
And with a general shout proclaimed him King; 60
Those very Jews who at their very best
Their humour more than loyalty exprest,
Now wondered why so long they had obeyed
An idol monarch which their hands had made;
Thought they might ruin him they could create
Or melt him to that golden calf, a State.
But these were random bolts; no formed design
Nor interest made the factious crowd to join:
The sober part of Israel, free from stain,
Well knew the value of a peaceful reign; 70
And looking backward with a wise affright
Saw seams of wounds dishonest to the sight,
In contemplation of whose ugly scars
They cursed the memory of civil wars.
The moderate sort of men, thus qualified,
Inclined the balance to the better side;
And David's mildness managed it so well,
The bad found no occasion to rebel.
But when to sin our biassed nature leans,
The careful Devil is still at hand with means 80
And providently pimps for ill desires;
The good old cause, revived, a plot requires.
Plots true or false are necessary things,
To raise up commonwealths and ruin kings.

 The inhabitants of old Jerusalem
Were Jebusites; the town so called from them
And theirs the native right.
But when the chosen people grew more strong,
The rightful cause at length became the wrong;

And every loss the men of Jebus bore, 90
They still were thought God's enemies the more.
Thus worn and weakened, well or ill content,
Submit they must to David's government:
Impoverished and deprived of all command,
Their taxes doubled as they lost their land;
And, what was harder yet to flesh and blood,
Their gods disgraced, and burnt like common wood.
This set the heathen priesthood in a flame,
For priests of all religions are the same.
Of whatsoe'er descent their godhead be, 100
Stock, stone, or other homely pedigree,
In his defence his servants are as bold,
As if he had been born of beaten gold.
The Jewish Rabbins, though their enemies,
In this conclude them honest men and wise:
For 'twas their duty, all the learned think,
To espouse his cause by whom they eat and drink.
From hence began that Plot, the nation's curse,
Bad in itself, but represented worse,
Raised in extremes, and in extremes decried, 110
With oaths affirmed, with dying vows denied,
Not weighed or winnowed by the multitude,
But swallowed in the mass, unchewed and crude.
Some truth there was, but dashed and brewed with lies
To please the fools and puzzle all the wise:
Succeeding times did equal folly call
Believing nothing or believing all.
The Egyptian rites the Jebusites embraced,
Where gods were recommended by their taste;
Such savoury deities must needs be good 120
As served at once for worship and for food.
By force they could not introduce these gods,
For ten to one in former days was odds:
So fraud was used, the sacrificer's trade;
Fools are more hard to conquer than persuade.
Their busy teachers mingled with the Jews
And raked for converts even the court and stews:
Which Hebrew priests the more unkindly took,
Because the fleece accompanies the flock.
Some thought they God's anointed meant to slay 130
By guns, invented since full many a day:
Our author swears it not; but who can know
How far the Devil and Jebusites may go?
This plot, which failed for want of common sense,
Had yet a deep and dangerous consequence;
For as, when raging fevers boil the blood,
The standing lake soon floats into a flood,
And every hostile humour which before
Slept quiet in its channels bubbles o'er;

So several factions from this first ferment   140
Work up to foam and threat the government.
Some by their friends, more by themselves thought wise,
Opposed the power to which they could not rise.
Some had in courts been great and, thrown from thence,
Like fiends were hardened in impenitence.
Some by their Monarch's fatal mercy grown
From pardoned rebels kinsmen to the throne
Were raised in power and public office high ;
Strong bands, if bands ungrateful men could tie.
Of these the false Achitophel was first,   150
A name to all succeeding ages curst :
For close designs and crooked counsels fit,
Sagacious, bold, and turbulent of wit,
Restless, unfixed in principles and place,
In power unpleased, impatient of disgrace ;
A fiery soul, which, working out its way,
Fretted the pigmy body to decay
And o'er-informed the tenement of clay.
A daring pilot in extremity,
Pleased with the danger, when the waves went high, 160
He sought the storms ; but, for a calm unfit,
Would steer too nigh the sands to boast his wit.
Great wits are sure to madness near allied
And thin partitions do their bounds divide ;
Else, why should he, with wealth and honour blest,
Refuse his age the needful hours of rest ?
Punish a body which he could not please,
Bankrupt of life, yet prodigal of ease ?
And all to leave what with his toil he won
To that unfeathered two-legged thing, a son,   170
Got, while his soul did huddled notions try,
And born a shapeless lump, like anarchy.
In friendship false, implacable in hate,
Resolved to ruin or to rule the state ;
To compass this the triple bond he broke,
The pillars of the public safety shook,
And fitted Israel for a foreign yoke ;
Then, seized with fear, yet still affecting fame,
Usurped a patriot's all-atoning name.
So easy still it proves in factious times   180
With public zeal to cancel private crimes.
How safe is treason and how sacred ill,
Where none can sin against the people's will,
Where crowds can wink and no offence be known,
Since in another's guilt they find their own !
Yet fame deserved no enemy can grudge ;
The statesman we abhor, but praise the judge.
In Israel's courts ne'er sat an Abbethdin
With more discerning eyes or hands more clean,

Unbribed, unsought, the wretched to redress,   190
Swift of despatch and easy of access.
Oh! had he been content to serve the crown
With virtues only proper to the gown,
Or had the rankness of the soil been freed
From cockle that oppressed the noble seed,
David for him his tuneful harp had strung
And Heaven had wanted one immortal song.
But wild ambition loves to slide, not stand,
And fortune's ice prefers to virtue's land.
Achitophel, grown weary to possess   200
A lawful fame and lazy happiness,
Disdained the golden fruit to gather free
And lent the crowd his arm to shake the tree.
Now, manifest of crimes contrived long since,
He stood at bold defiance with his Prince,
Held up the buckler of the people's cause
Against the crown, and skulked behind the laws.
The wished occasion of the Plot he takes;
Some circumstances finds, but more he makes;
By buzzing emissaries fills the ears   210
Of listening crowds with jealousies and fears
Of arbitrary counsels brought to light,
And proves the King himself a Jebusite.
Weak arguments! which yet he knew full well
Were strong with people easy to rebel.
For governed by the moon, the giddy Jews
Tread the same track when she the prime renews:
And once in twenty years their scribes record,
By natural instinct they change their lord.
Achitophel still wants a chief, and none   220
Was found so fit as warlike Absalon.
Not that he wished his greatness to create,
For politicians neither love nor hate;
But, for he knew his title not allowed
Would keep him still depending on the crowd,
That kingly power, thus ebbing out, might be
Drawn to the dregs of a democracy.
Him he attempts with studied arts to please
And sheds his venom in such words as these:

   'Auspicious prince, at whose nativity   230
Some royal planet ruled the southern sky,
Thy longing country's darling and desire,
Their cloudy pillar and their guardian fire,
Their second Moses, whose extended wand
Divides the seas and shows the promised land,
Whose dawning day in every distant age
Has exercised the sacred prophet's rage,
The people's prayer, the glad diviner's theme,
The young men's vision and the old men's dream,

Thee Saviour, thee the nation's vows confess,   240
And never satisfied with seeing bless :
Swift unbespoken pomps thy steps proclaim,
And stammering babes are taught to lisp thy name.
How long wilt thou the general joy detain,
Starve and defraud the people of thy reign ?
Content ingloriously to pass thy days,
Like one of virtue's fools that feeds on praise ;
Till thy fresh glories, which now shine so bright,
Grow stale and tarnish with our daily sight.
Believe me, royal youth, thy fruit must be   250
Or gathered ripe, or rot upon the tree.
Heaven has to all allotted, soon or late,
Some lucky revolution of their fate :
Whose motions if we watch and guide with skill,
(For human good depends on human will,)
Our fortune rolls as from a smooth descent
And from the first impression takes the bent ;
But, if unseized, she glides away like wind
And leaves repenting folly far behind.
Now, now she meets you with a glorious prize   260
And spreads her locks before her as she flies.
Had thus old David, from whose loins you spring,
Not dared, when fortune called him to be King,
At Gath an exile he might still remain,
And Heaven's anointing oil had been in vain.
Let his successful youth your hopes engage,
But shun the example of declining age.
Behold him setting in his western skies,
The shadows lengthening as the vapours rise ;
He is not now, as when, on Jordan's sand,   270
The joyful people thronged to see him land,
Covering the beach and blackening all the strand,
But like the Prince of Angels, from his height
Comes tumbling downward with diminished light :
Betrayed by one poor plot to public scorn,
(Our only blessing since his curst return,)
Those heaps of people, which one sheaf did bind,
Blown off and scattered by a puff of wind.
What strength can he to your designs oppose,
Naked of friends, and round beset with foes ?   280
If Pharaoh's doubtful succour he should use,
A foreign aid would more incense the Jews ;
Proud Egypt would dissembled friendship bring,
Foment the war, but not support the King ;
Nor would the royal party e'er unite
With Pharaoh's arms to assist the Jebusite ;
Or, if they should, their interest soon would break
And with such odious aid make David weak.
All sorts of men, by my successful arts
Abhorring kings, estrange their altered hearts   290

From David's rule: and 'tis the general cry,
Religion, commonwealth, and liberty.
If you, as champion of the public good,
Add to their arms a chief of royal blood,
What may not Israel hope, and what applause
Might such a general gain by such a cause?
Not barren praise alone, that gaudy flower,
Fair only to the sight, but solid power;
And nobler is a limited command,
Given by the love of all your native land,   300
Than a successive title, long and dark,
Drawn from the mouldy rolls of Noah's ark.'

    What cannot praise effect in mighty minds,
When flattery soothes and when ambition blinds?
Desire of power, on earth a vicious weed,
Yet sprung from high is of celestial seed;
In God 'tis glory, and when men aspire,
'Tis but a spark too much of heavenly fire.
The ambitious youth, too covetous of fame,
Too full of angel's metal in his frame,   310
Unwarily was led from virtue's ways,
Made drunk with honour and debauched with praise.
Half loth and half consenting to the ill,
For loyal blood within him struggled still,
He thus replied: 'And what pretence have I
To take up arms for public liberty?
My father governs with unquestioned right,
The faith's defender and mankind's delight,
Good, gracious, just, observant of the laws;
And Heaven by wonders has espoused his cause.   320
Whom has he wronged in all his peaceful reign?
Who sues for justice to his throne in vain?
What millions has he pardoned of his foes
Whom just revenge did to his wrath expose?
Mild, easy, humble, studious of our good,
Inclined to mercy and averse from blood.
If mildness ill with stubborn Israel suit,
His crime is God's beloved attribute.
What could he gain his people to betray
Or change his right for arbitrary sway?   330
Let haughty Pharaoh curse with such a reign
His fruitful Nile, and yoke a servile train.
If David's rule Jerusalem displease,
The dog-star heats their brains to this disease.
Why then should I, encouraging the bad,
Turn rebel and run popularly mad?
Were he a tyrant, who by lawless might
Oppressed the Jews and raised the Jebusite,
Well might I mourn; but nature's holy bands
Would curb my spirits and restrain my hands;   340

The people might assert their liberty,
But what was right in them were crime in me.
His favour leaves me nothing to require,
Prevents my wishes and outruns desire ;
What more can I expect while David lives ?
All but his kingly diadem he gives :
And that '—But there he paused, then sighing said,
' Is justly destined for a worthier head ;
For when my father from his toils shall rest
And late augment the number of the blest,   350
His lawful issue shall the throne ascend,
Or the collateral line, where that shall end.
His brother, though oppressed with vulgar spite,
Yet dauntless and secure of native right,
Of every royal virtue stands possest,
Still dear to all the bravest and the best.
His courage foes, his friends his truth proclaim,
His loyalty the King, the world his fame.
His mercy even the offending crowd will find,
For sure he comes of a forgiving kind.   360
Why should I then repine at Heaven's decree
Which gives me no pretence to royalty ?
Yet oh that Fate, propitiously inclined,
Had raised my birth or had debased my mind,
To my large soul not all her treasure lent,
And then betrayed it to a mean descent !
I find, I find my mounting spirits bold,
And David's part disdains my mother's mould.
Why am I scanted by a niggard birth ?
My soul disclaims the kindred of her earth,   370
And, made for empire, whispers me within,
Desire of greatness is a god-like sin.'

Him staggering so when Hell's dire agent found,
While fainting virtue scarce maintained her ground,
He pours fresh forces in, and thus replies :
' The eternal God, supremely good and wise,
Imparts not these prodigious gifts in vain.
What wonders are reserved to bless your reign !
Against your will your arguments have shown,
Such virtue's only given to guide a throne.   380
Not that your father's mildness I contemn,
But manly force becomes the diadem.
'Tis true he grants the people all they crave,
And more perhaps than subjects ought to have :
For lavish grants suppose a monarch tame
And more his goodness than his wit proclaim.
But when should people strive their bonds to break,
If not when kings are negligent or weak ?
Let him give on till he can give no more,
The thrifty Sanhedrin shall keep him poor ;   390

And every shekel which he can receive
Shall cost a limb of his prerogative.
To ply him with new plots shall be my care,
Or plunge him deep in some expensive war;
Which when his treasure can no more supply,
He must with the remains of kingship buy.
His faithful friends our jealousies and fears
Call Jebusites and Pharaoh's pensioners,
Whom when our fury from his aid has torn,
He shall be naked left to public scorn.   400
The next successor, whom I fear and hate,
My arts have made obnoxious to the State,
Turned all his virtues to his overthrow,
And gained our elders to pronounce a foe.
His right for sums of necessary gold
Shall first be pawned, and afterwards be sold;
Till time shall ever-wanting David draw
To pass your doubtful title into law.
If not, the people have a right supreme
To make their kings, for kings are made for them.   410
All empire is no more than power in trust,
Which, when resumed, can be no longer just.
Succession, for the general good designed,
In its own wrong a nation cannot bind:
If altering that the people can relieve,
Better one suffer than a nation grieve.
The Jews well know their power: ere Saul they chose
God was their King, and God they durst depose.
Urge now your piety, your filial name,
A father's right and fear of future fame,   420
The public good, that universal call,
To which even Heaven submitted, answers all.
Nor let his love enchant your generous mind;
'Tis Nature's trick to propagate her kind.
Our fond begetters, who would never die,
Love but themselves in their posterity.
Or let his kindness by the effects be tried,
Or let him lay his vain pretence aside.
God said, He loved your father; could He bring
A better proof than to anoint him King?   430
It surely showed, He loved the shepherd well
Who gave so fair a flock as Israel.
Would David have you thought his darling son?
What means he then to alienate the crown?
The name of godly he may blush to bear;
'Tis after God's own heart to cheat his heir.
He to his brother gives supreme command,
To you a legacy of barren land,
Perhaps the old harp on which he thrums his lays
Or some dull Hebrew ballad in your praise.   440

Then the next heir, a prince severe and wise,
Already looks on you with jealous eyes,
Sees through the thin disguises of your arts,
And marks your progress in the people's hearts ;
Though now his mighty soul its grief contains,
He meditates revenge who least complains ;
And like a lion, slumbering in the way
Or sleep dissembling, while he waits his prey,
His fearless foes within his distance draws,
Constrains his roaring and contracts his paws,   450
Till at the last, his time for fury found,
He shoots with sudden vengeance from the ground,
The prostrate vulgar passes o'er and spares,
But with a lordly rage his hunters tears ;
Your case no tame expedients will afford,
Resolve on death or conquest by the sword,
Which for no less a stake than life you draw,
And self-defence is Nature's eldest law.
Leave the warm people no considering time,
For then rebellion may be thought a crime.   460
Prevail yourself of what occasion gives,
But try your title while your father lives ;
And, that your arms may have a fair pretence,
Proclaim you take them in the King's defence ;
Whose sacred life each minute would expose
To plots from seeming friends and secret foes.
And who can sound the depth of David's soul ?
Perhaps his fear his kindness may control :
He fears his brother, though he loves his son,
For plighted vows too late to be undone.   470
If so, by force he wishes to be gained,
Like women's lechery to seem constrained.
Doubt not : but, when he most affects the frown,
Commit a pleasing rape upon the crown.
Secure his person to secure your cause :
They who possess the Prince possess the laws.'

   He said, and this advice above the rest
With Absalom's mild nature suited best ;
Unblamed of life (ambition set aside),
Not stained with cruelty nor puffed with pride,   480
How happy had he been, if Destiny
Had higher placed his birth or not so high !
His kingly virtues might have claimed a throne
And blessed all other countries but his own ;
But charming greatness since so few refuse,
'Tis juster to lament him than accuse.
Strong were his hopes a rival to remove,
With blandishments to gain the public love,
To head the faction while their zeal was hot,
And popularly prosecute the plot.   490

To further this, Achitophel unites
The malcontents of all the Israelites,
Whose differing parties he could wisely join
For several ends to serve the same design:
The best, (and of the princes some were such,)
Who thought the power of monarchy too much,
Mistaken men and patriots in their hearts,
Not wicked, but seduced by impious arts;
By these the springs of property were bent
And wound so high they cracked the government.   509
The next for interest sought to embroil the state,
To sell their duty at a dearer rate,
And make their Jewish markets of the throne,
Pretending public good to serve their own.
Others thought kings an useless heavy load,
Who cost too much and did too little good.
These were for laying honest David by
On principles of pure good husbandry.
With them joined all the haranguers of the throng
That thought to get preferment by the tongue.   516
Who follow next a double danger bring,
Not only hating David, but the King;
The Solymaean rout, well versed of old
In godly faction and in treason bold,
Cowering and quaking at a conqueror's sword,
But lofty to a lawful prince restored,
Saw with disdain an Ethnic plot begun
And scorned by Jebusites to be outdone.
Hot Levites headed these; who pulled before
From the ark, which in the Judges' days they bore, 520
Resumed their cant, and with a zealous cry
Pursued their old beloved theocracy,
Where Sanhedrin and priest enslaved the nation
And justified their spoils by inspiration;
For who so fit for reign as Aaron's race,
If once dominion they could found in grace?
These led the pack; though not of surest scent,
Yet deepest mouthed against the government.
A numerous host of dreaming saints succeed
Of the true old enthusiastic breed: 530
'Gainst form and order they their power employ,
Nothing to build and all things to destroy.
But far more numerous was the herd of such
Who think too little and who talk too much.
These out of mere instinct, they knew not why,
Adored their fathers' God and property,
And by the same blind benefit of Fate
The Devil and the Jebusite did hate:
Born to be saved even in their own despite,
Because they could not help believing right.   540

Such were the tools ; but a whole Hydra more
Remains of sprouting heads too long to score.
Some of their chiefs were princes of the land ;
In the first rank of these did Zimri stand,
A man so various that he seemed to be
Not one, but all mankind's epitome :
Stiff in opinions, always in the wrong,
Was everything by starts and nothing long ;
But in the course of one revolving moon
Was chymist, fiddler, statesman, and buffoon ;　550
Then all for women, painting, rhyming, drinking,
Besides ten thousand freaks that died in thinking.
Blest madman, who could every hour employ
With something new to wish or to enjoy !
Railing and praising were his usual themes,
And both, to show his judgment, in extremes :
So over violent or over civil
That every man with him was God or Devil.
In squandering wealth was his peculiar art ;
Nothing went unrewarded but desert.　560
Beggared by fools whom still he found too late,
He had his jest, and they had his estate.
He laughed himself from Court ; then sought relief
By forming parties, but could ne'er be chief :
For spite of him, the weight of business fell
On Absalom and wise Achitophel ;
Thus wicked but in will, of means bereft,
He left not faction, but of that was left.
　　Titles and names 'twere tedious to rehearse
Of lords below the dignity of verse.　570
Wits, warriors, commonwealth's-men were the best ;
Kind husbands and mere nobles all the rest.
And therefore in the name of dulness be
The well-hung Balaam and cold Caleb free ;
And canting Nadab let oblivion damn
Who made new porridge for the paschal lamb.
Let friendship's holy band some names assure,
Some their own worth, and some let scorn secure.
Nor shall the rascal rabble here have place
Whom kings no titles gave, and God no grace :　580
Not bull-faced Jonas, who could statutes draw
To mean rebellion and make treason law.
But he, though bad, is followed by a worse,
The wretch who Heaven's anointed dared to curse ;
Shimei, whose youth did early promise bring
Of zeal to God and hatred to his King,
Did wisely from expensive sins refrain
And never broke the Sabbath but for gain
Nor ever was he known an oath to vent
Or curse, unless against the government.　590

Thus heaping wealth by the most ready way
Among the Jews, which was to cheat and pray,
The City, to reward his pious hate
Against his master, chose him magistrate.
His hand a vare of justice did uphold,
His neck was loaded with a chain of gold.
During his office treason was no crime,
The sons of Belial had a glorious time;
For Shimei, though not prodigal of pelf,
Yet loved his wicked neighbour as himself.   600
When two or three were gathered to declaim
Against the monarch of Jerusalem,
Shimei was always in the midst of them:
And, if they cursed the King when he was by,
Would rather curse than break good company.
If any durst his factious friends accuse,
He packed a jury of dissenting Jews;
Whose fellow-feeling in the godly cause
Would free the suffering saint from human laws:
For laws are only made to punish those   610
Who serve the King, and to protect his foes.
If any leisure time he had from power,
Because 'tis sin to misemploy an hour,
His business was by writing to persuade
That kings were useless and a clog to trade:
And that his noble style he might refine,
No Rechabite more shunned the fumes of wine.
Chaste were his cellars, and his shrieval board
The grossness of a city feast abhorred:
His cooks with long disuse their trade forgot;   620
Cool was his kitchen, though his brains were hot.
Such frugal virtue malice may accuse;
But sure 'twas necessary to the Jews:
For towns once burnt such magistrates require
As dare not tempt God's providence by fire.
With spiritual food he fed his servants well,
But free from flesh that made the Jews rebel:
And Moses' laws he held in more account
For forty days of fasting in the mount.
To speak the rest, who better are forgot,   630
Would tire a well-breathed witness of the plot.
Yet, Corah, thou shalt from oblivion pass;
Erect thyself, thou monumental brass,
High as the serpent of thy metal made,
While nations stand secure beneath thy shade.
What though his birth were base, yet comets rise
From earthy vapours, ere they shine in skies.
Prodigious actions may as well be done
By weaver's issue as by prince's son.
This arch-attester for the public good   640

By that one deed ennobles all his blood.
Who ever asked the witnesses' high race
Whose oath with martyrdom did Stephen grace?
Ours was a Levite, and as times went then,
His tribe were God Almighty's gentlemen.
Sunk were his eyes, his voice was harsh and loud,
Sure signs he neither choleric was nor proud:
His long chin proved his wit, his saint-like grace
A church vermilion and a Moses' face.
His memory, miraculously great, 650
Could plots exceeding man's belief repeat;
Which therefore cannot be accounted lies,
For human wit could never such devise.
Some future truths are mingled in his book,
But where the witness failed, the prophet spoke:
Some things like visionary flights appear;
The spirit caught him up, the Lord knows where;
And gave him his Rabbinical degree
Unknown to foreign University.
His judgment yet his memory did excel, 660
Which pieced his wondrous evidence so well
And suited to the temper of the times,
Then groaning under Jebusitic crimes.
Let Israel's foes suspect his heavenly call
And rashly judge his writ apocryphal;
Our laws for such affronts have forfeits made,
He takes his life who takes away his trade.
Were I myself in witness Corah's place,
The wretch who did me such a dire disgrace
Should whet my memory, though once forgot, 670
To make him an appendix of my plot.
His zeal to Heaven made him his Prince despise,
And load his person with indignities.
But zeal peculiar privilege affords,
Indulging latitude to deeds and words:
And Corah might for Agag's murder call,
In terms as coarse as Samuel used to Saul.
What others in his evidence did join,
The best that could be had for love or coin,
In Corah's own predicament will fall, 680
For Witness is a common name to all.

Surrounded thus with friends of every sort,
Deluded Absalom forsakes the court;
Impatient of high hopes, urged with renown,
And fired with near possession of a crown.
The admiring crowd are dazzled with surprise
And on his goodly person feed their eyes.
His joy concealed, he sets himself to show,
On each side bowing popularly low,

His looks, his gestures, and his words he frames   690
And with familiar ease repeats their names.
Thus formed by nature, furnished out with arts,
He glides unfelt into their secret hearts.
Then with a kind compassionating look,
And sighs, bespeaking pity ere he spoke,
Few words he said, but easy those and fit,
More slow than Hybla-drops and far more sweet.
    ' I mourn, my countrymen, your lost estate,
Though far unable to prevent your fate :
Behold a banished man, for your dear cause   700
Exposed a prey to arbitrary laws!
Yet oh that I alone could be undone,
Cut off from empire, and no more a son !
Now all your liberties a spoil are made,
Egypt and Tyrus intercept your trade,
And Jebusites your sacred rites invade.
My father, whom with reverence yet I name,
Charmed into ease, is careless of his fame,
And, bribed with petty sums of foreign gold,
Is grown in Bathsheba's embraces old ;   710
Exalts his enemies, his friends destroys,
And all his power against himself employs.
He gives, and let him give, my right away ;
But why should he his own and yours betray ?
He, only he can make the nation bleed,
And he alone from my revenge is freed.
Take then my tears (with that he wiped his eyes),
'Tis all the aid my present power supplies :
No court-informer can these arms accuse ;
These arms may sons against their fathers use.   720
And 'tis my wish, the next successor's reign
May make no other Israelite complain.'

    Youth, beauty, graceful action seldom fail,
But common interest always will prevail ;
And pity never ceases to be shown
To him who makes the people's wrongs his own.
The crowd that still believe their kings oppress
With lifted hands their young Messiah bless :
Who now begins his progress to ordain
With chariots, horsemen, and a numerous train ;   730
From east to west his glories he displays
And, like the sun, the promised land surveys.
Fame runs before him as the morning star,
And shouts of joy salute him from afar ;
Each house receives him as a guardian god
And consecrates the place of his abode.
But hospitable treats did most commend
Wise Issachar, his wealthy western friend.

This moving court that caught the people's eyes,
And seemed but pomp, did other ends disguise;   740
Achitophel had formed it, with intent
To sound the depths and fathom, where it went,
The people's hearts, distinguish friends from foes,
And try their strength before they came to blows.
Yet all was coloured with a smooth pretence
Of specious love and duty to their prince.
Religion and redress of grievances,
Two names that always cheat and always please,
Are often urged; and good king David's life
Endangered by a brother and a wife.   750
Thus in a pageant show a plot is made,
And peace itself is war in masquerade.
Oh foolish Israel! never warned by ill!
Still the same bait, and circumvented still!
Did ever men forsake their present ease,
In midst of health imagine a disease,
Take pains contingent mischiefs to foresee,
Make heirs for monarchs, and for God decree?
What shall we think?   Can people give away
Both for themselves and sons their native sway?   760
Then they are left defenceless to the sword
Of each unbounded, arbitrary lord;
And laws are vain by which we right enjoy,
If kings unquestioned can those laws destroy.
Yet if the crowd be judge of fit and just,
And kings are only officers in trust,
Then this resuming covenant was declared
When kings were made, or is for ever barred.
If those who gave the sceptre could not tie
By their own deed their own posterity,   770
How then could Adam bind his future race?
How could his forfeit on mankind take place?
Or how could heavenly justice damn us all
Who ne'er consented to our father's fall?
Then kings are slaves to those whom they command
And tenants to their people's pleasure stand.
Add that the power, for property allowed,
Is mischievously seated in the crowd;
For who can be secure of private right,
If sovereign sway may be dissolved by might?   780
Nor is the people's judgment always true:
The most may err as grossly as the few,
And faultless kings run down by common cry
For vice, oppression, and for tyranny.
What standard is there in a fickle rout,
Which, flowing to the mark, runs faster out?
Nor only crowds but Sanhedrins may be
Infected with this public lunacy,

And share the madness of rebellious times,
To murder monarchs for imagined crimes.   790
If they may give and take whene'er they please,
Not kings alone, the Godhead's images,
But government itself at length must fall
To nature's state, where all have right to all.
Yet grant our lords, the people, kings can make,
What prudent men a settled throne would shake?
For whatsoe'er their sufferings were before,
That change they covet makes them suffer more.
All other errors but disturb a state,
But innovation is the blow of fate.   800
If ancient fabrics nod and threat to fall,
To patch the flaws and buttress up the wall,
Thus far 'tis duty: but here fix the mark;
For all beyond it is to touch our ark.
To change foundations, cast the frame anew,
Is work for rebels who base ends pursue,
At once divine and human laws control,
And mend the parts by ruin of the whole.
The tampering world is subject to this curse,
To physic their disease into a worse.   810

    Now what relief can righteous David bring?
How fatal 'tis to be too good a king!
Friends he has few, so high the madness grows;
Who dare be such must be the people's foes.
Yet some there were even in the worst of days;
Some let me name, and naming is to praise.

    In this short file Barzillai first appears,
Barzillai, crowned with honour and with years.
Long since the rising rebels he withstood
In regions waste beyond the Jordan's flood: 820
Unfortunately brave to buoy the state,
But sinking underneath his master's fate.
In exile with his godlike prince he mourned,
For him he suffered, and with him returned.
The court he practised, not the courtier's art:
Large was his wealth, but larger was his heart,
Which well the noblest objects knew to chuse,
The fighting warrior, and recording Muse.
His bed could once a fruitful issue boast;
Now more than half a father's name is lost.   830
His eldest hope, with every grace adorned,
By me, so Heaven will have it, always mourned
And always honoured, snatched in manhood's prime
By unequal fates and Providence's crime:
Yet not before the goal of honour won,
All parts fulfilled of subject and of son;
Swift was the race, but short the time to run.

Oh narrow circle, but of power divine,
Scanted in space, but perfect in thy line!
By sea, by land, thy matchless worth was known,   840
Arms thy delight, and war was all thy own:
Thy force infused the fainting Tyrians propped,
And haughty Pharaoh found his fortune stopped.
Oh ancient honour! oh unconquered hand,
Whom foes unpunished never could withstand!
But Israel was unworthy of thy name:
Short is the date of all immoderate fame.
It looks as Heaven our ruin had designed,
And durst not trust thy fortune and thy mind.
Now, free from earth, thy disencumbered soul   850
Mounts up, and leaves behind the clouds and starry pole:
From thence thy kindred legions mayest thou bring
To aid the guardian angel of thy King.
Here stop, my Muse, here cease thy painful flight;
No pinions can pursue immortal height:
Tell good Barzillai thou canst sing no more,
And tell thy soul she should have fled before:
Or fled she with his life, and left this verse
To hang on her departed patron's hearse?
Now take thy steepy flight from heaven, and see   860
If thou canst find on earth another he:
Another he would be too hard to find;
See then whom thou canst see not far behind.
Zadoc the priest, whom, shunning power and place,
His lowly mind advanced to David's grace.
With him the Sagan of Jerusalem,
Of hospitable soul and noble stem;
Him of the western dome, whose weighty sense
Flows in fit words and heavenly eloquence.
The Prophets' sons, by such example led,   870
To learning and to loyalty were bred:
For colleges on bounteous kings depend,
And never rebel was to arts a friend.
To these succeed the pillars of the laws,
Who best could plead, and best can judge a cause.
Next them a train of loyal peers ascend;
Sharp-judging Adriel, the Muses' friend,
Himself a Muse: in Sanhedrin's debate
True to his Prince, but not a slave of state;
Whom David's love with honours did adorn   880
That from his disobedient son were torn.
Jotham of piercing wit and pregnant thought,
Endued by nature and by learning taught
To move assemblies, who but only tried
The worse a while, then chose the better side,
Nor chose alone, but turned the balance too,
So much the weight of one brave man can do.

Hushai, the friend of David in distress,
In public storms of manly stedfastness;
By foreign treaties he informed his youth   890
And joined experience to his native truth.
His frugal care supplied the wanting throne,
Frugal for that, but bounteous of his own:
'Tis easy conduct when exchequers flow,
But hard the task to manage well the low.
For sovereign power is too depressed or high,
When kings are forced to sell or crowds to buy.
Indulge one labour more, my weary Muse,
For Amiel: who can Amiel's praise refuse?
Of ancient race by birth, but nobler yet   900
In his own worth and without title great:
The Sanhedrin long time as chief he ruled,
Their reason guided and their passion cooled:
So dexterous was he in the Crown's defence,
So formed to speak a loyal nation's sense,
That, as their band was Israel's tribes in small,
So fit was he to represent them all.
Now rasher charioteers the seat ascend,
Whose loose careers his steady skill commend:
They, like the unequal ruler of the day,   910
Misguide the seasons and mistake the way,
While he, withdrawn, at their mad labour smiles
And safe enjoys the sabbath of his toils.

  These were the chief, a small but faithful band
Of worthies in the breach who dared to stand
And tempt the united fury of the land.
With grief they viewed such powerful engines bent
To batter down the lawful government.
A numerous faction, with pretended frights,
In Sanhedrins to plume the regal rights;   920
The true successor from the Court removed;
The plot by hireling witnesses improved.
These ills they saw, and, as their duty bound,
They showed the King the danger of the wound;
That no concessions from the throne would please,
But lenitives fomented the disease;
That Absalom, ambitious of the crown,
Was made the lure to draw the people down;
That false Achitophel's pernicious hate
Had turned the plot to ruin Church and State;   930
The council violent, the rabble worse;
That Shimei taught Jerusalem to curse.

  With all these loads of injuries opprest,
And long revolving in his careful breast
The event of things, at last his patience tired,
Thus from his royal throne, by Heaven inspired.

The godlike David spoke; with awful fear
His train their Maker in their master hear.

'Thus long have I, by native mercy swayed,
My wrongs dissembled, my revenge delayed;   940
So willing to forgive the offending age;
So much the father did the king assuage.
But now so far my clemency they slight,
The offenders question my forgiving right.
That one was made for many, they contend;
But 'tis to rule, for that's a monarch's end.
They call my tenderness of blood my fear,
Though manly tempers can the longest bear.
Yet since they will divert my native course,
'Tis time to show I am not good by force.   950
Those heaped affronts that haughty subjects bring
Are burdens for a camel, not a king.
Kings are the public pillars of the State,
Born to sustain and prop the nation's weight:
If my young Samson will pretend a call
To shake the column, let him share the fall;
But oh that yet he would repent and live!
How easy 'tis for parents to forgive!
With how few tears a pardon might be won
From nature, pleading for a darling son!   960
Poor pitied youth, by my paternal care
Raised up to all the height his frame could bear!
Had God ordained his fate for empire born,
He would have given his soul another turn:
Gulled with a patriot's name, whose modern sense
Is one that would by law supplant his prince;
The people's brave, the politician's tool;
Never was patriot yet but was a fool.
Whence comes it that religion and the laws
Should more be Absalom's than David's cause?   970
His old instructor, ere he lost his place,
Was never thought endued with so much grace.
Good heavens, how faction can a patriot paint!
My rebel ever proves my people's saint.
Would they impose an heir upon the throne?
Let Sanhedrins be taught to give their own.
A king's at least a part of government,
And mine as requisite as their consent:
Without my leave a future king to choose
Infers a right the present to depose.   980
True, they petition me to approve their choice:
But Esau's hands suit ill with Jacob's voice.
My pious subjects for my safety pray,
Which to secure, they take my power away.
From plots and treasons Heaven preserve my years,
But save me most from my petitioners.

Unsatiate as the barren womb or grave,
God cannot grant so much as they can crave.
What then is left but with a jealous eye
To guard the small remains of royalty ?   990
The law shall still direct my peaceful sway,
And the same law teach rebels to obey :
Votes shall no more established power control,
Such votes as make a part exceed the whole.
No groundless clamours shall my friends remove
Nor crowds have power to punish ere they prove ;
For gods and godlike kings their care express
Still to defend their servants in distress.
Oh that my power to saving were confined !
Why am I forced, like Heaven, against my mind   1000
To make examples of another kind ?
Must I at length the sword of justice draw ?
Oh curst effects of necessary law !
How ill my fear they by my mercy scan !
Beware the fury of a patient man.
Law they require, let Law then show her face ;
They could not be content to look on Grace,
Her hinder parts, but with a daring eye
To tempt the terror of her front and die.
By their own arts, 'tis righteously decreed,   1010
Those dire artificers of death shall bleed.
Against themselves their witnesses will swear
Till, viper-like, their mother-plot they tear,
And suck for nutriment that bloody gore
Which was their principle of life before.
Their Belial with their Beelzebub will fight ;
Thus on my foes my foes shall do me right.
Nor doubt the event ; for factious crowds engage
In their first onset all their brutal rage.
Then let them take an unresisted course ;   1020
Retire and traverse, and delude their force :
But when they stand all breathless, urge the fight
And rise upon them with redoubled might :
For lawful power is still superior found,
When long driven back at length it stands the ground.'

   He said. The Almighty, nodding, gave consent ;
And peals of thunder shook the firmament.
Henceforth a series of new time began,
The mighty years in long procession ran ;
Once more the godlike David was restored,   1030
And willing nations knew their lawful lord.

TO MY DEAR FRIEND MR. CONGREVE

On his Comedy called The Double Dealer

WELL, then, the promised hour is come at last,
The present age of wit obscures the past:
Strong were our sires, and as they fought they writ,
Conquering with force of arms, and dint of wit:
Theirs was the giant race, before the flood;
And thus, when Charles returned, our empire stood.
Like Janus, he the stubborn soil manured,
With rules of husbandry the rankness cured;
Tamed us to manners when the stage was rude,
And boisterous English wit with art endued.   10
Our age was cultivated thus at length;
But what we gained in skill we lost in strength.
Our builders were with want of genius curst;
The second temple was not like the first;
Till you, the best Vitruvius, come at length,
Our beauties equal, but excel our strength.
Firm Doric pillars found your solid base;
The fair Corinthian crowns the higher space:
Thus all below is strength, and all above is grace.
In easy dialogue is Fletcher's praise;   20
He moved the mind, but had not power to raise:
Great Jonson did by strength of judgment please;
Yet, doubling Fletcher's force, he wants his ease.
In differing talents both adorned their age;
One for the study, t'other for the stage.
But both to Congreve justly shall submit,
One matched in judgment, both o'ermatched in wit.
In him all beauties of this age we see,   ⎫
Etherege his courtship, Southerne's purity,   ⎬
The satire, wit, and strength, of manly Wycherly.   ⎭   30
All this in blooming youth you have atchieved;
Nor are your foiled contemporaries grieved.
So much the sweetness of your manners move,
We cannot envy you, because we love.
Fabius might joy in Scipio, when he saw
A beardless consul made against the law,
And join his suffrage to the votes of Rome,
Though he with Hannibal was overcome.
Thus old Romano bowed to Raphael's fame,
And scholar to the youth he taught became.   40
  O that your brows my laurel had sustained!
Well had I been deposed, if you had reigned:
The father had descended for the son;
For only you are lineal to the throne.

G 3

Thus, when the state one Edward did depose,
A greater Edward in his room arose:
But now not I, but poetry, is cursed;
For Tom the second reigns like Tom the first.
But let them not mistake my patron's part,
Nor call his charity their own desert.   50
Yet this I prophecy,—Thou shalt be seen,
(Though with some short parenthesis between,)
High on the throne of wit, and, seated there,
Not mine,—that's little,—but thy laurel wear.
Thy first attempt an early promise made;
That early promise this has more than paid.
So bold, yet so judiciously you dare,
That your least praise is to be regular.
Time, place, and action, may with pains be wrought,
But genius must be born, and never can be taught.   60
This is your portion, this your native store;
Heaven, that but once was prodigal before,
To Shakespeare gave as much,—she could not give him more.

    Maintain your post; that's all the fame you need;
For 'tis impossible you should proceed.
Already I am worn with cares and age,
And just abandoning the ungrateful stage;
Unprofitably kept at Heaven's expence,
I live a rent-charge on his providence:
But you, whom every muse and grace adorn,   70
Whom I foresee to better fortune born,
Be kind to my remains; and O defend,
Against your judgment, your departed friend!
Let not the insulting foe my fame pursue,
But shade those laurels which descend to you:
And take for tribute what these lines express;
You merit more, nor could my love do less.

ALEXANDER'S FEAST, OR, THE
POWER OF MUSIC

1697

'TWAS at the royal feast for Persia won
    By Philip's warlike son—
    Aloft in awful state
    The godlike hero sate
    On his imperial throne;
    His valiant peers were placed around,
    Their brows with roses and with myrtles bound,
    (So should desert in arms be crown'd);

The lovely Thais by his side
Sate like a blooming eastern bride   10
In flower of youth and beauty's pride:—
Happy, happy, happy pair!
None but the brave
None but the brave
None but the brave deserves the fair!

Timotheus placed on high *musician!*
Amid the tuneful quire
With flying fingers touch'd the lyre:
The trembling notes ascend the sky
And heavenly joys inspire.   20
The song began from Jove
Who left his blissful seats above—
Such is the power of mighty love!
A dragon's fiery form belied the god;
Sublime on radiant spires he rode
When he to fair Olympia prest,
And while he sought her snowy breast,
Then round her slender waist he curl'd,
And stamp'd an image of himself, a sovereign of the world.
—The listening crowd admire the lofty sound!   30
A present deity! they shout around:
A present deity! the vaulted roofs rebound!
With ravish'd ears
The monarch hears,
Assumes the god;
Affects to nod
And seems to shake the spheres.

The praise of Bacchus then the sweet musician sung, *God Jovene*
Of Bacchus ever fair and ever young:
The jolly god in triumph comes!   40
Sound the trumpets, beat the drums!
Flush'd with a purple grace
He shows his honest face:
Now give the hautboys breath; he comes, he comes! *aboes*
Bacchus, ever fair and young,
Drinking joys did first ordain;   *Praise Jovene*
Bacchus' blessings are a treasure,
Drinking is the soldier's pleasure:
Rich the treasure,
Sweet the pleasure,   50
Sweet is pleasure after pain.

Soothed with the sound, the king grew vain;
Fought all his battles o'er again,
And thrice he routed all his foes, and thrice he slew the slain!
The master saw the madness rise, *musician*
His glowing cheeks, his ardent eyes;

And while he Heaven and Earth defied
Changed his hand and check'd his pride.
He chose a mournful Muse
Soft pity to infuse:
He sung Darius great and good, *Defeated by Alexander.*   60
By too severe a fate
Fallen, fallen, fallen, fallen,
Fallen from his high estate,
And weltering in his blood;
Deserted, at his utmost need,
By those his former bounty fed;
On the bare earth exposed he lies
With not a friend to close his eyes.
—With downcast looks the joyless victor sate,   70
Revolving in his alter'd soul
The various turns of Chance below;
And now and then a sigh he stole,
And tears began to flow.

The mighty master smiled to see
That love was in the next degree;
'Twas but a kindred-sound to move,
For pity melts the mind to love.
Softly sweet, in Lydian measures *soft sweet music.*
Soon he soothed his soul to pleasures.   80
War, he sung, is toil and trouble,
Honour but an empty bubble;
Never ending, still beginning,
Fighting still, and still destroying;
If the world be worth thy winning,
Think, O think, it worth enjoying:
Lovely Thais sits beside thee,
Take the good the gods provide thee!
—The many rend the skies with loud applause;
So Love was crown'd, but Music won the cause.   90
The prince, unable to conceal his pain,
Gazed on the fair
Who caused his care,
And sigh'd and look'd, sigh'd and look'd,
Sigh'd and look'd, and sigh'd again:
At length with love and wine at once opprest
The vanquish'd victor sunk upon her breast.

Now strike the golden lyre again:
A louder yet, and yet a louder strain!
Break his bands of sleep asunder   100
And rouse him like a rattling peal of thunder.
Hark, hark! the horrid sound
Has raised up his head:
As awaked from the dead

And amazed he stares around.
Revenge, revenge, Timotheus cries,
See the Furies arise!
See the snakes that they rear
How they hiss in their hair,
And the sparkles that flash from their eyes   110
Behold a ghastly band,
Each a torch in his hand!
Those are Grecian ghosts, that in battle were slain.
And unburied remain
Inglorious on the plain:
Give the vengeance due
To the valiant crew!
Behold how they toss their torches on high,
How they point to the Persian abodes
And glittering temples of their hostile gods.   120
—The princes applaud with a furious joy:
And the King seized a flambeau with zeal to destroy;
Thais led the way
To light him to his prey, *Persepolis*
And like another Helen, fired another Troy!

—Thus, long ago,
Ere heaving bellows learn'd to blow,
While organs yet were mute,
Timotheus, to his breathing flute
And sounding lyre   130
Could swell the soul to rage, or kindle soft desire.
At last divine Cecilia came,
Inventress of the vocal frame;
The sweet enthusiast from her sacred store
Enlarged the former narrow bounds,
And added length to solemn sounds,
With Nature's mother-wit, and arts unknown before.
—Let old Timotheus yield the prize
Or both divide the crown;
He raised a mortal to the skies: 140
She drew an angel down!

Persepolis is capital of Persia

Pity is akin to love.

ALEXANDER POPE

ELOISA TO ABELARD

ARGUMENT

ABELARD and Eloisa flourished in the twelfth Century; they were
two of the most distinguished Persons of their age in learning and beauty,
but for nothing more famous than for their unfortunate passion. After
a long course of calamities, they retired each to a several Convent,
and consecrated the remainder of their days to religion. It was many
years after this separation, that a letter of Abelard's to a Friend, which
contained the history of his misfortune, fell into the hands of Eloisa.
This awakening all her Tenderness, occasioned those celebrated letters
(out of which the following is partly extracted) which gives so lively
a picture of the struggles of grace and nature, virtue and passion.

IN these deep solitudes and awful cells,
Where heav'nly-pensive contemplation dwells,
And ever-musing melancholy reigns;
What means this tumult in a Vestal's veins?
Why rove my thoughts beyond this last retreat?
Why feels my heart its long-forgotten heat?
Yet, yet I love!—From Abelard it came,
And Eloïsa yet must kiss the name.
  Dear fatal name! rest ever unreveal'd,
Nor pass these lips in holy silence seal'd: 10
Hide it, my heart, within that close disguise,
Where mix'd with God's, his lov'd Idea lies:
O write it not, my hand—the name appears
Already written—wash it out, my tears!
In vain lost Eloïsa weeps and prays,
Her heart still dictates, and her hand obeys.
  Relentless walls! whose darksome round contains
Repentant sighs, and voluntary pains:
Ye rugged rocks! which holy knees have worn;
Ye grots and caverns shagg'd with horrid thorn!   20
Shrines! where their vigils pale-ey'd virgins keep,
And pitying saints, whose statues learn to weep!
Tho' cold like you, unmov'd and silent grown,
I have not yet forgot myself to stone.
All is not Heav'n's while Abelard has part,
Still rebel nature holds out half my heart;
Nor pray'rs nor fasts its stubborn pulse restrain,
Nor tears for ages taught to flow in vain.

Soon as thy letters trembling I unclose,
That well-known name awakens all my woes.   30
Oh name for ever sad ! for ever dear !
Still breath'd in sighs, still usher'd with a tear.
I tremble too, where'er my own I find,
Some dire misfortune follows close behind.
Line after line my gushing eyes o'erflow,
Led thro' a sad variety of woe :
Now warm in love, now with'ring in my bloom,
Lost in a convent's solitary gloom !
There stern Religion quench'd th' unwilling flame,
There died the best of passions, Love and Fame.   40
    Yet write, oh write me all, that I may join
Griefs to thy griefs, and echo sighs to thine.
Nor foes nor fortune take this pow'r away ;
And is my Abelard less kind than they ?
Tears still are mine, and those I need not spare,
Love but demands what else were shed in pray'r ;
No happier task these faded eyes pursue ;
To read and weep is all they now can do.
    Then share thy pain, allow that sad relief ;
Ah, more than share it, give me all thy grief.   50
Heav'n first taught létters for some wretch's aid,
Some banish'd lover, or some captive maid ;
They live, they speak, they breathe what love inspires,
Warm from the soul, and faithful to its fires,
The virgin's wish without her fears impart,
Excuse the blush, and pour out all the heart,
Speed the soft intercourse from soul to soul,
And waft a sigh from Indus to the Pole.
    Thou know'st how guiltless first I met thy flame,
When Love approach'd me under Friendship's name ;   60
My fancy form'd thee of angelic kind,
Some emanation of th' all-beauteous Mind.
Those smiling eyes, attemp'ring ev'ry ray,
Shone sweetly lambent with celestial day.
Guiltless I gaz'd ; heav'n listen'd while you sung ;
And truths divine came mended from that tongue.
From lips like those what precept fail'd to move ?
Too soon they taught me 'twas no sin to love :
Back thro' the paths of pleasing sense I ran,
Nor wish'd an Angel whom I lov'd a Man.   70
Dim and remote the joys of saints I see ;
Nor envy them that heav'n I lose for thee.
    How oft, when press'd to marriage, have I said,
Curse on all laws but those which Love has made ?
Love, free as air, at sight of human ties,
Spreads his light wings, and in a moment flies.
Let wealth, let honour, wait the wedded dame,
August her deed, and sacred be her fame ;

Before true passion all those views remove,
Fame, wealth, and honour! what are you to Love? 80
The jealous God, when we profane his fires,
Those restless passions in revenge inspires,
And bids them make mistaken mortals groan,
Who seek in love for aught but love alone.
Should at my feet the world's great master fall,
Himself, his throne, his world, I'd scorn 'em all:
Not Caesar's empress would I deign to prove;
No, make me mistress to the man I love;
If there be yet another name more free,
More fond than mistress, make me that to thee! 90
Oh! happy state! when souls each other draw,
When love is liberty, and nature, law:
All then is full, possessing, and possesst,
No craving void left aking in the breast:
Ev'n thought meets thought, ere from the lips it part,
And each warm wish springs mutual from the heart.
This sure is bliss (if bliss on earth there be)
And once the lot of Abelard and me.

　　Alas how chang'd! what sudden horrors rise!
A naked Lover bound and bleeding lies! 100
Where, where was Eloïse? her voice, her hand,
Her poniard had oppos'd the dire command.
Barbarian, stay! that bloody stroke restrain;
The crime was common, common be the pain.
I can no more; by shame, by rage suppress'd,
Let tears, and burning blushes speak the rest.

　　Canst thou forget that sad, that solemn day,
When victims at yon altar's foot we lay?
Canst thou forget what tears that moment fell,
When, warm in youth, I bade the world farewell? 110
As with cold lips I kiss'd the sacred veil,
The shrines all trembled, and the lamps grew pale:
Heav'n scarce believ'd the Conquest it survey'd,
And Saints with wonder heard the vows I made.
Yet then, to those dread altars as I drew,
Not on the Cross my eyes were fix'd, but you:
Not grace, or zeal, love only was my call,
And if I lose thy love, I lose my all.
Come! with thy looks, thy words, relieve my woe;
Those still at least are left thee to bestow. 120
Still on that breast enamour'd let me lie,
Still drink delicious poison from thy eye,
Pant on thy lip, and to thy heart be press'd;
Give all thou canst—and let me dream the rest.
Ah no! instruct me other joys to prize,
With other beauties charm my partial eyes,
Full in my view set all the bright abode,
And make my soul quit Abelard for God.

Ah think at least thy flock deserves thy care,
Plants of thy hand, and children of thy pray'r.   130
From the false world in early youth they fled,
By thee to mountains, wilds, and deserts led.
You rais'd these hallow'd walls; the desert smil'd,
And Paradise was open'd in the Wild.
No weeping orphan saw his father's stores
Our shrines irradiate, or emblaze the floors;
No silver saints, by dying misers giv'n,
Here brib'd the rage of ill-requited heav'n:
But such plain roofs as Piety could raise,
And only vocal with the Maker's praise.   140
In these lone walls (their days eternal bound)
These moss-grown domes with spiry turrets crown'd,
Where awful arches make a noon-day night,
And the dim windows shed a solemn light;
Thy eyes diffus'd a reconciling ray,
And gleams of glory brighten'd all the day.
But now no face divine contentment wears,
'Tis all blank sadness, or continual tears.
See how the force of others pray'rs I try,
(O pious fraud of am'rous charity!)   150
But why should I on others pray'rs depend?
Come thou, my father, brother, husband, friend!
Ah let thy handmaid, sister, daughter move,
And all those tender names in one, thy love!
The darksome pines that o'er yon rocks reclin'd
Wave high, and murmur to the hollow wind,
The wand'ring streams that shine between the hills,
The grots that echo to the tinkling rills,
The dying gales that pant upon the trees,
The lakes that quiver to the curling breeze;   160
No more these scenes my meditation aid,
Or lull to rest the visionary maid.
But o'er the twilight groves and dusky caves,
Long-sounding aisles, and intermingled graves,
Black Melancholy sits, and round her throws
A death-like silence, and a dead repose:
Her gloomy presence saddens all the scene,
Shades ev'ry flow'r, and darkens ev'ry green,
Deepens the murmur of the falling floods,
And breathes a browner horror on the woods.   170
Yet here for ever, ever must I stay;
Sad proof how well a lover can obey!
Death, only death, can break the lasting chain;
And here, ev'n then, shall my cold dust remain,
Here all its frailties, all its flames resign,
And wait till 'tis no sin to mix with thine.
Ah wretch! believ'd the spouse of God in vain,
Confess'd within the slave of love and man.

Assist me, heav'n! but whence arose that pray'r?
Sprung it from piety, or from despair?　　　　　180
Ev'n here, where frozen chastity retires,
Love finds an altar for forbidden fires.
I ought to grieve, but cannot what I ought;
I mourn the lover, not lament the fault;
I view my crime, but kindle at the view,
Repent old pleasures, and solicit new;
Now turn'd to heav'n, I weep my past offence,
Now think of thee, and curse my innocence.
Of all affliction taught a lover yet,
'Tis sure the hardest science to forget!　　　　190
How shall I lose the sin, yet keep the sense,
And love th' offender, yet detest th' offence?
How the dear object from the crime remove,
Or how distinguish penitence from love?
Unequal task! a passion to resign,
For hearts so touch'd, so pierc'd, so lost as mine.
Ere such a soul regains its peaceful state,
How often must it love, how often hate!
How often hope, despair, resent, regret,
Conceal, disdain,—do all things but forget.　　200
But let heav'n seize it, all at once 'tis fir'd;
Not touch'd, but rapt; not waken'd, but inspir'd!
Oh come! oh teach me nature to subdue,
Renounce my love, my life, myself—and you.
Fill my fond heart with God alone, for he
Alone can rival, can succeed to thee.
　How happy is the blameless Vestal's lot?
The world forgetting, by the world forgot:
Eternal sun-shine of the spotless mind!
Each pray'r accepted, and each wish resign'd;　210
Labour and rest, that equal periods keep;
'Obedient slumbers that can wake and weep;'
Desires compos'd, affections ever ev'n;
Tears that delight, and sighs that waft to heav'n.
Grace shines around her with serenest beams,
And whisp'ring Angels prompt her golden dreams.
For her th' unfading rose of Eden blooms,
And wings of Seraphs shed divine perfumes,
For her the Spouse prepares the bridal ring,
For her white virgins Hymenaeals sing,　　　220
To sounds of heav'nly harps she dies away,
And melts in visions of eternal day.
　Far other dreams my erring soul employ,
Far other raptures, of unholy joy:
When at the close of each sad, sorrowing day,
Fancy restores what vengeance snatch'd away,
Then conscience sleeps, and leaving nature free,
All my loose soul unbounded springs to thee.

O curst, dear horrors of all-conscious night!
How glowing guilt exalts the keen delight! 230
Provoking Daemons all restraint remove,
And stir within me ev'ry source of love.
I hear thee, view thee, gaze o'er all thy charms,
And round thy phantom glue my clasping arms.
I wake:—no more I hear, no more I view,
The phantom flies me, as unkind as you.
I call aloud; it hears not what I say:
I stretch my empty arms; it glides away.
To dream once more I close my willing eyes;
Ye soft illusions, dear deceits, arise! 240
Alas, no more! methinks we wand'ring go
Thro' dreary wastes, and weep each other's woe,
Where round some mould'ring tow'r pale ivy creeps,
And low-brow'd rocks hang nodding o'er the deeps.
Sudden you mount, you beckon from the skies;
Clouds interpose, waves roar, and winds arise.
I shriek, start up, the same sad prospect find,
And wake to all the griefs I left behind.

For thee the fates, severely kind, ordain
A cool suspense from pleasure and from pain; 250
Thy life a long dead calm of fix'd repose;
No pulse that riots, and no blood that glows.
Still as the sea, ere winds were taught to blow,
Or moving spirit bade the waters flow;
Soft as the slumbers of a saint forgiv'n,
And mild as op'ning gleams of promis'd heav'n.

Come, Abelard! for what hast thou to dread?
The torch of Venus burns not for the dead.
Nature stands check'd; Religion disapproves;
Ev'n thou art cold—yet Eloïsa loves. 260
Ah hopeless, lasting flames! like those that burn
To light the dead, and warm th' unfruitful urn.

What scenes appear where'er I turn my view?
The dear Ideas, where I fly, pursue,
Rise in the grove, before the altar rise,
Stain all my soul, and wanton in my eyes.
I waste the Matin lamp in sighs for thee,
Thy image steals between my God and me,
Thy voice I seem in ev'ry hymn to hear,
With ev'ry bead I drop too soft a tear. 270
When from the censer clouds of fragrance roll,
And swelling organs lift the rising soul,
One thought of thee puts all the pomp to flight,
Priests, tapers, temples, swim before my sight:
In seas of flame my plunging soul is drown'd,
While Altars blaze, and Angels tremble round.

While prostrate here in humble grief I lie,
Kind. virtuous drops just gath'ring in my eye,

While praying, trembling, in the dust I roll,
And dawning grace is op'ning on my soul: 280
Come, if thou dar'st, all charming as thou art!
Oppose thyself to heav'n; dispute my heart;
Come, with one glance of those deluding eyes
Blot out each bright Idea of the skies;
Take back that grace, those sorrows, and those tears;
Take back my fruitless penitence and pray'rs;
Snatch me, just mounting, from the blest abode;
Assist the fiends, and tear me from my God!
     No, fly me, fly me, far as Pole from Pole;
Rise Alps between us! and whole oceans roll!   290
Ah, come not, write not, think not once of me,
Nor share one pang of all I felt for thee.
Thy oaths I quit, thy memory resign;
Forget, renounce me, hate whate'er was mine.
Fair eyes, and tempting looks (which yet I view!)
Long lov'd, ador'd ideas, all adieu!
O Grace serene! oh virtue heav'nly fair!
Divine oblivion of low-thoughted care!
Fresh blooming Hope, gay daughter of the sky!
And Faith, our early immortality!   300
Enter, each mild, each amicable guest;
Receive, and wrap me in eternal rest!
     See in her cell sad Eloïsa spread,
Propt on some tomb, a neighbour of the dead.
In each low wind methinks a Spirit calls,
And more than Echoes talk along the walls.
Here, as I watch'd the dying lamps around,
From yonder shrine I heard a hollow sound.
'Come, sister, come!' (it said, or seem'd to say)
'Thy place is here, sad sister, come away!   310
Once like thyself, I trembled, wept, and pray'd,
Love's victim then, tho' now a sainted maid:
But all is calm in this eternal sleep;
Here grief forgets to groan, and love to weep,
Ev'n superstition loses ev'ry fear:
For God, not man, absolves our frailties here.'
     I come, I come! prepare your roseate bow'rs,
Celestial palms, and ever-blooming flow'rs.
Thither, where sinners may have rest, I go,
Where flames refin'd in breasts seraphic glow: 320
Thou, Abelard! the last sad office pay,
And smooth my passage to the realms of day;
See my lips tremble, and my eye-balls roll,
Suck my last breath, and catch my flying soul!
Ah no—in sacred vestments may'st thou stand,
The hallow'd taper trembling in thy hand,
Present the Cross before my lifted eye,
Teach me at once, and learn of me to die.

Ah then, thy once-lov'd Eloïsa see!
It will be then no crime to gaze on me.   330
See from my cheek the transient roses fly!
See the last sparkle languish in my eye!
'Till ev'ry motion, pulse, and breath be o'er;
And ev'n my Abelard be lov'd no more.
O Death all-eloquent! you only prove
What dust we dote on, when 'tis man we love.
    Then too, when fate shall thy fair frame destroy,
(That cause of all my guilt, and all my joy)
In trance extatic may thy pangs be drown'd,
Bright clouds descend, and Angels watch thee round, 340
From op'ning skies may streaming glories shine,
And Saints embrace thee with a love like mine.
    May one kind grave unite each hapless name,
And graft my love immortal on thy fame!
Then, ages hence, when all my woes are o'er,
When this rebellious heart shall beat no more;
If ever chance two wand'ring lovers brings
To Paraclete's white walls and silver springs,
O'er the pale marble shall they join their heads,
And drink the falling tears each other sheds;   350
Then sadly say, with mutual pity mov'd,
'Oh may we never love as these have lov'd!'
From the full choir when loud Hosannas rise,
And swell the pomp of dreadful sacrifice,
Amid that scene if some relenting eye
Glance on the stone where our cold relicks lie,
Devotion's self shall steal a thought from heav'n,
One human tear shall drop, and be forgiv'n.
And sure if fate some future bard shall join
In sad similitude of griefs to mine,   360
Condemn'd whole years in absence to deplore,
And image charms he must behold no more;
Such if there be, who loves so long, so well;
Let him our sad, our tender story tell;
The well-sung woes will sooth my pensive ghost;
He best can paint 'em who shall feel 'em most.

Nolueram, Belinda, tuos violare capillos;
    Sed iuvat hoc precibus me tribuisse tuis.—MARTIAL.

CANTO I

WHAT dire offence from amorous causes springs,
What mighty contests rise from trivial things,
I sing—This verse to CARYL, Muse! is due:
This, even Belinda may vouchsafe to view:
Slight is the subject, but not so the praise,
If she inspire, and he approve my lays.
    Say what strange motive, Goddess! could compel
A well-bred lord to assault a gentle belle?
O say what stranger cause, yet unexplored,
Could make a gentle belle reject a lord?   10
In tasks so bold, can little men engage,
And in soft bosoms dwells such mighty rage?
    Sol through white curtains shot a timorous ray,
And oped those eyes that must eclipse the day:
Now lap-dogs give themselves the rousing shake,
And sleepless lovers, just at twelve, awake:
Thrice rung the bell, the slipper knocked the ground,
And the pressed watch returned a silver sound.
Belinda still her downy pillow pressed,
Her guardian sylph prolonged the balmy rest: 20
'Twas he had summoned to her silent bed
The morning-dream that hovered o'er her head;
A youth more glittering than a birth-night beau,
(That even in slumber caused her cheek to glow)
Seemed to her ear his winning lips to lay,
And thus in whispers said, or seemed to say.
    ' Fairest of mortals, thou distinguished care
Of thousand bright inhabitants of air!
If e'er one vision touched thy infant thought,
Of all the nurse and all the priest have taught;   30
Of airy elves by moonlight shadows seen,
The silver token, and the circled green,
Or virgins visited by angel-powers,
With golden crowns and wreaths of heavenly flowers;
Hear and believe! thy own importance know,
Nor bound thy narrow views to things below.
Some secret truths, from learned pride concealed,
To maids alone and children are revealed:
What though no credit doubting wits may give!
The fair and innocent shall still believe.   40
Know, then, unnumbered spirits round thee fly,
The light militia of the lower sky:
These, though unseen, are ever on the wing,
Hang o'er the box, and hover round the ring.

Think what an equipage thou hast in air,
And view with scorn two pages and a chair.
As now your own, our beings were of old,
And once inclosed in woman's beauteous mould;
Thence, by a soft transition, we repair
From earthly vehicles to these of air.   50
Think not, when woman's transient breath is fled,
That all her vanities at once are dead;
Succeeding vanities she still regards,
And though she plays no more, o'erlooks the cards.
Her joy in gilded chariots, when alive,
And love of ombre, after death survive.
For when the fair in all their pride expire,
To their first elements their souls retire:
The sprites of fiery termagants in flame
Mount up, and take a salamander's name.   60
Soft yielding minds to water glide away,
And sip, with nymphs, their elemental tea.
The graver prude sinks downward to a gnome,
In search of mischief still on earth to roam.
The light coquettes in sylphs aloft repair,
And sport and flutter in the fields of air.
  ' Know further yet; whoever fair and chaste
Rejects mankind, is by some sylph embraced:
For spirits, freed from mortal laws, with ease
Assume what sexes and what shapes they please.   70
What guards the purity of melting maids,
In courtly balls, and midnight masquerades,
Safe from the treacherous friend, the daring spark,
The glance by day, the whisper in the dark,
When kind occasion prompts their warm desires,
When music softens, and when dancing fires ?
'Tis but their sylph, the wise celestials know,
Though honour is the word with men below.
  ' Some nymphs there are, too conscious of their face,
For life predestined to the gnomes' embrace.   80
These swell their prospects and exalt their pride,
When offers are disdained, and love denied:
Then gay ideas crowd the vacant brain,
While peers, and dukes, and all their sweeping train,
And garters, stars, and coronets appear,
And in soft sounds, " Your Grace " salutes their ear.
'Tis these that early taint the female soul,
Instruct the eyes of young coquettes to roll,
Teach infant-cheeks a hidden blush to know,
And little hearts to flutter at a beau.   90
  ' Oft, when the world imagine women stray,
The sylphs through mystic mazes guide their way,
Through all the giddy circle they pursue,
And old impertinence expel by new.

What tender maid but must a victim fall
To one man's treat, but for another's ball ?
When Florio speaks, what virgin could withstand,
If gentle Damon did not squeeze her hand ?
With varying vanities, from every part,
They shift the moving toyshop of their heart ;   100
Where wigs with wigs, with sword-knots sword-knots strive,
Beaux banish beaux, and coaches coaches drive.
This erring mortals levity may call ;
Oh blind to truth ! the sylphs contrive it all.
  ' Of these am I, who thy protection claim,
A watchful sprite, and Ariel is my name.
Late, as I ranged the crystal wilds of air,
In the clear mirror of thy ruling star
I saw, alas ! some dread event impend,
Ere to the main this morning sun descend,   110
But heaven reveals not what, or how, or where :
Warned by the sylph, oh pious maid, beware !
This to disclose is all thy guardian can :
Beware of all, but most beware of man ! '
  He said ; when Shock, who thought she slept too long,
Leaped up, and waked his mistress with his tongue.
'Twas then, Belinda, if report say true,
Thy eyes first opened on a billet-doux ;
Wounds, charms, and ardours were no sooner read,
But all the vision vanished from thy head.   120
  And now, unveiled, the toilet stands displayed,
Each silver vase in mystic order laid.
First, robed in white, the nymph intent adores,
With head uncovered, the cosmetic powers.
A heavenly image in the glass appears,
To that she bends, to that her eyes she rears ;
The inferior priestess, at her altar's side,
Trembling begins the sacred rites of pride.
Unnumbered treasures ope at once, and here
The various offerings of the world appear ;   130
From each she nicely culls with curious toil,
And decks the Goddess with the glittering spoil.
This casket India's glowing gems unlocks,
And all Arabia breathes from yonder box.
The tortoise here and elephant unite,
Transformed to combs, the speckled, and the white.
Here files of pins extend their shining rows,
Puffs, powders, patches, bibles, billet-doux.
Now awful beauty puts on all its arms ;
The fair each moment rises in her charms,   140
Repairs her smiles, awakens every grace,
And calls forth all the wonders of her face ;
Sees by degrees a purer blush arise,
And keener lightnings quicken in her eyes.

mock heroic

The busy sylphs surround their darling care,
These set the head, and those divide the hair,
Some fold the sleeve, whilst others plait the gown;
And Betty's praised for labours not her own.

CANTO II

NOT with more glories, in the ethereal plain,
The sun first rises o'er the purpled main,
Than, issuing forth, the rival of his beams
Launched on the bosom of the silver Thames.
Fair nymphs, and well-dressed youths around her shone,
But every eye was fixed on her alone.
On her white breast a sparkling cross she wore,
Which Jews might kiss, and infidels adore.
Her lively looks a sprightly mind disclose,
Quick as her eyes, and as unfixed as those: 10
Favours to none, to all she smiles extends;
Oft she rejects, but never once offends.
Bright as the sun, her eyes the gazers strike,
And, like the sun, they shine on all alike.
Yet graceful ease, and sweetness void of pride,
Might hide her faults, if belles had faults to hide:
If to her share some female errors fall,
Look on her face, and you'll forget 'em all. ✓
    This nymph, to the destruction of mankind,
Nourished two locks, which graceful hung behind   20
In equal curls, and well conspired to deck
With shining ringlets the smooth iv'ry neck.
Love in these labyrinths his slaves detains,
And mighty hearts are held in slender chains.
With hairy springes we the birds betray,
Slight lines of hair surprise the finny prey,
Fair tresses man's imperial race ensnare,
And beauty draws us with a single hair.
    The adventurous Baron the bright locks admired;
He saw, he wished, and to the prize aspired.   30
Resolved to win, he meditates the way,
By force to ravish, or by fraud betray;
For when success a lover's toil attends,
Few ask, if fraud or force attained his ends.
    For this, ere Phoebus rose, he had implored
Propitious heaven, and every power adored,
But chiefly Love—to Love an altar built,
Of twelve vast French romances, neatly gilt.
There lay three garters, half a pair of gloves;
And all the trophies of his former loves;   40
With tender billet-doux he lights the pyre,
And breathes three amorous sighs to raise the fire.

mock baron

Then prostrate falls, and begs with ardent eyes
Soon to obtain, and long possess the prize:
The powers gave ear, and granted half his prayer,
The rest the winds dispersed in empty air.
 But now secure the painted vessel glides,
The sun-beams trembling on the floating tides:
While melting music steals upon the sky,
And softened sounds along the waters die ;   50
Smooth flow the waves, the zephyrs gently play,
Belinda smiled, and all the world was gay.
All but the sylph—with careful thoughts oppressed,
The impending woe sat heavy on his breast.
He summons straight his denizens of air ;
The lucid squadrons round the sails repair:
Soft o'er the shrouds aërial whispers breathe,
That seemed but zephyrs to the train beneath.
Some to the sun their insect-wings unfold,
Waft on the breeze, or sink in clouds of gold ;   60
Transparent forms, too fine for mortal sight,
Their fluid bodies half dissolved in light,
Loose to the wind their airy garments flew,
Thin glittering textures of the filmy dew,
Dipt in the richest tincture of the skies,
Where light disports in ever-mingling dyes,
While every beam new transient colours flings,
Colours that change whene'er they wave their wings.
Amid the circle, on the gilded mast,
Superior by the head, was Ariel placed ;   70
His purple pinions opening to the sun,
He raised his azure wand, and thus begun.
 'Ye sylphs and sylphids, to your chief give ear !
Fays, fairies, genii, elves, and demons, hear !
Ye know the spheres and various tasks assigned
By laws eternal to the aërial kind.
Some in the fields of purest ether play,
And bask and whiten in the blaze of day.
Some guide the course of wandering orbs on high,
Or roll the planets through the boundless sky.   80
Some less refined, beneath the moon's pale light
Pursue the stars that shoot athwart the night,
Or suck the mists in grosser air below,
Or dip their pinions in the painted bow,
Or brew fierce tempests on the wintry main,
Or o'er the glebe distil the kindly rain.
Others on earth o'er human race preside,
Watch all their ways, and all their actions guide:
Of these the chief the care of nations own,
And guard with arms divine the British throne.   90
 'Our humbler province is to tend the fair,
Not a less pleasing, though less glorious care ;

To save the powder from too rude a gale,
Nor let the imprisoned essences exhale;
To draw fresh colours from the vernal flowers;
To steal from rainbows ere they drop in showers
A brighter wash; to curl their waving hairs,
Assist their blushes, and inspire their airs;
Nay oft, in dreams, invention we bestow,
To change a flounce, or add a furbelow.   100
  'This day, black omens threat the brightest fair,
That e'er deserved a watchful spirit's care;
Some dire disaster, or by force, or slight;
But what, or where, the fates have wrapt in night.
Whether the nymph shall break Diana's law,
Or some frail china jar receive a flaw;
Or stain her honour or her new brocade;
Forget her prayers, or miss a masquerade;
Or lose her heart, or necklace, at a ball;
Or whether Heaven has doom'd that Shock must fall. 110
Haste, then, ye spirits! to your charge repair:
The fluttering fan be Zephyretta's care;
The drops to thee, Brillante, we consign;
And, Momentilla, let the watch be thine;
Do thou, Crispissa, tend her favourite lock;
Ariel himself shall be the guard of Shock.
  'To fifty chosen sylphs, of special note,
We trust th' important charge, the petticoat:
Oft have we known that seven-fold fence to fail,
Though stiff with hoops, and armed with ribs of whale; 120
Form a strong line about the silver bound,
And guard the wide circumference around.
  'Whatever spirit, careless of his charge,
His post neglects, or leaves the fair at large,
Shall feel sharp vengeance soon o'ertake his sins,
Be stopped in vials, or transfixed with pins;
Or plunged in lakes of bitter washes lie,
Or wedged whole ages in a bodkin's eye:
Gums and pomatums shall his flight restrain,
While clogged he beats his silken wings in vain;   130
Or alum styptics with contracting power
Shrink his thin essence like a rivelled flower:
Or, as Ixion fixed, the wretch shall feel
The giddy motion of the whirling mill,
In fumes of burning chocolate shall glow,
And tremble at the sea that froths below!'
  He spoke; the spirits from the sails descend;
Some, orb in orb, around the nymph extend;
Some thrid the mazy ringlets of her hair;
Some hang upon the pendants of her ear: 140
With beating hearts the dire event they wait,
Anxious, and trembling for the birth of Fate.

CANTO III

CLOSE by those meads, for ever crowned with flowers,
Where Thames with pride surveys his rising towers,
There stands a structure of majestic frame,
Which from the neighb'ring Hampton takes its name.
Here Britain's statesmen oft the fall foredoom
Of foreign tyrants and of nymphs at home;
Here thou, great ANNA! whom three realms obey,
Dost sometimes counsel take—and sometimes tea.
    Hither the heroes and the nymphs resort,
To taste awhile the pleasures of a court; 10
In various talk the instructive hours they passed,
Who gave the ball, or paid the visit last;
One speaks the glory of the British queen,
And one describes a charming Indian screen;
A third interprets motions, looks, and eyes;
At every word a reputation dies.
Snuff, or the fan, supply each pause of chat,
With singing, laughing, ogling, and all that.
    Meanwhile, declining from the noon of day,
The sun obliquely shoots his burning ray; 20
The hungry judges soon the sentence sign,
And wretches hang that jury-men may dine;
The merchant from the Exchange returns in peace,
And the long labours of the toilet cease.
Belinda now, whom thirst of fame invites,
Burns to encounter two adventurous knights,
At ombre singly to decide their doom;
And swells her breast with conquests yet to come.
Straight the three bands prepare in arms to join,
Each band the number of the sacred nine. 30
Soon as she spreads her hand, the aërial guard
Descend, and sit on each important card:
First Ariel perched upon a Matadore,
Then each, according to the rank they bore;
For sylphs, yet mindful of their ancient race,
Are, as when women, wondrous fond of place.
    Behold, four kings in majesty revered,
With hoary whiskers and a forky beard;
And four fair queens whose hands sustain a flower,
The expressive emblem of their softer power; 40
Four knaves in garbs succinct, a trusty band,
Caps on their heads, and halberts in their hand;
And parti-coloured troops, a shining train,
Draw forth to combat on the velvet plain.
    The skilful nymph reviews her force with care:
Let spades be trumps! she said, and trumps they were.

Now move to war her sable Matadores,
In show like leaders of the swarthy Moors.
Spadillio first, unconquerable lord !
Led off two captive trumps, and swept the board.   50
As many more Manillio forced to yield,
And marched a victor from the verdant field.
Him Basto followed, but his fate more hard
Gained but one trump and one plebeian card.
With his broad sabre next, a chief in years,
The hoary majesty of spades appears,
Puts forth one manly leg, to sight revealed,
The rest, his many-coloured robe concealed.
The rebel knave, who dares his prince engage,
Proves the just victim of his royal rage.   60
Even mighty Pam, that kings and queens o'erthrew,
And mowed down armies in the fights of Lu,
Sad chance of war ! now destitute of aid,
Falls undistinguished by the victor spade !
    Thus far both armies to Belinda yield ;
Now to the Baron fate inclines the field.
His warlike Amazon her host invades,
The imperial consort of the crown of spades.
The club's black tyrant first her victim died,
Spite of his haughty mien, and barbarous pride :   70
What boots the regal circle on his head,
His giant limbs, in state unwieldy spread ;
That long behind he trails his pompous robe,
And, of all monarchs, only grasps the globe ?
    The Baron now his diamonds pours apace ;
The embroidered king who shows but half his face,
And his refulgent queen, with powers combined,
Of broken troops an easy conquest find.
Clubs, diamonds, hearts, in wild disorder seen,
With throngs promiscuous strow the level green.   80
Thus when dispersed a routed army runs,
Of Asia's troops, and Afric's sable sons,
With like confusion different nations fly,
Of various habit, and of various dye,
The pierced battalions disunited fall,
In heaps on heaps ; one fate o'erwhelms them all.
    The knave of diamonds tries his wily arts,
And wins (oh shameful chance !) the queen of hearts.
At this, the blood the virgin's cheek forsook,
A livid paleness spreads o'er all her look ;   90
She sees, and trembles at the approaching ill,
Just in the jaws of ruin, and codille.
And now (as oft in some distempered state)
On one nice trick depends the general fate :
An ace of hearts steps forth : the king unseen
Lurked in her hand, and mourned his captive queen :

He springs to vengeance with an eager pace,
And falls like thunder on the prostrate ace.
The nymph exulting fills with shouts the sky ;
The walls, the woods, and long canals reply. 100
    O thoughtless mortals ! ever blind to fate,
Too soon dejected, and too soon elate.
Sudden, these honours shall be snatched away,
And cursed for ever this victorious day.
    For lo ! the board with cups and spoons is crowned,
The berries crackle, and the mill turns round ;
On shining altars of Japan they raise
The silver lamp ; the fiery spirits blaze :
From silver spouts the grateful liquors glide,
While China's earth receives the smoking tide : 110
At once they gratify their scent and taste,
And frequent cups prolong the rich repast.
Straight hover round the fair her airy band ;
Some, as she sipped, the fuming liquor fanned,
Some o'er her lap their careful plumes displayed,
Trembling, and conscious of the rich brocade.
Coffee (which makes the politician wise,
And see through all things with his half-shut eyes)
Sent up in vapours to the Baron's brain
New stratagems, the radiant lock to gain. 120
Ah cease, rash youth ! desist ere 'tis too late,
Fear the just Gods, and think of Scylla's fate !
Changed to a bird, and sent to flit in air,
She dearly pays for Nisus' injured hair !
    But when to mischief mortals bend their will,
How soon they find fit instruments of ill !
Just then, Clarissa drew with tempting grace
A two-edged weapon from her shining case :
So ladies in romance assist their knight,
Present the spear, and arm him for the fight. 130
He takes the gift with reverence, and extends
The little engine on his fingers' ends ;
This just behind Belinda's neck he spread,
As o'er the fragrant steams she bends her head.
Swift to the lock a thousand sprites repair,
A thousand wings, by turns, blow back the hair :
And thrice they twitched the diamond in her ear :
Thrice she looked back, and thrice the foe drew near.
Just in that instant, anxious Ariel sought
The close recesses of the virgin's thought ; 140
As on the nosegay in her breast reclined,
He watched the ideas rising in her mind,
Sudden he viewed, in spite of all her art,
An earthly lover lurking at her heart.
Amazed, confused, he found his power expired,
Resigned to fate, and with a sigh retired.

The peer now spreads the glittering forfex wide,
To inclose the lock; now joins it, to divide.
Even then, before the fatal engine closed,
A wretched sylph too fondly interposed;   150
Fate urged the shears, and cut the sylph in twain,
(But airy substance soon unites again)
The meeting points the sacred hair dissever
From the fair head, for ever, and for ever!
  Then flashed the living lightning from her eyes,
And screams of horror rend the affrighted skies.
Not louder shrieks to pitying heaven are cast,
When husbands, or when lap-dogs breathe their last;
Or when rich China vessels fallen from high,
In glittering dust and painted fragments lie!   160
  'Let wreaths of triumph now my temples twine,'
(The victor cried) 'the glorious prize is mine!
While fish in streams, or birds delight in air,
Or in a coach and six the British fair,
As long as Atalantis shall be read,
Or the small pillow grace a lady's bed,
While visits shall be paid on solemn days,
When numerous wax-lights in bright order blaze,
While nymphs take treats, or assignations give,
So long my honour, name, and praise shall live!   170
What time would spare, from steel receives its date,
And monuments, like men, submit to fate!
Steel could the labour of the Gods destroy,
And strike to dust the imperial towers of Troy;
Steel could the works of mortal pride confound,
And hew triumphal arches to the ground.
What wonder then, fair nymph! thy hairs should feel
The conquering force of unresisted steel?'

CANTO IV

BUT anxious cares the pensive nymph oppressed,
And secret passions laboured in her breast.
Not youthful kings in battle seized alive,
Not scornful virgins who their charms survive,
Not ardent lovers robbed of all their bliss,
Not ancient ladies when refused a kiss,
Not tyrants fierce that unrepenting die,
Not Cynthia when her manteau's pinned awry,
E'er felt such rage, resentment, and despair,
As thou, sad virgin! for thy ravished hair.   10
  For, that sad moment, when the sylphs withdrew
And Ariel weeping from Belinda flew,

Umbriel, a dusky, melancholy sprite,
As ever sullied the fair face of light,
Down to the central earth, his proper scene,
Repaired to search the gloomy Cave of Spleen.
   Swift on his sooty pinions flits the gnome,
And in a vapour reached the dismal dome.
No cheerful breeze this sullen region knows,
The dreaded east is all the wind that blows.   20
Here in a grotto, sheltered close from air,
And screened in shades from day's detested glare,
She sighs for ever on her pensive bed,
Pain at her side, and Megrim at her head.
   Two handmaids wait the throne : alike in place,
But differing far in figure and in face.
Here stood Ill-nature like an ancient maid,
Her wrinkled form in black and white arrayed ;
With store of prayers, for mornings, nights, and noons,
Her hand is filled ; her bosom with lampoons.   30
   There Affectation, with a sickly mien,
Shows in her cheek the roses of eighteen,
Practised to lisp, and hang the head aside,
Faints into airs, and languishes with pride,
On the rich quilt sinks with becoming woe,
Wrapt in a gown, for sickness, and for show.
The fair ones feel such maladies as these,
When each new night-dress gives a new disease.
   A constant vapour o'er the palace flies ;
Strange phantoms rising as the mists arise ;   40
Dreadful, as hermit's dreams in haunted shades,
Or bright, as visions of expiring maids.
Now glaring fiends, and snakes on rolling spires,
Pale spectres, gaping tombs, and purple fires :
Now lakes of liquid gold, Elysian scenes,
And crystal domes, and angels in machines.
   Unnumbered throngs on every side are seen,
Of bodies changed to various forms by Spleen.
Here living tea-pots stand, one arm held out,
One bent ; the handle this, and that the spout :   50
A pipkin there, like Homer's tripod, walks ;
Here sighs a jar, and there a goose-pye talks ;
Men prove with child, as powerful fancy works,
And maids turned bottles, call aloud for corks.
   Safe passed the gnome through this fantastic band,
A branch of healing spleenwort in his hand.
Then thus address'd the power : ' Hail, wayward Queen !
Who rule the sex to fifty from fifteen :
Parent of vapours and of female wit,
Who give the hysteric, or poetic fit,   60
On various tempers act by various ways,
Make some take physic, others scribble plays ;

Who cause the proud their visits to delay,
And send the godly in a pet to pray.
A nymph there is, that all thy power disdains,
And thousands more in equal mirth maintains.
But oh! if e'er thy gnome could spoil a grace,
Or raise a pimple on a beauteous face,
Like citron-waters matrons' cheeks inflame,
Or change complexions at a losing game;   70
If e'er with airy horns I planted heads,
Or rumpled petticoats, or tumbled beds,
Or caused suspicion when no soul was rude,
Or discomposed the head-dress of a prude,
Or e'er to costive lap-dog gave disease,
Which not the tears of brightest eyes could ease:
Hear me, and touch Belinda with chagrin,
That single act gives half the world the spleen.'
    The Goddess with a discontented air
Seems to reject him, though she grants his prayer.   80
A wondrous bag with both her hands she binds,
Like that where once Ulysses held the winds;
There she collects the force of female lungs,
Sighs, sobs, and passions, and the war of tongues.
A vial next she fills with fainting fears,
Soft sorrows, melting griefs, and flowing tears.
The gnome rejoicing bears her gifts away,
Spreads his black wings, and slowly mounts to day.
    Sunk in Thalestris' arms the nymph he found,
Her eyes dejected and her hair unbound.   90
Full o'er their heads the swelling bag he rent,
And all the Furies issued at the vent.
Belinda burns with more than mortal ire,
And fierce Thalestris fans the rising fire.
' O wretched maid!' she spread her hands, and cried,
(While Hampton's echoes, ' Wretched maid!' replied)
' Was it for this you took such constant care
The bodkin, comb, and essence to prepare?
For this your locks in paper durance bound,
For this with torturing irons wreathed around?   100
For this with fillets strained your tender head,
And bravely bore the double loads of lead?
Gods! shall the ravisher display your hair,
While the fops envy, and the ladies stare!
Honour forbid! at whose unrivalled shrine
Ease, pleasure, virtue, all our sex resign.
Methinks already I your tears survey,
Already hear the horrid things they say,
Already see you a degraded toast,
And all your honour in a whisper lost!   110
How shall I, then, your hapless fame defend?
'Twill then be infamy to seem your friend!

And shall this prize, the inestimable prize,
Exposed through crystal to the gazing eyes,
And heightened by the diamond's circling rays,
On that rapacious hand for ever blaze ?
Sooner shall grass in Hyde-park Circus grow,
And wits take lodgings in the sound of Bow ;
Sooner let earth, air, sea, to chaos fall,
Men, monkeys, lap-dogs, parrots, perish all ! '   120
   She said ; then raging to Sir Plume repairs,
And bids her beau demand the precious hairs :
(Sir Plume of amber snuff-box justly vain,
And the nice conduct of a clouded cane)
With earnest eyes, and round unthinking face,
He first the snuff-box opened, then the case,
And thus broke out—' My Lord, why, what the devil ?
Zounds ! damn the lock ! 'fore Gad, you must be civil !
Plague on't ! 'tis past a jest—nay prithee, pox !
Give her the hair '—he spoke, and rapp'd his box.   130
   ' It grieves me much ' (replied the Peer again)
' Who speaks so well should ever speak in vain.
But by this lock, this sacred lock I swear,
(Which never more shall join its parted hair ;
Which never more its honours shall renew,
Clipped from the lovely head where late it grew)
That while my nostrils draw the vital air,
This hand, which won it, shall for ever wear.'
He spoke, and speaking, in proud triumph spread
The long-contended honours of her head.   140
   But Umbriel, hateful gnome ! forbears not so ;
He breaks the vial whence the sorrows flow.
Then see ! the nymph in beauteous grief appears,
Her eyes half-languishing, half-drowned in tears ;
On her heaved bosom hung her drooping head,
Which, with a sigh, she raised ; and thus she said.
   ' For ever cursed be this detested day,
Which snatched my best, my favourite curl away !
Happy ! ah ten times happy had I been,
If Hampton-Court these eyes had never seen !   150
Yet am not I the first mistaken maid,
By love of courts to numerous ills betrayed.
Oh had I rather un-admired remained
In some lone isle, or distant northern land ;
Where the gilt chariot never marks the way,
Where none learn ombre, or e'er taste bohea !
There kept my charms concealed from mortal eye,
Like roses, that in deserts bloom and die.
What moved my mind with youthful lords to roam ?
Oh had I stayed, and said my prayers at home !   160
'Twas this, the morning omens seemed to tell,
Thrice from my trembling hand the patch-box fell ;

The tottering China shook without a wind,
Nay, Poll sat mute, and Shock was most unkind !
A sylph too warned me of the threats of fate,
In mystic visions, now believed too late !
See the poor remnants of these slighted hairs !
My hands shall rend what ev'n thy rapine spares :
These in two sable ringlets taught to break,
Once gave new beauties to the snowy neck ; 170
The sister-lock now sits uncouth, alone,
And in its fellow's fate foresees its own ;
Uncurled it hangs, the fatal shears demands,
And tempts once more thy sacrilegious hands.
Oh hadst thou, cruel ! been content to seize
Hairs less in sight, or any hairs but these ! '

CANTO V

She said : the pitying audience melt in tears,
But fate and Jove had stopped the Baron's ears.
In vain Thalestris with reproach assails,
For who can move when fair Belinda fails ?
Not half so fixed the Trojan could remain,
While Anna begged and Dido raged in vain.
Then grave Clarissa graceful waved her fan ;
Silence ensued, and thus the nymph began.
  ' Say, why are beauties praised and honoured most,
The wise man's passion, and the vain man's toast ? 10
Why decked with all that land and sea afford,
Why Angels called, and Angel-like adored ?
Why round our coaches crowd the white-gloved beaux,
Why bows the side-box from its inmost rows ?
How vain are all these glories, all our pains,
Unless good sense preserve what beauty gains :
That men may say, when we the front-box grace :
" Behold the first in virtue as in face ! "
Oh ! if to dance all night, and dress all day,
Charmed the small-pox, or chased old-age away ; 20
Who would not scorn what housewife's cares produce,
Or who would learn one earthly thing of use ?
To patch, nay ogle, might become a saint,
Nor could it sure be such a sin to paint.
But since, alas ! frail beauty must decay,
Curled or uncurled, since locks will turn to grey ;
Since painted, or not painted, all shall fade,
And she who scorns a man, must die a maid ;
What then remains but well our power to use,
And keep good-humour still whate'er we lose ? 30

And trust me, dear! good-humour can prevail,
When airs, and flights, and screams, and scolding fail.
Beauties in vain their pretty eyes may roll;
Charms strike the sight, but merit wins the soul.'
  So spoke the dame, but no applause ensued;
Belinda frowned, Thalestris called her prude.
' To arms, to arms!' the fierce virago cries,
And swift as lightning to the combat flies.
All side in parties, and begin the attack;
Fans clap, silks rustle, and tough whalebones crack;   40
Heroes' and heroines' shouts confusedly rise,
And base and treble voices strike the skies.
No common weapons in their hands are found,
Like gods they fight, nor dread a mortal wound.
  So when bold Homer makes the gods engage,
And heavenly breasts with human passions rage;
'Gainst Pallas, Mars; Latona, Hermes arms;
And all Olympus rings with loud alarms:
Jove's thunder roars, heaven trembles all around,
Blue Neptune storms, the bellowing deeps resound: 50
Earth shakes her nodding towers, the ground gives way,
And the pale ghosts start at the flash of day!
  Triumphant Umbriel on a sconce's height
Clapped his glad wings, and sate to view the fight:
Propped on their bodkin spears, the sprites survey
The growing combat, or assist the fray.
  While through the press enraged Thalestris flies,
And scatters death around from both her eyes,
A beau and witling perished in the throng,
One died in metaphor, and one in song.   60
' O cruel nymph! a living death I bear,'
Cried Dapperwit, and sunk beside his chair.
A mournful glance Sir Fopling upwards cast,
' Those eyes are made so killing '—was his last.
Thus on Maeander's flowery margin lies
The expiring swan, and as he sings he dies.
  When bold Sir Plume had drawn Clarissa down,
Chloe stepped in, and killed him with a frown;
She smiled to see the doughty hero slain,
But, at her smile, the beau revived again.   70
  Now Jove suspends his golden scales in air,
Weighs the men's wits against the lady's hair;
The doubtful beam long nods from side to side;
At length the wits mount up, the hairs subside.
  See, fierce Belinda on the Baron flies,
With more than usual lightning in her eyes:
Nor feared the chief the unequal fight to try,
Who sought no more than on his foe to die.
But this bold lord with manly strength endued,
She with one finger and a thumb subdued: 80

Just where the breath of life his nostrils drew,
A charge of snuff the wily virgin threw ;
The gnomes direct, to every atom just,
The pungent grains of titillating dust.
Sudden, with starting tears each eye o'erflows,
And the high dome re-echoes to his nose.
  ' Now meet thy fate,' incensed Belinda cried,
And drew a deadly bodkin from her side.
(The same, his ancient personage to deck,
Her great great grandsire wore about his neck,   90
In three seal-rings ; which after, melted down,
Formed a vast buckle for his widow's gown :
Her infant grandame's whistle next it grew,
The bells she jingled, and the whistle blew ;
Then in a bodkin graced her mother's hairs,
Which long she wore, and now Belinda wears.)
  ' Boast not my fall ' (he cried) ' insulting foe !
Thou by some other shalt be laid as low,
Nor think, to die dejects my lofty mind :
All that I dread is leaving you behind !   100
Rather than so, ah let me still survive,
And burn in Cupid's flames—but burn alive.'
  ' Restore the lock ! ' she cries ; and all around
' Restore the lock ! ' the vaulted roofs rebound.
Not fierce Othello in so loud a strain
Roared for the handkerchief that caused his pain.
But see how oft ambitious aims are crossed,
And chiefs contend till all the prize is lost !
The lock, obtained with guilt, and kept with pain,
In every place is sought, but sought in vain :   110
With such a prize no mortal must be blest,
So heaven decrees ! with heaven who can contest ?
  Some thought it mounted to the lunar sphere,
Since all things lost on earth are treasured there.
There heroes' wits are kept in ponderous vases,
And beaux' in snuff-boxes and tweezer-cases.
There broken vows and death-bed alms are found,
And lovers' hearts with ends of ribband bound,
The courtier's promises, and sick men's prayers,
The smiles of harlots, and the tears of heirs,   120
Cages for gnats, and chains to yoke a flea,
Dried butterflies, and tomes of casuistry.
  But trust the Muse—she saw it upward rise,
Though marked by none but quick, poetic eyes :
(So Rome's great founder to the heavens withdrew,
To Proculus alone confessed in view)
A sudden star, it shot through liquid air,
And drew behind a radiant trail of hair.
Not Berenice's locks first rose so bright,
The heavens bespangling with dishevelled light.   130

The sylphs behold it kindling as it flies,
And pleased pursue its progress through the skies.
  This the beau monde shall from the Mall survey,
And hail with music its propitious ray.
This the blest lover shall for Venus take,
And send up vows from Rosamonda's lake.
This Partridge soon shall view in cloudless skies,
When next he looks through Galileo's eyes ;
And hence th' egregious wizard shall foredoom
The fate of Louis, and the fall of Rome.   140
  Then cease, bright nymph ! to mourn thy ravished hair,
Which adds new glory to the shining sphere !
Not all the tresses that fair head can boast,
Shall draw such envy as the lock you lost.
For, after all the murders of your eye,
When, after millions slain, yourself shall die :
When those fair suns shall set, as set they must,
And all those tresses shall be laid in dust,
This lock, the Muse shall consecrate to fame,
And 'midst the stars inscribe Belinda's name.   150

AN ESSAY ON CRITICISM

'TIS hard to say, if greater want of skill
Appear in writing or in judging ill ;
But of the two, less dang'rous is th' offence
To tire our patience, than mislead our sense.
Some few in that, but numbers err in this,
Ten censure wrong for one who writes amiss ;
A fool might once himself alone expose,
Now one in verse makes many more in prose.
  'Tis with our judgments as our watches, none
Go just alike, yet each believes his own.   10
In Poets as true genius is but rare,
True Taste as seldom is the Critic's share ;
Both must alike from Heav'n derive their light,
These born to judge, as well as those to write.
Let such teach others who themselves excel,
And censure freely who have written well.
Authors are partial to their wit, 'tis true,
But are not Critics to their judgment too ?
  Yet if we look more closely, we shall find
Most have the seeds of judgment in their mind :   20
Nature affords at least a glimm'ring light ;
The lines, tho' touch'd but faintly, are drawn right.
But as the slightest sketch, if justly trac'd,   ⎫
Is by ill-colouring but the more disgrac'd,   ⎬
So by false learning is good sense defac'd :   ⎭

Some are bewilder'd in the maze of schools,
And some made coxcombs Nature meant but fools.
In search of wit these lose their common sense,
And then turn Critics in their own defence:
Each burns alike, who can, or cannot write,   30
Or with a Rival's, or an Eunuch's spite.
All fools have still an itching to deride,
And fain would be upon the laughing side.
If Maevius scribble in Apollo's spight,
There are, who judge still worse than he can write.
    Some have at first for Wits, then Poets past,
Turn'd Critics next, and prov'd plain Fools at last.
Some neither can for Wits nor Critics pass,
As heavy mules are neither horse nor ass.
Those half-learn'd witlings, num'rous in our isle,   40
As half-form'd insects on the banks of Nile;
Unfinish'd things, one knows not what to call,
Their generation's so equivocal:
To tell 'em, would a hundred tongues require,
Or one vain wit's, that might a hundred tire.
    But you who seek to give and merit fame,
And justly bear a Critic's noble name,
Be sure yourself and your own reach to know,
How far your genius, taste, and learning go;
Launch not beyond your depth, but be discreet,   50
And mark that point where sense and dulness meet.
    Nature to all things fix'd the limits fit,
And wisely curb'd proud man's pretending wit.
As on the land while here the ocean gains,
In other parts it leaves wide sandy plains;
Thus in the soul while memory prevails,
The solid pow'r of understanding fails;
Where beams of warm imagination play,
The memory's soft figures melt away.
One science only will one genius fit;   60
So vast is art, so narrow human wit:
Not only bounded to peculiar arts,
But oft' in those confin'd to single parts.
Like kings we lose the conquests gain'd before,
By vain ambition still to make them more:
Each might his sev'ral province well command,
Would all but stoop to what they understand.
    First follow Nature, and your judgment frame
By her just standard, which is still the same:
Unerring NATURE, still divinely bright,   70
One clear, unchang'd, and universal light,
Life, force, and beauty, must to all impart,
At once the source, and end, and test of Art.
Art from that fund each just supply provides;
Works without show, and without pomp presides:

In some fair body thus th' informing soul
With spirits feeds, with vigour fills the whole,
Each motion guides, and ev'ry nerve sustains ;
Itself unseen, but in th' effects, remains.
Some, to whom Heav'n in wit has been profuse,   80
Want as much more, to turn it to its use ;
For wit and judgment often are at strife,
Tho' meant each other's aid, like man and wife.
'Tis more to guide, than spur the Muse's steed ;
Restrain his fury, than provoke his speed ;
The winged courser, like a gen'rous horse,
Shews most true mettle when you check his course.
    Those RULES of old discover'd, not devis'd,
Are Nature still, but Nature methodiz'd ;
Nature, like Liberty, is but restrain'd   90
By the same Laws which first herself ordain'd.
    Hear how learn'd Greece her useful rules indites,
When to repress, and when indulge our flights :
High on Parnassus' top her sons she show'd,
And pointed out those arduous paths they trod ;
Held from afar, aloft, th' immortal prize,
And urg'd the rest by equal steps to rise.
Just precepts thus from great examples giv'n,
She drew from them what they deriv'd from Heav'n.
The gen'rous Critic fann'd the Poet's fire,   100
And taught the world with Reason to admire.
Then Criticism the Muses handmaid prov'd,
To dress her charms, and make her more belov'd :
But following wits from that intention stray'd,
Who could not win the mistress, woo'd the maid ;
Against the Poets their own arms they turn'd,
Sure to hate most the men from whom they learn'd.
So modern 'Pothecaries, taught the art
By Doctor's bills to play the Doctor's part,
Bold in the practice of mistaken rules,   110
Prescribe, apply, and call their masters fools.
Some on the leaves of ancient authors prey,
Nor time nor moths e'er spoil'd so much as they :
Some drily plain, without invention's aid,
Write dull receipts how poems may be made.
These leave the sense, their learning to display,
And those explain the meaning quite away.
    You then whose judgment the right course would steer,
Know well each ANCIENT'S proper character ;
His Fable, Subject, scope in ev'ry page ;   120
Religion, Country, genius of his Age :
Without all these at once before your eyes,
Cavil you may, but never criticize.
Be Homer's works your study and delight,
Read them by day, and meditate by night ;

Thence form your judgment, thence your maxims bring,
And trace the Muses upward to their spring.
Still with itself compar'd, his text peruse ;
And let your comment be the Mantuan Muse.
   When first young Maro in his boundless mind   130
A work t' outlast immortal Rome design'd,
Perhaps he seem'd above the Critic's law,
And but from Nature's fountains scorn'd to draw :
But when t' examine ev'ry part he came,
Nature and Homer were, he found, the same.
Convinc'd, amaz'd, he checks the bold design :   ⎫
And rules as strict his labour'd verse confine,   ⎬
As if the Stagirite o'erlook'd each line.   ⎭
Learn hence for ancient rules a just esteem ;
To copy Nature is to copy them.   140
   Some beauties yet no Precepts can declare,
For there's a happiness as well as care.
Music resembles Poetry, in each   ⎫
Are nameless graces which no methods teach   ⎬
And which a master hand alone can reach.   ⎭
If, where the rules not far enough extend,
(Since rules were made but to promote their end)
Some lucky Licence answer to the full
Th' intent propos'd, that Licence is a rule.
Thus Pegasus, a nearer way to take,   150
May boldly deviate from the common track ;
From vulgar bounds with brave disorder part,
And snatch a grace beyond the reach of art,
Which without passing thro' the judgment, gains
The heart, and all its end at once attains.
In prospects thus, some objects please our eyes,   ⎫
Which out of nature's common order rise,   ⎬
The shapeless rock, or hanging precipice.   ⎭
Great Wits sometimes may gloriously offend,
And rise to faults true Critics dare not mend.   160
But tho' the Ancients thus their rules invade,
(As Kings dispense with laws themselves have made)
Moderns, beware ! or if you must offend
Against the precept, ne'er transgress its End ;
Let it be seldom, and compell'd by need ;
And have, at least, their precedent to plead.
The Critic else proceeds without remorse,
Seizes your frame, and puts his laws in force.
   I know there are, to whose presumptuous thoughts
Those freer beauties, ev'n in them, seem faults.   170
Some figures monstrous, and mis-shap'd appear,
Consider'd singly, or beheld too near,
Which, but proportion'd to their light, or place,
Due distance reconciles to form and grace.
A prudent chief not always must display
His pow'rs in equal ranks, and fair array,

But with th' occasion and the place comply,
Conceal his force, nay seem sometimes to fly.
Those oft are stratagems which errors seem,
Nor is it Homer nods, but we that dream.   180
　Still green with bays each ancient Altar stands,
Above the reach of sacrilegious hands ;
Secure from Flames, from Envy's fiercer rage,
Destructive War, and all-involving Age.
See from each clime the learn'd their incense bring !
Hear, in all tongues consenting Paeans ring !
In praise so just let ev'ry voice be join'd,
And fill the gen'ral chorus of mankind.
Hail, Bards triumphant ! born in happier days ;
Immortal heirs of universal praise !   190
Whose honours with increase of ages grow,
As streams roll down, enlarging as they flow ;
Nations unborn your mighty names shall sound,
And worlds applaud that must not yet be found !
O may some spark of your celestial fire,
The last, the meanest of your sons inspire,
(That on weak wings, from far, pursues your flights ;
Glows while he reads, but trembles as he writes)
To teach vain wits a science little known,
T' admire superior sense, and doubt their own !   200

　OF all the Causes which conspire to blind
Man's erring judgment, and misguide the mind,
What the weak head with strongest bias rules,
Is PRIDE, the nev'r-failing vice of fools.
Whatever Nature has in worth deny'd,
She gives in large recruits of needful Pride ;
For as in bodies, so in souls, we find
What wants in blood and spirits, swell'd with wind :
Pride, where Wit fails, steps in to our defence,
And fills up all the mighty Void of sense.   210
If once right reason drives that cloud away,
Truth breaks upon us with resistless day.
Trust not yourself ; but your defects to know,
Make use of ev'ry friend—and ev'ry foe.
A *little learning* is a dang'rous thing ;
Drink deep, or taste not the Pierian spring :
There shallow draughts intoxicate the brain,
And drinking largely sobers us again.
Fir'd at first sight with what the Muse imparts,
In fearless youth we tempt the heights of Arts,   220
While from the bounded level of our mind,
Short views we take, nor see the lengths behind ;
But more advanc'd, behold with strange surprise
New distant scenes of endless science rise !
So pleas'd at first the tow'ring Alps we try,
Mount o'er the vales, and seem to tread the sky,

Th' eternal snows appear already past,
And the first clouds and mountains seem the last;
But, those attain'd, we tremble to survey
The growing labours of the lengthen'd way,   230
Th' increasing prospects tires our wand'ring eyes,
Hills peep o'er hills, and Alps on Alps arise!
    A perfect Judge will read each work of Wit
With the same spirit that its author writ:
Survey the WHOLE, nor seek slight faults to find
Where nature moves, and rapture warms the mind;
Nor lose, for that malignant dull delight,
The gen'rous pleasure to be charm'd with wit.
But in such lays as neither ebb, nor flow,
Correctly cold, and regularly low,   240
That shunning faults, one quiet tenour keep;
We cannot blame indeed—but we may sleep.
In Wit, as Nature, what affects our hearts
Is not th' exactness of peculiar parts;
'Tis not a lip, or eye, we beauty call,
But the joint force and full result of all.
Thus when we view some well-proportion'd dome,
(The world's just wonder, and ev'n thine, O Rome!)
No single parts unequally surprize,
All comes united to th' admiring eyes;   250
No monstrous height, or breadth, or length appear;
The Whole at once is bold, and regular.
    Whoever thinks a faultless piece to see,
Thinks what ne'er was, nor is, nor e'er shall be.
In every work regard the writer's End,
Since none can compass more than they intend;
And if the means be just, the conduct true,
Applause, in spight of trivial faults, is due.
As men of breeding, sometimes men of wit,
T' avoid great errors, must the less commit: 260
Neglect the rules each verbal Critic lays,
For not to know some trifles, is a praise.
Most Critics, fond of some subservient art,
Still make the Whole depend upon a Part:
They talk of principles, but notions prize,
And all to one lov'd Folly sacrifice.
    Once on a time, La Mancha's Knight, they say,
A certain Bard encount'ring on the way,
Discours'd in terms as just, with looks as sage,
As e'er could Dennis, of the Grecian stage;   270
Concluding all were desp'rate sots and fools,
Who durst depart from Aristotle's rules.
Our Author happy in a judge so nice,
Produc'd his Play, and begg'd the Knight's advice;
Made him observe the subject, and the plot,
The manners, passions, unities; what not?

All which, exact to rule, were brought about,
Were but a combat in the lists left out.
' What ! leave the Combat out ? ' exclaims the Knight.
Yes, or we must renounce the Stagirite.   280
' Not so, by Heav'n ' (he answers in a rage),
' Knights, squires, and steeds, must enter on the stage.
So vast a throng the stage can ne'er contain.
' Then build a new, or act it in a plain.'
    Thus Critics, of less judgment than caprice,
Curious, not knowing, not exact but nice,
Form short Ideas ; and offend in arts
(As most in manners) by a love to parts.
    Some to *Conceit* alone their taste confine,
And glitt'ring thoughts struck out at ev'ry line ;   290
Pleas'd with a work where nothing's just or fit ;
One glaring Chaos and wild heap of wit.
Poets like painters, thus, unskill'd to trace
The naked nature and the living grace,
With gold and jewels cover ev'ry part,
And hide with ornaments their want of art.
True Wit is Nature to advantage dress'd,
What oft was thought, but ne'er so well express'd ;
Something, whose truth convinc'd at sight we find,
That gives us back the image of our mind.   300
As shades more sweetly recommend the light,
So modest plainness sets off sprightly wit.
For works may have more wit than does 'em good,
As bodies perish thro' excess of blood.
    Others for *Language* all their care express,
And value books, as women men, for Dress :
Their Praise is still,—the Style is excellent :
The Sense, they humbly take upon content.
Words are like leaves ; and where they most abound,
Much fruit of sense beneath is rarely found.   310
False eloquence, like the prismatic glass,
Its gaudy colours spreads on ev'ry place ;
The face of Nature we no more survey,
All glares alike, without distinction gay :
But true Expression, like th' unchanging Sun,
Clears and improves whate'er it shines upon,
It gilds all objects, but it alters none.
Expression is the dress of thought, and still
Appears more decent, as more suitable ;
A vile conceit in pompous words express'd,   320
Is like a clown in regal purple dress'd :
For diff'rent styles with diff'rent subjects sort,
As several garbs, with country, town, and court.
Some by old words to fame have made pretence,
Ancients in phrase, mere moderns in their sense ;
Such labour'd nothings, in so strange a style,
Amaze th' unlearn'd, and make the learned smile.

Unlucky, as Fungoso in the Play,
These sparks with aukward vanity display
What the fine gentleman wore yesterday ;   330
And but so mimic ancient wits at best,
As apes our grandsires, in their doublets drest.
In words, as fashions, the same rule will hold ;
Alike fantastic, if too new or old :
Be not the first by whom the new are try'd,
Not yet the last to lay the old aside.
  But most by Numbers judge a Poet's song ;
And smooth or rough, with them, is right or wrong :
In the bright Muse tho' thousand charms conspire,
Her Voice is all these tuneful fools admire ;   340
Who haunt Parnassus but to please their ear,
Not mend their minds ; as some to Church repair,
Not for the doctrine, but the music there.
These equal syllables alone require,
Tho' oft the ear the open vowels tire ;
While expletives their feeble aid do join ;
And ten low words oft creep in one dull line :
While they ring round the same unvary'd chimes,
With sure returns of still expected rhymes ;
Where'er you find ' the cooling western breeze,'   350
In the next line, it ' whispers thro' the trees : '
If crystal streams ' with pleasing murmurs creep,'
The reader's threat'n'd (not in vain) with ' sleep : '
Then, at the last and only couplet fraught
With some unmeaning thing they call a thought,
A needless Alexandrine ends the song,
That, like a wounded snake, drags its slow length along.
Leave such to tune their own dull rhymes, and know
What's roundly smooth, or languishingly slow ;
And praise the easy vigour of a line,   360
Where Denham's strength, and Waller's sweetness join.
True ease in writing comes from art, not chance,
As those move easiest who have learn'd to dance.
'Tis not enough no harshness gives offence,
The sound must seem an Echo to the sense :
Soft is the strain when Zephyr gently blows,
And the smooth stream in smoother numbers flows ;
But when loud surges lash the sounding shore,
The hoarse, rough verse should like the torrent roar.
When Ajax strives some rock's vast weight to throw, 370
The line too labours, and the words move slow :
Not so, when swift Camilla scours the plain,
Flies o'er th' unbending corn, and skims along the main.
Hear how Timotheus' varied lays surprize,
And bid alternate passions fall and rise !
While, at each change, the son of Libyan Jove
Now burns with glory, and then melts with love ;

Now his fierce eyes with sparkling fury glow,
Now sighs steal out, and tears begin to flow:
Persians and Greeks like turns of nature found,   380
And the world's victor stood subdu'd by Sound!
The pow'r of Music all our hearts allow,
And what Timotheus was, is DRYDEN now.

Avoid Extremes; and shun the fault of such,
Who still are pleas'd too little or too much.
At ev'ry trifle scorn to take offence,
That always shews great pride, or little sense:
Those heads, as stomachs, are not sure the best,
Which nauseate all, and nothing can digest.
Yet let not each gay Turn thy rapture move;   390
For fools admire, but men of sense approve:
As things seem large which we thro' mists descry,
Dulness is ever apt to magnify.

Some foreign writers, some our own despise;
The Ancients only, or the Moderns prize;
Thus Wit, like Faith, by each man is apply'd
To one small sect, and all are damn'd beside.
Meanly they seek the blessing to confine,
And force that sun but on a part to shine,
Which not alone the southern wit sublimes,   400
But ripens spirits in cold northern climes;
Which from the first has shone on ages past,
Enlights the present, and shall warm the last;
Tho' each may feel encreases and decays,
And see now clearer and now darker days.
Regard not then if Wit be old or new,
But blame the false, and value still the true.

Some ne'er advance a Judgment of their own,
But catch the spreading notion of the Town:
They reason and conclude by precedent,   410
And own stale nonsense which they ne'er invent.
Some judge of authors' names, not works, and then
Nor praise nor blame the writings, but the men.
Of all this servile herd, the worst is he
That in proud dulness joins with Quality.
A constant Critic at the great man's board,
To fetch and carry nonsense for my Lord.
What woful stuff this madrigal would be,
In some starv'd hackney sonneteer, or me?
But let a Lord once own the happy lines,   420
How the wit brightens! how the style refines!
Before his sacred name flies ev'ry fault,
And each exalted stanza teems with thought!

The Vulgar thus thro' Imitation err:
As oft the Learn'd by being singular;
So much they scorn the crowd, that if the throng
By chance go right, they purposely go wrong:

So Schismatics the plain believers quit,
And are but damn'd for having too much wit.
Some praise at morning what they blame at night;   430
But always think the last opinion right.
A Muse by these is like a mistress us'd,
This hour she's idoliz'd, the next abus'd;
While their weak heads like towns unfortify'd,
'Twixt sense and nonsense daily change their side.
Ask them the cause; they're wiser still, they say;
And still to-morrow's wiser than to-day.
We think our fathers fools; so wise we grow;
Our wiser sons, no doubt, will think us so.
Once School-divines this zealous isle o'er-spread;   440
Who knew most Sentences was deepest read:
Faith, Gospel, all, seem'd made to be disputed,
And none had sense enough to be confuted:
Scotists and Thomists, now, in peace remain,
Amidst their kindred cobwebs in Duck-lane.
If Faith itself has diff'rent dresses worn,
What wonder modes in Wit should take their turn?
Oft', leaving what is natural and fit,
The current folly proves the ready wit;
And authors think their reputation safe,   450
Which lives as long as fools are pleas'd to laugh.
   Some valuing those of their own side or mind,
Still make themselves the measure of mankind:
Fondly we think we honour merit then,
When we but praise ourselves in other men.
Parties in Wit attend on those of State,
And public faction doubles private hate.
Pride, Malice, Folly, against Dryden rose,
In various shapes of Parsons, Critics, Beaus:
But sense surviv'd, when merry jests were past;   460
For rising merit will buoy up at last.
Might he return, and bless once more our eyes,
New Blackmores and new Milbourns must arise:
Nay should great Homer lift his awful head,
Zoilus again would start up from the dead.
Envy will merit, as its shade, pursue;
But like a shadow, proves the substance true:
For envy'd Wit, like Sol eclips'd, makes known
Th' opposing body's grossness, not its own,
When first that sun too pow'rful beams displays,   470
It draws up vapours which obscure its rays;
But ev'n those clouds at last adorn its way,
Reflect new glories and augment the day.
   Be thou the first true merit to befriend;
His praise is lost, who stays 'till all commend.
Short is the date, alas, of modern rhymes,
And 'tis but just to let them live betimes.

No longer now that golden age appears,
When Patriarch-wits surviv'd a thousand years:
Now length of Fame (our second life) is lost,   480
And bare threescore is all ev'n that can boast;
Our sons their fathers' failing language see,
And such as Chaucer is, shall Dryden be.
So when the faithful pencil has design'd
Some bright Idea of the master's mind,
Where a new world leaps out at his command,
And ready Nature waits upon his hand;
When the ripe colours soften and unite,
And sweetly melt into just shade and light;
When mellowing years their full perfection give,   490
And each bold figure just begins to live,
The treach'rous colours the fair art betray,
And all the bright creation fades away!
    Unhappy Wit, like most mistaken things,
Atones not for that envy which it brings.
In youth alone its empty praise we boast,
But soon the short-liv'd vanity is lost:
Like some fair flow'r the early spring supplies,
That gaily blooms, but ev'n in blooming dies.
What is this Wit, which must our cares employ?   500
The owner's wife, that other men enjoy;
Then most our trouble still when most admir'd,
And still the more we give, the more requir'd;
Whose fame with pains we guard, but lose with ease,
Sure some to vex, but never all to please;
'Tis what the vicious fear, the virtuous shun,
By fools 'tis hated, and by knaves undone!
    If Wit so much from Ign'rance undergo,
Ah let not Learning too commence its foe!
Of old, those met rewards who could excell,   510
And such were prais'd, who but endeavour'd well:
Tho' triumphs were to gen'rals only due,
Crowns were reserv'd to grace the soldiers too,
Now, they who reach Parnassus' lofty crown,
Employ their pains to spurn some others down;
And while self-love each jealous writer rules,
Contending wits become the sport of fools:
But still the worst with most regret commend,
For each ill Author is as bad a Friend.
To what base ends, and by what abject ways,   520
Are mortals urg'd thro' sacred lust of praise!
Ah ne'er so dire a thirst of glory boast,
Nor in the Critic let the Man be lost.
Good-nature and good-sense must ever join:
To err is human, to forgive, divine.
    But if in noble minds some dregs remain
Not yet purg'd off, of spleen and sour disdain;

Discharge that rage on more provoking crimes,
Nor fear a dearth in these flagitious times.
No pardon vile Obscenity should find, 530
Tho' wit and art conspire to move your mind ;
But Dulness with Obscenity must prove
As shameful sure as impotence in love.
In the fat age of pleasure, wealth, and ease,
Sprung the rank weed, and thriv'd with large increase :
When love was all an easy Monarch's care ;
Seldom at council, never in a war :
Jilts rul'd the state, and statesmen farces writ ;
Nay wits had pensions, and young Lords had wit :
The Fair sate panting at a Courtier's play, 540
And not a Mask went unimprov'd away :
The modest fan was lifted up no more,
And Virgins smil'd at what they blush'd before.
The following license of a Foreign reign
Did all the dregs of bold Socinus drain ;
Then unbelieving Priests reform'd the nation,
And taught more pleasant methods of salvation ;
Where Heav'n's free subjects might their right dispute,
Lest God himself should seem too absolute :
Pulpits their sacred satire learn'd to spare, 550
And Vice admir'd to find a flatt'rer there !
Encourag'd thus, Wit's Titans brav'd the skies,
And the press groan'd with licens'd blasphemies.
These monsters, Critics ! with your darts engage,
Here point your thunder, and exhaust your rage !
Yet shun their fault, who, scandalously nice,
Will needs mistake an author into vice ;
All seems infected that th' infected spy,
As all looks yellow to the jaundic'd eye.

LEARN then what MORALS Critics ought to show, 560
For 'tis but half a Judge's task, to know.
'Tis not enough, taste, judgment, learning, join ;
In all you speak, let truth and candour shine :
That not alone what to your sense is due
All may allow ; but seek your friendship too.
Be silent always, when you doubt your sense ;
And speak, tho' sure, with seeming diffidence :
Some positive, persisting fops we know,
Who, if once wrong, will needs be always so ;
But you, with pleasure own your errors past, 570
And make each day a Critique on the last.
'Tis not enough your counsel still be true ;
Blunt truths more mischief than nice falsehoods do ;
Men must be taught as if you taught them not,
And things unknown propos'd as things forgot.
Without Good-Breeding, truth is disapprov'd ;
That only makes superior sense belov'd.

    Be niggards of advice on no pretence ;
For the worst avarice is that of sense.
With mean complacence ne'er betray your trust,   580
Nor be so civil as to prove unjust.
Fear not the anger of the wise to raise ;
Those best can bear reproof, who merit praise.
    'Twere well might Critics still this freedom take,
But Appius reddens at each word you speak,
And stares, tremendous, with a threat'ning eye,
Like some fierce Tyrant in old tapestry.
Fear most to tax an Honourable fool,
Whose right it is, uncensur'd, to be dull :
Such, without wit, are Poets when they please,   590
As without learning they can take Degrees.
Leave dang'rous truths to unsuccessful Satires,
And flattery to fulsome Dedicators,
Whom, when they praise, the World believes no more,
Than when they promise to give scribbling o'er.
'Tis best sometimes your censure to restrain,
And charitably let the dull be vain :
Your silence there is better than your spite,
For who can rail so long as they can write ?
Still humming on, their drouzy course they keep,   600
And lash'd so long, like tops, are lash'd asleep.
False steps but help them to renew the race,
As, after stumbling, Jades will mend their pace.
What crowds of these, impertinently bold,
In sounds and jingling syllables grown old,
Still run on Poets, in a raging vein,
Ev'n to the dregs and squeezings of the brain,
Strain out the last dull droppings of their sense,
And rhyme with all the rage of Impotence.
    Such shameless Bards we have ; and yet 'tis true, 610
There are as mad, abandon'd Critics too.
The bookful blockhead, ignorantly read,
With loads of learned lumber in his head,
With his own tongue still edifies his ears,
And always list'ning to himself appears.
All books he reads, and all he reads assails,
From Dryden's Fables down to Durfey's Tales.
With him, most authors steal their works, or buy ;
Garth did not write his own Dispensary.
Name a new Play, and he's the Poet's friend,   620
Nay show'd his faults—but when would Poets mend ?
No place so sacred from such fops is barr'd,
Nor is Paul's church more safe than Paul's churchyard :
Nay, fly to Altars ; there they'll talk you dead ;
For Fools rush in where Angels fear to tread.
Distrustful sense with modest caution speaks,   ⎫
It still looks home, and short excursions makes ;   ⎬
But rattling nonsense in full vollies breaks,   ⎭

And never shock'd, and never turn'd aside,
Bursts out, resistless, with a thund'ring tide.   630
But where's the man, who counsel can bestow,
Still pleas'd to teach, and yet not proud to know ?
Unbiass'd, or by favour, or by spite ;
Not dully prepossess'd, nor blindly right ;
Tho' learn'd, well-bred ; and tho' well-bred, sincere;
Modestly bold, and humanly severe :
Who to a friend his faults can freely show,
And gladly praise the merit of a foe ?
Blest with a taste exact, yet unconfin'd ;
A knowledge both of books and human kind ;   640
Gen'rous converse ; a soul exempt from pride ;
And love to praise, with reason on his side ?
   Such once were Critics ; such the happy few,
Athens and Rome in better ages knew.
The mighty Stagirite first left the shore,
Spread all his sails, and durst the deeps explore :
He steer'd securely, and discover'd far,
Led by the Light of the Maeonian Star.
Poets, a race long unconfin'd, and free,
Still fond and proud of savage liberty,   650
Receiv'd his laws ; and stood convinc'd 'twas fit,
Who conquer'd Nature, should preside o'er Wit.
   Horace still charms with graceful negligence,
And without method talks us into sense,
Will, like a friend, familiarly convey
The truest notions in the easiest way.
He, who supreme in judgment, as in wit,
Might boldly censure, as he boldly writ,
Yet judg'd with coolness, tho' he sung with fire ;
His Precepts teach but what his works inspire.   660
Our Critics take a contrary extreme,
They judge with fury, but they write with flegm :
Nor suffers Horace more in wrong Translations
By Wits, than Critics in as wrong Quotations.
   See Dionysius Homer's thoughts refine,
And call new beauties forth from ev'ry line !
   Fancy and art in gay Petronius please,
The scholar's learning, with the courtier's ease.
   In grave Quintilian's copious work we find
The justest rules, and clearest method join'd :   670
Thus useful arms in magazines we place,
All rang'd in order, and dispos'd with grace,
But less to please the eye than arm the hand,
Still fit for use, and ready at command.
   Thee, bold Longinus ! all the Nine inspire,
And bless their Critic with a Poet's fire.
An ardent Judge, who zealous in his trust,
With warmth gives sentence, yet is always just ;

Whose own example strengthens all his laws ;
And is himself that great Sublime he draws.   680
  Thus long succeeding Critics justly reign'd,
Licence repress'd, and useful laws ordain'd.
Learning and Rome alike in empire grew ;
And Arts still follow'd where her Eagles flew ;
From the same foes, at last, both felt their doom,
And the same age saw Learning fall, and Rome.
With Tyranny, then Superstition join'd,
As that the body, this enslav'd the mind ;
Much was believ'd, but little understood,
And to be dull was constru'd to be good ;   690
A second deluge Learning thus o'er-run,
And the Monks finish'd what the Goths begun.
  At length Erasmus, that great injur'd name,
(The glory of the Priesthood, and the shame !)
Stemm'd the wild torrent of a barb'rous age,
And drove those holy Vandals off the stage.
  But see ! each Muse, in LEO's golden days,
Starts from her trance, and trims her wither'd bays,
Rome's ancient Genius, o'er its ruins spread,
Shakes off the dust, and rears his rev'rend head.   700
Then Sculpture and her sister-arts revive :
Stones leap'd to form, and rocks began to live ;
With sweeter notes each rising Temple rung ;
A Raphael painted, and a Vida sung.
Immortal Vida : on whose honour'd brow
The Poet's bays and Critic's ivy grow :
Cremona now shall ever boast thy name,
As next in place to Mantua, next in fame !
  But soon by impious arms from Latium chas'd,
Their ancient bounds the banish'd Muses pass'd ;   710
Thence Arts o'er all the northern world advance,
But Critic-learning flourish'd most in France ;
The rules a nation, born to serve, obeys ;
And Boileau still in right of Horace sways.
But we, brave Britons, foreign laws despis'd,
And kept unconquer'd and unciviliz'd ;
Fierce for the liberties of wit, and bold,
We still defy'd the Romans, as of old.
Yet some there were, among the sounder few
Of those who less presum'd, and better knew,   720
Who durst assert the juster ancient cause,
And here restor'd Wit's fundamental laws.
Such was the Muse, whose rules and practice tell,
'Nature's chief Master-piece is writing well.'
Such was Roscommon, not more learn'd than good,
With manners gen'rous as his noble blood ;
To him the wit of Greece and Rome was known,
And ev'ry author's merit but his own.

Such late was Walsh—the Muse's judge and friend,
Who justly knew to blame or to commend ;   730
To failings mild, but zealous for desert ;
The clearest head, and the sincerest heart.
This humble praise, lamented shade ! receive,
This praise at least a grateful Muse may give :
The Muse, whose early voice you taught to sing,
Prescrib'd her heights, and prun'd her tender wing,
(Her guide now lost) no more attempts to rise,
But in low numbers short excursions tries :
Content, if hence th' unlearn'd their wants may view,
The learn'd reflect on what before they knew :   740
Careless of Censure, nor too fond of fame ;
Still pleas'd to praise, yet not afraid to blame ;
Averse alike, to flatter or offend ;
Not free from faults, nor yet too vain to mend.

ELEGY TO THE MEMORY OF AN
UNFORTUNATE LADY

WHAT beck'ning ghost, along the moonlight shade
Invites my steps, and points to yonder glade ?
'Tis she !—but why that bleeding bosom gored,
Why dimly gleams the visionary sword ?
O, ever beauteous, ever friendly ! tell,
Is it, in Heav'n, a crime to love too well ?
To bear too tender or too firm a heart,
To act a lover's or a Roman's part ?
Is there no bright reversion in the sky
For those who greatly think, or bravely die ?   10
    Why bade ye else, ye Pow'rs ! her soul aspire
Above the vulgar flight of low desire ?
Ambition first sprung from your blest abodes ;
The glorious fault of angels and of gods ;
Thence to their images on earth it flows,
And in the breasts of kings and heroes glows.
Most souls, 'tis true, but peep out once an age,
Dull sullen pris'ners in the body's cage :
Dim lights of life, that burn a length of years,
Useless, unseen, as lamps in sepulchres ;   20
Like Eastern kings a lazy state they keep,
And, close confined to their own palace, sleep.
    From these perhaps (ere Nature bade her die)
Fate snatch'd her early to the pitying sky.

As into air the purer spirits flow,
And sep'rate from their kindred dregs below,
So flew the soul to its congenial place,
Nor left one virtue to redeem her race.
  But thou, false guardian of a charge too good!
Thou, mean deserter of thy brother's blood!   30
See on these ruby lips the trembling breath,
These cheeks now fading at the blast of Death:
Cold is that breast which warm'd the world before,
And those love-darting eyes must roll no more.
Thus, if eternal Justice rules the ball,
Thus shall your wives, and thus your children fall;
On all the line a sudden vengeance waits,
And frequent herses shall besiege your gates.
There passengers shall stand, and pointing say
(While the long fun'rals blacken all the way),   40
'Lo! these were they whose souls the Furies steel'd
And cursed with hearts unknowing how to yield.'
Thus unlamented pass the proud away,
The gaze of fools, and pageant of a day!
So perish all whose breast ne'er learn'd to glow
For others' good, or melt at others' woe!
  What can atone (O ever-injured shade!)
Thy fate unpitied, and thy rites unpaid?
No friend's complaint, no kind domestic tear
Pleased thy pale ghost, or graced thy mournful bier. 50
By foreign hands thy dying eyes were closed,
By foreign hands thy decent limbs composed,
By foreign hands thy humble grave adorn'd,
By strangers honour'd, and by strangers mourn'd!
What tho' no friends in sable weeds appear,
Grieve for an hour, perhaps, then mourn a year,
And bear about the mockery of woe
To midnight dances, and the public show?
What tho' no weeping Loves thy ashes grace,
Nor polish'd marble emulate thy face?   60
What tho' no sacred earth allow thee room,
Nor hallow'd dirge be mutter'd o'er thy tomb?
Yet shall thy grave with rising flow'rs be drest,
And the green turf lie lightly on thy breast:
There shall the morn her earliest tears bestow,
There the first roses of the year shall blow;
While angels with their silver wings o'ershade
The ground now sacred by thy reliques made.
  So peaceful rests, without a stone, a name,
What once had beauty, titles, wealth, and fame. 70
How loved, how honour'd once, avails thee not,
To whom related, or by whom begot;
A heap of dust alone remains of thee,
'Tis all thou art, and all the proud shall be!

Poets themselves must fall, like those they sung,
Deaf the praised ear, and mute the tuneful tongue.
Ev'n he, whose soul now melts in mournful lays,
Shall shortly want the gen'rous tear he pays ;
Then from his closing eyes thy form shall part,
And the last pang shall tear thee from his heart ;   80
Life's idle business at one gasp be o'er,
The Muse forgot, and thou beloved no more !

SAMUEL JOHNSON

THE VANITY OF HUMAN WISHES

THE TENTH SATIRE OF JUVENAL, IMITATED

LET Observation, with extensive view,
Survey mankind from China to Peru ;
Remark each anxious toil, each eager strife,
And watch the busy scenes of crowded life ;
Then say how hope and fear, desire and hate,
O'erspread with snares the clouded maze of fate,
Where wav'ring man, betray'd by vent'rous pride
To tread the dreary paths without a guide,
As treach'rous phantoms in the mist delude,
Shuns fancied ills, or chases airy good :   10
How rarely reason guides the stubborn choice,
Rules the bold hand, or prompts the suppliant voice :
How nations sink, by darling schemes oppress'd,
When vengeance listens to the fool's request.
Fate wings with ev'ry wish th' afflictive dart,
Each gift of nature, and each grace of art :
With fatal heat impetuous courage glows,
With fatal sweetness elocution flows ;
Impeachment stops the speaker's pow'rful breath,
And restless fire precipitates on death.   20
　　But, scarce observ'd, the knowing and the bold
Fall in the gen'ral massacre of gold ;
Wide-wasting pest ! that rages unconfin'd,
And crowds with crimes the records of mankind.
For gold his sword the hireling ruffian draws,
For gold the hireling judge distorts the laws ;
Wealth heap'd on wealth nor truth nor safety buys,
The dangers gather as the treasures rise.
　　Let Hist'ry tell, where rival kings command,
And dubious title shakes the madded land,   30
When statutes glean the refuse of the sword,
How much more safe the vassal than the lord.
Low skulks the hind beneath the rage of pow'r,
And leaves the wealthy traitor in the Tow'r ;
Untouch'd his cottage, and his slumbers sound,
Tho' Confiscation's vultures hover round.
　　The needy traveller, serene and gay,
Walks the wild heath, and sings his toil away.

Does envy seize thee ? Crush th' upbraiding joy;
Increase his riches, and his peace destroy.   40
Now fears in dire vicissitude invade,
The rustling brake alarms, and quiv'ring shade ;
Nor light nor darkness bring his pain relief,
One shows the plunder, and one hides the thief.
    Yet still one gen'ral cry the skies assails,
And gain and grandeur load the tainted gales ;
Few know the toiling statesman's fear or care,
Th' insidious rival and the gaping heir.
    Once more, Democritus, arise on earth,
With cheerful wisdom and instructive mirth .   50
See motley life in modern trappings dress'd,
And feed with varied fools th' eternal jest.
Thou who could'st laugh, where want enchain'd caprice,
Toil crush'd conceit, and man was of a piece ;
Where wealth unlov'd without a mourner dy'd,
And scarce a sycophant was fed by pride ;
Where ne'er was known the form of mock debate,
Or seen a new-made mayor's unwieldy state ;
Where change of fav'rites make no change of laws,
And senates heard before they judg'd a cause ;   60
How would'st thou shake at Britain's modish tribe,
Dart the quick taunt, and edge the piercing gibe?
Attentive truth and nature to descry,
And pierce each scene with philosophic eye,
To thee were solemn toys, or empty show,
The robes of pleasure and the veils of woe :
All aid the farce, and all thy mirth maintain,
Whose joys are causeless, or whose griefs are vain.
    Such was the scorn that fill'd the sage's mind,
Renew'd at ev'ry glance on humankind ;   70
How just that scorn ere yet thy voice declare,
Search ev'ry state, and canvass ev'ry pray'r.
    Unnumber'd suppliants crowd Preferment's gate,
Athirst for wealth, and burning to be great ;
Delusive Fortune hears th' incessant call,
They mount, they shine, evaporate, and fall.
On ev'ry stage the foes of peace attend,
Hate dogs their flight, and insult mocks their end.
Love ends with hope, the sinking statesman's door
Pours in the morning worshipper no more ;   80
For growing names the weekly scribbler lies,
To growing wealth the dedicator flies ;
From ev'ry room descends the painted face,
That hung the bright palladium of the place,
And, smok'd in kitchens, or in auctions sold,
To better features yields the frame of gold :
For now no more we trace in ev'ry line
Heroic worth, benevolence divine :

The form distorted justifies the fall,
And detestation rids th' indignant wall.   90
  But will not Britain hear the last appeal,
Sign her foe's doom, or guard her fav'rite's zeal ?
Thro' Freedom's sons no more remonstrance rings,
Degrading nobles, and controlling kings ;
Our supple tribes repress their patriot throats,
And ask no questions but the price of votes ;
With weekly libels and septennial ale,
Their wish is full, to riot and to rail.
  In full-blown dignity, see Wolsey stand,
Law in his voice, and fortune in his hand :   100
To him the church, the realm, their pow'rs consign,
Thro' him the rays of regal bounty shine,
Turn'd by his nod the stream of honour flows,
His smile alone security bestows :
Still to new heights his restless wishes tow'r,
Claim leads to claim, and pow'r advances pow'r :
Till conquest unresisted ceas'd to please,
And rights submitted left him none to seize.
At length his sov'reign frowns—the train of state
Mark the keen glance, and watch the sign to hate.   110
Where'er he turns, he meets a stranger's eye,
His suppliants scorn him, and his followers fly :
Now drops at once the pride of awful state,
The golden canopy, the glitt'ring plate,
The regal palace, the luxurious board,
The liv'ried army, and the menial lord.
With age, with cares, with maladies oppress'd,
He seeks the refuge of monastic rest ;
Grief aids disease, remember'd folly stings,
And his last sighs reproach the faith of kings.   120
  Speak thou whose thoughts at humble peace repine,
Shall Wolsey's wealth, with Wolsey's end, be thine ?
Or liv'st thou now, with safer pride content,
The wisest justice on the banks of Trent ?
For why did Wolsey, near the steeps of fate,
On weak foundations raise th' enormous weight ?
Why, but to sink beneath misfortune's blow,
With louder ruin to the gulfs below ?
  What gave great Villiers to th' assassin's knife,
And fix'd disease on Harley's closing life ?   130
What murder'd Wentworth, and what exil'd Hyde,
By kings protected, and to kings ally'd ?
What but their wish indulg'd in courts to shine,
And pow'r too great to keep, or to resign ?
  When first the college rolls receive his name,
The young enthusiast quits his ease for fame ;
Thro' all his veins the fever of renown
Burns from the strong contagion of the gown :

O'er Bodley's dome his future labours spread,
And Bacon's mansion trembles o'er his head. 140
Are these thy views ? Proceed, illustrious youth,
And Virtue guard thee to the throne of Truth !
Yet should thy soul indulge the gen'rous heat
Till captive Science yields her last retreat ;
Should Reason guide thee with her brightest ray,
And pour on misty Doubt resistless day ;
Should no false kindness lure to loose delight,
Nor praise relax, nor difficulty fright ;
Should tempting Novelty thy cell refrain,
And Sloth effuse her opiate fumes in vain ; 150
Should Beauty blunt on fops her fatal dart,
Nor claim the triumph of a letter'd heart ;
Should no disease thy torpid veins invade,
Nor Melancholy's phantoms haunt thy shade ;
Yet hope not life from grief or danger free,
Nor think the doom of man revers'd for thee.
Deign on the passing world to turn thine eyes,
And pause awhile from letters to be wise ;
There mark what ills the scholar's life assail,
Toil, envy, want, the patron, and the jail. 160
See nations, slowly wise and meanly just,
To buried merit raise the tardy bust.
If dreams yet flatter, once again attend,
Hear Lydiat's life, and Galileo's end.
    Nor deem, when Learning her last prize bestows,
The glitt'ring eminence exempt from foes ;
See, when the vulgar 'scape, despis'd or aw'd,
Rebellion's vengeful talons seize on Laud.
From meaner minds tho' smaller fines content,
The plunder'd palace, or sequester'd rent ; 170
Mark'd out by dang'rous parts, he meets the shock,
And fatal Learning leads him to the block :
Around his tomb let Art and Genius weep,
But hear his death, ye blockheads, hear and sleep.
    The festal blazes, the triumphal show,
The ravish'd standard, and the captive foe,
The senate's thanks, the Gazette's pompous tale,
With force resistless o'er the brave prevail.
Such bribes the rapid Greek o'er Asia whirl'd,
For such the steady Romans shook the world ; 180
For such in distant lands the Britons shine,
And stain with blood the Danube or the Rhine ;
This pow'r has praise, that virtue scarce can warm
Till Fame supplies the universal charm.
Yet Reason frowns on War's unequal game,
Where wasted nations raise a single name ;
And mortgag'd states their grandsires' wreaths regret,
From age to age in everlasting debt ;

Wreaths which at last the dear-bought right convey
To rust on medals, or on stones decay.   190
  On what foundation stands the warrior's pride,
How just his hopes, let Swedish Charles decide.
A frame of adamant, a soul of fire,
No dangers fright him, and no labours tire ;
O'er love, o'er fear, extends his wide domain,
Unconquer'd lord of pleasure and of pain ;
No joys to him pacific sceptres yield,
War sounds the trump, he rushes to the field.
Behold surrounding kings their pow'rs combine,
And one capitulate, and one resign :   200
Peace courts his hand, but spreads her charms in vain ;
' Think nothing gain'd,' he cries, ' till nought remain,
On Moscow's walls till Gothic standards fly,
And all be mine beneath the polar sky.'
The march begins in military state,
And nations on his eye suspended wait ;
Stern Famine guards the solitary coast,
And Winter barricades the realms of Frost ;
He comes, nor want nor cold his course delay ;—
Hide, blushing glory, hide Pultowa's day :   210
The vanquish'd hero leaves his broken bands,
And shows his miseries in distant lands ;
Condemn'd a needy supplicant to wait,
While ladies interpose, and slaves debate.
But did not Chance at length her error mend ?
Did no subverted empire mark his end ?
Did rival monarchs give the fatal wound ?
Or hostile millions press him to the ground ?
His fall was destin'd to a barren strand,
A petty fortress, and a dubious hand ;   220
He left the name at which the world grew pale,
To point a moral, or adorn a tale.
  All times their scenes of pompous woes afford,
From Persia's tyrant to Bavaria's lord.
In gay hostility, and barb'rous pride,
With half mankind embattled at his side,
Great Xerxes comes to seize the certain prey,
And starves exhausted regions in his way.
Attendant Flatt'ry counts his myriads o'er,
Till counted myriads soothe his pride no more.   230
Fresh praise is try'd, till madness fires his mind,
The waves he lashes, and enchains the wind ;
New pow'rs are claim'd, new pow'rs are still bestow'd,
Till rude resistance lops the spreading god ;
The daring Greeks deride the martial show,
And heap their valleys with the gaudy foe ;
Th' insulted sea with humbler thoughts he gains,
A single skiff to speed his flight remains ;

Th' encumber'd oar scarce leaves the dreaded coast
Thro' purple billows and a floating host.　　　　240
　The bold Bavarian, in a luckless hour,
Tries the dread summits of Caesarean pow'r ;
With unexpected legions bursts away,
And sees defenceless realms receive his sway.
Short sway ! fair Austria spreads her mournful charms,
The queen, the beauty, sets the world in arms ;
From hill to hill the beacon's rousing blaze
Spreads wide the hope of plunder and of praise ;
The fierce Croatian, and the wild Hussar,
With all the sons of ravage, crowd the war :　　　250
The baffled prince, in honour's flatt'ring bloom,
Of hasty greatness finds the fatal doom ;
His foes' derision and his subjects' blame,
And steals to death from anguish and from shame.
　' Enlarge my life with multitude of days ! '
In health, in sickness, thus the suppliant prays :
Hides from himself his state, and shuns to know
That life protracted is protracted woe.
Time hovers o'er, impatient to destroy,
And shuts up all the passages of joy :　　　260
In vain their gifts the bounteous seasons pour,
The fruit autumnal, and the vernal flow'r ;
With listless eyes the dotard views the store,
He views, and wonders that they please no more ;
Now pall the tasteless meats and joyless wines,
And Luxury with sighs her slave resigns.
Approach, ye minstrels, try the soothing strain,
Diffuse the tuneful lenitives of pain :
No sounds, alas ! would touch th' impervious ear,
Though dancing mountains witness'd Orpheus near ;　270
Nor lute nor lyre his feeble pow'rs attend,
Nor sweeter music of a virtuous friend.
But everlasting dictates crowd his tongue,
Perversely grave, or positively wrong ;
The still returning tale, and ling'ring jest,
Perplex the fawning niece and pamper'd guest,
While growing hopes scarce awe the gath'ring sneer,
And scarce a legacy can bribe to hear :
The watchful guests still hint the last offence,
The daughter's petulance, the son's expense ;　　　280
Improve his heady rage with treach'rous skill,
And mould his passions till they make his will.
　Unnumber'd maladies his joints invade,
Lay siege to life, and press the dire blockade ;
But unextinguish'd av'rice still remains,
And dreaded losses aggravate his pains :
He turns, with anxious heart and crippled hands,
His bonds of debt, and mortgages of lands ;

Or views his coffers with suspicious eyes,
Unlocks his gold, and counts it till he dies.   290
    But grant, the virtues of a temp'rate prime
Bless with an age exempt from scorn or crime ;
An age that melts with unperceiv'd decay,
And glides in modest innocence away ;
Whose peaceful day Benevolence endears,
Whose night congratulating Conscience cheers ;
The gen'ral fav'rite, as the gen'ral friend :
Such age there is, and who shall wish its end ?
    Yet ev'n on this her load Misfortune flings,
To press the weary minutes' flagging wings ;   300
New sorrow rises as the day returns,
A sister sickens, or a daughter mourns.
Now kindred Merit fills the sable bier,
Now lacerated Friendship claims a tear.
Year chases year, decay pursues decay,
Still drops some joy from with'ring life away ;
New forms arise, and diff'rent views engage,
Superfluous lags the vet'ran on the stage,
Till pitying Nature signs the last release,
And bids afflicted worth retire to peace.   310
    But few there are whom hours like these await,
Who set unclouded in the gulfs of fate.
From Lydia's monarch should the search descend,
By Solon caution'd to regard his end,
In life's last scene what prodigies surprise,
Fears of the brave and follies of the wise !
From Marlb'rough's eyes the streams of dotage flow,
And Swift expires a driv'ler and a show.
    The teeming mother, anxious for her race,
Begs for each birth the fortune of a face ;   320
Yet Vane could tell what ills from beauty spring,
And Sedley curs'd the form that pleas'd a king.
Ye nymphs of rosy lips and radiant eyes,
Whom pleasure keeps too busy to be wise,
Whom joys with soft varieties invite,
By day the frolic, and the dance by night ;
Who frown with vanity, who smile with art,
And ask the latest fashion of the heart ;
What care, what rules, your heedless charms shall save,
Each nymph your rival, and each youth your slave ? 330
Against your fame with fondness hate combines,
The rival batters, and the lover mines.
With distant voice neglected Virtue calls,
Less heard and less, the faint remonstrance falls ;
Tir'd with contempt, she quits the slipp'ry reign,
And Pride and Prudence take her seat in vain.
In crowd at once, where none the pass defend,
The harmless freedom, and the private friend :

The guardians yield, by force superior ply'd,
To Int'rest, Prudence; and to Flatt'ry, Pride.   340
Here Beauty falls, betray'd, despis'd, distress'd,
And hissing Infamy proclaims the rest.
   Where then shall Hope and Fear their objects find?
Must dull suspense corrupt the stagnant mind?
Must helpless man, in ignorance sedate,
Roll darkling down the torrent of his fate?
Must no dislike alarm, no wishes rise,
No cries invoke the mercies of the skies?
Inquirer, cease: petitions yet remain,
Which Heav'n may hear: nor deem religion vain.   350
Still raise for good the supplicating voice,
But leave to Heav'n the measure and the choice.
Safe in his pow'r, whose eyes discern afar
The secret ambush of a specious pray'r,
Implore his aid, in his decisions rest,
Secure, whate'er he gives, he gives the best.
Yet when the sense of sacred presence fires,
And strong devotion to the skies aspires,
Pour forth thy fervours for a healthful mind,
Obedient passions, and a will resign'd;   360
For love, which scarce collective man can fill;
For patience, sov'reign o'er transmuted ill;
For faith, that, panting for a happier seat,
Counts death kind Nature's signal of retreat.
These goods for man the laws of Heav'n ordain,
These goods he grants, who grants the pow'r to gain;
With these celestial Wisdom calms the mind,
And makes the happiness she does not find.

[handwritten at top: 1760–1840. Industrial]

[handwritten: Didactic poem.]

OLIVER GOLDSMITH

THE DESERTED VILLAGE

[handwritten: Little village of his up]

SWEET AUBURN! loveliest village of the plain,
Where health and plenty cheer'd the labouring swain,
Where smiling spring its earliest visit paid,
And parting summer's ling'ring blooms delay'd:
Dear lovely bowers of innocence and ease,
Seats of my youth, when every sport could please,
How often have I loiter'd o'er thy green,
Where humble happiness endear'd each scene;
How often have I paus'd on every charm,
The shelter'd cot, the cultivated farm,   10
The never-failing brook, the busy mill,
The decent church that topp'd the neighbouring hill, *[handwritten: correct using... word. worth jile]*
The hawthorn bush, with seats beneath the shade,
For talking age and whisp'ring lovers made;
How often have I bless'd the coming day,
When toil remitting lent its turn to play, *[handwritten: condensed.]*
And all the village train, from labour free,
Led up their sports beneath the spreading tree;
While many a pastime circled in the shade,
The young contending as the old survey'd; *[handwritten: add antithesis]*   20
And many a gambol frolick'd o'er the ground,
And sleights of art and feats of strength went round;
And still as each repeated pleasure tir'd,
Succeeding sports the mirthful band inspir'd; *[handwritten: ? odd]*
The dancing pair that simply sought renown,
By holding out to tire each other down;
The swain mistrustless of his smutted face,
While secret laughter titter'd round the place;
The bashful virgin's side-long looks of love,
The matron's glance that would those looks reprove: 30
These were thy charms, sweet village; sports like these,
With sweet succession, taught e'en toil to please;
These round thy bowers their cheerful influence shed,
These were thy charms—But all these charms are fled.

Sweet smiling village, loveliest of the lawn,
Thy sports are fled, and all thy charms withdrawn;
Amidst thy bowers the tyrant's hand is seen,
And desolation saddens all thy green:
One only master grasps the whole domain,
And half a tillage stints thy smiling plain: 40

No more thy glassy brook reflects the day,
But chok'd with sedges, works its weedy way.
Along thy glades, a solitary guest,
The hollow-sounding bittern guards its nest;
Amidst thy desert walks the lapwing flies,
And tires their echoes with unvaried cries.
Sunk are thy bowers in shapeless ruin all,
And the long grass o'ertops the mould'ring wall;
And trembling, shrinking from the spoiler's hand,
Far, far away, thy children leave the land.　　　　50

Ill fares the land, to hast'ning ills a prey,
Where wealth accumulates, and men decay:
Princes and lords may flourish, or may fade;
A breath can make them, as a breath has made;
But a bold peasantry, their country's pride,
When once destroy'd, can never be supplied.

A time there was, ere England's griefs began,
When every rood of ground maintain'd its man;
For him light labour spread her wholesome store,
Just gave what life requir'd, but gave no more:　　　　60
His best companions, innocence and health;
And his best riches, ignorance of wealth.

But times are alter'd; trade's unfeeling train
Usurp the land and dispossess the swain;
Along the lawn, where scatter'd hamlets rose,
Unwieldy wealth, and cumbrous pomp repose;
And every want to opulence allied,
And every pang that folly pays to pride.
Those gentle hours that plenty bade to bloom,
Those calm desires that ask'd but little room,　　　　70
Those healthful sports that grac'd the peaceful scene,
Liv'd in each look, and brighten'd all the green;
These, far departing, seek a kinder shore,
And rural mirth and manners are no more.

Sweet AUBURN! parent of the blissful hour,
Thy glades forlorn confess the tyrant's power.
Here as I take my solitary rounds,
Amidst thy tangling walks, and ruin'd grounds,
And, many a year elaps'd, return to view
Where once the cottage stood, the hawthorn grew,　　　　80
Remembrance wakes with all her busy train,
Swells at my breast, and turns the past to pain.

In all my wand'rings round this world of care,
In all my griefs—and GOD has given my share—
I still had hopes my latest hours to crown,
Amidst these humble bowers to lay me down;

To husband out life's taper at the close,
And keep the flame from wasting by repose.
I still had hopes, for pride attends us still,
Amidst the swains to show my book-learn'd skill,   90
Around my fire an evening group to draw,
And tell of all I felt, and all I saw ;
And, as a hare, whom hounds and horns pursue,
Pants to the place from whence at first she flew,
I still had hopes, my long vexations pass'd, *nom. absolute*
Here to return—and die at home at last.

O blest retirement, friend to life's decline,
Retreats from care, that never must be mine,
How happy he who crowns in shades like these,
A youth of labour with an age of ease ;   100
Who quits a world where strong temptations try
And, since 'tis hard to combat, learns to fly !
For him no wretches, born to work and weep,
Explore the mine, or tempt the dangerous deep ;
No surly porter stands in guilty state
To spurn imploring famine from the gate ;
But on he moves to meet his latter end,
Angels around befriending Virtue's friend ;
Bends to the grave with unperceiv'd decay,
While Resignation gently slopes the way ;   110
And, all his prospects bright'ning to the last,
His Heaven commences ere the world be pass'd !

Sweet was the sound, when oft at evening's close
Up yonder hill the village murmur rose ;
There, as I pass'd with careless steps and slow,
The mingling notes came soften'd from below ;
The swain responsive as the milk-maid sung,
The sober herd that low'd to meet their young ;
The noisy geese that gabbled o'er the pool,
The playful children just let loose from school ;   120
The watchdog's voice that bay'd the whisp'ring wind,
And the loud laugh that spoke the vacant mind :
These all in sweet confusion sought the shade,
And fill'd each pause the nightingale had made.
But now the sounds of population fail,
No cheerful murmurs fluctuate in the gale,
No busy steps the grass-grown foot-way tread,
For all the bloomy flush of life is fled.
All but yon widow'd, solitary thing
That feebly bends beside the plashy spring ;   130
She, wretched matron, forc'd, in age, for bread,
To strip the brook with mantling cresses spread,
To pick her wintry faggot from the thorn,
To seek her nightly shed, and weep till morn ;
She only left of all the harmless train,
The sad historian of the pensive plain.

Near yonder copse, where once the garden smil'd,
And still where many a garden flower grows wild;
There, where a few torn shrubs the place disclose,
The village preacher's modest mansion rose.   140
A man he was to all the country dear,
And passing rich with forty pounds a year;
Remote from towns he ran his godly race,
Nor e'er had chang'd, nor wished to change his place;
Unpractis'd he to fawn, or seek for power,
By doctrines fashion'd to the varying hour;
Far other aims his heart had learned to prize,
More skill'd to raise the wretched than to rise.
His house was known to all the vagrant train,
He chid their wand'rings, but reliev'd their pain;   150
The long-remember'd beggar was his guest,
Whose beard descending swept his aged breast;
The ruin'd spendthrift, now no longer proud,
Claim'd kindred there, and had his claims allow'd;
The broken soldier, kindly bade to stay,
Sat by his fire, and talk'd the night away;
Wept o'er his wounds, or tales of sorrow done,
Shoulder'd his crutch, and show'd how fields were won.
Pleas'd with his guests, the good man learn'd to glow,
And quite forgot their vices in their woe;   160
Careless their merits, or their faults to scan,
His pity gave ere charity began.

Thus to relieve the wretched was his pride,
And e'en his failings lean'd to Virtue's side.
But in his duty prompt at every call,
He watch'd and wept, he pray'd and felt, for all;
And, as a bird each fond endearment tries
To tempt its new-fledg'd offspring to the skies,
He tried each art, reprov'd each dull delay,
Allur'd to brighter worlds, and led the way.   170

Beside the bed where parting life was laid,
And sorrow, guilt, and pain, by turns dismay'd,
The reverend champion stood. At his control,
Despair and Anguish fled the struggling soul;
Comfort came down the trembling wretch to raise,
And his last falt'ring accents whisper'd praise.

At church, with meek and unaffected grace,
His looks adorn'd the venerable place;
Truth from his lips prevail'd with double sway,
And fools, who came to scoff, remain'd to pray.   180
The service pass'd, around the pious man,
With steady zeal, each honest rustic ran;
Even children follow'd with endearing wile,
And pluck'd his gown, to share the good man's smile.

His ready smile a parent's warmth express'd,
Their welfare pleas'd him, and their cares distress'd ;
To them his heart, his love, his griefs were given,
But all his serious thoughts had rest in Heaven.
As some tall cliff, that lifts its awful form,
Swells from the vale, and midway leaves the storm,   190
Though round its breast the rolling clouds are spread,
Eternal sunshine settles on its head.

Beside yon straggling fence that skirts the way,
With blossom'd furze unprofitably gay,
There, in his noisy mansion, skill'd to rule,
The village master taught his little school ;
A man severe he was, and stern to view ;
I knew him well, and every truant knew ;
Well had the boding tremblers learn'd to trace
The day's disasters in his morning face ;   200
Full well they laugh'd, with counterfeited glee,
At all his jokes, for many a joke had he ;
Full well the busy whisper, circling round,
Convey'd the dismal tidings when he frown'd ;
Yet he was kind ; or if severe in aught,
The love he bore to learning was in fault ;
The village all declar'd how much he knew ;
'Twas certain he could write, and cypher too ;
Lands he could measure, terms and tides presage,
And e'en the story ran that he could gauge.   210
In arguing too, the parson own'd his skill,
For e'en though vanquish'd, he could argue still ;
While words of learned length and thund'ring sound
Amazed the gazing rustics rang'd around,
And still they gaz'd, and still the wonder grew,
That one small head could carry all he knew.

But past is all his fame. The very spot
Where many a time he triumph'd, is forgot.
Near yonder thorn, that lifts its head on high,
Where once the sign-post caught the passing eye,   220
Low lies that house where nut-brown draughts inspir'd,
Where grey-beard mirth and smiling toil retir'd,
Where village statesmen talk'd with looks profound,
And news much older than their ale went round.
Imagination fondly stoops to trace
The parlour splendours of that festive place ;
The white-wash'd wall, the nicely sanded floor,
The varnish'd clock that click'd behind the door ;
The chest contriv'd a double debt to pay,
A bed by night, a chest of drawers by day ;   230
The pictures plac'd for ornament and use,
The twelve good rules, the royal game of goose ;
The hearth, except when winter chill'd the day,
With aspen boughs, and flowers, and fennel gay ;

While broken tea-cups, wisely kept for show,
Rang'd o'er the chimney, glisten'd in a row.

Vain, transitory splendours! Could not all
Reprieve the tottering mansion from its fall!
Obscure it sinks, nor shall it more impart
An hour's importance to the poor man's heart;   240
Thither no more the peasant shall repair
To sweet oblivion of his daily care;
No more the farmer's news, the barber's tale,
No more the wood-man's ballad shall prevail;
No more the smith his dusky brow shall clear,
Relax his pond'rous strength, and lean to hear;
The host himself no longer shall be found
Careful to see the mantling bliss go round;
Nor the coy maid, half willing to be press'd,
Shall kiss the cup to pass it to the rest.   250

Yes! let the rich deride, the proud disdain,
These simple blessings of the lowly train;
To me more dear, congenial to my heart,
One native charm, than all the gloss of art;
Spontaneous joys, where Nature has its play,
The soul adopts, and owns their first-born sway;
Lightly they frolic o'er the vacant mind,
Unenvied, unmolested, unconfin'd:
But the long pomp, the midnight masquerade,
With all the freaks of wanton wealth array'd,   260
In these, ere triflers half their wish obtain,
The toiling pleasure sickens into pain;
And, e'en while fashion's brightest arts decoy,
The heart distrusting asks, if this be joy.

Ye friends to truth, ye statesmen, who survey
The rich man's joys increase, the poor's decay,
'Tis yours to judge, how wide the limits stand
Between a splendid and a happy land.
Proud swells the tide with loads of freighted ore,
And shouting Folly hails them from her shore;   270
Hoards, e'en beyond the miser's wish abound,
And rich men flock from all the world around.
Yet count our gains. This wealth is but a name
That leaves our useful products still the same.
Not so the loss. The man of wealth and pride
Takes up a space that many poor supplied;
Space for his lake, his park's extended bounds,
Space for his horses, equipage, and hounds,
The robe that wraps his limbs in silken sloth
Has robb'd the neighbouring fields of half their growth; 280
His seat, where solitary sports are seen,
Indignant spurns the cottage from the green;
Around the world each needful product flies,
For all the luxuries the world supplies:

While thus the land adorn'd for pleasure, all
In barren splendour feebly waits the fall.

As some fair female unadorn'd and plain,
Secure to please while youth confirms her reign,
Slights every borrow'd charm that dress supplies,
Nor shares with art the triumph of her eyes: 290
But when those charms are pass'd, for charms are frail,
When time advances, and when lovers fail,
She then shines forth, solicitous to bless,
In all the glaring impotence of dress.
Thus fares the land, by luxury betray'd,
In nature's simplest charms at first array'd ;
But verging to decline, its splendours rise,
Its vistas strike, its palaces surprise ;
While scourg'd by famine from the smiling land,
The mournful peasant leads his humble band ;   300
And while he sinks, without one arm to save,
The country blooms—a garden, and a grave.

Where then, ah ! where, shall poverty reside,
To 'scape the pressure of contiguous pride ?   *close*
If to some common's fenceless limits stray'd,
He drives his flock to pick the scanty blade,
Those fenceless fields the sons of wealth divide,
And e'en the bare-worn common is denied.
If to the city sped—What waits him there ?
To see profusion that he must not share ;   310
To see ten thousand baneful arts combin'd
To pamper luxury and thin mankind ;
To see those joys the sons of pleasure know
Extorted from his fellow creature's woe.
Here, while the courtier glitters in brocade,
There the pale artist plies the sickly trade ;
Here, while the proud their long-drawn pomps display,
There the black gibbet glooms beside the way.
The dome where Pleasure holds her midnight reign
Here, richly deck'd, admits the gorgeous train ;   320
Tumultuous grandeur crowds the blazing square,
The rattling chariots clash, the torches glare.
Sure scenes like these no troubles e'er annoy !
Sure these denote one universal joy !   *irony*
Are these thy serious thoughts ?—Ah, turn thine eyes
Where the poor houseless shiv'ring female lies.
She once, perhaps, in village plenty bless'd,
Has wept at tales of innocence distress'd ;
Her modest looks the cottage might adorn,
Sweet as the primrose peeps beneath the thorn ;   330
Now lost to all, her friends, her virtue fled,
Near her betrayer's door she lays her head,
And, pinch'd with cold, and shrinking from the shower,
With heavy heart deplores that luckless hour.

When idly first, ambitious of the town,
She left her wheel and robes of country brown.

Do thine, sweet AUBURN, thine, the loveliest train
Do thy fair tribes participate her pain?
E'en now, perhaps, by cold and hunger led,
At proud men's doors they ask a little bread!   340

Ah, no.   To distant climes, a dreary scene,
Where half the convex world intrudes between,
Through torrid tracts with fainting steps they go,
Where wild Altama murmurs to their woe.
Far different there from all that charm'd before,
The various terrors of that horrid shore;
Those blazing suns that dart a downward ray,
And fiercely shed intolerable day;
Those matted woods where birds forget to sing,
But silent bats in drowsy clusters cling;   350
Those pois'nous fields with rank luxuriance crown'd,
Where the dark scorpion gathers death around;
Where at each step the stranger fears to wake
The rattling terrors of the vengeful snake;
Where crouching tigers wait their hapless prey
And savage men more murd'rous still than they;
While oft in whirls the mad tornado flies,
Mingling the ravag'd landscape with the skies.
Far different these from every former scene,
The cooling brook, the grassy-vested green,   360
The breezy covert of the warbling grove,
That only shelter'd thefts of harmless love.

Good Heaven! what sorrows gloom'd that parting day,
That call'd them from their native walks away;
When the poor exiles, every pleasure pass'd,
Hung round their bowers, and fondly look'd their last,
And took a long farewell, and wish'd in vain
For seats like these beyond the western main;
And shudd'ring still to face the distant deep,
Return'd and wept, and still return'd to weep.   370
The good old sire the first prepar'd to go
To new-found worlds, and wept for others' woe;
But for himself, in conscious virtue brave,
He only wish'd for worlds beyond the grave.
His lovely daughter, lovelier in her tears,
The fond companion of his helpless years,
Silent went next, neglectful of her charms,
And left a lover's for a father's arms.
With louder plaints the mother spoke her woes,
And bless'd the cot where every pleasure rose,   380
And kiss'd her thoughtless babes with many a tear,
And clasp'd them close, in sorrow doubly dear;
Whilst her fond husband strove to lend relief
In all the silent manliness of grief.

O Luxury! thou curs'd by Heaven's decree,
How ill exchang'd are things like these for thee!
How do thy potions, with insidious joy
Diffuse their pleasures only to destroy!
Kingdoms by thee, to sickly greatness grown,
Boast of a florid vigour not their own;   390
At every draught more large and large they grow,
A bloated mass of rank unwieldy woe;
Till sapp'd their strength, and every part unsound,
Down, down they sink, and spread a ruin round.

E'en now the devastation is begun,
And half the business of destruction done;
E'en now, methinks, as pond'ring here I stand,
I see the rural virtues leave the land:
Down where yon anchoring vessel spreads the sail,
That idly waiting flaps with ev'ry gale,   400
Downward they move, a melancholy band,
Pass from the shore, and darken all the strand.
Contented toil, and hospitable care,
And kind connubial tenderness, are there;
And piety, with wishes plac'd above,
And steady loyalty, and faithful love.
And thou, sweet Poetry, thou loveliest maid,
Still first to fly where sensual joys invade;
Unfit in these degenerate times of shame,
To catch the heart, or strike for honest fame;   410
Dear charming nymph, neglected and decried,
My shame in crowds, my solitary pride;
Thou source of all my bliss, and all my woe,
That found'st me poor at first, and keep'st me so;
Thou guide by which the nobler arts excel,
Thou nurse of every virtue, fare thee well!
Farewell, and Oh! where'er thy voice be tried,
On Torno's cliffs, or Pambamarca's side,
Whether where equinoctial fervours glow,
Or winter wraps the polar world in snow,   420
Still let thy voice, prevailing over time,
Redress the rigours of th' inclement clime;
Aid slighted truth; with thy persuasive strain
Teach erring man to spurn the rage of gain;
Teach him, that states of native strength possess'd,
Though very poor, may still be very bless'd;
That trade's proud empire hastes to swift decay,
As ocean sweeps the labour'd mole away;
While self-dependent power can time defy,
As rocks resist the billows and the sky.   430

RETALIATION

A POEM

OF old, when Scarron his companions invited,
Each guest brought his dish, and the feast was united;
If our landlord supplies us with beef, and with fish,
Let each guest bring himself, and he brings the best dish:
Our Dean shall be venison, just fresh from the plains;
Our Burke shall be tongue, with a garnish of brains;
Our Will shall be wild-fowl, of excellent flavour,
And Dick with his pepper shall heighten their savour:
Our Cumberland's sweet-bread its place shall obtain,
And Douglas is pudding, substantial and plain:　　　　10
Our Garrick's a salad; for in him we see
Oil, vinegar, sugar, and saltness agree:
To make out the dinner, full certain I am,
That Ridge is anchovy, and Reynolds is lamb;
That Hickey's a capon, and by the same rule,
Magnanimous Goldsmith a gooseberry fool.
At a dinner so various, at such a repast,
Who'd not be a glutton, and stick to the last?
Here, waiter! more wine, let me sit while I'm able,
Till all my companions sink under the table;　　　　20
Then, with chaos and blunders encircling my head,
Let me ponder, and tell what I think of the dead.

　　Here lies the good Dean, re-united to earth,
Who mix'd reason with pleasure, and wisdom with mirth:
If he had any faults he has left us in doubt,
At least, in six weeks I could not find 'em out;
Yet some have declar'd, and it can't be denied 'em,
That sly-boots was cursedly cunning to hide 'em.

　　Here lies our good Edmund, whose genius was such,
We scarcely can praise it, or blame it too much;　　　　30
Who, born for the Universe, narrow'd his mind,
And to party gave up what was meant for mankind.
Though fraught with all learning, yet straining his throat
To persuade Tommy Townshend to lend him a vote;
Who, too deep for his hearers, still went on refining,
And thought of convincing, while they thought of dining;
Though equal to all things, for all things unfit,
Too nice for a statesman, too proud for a wit:
For a patriot, too cool; for a drudge, disobedient;
And too fond of the *right* to pursue the *expedient*.　　　　40
In short, 'twas his fate, unemploy'd, or in place, Sir,
To eat mutton cold, and cut blocks with a razor.

Here lies honest William, whose heart was a mint,
While the owner ne'er knew half the good that was in't;
The pupil of impulse, it forc'd him along,
His conduct still right, with his argument wrong;
Still aiming at honour, yet fearing to roam,
The coachman was tipsy, the chariot drove home;
Would you ask for his merits? alas! he had none;
What was good was spontaneous, his faults were his own.   50

Here lies honest Richard, whose fate I must sigh at;
Alas, that such frolic should now be so quiet!
What spirits were his! what wit and what whim!
Now breaking a jest, and now breaking a limb;
Now wrangling and grumbling to keep up the ball,
Now teasing and vexing, yet laughing at all!
In short, so provoking a devil was Dick,
That we wish'd him full ten times a day at Old Nick;
But, missing his mirth and agreeable vein,
As often we wish'd to have Dick back again.   60

Here Cumberland lies, having acted his parts,
The Terence of England, the mender of hearts;
A flattering painter, who made it his care
To draw men as they ought to be, not as they are.
His gallants are all faultless, his women divine,
And comedy wonders at being so fine;
Like a tragedy queen he has dizen'd her out,
Or rather like tragedy giving a rout.
His fools have their follies so lost in a crowd
Of virtues and feelings, that folly grows proud;   70
And coxcombs, alike in their failings alone,
Adopting his portraits, are pleas'd with their own.
Say, where has our poet this malady caught?
Or, wherefore his characters thus without fault?
Say, was it that vainly directing his view
To find out men's virtues, and finding them few,
Quite sick of pursuing each troublesome elf,
He grew lazy at last, and drew from himself?

Here Douglas retires, from his toils to relax,
The scourge of impostors, the terror of quacks: 80
Come, all ye quack bards, and ye quacking divines,
Come, and dance on the spot where your tyrant reclines:
When Satire and Censure encircl'd his throne,
I fear'd for your safety, I fear'd for my own;
But now he is gone, and we want a detector,
Our Dodds shall be pious, our Kenricks shall lecture;
Macpherson write bombast, and call it a style,
Our Townshend make speeches, and I shall compile;
New Lauders and Bowers the Tweed shall cross over,
No countryman living their tricks to discover;   90

Detection her taper shall quench to a spark,
And Scotchman meet Scotchman, and cheat in the dark.

Here lies David Garrick, describe me who can,
An abridgment of all that was pleasant in man ;
As an actor, confess'd without rival to shine :
As a wit, if not first, in the very first line :
Yet, with talents like these, and an excellent heart,
The man had his failings, a dupe to his art.
Like an ill-judging beauty, his colours he spread,
And beplaster'd with rouge his own natural red.   100
On the stage he was natural, simple, affecting ;
'Twas only that when he was off he was acting.
With no reason on earth to go out of his way,
He turn'd and he varied full ten times a day.
Though secure of our hearts, yet confoundedly sick
If they were not his own by finessing and trick,
He cast off his friends, as a huntsman his pack,
For he knew when he pleas'd he could whistle them back.
Of praise a mere glutton, he swallow'd what came,
And the puff of a dunce he mistook it for fame ;   110
Till his relish grown callous, almost to disease,
Who pepper'd the highest was surest to please.
But let us be candid, and speak out our mind,
If dunces applauded, he paid them in kind.
Ye Kenricks, ye Kellys, and Woodfalls so grave,
What a commerce was yours, while you got and you gave !
How did Grub-street re-echo the shouts that you rais'd,
While he was be-Roscius'd, and you were be-prais'd !
But peace to his spirit, wherever it flies,
To act as an angel, and mix with the skies :   120
Those poets, who owe their best fame to his skill,
Shall still be his flatterers, go where he will ;
Old Shakespeare receive him with praise and with love,
And Beaumonts and Bens be his Kellys above.

Here Hickey reclines, a most blunt, pleasant creature,
And slander itself must allow him good nature :
He cherish'd his friend, and he relish'd a bumper ;
Yet one fault he had, and that one was a thumper.
Perhaps you may ask if the man was a miser ?
I answer, no, no, for he always was wiser :   130
Too courteous, perhaps, or obligingly flat ?
His very worst foe can't accuse him of that :
Perhaps he confided in men as they go,
And so was too foolishly honest ? Ah no !
Then what was his failing ? come, tell it, and, burn ye !
He was, could he help it ?—a special attorney.

Here Reynolds is laid, and, to tell you my mind,
He has not left a better or wiser behind :

His pencil was striking, resistless, and grand ;
His manners were gentle, complying, and bland ;   140
Still born to improve us in every part,
His pencil our faces, his manners our heart :
To coxcombs averse, yet most civilly steering,
When they judg'd without skill he was still hard of hearing :
When they talk'd of their Raphaels, Correggios, and stuff,
He shifted his trumpet, and only took snuff.

THOMAS GRAY

ELEGY WRITTEN IN A COUNTRY CHURCHYARD

The Curfew tolls the knell of parting day,
The lowing herd wind slowly o'er the lea,
The plowman homeward plods his weary way,
And leaves the world to darkness and to me.

Now fades the glimmering landscape on the sight,
And all the air a solemn stillness holds,
Save where the beetle wheels his droning flight,
And drowsy tinklings lull the distant folds;

Save that from yonder ivy-mantled tow'r
The mopeing owl does to the moon complain   10
Of such, as wand'ring near her secret bow'r,
Molest her ancient solitary reign.

Beneath those rugged elms, that yew-tree's shade,
Where heaves the turf in many a mould'ring heap,
Each in his narrow cell for ever laid,
The rude Forefathers of the hamlet sleep.

The breezy call of incense-breathing Morn,
The swallow twitt'ring from the straw-built shed,
The cock's shrill clarion, or the echoing horn,
No more shall rouse them from their lowly bed.   20

For them no more the blazing hearth shall burn,
Or busy housewife ply her evening care:
No children run to lisp their sire's return,
Or climb his knees the envied kiss to share.

Oft did the harvest to their sickle yield,
Their furrow oft the stubborn glebe has broke;
How jocund did they drive their team afield!
How bow'd the woods beneath their sturdy stroke!

Let not Ambition mock their useful toil,
Their homely joys, and destiny obscure;   30
Nor Grandeur hear with a disdainful smile,
The short and simple annals of the poor.

The boast of heraldry, the pomp of pow'r,
And all that beauty, all that wealth e'er gave,
Awaits alike th' inevitable hour.
The paths of glory lead but to the grave.

Nor you, ye Proud, impute to These the fault,
If Mem'ry o'er their Tomb no Trophies raise,
Where thro' the long-drawn isle and fretted vault
The pealing anthem swells the note of praise.   40

Can storied urn or animated bust
Back to its mansion call the fleeting breath?
Can Honour's voice provoke the silent dust,
Or Flatt'ry sooth the dull cold ear of Death?

Perhaps in this neglected spot is laid
Some heart once pregnant with celestial fire;
Hands, that the rod of empire might have sway'd,
Or wak'd to extasy the living lyre.

But Knowledge to their eyes her ample page
Rich with the spoils of time did ne'er unroll;   50
Chill Penury repress'd their noble rage,
And froze the genial current of the soul.

Full many a gem of purest ray serene,
The dark unfathom'd caves of ocean bear:
Full many a flower is born to blush unseen,
And waste its sweetness on the desert air.

Some village-Hampden, that with dauntless breast
The little Tyrant of his fields withstood;
Some mute inglorious Milton here may rest,
Some Cromwell guiltless of his country's blood.   60

Th' applause of list'ning senates to command,
The threats of pain and ruin to despise,
To scatter plenty o'er a smiling land,
And read their hist'ry in a nation's eyes,

Their lot forbad: nor circumscrib'd alone
Their growing virtues, but their crimes confin'd;
Forbad to wade through slaughter to a throne,
And shut the gates of mercy on mankind,

The struggling pangs of conscious truth to hide,
To quench the blushes of ingenuous shame,   70
Or heap the shrine of Luxury and Pride
With incense kindled at the Muse's flame.

Far from the madding crowd's ignoble strife,
Their sober wishes never learn'd to stray;
Along the cool sequester'd vale of life
They kept the noiseless tenor of their way.

Yet ev'n these bones from insult to protect
Some frail memorial still erected nigh,
With uncouth rhimes and shapeless sculpture deck'd,
Implores the passing tribute of a sigh.   80

Their name, their years, spelt by th' unletter'd muse,
The place of fame and elegy supply :
And many a holy text around she strews,
That teach the rustic moralist to die.

For who, to dumb Forgetfulness a prey,
This pleasing anxious being e'er resign'd,
Left the warm precincts of the chearful day,
Nor cast one longing ling'ring look behind ?

On some fond breast the parting soul relies,
Some pious drops the closing eye requires ;   90
Ev'n from the tomb the voice of Nature cries,
Ev'n in our Ashes live their wonted Fires.

For thee, who mindful of th' unhonour'd Dead
Dost in these lines their artless tale relate ;
If chance, by lonely contemplation led,
Some kindred Spirit shall inquire thy fate,

Haply some hoary-headed Swain may say,
' Oft have we seen him at the peep of dawn
Brushing with hasty steps the dews away
To meet the sun upon the upland lawn.   100

' There at the foot of yonder nodding beech
That wreathes its old fantastic roots so high,
His listless length at noontide would he stretch,
And pore upon the brook that babbles by.

' Hard by yon wood, now smiling as in scorn,
Mutt'ring his wayward fancies he would rove,
Now drooping, woeful wan, like one forlorn,
Or craz'd with care, or cross'd in hopeless love.

' One morn I miss'd him on the custom'd hill,
Along the heath and near his fav'rite tree ;   110
Another came ; nor yet beside the rill,
Nor up the lawn, nor at the wood was he ;

' The next with dirges due in sad array
Slow thro' the church-way path we saw him born.
Approach and read (for thou can'st read) the lay,
Grav'd on the stone beneath yon aged thorn.'

THE EPITAPH

Here rests his head upon the lap of Earth
A Youth to Fortune and to Fame unknown.
Fair Science frown'd not on his humble birth,
And Melancholy mark'd him for her own.   120

Large was his bounty, and his soul sincere,
Heav'n did a recompence as largely send :
He gave to Mis'ry all he had, a tear,
He gain'd from Heav'n ('twas all he wish'd) a friend.

No farther seek his merits to disclose,
Or draw his frailties from their dread abode,
(There they alike in trembling hope repose,)
The bosom of his Father and his God.

THE PROGRESS OF POESY

A PINDARIC ODE

Φωνᾶντα συνετοῖσιν· ἐς δὲ τὸ πᾶν ἑρμηνέων
χατίζει.—PINDAR, *Olymp. ii.*

I 1

AWAKE, Æolian lyre, awake,
And give to rapture all thy trembling strings.
From Helicon's harmonious springs
A thousand rills their mazy progress take:
The laughing flowers, that round them blow,
Drink life and fragrance as they flow.
Now the rich stream of music winds along
Deep, majestic, smooth, and strong,
Thro' verdant vales, and Ceres' golden reign :
Now rowling down the steep amain,   10
Headlong, impetuous, see it pour :
The rocks, and nodding groves rebellow to the roar.

I 2

Oh ! Sovereign of the willing soul,
Parent of sweet and solemn-breathing airs,
Enchanting shell ! the sullen Cares,
And frantic Passions hear thy soft controul.
On Thracia's hills the Lord of War
Has curb'd the fury of his car,
And drop'd his thirsty lance at thy command.
Perching on the scept'red hand   20
Of Jove, thy magic lulls the feather'd king
With ruffled plumes, and flagging wing :
Quench'd in dark clouds of slumber lie
The terror of his beak, and light'nings of his eye.

I 3

Thee the voice, the dance, obey,
Temper'd to thy warbled lay.
O'er Idalia's velvet-green
The rosy-crowned Loves are seen
On Cytherea's day
With antic Sports, and blue-eyed Pleasures,　　　30
Frisking light in frolic measures ;
Now pursuing, now retreating,
Now in circling troops they meet :
To brisk notes in cadence beating
Glance their many-twinkling feet.
Slow melting strains their Queen's approach declare :
Where'er she turns the Graces homage pay.
With arms sublime, that float upon the air,
In gliding state she wins her easy way :
O'er her warm cheek, and rising bosom, move　　　40
The bloom of young Desire, and purple light of Love.

II 1

Man's feeble race what Ills await,
Labour, and Penury, the racks of Pain,
Disease, and Sorrow's weeping train,
And Death, sad refuge from the storms of Fate !
The fond complaint, my Song, disprove,
And justify the laws of Jove.
Say, has he giv'n in vain the heav'nly Muse ?
Night, and all her sickly dews,
Her Spectres wan, and Birds of boding cry,　　　50
He gives to range the dreary sky :
Till down the eastern cliffs afar
Hyperion's march they spy, and glitt'ring shafts of war.

II 2

In climes beyond the solar road,
Where shaggy forms o'er ice-built mountains roam,
The Muse has broke the twilight-gloom
To chear the shiv'ring Native's dull abode.
And oft, beneath the od'rous shade
Of Chili's boundless forests laid,
She deigns to hear the savage Youth repeat　　　60
In loose numbers wildly sweet
Their feather-cinctured Chiefs, and dusky Loves.
Her track, where'er the Goddess roves,
Glory pursue, and generous Shame,
Th' unconquerable Mind, and Freedom's holy flame.

II 3

Woods, that wave o'er Delphi's steep,
Isles, that crown th' Egaean deep,
Fields, that cool Ilissus laves,
Or where Maeander's amber waves
In lingering Lab'rinths creep,   70
How do your tuneful Echo's languish,
Mute, but to the voice of Anguish ?
Where each old poetic Mountain
Inspiration breath'd around :
Ev'ry shade and hallow'd Fountain
Murmur'd deep a solemn sound :
Till the sad Nine in Greece's evil hour
Left their Parnassus for the Latian plains.
Alike they scorn the pomp of tyrant-Power,
And coward Vice, that revels in her chains.   80
When Latium had her lofty spirit lost,
They sought, oh Albion ! next thy sea-encircled coast.

III 1

Far from the sun and summer-gale,
In thy green lap was Nature's Darling laid,
What time, where lucid Avon stray'd,
To Him the mighty Mother did unveil
Her aweful face : The dauntless Child
Stretch'd forth his little arms, and smiled.
This pencil take (she said) whose colours clear
Richly paint the vernal year :   90
Thine too these golden keys, immortal Boy !
This can unlock the gates of Joy ;
Of Horrour that, and thrilling Fears,
Or ope the sacred source of sympathetic Tears.

III 2

Nor second He, that rode sublime
Upon the seraph-wings of Extasy,
The secrets of th' Abyss to spy.
He pass'd the flaming bounds of Place and Time :
The living Throne, the saphire-blaze,
Where Angels tremble, while they gaze,   100
He saw ; but blasted with excess of light,
Closed his eyes in endless night.
Behold, where Dryden's less presumptuous car,
Wide o'er the fields of Glory bear
Two Coursers of ethereal race,
With necks in thunder cloath'd, and long-resounding pace.

III 3

Hark, his hands the lyre explore!
Bright-eyed Fancy hovering o'er
Scatters from her pictured urn
Thoughts, that breath, and words, that burn.   110
But ah! 'tis heard no more——
Oh! Lyre divine, what daring Spirit
Wakes thee now? tho' he inherit
Nor the pride, nor ample pinion,
That the Theban Eagle bear
Sailing with supreme dominion
Thro' the azure deep of air:
Yet oft before his infant eyes would run
Such forms, as glitter in the Muse's ray
With orient hues, unborrow'd of the Sun: 120
Yet shall he mount, and keep his distant way
Beyond the limits of a vulgar fate,
Beneath the Good how far—but far above the Great.

THE BARD

A PINDARIC ODE

Odes of Pindar
Classical odes.
regular.

1 1

' Ruin seize thee, ruthless King!
Confusion on thy banners wait,
Tho' fann'd by Conquest's crimson wing
They mock the air with idle state.
Helm, nor Hauberk's twisted mail,
Nor even thy virtues, Tyrant, shall avail
To save thy secret soul from nightly fears,
From Cambria's curse, from Cambria's tears!'
Such were the sounds, that o'er the crested pride
Of the first Edward scatter'd wild dismay,   10
As down the steep of Snowdon's shaggy side
He wound with toilsome march his long array.
Stout Glo'ster stood aghast in speechless trance:
To arms! cried Mortimer, and couch'd his quiv'ring lance.

strophe
personification

I 2

On a rock, whose haughty brow
Frowns o'er old Conway's foaming flood,
Robed in the sable garb of woe,
With haggard eyes the Poet stood;

antistrophe

(Loose his beard, and hoary hair
Stream'd, like a meteor, to the troubled air)   20
And with a Master's hand, and Prophet's fire,
Struck the deep sorrows of his lyre.
' Hark, how each giant-oak, and desert cave,
Sighs to the torrent's aweful voice beneath !
O'er thee, oh King ! their hundred arms they wave,
Revenge on thee in hoarser murmurs breath ;
Vocal no more, since Cambria's fatal day,
To high-born Hoel's harp, or soft Llewellyn's lay.

I 3

' Cold is Cadwallo's tongue,
That hush'd the stormy main :   30
Brave Urien sleeps upon his craggy bed :
Mountains, ye mourn in vain
Modred, whose magic song
Made huge Plinlimmon bow his cloud-top'd head.
On dreary Arvon's shore they lie,
Smear'd with gore, and ghastly pale :
Far, far aloof th' affrighted ravens sail ;
The famish'd Eagle screams, and passes by.
Dear lost companions of my tuneful art,
Dear, as the light that visits these sad eyes,   40
Dear, as the ruddy drops that warm my heart,
Ye died amidst your dying country's cries—
No more I weep. They do not sleep.
On yonder cliffs, a griesly band,
I see them sit, they linger yet,
Avengers of their native land :
With me in dreadful harmony they join,
And weave with bloody hands the tissue of thy line.'

II 1

" Weave the warp, and weave the woof,
The winding-sheet of Edward's race.   50
Give ample room, and verge enough
The characters of hell to trace.
Mark the year, and mark the night,
When Severn shall re-eccho with affright
The shrieks of death, thro' Berkley's roofs that ring,
Shrieks of an agonizing King !
She-Wolf of France, with unrelenting fangs,
That tear'st the bowels of thy mangled Mate,
From thee be born, who o'er thy country hangs
The scourge of Heav'n. What Terrors round him wait !   60
Amazement in his van, with Flight combined,
And sorrow's faded form, and solitude behind.

II 2

" Mighty Victor, mighty Lord,
Low on his funeral couch he lies ! *Black Prince* Ed IV
No pitying heart, no eye, afford
A tear to grace his obsequies.
Is the sable Warriour fled ?
Thy son is gone. He rests among the Dead.
The Swarm, that in thy noon-tide beam were born ?
Gone to salute the rising Morn. *Richard II*   70
Fair laughs the Morn, and soft the Zephyr blows,
While proudly riding o' er the azure realm
In gallant trim the gilded Vessel goes ;
Youth on the prow, and Pleasure at the helm ;
Regardless of the sweeping Whirlwind's sway,
That, hush'd in grim repose, expects his evening-prey.

II 3

" Fill high the sparkling bowl,
The rich repast prepare,
Reft of a crown, he yet may share the feast : *Bolingbroke*
Close by the regal chair
Fell Thirst and Famine scowl   80
A baleful smile upon their baffled Guest.
Heard ye the din of battle bray,
Lance to lance, and horse to horse ?
Long Years of havock urge their destined course,
And thro' the kindred squadrons mow their way.
Ye Towers of Julius, London's lasting shame,
With many a foul and midnight murther fed,
Revere his Consort's faith, his Father's fame,
And spare the meek Usurper's holy head.   90
Above, below, the rose of snow,
Twined with her blushing foe, we spread : *arms of Rd. III*
The bristled Boar in infant-gore *Coat of arms of Rd. III*
Wallows beneath the thorny shade.
Now, Brothers, bending o' er th' accursed loom,
Stamp we our vengeance deep, and ratify his doom.

III 1

" Edward, lo ! to sudden fate
(Weave we the woof. The thread is spun)
Half of thy heart we consecrate. *His Queen*
(The web is wove. The work is done.)"   100
' Stay, oh stay ! nor thus forlorn
Leave me unbless'd, unpitied, here to mourn :
In yon bright track, that fires the western skies,
They melt, they vanish from my eyes.
But oh ! what solemn scenes on Snowdon's height

Descending slow their glitt'ring skirts unroll?
Visions of glory, spare my aching sight,
Ye unborn Ages, crowd not on my soul!
No more our long-lost Arthur we bewail.
All-hail, ye genuine Kings, Britannia's Issue, hail!　110

III 2

'Girt with many a Baron bold
Sublime their starry fronts they rear;
And gorgeous Dames, and Statesmen old
In bearded majesty, appear.
In the midst a Form divine! *Owen Elizabeth*
Her eye proclaims her of the Briton-Line;
Her lyon-port, her awe-commanding face,
Attemper'd sweet to virgin-grace.
What strings symphonious tremble in the air, *lit & music*
What strains of vocal transport round her play!　120
Hear from the grave, great Taliessin, hear; *bard*
They breathe a soul to animate thy clay.
Bright Rapture calls, and soaring, as she sings,
Waves in the eye of Heav'n her many-colour'd wings.

III 3

'The verse adorn again
Fierce War, and faithful Love,
And Truth severe, by fairy Fiction drest. *Faerie Queen*
In buskin'd measures move
Pale Grief, and pleasing Pain,
With Horrour, Tyrant of the throbbing breast.　130
A Voice, as of the Cherub-Choir, *Paradise Lost.*
Gales from blooming Eden bear;
And distant warblings lessen on my ear,
That lost in long futurity expire.
Fond impious Man, think'st thou, yon sanguine cloud,
Rais'd by thy breath, has quench'd the Orb of day?
To-morrow he repairs the golden flood,
And warms the nations with redoubled ray.
Enough for me: With joy I see
The different doom our Fates assign.　140
Be thine Despair, and scept'red Care,
To triumph, and to die, are mine.'
He spoke, and headlong from the mountain's height
Deep in the roaring tide he plung'd to endless night.

WILLIAM COLLINS

AN ODE ON THE POPULAR SUPERSTITIONS OF THE HIGHLANDS OF SCOTLAND,

CONSIDERED AS THE SUBJECT OF POETRY

H——— thou return'st from Thames, whose Naiads long
  Have seen thee ling'ring, with a fond delay,
Mid those soft friends, whose hearts, some future day,
  Shall melt, perhaps, to hear thy tragic song.
Go, not unmindful of that cordial youth,
  Whom, long endear'd, thou leav'st by Lavant's side;
Together let us wish him lasting truth,
  And joy untainted with his destin'd bride.
Go! nor regardless, while these numbers boast
  My short-liv'd bliss, forget my social name;   10
But think far off how, on the southern coast,
  I met thy friendship with an equal flame!
Fresh to that soil thou turn'st, whose ev'ry vale
  Shall prompt the poet, and his song demand:
To thee thy copious subjects ne'er shall fail;
  Thou need'st but take the pencil to thy hand,
And paint what all believe who own thy genial land.

II

There must thou wake perforce thy Doric quill,
  'Tis Fancy's land to which thou sett'st thy feet;
Where still, 'tis said, the fairy people meet   20
  Beneath each birken shade on mead or hill.
There each trim lass that skims the milky store
  To the swart tribes their creamy bowl allots;
By night they sip it round the cottage-door,
  While airy minstrels warble jocund notes.
There every herd, by sad experience, knows
  How, wing'd with fate, their elf-shot arrows fly;
When the sick ewe her summer food foregoes,
  Or, stretch'd on earth, the heart-smit heifers lie.
Such airy beings awe th' untutor'd swain: 30
  Nor thou, though learn'd, his homelier thoughts neglect;
Let thy sweet muse the rural faith sustain;
  These are the themes of simple, sure effect,
That add new conquests to her boundless reign,
And fill, with double force, her heart-commanding strain.

III

Ev'n yet preserv'd, how often may'st thou hear,
  Where to the pole the Boreal mountains run,
Taught by the father to his list'ning son
  Strange lays, whose power had charm'd a SPENCER's ear.
At ev'ry pause, before thy mind possest,   40
  Old RUNIC bards shall seem to rise around,
With uncouth lyres, in many-coloured vest,
  Their matted hair with boughs fantastic crown'd:
Whether thou bid'st the well-taught hind repeat
  The choral dirge that mourns some chieftain brave,
When ev'ry shrieking maid her bosom beat,
  And strew'd with choicest herbs his scented grave;
Or whether, sitting in the shepherd's shiel,
  Thou hear'st some sounding tale of war's alarms;
When at the bugle's call, with fire and steel,   50
  The sturdy clans pour'd forth their bony swarms,
And hostile brothers met to prove each other's arms.

IV

'Tis thine to sing, how framing hideous spells
  In SKY's lone isle the gifted wizzard seer,
Lodged in the wintry cave with————,
  Or in the depth of Uist's dark forests dwells:
How they, whose sight such dreary dreams engross,
  With their own visions oft astonish'd droop,
When o'er the wat'ry strath or quaggy moss
  They see the gliding ghosts unbodied troop.   60
Or if in sports, or on the festive green,
  Their ———— glance some fated youth descry,
Who, now perhaps in lusty vigour seen
  And rosy health, shall soon lamented die.
For them the viewless forms of air obey,
  Their bidding heed, and at their beck repair.
They know what spirit brews the stormful day,
  And heartless, oft, like moody madness stare
To see the phantom train their secret work prepare.

VI

What though far off, from some dark dell espied,   70
  His glimm'ring mazes cheer th' excursive sight,
Yet turn, ye wand'rers, turn your steps aside,
  Nor trust the guidance of that faithless light;
For watchful, lurking 'mid th' unrustling reed,
  At those mirk hours the wily monster lies,
And listens oft to hear the passing steed,
  And frequent round him rolls his sullen eyes,
If chance his savage wrath may some weak wretch surprise.

VII

Ah, luckless swain, o'er all unblest indeed!
  Whom late bewilder'd in the dank, dark fen,   80
Far from his flocks and smoking hamlet then!
  To that sad spot ———————————:
On him enrag'd, the fiend, in angry mood,
  Shall never look with pity's kind concern,
But instant, furious, raise the whelming flood
  O'er its drown'd bank, forbidding all return.
Or, if he meditate his wish'd escape
  To some dim hill that seems uprising near,
To his faint eye the grim and grisly shape,
  In all its terrors clad, shall wild appear.   90
Meantime, the wat'ry surge shall round him rise,
  Pour'd sudden forth from ev'ry swelling source.
What now remains but tears and hopeless sighs?
  His fear-shook limbs have lost their youthly force,
And down the waves he floats, a pale and breathless corse.

VIII

For him, in vain, his anxious wife shall wait,
  Or wander forth to meet him on his way;
For him, in vain, at to-fall of the day,
  His babes shall linger at th' unclosing gate!
Ah, ne'er shall he return! Alone, if night   100
  Her travell'd limbs in broken slumbers steep,
With dropping willows drest, his mournful sprite
  Shall visit sad, perchance, her silent sleep:
Then he, perhaps, with moist and wat'ry hand,
  Shall fondly seem to press her shudd'ring cheek,
And with his blue swoln face before her stand,
  And, shiv'ring cold, these piteous accents speak:
Pursue, dear wife, thy daily toils pursue
  At dawn or dusk, industrious as before;
Nor e'er of me one hapless thought renew,   110
  While I lie welt'ring on the ozier'd shore,
Drown'd by the KAELPIE's wrath, nor e'er shall aid thee more!

IX

Unbounded is thy range; with varied stile
  Thy muse may, like those feath'ry tribes which spring
From their rude rocks, extend her skirting wing
  Round the moist marge of each cold Hebrid isle,
To that hoar pile which still its ruins shows:
  In whose small vaults a pigmy-folk is found,
Whose bones the delver with his spade upthrows,
  And culls them, wond'ring, from the hallow'd ground! 120
Or thither where beneath the show'ry west
  The mighty kings of three fair realms are laid;
Once foes, perhaps, together now they rest.
  No slaves revere them, and no wars invade:

Yet frequent now, at midnight's solemn hour,
  The rifted mounds their yawning cells unfold,
And forth the monarchs stalk with sov'reign pow'r
  In pageant robes, and wreath'd with sheeny gold,
And on their twilight tombs aerial council hold.

X

But O! o'er all, forget not KILDA's race,   130
  On whose bleak rocks, which brave the wasting tides,
Fair Nature's daughter, Virtue, yet abides.
  Go, just, as they, their blameless manners trace!
Then to my ear transmit some gentle song
  Of those whose lives are yet sincere and plain,
Their bounded walks the rugged cliffs along,
  And all their prospect but the wintry main.
With sparing temp'rance, at the needful time,
  They drain the sainted spring, or, hunger-prest,
Along th' Atlantic rock undreading climb,   140
  And of its eggs despoil the Solan's nest.
Thus blest in primal innocence they live,
  Suffic'd and happy with that frugal fare
Which tasteful toil and hourly danger give.
  Hard is their shallow soil, and bleak and bare:
Nor ever vernal bee was heard to murmur there!

XI

Nor need'st thou blush, that such false themes engage
  Thy gentle mind, of fairer stores possest;
For not alone they touch the village breast,
  But fill'd in elder time th' historic page.   150
There SHAKESPEARE's self, with ev'ry garland crown'd,
  In musing hour, his wayward sisters found,
And with their terrors drest the magic scene.
  From them he sung, when mid his bold design,
Before the Scot afflicted and aghast,
  The shadowy kings of BANQUO's fated line
Through the dark cave in gleamy pageant past.
  Proceed, nor quit the tales which, simply told,
Could once so well my answ'ring bosom pierce;
  Proceed, in forceful sounds and colours bold   160
The native legends of thy land rehearse;
To such adapt thy lyre and suit thy powerful verse.

XII

In scenes like these, which, daring to depart
  From sober truth, are still to nature true,
And call forth fresh delight to fancy's view,
  Th' heroic muse employ'd her TASSO's art!
How have I trembled, when, at TANCRED's stroke,
  Its gushing blood the gaping cypress pour'd;

When each live plant with mortal accents spoke,
   And the wild blast up-heav'd the vanish'd sword!   170
How have I sat, when pip'd the pensive wind,
   To hear his harp, by British FAIRFAX strung.
Prevailing poet, whose undoubting mind
   Believ'd the magic wonders which he sung!
Hence, at each sound, imagination glows;
   Hence his warm lay with softest sweetness flows:
Melting it flows, pure, num'rous, strong and clear,
   And fills th' impassion'd heart, and wins th' harmonious ear.

XIII

All hail, ye scenes that o'er my soul prevail,
   Ye ——— friths and lakes which, far away,   180
Are by smooth ANNAN fill'd, or past'ral TAY,
   Or DON'S romantic springs, at distance, hail!
The time shall come when I, perhaps, may tread
   Your lowly glens, o'erhung with spreading broom,
Or o'er your stretching heaths by fancy led:
Then will I dress once more the faded bow'r,
   Where JOHNSON sat in DRUMMOND'S —— shade;
Or crop from Tiviots dale each ———,
   And mourn on Yarrow's banks ———
Meantime, ye Pow'rs, that on the plains which bore   190
   The cordial youth, on LOTHIAN'S plains attend,
Where'er he dwell, on hill, or lowly muir,
   To him I lose, your kind protection lend,
And, touch'd with love like mine, preserve my absent friend.

WILLIAM COWPER

ON THE RECEIPT OF MY MOTHER'S PICTURE OUT OF NORFOLK

THE GIFT OF MY COUSIN ANN BODHAM

OH that those lips had language! Life has pass'd
With me but roughly since I heard thee last.
Those lips are thine—thy own sweet smiles I see,
The same that oft in childhood solaced me;
Voice only fails, else, how distinct they say,
'Grieve not, my child, chase all thy fears away!'
The meek intelligence of those dear eyes
(Blest be the art that can immortalize,
The art that baffles time's tyrannic claim
To quench it) here shines on me still the same. 10
    Faithful remembrancer of one so dear,
Oh welcome guest, though unexpected, here!
Who bidd'st me honour with an artless song,
Affectionate, a mother lost so long,
I will obey, not willingly alone,
But gladly, as the precept were her own;
And, while that face renews my filial grief,
Fancy shall weave a charm for my relief—
Shall steep me in Elysian reverie,
A momentary dream, that thou art she. 20
    My mother, when I learn'd that thou wast dead,
Say, wast thou conscious of the tears I shed?
Hover'd thy spirit o'er thy sorrowing son,
Wretch even then, life's journey just begun?
Perhaps thou gav'st me, though unseen, a kiss;
Perhaps a tear, if souls can weep in bliss—
Ah that maternal smile! it answers—Yes.
I heard the bell toll'd on thy burial day,
I saw the hearse that bore thee slow away,
And, turning from my nurs'ry window, drew 30
A long, long sigh, and wept a last adieu!
But was it such?—It was.—Where thou art gone
Adieus and farewells are a sound unknown.
May I but meet thee on that peaceful shore,
The parting sound shall pass my lips no more!
Thy maidens griev'd themselves at my concern,
Oft gave me promise of a quick return.

What ardently I wish'd, I long believ'd,
And, disappointed still, was still deceiv'd;
By disappointment every day beguil'd,　　　　　40
Dupe of *to-morrow* even from a child.
Thus many a sad to-morrow came and went,
Till, all my stock of infant sorrow spent,
I learn'd at last submission to my lot:
But, though I less deplor'd thee, ne'er forgot.
　Where once we dwelt our name is heard no more,
Children not thine have trod my nurs'ry floor;
And where the gard'ner Robin, day by day,
Drew me to school along the public way,
Delighted with my bauble coach, and wrapt　　　50
In scarlet mantle warm, and velvet capt,
'Tis now become a history little known,
That once we call'd the past'ral house our own.
Short-liv'd possession! but the record fair
That mem'ry keeps of all thy kindness there,
Still outlives many a storm that has effac'd
A thousand other themes less deeply trac'd.
Thy nightly visits to my chamber made,
That thou might'st know me safe and warmly laid;
Thy morning bounties ere I left my home,　　　60
The biscuit, or confectionary plum;
The fragrant waters on my cheeks bestow'd
By thy own hand, till fresh they shone and glow'd;
All this, and more endearing still than all,
Thy constant flow of love, that knew no fall,
Ne'er roughen'd by those cataracts and brakes
That humour interpos'd too often makes;
All this still legible in mem'ry's page,
And still to be so, to my latest age,
Adds joy to duty, makes me glad to pay　　　70
Such honours to thee as my numbers may;
Perhaps a frail memorial, but sincere,
Not scorn'd in heav'n, though little notic'd here.
　Could time, his flight revers'd, restore the hours,
When, playing with thy vesture's tissued flow'rs,
The violet, the pink, and jessamine,
I prick'd them into paper with a pin,
(And thou wast happier than myself the while,
Would'st softly speak, and stroke my head and smile)
Could those few pleasant hours again appear,　　80
Might one wish bring them, would I wish them here?
I would not trust my heart—the dear delight
Seems so to be desir'd, perhaps I might.—
But no—what here we call our life is such,
So little to be lov'd, and thou so much,
That I should ill requite thee to constrain
Thy unbound spirit into bonds again.

Thou, as a gallant bark from Albion's coast
(The storms all weather'd and the ocean cross'd)
Shoots into port at some well-haven'd isle,   90
Where spices breathe and brighter seasons smile,
There sits quiescent on the floods that show
Her beauteous form reflected clear below,
While airs impregnated with incense play
Around her, fanning light her streamers gay ;
So thou, with sails how swift ! hast reach'd the shore
' Where tempests never beat nor billows roar,'
And thy lov'd consort on the dang'rous tide
Of life, long since, has anchor'd at thy side.
But me, scarce hoping to attain that rest,   100
Always from port withheld, always distress'd—
Me howling winds drive devious, tempest toss'd,
Sails ript, seams op'ning wide, and compass lost,
And day by day some current's thwarting force
Sets me more distant from a prosp'rous course.
But oh the thought, that thou art safe, and he !
That thought is joy, arrive what may to me.
My boast is not that I deduce my birth
From loins enthron'd, and rulers of the earth ;
But higher far my proud pretensions rise—   110
The son of parents pass'd into the skies.
And now, farewell—time, unrevok'd, has run
His wonted course, yet what I wish'd is done.
By contemplation's help, not sought in vain,
I seem t' have liv'd my childhood o'er again ;
To have renew'd the joys that once were mine,
Without the sin of violating thine :
And, while the wings of fancy still are free,
And I can view this mimic shew of thee,
Time has but half succeeded in his theft—   120
Thyself remov'd, thy power to sooth me left.

ROBERT BURNS

TAM O' SHANTER

WHEN chapman billies leave the street,
And drouthy neibors neibors meet,
As market-days are wearing late,
An' folk begin to tak the gate;
While we sit bousing at the nappy,
An' getting fou and unco happy,
We think na on the lang Scots miles,
The mosses, waters, slaps, and styles,
That lie between us and our hame,
Where sits our sulky sullen dame,   10
Gathering her brows like gathering storm,
Nursing her wrath to keep it warm.
　This truth fand honest Tam o' Shanter,
As he frae Ayr ae night did canter—
(Auld Ayr, wham ne'er a town surpasses
For honest men and bonnie lasses).
　O Tam! hadst thou but been sae wise
As ta'en thy ain wife Kate's advice!
She tauld thee weel thou was a skellum,
A bletherin', blusterin', drunken blellum;   20
That frae November till October,
Ae market-day thou was na sober;
That ilka melder wi' the miller
Thou sat as lang as thou had siller;
That every naig was ca'd a shoe on,
The smith and thee gat roarin' fou on;
That at the Lord's house, even on Sunday,
Thou drank wi' Kirkton Jean till Monday.
She prophesied that, late or soon,
Thou would be found deep drown'd in Doon;   30
Or catch'd wi' warlocks in the mirk
By Alloway's auld haunted kirk.
　Ah, gentle dames! it gars me greet
To think how mony counsels sweet,
How mony lengthen'd sage advices,
The husband frae the wife despises!
　But to our tale: Ae market night,
Tam had got planted unco right,
Fast by an ingle, bleezing finely,
Wi' reaming swats, that drank divinely;   40

And at his elbow, Souter Johnny,
His ancient, trusty, drouthy crony ;
Tam lo'ed him like a very brither ;
They had been fou for weeks thegither.
The night drave on wi' sangs and clatter,
And aye the ale was growing better :
The landlady and Tam grew gracious,
Wi' favours secret, sweet, and precious ;
The souter tauld his queerest stories ;
The landlord's laugh was ready chorus :   50
The storm without might rair and rustle,
Tam did na mind the storm a whistle.
    Care, mad to see a man sae happy,
E'en drown'd himsel amang the nappy ;
As bees flee hame wi' lades o' treasure,
The minutes wing'd their way wi' pleasure ;
Kings may be blest, but Tam was glorious,
O'er a' the ills o' life victorious !
    But pleasures are like poppies spread—
You seize the flow'r, its bloom is shed ;   60
Or like the snow falls in the river—
A moment white—then melts for ever ;
Or like the borealis race,
That flit ere you can point their place ;
Or like the rainbow's lovely form
Evanishing amid the storm.
Nae man can tether time or tide ;
The hour approaches Tam maun ride ;
That hour, o' night's black arch the key-stane,
That dreary hour he mounts his beast in ;   70
And sic a night he taks the road in,
As ne'er poor sinner was abroad in.
    The wind blew as 'twad blawn its last ;
The rattling show'rs rose on the blast ;
The speedy gleams the darkness swallow'd ;
Loud, deep, and lang, the thunder bellow'd :
That night, a child might understand,
The Deil had business on his hand.
    Weel mounted on his gray mare, Meg,
A better never lifted leg,   80
Tam skelpit on thro' dub and mire,
Despising wind, and rain, and fire ;
Whiles holding fast his gude blue bonnet ;
Whiles crooning o'er some auld Scots sonnet ;
Whiles glow'ring round wi' prudent cares,
Lest bogles catch him unawares :
Kirk-Alloway was drawing nigh,
Whare ghaists and houlets nightly cry.
    By this time he was cross the ford,
Where in the snaw the chapman smoor'd ;   90

And past the birks and meikle stane,
Where drunken Charlie brak's neck-bane;
And thro' the whins, and by the cairn,
Where hunters fand the murder'd bairn;
And near the thorn, aboon the well,
Where Mungo's mither hang'd hersel.
Before him Doon pours all his floods;
The doubling storm roars thro' the woods;
The lightnings flash from pole to pole;
Near and more near the thunders roll: 100
When, glimmering thro' the groaning trees,
Kirk-Alloway seem'd in a bleeze;
Thro' ilka bore the beams were glancing;
And loud resounded mirth and dancing.
    Inspiring bold John Barleycorn!
What dangers thou canst make us scorn!
Wi' tippenny, we fear nae evil;
Wi' usquebae, we'll face the devil!
The swats sae ream'd in Tammie's noddle,
Fair play, he car'd na deils a boddle!   110
But Maggie stood right sair astonish'd,
Till, by the heel and hand admonish'd,
She ventur'd forward on the light;
And, wow! Tam saw an unco sight!
    Warlocks and witches in a dance!
Nae cotillon brent new frae France,
But hornpipes, jigs, strathspeys, and reels,
Put life and mettle in their heels.
A winnock-bunker in the east,
There sat auld Nick, in shape o' beast—   120
A touzie tyke, black, grim, and large!
To gie them music was his charge:
He screw'd the pipes and gart them skirl,
Till roof and rafters a' did dirl.—
Coffins stood round like open presses,
That shaw'd the dead in their last dresses;
And by some devilish cantraip sleight
Each in its cauld hand held a light,
By which heroic Tam was able
To note upon the haly table   130
A murderer's banes in gibbet-airns;
Twa span-lang, wee, unchristen'd bairns;
A thief new-cutted frae a rape—
Wi' his last gasp his gab did gape;
Five tomahawks, wi' blude red rusted;
Five scymitars, wi' murder crusted;
A garter, which a babe had strangled;
A knife, a father's throat had mangled,
Whom his ain son o' life bereft,
The gray hairs yet stack to the heft;   140

Wi' mair of horrible and awefu',
Which even to name wad be unlawfu'.
   As Tammie glowr'd, amaz'd, and curious,
The mirth and fun grew fast and furious:
The piper loud and louder blew;
The dancers quick and quicker flew;
They reel'd, they set, they cross'd, they cleekit,
Till ilka carlin swat and reekit,
And coost her duddies to the wark,
And linkit at it in her sark!   150
   Now Tam, O Tam! had thae been queans,
A' plump and strapping in their teens;
Their sarks, instead o' creeshie flannen,
Been snaw-white seventeen hunder linen!
Thir breeks o' mine, my only pair,
That ance were plush, o' gude blue hair,
I wad hae gi'en them off my hurdies,
For ae blink o' the bonnie burdies!
   But wither'd beldams, auld and droll,
Rigwoodie hags wad spean a foal,   160
Louping and flinging on a crummock,
I wonder didna turn thy stomach.
   But Tam kend what was what fu' brawlie:
There was ae winsome wench and walie
That night enlisted in the core,
(Lang after kend on Carrick shore!
For mony a beast to dead she shot,
And perish'd mony a bonnie boat,
And shook baith meikle corn and bear,
And kept the country-side in fear.)   170
Her cutty sark, o' Paisley harn,
That while a lassie she had worn,
In longitude tho' sorely scanty,
It was her best, and she was vauntie—
Ah! little kend thy reverend grannie
That sark she coft for her wee Nannie
Wi' twa pund Scots ('twas a' her riches)
Wad ever grac'd a dance of witches!
   But here my Muse her wing maun cour,
Sic flights are far beyond her pow'r—   180
To sing how Nannie lap and flang,
(A souple jad she was, and strang);
And how Tam stood, like ane bewitch'd,
And thought his very een enrich'd;
Even Satan glowr'd, and fidg'd fu' fain,
And hotch'd and blew wi' might and main;
Till first ae caper, syne anither,
Tam tint his reason a' thegither,
And roars out ' Weel done, Cutty-sark!'
And in an instant all was dark!   190

And scarcely had he Maggie rallied,
When out the hellish legion sallied.
  As bees bizz out wi' angry fyke
When plundering herds assail their byke,
As open pussie's mortal foes
When pop! she starts before their nose,
As eager runs the market-crowd
When 'Catch the thief!' resounds aloud.
So Maggie runs—the witches follow,
Wi' mony an eldritch skriech and hollo.   200
  Ah, Tam! ah, Tam! thou'll get thy fairin!
In hell they'll roast thee like a herrin!
In vain thy Kate awaits thy comin!
Kate soon will be a woefu' woman!
Now do thy speedy utmost, Meg,
And win the key-stane o' the brig:
There at them thou thy tail may toss,
A running stream they dare na cross.
But ere the key-stane she could make,
The fient a tail she had to shake!   210
For Nannie, far before the rest,
Hard upon noble Maggie prest,
And flew at Tam wi' furious ettle;
But little wist she Maggie's mettle!
Ae spring brought off her master hale,
But left behind her ain gray tail:
The carlin claught her by the rump,
And left poor Maggie scarce a stump.
  Now, wha this tale o' truth shall read,
Each man and mother's son, take heed;   220
Whene'er to drink you are inclin'd,
Or cutty-sarks run in your mind,
Think, ye may buy the joys o'er dear;
Remember TAM O' SHANTER'S MEARE!

TO WILLIAM SIMPSON OF OCHILTREE
MAY, 1785

I GAT your letter, winsome *Willie*;
Wi' gratefu' heart I thank you brawlie;
Tho' I maun say't, I wad be silly,
    An' unco vain,
Should I believe, my coaxin billie,
    Your flatterin strain.

But I'se believe ye kindly meant it,
I sud be laith to think ye hinted
Ironic satire, sidelins sklented
    On my poor Musie;   10
Tho' in sic phraisin terms ye've penn'd it,
    I scarce excuse ye.

My senses wad be in a creel,
Should I but dare a *hope* to speel.
Wi' *Allan*, or wi' *Gilbertfield*,
    The braes o' fame ;
Or *Ferguson*, the writer-chiel,
    A deathless name.

(O *Ferguson* ! thy glorious parts
Ill suited law's dry, musty arts !   20
My curse upon your whunstane hearts,
    Ye Enbrugh Gentry !
The tythe o' what ye waste at cartes
    Wad stow'd his pantry !)

Yet when a tale comes i' my head,
Or lasses gie my heart a screed,
As whiles they're like to be my dead,
    (O sad disease !)
I kittle up my *rustic reed* ;
    It gies me ease.   30

Auld *Coila*, now, may fidge fu' fain,
She 's gotten *Poets* o' her ain,
Chiels wha their chanters winna hain,
    But tune their lays,
Till echoes a' resound again
    Her weel-sung praise.

Nae Poet thought her worth his while,
To set her name in measur'd style ;
She lay like some unkend-of isle,
    Beside *New Holland*,   40
Or whare wild-meeting oceans boil
    Besouth *Magellan*.

Ramsay an' famous *Ferguson*
Gied *Forth* an' *Tay* a lift aboon ;
Yarrow an' *Tweed*, to mony a tune,
    Owre Scotland rings,
While *Irwin*, *Lugar*, *Ayr*, an' *Doon*,
    Naebody sings.

Th' *Ilissus*, *Tiber*, *Thames*, an' *Seine*,
Glide sweet in mony a tunefu' line ;   50
But, *Willie*, set your fit to mine,
    An' cock your crest,
We'll gar our streams an' burnies shine
    Up wi' the best.

We'll sing auld *Coila's* plains an' fells,
Her moors red-brown wi' heather bells,
Her banks an' braes, her dens an' dells,
    Where glorious *Wallace*
Aft bure the gree, as story tells,
    Frae Southron billies.   60

At *Wallace*' name, what Scottish blood
But boils up in a spring-tide flood!
Oft have our fearless fathers strode
  By *Wallace*' side,
Still pressing onward, red-wat shod,
  Or glorious died.

O, sweet are *Coila's* haughs an' woods,
When lintwhites chant amang the buds,
And jinkin hares, in amorous whids,
  Their loves enjoy,   70
While thro' the braes the cushat croods
  Wi' wailfu' cry!

Ev'n Winter bleak has charms to me
When winds rave thro' the naked tree;
Or frost on hills of *Ochiltree*
  Are hoary gray;
Or blinding drifts wild-furious flee,
  Dark'ning the day!

O *Nature*! a' thy shews an' forms
To feeling, pensive hearts hae charms! 80
Whether the Summer kindly warms,
  Wi' life an' light,
Or Winter howls, in gusty storms,
  The lang, dark night!

The Muse, nae Poet ever fand her,
Till by himsel he learn'd to wander
Adown some trottin' burn's meander,
  An' no think lang;
O sweet, to stray an' pensive ponder
  A heart-felt sang!   90

The warly race may drudge an' drive,
Hog-shouther, jundie, stretch, an' strive:
Let me fair *Nature's* face descrive,
  And I, wi' pleasure,
Shall let the busy, grumbling hive
  Bum owre their treasure.

Fareweel, ' my rhyme-composing ' brither!
We've been owre lang unkenn'd to ither:
Now let us lay our heads thegither,
  In love fraternal;   100
May *Envy* wallop in a tether,
  Black fiend infernal!

While Highlandmen hate tolls an' taxes;
While moorlan herds like guid fat braxies:
While Terra Firma, on her axis,
  Diurnal turns,
Count on a friend, in faith an' practice,
  In *Robert Burns*.

ADDRESS TO THE DEIL

O Prince! O Chief of many thronèd Pow'rs
That led the embattl'd Seraphim to war—MILTON.

O THOU! whatever title suit thee,
Auld Hornie, Satan, Nick, or Clootie,
Wha in yon cavern grim an' sootie,
   Clos'd under hatches,
Spairges about the brunstane cootie,
   To scaud poor wretches!

Hear me, auld *Hangie*, for a wee,
An' let poor damnèd bodies be;
I'm sure sma' pleasure it can gie,
   Ev'n to a *deil*,   10
To skelp an' scaud poor dogs like me,
   An' hear us squeal!

Great is thy pow'r, an' great thy fame;
Far kend an' noted is thy name;
An', tho' yon lowin heugh 's thy hame,
   Thou travels far;
An' faith! thou 's neither lag nor lame,
   Nor blate nor scaur.

Whyles, rangin' like a roarin' lion
For prey, a' holes an' corners tryin;   20
Whyles, on the strong-wing'd tempest flyin,
   Tirlin the kirks;
Whyles, in the human bosom pryin,
   Unseen thou lurks.

I've heard my reverend *Graunie* say,
In lanely glens ye like to stray;
Or where auld, ruin'd castles gray
   Nod to the moon,
Ye fright the nightly wand'rer's way,
   Wi' eldritch croon.   30

When twilight did my *Graunie* summon
To say her pray'rs, douce, honest woman!
Aft yont the dyke she 's heard you bummin,
   Wi' eerie drone;
Or, rustlin, thro' the boortrees comin,
   Wi' heavy groan.

Ae dreary, windy, winter night
The stars shot down wi' sklentin light,
Wi' you mysel I gat a fright
            Ayont the lough ;   40
Ye like a rash-buss stood in sight
            Wi' waving sough.

The cudgel in my nieve did shake,
Each bristled hair stood like a stake,
When wi' an eldritch stoor quaick, quaick,
            Amang the springs,
Awa ye squatter'd like a drake
            On whistling wings.

Let *warlocks* grim, an' wither'd *hags*,
Tell how wi' you on ragweed nags   50
They skim the muirs an' dizzy crags,
            Wi' wicked speed ;
And in kirk-yards renew their leagues,
            Owre howkit dead.

Thence countra wives, wi' toil an' pain,
May plunge an' plunge the kirn in vain ;
For O ! the yellow treasure 's taen
            By witching skill ;
An' dawtit twal-pint *Hawkie*'s gane
            As yell 's the Bill.   60

When thowes dissolve the snawy hoord,
An' float the jinglin icy-boord,
Then *Water-kelpies* haunt the foord,
            By your direction,
An' 'nighted trav'llers are allur'd
            To their destruction.

An' aft your moss-traversing *Spunkies*
Decoy the wight that late an' drunk is :
The bleezin, curst, mischievous monkies
            Delude his eyes,   70
Till in some miry slough he sunk is,
            Ne'er mair to rise.

When *Masons*' mystic *word* an' *grip*
In storms an' tempests raise you up,
Some cock or cat your rage maun stop,
            Or, strange to tell !
The youngest Brother ye wad whip
            Aff straught to hell.

Lang syne, in *Eden's* bonnie yard,
When youthfu' lovers first were pair'd, 80
And all the Soul of Love they shar'd,
      The raptur'd hour,
Sweet on the fragrant, flow'ry swaird,
      In shady bow'r ;

Then you, ye auld snick-drawing dog !
Ye cam to Paradise incog.
An' play'd on man a cursed brogue,
      (Black be your fa !)
An' gied the infant warld a shog,
      'Maist ruin'd a'. 90

D'ye mind that day, when in a bizz,
Wi' reekit duds, an' reestit gizz,
Ye did present your smoutie phiz
      'Mang better folk,
An' sklented on the *man of Uzz*
      Your spitefu' joke ?

An' how ye gat him i' your thrall,
An' brak him out o' house an' hal',
While scabs an' blotches did him gall
      Wi' bitter claw, 100
An' lows'd his ill-tongu'd wicked Scawl,
      Was warst ava ?

But a' your doings to rehearse,
Your wily snares an' fechtin fierce,
Sin' that day *Michael* did you pierce,
      Down to this time,
Wad ding a' Lallan tongue, or Erse,
      In prose or rhyme.

An' now, auld *Cloots*, I ken ye're thinkin,
A certain Bardie 's rantin, drinkin, 110
Some luckless hour will send him linkin,
      To your black pit ;
But faith ! he'll turn a corner jinkin,
      An' cheat you yet.

But fare you weel, auld *Nickie-ben* !
O wad ye tak a thought an' men' !
Ye aiblins might—I dinna ken—
      Still hae a *stake* :
I'm wae to think upo' yon den,
      Ev'n for your sake ! 120

EPISTLE TO JAMES SMITH

Friendship! mysterious cement of the soul!
Sweet'ner of Life and solder of Society!
   I owe thee much.—BLAIR.

DEAR Smith, the sleeest pawkie thief
That e'er attempted stealth or rief,
Ye surely hae some warlock-breef
        Owre human hearts;
For ne'er a bosom yet was prief
        Against your arts.

For me, I swear by sun an' moon,
And ev'ry star that blinks aboon,
Ye've cost me twenty pair o' shoon
        Just gaun to see you;   10
And ev'ry ither pair that's done,
        Mair taen I'm wi' you.

That auld capricious carlin, Nature,
To mak amends for scrimpit stature,
She's turn'd you aff, a human creature
        On her *first* plan,
And in her freaks, on ev'ry feature,
        She's wrote, *the Man.*

Just now I've taen the fit o' rhyme,
My barmie noddle's working prime,   20
My fancy yerkit up sublime
        Wi' hasty summon:
Hae ye a leisure-moment's time
        To hear what's comin?

Some rhyme a neebor's name to lash;
Some rhyme (vain thought!) for needfu' cash;
Some rhyme to court the countra clash,
        An' raise a din;
For me, an aim I never fash;
        I rhyme for fun.   30

The star that rules my luckless lot,
Has fated me the russet coat,
An' damn'd my fortune to the groat;
        But, in requit,
Has blest me with a random shot
        O' countra wit.

This while my notion's taen a sklent,
To try my fate in guid, black *prent*;
But still the mair I'm that way bent,
        Something cries ' Hoolie!   40
I red you, honest man, tak tent!
        Ye'll shaw your folly.

'There's ither Poets, much your betters,
Far seen in *Greek*, deep men o' letters,
Hae thought they had ensured their debtors
   A' future ages ;
Now moths deform in shapeless tatters
   Their unknown pages.'

Then farewel hopes o' laurel-boughs,
To garland my poetic brows !   50
Henceforth I'll rove where busy ploughs
   Are whistling thrang,
An' teach the lanely heights an' howes
   My rustic sang.

I'll wander on, wi' tentless heed
How never-halting moments speed,
Till fate shall snap the brittle thread ;
   Then, all unknown,
I'll lay me with th' inglorious dead,   60
   Forgot and gone !

But why o' Death begin a tale ?
Just now we're living, sound an' hale ;
Then top and maintop crowd the sail,
   Heave *Care* o'er side !
And large, before Enjoyment's gale,
   Let's tak the tide.

This life, sae far's I understand,
Is a' enchanted fairy-land,
Where Pleasure is the Magic Wand,
   That, wielded right,   70
Maks Hours like Minutes, hand in hand,
   Dance by fu' light.

The magic wand then let us wield :
For, ance that five-an'-forty's speel'd,
See, crazy, weary, joyless Eild,
   Wi' wrinkled face,
Comes hostin, hirplin owre the field,
   Wi' creepin pace.

When ance *life's day* draws near the gloamin,
Then fareweel vacant careless roamin ;   80
An' fareweel cheerfu' tankards foamin,
   An' social noise ;
An' fareweel dear deluding *woman*,
   The joy of joys !

O Life! how pleasant in thy morning,
Young Fancy's rays the hills adorning!
Cold-pausing Caution's lesson scorning,
   We frisk away,
Like schoolboys, at th' expected warning,
   To joy and play.   90

We wander there, we wander here,
We eye the rose upon the brier,
Unmindful that the thorn is near,
   Among the leaves:
And tho' the puny wound appear,
   Short while it grieves.

Some, lucky, find a flow'ry spot,
For which they never toil'd nor swat;
They drink the sweet and eat the fat,
   But care or pain;   100
And, haply, eye the barren hut
   With high disdain.

With steady aim, some Fortune chase;
Keen hope does ev'ry sinew brace;
Thro' fair, thro' foul, they urge the race,
   And seize the prey;
Then cannie, in some cozie place,
   They close the *day*.

And others, like your humble servan',
Poor wights! nae rules nor roads observin, 110
To right or left, eternal swervin,
   They zig-zag on;
Till curst with age, obscure an' starvin,
   They aften groan.

Alas! what bitter toil an' straining—
But truce with peevish, poor complaining.
Is Fortune's fickle *Luna* waning?
   E'en let her gang!
Beneath what light she has remaining,
   Let's sing our sang.   120

My pen I here fling to the door,
And kneel 'Ye Pow'rs!' and warm implore,
'Tho' I should wander *Terra* o'er,
   In all her climes,
Grant me but this, I ask no more,
   Aye rowth o' rhymes.

'Gie dreeping roasts to countra Lairds,
Till icicles hing frae their beards;
Gie fine braw claes to fine Life-guards,
   And Maids of Honour; 130
And yill an' whisky gie to Cairds,
   Until they sconner.

' A title, *Dempster* merits it ;
A garter gie to *Willie Pitt* ;
Gie Wealth to some be-ledger'd Cit,
   In cent per cent ;
But gie me real, Sterling Wit,
   And I'm content.

' While Ye are pleased to keep me hale,
I'll sit down o'er my scanty meal,   140
Be 't *water-brose*, or *muslin-kail*,
   Wi' cheerfu' face,
As lang's the Muses dinna fail
   To say the grace.'

An anxious e'e I never throws
Behint my lug, or by my nose ;
I jouk beneath Misfortune's blows
   As weel 's I may ;
Sworn foe to Sorrow, Care, and Prose,
   I rhyme away.   150

O ye douce folk, that live by rule,
Grave, tideless-blooded, calm, and cool,
Compar'd wi' you—O fool ! fool ! fool !
   How much unlike !
Your hearts are just a standing pool,
   Your lives a dyke !

Nae hare-brain'd sentimental traces,
In your unletter'd, nameless faces !
In *arioso* trills and graces
   Ye never stray,   160
But *gravissimo*, solemn basses,
   Ye hum away.

Ye are sae *grave*, nae doubt ye're *wise* ;
Nae ferly tho' ye do despise
The hairum-scairum, ram-stam boys,
   The rattlin' squad :
I see ye upward cast your eyes—
   Ye ken the road.

Whilst I—but I shall haud me there—
Wi' you I'll scarce gang *ony where*—   170
Then, *Jamie*, I shall say nae mair,
   But quat my sang,
Content with *You* to mak a pair,
   Whare'er I gang.

GEORGE CRABBE

THE VILLAGE

BOOK I

THE Village Life, and every care that reigns
O'er youthful peasants and declining swains;
What labour yields, and what, that labour past,
Age, in its hour of languor, finds at last;
What form the real picture of the poor,
Demand a song—the Muse can give no more.
　Fled are those times, when, in harmonious strains,
The rustic poet praised his native plains:
No shepherds now, in smooth alternate verse,
Their country's beauty or their nymphs' rehearse;　　　**10**
Yet still for these we frame the tender strain,
Still in our lays fond Corydons complain,
And shepherds' boys their amorous pains reveal,
The only pains, alas! they never feel.
　On Mincio's banks, in Caesar's bounteous reign,
If Tityrus found the Golden Age again,
Must sleepy bards the flattering dream prolong,
Mechanic echoes of the Mantuan song?
From Truth and Nature shall we widely stray,
Where Virgil, not where Fancy, leads the way?　　　**20**
　Yes, thus the Muses sing of happy swains,
Because the Muses never knew their pains:
They boast their peasants' pipes; but peasants now
Resign their pipes and plod behind the plough;
And few, amid the rural-tribe, have time
To number syllables, and play with rhyme;
Save honest Duck, what son of verse could share
The poet's rapture, and the peasant's care?
Or the great labours of the field degrade,
With the new peril of a poorer trade?　　　**30**
　From this chief cause these idle praises spring,
That themes so easy few forbear to sing;
For no deep thought the trifling subjects ask;
To sing of shepherds is an easy task:
The happy youth assumes the common strain,
A nymph his mistress, and himself a swain;
With no sad scenes he clouds his tuneful prayer,
But all, to look like her, is painted fair.
　I grant indeed that fields and flocks have charms
For him that grazes or for him that farms;　　　**40**
But when amid such pleasing scenes I trace
The poor laborious natives of the place,
And see the mid-day sun, with fervid ray,
On their bare heads and dewy temples play;

While some, with feebler heads and fainter hearts,
Deplore their fortune, yet sustain their parts—
Then shall I dare these real ills to hide
In tinsel trappings of poetic pride ?
  No ; cast by Fortune on a frowning coast,   50
Which neither groves nor happy valleys boast ;
Where other cares than those the Muse relates,
And other shepherds dwell with other mates ;
By such examples taught, I paint the Cot,
As Truth will paint it, and as Bards will not :
Nor you, ye poor, of letter'd scorn complain,
To you the smoothest song is smooth in vain ;
O'ercome by labour, and bow'd down by time,
Feel you the barren flattery of a rhyme ?
Can poets soothe you, when you pine for bread,
By winding myrtles round your ruin'd shed ?   60
Can their light tales your weighty griefs o'erpower,
Or glad with airy mirth the toilsome hour ?
  Lo ! where the heath, with withering brake grown o'er,
Lends the light turf that warms the neighbouring poor ;
From thence a length of burning sand appears,
Where the thin harvest waves its wither'd ears ;
Rank weeds, that every art and care defy,
Reign o'er the land, and rob the blighted rye :
There thistles stretch their prickly arms afar,
And to the ragged infant threaten war ;   70
There poppies nodding, mock the hope of toil ;
There the blue bugloss paints the sterile soil ;
Hardy and high, above the slender sheaf,
The slimy mallow waves her silky leaf ;
O'er the young shoot the charlock throws a shade,
And clasping tares cling round the sickly blade ;
With mingled tints the rocky coasts abound,
And a sad splendour vainly shines around.
So looks the nymph whom wretched arts adorn,
Betray'd by Man, then left for Man to scorn ;   80
Whose cheek in vain assumes the mimic rose,
While her sad eyes the troubled breast disclose ;
Whose outward splendour is but folly's dress,
Exposing most, when most it gilds distress.
  Here joyless roam a wild amphibious race,
With sullen woe display'd in every face ;
Who, far from civil arts and social fly,
And scowl at strangers with suspicious eye.
  Here too the lawless merchant of the main
Draws from his plough th' intoxicated swain ;   90
Want only claim'd the labour of the day,
But vice now steals his nightly rest away.
  Where are the swains, who, daily labour done,
With rural games play'd down the setting sun ;

Who struck with matchless force the bounding ball,
Or made the pond'rous quoit obliquely fall;
While some huge Ajax, terrible and strong,
Engaged some artful stripling of the throng,
And fell beneath him, foil'd, while far around
Hoarse triumph rose, and rocks return'd the sound？ 100
Where now are these？—Beneath yon cliff they stand,
To show the freighted pinnace where to land;
To load the ready steed with guilty haste,
To fly in terror o'er the pathless waste,
Or, when detected, in their straggling course,
To foil their foes by cunning or by force;
Or, yielding part (which equal knaves demand),
To gain a lawless passport through the land.
   Here, wand'ring long, amid these frowning fields,
I sought the simple life that Nature yields;   110
Rapine and Wrong and Fear usurp'd her place,
And a bold, artful, surly, savage race;
Who, only skill'd to take the finny tribe,
The yearly dinner, or septennial bribe,
Wait on the shore, and, as the waves run high,
On the tost vessel bend their eager eye,
Which to their coast directs its vent'rous way;
Theirs, or the ocean's, miserable prey.
   As on their neighbouring beach yon swallows stand,
And wait for favouring winds to leave the land;   120
While still for flight the ready wing is spread:
So waited I the favouring hour, and fled;
Fled from these shores where guilt and famine reign,
And cried, Ah! hapless they who still remain;
Who still remain to hear the ocean roar,
Whose greedy waves devour the lessening shore;
Till some fierce tide, with more imperious sway,
Sweeps the low hut and all it holds away;
When the sad tenant weeps from door to door,
And begs a poor protection from the poor!   130
   But these are scenes where Nature's niggard hand
Gave a spare portion to the famish'd land;
Hers is the fault, if here mankind complain
Of fruitless toil and labour spent in vain;
But yet in other scenes more fair in view,
Where Plenty smiles—alas! she smiles for few—
And those who taste not, yet behold her store,
Are as the slaves that dig the golden ore,—
The wealth around them makes them doubly poor.
   Or will you deem them amply paid in health,   140
Labour's fair child, that languishes with wealth？
Go then! and see them rising with the sun,
Through a long course of daily toil to run;
See them beneath the dog-star's raging heat,
When the knees tremble and the temples beat;

Behold them, leaning on their scythes, look o'er
The labour past, and toils to come explore;
See them alternate suns and showers engage,
And hoard up aches and anguish for their age;
Through fens and marshy moors their steps pursue, 150
When their warm pores imbibe the evening dew;
Then own that labour may as fatal be
To these thy slaves, as thine excess to thee.

 Amid this tribe too oft a manly pride
Strives in strong toil the fainting heart to hide;
There may you see the youth of slender frame
Contend with weakness, weariness, and shame;
Yet, urged along, and proudly loth to yield,
He strives to join his fellows of the field.
Till long-contending nature droops at last, 160
Declining health rejects his poor repast,
His cheerless spouse the coming danger sees,
And mutual murmurs urge the slow disease.

 Yet grant them health, 'tis not for us to tell,
Though the head droops not, that the heart is well;
Or will you praise that homely, healthy fare,
Plenteous and plain, that happy peasants share!
Oh! trifle not with wants you cannot feel,
Nor mock the misery of a stinted meal;
Homely, not wholesome, plain, not plenteous, such 170
As you who praise would never deign to touch.

 Ye gentle souls, who dream of rural ease,
Whom the smooth stream and smoother sonnet please;
Go! if the peaceful cot your praises share,
Go look within, and ask if peace be there;
If peace be his—that drooping weary sire,
Or theirs, that offspring round their feeble fire;
Or hers, that matron pale, whose trembling hand
Turns on the wretched hearth th' expiring brand!

 Nor yet can Time itself obtain for these 180
Life's latest comforts, due respect and ease;
For yonder see that hoary swain, whose age
Can with no cares except his own engage;
Who, propp'd on that rude staff, looks up to see
The bare arms broken from the withering tree,
On which, a boy, he climb'd the loftiest bough,
Then his first joy, but his sad emblem now.

 He once was chief in all the rustic trade;
His steady hand the straightest furrow made;
Full many a prize he won, and still is proud 190
To find the triumphs of his youth allow'd;
A transient pleasure sparkles in his eyes,
He hears and smiles, then thinks again and sighs:
For now he journeys to his grave in pain;
The rich disdain him; nay, the poor disdain:

Alternate masters now their slave command,
Urge the weak efforts of his feeble hand,
And, when his age attempts its task in vain,
With ruthless taunts, of lazy poor complain.
  Oft may you see him, when he tends the sheep,   200
His winter-charge, beneath the hillock weep,
Oft hear him murmur to the winds that blow
O'er his white locks and bury them in snow,
When, roused by rage and muttering in the morn,
He mends the broken hedge with icy thorn :—
  'Why do I live, when I desire to be
At once from life and life's long labour free ?
Like leaves in spring, the young are blown away,
Without the sorrows of a slow decay ;
I, like yon wither'd leaf, remain behind,   210
Nipp'd by the frost, and shivering in the wind ;
There it abides till younger buds come on,
As I, now all my fellow-swains are gone ;
Then, from the rising generation thrust,
It falls, like me, unnoticed to the dust.
  'These fruitful fields, these numerous flocks I see,
Are others' gain, but killing cares to me :
To me the children of my youth are lords,
Cool in their looks, but hasty in their words :
Wants of their own demand their care ; and who   220
Feels his own want and succours others too ?
A lonely, wretched man, in pain I go,
None need my help, and none relieve my wo ;
Then let my bones beneath the turf be laid,
And men forget the wretch they would not aid.'
  Thus groan the old, till, by disease oppress'd,
They taste a final woe, and then they rest.
  Theirs is yon House that holds the parish-poor,
Whose walls of mud scarce bear the broken door ;
There, where the putrid vapours, flagging, play,   230
And the dull wheel hums doleful through the day ;—
There children dwell who know no parents' care ;
Parents, who know no children's love, dwell there !
Heart-broken matrons on their joyless bed,
Forsaken wives, and mothers never wed ;
Dejected widows with unheeded tears,
And crippled age with more than childhood fears ;
The lame, the blind, and, far the happiest they !
The moping idiot and the madman gay.
  Here too the sick their final doom receive,   240
Here brought, amid the scenes of grief, to grieve,
Where the loud groans from some sad chamber flow,
Mix'd with the clamours of the crowd below ;
Here, sorrowing, they each kindred sorrow scan,
And the cold charities of man to man :

Whose laws indeed for ruin'd age provide,
And strong compulsion plucks the scrap from pride;
But still that scrap is bought with many a sigh,
And pride embitters what it can't deny.
   Say ye, oppress'd by some fantastic woes,   250
Some jarring nerve that baffles your repose;
Who press the downy couch, while slaves advance
With timid eye, to read the distant glance;
Who with sad prayers the weary doctor tease,
To name the nameless ever-new disease;
Who with mock patience dire complaints endure,
Which real pain and that alone can cure;
How would ye bear in real pain to lie,
Despised, neglected, left alone to die?
How would ye bear to draw your latest breath,   260
Where all that's wretched paves the way for death?
   Such is that room which one rude beam divides,
And naked rafters form the sloping sides;
Where the vile bands that bind the thatch are seen,
And lath and mud are all that lie between;
Save one dull pane, that, coarsely patch'd, gives way
To the rude tempest, yet excludes the day:
Here, on a matted flock, with dust o'erspread,
The drooping wretch reclines his languid head;
For him no hand the cordial cup applies,   270
Or wipes the tear that stagnates in his eyes;
No friends with soft discourse his pain beguile,
Or promise hope till sickness wears a smile.
   But soon a loud and hasty summons calls,
Shakes the thin roof, and echoes round the walls;
Anon, a figure enters, quaintly neat,
All pride and business, bustle and conceit;
With looks unalter'd by these scenes of wo,
With speed that, entering, speaks his haste to go,
He bids the gazing throng around him fly,   280
And carries fate and physic in his eye:
A potent quack, long versed in human ills,
Who first insults the victim whom he kills;
Whose murd'rous hand a drowsy Bench protect,
And whose most tender mercy is neglect.
   Paid by the parish for attendance here,
He wears contempt upon his sapient sneer;
In haste he seeks the bed where Misery lies,
Impatience mark'd in his averted eyes;
And, some habitual queries hurried o'er,   290
Without reply, he rushes on the door:
His drooping patient, long inured to pain,
And long unheeded, knows remonstrance vain;
He ceases now the feeble help to crave
Of man; and silent sinks into the grave.

But ere his death some pious doubts arise,
Some simple fears, which ' bold bad ' men despise ;
Fain would he ask the parish-priest to prove
His title certain to the joys above :
For this he sends the murmuring nurse, who calls   300
The holy stranger to these dismal walls :
And doth not he, the pious man, appear,
He, ' passing rich with forty pounds a year ' ?
Ah ! no ; a shepherd of a different stock,
And far unlike him, feeds this little flock :
A jovial youth, who thinks his Sunday's task
As much as God or man can fairly ask ;
The rest he gives to loves and labours light,
To fields the morning, and to feasts the night ;
None better skill'd the noisy pack to guide,   310
To urge their chase, to cheer them or to chide ;
A sportsman keen, he shoots through half the day,
And, skill'd at whist, devotes the night to play :
Then, while such honours bloom around his head,
Shall he sit sadly by the sick man's bed,
To raise the hope he feels not, or with zeal
To combat fears that e'en the pious feel ?
  Now once again the gloomy scene explore,
Less gloomy now ; the bitter hour is o'er,
The man of many sorrows sighs no more.—   320
Up yonder hill, behold how sadly slow
The bier moves winding from the vale below ;
There lie the happy dead, from trouble free,
And the glad parish pays the frugal fee :
No more, O Death ! thy victim starts to hear
Churchwarden stern, or kingly overseer ;
No more the farmer claims his humble bow,
Thou art his lord, the best of tyrants thou !
  Now to the church behold the mourners come,
Sedately torpid and devoutly dumb ;   330
The village children now their games suspend,
To see the bier that bears their ancient friend ;
For he was one in all their idle sport,
And like a monarch ruled their little court.
The pliant bow he form'd, the flying ball,
The bat, the wicket, were his labours all ;
Him now they follow to his grave, and stand
Silent and sad, and gazing, hand in hand ;
While bending low, their eager eyes explore
The mingled relics of the parish poor :   340
The bell tolls late, the moping owl flies round,
Fear marks the flight and magnifies the sound ;
The busy priest, detain'd by weightier care,
Defers his duty till the day of prayer ;
And, waiting long, the crowd retire distress'd,
To think a poor man's bones should lie unbless'd.

BOOK II

No longer truth, though shown in verse, disdain,
But own the Village Life a life of pain:
I too must yield, that oft amid these woes
Are gleams of transient mirth and hours of sweet repose,
Such as you find on yonder sportive Green,
The 'squire's tall gate and churchway-walk between;
Where loitering stray a little tribe of friends,
On a fair Sunday when the sermon ends:
Then rural beaux their best attire put on,
To win their nymphs, as other nymphs are won;   10
While those long wed go plain, and by degrees,
Like other husbands, quit their care to please.
Some of the sermon talk, a sober crowd,
And loudly praise, if it were preach'd aloud;
Some on the labours of the week look round;
Feel their own worth, and think their toil renown'd;
While some, whose hopes to no renown extend,
Are only pleased to find their labours end.
    Thus, as their hours glide on, with pleasure fraught,
Their careful masters brood the painful thought;   20
Much in their mind they murmur and lament,
That one fair day should be so idly spent;
And think that Heaven deals hard, to tithe their store
And tax their time for preachers and the poor.
    Yet still, ye humbler friends, enjoy your hour,
This is your portion, yet unclaim'd of power;
This is Heaven's gift to weary men oppress'd,
And seems the type of their expected rest:
But yours, alas! are joys that soon decay;
Frail joys, begun and ended with the day;   30
Or yet, while day permits those joys to reign,
The village vices drive them from the plain.
    See the stout churl, in drunken fury great,
Strike the bare bosom of his teeming mate!
His naked vices, rude and unrefined,
Exert their open empire o'er the mind;
But can we less the senseless rage despise,
Because the savage acts without disguise?
    Yet here disguise, the city's vice, is seen,
And Slander steals along and taints the Green: 40
At her approach domestic peace is gone,
Domestic broils at her approach come on;
She to the wife the husband's crime conveys,
She tells the husband when his consort strays;
Her busy tongue, through all the little state,
Diffuses doubt, suspicion, and debate;
Peace, tim'rous goddess! quits her old domain,
In sentiment and song content to reign.

Nor are the nymphs that breathe the rural air
So fair as Cynthia's, nor so chaste as fair :   50
These to the town afford each fresher face,
And the clown's trull receives the peer's embrace ;
From whom, should chance again convey her down,
The peer's disease in turn attacks the clown.
Here too the 'squires, or 'squire-like farmers, talk,
How round their regions nightly pilferers walk ;
How from their ponds the fish are borne, and all
The rip'ning treasures from their lofty wall ;
How meaner rivals in their sports delight,
Just rich enough to claim a doubtful right ;   60
Who take a licence round their fields to stray,
A mongrel race ! the poachers of the day.
And hark ! the riots of the Green begin,
That sprang at first from yonder noisy inn ;
What time the weekly pay was vanish'd all,
And the slow hostess scored the threat'ning wall ;
What time they ask'd, their friendly feast to close,
A final cup, and that will make them foes ;
When blows ensue that break the arm of toil,
And rustic battle ends the boobies' broil.   70
Save when to yonder Hall they bend their way,
Where the grave justice ends the grievous fray ;
He who recites, to keep the poor in awe,
The law's vast volume—for he knows the law :—
To him with anger or with shame repair
The injured peasant and deluded fair.
Lo ! at his throne the silent nymph appears,
Frail by her shape, but modest in her tears ;
And while she stands abash'd, with conscious eye,
Some favourite female of her judge glides by,   80
Who views with scornful glance the strumpet's fate,
And thanks the stars that made her keeper great ;
Near her the swain, about to bear for life
One certain evil, doubts 'twixt war and wife ;
But, while the falt'ring damsel takes her oath,
Consents to wed, and so secures them both.
Yet why, you ask, these humble crimes relate,
Why make the Poor as guilty as the Great ?
To show the great, those mightier sons of pride,
How near in vice the lowest are allied ;   90
Such are their natures and their passions such,
But these disguise too little, those too much :
So shall the man of power and pleasure see
In his own slave as vile a wretch as he ;
In his luxurious lord the servant find
His own low pleasures and degenerate mind :
And each in all the kindred vices trace,
Of a poor, blind, bewilder'd, erring race ;

Who, a short time in varied fortune past,
Die, and are equal in the dust at last.   100
   And you, ye Poor, who still lament your fate,
Forbear to envy those you call the Great;
And know, amid those blessings they possess,
They are, like you, the victims of distress;
While Sloth with many a pang torments her slave,
Fear waits on guilt, and Danger shakes the brave.
   Oh! if in life one noble chief appears,
Great in his name, while blooming in his years;
Born to enjoy whate'er delights mankind,
And yet to all you feel or fear resign'd;   110
Who gave up joys and hopes to you unknown,
For pains and dangers greater than your own:
If such there be, then let your murmurs cease,
Think, think of him, and take your lot in peace.
   And such there was:—Oh! grief, that checks our pride,
Weeping we say there was,—for MANNERS died:
Beloved of Heaven, these humble lines forgive,
That sing of Thee, and thus aspire to live.
   As the tall oak, whose vigorous branches form
An ample shade and brave the wildest storm,   120
High o'er the subject wood is seen to grow,
The guard and glory of the trees below;
Till on its head the fiery bolt descends,
And o'er the plain the shatter'd trunk extends;
Yet then it lies, all wond'rous as before,
And still the glory, though the guard no more:
   So THOU, when every virtue, every grace,
Rose in thy soul, or shone within thy face;
When, though the son of GRANBY, thou were known
Less by thy father's glory than thy own;   130
When Honour lov'd and gave thee every charm,
Fire to thy eye and vigour to thy arm;
Then from our lofty hopes and longing eyes,
Fate and thy virtues call'd thee to the skies;
Yet still we wonder at thy tow'ring fame,
And losing thee, still dwell upon thy name.
   Oh! ever honour'd, ever valued! say,
What verse can praise thee, or what work repay?
Yet verse (in all we can) thy worth repays,
Nor trusts the tardy zeal of future days;—   140
Honours for thee thy country shall prepare,
Thee in their hearts, the good, the brave shall bear;
To deeds like thine shall noblest chiefs aspire,
The Muse shall mourn thee, and the world admire.
   In future times, when smit with Glory's charms,
The untried youth first quits a father's arms;—
'Oh! be like him,' the weeping sire shall say;
'Like MANNERS walk, who walk'd in Honour's way;

In danger foremost, yet in death sedate,
Oh! be like him in all things, but his fate!'   150
  If for that fate such public tears be shed,
That Victory seems to die now THOU art dead;
How shall a friend his nearer hope resign,
That friend a brother, and whose soul was thine?
By what bold lines shall we his grief express,
Or by what soothing numbers make it less?
  'Tis not, I know, the chiming of a song,
Nor all the powers that to the Muse belong,
Words aptly cull'd and meanings well express'd,
Can calm the sorrows of a wounded breast;   160
But Virtue, soother of the fiercest pains,
Shall heal that bosom, RUTLAND, where she reigns.
  Yet hard the task to heal the bleeding heart,
To bid the still-recurring thoughts depart,
Tame the fierce grief and stem the rising sigh,
And curb rebellious passion, with reply;
Calmly to dwell on all that pleased before,
And yet to know that all shall please no more;—
Oh! glorious labour of the soul, to save
Her captive powers, and bravely mourn the brave.   170
  To such these thoughts will lasting comfort give—
Life is not measured by the time we live:
'Tis not an even course of threescore years,
A life of narrow views and paltry fears,
Gray hairs and wrinkles and the cares they bring,
That take from death the terrors or the sting;
But 'tis the gen'rous spirit, mounting high
Above the world, that native of the sky;
The noble spirit, that, in dangers brave,
Calmly looks on, or looks beyond the grave:—   180
Such MANNERS was, so he resign'd his breath,
If in a glorious, then a timely death.
  Cease then that grief and let those tears subside;
If Passion rule us, be that passion pride;
If Reason, Reason bids us strive to raise
Our fallen hearts, and be like him we praise;
Or if Affection still the soul subdue,
Bring all his virtues, all his worth in view,
And let Affection find its comfort too:
For how can Grief so deeply wound the heart,   190
When Admiration claims so large a part?
  Grief is a foe,—expel him then thy soul;
Let nobler thoughts the nearer views control!
Oh! make the age to come thy better care,
See other RUTLANDS, other GRANBYS there!
And, as thy thoughts through streaming ages glide,
See other heroes die as MANNERS died:
And from their fate, thy race shall nobler grow,
As trees shoot upwards that are pruned below;

Or as old Thames, borne down with decent pride,   200
Sees his young streams run warbling at his side;
Though some, by art cut off, no longer run,
And some are lost beneath the summer's sun—
Yet the pure stream moves on, and, as it moves,
Its power increases and its use improves;
While plenty round its spacious waves bestow,
Still it flows on, and shall for ever flow.

PETER GRIMES

OLD Peter Grimes made fishing his employ,
His wife he cabin'd with him and his boy,
And seem'd that life laborious to enjoy:
To town came quiet Peter with his fish,
And had of all a civil word and wish.
He left his trade upon the sabbath-day,
And took young Peter in his hand to pray:
But soon the stubborn boy from care broke loose,
At first refused, then added his abuse:
His father's love he scorn'd, his power defied,   10
But being drunk, wept sorely when he died.
  Yes! then he wept, and to his mind there came
Much of his conduct, and he felt the shame,—
How he had oft the good old man reviled,
And never paid the duty of a child;
How, when the father in his Bible read,
He in contempt and anger left the shed:
'It is the word of life,' the parent cried;
—'This is the life itself,' the boy replied;
And while old Peter in amazement stood,   20
Gave the hot spirit to his boiling blood:—
How he, with oath and furious speech, began
To prove his freedom and assert the man;
And when the parent check'd his impious rage,
How he had cursed the tyranny of age,—
Nay, once had dealt the sacrilegious blow
On his bare head, and laid his parent low;
The father groan'd—'If thou art old,' said he,
'And hast a son—thou wilt remember me:
Thy mother left me in a happy time,   30
Thou kill'dst not her—Heav'n spares the double crime.'
  On an inn-settle, in his maudlin grief,
This he revolved, and drank for his relief.
  Now lived the youth in freedom, but debarr'd
From constant pleasure, and he thought it hard;
Hard that he could not every wish obey,
But must awhile relinquish ale and play;

Hard! that he could not to his cards attend,
But must acquire the money he would spend.
  With greedy eye he look'd on all he saw,   40
He knew not justice, and he laugh'd at law;
On all he mark'd he stretch'd his ready hand;
He fish'd by water, and he filch'd by land:
Oft in the night has Peter dropp'd his oar,
Fled from his boat and sought for prey on shore;
Oft up the hedge-row glided, on his back
Bearing the orchard's produce in a sack,
Or farm-yard load, tugg'd fiercely from the stack;
And as these wrongs to greater numbers rose,
The more he look'd on all men as his foes.   50
  He built a mud-wall'd hovel, where he kept
His various wealth, and there he oft-times slept;
But no success could please his cruel soul,
He wish'd for one to trouble and control;
He wanted some obedient boy to stand
And bear the blow of his outrageous hand;
And hoped to find in some propitious hour
A feeling creature subject to his power.
  Peter had heard there were in London then,—
Still have they being!—workhouse-clearing men,   60
Who, undisturb'd by feelings just or kind,
Would parish-boys to needy tradesmen bind:
They in their want a trifling sum would take,
And toiling slaves of piteous orphans make.
  Such Peter sought, and when a lad was found,
The sum was dealt him, and the slave was bound.
Some few in town observed in Peter's trap
A boy, with jacket blue and woollen cap;
But none inquired how Peter used the rope,
Or what the bruise, that made the stripling stoop;   70
None could the ridges on his back behold,
None sought him shiv'ring in the winter's cold;
None put the question,—'Peter, dost thou give
The boy his food?—What, man! the lad must live:
Consider, Peter, let the child have bread,
He'll serve thee better if he's stroked and fed.'
None reason'd thus—and some, on hearing cries,
Said calmly, 'Grimes is at his exercise.'
  Pinn'd, beaten, cold, pinch'd, threaten'd, and abused—
His efforts punish'd and his food refused,—   80
Awake tormented,—soon aroused from sleep,—
Struck if he wept, and yet compell'd to weep,
The trembling boy dropp'd down and strove to pray,
Received a blow, and trembling turn'd away,
Or sobb'd and hid his piteous face:—while he,
The savage master, grinn'd in horrid glee:
He'd now the power he ever loved to show,
A feeling being subject to his blow.

Thus lived the lad, in hunger, peril, pain,
His tears despised, his supplications vain: 90
Compell'd by fear to lie, by need to steal,
His bed uneasy and unbless'd his meal,
For three sad years the boy his tortures bore,
And then his pains and trials were no more.
  ' How died he, Peter ? ' when the people said,
He growl'd—' I found him lifeless in his bed ; '
Then tried for softer tone, and sigh'd, ' Poor Sam is dead.'
Yet murmurs were there, and some questions ask'd,—
How he was fed, how punish'd, and how task'd ?
Much they suspected, but they little proved,   100
And Peter pass'd untroubled and unmoved.
  Another boy with equal ease was found,
The money granted, and the victim bound ;
And what his fate ?—One night it chanced he fell
From the boat's mast and perish'd in her well,
Where fish were living kept, and where the boy
(So reason'd men) could not himself destroy :—
  ' Yes ! so it was,' said Peter, ' in his play,
(For he was idle both by night and day,)
He climb'd the main-mast and then fell below ; '—   110
Then show'd his corpse and pointed to the blow :
' What said the jury ? '—they were long in doubt
But sturdy Peter faced the matter out :
So they dismiss'd him, saying at the time,
' Keep fast your hatchway when you've boys who climb.'
This hit the conscience, and he colour'd more
Than for the closest questions put before.
  Thus all his fears the verdict set aside,
And at the slave-shop Peter still applied.
  Then came a boy, of manners soft and mild,—   120
Our seamen's wives with grief beheld the child ;
All thought (the poor themselves) that he was one
Of gentle blood, some noble sinner's son,
Who had, belike, deceived some humble maid,
Whom he had first seduced and then betray'd :—
However this, he seem'd a gracious lad,
In grief submissive and with patience sad.
  Passive he labour'd, till his slender frame
Bent with his loads, and he at length was lame :
Strange that a frame so weak could bear so long   130
The grossest insult and the foulest wrong ;
But there were causes—in the town they gave
Fire, food, and comfort, to the gentle slave ;
And though stern Peter, with a cruel hand,
And knotted rope, enforced the rude command,
Yet he consider'd what he'd lately felt,
And his vile blows with selfish pity dealt.
  One day such draughts the cruel fisher made,
He could not vend them in his borough-trade,

But sail'd for London-mart: the boy was ill,   140
But ever humbled to his master's will;
And on the river, where they smoothly sail'd,
He strove with terror and awhile prevail'd;
But new to danger on the angry sea,
He clung affrighten'd to his master's knee:
The boat grew leaky and the wind was strong,
Rough was the passage and the time was long;
His liquor fail'd, and Peter's wrath arose,—
No more is known—the rest we must suppose,
Or learn of Peter;—Peter says, he 'spied   150
The stripling's danger and for harbour tried;
Meantime the fish, and then th' apprentice died.'

The pitying women raised a clamour round,
And weeping said, 'Thou hast thy 'prentice drown'd.'

Now the stern man was summon'd to the hall,
To tell his tale before the burghers all:
He gave th' account; profess'd the lad he loved,
And kept his brazen features all unmoved.

The mayor himself with tone severe replied,—
'Henceforth with thee shall never boy abide;   160
Hire thee a freeman, whom thou durst not beat,
But who, in thy despite, will sleep and eat:
Free thou art now!—again shouldst thou appear,
Thou'lt find thy sentence, like thy soul, severe.'

Alas! for Peter not a helping hand,
So was he hated, could he now command;
Alone he row'd his boat, alone he cast
His nets beside, or made his anchor fast;
To hold a rope or hear a curse was none,—
He toil'd and rail'd; he groan'd and swore alone.   170

Thus by himself compell'd to live each day,
To wait for certain hours the tide's delay;
At the same times the same dull views to see,
The bounding marsh-bank and the blighted tree;
The water only, when the tides were high,
When low, the mud half-cover'd and half-dry;
The sun-burnt tar that blisters on the planks,
And bank-side stakes in their uneven ranks;
Heaps of entangled weeds that slowly float,
As the tide rolls by the impeded boat.   180

When tides were neap, and, in the sultry day,
Through the tall bounding mud-banks made their way,
Which on each side rose swelling, and below
The dark warm flood ran silently and slow;
There anchoring, Peter chose from man to hide,
There hang his head, and view the lazy tide
In its hot slimy channel slowly glide;
Where the small eels that left the deeper way
For the warm shore, within the shallows play;

Where gaping mussels, left upon the mud,   190
Slope their slow passage to the fallen flood ;—
Here dull and hopeless he'd lie down and trace
How sidelong crabs had scrawl'd their crooked race ;
Or sadly listen to the tuneless cry
Of fishing gull or clanging golden-eye ;
What time the sea-birds to the marsh would come,
And the loud bittern, from the bulrush home,
Gave from the salt-ditch side the bellowing boom :
He nursed the feelings these dull scenes produce,
And loved to stop beside the opening sluice ;   200
Where the small stream, confined in narrow bound,
Ran with a dull, unvaried, sadd'ning sound ;
Where all, presented to the eye or ear,
Oppress'd the soul with misery, grief, and fear.
   Besides these objects, there were places three,
Which Peter seem'd with certain dread to see ;
When he drew near them he would turn from each,
And loudly whistle till he pass'd the reach.
   A change of scene to him brought no relief ;
In town, 'twas plain, men took him for a thief :   210
The sailors' wives would stop him in the street,
And say, ' Now, Peter, thou'st no boy to beat : '
Infants at play, when they perceived him, ran,
Warning each other—' That 's the wicked man : '
He growl'd an oath, and in an angry tone
Cursed the whole place and wish'd to be alone.
   Alone he was, the same dull scenes in view,
And still more gloomy in his sight they grew :
Though man he hated, yet employ'd alone
At bootless labour, he would swear and groan,   220
Cursing the shoals that glided by the spot,
And gulls that caught them when his arts could not.
   Cold nervous tremblings shook his sturdy frame,
And strange disease—he couldn't say the name ;
Wild were his dreams, and oft he rose in fright,
Waked by his view of horrors in the night,—
Horrors that would the sternest minds amaze,
Horrors that demons might be proud to raise :
And though he felt forsaken, grieved at heart,
To think he lived from all mankind apart ;   230
Yet, if a man approach'd, in terrors he would start.
   A winter pass'd since Peter saw the town,
And summer-lodgers were again come down ;
These, idly curious, with their glasses spied
The ships in bay as anchor'd for the tide,—
The river's craft,—the bustle of the quay,—
And sea-port views, which landmen love to see.
   One, up the river, had a man and boat
Seen day by day, now anchor'd, now afloat ;

Fisher he seem'd, yet used no net nor hook; 240
Of sea-fowl swimming by no heed he took,
But on the gliding waves still fix'd his lazy look:
At certain stations he would view the stream,
As if he stood bewilder'd in a dream,
Or that some power had chain'd him for a time,
To feel a curse or meditate on crime.

This known, some curious, some in pity went,
And others question'd—'Wretch, dost thou repent?'
He heard, he trembled, and in fear resign'd
His boat: new terror fill'd his restless mind; 250
Furious he grew, and up the country ran,
And there they seized him—a distemper'd man:—
Him we received, and to a parish-bed,
Follow'd and curs'd, the groaning man was led.

Here when they saw him, whom they used to shun,
A lost, lone man, so harass'd and undone;
Our gentle females, ever prompt to feel,
Perceived compassion on their anger steal;
His crimes they could not from their memories blot,
But they were grieved, and trembled at his lot. 260

A priest too came, to whom his words are told;
And all the signs they shudder'd to behold.
'Look! look!' they cried; 'his limbs with horror shake,
And as he grinds his teeth, what noise they make!
How glare his angry eyes, and yet he's not awake:
See! what cold drops upon his forehead stand,
And how he clenches that broad bony hand.'

The priest attending, found he spoke at times
As one alluding to his fears and crimes:
'It was the fall,' he mutter'd, 'I can show 270
The manner how—I never struck a blow:'—
And then aloud—'Unhand me, free my chain;
On oath, he fell—it struck him to the brain:—
Why ask my father?—that old man will swear
Against my life; besides, he wasn't there:—
What, all agreed?—Am I to die to-day?—
My Lord, in mercy, give me time to pray.'

Then, as they watch'd him, calmer he became,
And grew so weak he couldn't move his frame,
But murmuring spake,—while they could see and hear 280
The start of terror and the groan of fear;
See the large dew-beads on his forehead rise,
And the cold death-drop glaze his sunken eyes;
Nor yet he died, but with unwonted force
Seem'd with some fancied being to discourse:
He knew not us, or with accustom'd art
He hid the knowledge, yet exposed his heart;
'Twas part confession and the rest defence,
A madman's tale, with gleams of waking sense.

'I'll tell you all,' he said, 'the very day   290
When the old man first placed them in my way:
My father's spirit—he who always tried
To give me trouble, when he lived and died—
When he was gone, he could not be content
To see my days in painful labour spent,
But would appoint his meetings, and he made
Me watch at these, and so neglect my trade.
 ''Twas one hot noon, all silent, still, serene,
No living being had I lately seen;
I paddled up and down and dipp'd my net,   300
But (such his pleasure) I could nothing get,—
A father's pleasure, when his toil was done,
To plague and torture thus an only son!
And so I sat and look'd upon the stream,
How it ran on, and felt as in a dream:
But dream it was not; no!—I fix'd my eyes
On the mid stream and saw the spirits rise;
I saw my father on the water stand,
And hold a thin pale boy in either hand;
And there they glided ghastly on the top   310
Of the salt flood, and never touch'd a drop:
I would have struck them, but they knew th' intent,
And smiled upon the oar, and down they went.
 'Now, from that day, whenever I began
To dip my net, there stood the hard old man—
He and those boys: I humbled me and pray'd
They would be gone;—they heeded not, but stay'd:
Nor could I turn, nor would the boat go by,
But gazing on the spirits, there was I:
They bade me leap to death, but I was loth to die: 320
And every day, as sure as day arose,
Would these three spirits meet me ere the close;
To hear and mark them daily was my doom,
And "Come," they said, with weak, sad voices, "come."
To row away with all my strength I try'd,
But there were they, hard by me in the tide,
The three unbodied forms—and "Come," still "come," they
      cried.
 'Fathers should pity—but this old man shook
His hoary locks, and froze me by a look:
Thrice, when I struck them, through the water came 330
A hollow groan, that weaken'd all my frame:
"Father!" said I, "have mercy:"—He replied,
I know not what—the angry spirit lied,—
"Didst thou not draw thy knife?" said he:—'Twas
      true,
But I had pity and my arm withdrew:
He cried for mercy which I kindly gave,
But he has no compassion in his grave.

'There were three places, where they ever rose,—
The whole long river has not such as those,—
Places accursed, where, if a man remain,   340
He'll see the things which strike him to the brain;
And there they made me on my paddle lean,
And look at them for hours;—accursed scene!
When they would glide to that smooth eddy-space,
Then bid me leap and join them in the place;
And at my groans each little villain sprite
Enjoy'd my pains and vanish'd in delight.
'In one fierce summer-day, when my poor brain
Was burning hot, and cruel was my pain,
Then came this father-foe, and there he stood   350
With his two boys again upon the flood;
There was more mischief in their eyes, more glee
In their pale faces when they glared at me:
Still did they force me on the oar to rest,
And when they saw me fainting and oppress'd,
He, with his hand, the old man, scoop'd the flood,
And there came flame about him mix'd with blood;
He bade me stoop and look upon the place,
Then flung the hot-red liquor in my face;
Burning it blazed, and then I roar'd for pain,   360
I thought the demons would have turn'd my brain.
'Still there they stood, and forced me to behold
A place of horrors—they cannot be told—
Where the flood open'd, there I heard the shriek
Of tortured guilt—no earthly tongue can speak:
"All days alike! for ever!" did they say,
"And unremitted torments every day"—
Yes, so they said:'—But here he ceased and gazed
On all around, affrighten'd and amazed;
And still he tried to speak, and look'd in dread   370
Of frighten'd females gathering round his bed;
Then dropp'd exhausted, and appear'd at rest,
Till the strong foe the vital powers possess'd:
Then with an inward, broken voice he cried,
'Again they come,' and mutter'd as he died.

WILLIAM WORDSWORTH

LINES

COMPOSED A FEW MILES ABOVE TINTERN ABBEY, ON REVISITING
THE BANKS OF THE WYE DURING A TOUR.   JULY 13, 1798.

FIVE years have past ; five summers, with the length
Of five long winters ! and again I hear
These waters, rolling from their mountain-springs
With a soft inland murmur.—Once again
Do I behold these steep and lofty cliffs,
That on a wild secluded scene impress
Thoughts of more deep seclusion ; and connect
The landscape with the quiet of the sky.
The day is come when I again repose
Here, under this dark sycamore, and view   10
These plots of cottage-ground, these orchard-tufts,
Which at this season, with their unripe fruits,
Are clad in one green hue, and lose themselves
'Mid groves and copses. Once again I see
These hedge-rows, hardly hedge-rows, little lines
Of sportive wood run wild : these pastoral farms,
Green to the very door ; and wreaths of smoke
Sent up, in silence, from among the trees !
With some uncertain notice, as might seem
Of vagrant dwellers in the houseless woods,   20
Or of some Hermit's cave, where by his fire.
The Hermit sits alone.

                  These beauteous forms,
Through a long absence, have not been to me
As is a landscape to a blind man's eye :
But oft, in lonely rooms, and 'mid the din
Of towns and cities, I have owed to them,
In hours of weariness, sensations sweet,
Felt in the blood, and felt along the heart ;
And passing even into my purer mind,
With tranquil restoration :—feelings too   30
Of unremembered pleasure : such, perhaps,
As have no slight or trivial influence
On that best portion of a good man's life,
His little, nameless, unremembered, acts
Of kindness and of love. Nor less, I trust,
To them I may have owed another gift,
Of aspect more sublime ; that blessed mood,

In which the burthen of the mystery,
In which the heavy and the weary weight
Of all this unintelligible world,   40
Is lightened :—that serene and blessed mood,
In which the affections gently lead us on,—
Until, the breath of this corporeal frame
And even the motion of our human blood
Almost suspended, we are laid asleep
In body, and become a living soul :
While with an eye made quiet by the power
Of harmony, and the deep power of joy,
We see into the life of things.
                       If this
Be but a vain belief, yet, oh ! how oft—   50
In darkness and amid the many shapes
Of joyless daylight ; when the fretful stir
Unprofitable, and the fever of the world,
Have hung upon the beatings of my heart—
How oft, in spirit, have I turned to thee,
O sylvan Wye ! thou wanderer thro' the woods,
How often has my spirit turned to thee !

   And now, with gleams of half-extinguished thought,
With many recognitions dim and faint,
And somewhat of a sad perplexity,   60
The picture of the mind revives again :
While here I stand, not only with the sense
Of present pleasure, but with pleasing thoughts
That in this moment there is life and food
For future years. And so I dare to hope,
Though changed, no doubt, from what I was when first
I came among these hills ; when like a roe
I bounded o'er the mountains, by the sides
Of the deep rivers, and the lonely streams,
Wherever nature led : more like a man   70
Flying from something that he dreads, than one
Who sought the thing he loved. For nature then
(The coarser pleasures of my boyish days,
And their glad animal movements all gone by)
To me was all in all.—I cannot paint
What then I was. The sounding cataract
Haunted me like a passion : the tall rock,
The mountain, and the deep and gloomy wood,
Their colours and their forms, were then to me
An appetite ; a feeling and a love,   80
That had no need of a remoter charm,
By thought supplied, nor any interest
Unborrowed from the eye.—That time is past,
And all its aching joys are now no more,
And all its dizzy raptures. Not for this
Faint I, nor mourn nor murmur ; other gifts

Have followed ; for such loss, I would believe,
Abundant recompense.   For I have learned
To look on nature, not as in the hour
Of thoughtless youth ; but hearing oftentimes   90
The still, sad music of humanity,
Nor harsh nor grating, though of ample power
To chasten and subdue.   And I have felt
A presence that disturbs me with the joy
Of elevated thoughts ; a sense sublime
Of something far more deeply interfused,
Whose dwelling is the light of setting suns,
And the round ocean and the living air,
And the blue sky, and in the mind of man :
A motion and a spirit, that impels   100
All thinking things, all objects of all thought,
And rolls through all things.   Therefore am I still
A lover of the meadows and the woods,
And mountains ; and of all that we behold
From this green earth ; of all the mighty world
Of eye, and ear,—both what they half create,
And what perceive ; well pleased to recognise
In nature and the language of the sense
The anchor of my purest thoughts, the nurse,
The guide, the guardian of my heart, and soul   110
Of all my moral being.
                              Nor perchance,
If I were not thus taught, should I the more
Suffer my genial spirits to decay :
For thou art with me here upon the banks
Of this fair river ; thou my dearest Friend,
My dear, dear Friend ; and in thy voice I catch
The language of my former heart, and read
My former pleasures in the shooting lights
Of thy wild eyes.   Oh ! yet a little while
May I behold in thee what I was once,   120
My dear, dear Sister ! and this prayer I make,
Knowing that Nature never did betray
The heart that loved her ; 'tis her privilege,
Through all the years of this our life, to lead
From joy to joy : for she can so inform
The mind that is within us, so impress
With quietness and beauty, and so feed
With lofty thoughts, that neither evil tongues,
Rash judgments, nor the sneers of selfish men,
Nor greetings where no kindness is, nor all   130
The dreary intercourse of daily life,
Shall e'er prevail against us, or disturb
Our cheerful faith, that all which we behold
Is full of blessings Therefore let the moon
Shine on thee in thy solitary walk ;
And let the misty mountain-winds be free

To blow against thee : and, in after years,
When these wild ecstasies shall be matured
Into a sober pleasure ; when thy mind
Shall be a mansion for all lovely forms,　　　　　140
Thy memory be as a dwelling-place
For all sweet sounds and harmonies ; oh ! then,
If solitude, or fear, or pain, or grief,
Should be thy portion, with what healing thoughts
Of tender joy wilt thou remember me,
And these my exhortations ! Nor, perchance—
If I should be where I no more can hear
Thy voice, nor catch from thy wild eyes these gleams
Of past existence—wilt thou then forget
That on the banks of this delightful stream　　　150
We stood together ; and that I, so long
A worshipper of Nature, hither came
Unwearied in that service : rather say
With warmer love—oh ! with far deeper zeal
Of holier love.　Nor wilt thou then forget
That after many wanderings, many years
Of absence, these steep woods and lofty cliffs,
And this green pastoral landscape, were to me
More dear, both for themselves and for thy sake !

THE SIMPLON PASS

——————Brook and road
Were fellow-travellers in this gloomy Pass,
And with them did we journey several hours
At a slow step.　The immeasurable height
Of woods decaying, never to be decayed,
The stationary blasts of waterfalls,
And in the narrow rent, at every turn,
Winds thwarting winds bewildered and forlorn,
The torrents shooting from the clear blue sky,
The rocks that muttered close upon our ears,　　　10
Black drizzling crags that spake by the wayside
As if a voice were in them, the sick sight
And giddy prospect of the raving stream,
The unfettered clouds and region of the heavens,
Tumult and peace, the darkness and the light—
Were all like workings of one mind, the features
Of the same face, blossoms upon one tree,
Characters of the great Apocalypse,
The types and symbols of Eternity,
Of first, and last, and midst, and without end.　　　20

INFLUENCE OF NATURAL OBJECTS

IN CALLING FORTH AND STRENGTHENING THE IMAGINATION IN BOYHOOD AND EARLY YOUTH

WRITTEN IN GERMANY

WISDOM and Spirit of the universe!
Thou Soul, that art the Eternity of thought!
And giv'st to forms and images a breath
And everlasting motion! not in vain,
By day or star-light, thus from my first dawn
Of childhood didst thou intertwine for me
The passions that build up our human soul;
Not with the mean and vulgar works of Man;
But with high objects, with enduring things,
With life and nature; purifying thus   10
The elements of feeling and of thought,
And sanctifying by such discipline
Both pain and fear,—until we recognise
A grandeur in the beatings of the heart.

Nor was this fellowship vouchsafed to me
With stinted kindness. In November days,
When vapours rolling down the valleys made
A lonely scene more lonesome; among woods
At noon; and 'mid the calm of summer nights,
When, by the margin of the trembling lake,   20
Beneath the gloomy hills, homeward I went
In solitude, such intercourse was mine:
Mine was it in the fields both day and night,
And by the waters, all the summer long.
And in the frosty season, when the sun
Was set, and, visible for many a mile,
The cottage-windows through the twilight blazed,
I heeded not the summons: happy time
It was indeed for all of us; for me
It was a time of rapture! Clear and loud   30
The village-clock tolled six—I wheeled about,
Proud and exulting like an untired horse
That cares not for his home.—All shod with steel
We hissed along the polished ice, in games
Confederate, imitative of the chase
And woodland pleasures,—the resounding horn,
The pack loud-chiming, and the hunted hare.
So through the darkness and the cold we flew,
And not a voice was idle: with the din
Smitten, the precipices rang aloud;   40

The leafless trees and every icy crag
Tinkled like iron; while far-distant hills
Into the tumult sent an alien sound
Of melancholy, not unnoticed while the stars,
Eastward, were sparkling clear, and in the west
The orange sky of evening died away.

Not seldom from the uproar I retired
Into a silent bay, or sportively
Glanced sideway, leaving the tumultuous throng,
To cut across the reflex of a star;   50
Image that, flying still before me, gleamed
Upon the glassy plain: and oftentimes,
When we had given our bodies to the wind,
And all the shadowy banks on either side
Came sweeping through the darkness, spinning still
The rapid line of motion, then at once
Have I, reclining back upon my heels,
Stopped short; yet still the solitary cliffs
Wheeled by me—even as if the earth had rolled
With visible motion her diurnal round!   60
Behind me did they stretch in solemn train,
Feebler and feebler, and I stood and watched
Till all was tranquil as a summer sea.

THERE WAS A BOY

THERE was a Boy; ye knew him well, ye cliffs
And islands of Winander!—many a time,
At evening, when the earliest stars began
To move along the edges of the hills,
Rising or setting, would he stand alone,
Beneath the trees, or by the glimmering lake;
And there, with fingers interwoven, both hands
Pressed closely palm to palm and to his mouth
Uplifted, he, as through an instrument,
Blew mimic hootings to the silent owls,   10
That they might answer him.—And they would shout
Across the watery vale, and shout again,
Responsive to his call,—with quivering peals,
And long halloos, and screams, and echoes loud
Redoubled and redoubled; concourse wild
Of jocund din! And, when there came a pause
Of silence such as baffled his best skill:
Then sometimes, in that silence, while he hung
Listening, a gentle shock of mild surprise
Has carried far into his heart the voice   20
Of mountain-torrents; or the visible scene

Would enter unawares into his mind
With all its solemn imagery, its rocks,
Its woods, and that uncertain heaven received
Into the bosom of the steady lake.

   This boy was taken from his mates, and died
In childhood, ere he was full twelve years old.
Pre-eminent in beauty is the vale
Where he was born and bred : the churchyard hangs
Upon a slope above the village-school ;   30
And through that churchyard when my way has led
On summer-evenings, I believe that there
A long half-hour together I have stood
Mute—looking at the grave in which he lies !

NUTTING

————————————It seems a day
(I speak of one from many singled out)
One of those heavenly days that cannot die ;
When, in the eagerness of boyish hope,
I left our cottage-threshold, sallying forth
With a huge wallet o'er my shoulders slung,
A nutting-crook in hand ; and turned my steps
Tow'rd some far-distant wood, a Figure quaint,
Tricked out in proud disguise of cast-off weeds
Which for that service had been husbanded,   10
By exhortation of my frugal Dame—
Motley accoutrement, of power to smile
At thorns, and brakes, and brambles,—and in truth
More ragged than need was ! O'er pathless rocks,
Through beds of matted fern, and tangled thickets,
Forcing my way, I came to one dear nook
Unvisited, where not a broken bough
Drooped with its withered leaves, ungracious sign
Of devastation ; but the hazels rose
Tall and erect, with tempting clusters hung,   20
A virgin scene !—A little while I stood,
Breathing with such suppression of the heart
As joy delights in ; and with wise restraint
Voluptuous, fearless of a rival, eyed
The banquet ;—or beneath the trees I sate
Among the flowers, and with the flowers I played ;
A temper known to those who, after long
And weary expectation, have been blest
With sudden happiness beyond all hope.
Perhaps it was a bower beneath whose leaves   30
The violets of five seasons re-appear
And fade, unseen by any human eye ;

Where fairy water-breaks do murmur on
For ever ; and I saw the sparkling foam,
And—with my cheek on one of those green stones
That, fleeced with moss, under the shady trees,
Lay round me, scattered like a flock of sheep—
I heard the murmur and the murmuring sound,
In that sweet mood when pleasure loves to pay
Tribute to ease ; and, of its joy secure,   40
The heart luxuriates with indifferent things,
Wasting its kindliness on stocks and stones,
And on the vacant air.   Then up I rose,
And dragged to earth both branch and bough, with crash
And merciless ravage : and the shady nook
Of hazels, and the green and mossy bower,
Deformed and sullied, patiently gave up
Their quiet being : and unless I now
Confound my present feelings with the past,
Ere from the mutilated bower I turned   50
Exulting, rich beyond the wealth of kings,
I felt a sense of pain when I beheld
The silent trees, and saw the intruding sky.—
Then, dearest Maiden, move along these shades
In gentleness of heart ; with gentle hand
Touch—for there is a spirit in the woods.

MICHAEL

A PASTORAL POEM

If from the public way you turn your steps
Up the tumultuous brook of Green-head Ghyll,
You will suppose that with an upright path
Your feet must struggle ; in such bold ascent
The pastoral mountains front you, face to face.
But, courage ! for around that boisterous brook
The mountains have all opened out themselves,
And made a hidden valley of their own.
No habitation can be seen ; but they
Who journey thither find themselves alone   10
With a few sheep, with rocks and stones, and kites
That overhead are sailing in the sky.
It is in truth an utter solitude ;
Nor should I have made mention of this Dell
But for one object which you might pass by,
Might see and notice not.   Beside the brook
Appears a straggling heap of unhewn stones !
And to that simple object appertains
A story—unenriched with strange events,
Yet not unfit, I deem, for the fireside,   20
Or for the summer shade.   It was the first

Of those domestic tales that spake to me
Of Shepherds, dwellers in the valleys, men
Whom I already loved ;—not verily
For their own sakes, but for the fields and hills
Where was their occupation and abode.
And hence this Tale, while I was yet a Boy,
Careless of books, yet having felt the power
Of Nature, by the gentle agency
Of natural objects, led me on to feel   30
For passions that were not my own, and think
(At random and imperfectly indeed)
On man, the heart of man, and human life.
Therefore, although it be a history
Homely and rude, I will relate the same
For the delight of a few natural hearts ;
And, with yet fonder feeling, for the sake
Of youthful Poets, who among these hills
Will be my second self when I am gone.

UPON the forest-side in Grasmere Vale   40
There dwelt a Shepherd, Michael was his name ;
An old man, stout of heart, and strong of limb.
His bodily frame had been from youth to age
Of an unusual strength : his mind was keen,
Intense, and frugal, apt for all affairs,
And in his shepherd's calling he was prompt
And watchful more than ordinary men.
Hence had he learned the meaning of all winds,
Of blasts of every tone ; and oftentimes,
When others heeded not, He heard the South   50
Make subterraneous music, like the noise
Of bagpipers on distant Highland hills.
The Shepherd, at such warning, of his flock
Bethought him, and he to himself would say,
' The winds are now devising work for me ! '
And, truly, at all times, the storm, that drives
The traveller to a shelter, summoned him
Up to the mountains : he had been alone
Amid the heart of many thousand mists,
That came to him, and left him, on the heights.   60
So lived he till his eightieth year was past.
And grossly that man errs, who should suppose
That the green valleys, and the streams and rocks,
Were things indifferent to the Shepherd's thoughts.
Fields, where with cheerful spirits he had breathed
The common air ; hills, which with vigorous step
He had so often climbed ; which had impressed
So many incidents upon his mind
Of hardship, skill or courage, joy or fear ;
Which, like a book, preserved the memory   70
Of the dumb animals, whom he had saved,

Had fed or sheltered, linking to such acts
The certainty of honourable gain;
Those fields, those hills—what could they less? had laid
Strong hold on his affections, were to him
A pleasurable feeling of blind love,
The pleasure which there is in life itself.

His days had not been passed in singleness.
His Helpmate was a comely matron, old—
Though younger than himself full twenty years.   80
She was a woman of a stirring life,
Whose heart was in her house: two wheels she had
Of antique form; this large, for spinning wool;
That small, for flax; and, if one wheel had rest,
It was because the other was at work.
The Pair had but one inmate in their house,
An only Child, who had been born to them
When Michael, telling o'er his years, began
To deem that he was old,—in shepherd's phrase,
With one foot in the grave. This only Son,   90
With two brave sheep-dogs tried in many a storm,
The one of an inestimable worth,
Made all their household. I may truly say,
That they were as a proverb in the vale
For endless industry. When day was gone,
And from their occupations out of doors
The Son and Father were come home, even then,
Their labour did not cease; unless when all
Turned to the cleanly supper-board, and there,
Each with a mess of pottage and skimmed milk,   100
Sat round the basket piled with oaten cakes,
And their plain home-made cheese. Yet when the meal
Was ended, Luke (for so the Son was named)
And his old Father both betook themselves
To such convenient work as might employ
Their hands by the fire-side; perhaps to card
Wool for the Housewife's spindle, or repair
Some injury done to sickle, flail, or scythe,
Or other implement of house or field.

Down from the ceiling, by the chimney's edge,   110
That in our ancient uncouth country style
With huge and black projection over-browed
Large space beneath, as duly as the light
Of day grew dim the Housewife hung a lamp;
An aged utensil, which had performed
Service beyond all others of its kind.
Early at evening did it burn—and late,
Surviving comrade of uncounted hours,
Which, going by from year to year, had found,
And left, the couple neither gay perhaps   120

Nor cheerful, yet with objects and with hopes,
Living a life of eager industry.
And now, when Luke had reached his eighteenth year,
There by the light of this old lamp they sate,
Father and Son, while far into the night
The Housewife plied her own peculiar work,
Making the cottage through the silent hours
Murmur as with the sound of summer flies.
This light was famous in its neighbourhood,
And was a public symbol of the life   130
That thrifty Pair had lived. For, as it chanced,
Their cottage on a plot of rising ground
Stood single, with large prospect, north and south,
High into Easedale, up to Dunmail-Raise,
And westward to the village near the lake ;
And from this constant light, so regular,
And so far seen, the House itself, by all
Who dwelt within the limits of the vale,
Both old and young, was named THE EVENING STAR.

Thus living on through such a length of years,   140
The Shepherd, if he loved himself, must needs
Have loved his Helpmate ; but to Michael's heart
This son of his old age was yet more dear—
Less from instinctive tenderness, the same
Fond spirit that blindly works in the blood of all—
Than that a child, more than all other gifts
That earth can offer to declining man,
Brings hope with it, and forward-looking thoughts,
And stirrings of inquietude, when they
By tendency of nature needs must fail.   150
Exceeding was the love he bare to him,
His heart and his heart's joy ! For oftentimes
Old Michael, while he was a babe in arms,
Had done him female service, not alone
For pastime and delight, as is the use
Of fathers, but with patient mind enforced
To acts of tenderness ; and he had rocked
His cradle, as with a woman's gentle hand.

And in a later time, ere yet the Boy
Had put on boy's attire, did Michael love,   160
Albeit of a stern unbending mind,
To have the Young-one in his sight, when he
Wrought in the field, or on his shepherd's stool
Sate with a fettered sheep before him stretched
Under the large old oak, that near his door
Stood single, and, from matchless depth of shade,
Chosen for the Shearer's covert from the sun,
Thence in our rustic dialect was called
The CLIPPING TREE, a name which yet it bears.

There, while they two were sitting in the shade,   170
With others round them, earnest all and blithe,
Would Michael exercise his heart with looks
Of fond correction and reproof bestowed
Upon the Child, if he disturbed the sheep
By catching at their legs, or with his shouts
Scared them, while they lay still beneath the shears.

And when by Heaven's good grace the boy grew up
A healthy Lad, and carried in his cheek
Two steady roses that were five years old ;
Then Michael from a winter coppice cut   180
With his own hand a sapling, which he hooped
With iron, making it throughout in all
Due requisites a perfect shepherd's staff,
And gave it to the Boy ; wherewith equipt
He as a watchman oftentimes was placed
At gate or gap, to stem or turn the flock ;
And, to his office prematurely called,
There stood the urchin, as you will divine,
Something between a hindrance and a help ;
And for this cause not always, I believe,   190
Receiving from his Father hire of praise ;
Though nought was left undone which staff, or voice,
Or looks, or threatening gestures, could perform.

But soon as Luke, full ten years old, could stand
Against the mountain blasts ; and to the heights,
Not fearing toil, nor length of weary ways,
He with his Father daily went, and they
Were as companions, why should I relate
That objects which the Shepherd loved before
Were dearer now ? that from the Boy there came   200
Feelings and emanations—things which were
Light to the sun and music to the wind ;
And that the old Man's heart seemed born again ?

Thus in his Father's sight the Boy grew up :
And now, when he had reached his eighteenth year,
He was his comfort and his daily hope.

While in this sort the simple household lived
From day to day, to Michael's ear there came
Distressful tidings. Long before the time
Of which I speak, the Shepherd had been bound   210
In surety for his brother's son, a man
Of an industrious life, and ample means ;
But unforeseen misfortunes suddenly
Had prest upon him ; and old Michael now
Was summoned to discharge the forfeiture,
A grievous penalty, but little less

Than half his substance. This unlooked-for claim,
At the first hearing, for a moment took
More hope out of his life than he supposed
That any old man ever could have lost.   220
As soon as he had armed himself with strength
To look his trouble in the face, it seemed
The Shepherd's sole resource to sell at once
A portion of his patrimonial fields.
Such was his first resolve; he thought again,
And his heart failed him. 'Isabel,' said he,
Two evenings after he had heard the news,
'I have been toiling more than seventy years,
And in the open sunshine of God's love
Have we all lived; yet, if these fields of ours   230
Should pass into a stranger's hand, I think
That I could not lie quiet in my grave.
Our lot is a hard lot; the sun himself
Has scarcely been more diligent than I;
And I have lived to be a fool at last
To my own family. An evil man
That was, and made an evil choice, if he
Were false to us; and, if he were not false,
There are ten thousand to whom loss like this
Had been no sorrow. I forgive him;—but   240
'Twere better to be dumb than to talk thus.

    When I began, my purpose was to speak
Of remedies and of a cheerful hope.
Our Luke shall leave us, Isabel; the land
Shall not go from us, and it shall be free;
He shall possess it, free as is the wind
That passes over it. We have, thou know'st,
Another kinsman—he will be our friend
In this distress. He is a prosperous man,
Thriving in trade—and Luke to him shall go,   250
And with his kinsman's help and his own thrift
He quickly will repair this loss, and then
He may return to us. If here he stays,
What can be done? Where every one is poor,
What can be gained?'
                        At this the old Man paused,
And Isabel sat silent, for her mind
Was busy, looking back into past times.
There's Richard Bateman, thought she to herself,
He was a parish-boy—at the church-door
They made a gathering for him, shillings, pence,   260
And halfpennies, wherewith the neighbours bought
A basket, which they filled with pedlar's wares;
And, with this basket on his arm, the lad
Went up to London, found a master there,
Who, out of many, chose the trusty boy
To go and overlook his merchandise

Beyond the seas; where he grew wondrous rich,
And left estates and monies to the poor,
And, at his birth-place, built a chapel floored
With marble, which he sent from foreign lands.   270
These thoughts, and many others of like sort,
Passed quickly through the mind of Isabel,
And her face brightened. The old Man was glad,
And thus resumed :—' Well, Isabel ! this scheme
These two days has been meat and drink to me.
Far more than we have lost is left us yet.
   We have enough—I wish indeed that I
Were younger ;—but this hope is a good hope.
Make ready Luke's best garments, of the best
Buy for him more, and let us send him forth   280
To-morrow, or the next day, or to-night :
   If he *could* go, the Boy should go to-night.

   Here Michael ceased, and to the fields went forth
With a light heart. The Housewife for five days
Was restless morn and night, and all day long
Wrought on with her best fingers to prepare
Things needful for the journey of her son.
But Isabel was glad when Sunday came
To stop her in her work : for, when she lay
By Michael's side, she through the last two nights   290
Heard him, how he was troubled in his sleep :
And when they rose at morning she could see
That all his hopes were gone. That day at noon
She said to Luke, while they two by themselves
Were sitting at the door, ' Thou must not go :
We have no other Child but thee to lose,
None to remember—do not go away,
For if thou leave thy Father he will die.'
The Youth made answer with a jocund voice ;
And Isabel, when she had told her fears,   300
Recovered heart. That evening her best fare
Did she bring forth, and all together sat
Like happy people round a Christmas fire.

   With daylight Isabel resumed her work ;
And all the ensuing week the house appeared
As cheerful as a grove in Spring : at length
The expected letter from their kinsman came,
With kind assurances that he would do
His utmost for the welfare of the Boy ;
To which, requests were added, that forthwith   310
He might be sent to him. Ten times or more
The letter was read over ; Isabel
Went forth to show it to the neighbours round ;
Nor was there at that time on English land
A prouder heart than Luke's. When Isabel

Had to her house returned, the old Man said,
'He shall depart to-morrow.' To this word
The Housewife answered, talking much of things
Which, if at such short notice he should go,
Would surely be forgotten. But at length   320
She gave consent, and Michael was at ease.

Near the tumultuous brook of Green-head Ghyll,
In that deep valley, Michael had designed
To build a Sheep-fold; and, before he heard
The tidings of his melancholy loss,
For this same purpose he had gathered up
A heap of stones, which by the streamlet's edge
Lay thrown together, ready for the work.
With Luke that evening thitherward he walked:
And soon as they had reached the place he stopped,   330
And thus the old Man spake to him:—'My son,
To-morrow thou wilt leave me: with full heart
I look upon thee, for thou art the same
That wert a promise to me ere thy birth,
And all thy life hast been my daily joy.
I will relate to thee some little part
Of our two histories; 'twill do thee good
When thou art from me, even if I should touch
On things thou canst not know of.——After thou
First cam'st into the world—as oft befalls   340
To new-born infants—thou didst sleep away
Two days, and blessings from thy Father's tongue
Then fell upon thee. Day by day passed on,
And still I loved thee with increasing love.
Never to living ear came sweeter sounds
Than when I heard thee by our own fireside
First uttering, without words, a natural tune;
While thou, a feeding babe, didst in thy joy
Sing at thy Mother's breast. Month followed month,
And in the open fields my life was passed   350
And on the mountains; else I think that thou
Hadst been brought up upon thy Father's knees.
But we were playmates, Luke: among these hills,
As well thou knowest, in us the old and young
Have played together, nor with me didst thou
Lack any pleasure which a boy can know.'
Luke had a manly heart; but at these words
He sobbed aloud. The old Man grasped his hand.
And said, 'Nay, do not take it so—I see
That these are things of which I need not speak.   360
—Even to the utmost I have been to thee
A kind and a good Father: and herein
I but repay a gift which I myself
Received at others' hands; for, though now old
Beyond the common life of man, I still

Remember them who loved me in my youth.
Both of them sleep together : here they lived,
As all their Forefathers had done ; and, when
At length their time was come, they were not loth
To give their bodies to the family mould.   370
I wished that thou shouldst live the life they lived,
But 'tis a long time to look back, my Son,
And see so little gain from threescore years.
These fields were burthened when they came to me ;
Till I was forty years of age, not more
Than half of my inheritance was mine.
I toiled and toiled ; God blessed me in my work,
And till these three weeks past the land was free.
—It looks as if it never could endure
Another Master. Heaven forgive me, Luke,   380
If I judge ill for thee, but it seems good
That thou shouldst go.'
                   At this the old Man paused ;
Then, pointing to the stones near which they stood,
Thus, after a short silence, he resumed :
'This was a work for us ; and now, my Son,
It is a work for me. But, lay one stone—
Here, lay it for me, Luke, with thine own hands.
Nay, Boy, be of good hope ;—we both may live
To see a better day. At eighty-four
I still am strong and hale ;—do thou thy part ;   390
I will do mine.—I will begin again
With many tasks that were resigned to thee :
Up to the heights, and in among the storms,
Will I without thee go again, and do
All works which I was wont to do alone,
Before I knew thy face.—Heaven bless thee, Boy !
Thy heart these two weeks has been beating fast
With many hopes ; it should be so—yes—yes—
I knew that thou couldst never have a wish
To leave me, Luke : thou hast been bound to me   400
Only by links of love : when thou art gone,
What will be left to us !—But I forget
My purposes. Lay now the corner-stone,
As I requested ; and hereafter, Luke,
When thou art gone away, should evil men
Be thy companions, think of me, my Son,
And of this moment ; hither turn thy thoughts,
And God will strengthen thee : amid all fear
And all temptation, Luke, I pray that thou
May'st bear in mind the life thy Fathers lived,   410
Who, being innocent, did for that cause
Bestir them in good deeds. Now, fare thee well—
When thou return'st, thou in this place wilt see
A work which is not here : a covenant
'Twill be between us ; but, whatever fate

Befall thee, I shall love thee to the last,
And bear thy memory with me to the grave.'

The Shepherd ended here ; and Luke stooped down,
And, as his Father had requested, laid
The first stone of the Sheep-fold. At the sight   420
The old Man's grief broke from him ; to his heart
He pressed his Son, he kissèd him and wept ;
And to the house together they returned.
—Hushed was that House in peace, or seeming peace,
Ere the night fell:—with morrow's dawn the Boy
Began his journey, and, when he had reached
The public way, he put on a bold face ;
And all the neighbours, as he passed their doors,
Came forth with wishes and with farewell prayers,
That followed him till he was out of sight.   430

A good report did from their Kinsman come,
Of Luke and his well-doing : and the Boy
Wrote loving letters, full of wondrous news,
Which, as the Housewife phrased it, were throughout
' The prettiest letters that were ever seen.'
Both parents read them with rejoicing hearts.
So, many months passed on : and once again
The Shepherd went about his daily work
With confident and cheerful thoughts ; and now
Sometimes when he could find a leisure hour   440
He to that valley took his way, and there
Wrought at the Sheep-fold. Meantime Luke began
To slacken in his duty ; and, at length,
He in the dissolute city gave himself
To evil courses : ignominy and shame
Fell on him, so that he was driven at last
To seek a hiding-place beyond the seas.

There is a comfort in the strength of love ;
'Twill make a thing endurable, which else
Would overset the brain, or break the heart :   450
I have conversed with more than one who well
Remember the old Man, and what he was
Years after he had heard this heavy news.
His bodily frame had been from youth to age
Of an unusual strength. Among the rocks
He went, and still looked up to sun and cloud,
And listened to the wind ; and, as before,
Performed all kinds of labour for his sheep,
And for the land, his small inheritance.
And to that hollow dell from time to time   460
Did he repair, to build the Fold of which
His flock had need. 'Tis not forgotten yet
The pity which was then in every heart

For the old Man—and 'tis believed by all
That many and many a day he thither went,
And never lifted up a single stone.

There, by the Sheep-fold, sometimes was he seen
Sitting alone, or with his faithful Dog,
Then old, beside him, lying at his feet.
The length of full seven years, from time to time,   470
He at the building of this Sheep-fold wrought,
And left the work unfinished when he died.
Three years, or little more, did Isabel
Survive her Husband : at her death the estate
Was sold, and went into a stranger's hand.
The Cottage which was named THE EVENING STAR
Is gone—the ploughshare has been through the ground
On which it stood ; great changes have been wrought
In all the neighbourhood :—yet the oak is left
That grew beside their door ; and the remains   480
Of the unfinished Sheep-fold may be seen
Beside the boisterous brook of Green-head Ghyll.

RESOLUTION AND INDEPENDENCE

I

THERE was a roaring in the wind all night ;
The rain came heavily and fell in floods ;
But now the sun is rising calm and bright ;
The birds are singing in the distant woods ;
Over his own sweet voice the Stock-dove broods ;
The Jay makes answer as the Magpie chatters ;
And all the air is filled with pleasant noise of waters.

II

All things that love the sun are out of doors ;
The sky rejoices in the morning's birth ;
The grass is bright with rain-drops ;—on the moors   10
The hare is running races in her mirth ;
And with her feet she from the plashy earth
Raises a mist ; that, glittering in the sun,
Runs with her all the way, wherever she doth run.

III

I was a Traveller then upon the moor ;
I saw the hare that raced about with joy ;
I heard the woods and distant waters roar ;
Or heard them not, as happy as a boy :
The pleasant season did my heart employ :
My old remembrances went from me wholly ;   20
And all the ways of men, so vain and melancholy.

IV

But, as it sometimes chanceth, from the might
Of joy in minds that can no further go,
As high as we have mounted in delight
In our dejection do we sink as low ;
To me that morning did it happen so ;
And fears and fancies thick upon me came ;
Dim sadness—and blind thoughts, I knew not, nor could name.

V

I heard the sky-lark warbling in the sky ;
And I bethought me of the playful hare :   30
Even such a happy Child of earth am I ;
Even as these blissful creatures do I fare ;
Far from the world I walk, and from all care ;
But there may come another day to me—
Solitude, pain of heart, distress, and poverty.

VI

My whole life I have lived in pleasant thought,
As if life's business were a summer mood ;
As if all needful things would come unsought
To genial faith, still rich in genial good ;
But how can He expect that others should   40
Build for him, sow for him, and at his call
Love him, who for himself will take no heed at all ?

VII

I thought of Chatterton, the marvellous Boy,
The sleepless Soul that perished in his pride ;
Of Him who walked in glory and in joy
Following his plough, along the mountain-side :
By our own spirits are we deified :
We Poets in our youth begin in gladness ;
But thereof come in the end despondency and madness.

VIII

Now, whether it were by peculiar grace,   50
A leading from above, a something given,
Yet it befell that, in this lonely place,
When I with these untoward thoughts had striven,
Beside a pool bare to the eye of heaven
I saw a Man before me unawares :
The oldest man he seemed that ever wore grey hairs.

IX

As a huge stone is sometimes seen to lie
Couched on the bald top of an eminence ;
Wonder to all who do the same espy,
By what means it could thither come, and whence ;   60
So that it seems a thing endued with sense :
Like a sea-beast crawled forth, that on a shelf
Of rock or sand reposeth, there to sun itself ;

X

Such seemed this Man, not all alive nor dead,
Nor all asleep—in his extreme old age:
His body was bent double, feet and head
Coming together in life's pilgrimage;
As if some dire constraint of pain, or rage
Of sickness felt by him in times long past,
A more than human weight upon his frame had cast.   70

XI

Himself he propped, limbs, body, and pale face,
Upon a long grey staff of shaven wood:
And, still as I drew near with gentle pace,
Upon the margin of that moorish flood
Motionless as a cloud the old Man stood,
That heareth not the loud winds when they call;
And moveth all together, if it move at all.

XII

At length, himself unsettling, he the pond
Stirred with his staff, and fixedly did look
Upon the muddy water, which he conned,   80
As if he had been reading in a book:
And now a stranger's privilege I took;
And, drawing to his side, to him did say,
'This morning gives us promise of a glorious day.'

XIII

A gentle answer did the old Man make,
In courteous speech which forth he slowly drew:
And him with further words I thus bespake,
'What occupation do you there pursue?
This is a lonesome place for one like you.'
Ere he replied, a flash of mild surprise   90
Broke from the sable orbs of his yet-vivid eyes.

XIV

His words came feebly, from a feeble chest,
But each in solemn order followed each,
With something of a lofty utterance drest—
Choice word and measured phrase, above the reach
Of ordinary men; a stately speech;
Such as grave Livers do in Scotland use,
Religious men, who give to God and man their dues.

XV

He told, that to these waters he had come
To gather leeches, being old and poor: 100
Employment hazardous and wearisome!
And he had many hardships to endure:
From pond to pond he roamed, from moor to moor;
Housing, with God's good help, by choice or chance;
And in this way he gained an honest maintenance.

XVI

The old Man still stood talking by my side;
But now his voice to me was like a stream
Scarce heard; nor word from word could I divide;
And the whole body of the Man did seem
Like one whom I had met with in a dream;   110
Or like a man from some far region sent,
To give me human strength, by apt admonishment.

XVII

My former thoughts returned: the fear that kills;
And hope that is unwilling to be fed;
Cold, pain, and labour, and all fleshly ills;
And mighty Poets in their misery dead.
—Perplexed, and longing to be comforted,
My question eagerly did I renew,
'How is it that you live, and what is it you do?'

XVIII

He with a smile did then his words repeat;   120
And said that, gathering leeches, far and wide
He travelled; stirring thus about his feet
The waters of the pools where they abide.
'Once I could meet with them on every side;
But they have dwindled long by slow decay;
Yet still I persevere, and find them where I may.'

XIX

While he was talking thus, the lonely place,
The old Man's shape, and speech—all troubled me:
In my mind's eye I seemed to see him pace
About the weary moors continually,   130
Wandering about alone and silently.
While I these thoughts within myself pursued,
He, having made a pause, the same discourse renewed.

XX

And soon with this he other matter blended,
Cheerfully uttered, with demeanour kind,
But stately in the main; and, when he ended,
I could have laughed myself to scorn to find
In that decrepit Man so firm a mind.
'God,' said I, 'be my help and stay secure;
I'll think of the Leech-gatherer on the lonely moor!' 140

YEW-TREES

THERE is a Yew-tree, pride of Lorton Vale,
Which to this day stands single, in the midst
Of its own darkness, as it stood of yore :
Not loth to furnish weapons for the bands
Of Umfraville or Percy ere they marched
To Scotland's heaths ; or those that crossed the sea
And drew their sounding bows at Azincour,
Perhaps at earlier Crecy, or Poictiers.
Of vast circumference and gloom profound
This solitary Tree ! a living thing   10
Produced too slowly ever to decay ;
Of form and aspect too magnificent
To be destroyed. But worthier still of note
Are those fraternal Four of Borrowdale,
Joined in one solemn and capacious grove ;
Huge trunks ! and each particular trunk a growth
Of intertwisted fibres serpentine
Up-coiling, and inveterately convolved ;
Nor uninformed with Phantasy, and looks
That threaten the profane ; a pillared shade,   20
Upon whose grassless floor of red-brown hue,
By sheddings from the pining umbrage tinged
Perennially—beneath whose sable roof
Of boughs, as if for festal purpose decked
With unrejoicing berries—ghostly Shapes
May meet at noontide ; Fear and trembling Hope,
Silence and Foresight ; Death the Skeleton
And Time the Shadow ;—there to celebrate,
As in a natural temple scattered o'er
With altars undisturbed of mossy stone,   30
United worship ; or in mute repose
To lie, and listen to the mountain flood
Murmuring from Glaramara's inmost caves.

AT THE GRAVE OF BURNS

SEVEN YEARS AFTER HIS DEATH

I SHIVER, Spirit fierce and bold,
At thought of what I now behold :
As vapours breathed from dungeons cold
    Strike pleasure dead,
So sadness comes from out the mould
    Where Burns is laid.

And have I then thy bones so near.
And thou forbidden to appear ?
As if it were thyself that 's here
     I shrink with pain ;   10
And both my wishes and my fear
      Alike are vain.

Off weight—nor press on weight !—away
Dark thoughts !—they came, but not to stay ;
With chastened feelings would I pay
     The tribute due
To him, and aught that hides his clay
      From mortal view.

Fresh as the flower, whose modest worth
He sang, his genius 'glinted' forth,   20
Rose like a star that touching earth,
     For so it seems,
Doth glorify its humble birth
      With matchless beams.

The piercing eye, the thoughtful brow,
The struggling heart, where be they now ?—
Full soon the Aspirant of the plough,
     The prompt, the brave,
Slept, with the obscurest, in the low
      And silent grave.   30

I mourned with thousands, but as one
More deeply grieved, for He was gone
Whose light I hailed when first it shone,
     And showed my youth
How Verse may build a princely throne
      On humble truth.

Alas ! where'er the current tends,
Regret pursues and with it blends,—
Huge Criffel's hoary top ascends   40
     By Skiddaw seen,—
Neighbours we were, and loving friends
      We might have been ;

True friends though diversely inclined ;
But heart with heart and mind with mind,
Where the main fibres are entwined,
     Through Nature's skill,
May even by contraries be joined
      More closely still.

The tear will start, and let it flow ;
Thou 'poor Inhabitant below,'   50
At this dread moment—even so—
     Might we together
Have sate and talked where gowans blow,
      Or on wild heather.

What treasures would have then been placed
Within my reach ; of knowledge graced
By fancy what a rich repast !
        But why go on ?—
Oh ! spare to sweep, thou mournful blast,
       His grave grass-grown.　　　　　60

There, too, a Son, his joy and pride,
(Not three weeks past the Stripling died,)
Lies gathered to his Father's side,
        Soul-moving sight !
Yet one to which is not denied
       Some sad delight.

For *he* is safe, a quiet bed
Hath early found among the dead,
Harboured where none can be misled,
        Wronged, or distrest ;　　　　　70
And surely here it may be said
       That such are blest.

And oh for Thee, by pitying grace
Checked oft-times in a devious race,
May He, who halloweth the place
        Where Man is laid,
Receive thy Spirit in the embrace
       For which it prayed !

Sighing I turned away ; but ere
Night fell I heard, or seemed to hear,　　80
Music that sorrow comes not near,
        A ritual hymn,
Chanted in love that casts out fear
       By Seraphim.

THOUGHTS

SUGGESTED THE DAY FOLLOWING, ON THE BANKS OF NITH, NEAR THE POET'S RESIDENCE

Too frail to keep the lofty vow
That must have followed when his brow
Was wreathed—' The Vision ' tells us how—
        With holly spray,
He faltered, drifted to and fro,
       And passed away.

Well might such thoughts, dear Sister, throng
Our minds when, lingering all too long,
Over the grave of Burns we hung
    In social grief—   10
Indulged as if it were a wrong
    To seek relief.

But, leaving each unquiet theme
Where gentlest judgments may misdeem,
And prompt to welcome every gleam
    Of good and fair,
Let us beside the limpid Stream
    Breathe hopeful air.

Enough of sorrow, wreck, and blight;
Think rather of those moments bright   20
When to the consciousness of right
    His course was true,
When Wisdom prospered in his sight
    And virtue grew.

Yes, freely let our hearts expand,
Freely as in youth's season bland,
When side by side, his Book in hand,
    We wont to stray,
Our pleasure varying at command
    Of each sweet Lay.   30

How oft inspired must he have trod
These pathways, yon far-stretching road!
There lurks his home; in that Abode,
    With mirth elate,
Or in his nobly-pensive mood,
    The Rustic sate.

Proud thoughts that Image overawes,
Before it humbly let us pause,
And ask of Nature from what cause
    And by what rules   40
She trained her Burns to win applause
    That shames the Schools.

Through busiest street and loneliest glen
Are felt the flashes of his pen;
He rules 'mid winter snows, and when
    Bees fill their hives;
Deep in the general heart of men
    His power survives.

What need of fields in some far clime
Where Heroes, Sages, Bards sublime,   50
And all that fetched the flowing rhyme
    From genuine springs,
Shall dwell together till old Time
    Folds up his wings?

Sweet Mercy! to the gates of Heaven
This Minstrel lead, his sins forgiven ;
The rueful conflict, the heart riven
          With vain endeavour,
And memory of Earth's bitter leaven,
          Effaced for ever.   60

But why to Him confine the prayer,
When kindred thoughts and yearnings bear
On the frail heart the purest share
          With all that live ?—
The best of what we do and are,
          Just God, forgive !

FRENCH REVOLUTION

AS IT APPEARED TO ENTHUSIASTS AT ITS COMMENCEMENT

Oh ! pleasant exercise of hope and joy !
For mighty were the auxiliars which then stood
Upon our side, we who were strong in love !
Bliss was it in that dawn to be alive,
But to be young was very heaven !—Oh ! times,
In which the meagre, stale, forbidding ways
Of custom, law, and statute, took at once
The attraction of a country in romance !
When Reason seemed the most to assert her rights,
When most intent on making of herself   10
A prime Enchantress—to assist the work
Which then was going forward in her name !
Not favoured spots alone, but the whole earth,
The beauty wore of promise, that which sets
(As at some moment might not be unfelt
Among the bowers of paradise itself)
The budding rose above the rose full blown.
What temper at the prospect did not wake
To happiness unthought of ? The inert
Were roused, and lively natures rapt away !   20
They who had fed their childhood upon dreams,
The playfellows of fancy, who had made
All powers of swiftness, subtilty, and strength
Their ministers,—who in lordly wise had stirred
Among the grandest objects of the sense,
And dealt with whatsoever they found there
As if they had within some lurking right
To wield it ;—they, too, who, of gentle mood,
Had watched all gentle motions, and to these
Had fitted their own thoughts, schemers more mild, 30

And in the region of their peaceful selves ;—
Now was it that both found, the meek and lofty
Did both find, helpers to their heart's desire,
And stuff at hand, plastic as they could wish ;
Were called upon to exercise their skill,
Not in Utopia, subterranean fields,
Or some secreted island, Heaven knows where !
But in the very world, which is the world
Of all of us,—the place where in the end
We find our happiness, or not at all !   40

CHARACTER OF THE HAPPY WARRIOR

WHO is the happy Warrior ? Who is he
That every man in arms should wish to be ?
—It is the generous Spirit, who, when brought
Among the tasks of real life, hath wrought
Upon the plan that pleased his boyish thought :
Whose high endeavours are an inward light
That makes the path before him always bright :
Who, with a natural instinct to discern
What knowledge can perform, is diligent to learn,
Abides by this resolve, and stops not there,   10
But makes his moral being his prime care ;
Who, doomed to go in company with Pain,
And Fear, and Bloodshed, miserable train !
Turns his necessity to glorious gain ;
In face of these doth exercise a power
Which is our human nature's highest dower ;
Controls them and subdues, transmutes, bereaves
Of their bad influence, and their good receives :
By objects, which might force the soul to abate
Her feeling, rendered more compassionate ;   20
Is placable—because occasions rise
So often that demand such sacrifice ;
More skilful in self-knowledge, even more pure,
As tempted more ; more able to endure,
As more exposed to suffering and distress ;
Thence, also, more alive to tenderness.
—'Tis he whose law is reason : who depends
Upon that law as on the best of friends ;
Whence, in a state where men are tempted still
To evil for a guard against worse ill,   30
And what in quality or act is best
Doth seldom on a right foundation rest,
He labours good on good to fix, and owes
To virtue every triumph that he knows :
—Who, if he rise to station of command,
Rises by open means ; and there will stand

On honourable terms, or else retire,
And in himself possess his own desire;
Who comprehends his trust, and to the same
Keeps faithful with a singleness of aim;⁣   40
And therefore does not stoop, nor lie in wait
For wealth, or honours, or for worldly state;
Whom they must follow; on whose head must fall,
Like showers of manna, if they come at all:
Whose powers shed round him in the common strife,
Or mild concerns of ordinary life,
A constant influence, a peculiar grace;
But who, if he be called upon to face
Some awful moment to which Heaven has joined
Great issues, good or bad for human kind,   50
Is happy as a Lover; and attired
With sudden brightness, like a Man inspired;
And, through the heat of conflict, keeps the law
In calmness made, and sees what he foresaw;
Or if an unexpected call succeed,
Come when it will, is equal to the need:
—He who, though thus endued as with a sense
And faculty for storm and turbulence,
Is yet a Soul whose master-bias leans
To homefelt pleasures and to gentle scenes;   60
Sweet images! which, wheresoe'er he be,
Are at his heart; and such fidelity
It is his darling passion to approve;
More brave for this, that he hath much to love:——
'Tis, finally, the Man, who, lifted high,
Conspicuous object in a Nation's eye,
Or left unthought-of in obscurity,—
Who, with a toward or untoward lot,
Prosperous or adverse, to his wish or not—
Plays, in the many games of life, that one   70
Where what he most doth value must be won:
Whom neither shape of danger can dismay,
Nor thought of tender happiness betray;
Who, not content that former worth stand fast,
Looks forward, persevering to the last,
From well to better, daily self-surpast:
Who, whether praise of him must walk the earth
For ever, and to noble deeds give birth,
Or he must fall, to sleep without his fame,
And leave a dead unprofitable name—   80
Finds comfort in himself and in his cause;
And, while the mortal mist is gathering, draws
His breath in confidence of Heaven's applause:
This is the happy Warrior; this is He
That every Man in arms should wish to be.

ODE

INTIMATIONS OF IMMORTALITY FROM RECOLLEC-
TIONS OF EARLY CHILDHOOD

> The Child is father of the Man;
> And I could wish my days to be
> Bound each to each by natural piety.

I

THERE was a time when meadow, grove, and stream,
The earth, and every common sight,
        To me did seem
        Apparelled in celestial light,
The glory and the freshness of a dream.
It is not now as it hath been of yore ;—
        Turn wheresoe'er I may
        By night or day,
The things which I have seen I now can see no more.

II

        The Rainbow comes and goes,   10
        And lovely is the Rose,
        The Moon doth with delight
    Look round her when the heavens are bare,
        Waters on a starry night
        Are beautiful and fair ;
    The sunshine is a glorious birth ;
    But yet I know, where'er I go,
That there hath past away a glory from the earth.

III

Now, while the birds thus sing a joyous song,
    And while the young lambs bound   20
        As to the tabor's sound,
To me alone there came a thought of grief :
A timely utterance gave that thought relief,
        And I again am strong :
The cataracts blow their trumpets from the steep :
No more shall grief of mine the season wrong ;
I hear the Echoes through the mountains throng,
The Winds come to me from the fields of sleep,
        And all the earth is gay ;
            Land and sea   30
    Give themselves up to jollity,
        And with the heart of May

Doth every Beast keep holiday ;—
  Thou Child of Joy,
Shout round me, let me hear thy shouts, thou happy Shepherd-
      boy !

IV

Ye blessèd Creatures, I have heard the call
  Ye to each other make ; I see
The heavens laugh with you in your jubilee :
    My heart is at your festival,
    My head hath its coronal,   40
The fulness of your bliss, I feel—I feel it all.
      Oh evil day ! if I were sullen
      While Earth herself is adorning,
        This sweet May-morning,
      And the Children are culling
        On every side,
      In a thousand valleys far and wide,
      Fresh flowers ; while the sun shines warm,
And the Babe leaps up on his Mother's arm:—
      I hear, I hear, with joy I hear !   50
  —But there 's a Tree, of many, one,
A single Field which I have looked upon,
Both of them speak of something that is gone:
      The Pansy at my feet
      Doth the same tale repeat :
Whither is fled the visionary gleam ?
Where is it now, the glory and the dream ?

V

Our birth is but a sleep and a forgetting :
The Soul that rises with us, our life's Star,
      Hath had elsewhere its setting,   60
      And cometh from afar :
      Not in entire forgetfulness,
      And not in utter nakedness,
But trailing clouds of glory do we come
      From God, who is our home :
Heaven lies about us in our infancy !
Shades of the prison-house begin to close
      Upon the growing Boy,
But He beholds the light, and whence it flows,
      He sees it in his joy ;   70
The Youth, who daily farther from the east
      Must travel, still is Nature's Priest,
      And by the vision splendid
      Is on his way attended ;
At length the Man perceives it die away,
And fade into the light of common day.

VI

Earth fills her lap with pleasures of her own;
Yearnings she hath in her own natural kind,
And, even with something of a Mother's mind.
          And no unworthy aim,
          The homely Nurse doth all she can
To make her Foster-child, her Inmate Man,
          Forget the glories he hath known,
And that imperial palace whence he came.   80

VII

Behold the Child among his new-born blisses,
A six years' Darling of a pigmy size!
See, where 'mid work of his own hand he lies,
Fretted by sallies of his mother's kisses,
With light upon him from his father's eyes!
See, at his feet, some little plan or chart,   90
Some fragment from his dream of human life,
Shaped by himself with newly-learned art;
          A wedding or a festival,
          A mourning or a funeral;
          And this hath now his heart,
          And unto this he frames his song:
          Then will he fit his tongue
To dialogues of business, love, or strife;
          But it will not be long
    •   Ere this be thrown aside,   100
          And with new joy and pride
The little Actor cons another part;
Filling from time to time his 'humorous stage'
With all the Persons, down to palsied Age,
That Life brings with her in her equipage;
          As if his whole vocation
          Were endless imitation.

VIII

Thou, whose exterior semblance doth belie
          Thy Soul's immensity;
Thou best Philosopher, who yet dost keep   110
Thy heritage, thou Eye among the blind,
That, deaf and silent, read'st the eternal deep,
Haunted for ever by the eternal mind,—
          Mighty Prophet! Seer blest!
          On whom those truths do rest,
Which we are toiling all our lives to find,
In darkness lost, the darkness of the grave;
Thou, over whom thy Immortality
Broods like the Day, a Master o'er a Slave,
A Presence which is not to be put by;   120

Thou little Child, yet glorious in the might
Of heaven-born freedom on thy being's height,
Why with such earnest pains dost thou provoke
The years to bring the inevitable yoke,
Thus blindly with thy blessedness at strife ?
Full soon thy Soul shall have her earthly freight,
And custom lie upon thee with a weight,
Heavy as frost, and deep almost as life !

IX

O joy ! that in our embers
Is something that doth live,   130
That nature yet remembers
What was so fugitive !
The thought of our past years in me doth breed
Perpetual benediction : not indeed
For that which is most worthy to be blest—
Delight and liberty, the simple creed
Of Childhood, whether busy or at rest,
With new-fledged hope still fluttering in his breast :—
Not for these I raise
The song of thanks and praise ;   140
But for those obstinate questionings
Of sense and outward things,
Fallings from us, vanishings ;
Blank misgivings of a Creature
Moving about in worlds not realised,
High instincts before which our mortal Nature
Did tremble like a guilty Thing surprised :
But for those first affections,
Those shadowy recollections,
Which, be they what they may,   150
Are yet the fountain-light of all our day,
Are yet a master-light of all our seeing ;
Uphold us, cherish, and have power to make
Our noisy years seem moments in the being
Of the eternal Silence : truths that wake,
To perish never :
Which neither listlessness, nor mad endeavour,
Nor Man nor Boy,
Nor all that is at enmity with joy,
Can utterly abolish or destroy !   160
Hence in a season of calm weather
Though inland far we be,
Our Souls have sight of that immortal sea
Which brought us hither,
Can in a moment travel thither,
And see the Children sport upon the shore,
And hear the mighty waters rolling evermore.

X

Then sing, ye Birds, sing, sing a joyous song!
    And let the young Lambs bound
    As to the tabor's sound! 170
We in thought will join your throng,
    Ye that pipe and ye that play,
    Ye that through your hearts to-day
    Feel the gladness of the May!
What though the radiance which was once so bright
Be now for ever taken from my sight,
    Though nothing can bring back the hour
Of splendour in the grass, of glory in the flower;
    We will grieve not, rather find
    Strength in what remains behind; 180
    In the primal sympathy
    Which having been must ever be;
    In the soothing thoughts that spring
    Out of human suffering;
    In the faith that looks through death,
In years that bring the philosophic mind.

XI

And O, ye Fountains, Meadows, Hills, and Groves,
Forebode not any severing of our loves!
Yet in my heart of hearts I feel your might;
I only have relinquished one delight 190
To live beneath your more habitual sway.
I love the Brooks which down their channels fret,
Even more than when I tripped lightly as they;
The innocent brightness of a new-born Day
    Is lovely yet;
The Clouds that gather round the setting sun
Do take a sober colouring from an eye
That hath kept watch o'er man's mortality;
Another race hath been, and other palms are won.
Thanks to the human heart by which we live, 200
Thanks to its tenderness, its joys, and fears,
To me the meanest flower that blows can give
Thoughts that do often lie too deep for tears.

LAODAMIA

' WITH sacrifice before the rising morn
Vows have I made by fruitless hope inspired;
And from the infernal Gods, 'mid shades forlorn
Of night, my slaughtered Lord have I required:
Celestial pity I again implore;—
Restore him to my sight—great Jove, restore!'

So speaking, and by fervent love endowed
With faith, the Suppliant heavenward lifts her hands ;
While, like the sun emerging from a cloud,
Her countenance brightens—and her eye expands ;   10
Her bosom heaves and spreads, her stature grows ;
And she expects the issue in repose.

O terror ! what hath she perceived ?—O joy !
What doth she look on ?—whom doth she behold ?
Her Hero slain upon the beach of Troy ?
His vital presence ? his corporeal mould ?
It is—if sense deceive her not—'tis He !
And a God leads him, wingèd Mercury !

Mild Hermes spake—and touched her with his wand
That calms all fear ; ' Such grace hath crowned thy prayer,
Laodamía ! that at Jove's command   21
Thy Husband walks the paths of upper air :
He comes to tarry with thee three hours' space ;
Accept the gift, behold him face to face ! '

Forth sprang the impassioned Queen her Lord to clasp ;
Again that consummation she essayed ;
But unsubstantial Form eludes her grasp
As often as that eager grasp was made.
The Phantom parts—but parts to re-unite,
And re-assume his place before her sight.   30

' Protesiláus, lo ! thy guide is gone !
Confirm, I pray, the vision with thy voice :
This is our palace,—yonder is thy throne ;
Speak, and the floor thou tread'st on will rejoice.
Not to appal me have the gods bestowed
This precious boon ; and blest a sad abode.'

' Great Jove, Laodamía ! doth not leave
His gifts imperfect :—Spectre though I be,
I am not sent to scare thee or deceive ;
But in reward of thy fidelity.   40
And something also did my worth obtain ;
For fearless virtue bringeth boundless gain.

' Thou knowest, the Delphic oracle foretold
That the first Greek who touched the Trojan strand
Should die ; but me the threat could not withhold :
A generous cause a victim did demand ;
And forth I leapt upon the sandy plain ;
A self-devoted chief—by Hector slain.'

' Supreme of Heroes—bravest, noblest, best !
Thy matchless courage I bewail no more,   50
Which then, when tens of thousands were deprest
By doubt, propelled thee to the fatal shore ;
Thou found'st—and I forgive thee—here thou art—
A nobler counsellor than my poor heart.

But thou, though capable of sternest deed,
Wert kind as resolute, and good as brave;
And he, whose power restores thee, hath decreed
Thou shouldst elude the malice of the grave:
Redundant are thy locks, thy lips as fair
As when their breath enriched Thessalian air.   60

'No Spectre greets me,—no vain Shadow this;
Come, blooming Hero, place thee by my side!
Give, on this well-known couch, one nuptial kiss
To me, this day, a second time thy bride!'
Jove frowned in heaven: the conscious Parcae threw
Upon those roseate lips a Stygian hue.

'This visage tells thee that my doom is past:
Nor should the change be mourned, even if the joys
Of sense were able to return as fast
And surely as they vanish. Earth destroys   70
Those raptures duly—Erebus disdains:
Calm pleasures there abide—majestic pains.

'Be taught, O faithful Consort, to control
Rebellious passion: for the Gods approve
The depth, and not the tumult, of the soul;
A fervent, not ungovernable, love.
Thy transports moderate; and meekly mourn
When I depart, for brief is my sojourn—'

'Ah wherefore?—Did not Hercules by force
Wrest from the guardian Monster of the tomb   80
Alcestis, a reanimated corse,
Given back to dwell on earth in vernal bloom?
Medea's spells dispersed the weight of years,
And Aeson stood a youth 'mid youthful peers.

'The Gods to us are merciful—and they
Yet further may relent: for mightier far
Than strength of nerve and sinew, or the sway
Of magic potent over sun and star,
Is love, though oft to agony distrest,
And though his favourite seat be feeble woman's breast.   90

'But if thou goest, I follow—' 'Peace!' he said,—
She looked upon him and was calmed and cheered;
The ghastly colour from his lips had fled;
In his deportment, shape, and mien, appeared
Elysian beauty, melancholy grace,
Brought from a pensive though a happy place.

He spake of love, such love as Spirits feel
In worlds whose course is equable and pure;
No fears to beat away—no strife to heal—
The past unsighed for, and the future sure;   100
Spake of heroic arts in graver mood
Revived, with finer harmony pursued;

Of all that is most beauteous—imaged there
In happier beauty ; more pellucid streams,
An ampler ether, a diviner air,
And fields invested with purpureal gleams ;
Climes which the sun, who sheds the brightest day
Earth knows, is all unworthy to survey.

Yet there the Soul shall enter which hath earned
That privilege by virtue.—' Ill', said he,   110
' The end of man's existence I discerned,
Who from ignoble games and revelry
Could draw, when we had parted, vain delight,
While tears were thy best pastime, day and night ;

' And while my youthful peers before my eyes
(Each hero following his peculiar bent)
Prepared themselves for glorious enterprise
By martial sports,—or, seated in the tent,
Chieftains and kings in council were detained ;
What time the fleet at Aulis lay enchained.   120

' The wished-for wind was given :—I then revolved
The oracle, upon the silent sea ;
And, if no worthier led the way, resolved
That, of a thousand vessels, mine should be
The foremost prow in pressing to the strand,—
Mine the first blood that tinged the Trojan sand.

' Yet bitter, oft-times bitter, was the pang
When of thy loss I thought, belovèd Wife !
On thee too fondly did my memory hang,
And on the joys we shared in mortal life,—   130
The paths which we had trod—these fountains, flowers ;
My new-planned cities, and unfinished towers.

' But should suspense permit the Foe to cry,
" Behold they tremble !—haughty their array,
Yet of their number no one dares to die ? "
In soul I swept the indignity away :
Old frailties then recurred :—but lofty thought,
In act embodied, my deliverance wrought.

' And Thou, though strong in love, art all too weak
In reason, in self-government too slow ;   140
I counsel thee by fortitude to seek
Our blest re-union in the shades below.
The invisible world with thee hath sympathised ;
Be thy affections raised and solemnised.

' Learn, by a mortal yearning, to ascend—
Seeking a higher object. Love was given,
Encouraged, sanctioned, chiefly for that end ;
For this the passion to excess was driven—
That self might be annulled : her bondage prove
The fetters of a dream opposed to love.'—   150

Aloud she shrieked! for Hermes reappears!
Round the dear Shade she would have clung—'tis vain:
The hours are past—too brief had they been years;
And him no mortal effort can detain:
Swift, toward the realms that know not earthly day,
He through the portal takes his silent way,
And on the palace-floor a lifeless corse She lay.

Thus, all in vain exhorted and reproved,
She perished; and, as for a wilful crime,
By the just Gods whom no weak pity moved,   160
Was doomed to wear out her appointed time,
Apart from happy Ghosts, that gather flowers
Of blissful quiet 'mid unfading bowers.

—Yet tears to human suffering are due;
And mortal hopes defeated and o'erthrown
Are mourned by man, and not by man alone,
As fondly he believes.—Upon the side
Of Hellespont (such faith was entertained)
A knot of spiry trees for ages grew
From out the tomb of him for whom she died;   170
And ever, when such stature they had gained
That Ilium's walls were subject to their view,
The trees' tall summits withered at the sight;
A constant interchange of growth and blight!

COMPOSED UPON AN EVENING OF
EXTRAORDINARY SPLENDOUR AND BEAUTY

I

HAD this effulgence disappeared
With flying haste, I might have sent,
Among the speechless clouds, a look
Of blank astonishment;
But 'tis endued with power to stay,
And sanctify one closing day,
That frail Mortality may see—
What is?—ah no, but what *can* be!
Time was when field and watery cove
With modulated echoes rang,   10
While choirs of fervent Angels sang
Their vespers in the grove;
Or, crowning, star-like, each some sovereign height,
Warbled, for heaven above and earth below,
Strains suitable to both.—Such holy rite,
Methinks, if audibly repeated now

From hill or valley, could not move
Sublimer transport, purer love,
Than doth this silent spectacle—the gleam—
The shadow—and the peace supreme!   20

II

No sound is uttered,—but a deep
And solemn harmony pervades
The hollow vale from steep to steep,
And penetrates the glades.
Far-distant images draw nigh,
Called forth by wondrous potency
Of beamy radiance, that imbues
Whate'er it strikes with gem-like hues!
In vision exquisitely clear,
Herds range along the mountain side;   30
And glistening antlers are descried;
And gilded flocks appear.
Thine is the tranquil hour, purpureal Eve!
But long as god-like wish, or hope divine,
Informs my spirit, ne'er can I believe
That this magnificence is wholly thine!
—From worlds not quickened by the sun
A portion of the gift is won;
An intermingling of Heaven's pomp is spread
On ground which British shepherds tread!   40

III

And if there be whom broken ties
Afflict, or injuries assail,
Yon hazy ridges to their eyes
Present a glorious scale,
Climbing suffused with sunny air,
To stop—no record hath told where!
And tempting Fancy to ascend,
And with immortal Spirits blend!
—Wings at my shoulders seem to play;
But, rooted here, I stand and gaze   50
On those bright steps that heavenward raise
Their practicable way.
Come forth, ye drooping old men, look abroad,
And see to what fair countries ye are bound!
And if some traveller, weary of his road,
Hath slept since noon-tide on the grassy ground,
Ye Genii! to his covert speed;
And wake him with such gentle heed
As may attune his soul to meet the dower
Bestowed on this transcendent hour!   60

IV

Such hues from their celestial Urn
Were wont to stream before mine eye,
Where'er it wandered in the morn
Of blissful infancy.
This glimpse of glory, why renewed ?
Nay, rather speak with gratitude ;
For, if a vestige of those gleams
Survived, 'twas only in my dreams.
Dread Power ! whom peace and calmness serve
No less than Nature's threatening voice,　　　　　　70
If aught unworthy be my choice,
From THEE if I would swerve ;
Oh, let Thy grace remind me of the light
Full early lost, and fruitlessly deplored ;
Which, at this moment, on my waking sight
Appears to shine, by miracle restored ;
My soul, though yet confined to earth,
Rejoices in a second birth !
—'Tis past, the visionary splendour fades ;
And night approaches with her shades.　　　　　　80

WRITTEN IN A BLANK LEAF OF
MACPHERSON'S OSSIAN

OFT have I caught, upon a fitful breeze,
Fragments of far-off melodies,
With ear not coveting the whole,
A part so charmed the pensive soul :
While a dark storm before my sight
Was yielding, on a mountain height
Loose vapours have I watched, that won
Prismatic colours from the sun ;
Nor felt a wish that heaven would show
The image of its perfect bow.　　　　　　10
What need, then, of these finished Strains ?
Away with counterfeit Remains !
An abbey in its lone recess,
A temple of the wilderness,
Wrecks though they be, announce with feeling
The majesty of honest dealing.
Spirit of Ossian ! if imbound
In language thou may'st yet be found,
If aught (intrusted to the pen
Or floating on the tongues of men,　　　　　　20
Albeit shattered and impaired)
Subsist thy dignity to guard,

In concert with memorial claim
Of old grey stone, and high-born name
That cleaves to rock or pillared cave
Where moans the blast, or beats the wave,
Let Truth, stern arbitress of all,
Interpret that Original,
And for presumptuous wrongs atone ;—
Authentic words be given, or none !   30
Time is not blind ;—yet He, who spares
Pyramid pointing to the stars,
Hath preyed with ruthless appetite
On all that marked the primal flight
Of the poetic ecstasy
Into the land of mystery.
No tongue is able to rehearse
One measure, Orpheus ! of thy verse ;
Musaeus, stationed with his lyre
Supreme among the Elysian quire,   40
Is, for the dwellers upon earth,
Mute as a lark ere morning's birth.
Why grieve for these, though past away
The music, and extinct the lay ?
When thousands, by severer doom,
Full early to the silent tomb
Have sunk, at Nature's call ; or strayed
From hope and promise, self-betrayed ;
The garland withering on their brows ;
Stung with remorse for broken vows ;   50
Frantic—else how might they rejoice ?
And friendless, by their own sad choice !

Hail, Bards of mightier grasp ! on you
I chiefly call, the chosen Few,
Who cast not off the acknowledged guide,
Who faltered not, nor turned aside ;
Whose lofty genius could survive
Privation, under sorrow thrive ;
In whom the fiery Muse revered
The symbol of a snow-white beard,   60
Bedewed with meditative tears
Dropped from the lenient cloud of years.

Brothers in soul ! though distant times
Produced you nursed in various climes,
Ye, when the orb of life had waned,
A plenitude of love retained :
Hence, while in you each sad regret
By corresponding hope was met,
Ye lingered among human kind,
Sweet voices for the passing wind ;   70
Departing sunbeams, loth to stop,
Though smiling on the last hill-top !

Such to the tender-hearted maid
Even ere her joys begin to fade;
Such, haply, to the rugged chief
By fortune crushed, or tamed by grief;
Appears, on Morven's lonely shore,
Dim-gleaming through imperfect lore,
The Son of Fingal; such was blind
Maeonides of ampler mind;   80
Such Milton, to the fountain-head
Of glory by Urania led!

SAMUEL TAYLOR COLERIDGE

THE RIME OF THE ANCIENT MARINER

IN SEVEN PARTS

Facile credo, plures esse Naturas invisibiles quam visibiles in rerum universitate. Sed horum omnium familiam quis nobis enarrabit ? et gradus et cognationes et discrimina et singulorum munera ? Quid agunt ? quae loca habitant ? Harum rerum notitiam semper ambivit ingenium humanum, nunquam attigit. Juvat, interea, non diffiteor, quandoque in animo, tanquam in tabula, majoris et melioris mundi imaginem contemplari : ne mens assuefacta hodiernae vitae minutiis se contrahat nimis, et tota subsidat in pusillas cogitationes. Sed veritati interea invigilandum est, modusque servandus, ut certa ab incertis, diem a nocte, distinguamus.—T. BURNET, *Archaeol. Phil.* p. 68.

ARGUMENT

How a Ship having passed the Line was driven by storms to the cold Country towards the South Pole ; and how from thence she made her course to the tropical Latitude of the Great Pacific Ocean ; and of the strange things that befell ; and in what manner the Ancyent Marinere came back to his own Country. [1798.]

PART THE FIRST

An ancient Mariner meeteth three Gallants bidden to a wedding-feast, and detaineth one.

It is an ancient Mariner,
And he stoppeth one of three.
' By thy long grey beard and glittering eye,
Now wherefore stopp'st thou me ?

' The Bridegroom's doors are opened wide,
And I am next of kin ;
The guests are met, the feast is set :
May'st hear the merry din.'

He holds him with his skinny hand,
' There was a ship,' quoth he.   10
' Hold off ! unhand me, greybeard loon ! '
Eftsoons his hand dropt he.

The wedding-guest is spell-bound by the eye of the old

He holds him with his glittering eye—
The Wedding-Guest stood still,
And listens like a three years' child :
The Mariner hath his will.

The Wedding-Guest sat on a stone :
He cannot choose but hear ;
And thus spake on that ancient man,
The bright-eyed Mariner.   20

sea-faring
man, and con-
strained to
hear his tale.

The ship was cheered, the harbour cleared,
Merrily did we drop
Below the kirk, below the hill,
Below the lighthouse top.

The sun came up upon the left,
Out of the sea came he !
And he shone bright, and on the right
Went down into the sea.

Higher and higher every day,
Till over the mast at noon—   30
The Wedding-Guest here beat his breast,
For he heard the loud bassoon.

The Mariner
tells how the
ship sailed
southward
with a good
wind and fair
weather, till it
reached the
line.

The bride hath paced into the hall,
Red as a rose is she ;
Nodding their heads before her goes
The merry minstrelsy.

The wedding-
guest heareth
the bridal
music ; but
the mariner
continueth his
tale.

The Wedding-Guest he beat his breast,
Yet he cannot choose but hear ;
And thus spake on that ancient man,
The bright-eyed Mariner.   40

And now the Storm-blast came, and he
Was tyrannous and strong :
He struck with his o'ertaking wings,
And chased us south along.

The ship driven
by a storm
toward the
South Pole.

With sloping masts and dipping prow,
As who pursued with yell and blow
Still treads the shadow of his foe,
And forward bends his head,
The ship drove fast, loud roared the blast,
And southward aye we fled.   50

And now there came both mist and snow
And it grew wondrous cold :
And ice, mast-high, came floating by,
As green as emerald.

The land of ice,
and of fearful
sounds, where
no living thing
was to be seen.

And through the drifts the snowy clifts
Did send a dismal sheen :
Nor shapes of men nor beasts we ken—
The ice was all between.

The ice was here, the ice was there,
The ice was all around :   60
It cracked and growled, and roared and howled,
Like noises in a swound !

Till a great
sea-bird, called
the Albatross,
came through
the snow-fog,
and was re-
ceived with
great joy and
hospitality.

At length did cross an Albatross :
Thorough the fog it came ;
As if it had been a Christian soul,
We hailed it in God's name.

It ate the food it ne'er had eat,
And round and round it flew.
The ice did split with a thunder-fit;
The helmsman steered us through !   70

And lo ! the
Albatross
proveth a bird
of good omen,
and followeth
the ship as it
returned
northward
through fog
and floating
ice.

And a good south wind sprung up behind ;
The Albatross did follow,
And every day, for food or play,
Came to the mariner's hollo !

In mist or cloud, on mast or shroud,
It perched for vespers nine ;
Whiles all the night, through fog-smoke white,
Glimmered the white moonshine.

The ancient
Mariner in-
hospitably
killeth the
pious bird of
good omen.

' God save thee, ancient Mariner !
From the fiends, that plague thee thus !—   80
Why look'st thou so ? '—With my cross-bow
I shot the Albatross.

PART THE SECOND

The Sun now rose upon the right :
Out of the sea came he,
Still hid in mist, and on the left
Went down into the sea.

And the good south wind still blew behind,
But no sweet bird did follow,
Nor any day for food or play
Came to the mariner's hollo !   90

His shipmates
cry out against
the ancient
Mariner, for
killing the bird
of good luck.

And I had done an hellish thing,
And it would work 'em woe :
For all averred, I had killed the bird
That made the breeze to blow.
Ah wretch ! said they, the bird to slay,
That made the breeze to blow !

But when the
fog cleared off,
they justify
the same, and
thus make
themselves ac-
complices in
the crime.

Nor dim nor red, like God's own head,
The glorious Sun uprist :
Then all averred, I had killed the bird
That brought the fog and mist.   100
'Twas right, said they, such birds to slay,
That bring the fog and mist.

The fair breeze blew, the white foam flew,
The furrow followed free;
We were the first that ever burst
Into that silent sea.

Down dropt the breeze, the sails dropt down,
'Twas sad as sad could be;
And we did speak only to break
The silence of the sea!   110

All in a hot and copper sky,
The bloody Sun, at noon,
Right up above the mast did stand,
No bigger than the Moon.

Day after day, day after day,
We stuck, nor breath nor motion;
As idle as a painted ship
Upon a painted ocean.

Water, water, everywhere,
And all the boards did shrink;   120
Water, water, everywhere,
Nor any drop to drink.

The very deep did rot: O Christ!
That ever this should be!
Yea, slimy things did crawl with legs
Upon the slimy sea.

About, about, in reel and rout
The death-fires danced at night;
The water, like a witch's oils,
Burnt green, and blue and white.   130

And some in dreams assured were
Of the spirit that plagued us so;
Nine fathom deep he had followed us
From the land of mist and snow.

planet, neither departed souls nor angels; concerning whom the learned Jew, Josephus, and the Platonic Constantinopolitan, Michael Psellus, may be consulted. They are very numerous, and there is no climate or element without one or more.

And every tongue, through utter drought,
Was withered at the root;
We could not speak, no more than if
We had been choked with soot.

Ah! well-a-day! what evil looks
Had I from old and young!   140
Instead of the cross, the Albatross
About my neck was hung.

the ancient Mariner: in sign whereof they hang the dead sea-bird round his neck.

The fair breeze continues; the ship enters the Pacific Ocean and sails northward, even till it reaches the Line.

The ship hath been suddenly becalmed.

And the Albatross begins to be avenged.

A spirit had followed them; one of the invisible inhabitants of this

The shipmates, in their sore distress, would fain throw the whole guilt on

PART THE THIRD

There passed a weary time. Each throat
Was parched, and glazed each eye.
A weary time ! a weary time !
How glazed each weary eye,
When looking westward, I beheld
A something in the sky.

The ancient Mariner beholdeth a sign in the element afar off.

At first it seemed a little speck,
And then it seemed a mist ;   150
It moved and moved, and took at last
A certain shape, I wist.

A speck, a mist, a shape, I wist !
And still it neared and neared :
As if it dodged a water-sprite,
It plunged and tacked and veered.

At its nearer approach, it seemeth him to be a ship; and at a dear ransom he freeth his speech from the bonds of thirst.
A flash of joy;

With throats unslaked, with black lips baked,
We could not laugh nor wail ;
Through utter drought all dumb we stood !
I bit my arm, I sucked the blood,   160
And cried, A sail ! a sail !

With throats unslaked, with black lips baked,
Agape they heard me call :
Gramercy ! they for joy did grin,
And all at once their breath drew in,
As they were drinking all.

And horror follows. For can it be a ship that comes onward without wind or tide ?

See ! See ! (I cried) she tacks no more !
Hither to work us weal ;
Without a breeze, without a tide,
She steadies with upright keel !   170

The western wave was all aflame.
The day was well nigh done !
Almost upon the western wave
Rested the broad bright Sun ;
When that strange shape drove suddenly
Betwixt us and the Sun.

It seemeth him but the skeleton of a ship.
And its ribs are seen as bars on the face of the setting Sun.

And straight the Sun was flecked with bars,
(Heaven's Mother send us grace !)
As if through a dungeon-grate he peered
With broad and burning face.   180

Alas ! (thought I, and my heart beat loud)
How fast she nears and nears !
Are those *her* sails that glance in the Sun,
Like restless gossameres !

Are those *her* ribs through which the Sun
Did peer, as through a grate?
And is that Woman all her crew?
Is that a Death? and are there two?
Is Death that woman's mate?

Her lips were red, *her* looks were free,   190
Her locks were yellow as gold:
Her skin was as white as leprosy,
The Nightmare Life-in-Death was she,
Who thicks man's blood with cold.

The naked hulk alongside came,
And the twain were casting dice;
'The game is done! I've won, I've won!'
Quoth she, and whistles thrice.

The Sun's rim dips; the stars rush out:
At one stride comes the dark;   200
With far-heard whisper, o'er the sea,
Off shot the spectre-bark.

We listened and looked sideways up!
Fear at my heart, as at a cup,
My life-blood seemed to sip!
The stars were dim, and thick the night,
The steersman's face by his lamp gleamed white;
From the sails the dew did drip—
Till clomb above the eastern bar
The horned Moon, with one bright star   210
Within the nether tip.

One after one, by the star-dogged Moon,
Too quick for groan or sigh,
Each turned his face with a ghastly pang,
And cursed me with his eye.

Four times fifty living men,
(And I heard nor sigh nor groan)
With heavy thump, a lifeless lump,
They dropped down one by one.

The souls did from their bodies fly,—   220
They fled to bliss or woe!
And every soul, it passed me by,
Like the whizz of my cross-bow!

PART THE FOURTH

'I fear thee, ancient Mariner!
I fear thy skinny hand!
And thou art long, and lank, and brown,
As is the ribbed sea-sand.

Marginal glosses:

The Spectre-Woman and her Death-mate, and no other on board the skeleton-ship. Like vessel, like crew!

Death and Life-in-Death have diced for the ship's crew, and she (the latter) winneth the ancient Mariner.

No twilight within the courts of the Sun.

At the rising of the Moon,

one after another,

his shipmates drop down dead;

but Life-in-Death begins her work on the ancient Mariner.

The wedding-guest feareth that a spirit is talking to him;

'I fear thee and thy glittering eye,
And thy skinny hand, so brown.'—
Fear not, fear not, thou Wedding-Guest!   230
This body dropt not down.

But the ancient Mariner assureth him of his bodily life, and proceedeth to relate his horrible penance.

Alone, alone, all, all alone,
Alone on a wide wide sea!
And never a saint took pity on
My soul in agony.

He despiseth the creatures of the calm. And envieth that they should live, and so many lie dead.

The many men, so beautiful!
And they all dead did lie:
And a thousand thousand slimy things
Lived on; and so did I.

I looked upon the rotting sea,   240
And drew my eyes away;
I looked upon the rotting deck,
And there the dead men lay.

I looked to heaven, and tried to pray;
But or ever a prayer had gusht,
A wicked whisper came, and made
My heart as dry as dust.

I closed my lids, and kept them close,
And the balls like pulses beat;   249
For the sky and the sea, and the sea and the sky
Lay like a load on my weary eye,
And the dead were at my feet.

But the curse liveth for him in the eye of the dead men.

The cold sweat melted from their limbs,
Nor rot nor reek did they;
The look with which they looked on me
Had never passed away.

An orphan's curse would drag to hell
A spirit from on high;
But oh! more horrible than that
Is a curse in a dead man's eye!   260
Seven days, seven nights, I saw that curse,
And yet I could not die.

In his loneliness and fixedness he yearneth towards the journeying Moon, and the stars that still sojourn, yet still move onward; and everywhere the blue sky belongs to them, and is their appointed rest, and their native country and their own natural homes, which they enter unannounced, as lords that are certainly expected, and yet there is a silent joy at their arrival.

The moving Moon went up the sky,
And nowhere did abide:
Softly she was going up,
And a star or two beside—

Her beams bemocked the sultry main,
Like April hoar-frost spread ;
But where the ship's huge shadow lay,
The charmed water burnt alway   270
A still and awful red.

Beyond the shadow of the ship,
I watched the water-snakes :
They moved in tracks of shining white,
And when they reared, the elfish light
Fell off in hoary flakes.

By the light of the Moon he beholdeth God's creatures of the great calm.

Within the shadow of the ship
I watched their rich attire :
Blue, glossy green, and velvet black,
They coiled and swam ; and every track 280
Was a flash of golden fire.

O happy living things ! no tongue
Their beauty might declare :
A spring of love gushed from my heart,
And I blessed them unaware :
Sure my kind saint took pity on me,
And I blessed them unaware.

Their beauty and their happiness.

He blesseth them in his heart.

The selfsame moment I could pray ;
And from my neck so free
The Albatross fell off, and sank   290
Like lead into the sea.

The spell begins to break.

PART THE FIFTH

Oh sleep ! it is a gentle thing,
Beloved from pole to pole !
To Mary Queen the praise be given !
She sent the gentle sleep from Heaven,
That slid into my soul.

The silly buckets on the deck,
That had so long remained,
I dreamt that they were filled with dew ;
And when I awoke, it rained.   300

By grace of the holy Mother, the ancient Mariner is refreshed with rain.

My lips were wet, my throat was cold,
My garments all were dank ;
Sure I had drunken in my dreams,
And still my body drank.

I moved, and could not feel my limbs :
I was so light—almost
I thought that I had died in sleep
And was a blessed ghost.

And soon I heard a roaring wind:
It did not come anear;   310
But with its sound it shook the sails,
That were so thin and sere.

The upper air burst into life!
And a hundred fire-flags sheen,
To and fro they were hurried about!
And to and fro, and in and out,
The wan stars danced between.

And the coming wind did roar more loud,
And the sails did sigh like sedge;   319
And the rain poured down from one black cloud;
The Moon was at its edge.

The thick black cloud was cleft, and still
The Moon was at its side:
Like waters shot from some high crag,
The lightning fell with never a jag,
A river steep and wide.

The loud wind never reached the ship,
Yet now the ship moved on!
Beneath the lightning and the Moon
The dead men gave a groan.   330

They groaned, they stirred, they all uprose,
Nor spake, nor moved their eyes;
It had been strange, even in a dream,
To have seen those dead men rise.

The helmsman steered, the ship moved on;
Yet never a breeze up blew;
The mariners all 'gan work the ropes,
Where they were wont to do;
They raised their limbs like lifeless tools—
We were a ghastly crew.   340

The body of my brother's son
Stood by me, knee to knee:
The body and I pulled at one rope,
But he said nought to me.

'I fear thee, ancient Mariner!'
Be calm, thou Wedding-Guest!
'Twas not those souls that fled in pain,
Which to their corses came again,
But a troop of spirits blest:

For when it dawned—they dropt their arms, 350
And clustered round the mast;
Sweet sounds rose slowly through their mouths,
And from their bodies passed.

Around, around, flew each sweet sound,
Then darted to the Sun;
Slowly the sounds came back again,
Now mixed, now one by one.

Sometimes a-dropping from the sky
I heard the skylark sing;
Sometimes all little birds that are,   360
How they seemed to fill the sea and air
With their sweet jargoning!

And now 'twas like all instruments,
Now like a lonely flute;
And now it is an angel's song,
That makes the heavens be mute.

It ceased; yet still the sails made on
A pleasant noise till noon,
A noise like of a hidden brook
In the leafy month of June,   370
That to the sleeping woods all night
Singeth a quiet tune.

Till noon we quietly sailed on,
Yet never a breeze did breathe:
Slowly and smoothly went the ship,
Moved onward from beneath.

Under the keel nine fathom deep,
From the land of mist and snow,
The spirit slid: and it was he
That made the ship to go.   380
The sails at noon left off their tune,
And the ship stood still also.

The lonesome spirit from the South Pole carries on the ship as far as the Line, in obedience to the angelic troop, but still requireth vengeance.

The Sun, right up above the mast,
Had fixed her to the ocean:
But in a minute she 'gan stir,
With a short uneasy motion—
Backwards and forwards half her length
With a short uneasy motion.

Then, like a pawing horse let go,
She made a sudden bound: 390
It flung the blood into my head,
And I fell down in a swound.

How long in that same fit I lay,
I have not to declare;
But ere my living life returned,
I heard and in my soul discerned
Two voices in the air.

The Polar Spirit's fellow daemons, the invisible inhabitants of the element,

take part in
his wrong; and
two of them
relate, one to
the other, that
penance long
and heavy for
the ancient
Mariner hath
been accorded
to the Polar
Spirit, who
returneth
southward.

'Is it he?' quoth one, 'Is this the man?
By him who died on cross,
With his cruel bow he laid full low   400
The harmless Albatross.

'The spirit who bideth by himself
In the land of mist and snow,
He loved the bird that loved the man
Who shot him with his bow.'

The other was a softer voice,
As soft as honeydew:
Quoth he, 'The man hath penance done,
And penance more will do.'

PART THE SIXTH

First Voice.

'But tell me, tell me! speak again,   410
Thy soft response renewing—
What makes that ship drive on so fast?
What is the ocean doing?'

Second Voice.

'Still as a slave before his lord,
The ocean hath no blast;
His great bright eye most silently
Up to the Moon is cast—

'If he may know which way to go;
For she guides him smooth or grim.
See, brother, see! how graciously   420
She looketh down on him.'

First Voice.

The Mariner
hath been cast
into a trance;
for the angelic
power causeth
the vessel to
drive north-
ward faster
than human
life could en-
dure.

'But why drives on that ship so fast,
Without or wave or wind?'

Second Voice.

'The air is cut away before,
And closes from behind.

'Fly, brother, fly! more high, more high!
Or we shall be belated:
For slow and slow that ship will go,
When the Mariner's trance is abated.'

The super-
natural motion
is retarded;
the Mariner
awakes, and
his penance
begins anew.

I woke, and we were sailing on   430
As in a gentle weather:
'Twas night, calm night, the Moon was high;
The dead men stood together.

All stood together on the deck,
For a charnel-dungeon fitter:
All fixed on me their stony eyes,
That in the Moon did glitter.

The pang, the curse, with which they died,
Had never passed away:
I could not draw my eyes from theirs,   440
Nor turn them up to pray.

And now this spell was snapt: once more
I viewed the ocean green,
And looked far forth, yet little saw
Of what had else been seen—

The curse is finally expiated.

Like one, that on a lonesome road
Doth walk in fear and dread,
And having once turned round walks on,
And turns no more his head;
Because he knows, a frightful fiend   450
Doth close behind him tread.

But soon there breathed a wind on me,
Nor sound nor motion made:
Its path was not upon the sea,
In ripple or in shade.

It raised my hair, it fanned my cheek
Like a meadow-gale of spring—
It mingled strangely with my fears,
Yet it felt like a welcoming.

Swiftly, swiftly flew the ship,   460
Yet she sailed softly too:
Sweetly, sweetly blew the breeze—
On me alone it blew.

Oh! dream of joy! is this indeed
The lighthouse top I see?
Is this the hill? is this the kirk?
Is this mine own countree?

And the ancient Mariner beholdeth his native country.

We drifted o'er the harbour-bar,
And I with sobs did pray—
O let me be awake, my God!   470
Or let me sleep alway.

The harbour-bay was clear as glass,
So smoothly it was strewn!
And on the bay the moonlight lay,
And the shadow of the Moon.

The rock shone bright, the kirk no less,
That stands above the rock:
The moonlight steeped in silentness
The steady weathercock.

And the bay was white with silent light,   480
Till rising from the same,
Full many shapes, that shadows were,
In crimson colours came.

The angelic spirits leave

A little distance from the prow
Those crimson shadows were:
I turned my eyes upon the deck—
Oh, Christ! what saw I there!

Each corse lay flat, lifeless and flat,
And, by the holy rood!
A man all light, a seraph-man,   490
On every corse there stood.

This seraph-band, each waved his hand:
It was a heavenly sight!
They stood as signals to the land,
Each one a lovely light;

This seraph-band, each waved his hand,
No voice did they impart—
No voice; but oh! the silence sank
Like music on my heart.

But soon I heard the dash of oars,   500
I heard the Pilot's cheer;
My head was turned perforce away,
And I saw a boat appear.

The Pilot and the Pilot's boy,
I heard them coming fast:
Dear Lord in Heaven! it was a joy
The dead men could not blast.

I saw a third—I heard his voice:
It is the Hermit good!
He singeth loud his godly hymns   510
That he makes in the wood.
He'll shrive my soul, he'll wash away
The Albatross's blood.

PART THE SEVENTH

This Hermit good lives in that wood
Which slopes down to the sea.
How loudly his sweet voice he rears!
He loves to talk with marineres
That come from a far countree.

He kneels at morn, and noon, and eve—
He hath a cushion plump: 520
It is the moss that wholly hides
The rotted old oak-stump.

The skiff-boat neared: I heard them talk,
' Why this is strange, I trow!
Where are those lights so many and fair,
That signal made but now?'

'Strange, by my faith!' the Hermit said—
'And they answered not our cheer!
The planks look warped! and see those sails,
How thin they are and sere!   530
I never saw aught like to them,
Unless perchance it were

'Brown skeletons of leaves that lag
My forest-brook along;
When the ivy-tod is heavy with snow,
And the owlet whoops to the wolf below,
That eats the she-wolf's young.'

'Dear Lord! it hath a fiendish look—'
(The Pilot made reply)
'I am a-feared'—'Push on, push on!'   540
Said the Hermit cheerily.

The boat came closer to the ship,
But I nor spake nor stirred;
The boat came close beneath the ship,
And straight a sound was heard.

Under the water it rumbled on,
Still louder and more dread:
It reached the ship, it split the bay;
The ship went down like lead.

Stunned by that loud and dreadful sound, 550
Which sky and ocean smote,
Like one that hath been seven days drowned
My body lay afloat;
But swift as dreams, myself I found
Within the Pilot's boat.

Upon the whirl, where sank the ship,
The boat spun round and round;
And all was still, save that the hill
Was telling of the sound.

I moved my lips—the Pilot shrieked   560
And fell down in a fit;
The holy Hermit raised his eyes,
And prayed where he did sit.

I took the oars: the Pilot's boy,
Who now doth crazy go,
Laughed loud and long, and all the while
His eyes went to and fro.
'Ha! ha!' quoth he, 'full plain I see,
The Devil knows how to row.'

And now, all in my own countree,   570
I stood on the firm land!
The Hermit stepped forth from the boat,
And scarcely he could stand.

approacheth the ship with wonder.

The ship suddenly sinketh

The ancient Mariner is saved in the Pilot's boat.

' O shrive me, shrive me, holy man!'
The Hermit crossed his brow.
'Say quick,' quoth he, 'I bid thee say—
What manner of man art thou?'

Forthwith this frame of mine was wrenched
With a woeful agony,
Which forced me to begin my tale;   580
And then it left me free.

Since then, at an uncertain hour,
That agony returns:
And till my ghastly tale is told,
This heart within me burns.

I pass, like night, from land to land;
I have strange power of speech;
That moment that his face I see,
I know the man that must hear me:
To him my tale I teach.   590

What loud uproar bursts from that door!
The wedding-guests are there:
But in the garden-bower the bride
And bride-maids singing are:
And hark the little vesper bell,
Which biddeth me to prayer!

O Wedding-Guest! this soul hath been
Alone on a wide wide sea:
So lonely 'twas, that God Himself
Scarce seemed there to be.   600

O sweeter than the marriage-feast,
'Tis sweeter far to me,
To walk together to the kirk
With a goodly company!—

To walk together to the kirk,
And all together pray,
While each to his great Father bends,
Old men, and babes, and loving friends,
And youths and maidens gay!

Farewell, farewell! but this I tell   610
To thee, thou Wedding-Guest!
He prayeth well, who loveth well
Both man and bird and beast.

He prayeth best, who loveth best
All things both great and small;
For the dear God who loveth us,
He made and loveth all.

The Mariner, whose eye is bright,
Whose beard with age is hoar,
Is gone: and now the Wedding-Guest   620
Turned from the bridegroom's door.

He went like one that hath been stunned,
And is of sense forlorn:
A sadder and a wiser man,
He rose the morrow morn.

CHRISTABEL

PART THE FIRST

'TIS the middle of night by the castle clock,
And the owls have awakened the crowing cock;
Tu—whit!——Tu—whoo!
And hark, again! the crowing cock,
How drowsily it crew.

Sir Leoline, the Baron rich,
Hath a toothless mastiff, which
From her kennel beneath the rock
Maketh answer to the clock,
Four for the quarters, and twelve for the hour;   10
Ever and aye, by shine and shower,
Sixteen short howls, not over loud;
Some say, she sees my lady's shroud.

Is the night chilly and dark?
The night is chilly, but not dark.
The thin grey cloud is spread on high,
It covers but not hides the sky.
The moon is behind, and at the full;
And yet she looks both small and dull.
The night is chill, the cloud is grey: 20
'Tis a month before the month of May,
And the Spring comes slowly up this way.

The lovely lady, Christabel,
Whom her father loves so well,
What makes her in the wood so late,
A furlong from the castle gate?
She had dreams all yesternight
Of her own betrothed knight;
And she in the midnight wood will pray
For the weal of her lover that's far away.   30

She stole along, she nothing spoke,
The sighs she heaved were soft and low,
And naught was green upon the oak,
But moss and rarest mistletoe:
She kneels beneath the huge oak tree,
And in silence prayeth she.

The lady sprang up suddenly,
The lovely lady, Christabel!
It moaned as near, as near can be,
But what it is, she cannot tell.—   40
On the other side it seems to be,
Of the huge, broad-breasted, old oak tree.

The night is chill; the forest bare;
Is it the wind that moaneth bleak?
There is not wind enough in the air
To move away the ringlet curl
From the lovely lady's cheek—
There is not wind enough to twirl
The one red leaf, the last of its clan,
That dances as often as dance it can,   50
Hanging so light, and hanging so high,
On the topmost twig that looks up at the sky.

Hush, beating heart of Christabel!
Jesu, Maria, shield her well!
She folded her arms beneath her cloak,
And stole to the other side of the oak.
    What sees she there?

There she sees a damsel bright,
Drest in a silken robe of white,
That shadowy in the moonlight shone: 60
The neck that made that white robe wan,
Her stately neck, and arms were bare;
Her blue-veined feet unsandal'd were
And wildly glittered here and there
The gems entangled in her hair.
I guess, 'twas frightful there to see
A lady so richly clad as she—
Beautiful exceedingly!

'Mary mother, save me now!'
(Said Christabel) 'And who art thou?'   70

The lady strange made answer meet,
And her voice was faint and sweet:—
'Have pity on my sore distress,
I scarce can speak for weariness:
Stretch forth thy hand, and have no fear!'
Said Christabel, 'How camest thou here?'
And the lady, whose voice was faint and sweet,
Did thus pursue her answer meet:—

'My sire is of a noble line,
And my name is Geraldine: 80
Five warriors seized me yestermorn,
Me, even me, a maid forlorn:
They choked my cries with force and fright,
And tied me on a palfrey white.

The palfrey was as fleet as wind,
And they rode furiously behind.
They spurred amain, their steeds were white;
And once we crossed the shade of night.
As sure as Heaven shall rescue me,
I have no thought what men they be;   90
Nor do I know how long it is
(For I have lain entranced I wis)
Since one, the tallest of the five,
Took me from the palfrey's back,
A weary woman, scarce alive.
Some muttered words his comrades spoke:
He placed me underneath this oak,
He swore they would return with haste;
Whither they went I cannot tell—
I thought I heard, some minutes past,   100
Sounds as of a castle-bell.
Stretch forth thy hand' (thus ended she),
'And help a wretched maid to flee.'

Then Christabel stretched forth her hand
And comforted fair Geraldine:
' O well, bright dame ! may you command
The service of Sir Leoline;
And gladly our stout chivalry
Will he send forth and friends withal
To guide and guard you safe and free   110
Home to your noble father's hall.'

She rose: and forth with steps they passed
That strove to be, and were not, fast.
Her gracious stars the lady blest,
And thus spake on sweet Christabel:
'All our household are at rest,
The hall as silent as the cell;
Sir Leoline is weak in health
And may not well awakened be,
But we will move as if in stealth   120
And I beseech your courtesy,
This night to share your couch with me.'

They crossed the moat, and Christabel
Took the key that fitted well;
A little door she opened straight,
All in the middle of the gate;
The gate that was ironed within and without,
Where an army in battle array had marched out.
The lady sank, belike through pain,
And Christabel with might and main   130
Lifted her up, a weary weight,
Over the threshold of the gate:
Then the lady rose again,
And moved, as she were not in pain.

So free from danger, free from fear,
They crossed the court : right glad they were.
And Christabel devoutly cried
To the lady by her side,
'Praise we the Virgin all divine   140
Who hath rescued thee from thy distress ! '
' Alas, alas ! ' said Geraldine,
' I cannot speak for weariness.'
So free from danger, free from fear,
They crossed the court : right glad they were.

Outside her kennel, the mastiff old
Lay fast asleep, in moonshine cold.
The mastiff old did not awake,
Yet she an angry moan did make !
And what can ail the mastiff bitch ?
Never till now she uttered yell   150
Beneath the eye of Christabel.
Perhaps it is the owlet's scritch :
For what can ail the mastiff bitch ?

They passed the hall, that echoes still,
Pass as lightly as you will !
The brands were flat, the brands were dying,
Amid their own white ashes lying ;
But when the lady passed, there came
A tongue of light, a fit of flame ;
And Christabel saw the lady's eye,   160
And nothing else saw she thereby,
Save the boss of the shield of Sir Leoline tall,
Which hung in a murky old niche in the wall.
' O softly tread,' said Christabel,
' My father seldom sleepeth well.'

Sweet Christabel her feet doth bare,
And jealous of the listening air
They steal their way from stair to stair,
Now in glimmer, and now in gloom,
And now they pass the Baron's room,   170
As still as death, with stifled breath !
And now have reached her chamber door ;
And now doth Geraldine press down
The rushes of the chamber floor.

The moon shines dim in the open air,
And not a moonbeam enters here.
But they without its light can see
The chamber carved so curiously,
Carved with figures strange and sweet,
All made out of the carver's brain,   180
For a lady's chamber meet :
The lamp with twofold silver chain
Is fastened to an angel's feet.

The silver lamp burns dead and dim;
But Christabel the lamp will trim.
She trimmed the lamp, and made it bright,
And left it swinging to and fro,
While Geraldine, in wretched plight,
Sank down upon the floor below.

'O weary lady, Geraldine, 190
I pray you, drink this cordial wine!
It is a wine of virtuous powers;
My mother made it of wild flowers.'

'And will your mother pity me,
Who am a maiden most forlorn?'
Christabel answered—'Woe is me!
She died the hour that I was born.
I have heard the grey-haired friar tell,
How on her deathbed she did say,
That she should hear the castle-bell 200
Strike twelve upon my wedding-day.
O mother dear! that thou wert here!'
'I would,' said Geraldine, 'she were!'

But soon with altered voice, said she—
'Off, wandering mother! Peak and pine,
I have power to bid thee flee.'
Alas! what ails poor Geraldine?
Why stares she with unsettled eye?
Can she the bodiless dead espy?
And why with hollow voice cries she, 210
'Off, woman, off! this hour is mine—
Though thou her guardian spirit be,
Off, woman, off! 'tis given to me.'

Then Christabel knelt by the lady's side,
And raised to heaven her eyes so blue—
'Alas!' said she, 'this ghastly ride—
Dear lady! it hath wildered you!'
The lady wiped her moist cold brow,
And faintly said, ''Tis over now!'

Again the wild-flower wine she drank: 220
Her fair large eyes 'gan glitter bright,
And from the floor whereon she sank,
The lofty lady stood upright;
She was most beautiful to see,
Like a lady of a far countrée.

And thus the lofty lady spake—
'All they who live in the upper sky,
Do love you, holy Christabel!
And you love them, and for their sake
And for the good which me befell, 230
Even I in my degree will try,

Fair maiden, to requite you well.
But now unrobe yourself; for I
Must pray, ere yet in bed I lie.'

Quoth Christabel, 'So let it be!'
And as the lady bade, did she.
Her gentle limbs did she undress,
And lay down in her loveliness.

But through her brain of weal and woe
So many thoughts moved to and fro,   240
That vain it were her lids to close;
So half-way from the bed she rose,
And on her elbow did recline
To look at the lady Geraldine.

Beneath the lamp the lady bowed,
And slowly rolled her eyes around;
Then drawing in her breath aloud,
Like one that shuddered, she unbound
The cincture from beneath her breast:
Her silken robe, and inner vest,   250
Dropt to her feet, and full in view,
Behold! her bosom and half her side——
A sight to dream of, not to tell!
O shield her! shield sweet Christabel!

Yet Geraldine nor speaks nor stirs;
Ah! what a stricken look was hers!
Deep from within she seems half-way
To lift some weight with sick assay,
And eyes the maid and seeks delay;
Then suddenly as one defied   260
Collects herself in scorn and pride,
And lay down by the Maiden's side!—
And in her arms the maid she took,
        Ah wel-a-day!
And with low voice and doleful look
These words did say:
'In the touch of this bosom there worketh a spell,
Which is lord of thy utterance, Christabel!
Thou knowest to-night, and wilt know to-morrow,
This mark of my shame, this seal of my sorrow;   270
        But vainly thou warrest,
            For this is alone in
        Thy power to declare,
            That in the dim forest
        Thou heard'st a low moaning,
And found'st a bright lady, surpassingly fair:
And didst bring her home with thee in love and in charity,
To shield her and shelter her from the damp air.'

THE CONCLUSION TO PART THE FIRST

It was a lovely sight to see
The lady Christabel, when she 280
Was praying at the old oak tree.
    Amid the jagged shadows
    Of mossy leafless boughs,
    Kneeling in the moonlight,
    To make her gentle vows;
Her slender palms together prest,
Heaving sometimes on her breast;
Her face resigned to bliss or bale—
Her face, oh call it fair not pale,
And both blue eyes more bright than clear. 290
Each about to have a tear.

With open eyes (ah woe is me!)
Asleep, and dreaming fearfully,
Fearfully dreaming, yet I wis,
Dreaming that alone, which is—
O sorrow and shame! Can this be she,
The lady, who knelt at the old oak tree?
And lo! the worker of these harms,
That holds the maiden in her arms,
Seems to slumber still and mild, 300
As a mother with her child.

A star hath set, a star hath risen,
O Geraldine! since arms of thine
Have been the lovely lady's prison.
O Geraldine! one hour was thine—
Thou'st had thy will! By tairn and rill,
The night-birds all that hour were still.
But now they are jubilant anew,
From cliff and tower, tu—whoo! tu—whoo!
Tu—whoo! tu—whoo! from wood and fell! 310

And see! the lady Christabel
Gathers herself from out her trance;
Her limbs relax, her countenance
Grows sad and soft; the smooth thin lids
Close o'er her eyes; and tears she sheds—
Large tears that leave the lashes bright!
And oft the while she seems to smile
As infants at a sudden light!

Yea, she doth smile, and she doth weep,
Like a youthful hermitess, 320
Beauteous in a wilderness,
Who, praying always, prays in sleep.
And, if she move unquietly,
Perchance, 'tis but the blood so free,

Comes back and tingles in her feet.
No doubt, she hath a vision sweet.
What if her guardian spirit 'twere,
What if she knew her mother near ?
But this she knows, in joys and woes,
That saints will aid if men will call :   330
For the blue sky bends over all !

PART THE SECOND

' Each matin bell,' the Baron saith,
' Knells us back to a world of death.'
These words Sir Leoline first said,
When he rose and found his lady dead :
These words Sir Leoline will say,
Many a morn to his dying day !

And hence the custom and law began,
That still at dawn the sacristan,
Who duly pulls the heavy bell,   340
Five and forty beads must tell
Between each stroke—a warning knell,
Which not a soul can choose but hear
From Bratha Head to Wyndermere.

Saith Bracy the bard, ' So let it knell !
And let the drowsy sacristan
Still count as slowly as he can !
There is no lack of such, I ween
As well fill up the space between.
In Langdale Pike and Witch's Lair,   350
And Dungeon-ghyll so foully rent,
With ropes of rock and bells of air
Three sinful sextons' ghosts are pent,
Who all give back, one after t'other,
The death-note to their living brother ;
And oft too, by the knell offended,
Just as their one ! two ! three ! is ended,
The devil mocks the doleful tale
With a merry peal from Borrowdale.'

The air is still ! through mist and cloud   360
That merry peal comes ringing loud ;
And Geraldine shakes off her dread,
And rises lightly from the bed ;
Puts on her silken vestments white,
And tricks her hair in lovely plight,
And nothing doubting of her spell
Awakens the lady Christabel.
' Sleep you, sweet lady Christabel ?
I trust that you have rested well.'

And Christabel awoke and spied   370
The same who lay down by her side—

O rather say, the same whom she
Raised up beneath the old oak tree!
Nay, fairer yet! and yet more fair!
For she belike hath drunken deep
Of all the blessedness of sleep!
And while she spake, her looks, her air
Such gentle thankfulness declare,
That (so it seemed) her girded vests
Grew tight beneath her heaving breasts. 380
'Sure I have sinned!' said Christabel,
 Now heaven be praised if all be well!'
And in low faltering tones, yet sweet,
Did she the lofty lady greet
With such perplexity of mind
As dreams too lively leave behind.

So quickly she rose, and quickly arrayed
Her maiden limbs, and having prayed
That He, who on the cross did groan,
Might wash away her sins unknown, 390
She forthwith led fair Geraldine
To meet her sire, Sir Leoline.

The lovely maid and the lady tall
Are pacing both into the hall,
And pacing on through page and groom
Enter the Baron's presence-room.

The Baron rose, and while he prest
His gentle daughter to his breast,
With cheerful wonder in his eyes
The lady Geraldine espies, 400
And gave such welcome to the same,
As might beseem so bright a dame!

But when he heard the lady's tale,
And when she told her father's name,
Why waxed Sir Leoline so pale,
Murmuring o'er the name again,
'Lord Roland de Vaux of Tryermaine?'

Alas! they had been friends in youth;
But whispering tongues can poison truth;
And constancy lives in realms above; 410
And life is thorny; and youth is vain:
And to be wroth with one we love,
Doth work like madness in the brain.
And thus it chanced, as I divine,
With Roland and Sir Leoline.
Each spake words of high disdain.
And insult to his heart's best brother:
They parted—ne'er to meet again!
But never either found another
To free the hollow heart from paining— 420

They stood aloof, the scars remaining,
Like cliffs which had been rent asunder;
A dreary sea now flows between.
But neither heat, nor frost, nor thunder,
Shall wholly do away, I ween,
The marks of that which once hath been.

Sir Leoline, a moment's space,
Stood gazing on the damsel's face.
And the youthful Lord of Tryermaine
Came back upon his heart again. 430

O then the Baron forgot his age,
His noble heart swelled high with rage;
He swore by the wounds in Jesu's side,
He would proclaim it far and wide
With trump and solemn heraldry,
That they, who thus had wronged the dame,
Were base as spotted infamy!
'And if they dare deny the same,
My herald shall appoint a week
And let the recreant traitors seek 440
My tourney court—that there and then
I may dislodge their reptile souls
From the bodies and forms of men!'
He spake: his eye in lightning rolls!
For the lady was ruthlessly seized; and he kenned
In the beautiful lady the child of his friend!

And now the tears were on his face,
And fondly in his arms he took
Fair Geraldine, who met the embrace,
Prolonging it with joyous look. 450
Which, when she viewed, a vision fell
Upon the soul of Christabel,
The vision of fear, the touch and pain!
She shrunk and shuddered, and saw again—
(Ah, woe is me! Was it for thee,
Thou gentle maid! such sights to see?)

Again she saw that bosom old,
Again she felt that bosom cold,
And drew in her breath with a hissing sound:
Whereat the Knight turned wildly round, 460
And nothing saw, but his own sweet maid
With eyes upraised, as one that prayed.

The touch, the sight, had passed away,
And in its stead that vision blest,
Which comforted her after-rest,
While in the lady's arms she lay,
Had put a rapture in her breast,
And on her lips and o'er her eyes
Spread smiles like light!

With new surprise,

'What ails then my beloved child?'
The Baron said—His daughter mild
Made answer, 'All will yet be well!'
I ween, she had no power to tell
Aught else: so mighty was the spell.

Yet he, who saw this Geraldine,
Had deemed her such a thing divine.
Such sorrow with such grace she blended,
As if she feared she had offended
Sweet Christabel, that gentle maid!
And with such lowly tones she prayed.
She might be sent without delay
Home to her father's mansion.

'Nay!

Nay, by my soul!' said Leoline.
'Ho! Bracy the bard, the charge be thine!
Go thou, with music sweet and loud,
And take two steeds with trappings proud,
And take the youth whom thou lov'st best
To bear thy harp, and learn thy song,
And clothe you both in solemn vest,
And over the mountains haste along,
Lest wandering folk, that are abroad,
Detain you on the valley road.

'And when he has crossed the Irthing flood,
My merry bard! he hastes, he hastes
Up Knorren Moor, through Halegarth Wood,
And reaches soon that castle good
Which stands and threatens Scotland's wastes.

'Bard Bracy! bard Bracy! your horses are fleet,
Ye must ride up the hall, your music so sweet,
More loud than your horses' echoing feet!
And loud and loud to Lord Roland call,
"Thy daughter is safe in Langdale hall!
Thy beautiful daughter is safe and free—
Sir Leoline greets thee thus through me.
He bids thee come without delay
With all thy numerous array;
And take thy lovely daughter home:
And he will meet thee on the way
With all his numerous array
White with their panting palfreys' foam":
And by mine honour! I will say,
That I repent me of the day
When I spake words of fierce disdain
To Roland de Vaux of Tryermaine!—
—For since that evil hour hath flown,
Many a summer's sun hath shone;
Yet ne'er found I a friend again
Like Roland de Vaux of Tryermaine.'

The lady fell, and clasped his knees,
Her face upraised, her eyes o'erflowing;   520
And Bracy replied, with faltering voice,
His gracious hail on all bestowing;—
'Thy words, thou sire of Christabel,
Are sweeter than my harp can tell;
Yet might I gain a boon of thee,
This day my journey should not be,
So strange a dream hath come to me;
That I had vowed with music loud
To clear yon wood from thing unblest,
Warned by a vision in my rest!   530
For in my sleep I saw that dove,
That gentle bird, whom thou dost love,
And call'st by thy own daughter's name—
Sir Leoline! I saw the same,
Fluttering, and uttering fearful moan,
Among the green herbs in the forest alone.
Which when I saw and when I heard,
I wonder'd what might ail the bird:
For nothing near it could I see,
Save the grass and green herbs underneath the old tree.

'And in my dream, methought, I went   541
To search out what might there be found;
And what the sweet bird's trouble meant,
That thus lay fluttering on the ground.
I went and peered, and could descry
No cause for her distressful cry;
But yet for her dear lady's sake
I stooped, methought, the dove to take,
When lo! I saw a bright green snake
Coiled around its wings and neck.   550
Green as the herbs on which it couched,
Close by the dove's its head it crouched;
And with the dove it heaves and stirs,
Swelling its neck as she swelled hers!
I woke; it was the midnight hour,
The clock was echoing in the tower;
But though my slumber was gone by,
This dream it would not pass away—
It seems to live upon the eye!
And thence I vowed this selfsame day,   560
With music strong and saintly song
To wander through the forest bare,
Lest aught unholy loiter there.'

Thus Bracy said: the Baron, the while,
Half-listening heard him with a smile;
Then turned to Lady Geraldine,
His eyes made up of wonder and love;

And said in courtly accents fine,
'Sweet maid, Lord Roland's beauteous dove,
With arms more strong than harp or song, 570
Thy sire and I will crush the snake!'
He kissed her forehead as he spake,
And Geraldine in maiden wise,
Casting down her large bright eyes,
With blushing cheek and courtesy fine
She turned her from Sir Leoline;
Softly gathering up her train,
That o'er her right arm fell again;
And folded her arms across her chest,
And couched her head upon her breast, 580
And looked askance at Christabel——
Jesu, Maria, shield her well!

A snake's small eye blinks dull and shy,
And the lady's eyes they shrunk in her head,
Each shrunk up to a serpent's eye,
And with somewhat of malice, and more of dread,
At Christabel she looked askance!—
One moment—and the sight was fled!
But Christabel in dizzy trance
Stumbling on the unsteady ground 590
Shuddered aloud, with a hissing sound;
And Geraldine again turned round,
And like a thing, that sought relief,
Full of wonder and full of grief,
She rolled her large bright eyes divine
Wildly on Sir Leoline.

The maid, alas! her thoughts are gone,
She nothing sees—no sight but one!
The maid, devoid of guile and sin,
I know not how, in fearful wise 600
So deeply had she drunken in
That look, those shrunken serpent eyes,
That all her features were resigned
To this sole image in her mind:
And passively did imitate
That look of dull and treacherous hate!
And thus she stood, in dizzy trance,
Still picturing that look askance
With forced unconscious sympathy
Full before her father's view—— 610
As far as such a look could be,
In eyes so innocent and blue!

And when the trance was o'er, the maid
Paused awhile, and inly prayed:
Then falling at the Baron's feet,
'By my mother's soul do I entreat
That thou this woman send away!'

She said: and more she could not say:
For what she knew she could not tell,
O'er-mastered by the mighty spell.   620

Why is thy cheek so wan and wild,
Sir Leoline? Thy only child
Lies at thy feet, thy joy, thy pride,
So fair, so innocent, so mild;
The same, for whom thy lady died!
O by the pangs of her dear mother
Think thou no evil of thy child!
For her, and thee, and for no other,
She prayed the moment ere she died:
Prayed that the babe, for whom she died,   630
Might prove her dear lord's joy and pride!
    That prayer her deadly pangs beguiled,
            Sir Leoline!
    And wouldst thou wrong thy only child,
            Her child and thine?

Within the Baron's heart and brain
If thoughts like these had any share,
They only swelled his rage and pain,
And did but work confusion there.
His heart was cleft with pain and rage,   640
His cheeks they quivered, his eyes were wild,
Dishonour'd thus in his old age;
Dishonour'd by his only child,
And all his hospitality
To the insulted daughter of his friend
By more than woman's jealousy
Brought thus to a disgraceful end—
He rolled his eye with stern regard
Upon the gentle minstrel bard,
And said in tones abrupt, austere—   650
'Why, Bracy! dost thou loiter here?
I bade thee hence!' The bard obeyed;
And turning from his own sweet maid,
The aged knight, Sir Leoline,
Led forth the lady Geraldine!

THE CONCLUSION TO PART THE SECOND

A little child, a limber elf,
Singing, dancing to itself,
A fairy thing with red round cheeks
That always finds, and never seeks,
Makes such a vision to the sight   660
As fills a father's eyes with light;
And pleasures flow in so thick and fast
Upon his heart, that he at last

Must needs express his love's excess
With words of unmeant bitterness.
Perhaps 'tis pretty to force together
Thoughts so all unlike each other;
To mutter and mock a broken charm,
To dally with wrong that does no harm.
Perhaps 'tis tender too and pretty   670
At each wild word to feel within
A sweet recoil of love and pity.
And what, if in a world of sin
(O sorrow and shame should this be true!)
Such giddiness of heart and brain
Comes seldom save from rage and pain,
So talks as it's most used to do.

KUBLA KHAN

OR, A VISION IN A DREAM

The following fragment is here published at the request of a poet of great and deserved celebrity, and as far as the Author's own opinions are concerned, rather as a psychological curiosity, than on the ground of any supposed *poetic* merits.

In the summer of the year 1797, the Author, then in ill health, had retired to a lonely farm-house between Porlock and Linton, on the Exmoor confines of Somerset and Devonshire. In consequence of a slight indisposition, an anodyne had been prescribed, from the effects of which he fell asleep in his chair at the moment that he was reading the following sentence, or words of the same substance, in *Purchas's Pilgrimage*: 'Here the Khan Kubla commanded a palace to be built, and a stately garden thereunto: and thus ten miles of fertile ground were inclosed with a wall.' The author continued for about three hours in a profound sleep, at least of the external senses, during which time he has the most vivid confidence, that he could not have composed less than from two to three hundred lines; if that indeed can be called composition in which all the images rose up before him as *things*, with a parallel production of the correspondent expressions, without any sensation or consciousness of effort. On awaking he appeared to himself to have a distinct recollection of the whole, and taking his pen, ink, and paper, instantly and eagerly wrote down the lines that are here preserved. At this moment he was unfortunately called out by a person on business from Porlock, and detained by him above an hour, and on his return to his room, found to his no small surprise and mortification, that though he still retained some vague and dim recollection of the general purport of the vision, yet, with the exception of some eight or ten scattered lines and images, all the rest had passed away like the images

on the surface of a stream into which a stone had been cast, but, alas!
without the after restoration of the latter

                     Then all the charm
Is broken—all that phantom-world so fair
Vanishes, and a thousand circlets spread,
And each mis-shape the other. Stay awhile,
Poor youth! who scarcely darest lift up thine eyes—
The stream will soon renew its smoothness, soon
The visions will return! And lo, he stays,
And soon the fragments dim of lovely forms
Come trembling back, unite, and now once more
The pool becomes a mirror.

Yet from the still surviving recollections in his mind, the Author has
frequently purposed to finish for himself what had been originally
as it were, given to him. σάμερον ἄδιον ᾄσω[1]: but the to-morrow is yet
to come.

KUBLA KHAN

In Xanadu did Kubla Khan
A stately pleasure-dome decree:
Where Alph, the sacred river, ran
Through caverns measureless to man
     Down to a sunless sea.
So twice five miles of fertile ground
With walls and towers were girdled round:
And here were gardens bright with sinuous rills,
Where blossomed many an incense-bearing tree;
And here were forests ancient as the hills,   10
Enfolding sunny spots of greenery.

But oh! that deep romantic chasm which slanted
Down the green hill athwart a cedarn cover!
A savage place! as holy and enchanted
As e'er beneath a waning moon was haunted
By woman wailing for her demon-lover!
And from this chasm, with ceaseless turmoil seething,
As if this earth in fast thick pants were breathing,
A mighty fountain momently was forced:
Amid whose swift half-intermitted burst   20
Huge fragments vaulted like rebounding hail,
Or chaffy grain beneath the thresher's flail:
And mid these dancing rocks at once and ever
It flung up momently the sacred river.
Five miles meandering with a mazy motion
Through wood and dale the sacred river ran,
Then reached the caverns measureless to man,
And sank in tumult to a lifeless ocean:
And 'mid this tumult Kubla heard from far
Ancestral voices prophesying war!   30

[1] Altered in 1834 to αὔριον ἄδιον ᾄσω.

The shadow of the dome of pleasure
Floated midway on the waves;
Where was heard the mingled measure
From the fountain and the caves,
It was a miracle of rare device,
A sunny pleasure-dome with caves of ice!

A damsel with a dulcimer
In a vision once I saw:
It was an Abyssinian maid,
And on her dulcimer she played,   40
Singing of Mount Abora.
Could I revive within me
Her symphony and song,
To such a deep delight 'twould win me,
That with music loud and long,
I would build that dome in air,
That sunny dome! those caves of ice!
And all who heard should see them there,
And all should cry, Beware! Beware!
His flashing eyes, his floating hair!   50
Weave a circle round him thrice,
And close your eyes with holy dread,
For he on honey-dew hath fed,
And drunk the milk of Paradise.

TO A GENTLEMAN

[WILLIAM WORDSWORTH]

COMPOSED ON THE NIGHT AFTER HIS RECITATION OF A POEM ON THE GROWTH OF AN INDIVIDUAL MIND

FRIEND of the wise! and teacher of the good!
Into my heart have I received that lay
More than historic, that prophetic lay
Wherein (high theme by thee first sung aright)
Of the foundations and the building up
Of a Human Spirit thou hast dared to tell
What may be told, to the understanding mind
Revealable; and what within the mind
By vital breathings secret as the soul
Of vernal growth, oft quickens in the heart   10
Thoughts all too deep for words!—

                    Theme hard as high!
Of smiles spontaneous, and mysterious fears
(The firstborn they of Reason and twin-birth),
Of tides obedient to external force,
And currents self-determined, as might seem,
Or by some inner Power; of moments awful,

Now in thy inner life, and now abroad,
When Power streamed from thee, and thy soul received
The light reflected, as a light bestowed—
Of Fancies fair, and milder hours of youth,   20
Hyblaean murmurs of poetic thought
Industrious in its joy, in vales and glens
Native or outland, lakes and famous hills!
Or on the lonely high-road, when the stars
Were rising; or by secret mountain-streams,
The guides and the companions of thy way!

Of more than Fancy, of the Social Sense
Distending wide, and Man beloved as Man,
Where France in all her towns lay vibrating
Like some becalmed bark beneath the burst   30
Of Heaven's immediate thunder, when no cloud
Is visible, or shadow on the main.
For thou wert there, thine own brows garlanded,
Amid the tremor of a realm aglow,
Amid a mighty nation jubilant,
When from the general Heart of Human kind
Hope sprang forth like a full-born Deity!
——Of that dear Hope afflicted and struck down,
So summoned homeward, thenceforth calm and sure
From the dread watch-tower of man's absolute Self,   40
With light unwaning on her eyes, to look
Far on—herself a glory to behold,
The Angel of the vision!   Then (last strain)
Of Duty, chosen laws controlling choice,
Action and joy!—An Orphic song indeed,
A song divine of high and passionate thoughts,
To their own music chanted!

                              O great Bard!
Ere yet that last strain dying awed the air,
With steadfast eye I viewed thee in the choir
Of ever-enduring men.   The truly Great   50
Have all one age, and from one visible space
Shed influence!   They, both in power and act,
Are permanent, and Time is not with *them*,
Save as it worketh *for* them, they *in* it,
Nor less a sacred roll, than those of old,
And to be placed, as they, with gradual fame
Among the Archives of Mankind, thy work
Makes audible a linked lay of Truth,
Of Truth profound a sweet continuous lay,
Not learnt, but native, her own natural notes!   60
Ah! as I listen'd with a heart forlorn,
The pulses of my being beat anew:
And even as life returns upon the drowned,
Life's joy rekindling roused a throng of pains—
Keen pangs of Love, awakening as a babe

Turbulent, with an outcry in the heart ;
And fears self-willed, that shunned the eye of Hope ;
And Hope that scarce would know itself from Fear ;
Sense of past Youth, and Manhood come in vain ;   70
And Genius given, and knowledge won in vain ;
And all which I had culled in wood-walks wild,
And all which patient toil had reared, and all,
Commune with *thee* had opened out—but flowers
Strewed on my corse, and borne upon my bier,
In the same coffin, for the selfsame grave !

That way no more ! and ill beseems it me,
Who came a welcomer in herald's guise,
Singing of Glory, and Futurity,
To wander back on such unhealthful road,
Plucking the poisons of self-harm ! And ill   80
Such intertwine beseems triumphal wreaths
Strew'd before *thy* advancing !

                                        Nor do thou,
Sage Bard ! impair the memory of that hour
Of thy communion with my nobler mind
By pity or grief, already felt too long !
Nor let my words import more blame than needs.
The tumult rose and ceased : for peace is nigh
Where wisdom's voice has found a listening heart.
Amid the howl of more than wintry storms,
The Halcyon hears the voice of vernal hours   90
Already on the wing.

                                    Eve following eve,
Dear tranquil time, when the sweet sense of Home
Is sweetest ! moments for their own sake hailed
And more desired, more precious for thy song,
In silence listening, like a devout child,
My soul lay passive, by thy various strain
Driven as in surges now beneath the stars,
With momentary stars of my own birth,
Fair constellated foam, still darting off
Into the darkness ; now a tranquil sea,   100
Outspread and bright, yet swelling to the moon.

And when—O Friend ! my comforter and guide !
Strong in thyself, and powerful to give strength !—
Thy long sustained Song finally closed,
And thy deep voice had ceased—yet thou thyself
Wert still before my eyes, and round us both
That happy vision of beloved faces—
Scarce conscious, and yet conscious of its close
I sate, my being blended in one thought
(Thought was it ? or aspiration ? or resolve ?)   110
Absorbed, yet hanging still upon the sound—
And when I rose, I found myself in prayer.

LORD BYRON

CHILDE HAROLD'S PILGRIMAGE

CANTO THE THIRD

'Afin que cette application vous forçât de penser à autre chose; il
n'y a en vérité de remède que celui-là et le temps.'
Lettre du Roi de Prusse à D'Alembert, Sept. 7, 1776.

I

Is thy face like thy mother's, my fair child!
ADA! sole daughter of my house and heart?
When last I saw thy young blue eyes they smiled,
And then we parted,—not as now we part,
But with a hope.—
        Awaking with a start,
The waters heave around me; and on high
The winds lift up their voices: I depart,
Whither I know not; but the hour 's gone by,
When Albion's lessening shores could grieve or glad mine eye.

II

Once more upon the waters! yet once more!   10
And the waves bound beneath me as a steed
That knows his rider. Welcome to their roar!
Swift be their guidance, wheresoe'er it lead!
Though the strain'd mast should quiver as a reed,
And the rent canvas fluttering strew the gale,
Still must I on; for I am as a weed,
Flung from the rock, on Ocean's foam to sail
Where'er the surge may sweep, the tempest's breath prevail.

III

In my youth's summer I did sing of One,
The wandering outlaw of his own dark mind;   20
Again I seize the theme, then but begun,
And bear it with me, as the rushing wind
Bears the cloud onwards: in that Tale I find
The furrows of long thought, and dried-up tears,
Which, ebbing, leave a sterile track behind,
O'er which all heavily the journeying years
Plod the last sands of life,—where not a flower appears.

IV

Since my young days of passion—joy, or pain,
Perchance my heart and harp have lost a string,
And both may jar: it may be, that in vain   30
I would essay as I have sung to sing.
Yet, though a dreary strain, to this I cling;
So that it wean me from the weary dream
Of selfish grief or gladness—so it fling
Forgetfulness around me—it shall seem
To me, though to none else, a not ungrateful theme.

V

He, who grown aged in this world of woe,
In deeds, not years, piercing the depths of life,
So that no wonder waits him ; nor below
Can love or sorrow, fame, ambition, strife,   40
Cut to his heart again with the keen knife
Of silent, sharp endurance : he can tell
Why thought seeks refuge in lone caves, yet rife
With airy images, and shapes which dwell
Still unimpair'd, though old, in the soul's haunted cell.

VI

'Tis to create, and in creating live
A being more intense, that we endow
With form our fancy, gaining as we give
The life we image, even as I do now.
What am I ? Nothing : but not so art thou,   50
Soul of my thought ! with whom I traverse earth,
Invisible but gazing, as I glow
Mix'd with thy spirit, blended with thy birth,
And feeling still with thee in my crush'd feelings' dearth.

VII

Yet must I think less wildly :—I *have* thought
Too long and darkly, till my brain became,
In its own eddy boiling and o'erwrought,
A whirling gulf of phantasy and flame :
And thus, untaught in youth my heart to tame,
My springs of life were poison'd. 'Tis too late !   60
Yet am I changed ; though still enough the same
In strength to bear what time can not abate,
And feed on bitter fruits without accusing Fate.

VIII

Something too much of this :—but now 'tis past,
And the spell closes with its silent seal.
Long absent HAROLD re-appears at last ;
He of the breast which fain no more would feel,
Wrung with the wounds which kill not, but ne'er heal ;
Yet Time, who changes all, had alter'd him
In soul and aspect as in age : years steal   70
Fire from the mind as vigour from the limb ;
And life's enchanted cup but sparkles near the brim.

IX

His had been quaff'd too quickly, and he found
The dregs were wormwood; but he fill'd again,
And from a purer fount, on holier ground,
And deem'd its spring perpetual; but in vain!
Still round him clung invisibly a chain
Which gall'd for ever, fettering though unseen,
And heavy though it clank'd not; worn with pain,
Which pined although it spoke not, and grew keen,   80
Entering with every step he took through many a scene.

X

Secure in guarded coldness, he had mix'd
Again in fancied safety with his kind,
And deem'd his spirit now so firmly fix'd
And sheath'd with an invulnerable mind,
That, if no joy, no sorrow lurk'd behind;
And he, as one, might 'midst the many stand
Unheeded, searching through the crowd to find
Fit speculation; such as in strange land
He found in wonder-works of God and Nature's hand.   90

XI

But who can view the ripen'd rose, nor seek
To wear it? who can curiously behold
The smoothness and the sheen of beauty's cheek,
Nor feel the heart can never all grow old?
Who can contemplate Fame through clouds unfold
The star which rises o'er her steep, nor climb?
Harold, once more within the vortex, roll'd
On with the giddy circle, chasing Time,
Yet with a nobler aim than in his youth's fond prime.

XII

But soon he knew himself the most unfit   100
Of men to herd with Man; with whom he held
Little in common; untaught to submit
His thoughts to others, though his soul was quell'd,
In youth by his own thoughts; still uncompell'd,
He would not yield dominion of his mind
To spirits against whom his own rebell'd;
Proud though in desolation; which could find
A life within itself, to breathe without mankind.

XIII

Where rose the mountains, there to him were friends;
Where roll'd the ocean, thereon was his home;   110
Where a blue sky, and glowing clime, extends,
He had the passion and the power to roam;
The desert, forest, cavern, breaker's foam,
Were unto him companionship; they spake
A mutual language, clearer than the tome
Of his land's tongue, which he would oft forsake
For Nature's pages glass'd by sunbeams on the lake.

XIV

Like the Chaldean, he could watch the stars,
Till he had peopled them with beings bright
As their own beams; and earth, and earth-born jars, 120
And human frailties, were forgotten quite:
Could he have kept his spirit to that flight
He had been happy; but this clay will sink
Its spark immortal, envying it the light
To which it mounts, as if to break the link
That keeps us from yon heaven which woos us to its brink.

XV

But in Man's dwellings he became a thing
Restless and worn, and stern and wearisome,
Droop'd as a wild-born falcon with clipt wing,
To whom the boundless air alone were home: 130
Then came his fit again, which to o'ercome,
As eagerly the barr'd-up bird will beat
His breast and beak against his wiry dome
Till the blood tinge his plumage, so the heat
Of his impeded soul would through his bosom eat.

XVI

Self-exiled Harold wanders forth again,
With nought of hope left, but with less of gloom;
The very knowledge that he lived in vain,
That all was over on this side the tomb,
Had made Despair a smilingness assume,   140
Which, though 'twere wild,—as on the plunder'd wreck
When mariners would madly meet their doom
With draughts intemperate on the sinking deck,—
Did yet inspire a cheer, which he forbore to check.

XVII

Stop!—for thy tread is on an Empire's dust!
An Earthquake's spoil is sepulchred below!
Is the spot mark'd with no colossal bust?
Nor column trophied for triumphal show?
None; but the moral's truth tells simpler so,
As the ground was before, thus let it be;—   150
How that red rain hath made the harvest grow!
And is this all the world has gain'd by thee,
Thou first and last of fields! king-making Victory?

XVIII

And Harold stands upon this place of skulls,
The grave of France, the deadly Waterloo!
How in an hour the power which gave annuls
Its gifts, transferring fame as fleeting too!
In ' pride of place ' here last the eagle flew,
Then tore with bloody talon the rent plain,
Pierced by the shaft of banded nations through;   160
Ambition's life and labours all were vain;
He wears the shatter'd links of the world's broken chain.

XIX

Fit retribution ! Gaul may champ the bit
And foam in fetters ;—but is Earth more free ?
Did nations combat to make *One* submit ;
Or league to teach all kings true sovereignty ?
What ! shall reviving Thraldom again be
The patch'd-up idol of enlighten'd days ?
Shall we, who struck the Lion down, shall we
Pay the Wolf homage ? proffering lowly gaze   170
And servile knees to thrones ? No ; *prove* before ye praise!

XX

If not, o'er one fallen despot boast no more !
In vain fair cheeks were furrow'd with hot tears
For Europe's flowers long rooted up before
The trampler of her vineyards ; in vain years
Of death, depopulation, bondage, fears,
Have all been borne, and broken by the accord
Of roused-up millions ; all that most endears
Glory, is when the myrtle wreathes a sword
Such as Harmodius drew on Athens' tyrant lord.   180

XXI

There was a sound of revelry by night,
And Belgium's capital had gather'd then
Her Beauty and her Chivalry, and bright
The lamps shone o'er fair women and brave men ;
A thousand hearts beat happily ; and when
Music arose with its voluptuous swell,
Soft eyes look'd love to eyes which spake again,
And all went merry as a marriage bell ;
But hush ! hark ! a deep sound strikes like a rising knell !

XXII

Did ye not hear it ?—No ; 'twas but the wind,   190
Or the car rattling o'er the stony street ;
On with the dance ! let joy be unconfined ;
No sleep till morn, when Youth and Pleasure meet
To chase the glowing Hours with flying feet—
But hark !—that heavy sound breaks in once more,
As if the clouds its echo would repeat ;
And nearer, clearer, deadlier than before !
Arm ! Arm ! it is—it is—the cannon's opening roar !

XXIII

Within a window'd niche of that high hall
Sate Brunswick's fated chieftain ; he did hear   200
That sound the first amidst the festival,
And caught its tone with Death's prophetic ear ;
And when they smiled because he deem'd it near
His heart more truly knew that peal too well
Which stretch'd his father on a bloody bier,
And roused the vengeance blood alone could quell;
He rush'd into the field, and, foremost fighting, fell.

XXIV

Ah ! then and there was hurrying to and fro,
And gathering tears, and tremblings of distress,
And cheeks all pale, which but an hour ago   210
Blush'd at the praise of their own loveliness ;
And there were sudden partings, such as press
The life from out young hearts, and choking sighs
Which ne'er might be repeated ; who could guess
If ever more should meet those mutual eyes,
Since upon night so sweet such awful morn could rise !

XXV

And there was mounting in hot haste : the steed,
The mustering squadron, and the clattering car,
Went pouring forward with impetuous speed,
And swiftly forming in the ranks of war ;   220
And the deep thunder peal on peal afar ;
And near, the beat of the alarming drum
Roused up the soldier ere the morning star ;
While throng'd the citizens with terror dumb,
Or whispering, with white lips—'The foe ! they come ! they come !'

XXVI

And wild and high the ' Cameron's gathering ' rose !
The war-note of Lochiel, which Albyn's hills
Have heard, and heard, too, have her Saxon foes :—
How in the noon of night that pibroch thrills,
Savage and shrill ! But with the breath which fills   230
Their mountain-pipe, so fill the mountaineers
With the fierce native daring which instils
The stirring memory of a thousand years,
And Evan's, Donald's fame rings in each clansman's ears !

XXVII

And Ardennes waves above them her green leaves,
Dewy with nature's tear-drops as they pass,
Grieving, if aught inanimate e'er grieves,
Over the unreturning brave,—alas !
Ere evening to be trodden like the grass
Which now beneath them, but above shall grow   240
In its next verdure, when this fiery mass
Of living valour, rolling on the foe
And burning with high hope, shall moulder cold and low.

XXVIII

Last noon beheld them full of lusty life,
Last eve in Beauty's circle proudly gay,
The midnight brought the signal-sound of strife,
The morn the marshalling in arms,—the day
Battle's magnificently stern array !
The thunder-clouds close o'er it, which when rent
The earth is cover'd thick with other clay,   250
Which her own clay shall cover, heap'd and pent,
Rider and horse,—friend, foe,—in one red burial blent !

XXIX

Their praise is hymn'd by loftier harps than mine:
Yet one I would select from that proud throng,
Partly because they blend me with his line,
And partly that I did his sire some wrong,
And partly that bright names will hallow song;
And his was of the bravest, and when shower'd
The death-bolts deadliest the thinn'd files along,
Even where the thickest of war's tempest lower'd,   260
They reach'd no nobler breast than thine, young, gallant Howard!

XXX

There have been tears and breaking hearts for thee,
And mine were nothing had I such to give;
But when I stood beneath the fresh green tree,
Which living waves where thou didst cease to live,
And saw around me the wide field revive
With fruits and fertile promise, and the Spring
Came forth her work of gladness to contrive,
With all her reckless birds upon the wing,
I turn'd from all she brought to those she could not bring.   270

XXXI

I turn'd to thee, to thousands, of whom each
And one as all a ghastly gap did make
In his own kind and kindred, whom to teach
Forgetfulness were mercy for their sake;
The Archangel's trump, not Glory's, must awake
Those whom they thirst for; though the sound of Fame
May for a moment soothe, it cannot slake
The fever of vain longing, and the name
So honour'd but assumes a stronger, bitterer claim.

XXXII

They mourn, but smile at length; and, smiling, mourn:
The tree will wither long before it fall;   281
The hull drives on, though mast and sail be torn;
The roof-tree sinks, but moulders on the hall
In massy hoariness; the ruin'd wall
Stands when its wind-worn battlements are gone;
The bars survive the captive they enthral;
The day drags through, though storms keep out the sun;
And thus the heart will break, yet brokenly live on:

XXXIII

Even as a broken mirror, which the glass
In every fragment multiplies; and makes   290
A thousand images of one that was,
The same, and still the more, the more it breaks;
And thus the heart will do which not forsakes,
Living in shatter'd guise; and still, and cold,
And bloodless, with its sleepless sorrow aches,
Yet withers on till all without is old,
Showing no visible sign, for such things are untold.

XXXIV

There is a very life in our despair,
Vitality of poison,—a quick root
Which feeds these deadly branches ; for it were   330
As nothing did we die ; but Life will suit
Itself to Sorrow's most detested fruit,
Like to the apples on the Dead Sea's shore,
All ashes to the taste : Did man compute
Existence by enjoyment, and count o'er
Such hours 'gainst years of life,—say, would he name three-score?

XXXV

The Psalmist number'd out the years of man :
They are enough ; and if thy tale be *true*,
Thou, who didst grudge him even that fleeting span,
More than enough, thou fatal Waterloo !   310
Millions of tongues record thee, and anew
Their children's lips shall echo them, and say—
' Here, where the sword united nations drew,
Our countrymen were warring on that day ! '
And this is much, and all which will not pass away.

XXXVI

There sunk the greatest, nor the worst of men,
Whose spirit, antithetically mixt,
One moment of the mightiest, and again
On little objects with like firmness fixt,
Extreme in all things ! Hadst thou been betwixt,   320
Thy throne had still been thine, or never been ;
For daring made thy rise as fall : thou seek'st
Even now to re-assume the imperial mien,
And shake again the world, the Thunderer of the scene !

XXXVII

Conqueror and captive of the earth art thou !
She trembles at thee still, and thy wild name
Was ne'er more bruited in men's minds than now
That thou art nothing, save the jest of Fame,
Who woo'd thee once, thy vassal, and became
The flatterer of thy fierceness, till thou wert   330
A god unto thyself ; nor less the same
To the astounded kingdoms all inert,
Who deem'd thee for a time whate'er thou didst assert.

XXXVIII

Oh, more or less than man—in high or low,
Battling with nations, flying from the field ;
Now making monarchs' necks thy footstool, now
More than thy meanest soldier taught to yield ;
An empire thou couldst crush, command, rebuild,
But govern not thy pettiest passion, nor,
However deeply in men's spirits skill'd,   340
Look through thine own, nor curb the lust of war,
Nor learn that tempted Fate will leave the loftiest star.

XXXIX

Yet well thy soul hath brook'd the turning tide
With that untaught, innate philosophy,
Which, be it wisdom, coldness, or deep pride,
Is gall and wormwood to an enemy.
When the whole host of hatred stood hard by,
To watch and mock thee shrinking, thou hast smiled
With a sedate and all-enduring eye;—
When Fortune fled her spoil'd and favourite child,   350
He stood unbow'd beneath the ills upon him piled.

XL

Sager than in thy fortunes; for in them
Ambition steel'd thee on too far to show
That just, habitual scorn, which could contemn
Men and their thoughts; 'twas wise to feel, not so
To wear it ever on thy lip and brow,
And spurn the instruments thou wert to use,
Till they were turn'd unto thine overthrow:
'Tis but a worthless world to win or lose;
So hath it proved to thee, and all such lot who choose. 360

XLI

If, like a tower upon a headland rock,
Thou hadst been made to stand or fall alone,
Such scorn of man had help'd to brave the shock;
But men's thoughts were the steps which paved thy throne,
Their admiration thy best weapon shone;
The part of Philip's son was thine, not then
(Unless aside thy purple had been thrown)
Like stern Diogenes to mock at men;
For sceptred cynics earth were far too wide a den.

XLII

But quiet to quick bosoms is a hell,   370
And *there* hath been thy bane; there is a fire
And motion of the soul which will not dwell
In its own narrow being, but aspire
Beyond the fitting medium of desire;
And, but once kindled, quenchless evermore,
Preys upon high adventure, nor can tire
Of aught but rest; a fever at the core,
Fatal to him who bears, to all who ever bore.

XLIII

This makes the madmen who have made men mad
By their contagion; Conquerors and Kings,   380
Founders of sects and systems, to whom add
Sophists, Bards, Statesmen, all unquiet things
Which stir too strongly the soul's secret springs,
And are themselves the fools to those they fool;
Envied, yet how unenviable! what stings
Are theirs! One breast laid open were a school
Which would unteach mankind the lust to shine or rule:

XLIV

Their breath is agitation, and their life
A storm whereon they ride, to sink at last,
And yet so nursed and bigoted to strife,
That should their days, surviving perils past,
Melt to calm twilight, they feel overcast
With sorrow and supineness, and so die ;
Even as a flame unfed, which runs to waste
With its own flickering, or a sword laid by,
Which eats into itself, and rusts ingloriously.

XLV

He who ascends to mountain-tops, shall find
The loftiest peaks most wrapt in clouds and snow ;
He who surpasses or subdues mankind,
Must look down on the hate of those below.
Though high *above* the sun of glory glow,
And far *beneath* the earth and ocean spread,
Round him are icy rocks, and loudly blow
Contending tempests on his naked head,
And thus reward the toils which to those summits led.

XLVI

Away with these ! true Wisdom's world will be
Within its own creation, or in thine,
Maternal Nature ! for who teems like thee,
Thus on the banks of thy majestic Rhine ?
There Harold gazes on a work divine,
A blending of all beauties ; streams and dells,
Fruit, foliage, crag, wood, cornfield, mountain, vine,
And chiefless castles breathing stern farewells
From gray but leafy walls, where Ruin greenly dwells.

XLVII

And there they stand, as stands a lofty mind,
Worn, but unstooping to the baser crowd,
All tenantless, save to the crannying wind,
Or holding dark communion with the crowd.
There was a day when they were young and proud ;
Banners on high, and battles pass'd below ;
But they who fought are in a bloody shroud,
And those which waved are shredless dust ere now,
And the bleak battlements shall bear no future blow.

XLVIII

Beneath those battlements, within those walls,
Power dwelt amidst her passions ; in proud state
Each robber chief upheld his armed halls,
Doing his evil will, nor less elate
Than mightier heroes of a longer date.
What want these outlaws conquerors should have
But history's purchased page to call them great ?
A wider space, an ornamented grave ?
Their hopes were not less warm, their souls were full as brave.

390

400

410

420

430

XLIX

In their baronial feuds and single fields,
What deeds of prowess unrecorded died !
And Love, which lent a blazon to their shields,
With emblems well devised by amorous pride,
Through all the mail of iron hearts would glide ;
But still their flame was fierceness, and drew on
Keen contest and destruction near allied,
And many a tower for some fair mischief won,   440
Saw the discolour'd Rhine beneath its ruin run.

L

But Thou, exulting and abounding river !
Making thy waves a blessing as they flow
Through banks whose beauty would endure for ever
Could man but leave thy bright creation so,
Nor its fair promise from the surface mow
With the sharp scythe of conflict,—then to see
Thy valley of sweet waters, were to know
Earth paved like Heaven ; and to seem such to me,
Even now what wants thy stream ?—that it should Lethe be.

LI

A thousand battles have assail'd thy banks,   451
But these and half their fame have pass'd away,
And Slaughter heap'd on high his weltering ranks ;
Their very graves are gone, and what are they ?
Thy tide wash'd down the blood of yesterday,
And all was stainless, and on thy clear stream
Glass'd, with its dancing light, the sunny ray ;
But o'er the blacken'd memory's blighting dream
Thy waves would vainly roll, all sweeping as they seem.

LII

Thus Harold inly said, and pass'd along,   460
Yet not insensible to all which here
Awoke the jocund birds to early song
In glens which might have made even exile dear :
Though on his brow were graven lines austere,
And tranquil sternness, which had ta'en the place
Of feelings fierier far but less severe,
Joy was not always absent from his face,
But o'er it in such scenes would steal with transient trace.

LIII

Nor was all love shut from him, though his days
Of passion had consumed themselves to dust.   470
It is in vain that we would coldly gaze
On such as smile upon us ; the heart must
Leap kindly back to kindness, though disgust
Hath wean'd it from all worldlings : thus he felt,
For there was soft remembrance, and sweet trust
In one fond breast, to which his own would melt,
And in its tenderer hour on that his bosom dwelt.

LIV

And he had learn'd to love,—I know not why,
For this in such as him seems strange of mood,—
The helpless looks of blooming infancy,   480
Even in its earliest nurture ; what subdued,
To change like this, a mind so far imbued
With scorn of man, it little boots to know ;
But thus it was ; and though in solitude
Small power the nipp'd affections have to grow,
In him this glow'd when all beside had ceased to glow.

LV

And there was one soft breast, as hath been said,
Which unto his was bound by stronger ties
Than the church links withal ; and, though unwed,
That love was pure, and, far above disguise,   490
Had stood the test of mortal enmities
Still undivided, and cemented more
By peril, dreaded most in female eyes ;
But this was firm, and from a foreign shore
Well to that heart might his these absent greetings pour !

1

The castled crag of Drachenfels
Frowns o'er the wide and winding Rhine,
Whose breast of waters broadly swells
Between the banks which bear the vine,
And hills all rich with blossom'd trees,   500
And fields which promise corn and wine,
And scatter'd cities crowning these,
Whose far white walls along them shine,
Have strew'd a scene, which I should see
With double joy wert *thou* with me.

2

And peasant girls, with deep blue eyes,
And hands which offer early flowers,
Walk smiling o'er this paradise ;
Above, the frequent feudal towers
Through green leaves lift their walls of gray ;   510
And many a rock which steeply lowers,
And noble arch in proud decay,
Look o'er this vale of vintage-bowers;
But one thing want these banks of Rhine,—
Thy gentle hand to clasp in mine !

3

I send the lilies given to me ;
Though long before thy hand they touch,
I know that they must wither'd be,
But yet reject them not as such ;

For I have cherish'd them as dear,   520
Because they yet may meet thine eye,
And guide thy soul to mine even here,
When thou behold'st them drooping nigh,
And know'st them gather'd by the Rhine,
And offer'd from my heart to thine!

4

The river nobly foams and flows,
The charm of this enchanted ground,
And all its thousand turns disclose
Some fresher beauty varying round:
The haughtiest breast its wish might bound   530
Through life to dwell delighted here;
Nor could on earth a spot be found
To nature and to me so dear,
Could thy dear eyes in following mine
Still sweeten more these banks of Rhine!

LVI

By Coblentz, on a rise of gentle ground,
There is a small and simple pyramid,
Crowning the summit of the verdant mound;
Beneath its base are heroes' ashes hid,
Our enemy's—but let not that forbid   540
Honour to Marceau! o'er whose early tomb
Tears, big tears, gush'd from the rough soldier's lid,
Lamenting and yet envying such a doom,
Falling for France, whose rights he battled to resume.

LVII

Brief, brave, and glorious was his young career,—
His mourners were two hosts, his friends and foes;
And fitly may the stranger lingering here
Pray for his gallant spirit's bright repose;
For he was Freedom's champion, one of those,
The few in number, who had not o'erstept   550
The charter to chastise which she bestows
On such as wield her weapons; he had kept
The whiteness of his soul, and thus men o'er him wept.

LVIII

Here Ehrenbreitstein, with her shatter'd wall
Black with the miner's blast, upon her height
Yet shows of what she was, when shell and ball
Rebounding idly on her strength did light:
A tower of victory! from whence the flight
Of baffled foes was watch'd along the plain:
But Peace destroy'd what War could never blight,   560
And laid those proud roofs bare to Summer's rain—
On which the iron shower for years had pour'd in vain.

LIX

Adieu to thee, fair Rhine! How long delighted
The stranger fain would linger on his way!
Thine is a scene alike where souls united
Or lonely Contemplation thus might stray;
And could the ceaseless vultures cease to prey
On self-condemning bosoms, it were here,
Where Nature, nor too sombre nor too gay,
Wild but not rude, awful yet not austere,   570
Is to the mellow Earth as Autumn to the year.

LX

Adieu to thee again! a vain adieu!
There can be no farewell to scene like thine;
The mind is colour'd by thy every hue;
And if reluctantly the eyes resign
Their cherish'd gaze upon thee, lovely Rhine!
'Tis with the thankful heart of parting praise;
More mighty spots may rise, more glaring shine,
But none unite in one attaching maze
The brilliant, fair, and soft,—the glories of old days.   580

LXI

The negligently grand, the fruitful bloom
Of coming ripeness, the white city's sheen,
The rolling stream, the precipice's gloom,
The forest's growth, and Gothic walls between,
The wild rocks shaped as they had turrets been,
In mockery of man's art; and these withal
A race of faces happy as the scene,
Whose fertile bounties here extend to all,
Still springing o'er thy banks, though Empires near them fall.

LXII

But these recede. Above me are the Alps,   590
The palaces of Nature, whose vast walls
Have pinnacled in clouds their snowy scalps,
And throned Eternity in icy halls
Of cold sublimity, where forms and falls
The avalanche—the thunderbolt of snow!
All that expands the spirit, yet appals,
Gather around these summits, as to show
How Earth may pierce to Heaven, yet leave vain man below.

LXIII

But ere these matchless heights I dare to scan,
There is a spot should not be pass'd in vain,—   600
Morat! the proud, the patriot field! where man
May gaze on ghastly trophies of the slain,
Nor blush for those who conquer'd on that plain;
Here Burgundy bequeath'd his tombless host,
A bony heap, through ages to remain,
Themselves their monument;—the Stygian coast
Unsepulchred they roam'd, and shriek'd each wandering ghost.

LXIV

While Waterloo with Cannae's carnage vies,
Morat and Marathon twin names shall stand ;
They were true Glory's stainless victories,   610
Won by the unambitious heart and hand
Of a proud, brotherly, and civic band,
All unbought champions in no princely cause
Of vice-entail'd Corruption ; they no land
Doom'd to bewail the blasphemy of laws
Making kings' rights divine, by some Draconic clause.

LXV

By a lone wall a lonelier column rears
A gray and grief-worn aspect of old days ;
'Tis the last remnant of the wreck of years,
And looks as with the wild-bewilder'd gaze   620
Of one to stone converted by amaze,
Yet still with consciousness ; and there it stands
Making a marvel that it not decays,
When the coeval pride of human hands,
Levell'd Adventicum, hath strew'd her subject lands.

LXVI

And there—oh ! sweet and sacred be the name !—
Julia—the daughter, the devoted—gave
Her youth to Heaven ; her heart, beneath a claim
Nearest to Heaven's, broke o'er a father's grave.
Justice is sworn 'gainst tears, and hers would crave   630
The life she lived in ; but the judge was just,
And then she died on him she could not save.
Their tomb was simple, and without a bust,
And held within their urn one mind, one heart, one dust.

LXVII

But these are deeds which should not pass away,
And names that must not wither, though the earth
Forgets her empires with a just decay,
The enslavers and the enslaved, their death and birth ;
The high, the mountain-majesty of worth
Should be, and shall, survivor of its woe,   640
And from its immortality look forth
In the sun's face, like yonder Alpine snow,
Imperishably pure beyond all things below.

LXVIII

Lake Leman woos me with its crystal face,
The mirror where the stars and mountains view
The stillness of their aspect in each trace
Its clear depth yields of their far height and hue :
There is too much of man here, to look through
With a fit mind the might which I behold ;
But soon in me shall Loneliness renew   650
Thoughts hid, but not less cherish'd than of old,
Ere mingling with the herd had penn'd me in their fold.

LXIX

To fly from, need not be to hate, mankind :
All are not fit with them to stir and toil,
Nor is it discontent to keep the mind
Deep in its fountain, lest it overboil
In the hot throng, where we become the spoil
Of our infection, till too late and long
We may deplore and struggle with the coil
In wretched interchange of wrong for wrong   660
Midst a contentious world, striving where none are strong.

LXX

There, in a moment we may plunge our years
In fatal penitence, and in the blight
Of our own soul turn all our blood to tears,
And colour things to come with hues of Night ;
The race of life becomes a hopeless flight
To those that walk in darkness : on the sea
The boldest steer but where their ports invite ;
But there are wanderers o'er Eternity
Whose bark drives on and on, and anchor'd ne'er shall be. 670

LXXI

Is it not better, then, to be alone,
And love Earth only for its earthly sake ?
By the blue rushing of the arrowy Rhone,
Or the pure bosom of its nursing lake,
Which feeds it as a mother who doth make
A fair but froward infant her own care,
Kissing its cries away as these awake ;—
Is it not better thus our lives to wear,
Than join the crushing crowd, doom'd to inflict or bear ?

LXXII

I live not in myself, but I become   680
Portion of that around me ; and to me
High mountains are a feeling, but the hum
Of human cities torture : I can see
Nothing to loathe in nature, save to be
A link reluctant in a fleshly chain,
Class'd among creatures, when the soul can flee,
And with the sky, the peak, the heaving plain
Of ocean, or the stars, mingle, and not in vain.

LXXIII

And thus I am absorb'd, and this is life :
I look upon the peopled desert past,   690
As on a place of agony and strife,
Where, for some sin, to sorrow I was cast,
To act and suffer, but remount at last
With a fresh pinion ; which I feel to spring,
Though young, yet waxing vigorous as the blast
Which it would cope with, on delighted wing,
Spurning the clay-cold bonds which round our being cling.

LXXIV

And when, at length, the mind shall be all free
From what it hates in this degraded form,
Reft of its carnal life, save what shall be   700
Existent happier in the fly and worm,—
When elements to elements conform,
And dust is as it should be, shall I not
Feel all I see, less dazzling, but more warm ?
The bodiless thought ? the Spirit of each spot ?
Of which, even now, I share at times the immortal lot ?

LXXV

Are not the mountains, waves, and skies, a part
Of me and of my soul, as I of them ?
Is not the love of these deep in my heart
With a pure passion ? should I not contemn   710
All objects, if compared with these ? and stem
A tide of suffering, rather than forego
Such feelings for the hard and worldly phlegm
Of those whose eyes are only turn'd below,
Gazing upon the ground, with thoughts which dare not glow ?

LXXVI

But this is not my theme ; and I return
To that which is immediate, and require
Those who find contemplation in the urn,
To look on One, whose dust was once all fire,
A native of the land where I respire   720
The clear air for a while—a passing guest,
Where he became a being,—whose desire
Was to be glorious ; 'twas a foolish quest,
The which to gain and keep, he sacrificed all rest.

LXXVII

Here the self-torturing sophist, wild Rousseau,
The apostle of affliction, he who threw
Enchantment over passion, and from woe
Wrung overwhelming eloquence, first drew
The breath which made him wretched ; yet he knew
How to make madness beautiful, and cast   730
O'er erring deeds and thoughts a heavenly hue
Of words, like sunbeams, dazzling as they past
The eyes, which o'er them shed tears feelingly and fast.

LXXVIII

His love was passion's essence :—as a tree
On fire by lightning, with ethereal flame
Kindled he was, and blasted ; for to be
Thus, and enamour'd, were in him the same.
But his was not the love of living dame,
Nor of the dead who rise upon our dreams,
But of ideal beauty, which became   740
In him existence, and o'erflowing teems
Along his burning page, distemper'd though it seems.

LXXIX

This breathed itself to life in Julie, *this*
Invested her with all that's wild and sweet;
This hallow'd, too, the memorable kiss
Which every morn his fever'd lip would greet,
From hers, who but with friendship his would meet;
But to that gentle touch through brain and breast
Flash'd the thrill'd spirit's love-devouring heat;
In that absorbing sigh perchance more blest   750
Than vulgar minds may be with all they seek possest.

LXXX

His life was one long war with self-sought foes,
Or friends by him self-banish'd; for his mind
Had grown Suspicion's sanctuary, and chose,
For its own cruel sacrifice, the kind,
'Gainst whom he raged with fury strange and blind.
But he was phrensied,—wherefore, who may know?
Since cause might be which skill could never find;
But he was phrensied by disease or woe,
To that worst pitch of all, which wears a reasoning show.   760

LXXXI

For then he was inspired, and from him came,
As from the Pythian's mystic cave of yore,
Those oracles which set the world in flame,
Nor ceased to burn till kingdoms were no more:
Did he not this for France? which lay before
Bow'd to the inborn tyranny of years?
Broken and trembling to the yoke she bore,
Till by the voice of him and his compeers
Roused up to too much wrath, which follows o'ergrown fears?

LXXXII

They made themselves a fearful monument!   770
The wreck of old opinions—things which grew,
Breathed from the birth of time: the veil they rent,
And what behind it lay, all earth shall view.
But good with ill they also overthrew,
Leaving but ruins, wherewith to rebuild
Upon the same foundation, and renew
Dungeons and thrones, which the same hour refill'd,
As heretofore, because ambition was self-will'd.

LXXXIII

But this will not endure, nor be endured!
Mankind have felt their strength, and made it felt.   780
They might have used it better, but, allured
By their new vigour, sternly have they dealt
On one another; pity ceased to melt
With her once natural charities. But they,
Who in oppression's darkness caved had dwelt,
They were not eagles, nourish'd with the day;
What marvel then, at times, if they mistook their prey?

LXXXIV

What deep wounds ever closed without a scar?
The heart's bleed longest, and but heal to wear
That which disfigures it; and they who war   790
With their own hopes, and have been vanquish'd, bear
Silence, but not submission: in his lair
Fix'd Passion holds his breath, until the hour
Which shall atone for years; none need despair:
It came, it cometh, and will come,—the power
To punish or forgive—in *one* we shall be slower.

LXXXV

Clear, placid Leman! thy contrasted lake,
With the wild world I dwelt in, is a thing
Which warns me, with its stillness, to forsake
Earth's troubled waters for a purer spring.   800
This quiet sail is as a noiseless wing
To waft me from distraction; once I loved
Torn ocean's roar, but thy soft murmuring
Sounds sweet as if a Sister's voice reproved,
That I with stern delights should e'er have been so mov'd.

LXXXVI

It is the hush of night, and all between
Thy margin and the mountains, dusk, yet clear,
Mellow'd and mingling, yet distinctly seen,
Save darken'd Jura, whose capt heights appear
Precipitously steep; and drawing near,   810
There breathes a living fragrance from the shore,
Of flowers yet fresh with childhood; on the ear
Drops the light drip of the suspended oar,
Or chirps the grasshopper one good-night carol more;

LXXXVII

He is an evening reveller, who makes
His life an infancy, and sings his fill;
At intervals, some bird from out the brakes
Starts into voice a moment, then is still.
There seems a floating whisper on the hill,
But that is fancy, for the starlight dews   820
All silently their tears of love instil,
Weeping themselves away, till they infuse
Deep into nature's breast the spirit of her hues.

LXXXVIII

Ye stars! which are the poetry of heaven!
If in your bright leaves we would read the fate
Of men and empires,—'tis to be forgiven,
That in our aspirations to be great,
Our destinies o'erleap their mortal state,
And claim a kindred with you; for ye are
A beauty and a mystery, and create   830
In us such love and reverence from afar,
That fortune, fame, power, life, have named themselves a star.

LXXXIX

All heaven and earth are still—though not in sleep,
But breathless, as we grow when feeling most;
And silent, as we stand in thoughts too deep :—
All heaven and earth are still : From the high host
Of stars, to the lull'd lake and mountain-coast,
All is concenter'd in a life intense,
Where not a beam, nor air, nor leaf is lost,
But hath a part of being, and a sense   840
Of that which is of all Creator and defence.

XC

Then stirs the feeling infinite, so felt
In solitude, where we are *least* alone ;
A truth, which through our being then doth melt,
And purifies from self : it is a tone,
The soul and source of music, which makes known
Eternal harmony, and sheds a charm
Like to the fabled Cytherea's zone,
Binding all things with beauty ;—'twould disarm
The spectre Death, had he substantial power to harm.   850

XCI

Not vainly did the early Persian make
His altar the high places, and the peak
Of earth-o'ergazing mountains, and thus take
A fit and unwall'd temple, there to seek
The Spirit, in whose honour shrines are weak,
Uprear'd of human hands. Come, and compare
Columns and idol-dwellings, Goth or Greek,
With Nature's realms of worship, earth and air,
Nor fix on fond abodes to circumscribe thy pray'r !

XCII

The sky is changed !—and such a change ! Oh night,   860
And storm, and darkness, ye are wondrous strong,
Yet lovely in your strength, as is the light
Of a dark eye in woman !   Far along,
From peak to peak, the rattling crags among
Leaps the live thunder ! Not from one lone cloud,
But every mountain now hath found a tongue,
And Jura answers, through her misty shroud,
Back to the joyous Alps, who call to her aloud !

XCIII

And this is in the night :—Most glorious night !
Thou wert not sent for slumber ! let me be   870
A sharer in thy fierce and far delight,—
A portion of the tempest and of thee !
How the lit lake shines, a phosphoric sea,
And the big rain comes dancing to the earth !
And now again 'tis black,—and now, the glee
Of the loud hills shakes with its mountain-mirth,
As if they did rejoice o'er a young earthquake's birth.

XCIV

Now, where the swift Rhone cleaves his way between
Heights which appear as lovers who have parted
In hate, whose mining depths so intervene,   880
That they can meet no more, though broken-hearted ;
Though in their souls, which thus each other thwarted,
Love was the very root of the fond rage
Which blighted their life's bloom, and then departed :
Itself expired, but leaving them an age
Of years all winters,—war within themselves to wage.

XCV

Now, where the quick Rhone thus hath cleft his way,
The mightiest of the storms hath ta'en his stand :
For here, not one, but many, make their play,
And fling their thunder-bolts from hand to hand,   890
Flashing and cast around ; of all the band,
The brightest through these parted hills hath fork'd
His lightnings,—as if he did understand,
That in such gaps as desolation work'd,
There the hot shaft should blast whatever therein lurk'd.

XCVI

Sky, mountains, river, winds, lake, lightnings ! ye !
With night, and clouds, and thunder, and a soul
To make these felt and feeling, well may be
Things that have made me watchful ; the far roll
Of your departing voices, is the knoll   900
Of what in me is sleepless,—if I rest.
But where of ye, O tempests ! is the goal ?
Are ye like those within the human breast ?
Or do ye find, at length, like eagles, some high nest ?

XCVII

Could I embody and unbosom now
That which is most within me,—could I wreak
My thoughts upon expression, and thus throw
Soul, heart, mind, passions, feelings, strong or weak,
All that I would have sought, and all I seek,
Bear, know, feel, and yet breathe—into *one* word,   910
And that one word were Lightning, I would speak ;
But as it is, I live and die unheard,
With a most voiceless thought, sheathing it as a sword.

XCVIII

The morn is up again, the dewy morn,
With breath all incense, and with cheek all bloom,
Laughing the clouds away with playful scorn,
And living as if earth contain'd no tomb,—
And glowing into day : we may resume
The march of our existence : and thus I,
Still on thy shores, fair Leman ! may find room   920
And food for meditation, nor pass by
Much, that may give us pause, if ponder'd fittingly.

XCIX

Clarens ! sweet Clarens, birthplace of deep Love !
Thine air is the young breath of passionate thought ;
Thy trees take root in Love ; the snows above
The very Glaciers have his colours caught,
And sun-set into rose-hues sees them wrought
By rays which sleep there lovingly : the rocks,
The permanent crags, tell here of Love, who sought
In them a refuge from the worldly shocks,   930
Which stir and sting the soul with hope that woos, then mocks.

C

Clarens ! by heavenly feet thy paths are trod,—
Undying Love's, who here ascends a throne
To which the steps are mountains ; where the god
Is a pervading life and light,—so shown
Not on those summits solely, nor alone
In the still cave and forest ; o'er the flower
His eye is sparkling, and his breath hath blown,
His soft and summer breath, whose tender power
Passes the strength of storms in their most desolate hour. 940

CI

All things are here of *him* ; from the black pines,
Which are his shade on high, and the loud roar
Of torrents, where he listeneth, to the vines
Which slope his green path downward to the shore,
Where the bow'd waters meet him, and adore,
Kissing his feet with murmurs ; and the wood,
The covert of old trees, with trunks all hoar,
But light leaves, young as joy, stands where it stood,
Offering to him, and his, a populous solitude.

CII

A populous solitude of bees and birds,   950
And fairy-form'd and many-colour'd things,
Who worship him with notes more sweet than words,
And innocently open their glad wings,
Fearless and full of life : the gush of springs,
And fall of lofty fountains, and the bend
Of stirring branches, and the bud which brings
The swiftest thought of beauty, here extend,
Mingling, and made by Love, unto one mighty end.

CIII

He who hath loved not, here would learn that lore,
And make his heart a spirit ; he who knows   960
That tender mystery, will love the more ;
For this is Love's recess, where vain men's woes,
And the world's waste, have driven him far from those,
For 'tis his nature to advance or die ;
He stands not still, but or decays, or grows
Into a boundless blessing, which may vie
With the immortal lights, in its eternity !

CIV

'Twas not for fiction chose Rousseau this spot,
Peopling it with affections ; but he found
It was the scene which Passion must allot   970
To the mind's purified beings ; 'twas the ground
Where early Love his Psyche's zone unbound,
And hallow'd it with loveliness : 'tis lone,
And wonderful, and deep, and hath a sound,
And sense, and sight of sweetness ; here the Rhone
Hath spread himself a couch, the Alps have rear'd a throne.

CV

Lausanne ! and Ferney ! ye have been the abodes
Of names which unto you bequeath'd a name ;
Mortals, who sought and found, by dangerous roads,
A path to perpetuity of fame :   980
They were gigantic minds, and their steep aim
Was, Titan-like, on daring doubts to pile
Thoughts which should call down thunder, and the flame
Of Heaven again assail'd, if Heaven the while
On man and man's research could deign do more than smile.

CVI

The one was fire and fickleness, a child
Most mutable in wishes, but in mind
A wit as various,—gay, grave, sage, or wild,—
Historian, bard, philosopher, combined ;
He multiplied himself among mankind,   990
The Proteus of their talents : But his own
Breathed most in ridicule,—which, as the wind,
Blew where it listed, laying all things prone,—
Now to o'erthrow a fool, and now to shake a throne.

CVII

The other, deep and slow, exhausting thought,
And hiving wisdom with each studious year,
In meditation dwelt, with learning wrought,
And shaped his weapon with an edge severe,
Sapping a solemn creed with solemn sneer ;
The lord of irony,—that master-spell,   1000
Which stung his foes to wrath, which grew from fear,
And doom'd him to the zealot's ready Hell,
Which answers to all doubts so eloquently well.

CVIII

Yet, peace be with their ashes,—for by them,
If merited, the penalty is paid ;
It is not ours to judge,—far less condemn ;
The hour must come when such things shall be made
Known unto all, or hope and dread allay'd
By slumber, on one pillow, in the dust,
Which, thus much we are sure, must lie decay'd ; 1010
And when it shall revive, as is our trust,
'Twill be to be forgiven, or suffer what is just.

CIX

But let me quit man's works, again to read
His Maker's, spread around me, and suspend
This page, which from my reveries I feed,
Until it seems prolonging without end.
The clouds above me to the white Alps tend,
And I must pierce them, and survey whate'er
May be permitted, as my steps I bend
To their most great and growing region, where   1020
The earth to her embrace compels the powers of air.

CX

Italia! too, Italia! looking on thee,
Full flashes on the soul the light of ages,
Since the fierce Carthaginian almost won thee,
To the last halo of the chiefs and sages
Who glorify thy consecrated pages ;
Thou wert the throne and grave of empires ; still,
The fount at which the panting mind assuages
Her thirst of knowledge, quaffing there her fill,
Flows from the eternal source of Rome's imperial hill. 1030

CXI

Thus far have I proceeded in a theme
Renew'd with no kind auspices :—to feel
We are not what we have been, and to deem
We are not what we should be, and to steel
The heart against itself ; and to conceal,
With a proud caution, love, or hate, or aught,—
Passion or feeling, purpose, grief or zeal,—
Which is the tyrant spirit of our thought,
Is a stern task of soul :—No matter,—it is taught.

CXII

And for these words, thus woven into song,   1040
It may be that they are a harmless wile,—
The colouring of the scenes which fleet along,
Which I would seize, in passing, to beguile
My breast, or that of others, for a while.
Fame is the thirst of youth, but I am not
So young as to regard men's frown or smile,
As loss or guerdon of a glorious lot ;
I stood and stand alone,—remember'd or forgot.

CXIII

I have not loved the world, nor the world me ;
I have not flatter'd its rank breath, nor bow'd   1050
To its idolatries a patient knee,—
Nor coin'd my cheek to smiles,—nor cried aloud
In worship of an echo ; in the crowd
They could not deem me one of such ; I stood
Among them, but not of them ; in a shroud
Of thoughts which were not their thoughts, and still could,
Had I not filed my mind, which thus itself subdued.

CXIV

I have not loved the world, nor the world loved me,—
But let us part fair foes; I do believe,
Though I have found them not, that there may be 1060
Words which are things, hopes which will not deceive,
And virtues which are merciful, nor weave
Snares for the failing; I would also deem
O'er others' griefs that some sincerely grieve;
That two, or one, are almost what they seem,
That goodness is no name, and happiness no dream.

CXV

My daughter! with thy name this song begun;
My daughter! with thy name thus much shall end;
I see thee not, I hear thee not, but none
Can be so wrapt in thee; thou art the friend   1070
To whom the shadows of far years extend:
Albeit my brow thou never shouldst behold,
My voice shall with thy future visions blend,
And reach into thy heart, when mine is cold,
A token and a tone, even from thy father's mould.

CXVI

To aid thy mind's development, to watch
Thy dawn of little joys, to sit and see
Almost thy very growth, to view thee catch
Knowledge of objects,—wonders yet to thee!
To hold thee lightly on a gentle knee,   1080
And print on thy soft cheek a parent's kiss,—
This, it should seem, was not reserved for me;
Yet this was in my nature: as it is,
I know not what is there, yet something like to this.

CXVII

Yet, though dull Hate as duty should be taught,
I know that thou wilt love me; though my name
Should be shut from thee, as a spell still fraught
With desolation, and a broken claim:
Though the grave closed between us,—'twere the same,
I know that thou wilt love me; though to drain 1090
My blood from out thy being were an aim,
And an attainment,—all would be in vain,—
Still thou wouldst love me, still that more than life retain.

CXVIII

The child of love, though born in bitterness,
And nurtured in convulsion. Of thy sire
These were the elements, and thine no less.
As yet such are around thee, but thy fire
Shall be more temper'd, and thy hope far higher.
Sweet be thy cradled slumbers! O'er the sea
And from the mountains where I now respire,   1100
Fain would I waft such blessing upon thee,
As, with a sigh, I deem thou might'st have been to me.

CANTO THE FOURTH

' Visto ho Toscana, Lombardia, Romagna,
Quel Monte che divide, e quel che serra
Italia, e un mare e l' altro, che la bagna.'
Ariosto, Satira iii.

I

I STOOD in Venice, on the Bridge of Sighs ;
A palace and a prison on each hand :
I saw from out the wave her structures rise
As from the stroke of the enchanter's wand :
A thousand years their cloudy wings expand
Around me, and a dying Glory smiles
O'er the far times, when many a subject land
Look'd to the winged Lion's marble piles,
Where Venice sate in state, throned on her hundred isles !

II

She looks a sea Cybele, fresh from ocean,   10
Rising with her tiara of proud towers
At airy distance, with majestic motion,
A ruler of the waters and their powers :
And such she was ;—her daughters had their dowers
From spoils of nations, and the exhaustless East
Pour'd in her lap all gems in sparkling showers.
In purple was she robed, and of her feast
Monarchs partook, and deem'd their dignity increased.

III

In Venice Tasso's echoes are no more,
And silent rows the songless gondolier ;   20
Her palaces are crumbling to the shore,
And music meets not always now the ear :
Those days are gone—but Beauty still is here.
States fall, arts fade—but Nature doth not die,
Nor yet forget how Venice once was dear,
The pleasant place of all festivity,
The revel of the earth, the masque of Italy !

IV

But unto us she hath a spell beyond
Her name in story, and her long array
Of mighty shadows, whose dim forms despond   30
Above the dogeless city's vanish'd sway ;
Ours is a trophy which will not decay
With the Rialto ; Shylock and the Moor,
And Pierre, cannot be swept or worn away—
The keystones of the arch ! though all were o'er,
For us repeopled were the solitary shore.

V

The beings of the mind are not of clay ;
Essentially immortal, they create
And multiply in us a brighter ray
And more beloved existence : that which Fate   40
Prohibits to dull life, in this our state
Of mortal bondage, by these spirits supplied,
First exiles, then replaces what we hate ;
Watering the heart whose early flowers have died,
And with a fresher growth replenishing the void.

VI

Such is the refuge of our youth and age,
The first from Hope, the last from Vacancy ;
And this worn feeling peoples many a page,
And, may be, that which grows beneath mine eye :
Yet there are things whose strong reality   50
Outshines our fairy-land ; in shape and hues
More beautiful than our fantastic sky,
And the strange constellations which the Muse
O'er her wild universe is skilful to diffuse :

VII

I saw or dream'd of such,—but let them go,—
They came like truth, and disappear'd like dreams ;
And whatsoe'er they were—are now but so :
I could replace them if I would ; still teems
My mind with many a form which aptly seems
Such as I sought for, and at moments found ;   60
Let these too go—for waking Reason deems
Such overweening phantasies unsound,
And other voices speak, and other sights surround.

VIII

I've taught me other tongues, and in strange eyes
Have made me not a stranger ; to the mind
Which is itself, no changes bring surprise ;
Nor is it harsh to make, nor hard to find
A country with—ay, or without mankind ;
Yet was I born where men are proud to be,—
Not without cause ; and should I leave behind   70
The inviolate island of the sage and free,
And seek me out a home by a remoter sea,

IX

Perhaps I loved it well : and should I lay
My ashes in a soil which is not mine,
My spirit shall resume it—if we may
Unbodied choose a sanctuary. I twine
My hopes of being remember'd in my line
With my land's language : if too fond and far
These aspirations in their scope incline,—   80
If my fame should be, as my fortunes are,
Of hasty growth and blight, and dull Oblivion bar

X

My name from out the temple where the dead
Are honour'd by the nations—let it be—
And light the laurels on a loftier head!
And be the Spartan's epitaph on me—
'Sparta hath many a worthier son than he.'
Meantime I seek no sympathies, nor need;
The thorns which I have reap'd are of the tree
I planted: they have torn me, and I bleed:
I should have known what fruit would spring from such a seed.

XI

The spouseless Adriatic mourns her lord;   91
And, annual marriage now no more renew'd,
The Bucentaur lies rotting unrestored,
Neglected garment of her widowhood!
St. Mark yet sees his lion where he stood
Stand, but in mockery of his wither'd power,
Over the proud Place where an Emperor sued,
And monarchs gazed and envied in the hour
When Venice was a queen with an unequall'd dower.

XII

The Suabian sued, and now the Austrian reigns—   100
An Emperor tramples where an Emperor knelt;
Kingdoms are shrunk to provinces, and chains
Clank over sceptred cities; nations melt
From power's high pinnacle, when they have felt
The sunshine for a while, and downward go
Like lauwine loosen'd from the mountain's belt;
Oh for one hour of blind old Dandolo!
Th' octogenarian chief, Byzantium's conquering foe.

XIII

Before St. Mark still glow his steeds of brass,
Their gilded collars glittering in the sun;   110
But is not Doria's menace come to pass?
Are they not *bridled?*—Venice, lost and won,
Her thirteen hundred years of freedom done,
Sinks, like a seaweed, into whence she rose!
Better be whelm'd beneath the waves, and shun,
Even in destruction's depth, her foreign foes,
From whom submission wrings an infamous repose.

XIV

In youth she was all glory,—a new Tyre;
Her very by-word sprung from victory,
The 'Planter of the Lion,' which through fire   120
And blood she bore o'er subject earth and sea;
Though making many slaves, herself still free,
And Europe's bulwark 'gainst the Ottomite;
Witness Troy's rival, Candia! Vouch it, ye
Immortal waves that saw Lepanto's fight!
For ye are names no time nor tyranny can blight.

XV

Statues of glass—all shiver'd—the long file
Of her dead Doges are declined to dust;
But where they dwelt, the vast and sumptuous pile
Bespeaks the pageant of their splendid trust;   130
Their sceptre broken, and their sword in rust,
Have yielded to the stranger: empty halls,
Thin streets, and foreign aspects, such as must
Too oft remind her who and what inthrals,
Have flung a desolate cloud o'er Venice' lovely walls.

XVI

When Athens' armies fell at Syracuse,
And fetter'd thousands bore the yoke of war,
Redemption rose up in the Attic Muse,
Her voice their only ransom from afar:
See! as they chant the tragic hymn, the car   140
Of the o'ermaster'd victor stops, the reins
Fall from his hands, his idle scimitar
Starts from its belt—he rends his captive's chains,
And bids him thank the bard for freedom and his strains.

XVII

Thus, Venice, if no stronger claim were thine,
Were all thy proud historic deeds forgot,
Thy choral memory of the Bard divine,
Thy love of Tasso, should have cut the knot
Which ties thee to thy tyrants; and thy lot
Is shameful to the nations,—most of all,   150
Albion! to thee: the Ocean queen should not
Abandon Ocean's children; in the fall
Of Venice think of thine, despite thy watery wall.

XVIII

I loved her from my boyhood; she to me
Was as a fairy city of the heart,
Rising like water-columns from the sea,
Of joy the sojourn, and of wealth the mart;
And Otway, Radcliffe, Schiller, Shakespeare's art,
Had stamp'd her image in me, and even so,
Although I found her thus, we did not part;   160
Perchance even dearer in her day of woe,
Than when she was a boast, a marvel, and a show.

XIX

I can repeople with the past—and of
The present there is still for eye and thought,
And meditation chasten'd down, enough;
And more, it may be, than I hoped or sought;
And of the happiest moments which were wrought
Within the web of my existence, some
From thee, fair Venice! have their colours caught:
There are some feelings Time cannot benumb,   170
Nor Torture shake, or mine would now be cold and dumb.

XX

But from their nature will the tannen grow
Loftiest on loftiest and least shelter'd rocks,
Rooted in barrenness, where nought below
Of soil supports them 'gainst the Alpine shocks
Of eddying storms ; yet springs the trunk, and mocks
The howling tempest, till its height and frame
Are worthy of the mountains from whose blocks
Of bleak, gray granite into life it came,
And grew a giant tree ;—the mind may grow the same. 180

XXI

Existence may be borne, and the deep root
Of life and sufferance make its firm abode
The bare and desolated bosoms : mute
The camel labours with the heaviest load,
And the wolf dies in silence,—not bestow'd
In vain should such example be ; if they,
Things of ignoble or of savage mood,
Endure and shrink not, we of nobler clay
May temper it to bear,—it is but for a day.

XXII

All suffering doth destroy, or is destroy'd,   190
Even by the sufferer ; and, in each event,
Ends :—Some, with hope replenish'd and rebuoy'd,
Return to whence they came—with like intent,
And weave their web again ; some, bow'd and bent,
Wax gray and ghastly, withering ere their time,
And perish with the reed on which they leant ;
Some seek devotion, toil, war, good or crime,
According as their souls were form'd to sink or climb.

XXIII

But ever and anon of griefs subdued
There comes a token like a scorpion's sting,   200
Scarce seen, but with fresh bitterness imbued ;
And slight withal may be the things which bring
Back on the heart the weight which it would fling
Aside for ever : it may be a sound—
A tone of music—summer's eve—or spring—
A flower—the wind—the ocean—which shall wound,
Striking the electric chain wherewith we are darkly bound ;

XXIV

And how and why we know not, nor can trace
Home to its cloud this lightning of the mind,
But feel the shock renew'd, nor can efface   210
The blight and blackening which it leaves behind
Which out of things familiar, undesign'd,
When least we deem of such, calls up to view
The spectres whom no exorcism can bind,—
The cold, the changed, perchance the dead—anew,
The mourn'd, the loved, the lost—too many ! yet how few !

XXV

But my soul wanders ; I demand it back
To meditate amongst decay, and stand
A ruin amidst ruins ; there to track
Fall'n states and buried greatness, o'er a land   220
Which *was* the mightiest in its old command,
And *is* the loveliest, and must ever be
The master-mould of Nature's heavenly hand ;
Wherein were cast the heroic and the free,
The beautiful, the brave, the lords of earth and sea,

XXVI

The commonwealth of kings, the men of Rome !
And even since, and now, fair Italy !
Thou art the garden of the world, the home
Of all Art yields, and Nature can decree ;
Even in thy desert, what is like to thee ?   230
Thy very weeds are beautiful, thy waste
More rich than other climes' fertility ;
Thy wreck a glory, and thy ruin graced
With an immaculate charm which cannot be defaced.

XXVII

The moon is up, and yet it is not night ;
Sunset divides the sky with her ; a sea
Of glory streams along the Alpine height
Of blue Friuli's mountains ; Heaven is free
From clouds, but of all colours seems to be,—
Melted to one vast Iris of the West,—   240
Where the Day joins the past Eternity ,
While, on the other hand, meek Dian's crest
Floats through the azure air—an island of the blest !

XXVIII

A single star is at her side, and reigns
With her o'er half the lovely heaven ; but still
Yon sunny sea heaves brightly, and remains
Roll'd o'er the peak of the far Rhaetian hill,
As Day and Night contending were, until
Nature reclaim'd her order :—gently flows
The deep-dyed Brenta, where their hues instil   250
The odorous purple of a new-born rose,
Which streams upon her stream, and glass'd within it glows,

XXIX

Fill'd with the face of heaven, which, from afar,
Comes down upon the waters ; all its hues,
From the rich sunset to the rising star,
Their magical variety diffuse :
And now they change ; a paler shadow strews
Its mantle o'er the mountains ; parting day
Dies like the dolphin, whom each pang imbues
With a new colour as it gasps away,   260
The last still loveliest, till—'tis gone—and all is gray.

XXX

There is a tomb in Arqua;—rear'd in air,
Pillar'd in their sarcophagus, repose
The bones of Laura's lover : here repair
Many familiar with his well-sung woes,
The pilgrims of his genius. He arose
To raise a language, and his land reclaim
From the dull yoke of her barbaric foes :
Watering the tree which bears his lady's name
With his melodious tears, he gave himself to fame.   270

XXXI

They keep his dust in Arqua, where he died ;
The mountain-village where his latter days
Went down the vale of years ; and 'tis their pride—
An honest pride—and let it be their praise,
To offer to the passing stranger's gaze
His mansion and his sepulchre ; both plain
And venerably simple, such as raise
A feeling more accordant with his strain
Than if a pyramid form'd his monumental fane.

XXXII

And the soft quiet hamlet where he dwelt   280
Is one of that complexion which seems made
For those who their mortality have felt,
And sought a refuge from their hopes decay'd
In the deep umbrage of a green hill's shade,
Which shows a distant prospect far away
Of busy cities, now in vain display'd,
For they can lure no further ; and the ray
Of a bright sun can make sufficient holiday,

XXXIII

Developing the mountains, leaves, and flowers,
And shining in the brawling brook, whereby,   290
Clear as its current, glide the sauntering hours
With a calm languor, which, though to the eye
Idlesse it seem, hath its morality.
If from society we learn to live,
'Tis solitude should teach us how to die ;
It hath no flatterers ; vanity can give
No hollow aid ; alone—man with his God must strive :

XXXIV

Or, it may be, with demons, who impair
The strength of better thoughts, and seek their prey
In melancholy bosoms, such as were   300
Of moody texture from their earliest day,
And loved to dwell in darkness and dismay,
Deeming themselves predestined to a doom
Which is not of the pangs that pass away ;
Making the sun like blood, the earth a tomb,
The tomb a hell, and hell itself a murkier gloom.

XXXV

Ferrara! in thy wide and grass-grown streets,
Whose symmetry was not for solitude,
There seems as 'twere a curse upon the seats
Of former sovereigns, and the antique brood   310
Of Este, which for many an age made good
Its strength within thy walls, and was of yore
Patron or tyrant, as the changing mood
Of petty power impell'd, of those who wore
The wreath which Dante's brow alone had worn before.

XXXVI

And Tasso is their glory and their shame.
Hark to his strain! and then survey his cell!
And see how dearly earn'd Torquato's fame,
And where Alfonso bade his poet dwell:
The miserable despot could not quell   320
The insulted mind he sought to quench, and blend
With the surrounding maniacs, in the hell
Where he had plunged it. Glory without end
Scatter'd the clouds away; and on that name attend

XXXVII

The tears and praises of all time; while thine
Would rot in its oblivion—in the sink
Of worthless dust, which from thy boasted line
Is shaken into nothing—but the link
Thou formest in his fortunes bids us think
Of thy poor malice, naming thee with scorn: 330
Alfonso! how thy ducal pageants shrink
From thee! if in another station born,
Scarce fit to be the slave of him thou madest to mourn:

XXXVIII

Thou! form'd to eat, and be despised, and die,
Even as the beasts that perish, save that thou
Hadst a more splendid trough and wider sty:
He! with a glory round his furrow'd brow,
Which emanated then, and dazzles now,
In face of all his foes, the Cruscan quire,
And Boileau, whose rash envy could allow   340
No strain which shamed his country's creaking lyre,
That whetstone of the teeth—monotony in wire!

XXXIX

Peace to Torquato's injured shade! 'twas his
In life and death to be the mark where Wrong
Aim'd with her poison'd arrows,—but to miss.
Oh, victor unsurpass'd in modern song!
Each year brings forth its millions; but how long
The tide of generations shall roll on,
And not the whole combined and countless throng
Compose a mind like thine? though all in one   350
Condensed their scatter'd rays, they would not form a sun.

XL

Great as thou art, yet parallel'd by those,
Thy countrymen, before thee born to shine,
The Bards of Hell and Chivalry : first rose
The Tuscan father's comedy divine ;
Then, not unequal to the Florentine,
The southern Scott, the minstrel who call'd forth
A new creation with his magic line,
And, like the Ariosto of the North,
Sang ladye-love and war, romance and knightly worth.   360

XLI

The lightning rent from Ariosto's bust
The iron crown of laurel's mimick'd leaves ;
Nor was the ominous element unjust,
For the true laurel-wreath which Glory weaves
Is of the tree no bolt of thunder cleaves,
And the false semblance but disgraced his brow ;
Yet still, if fondly Superstition grieves,
Know, that the lightning sanctifies below
Whate'er it strikes ;—yon head is doubly sacred now.

XLII

Italia ! oh Italia ! thou who hast   370
The fatal gift of beauty, which became
A funeral dower of present woes and past,
On thy sweet brow is sorrow plough'd by shame,
And annals graved in characters of flame.
Oh, God ! that thou wert in thy nakedness
Less lovely or more powerful, and couldst claim
Thy right, and awe the robbers back, who press
To shed thy blood, and drink the tears of thy distress ;

XLIII

Then might'st thou more appal ; or, less desired,
Be homely and be peaceful, undeplored   380
For thy destructive charms ; then, still untired,
Would not be seen the armed torrents pour'd
Down the deep Alps ; nor would the hostile horde
Of many-nation'd spoilers from the Po
Quaff blood and water ; nor the stranger's sword
Be thy sad weapon of defence, and so,
Victor or vanquish'd, thou the slave of friend or foe.

XLIV

Wandering in youth, I traced the path of him,
The Roman friend of Rome's least-mortal mind,
The friend of Tully : as my bark did skim   390
The bright blue waters with a fanning wind,
Came Megara before me, and behind
Aegina lay, Piraeus on the right,
And Corinth on the left ; I lay reclined
Along the prow, and saw all these unite
In ruin, even as he had seen the desolate sight ;

XLV

For Time hath not rebuilt them, but uprear'd
Barbaric dwellings on their shatter'd site,
Which only make more mourn'd and more endear'd
The few last rays of their far-scatter'd light,   400
And the crush'd relics of their vanish'd might.
The Roman saw these tombs in his own age,
These sepulchres of cities, which excite
Sad wonder, and his yet surviving page
The moral lesson bears, drawn from such pilgrimage.

XLVI

That page is now before me, and on mine
His country's ruin added to the mass
Of perish'd states he mourn'd in their decline,
And I in desolation : all that *was*
Of then destruction *is ;* and now, alas !   410
Rome—Rome imperial, bows her to the storm,
In the same dust and blackness, and we pass
The skeleton of her Titanic form,
Wrecks of another world, whose ashes still are warm.

XLVII

Yet, Italy ! through every other land
Thy wrongs should ring, and shall, from side to side ;
Mother of Arts ! as once of arms ; thy hand
Was then our guardian, and is still our guide ;
Parent of our religion ! whom the wide
Nations have knelt to for the keys of heaven !   420
Europe, repentant of her parricide,
Shall yet redeem thee, and, all backward driven,
Roll the barbarian tide, and sue to be forgiven.

XLVIII

But Arno wins us to the fair white walls,
Where the Etrurian Athens claims and keeps
A softer feeling for her fairy halls.
Girt by her theatre of hills, she reaps
Her corn, and wine, and oil, and Plenty leaps
To laughing life, with her redundant horn.
Along the banks where smiling Arno sweeps   430
Was modern Luxury of Commerce born,
And buried Learning rose, redeem'd to a new morn.

XLIX

There, too, the Goddess loves in stone, and fills
The air around with beauty ; we inhale
The ambrosial aspect, which, beheld, instils
Part of its immortality ; the veil
Of heaven is half undrawn ; within the pale
We stand, and in that form and face behold
What Mind can make, when Nature's self would fail ;
And to the fond idolaters of old   440
Envy the innate flash which such a soul could mould :

L

We gaze and turn away, and know not where,
Dazzled and drunk with beauty, till the heart,
Reels with its fulness ; there—for ever there—
Chain'd to the chariot of triumphal Art,
We stand as captives, and would not depart.
Away !—there need no words nor terms precise,
The paltry jargon of the marble mart,
Where Pedantry gulls Folly—we have eyes :
Blood, pulse, and breast confirm the Dardan Shepherd's prize.

LI

Appear'dst thou not to Paris in this guise ?   451
Or to more deeply blest Anchises ? or,
In all thy perfect goddess-ship, when lies
Before thee thy own vanquish'd Lord of War ?
And gazing in thy face as toward a star,
Laid on thy lap, his eyes to thee upturn,
Feeding on thy sweet cheek ! while thy lips are
With lava kisses melting while they burn,
Shower'd on his eyelids, brow, and mouth, as from an urn ?

LII

Glowing, and circumfused in speechless love   460
Their full divinity inadequate
That feeling to express, or to improve,
The gods become as mortals, and man's fate
Has moments like their brightest ; but the weight
Of earth recoils upon us ;—let it go !
We can recall such visions, and create,
From what has been, or might be, things which grow
Into thy statue's form, and look like gods below.

LIII

I leave to learned fingers and wise hands,
The artist and his ape, to teach and tell   470
How well his connoisseurship understands
The graceful bend, and the voluptuous swell :
Let these describe the undescribable :
I would not their vile breath should crisp the stream
Wherein that image shall for ever dwell ;
The unruffled mirror of the loveliest dream
That ever left the sky on the deep soul to beam.

LIV

In Santa Croce's holy precincts lie
Ashes which make it holier, dust which is
Even in itself an immortality,   480
Though there were nothing save the past, and this,
The particle of those sublimities
Which have relapsed to chaos : her repose
Angelo's, Alfieri's bones, and his,
The starry Galileo, with his woes ;
Here Machiavelli's earth return'd to whence it rose.

LV

These are four minds, which, like the elements,
Might furnish forth creation :—Italy !
Time, which hath wrong'd thee with ten thousand rents
Of thine imperial garment, shall deny,   490
And hath denied, to every other sky,
Spirits which soar from ruin : thy decay
Is still impregnate with divinity,
Which gilds it with revivifying ray ;
Such as the great of yore, Canova is to-day.

LVI

But where repose the all Etruscan three—
Dante, and Petrarch, and, scarce less than they,
The Bard of Prose, creative spirit ! he
Of the Hundred Tales of love—where did they lay
Their bones, distinguish'd from our common clay   500
In death as life ?   Are they resolved to dust,
And have their country's marbles nought to say ?
Could not her quarries furnish forth one bust ?
Did they not to her breast their filial earth intrust ?

LVII

Ungrateful Florence ! Dante sleeps afar,
Like Scipio, buried by the upbraiding shore :
Thy factions, in their worse than civil war,
Proscribed the bard whose name for evermore
Their children's children would in vain adore
With the remorse of ages ; and the crown   510
Which Petrarch's laureate brow supremely wore,
Upon a far and foreign soil had grown,
His life, his fame, his grave, though rifled—not thine own.

LVIII

Boccaccio to his parent earth bequeath'd
His dust,—and lies it not her great among,
With many a sweet and solemn requiem breathed
O'er him who form'd the Tuscan's siren tongue ?
That music in itself, whose sounds are song,
The poetry of speech ? No ;—even his tomb
Uptorn, must bear the hyaena bigot's wrong,   520
No more amidst the meaner dead find room,
Nor claim a passing sigh, because it told for *whom !*

LIX

And Santa Croce wants their mighty dust ;
Yet for this want more noted, as of yore
The Caesar's pageant, shorn of Brutus' bust,
Did but of Rome's best Son remind her more :
Happier Ravenna ! on thy hoary shore,
Fortress of falling empire ! honour'd sleeps
The immortal exile ;—Arqua, too, her store
Of tuneful relics proudly claims and keeps,   530
While Florence vainly begs her banish'd dead and weeps.

LX

What is her pyramid of precious stones ?
Of porphyry, jasper, agate, and all hues
Of gem and marble, to incrust the bones
Of merchant-dukes ? the momentary dews
Which, sparkling to the twilight stars, infuse
Freshness in the green turf that wraps the dead,
Whose names are mausoleums of the Muse,
Are gently prest with far more reverent tread
Than ever paced the slab which paves the princely head. 540

LXI

There be more things to greet the heart and eyes
In Arno's dome of Art's most princely shrine,
Where Sculpture with her rainbow sister vies ;
There be more marvels yet—but not for mine ;
For I have been accustom'd to entwine
My thoughts with Nature rather in the fields,
Than Art in galleries ; though a work divine
Calls for my spirit's homage, yet it yields
Less than it feels, because the weapon which it wields

LXII

Is of another temper, and I roam   550
By Thrasimene's lake, in the defiles
Fatal to Roman rashness, more at home ;
For there the Carthaginian's warlike wiles
Come back before me, as his skill beguiles
The host between the mountains and the shore,
Where Courage falls in her despairing files,
And torrents, swoll'n to rivers with their gore,
Reek through the sultry plain, with legions scatter'd o'er,

LXIII

Like to a forest fell'd by mountain winds ;
And such the storm of battle on this day,   560
And such the frenzy, whose convulsion blinds
To all save carnage, that, beneath the fray,
An earthquake reel'd unheededly away !
None felt stern Nature rocking at his feet,
And yawning forth a grave for those who lay
Upon their bucklers for a winding-sheet ;
Such is the absorbing hate when warring nations meet !

LXIV

The Earth to them was as a rolling bark
Which bore them to Eternity ; they saw
The Ocean round, but had no time to mark   570
The motions of their vessel ; Nature's law,
In them suspended, reck'd not of the awe
Which reigns when mountains tremble, and the birds
Plunge in the clouds for refuge, and withdraw
From their down-toppling nests ; and bellowing herds
Stumble o'er heaving plains, and man's dread hath no words.

LXV

Far other scene is Thrasimene now;
Her lake a sheet of silver, and her plain
Rent by no ravage save the gentle plough;
Her aged trees rise thick as once the slain   580
Lay where their roots are; but a brook hath ta'en—
A little rill of scanty stream and bed—
A name of blood from that day's sanguine rain;
And Sanguinetto tells ye where the dead
Made the earth wet, and turn'd the unwilling waters red.

LXVI

But thou, Clitumnus! in thy sweetest wave
Of the most living crystal that was e'er
The haunt of river nymph, to gaze and lave
Her limbs where nothing hid them, thou dost rear
Thy grassy banks whereon the milk-white steer   590
Grazes; the purest god of gentle waters!
And most serene of aspect, and most clear;
Surely that stream was unprofaned by slaughters,
A mirror and a bath for Beauty's youngest daughters!

LXVII

And on thy happy shore a Temple still,
Of small and delicate proportion, keeps,
Upon a mild declivity of hill,
Its memory of thee; beneath it sweeps
Thy current's calmness; oft from out it leaps
The finny darter with the glittering scales,   600
Who dwells and revels in thy glassy deeps;
While, chance, some scatter'd water-lily sails
Down where the shallower wave still tells its bubbling tales.

LXVIII

Pass not unblest the Genius of the place!
If through the air a zephyr more serene
Win to the brow, 'tis his; and if ye trace
Along his margin a more eloquent green,
If on the heart the freshness of the scene
Sprinkle its coolness, and from the dry dust
Of weary life a moment lave it clean   610
With Nature's baptism,—'tis to him ye must
Pay orisons for this suspension of disgust.

LXIX

The roar of waters!—from the headlong height
Velino cleaves the wave-worn precipice;
The fall of waters! rapid as the light
The flashing mass foams shaking the abyss;
The hell of waters! where they howl and hiss,
And boil in endless torture; while the sweat
Of their great agony, wrung out from this
Their Phlegethon, curls round the rocks of jet   620
That guard the gulf around, in pitiless horror set,

LXX

And mounts in spray the skies, and thence again
Returns in an unceasing shower, which round,
With its unemptied cloud of gentle rain,
Is an eternal April to the ground,
Making it all one emerald :—how profound
The gulf ! and how the giant element
From rock to rock leaps with delirious bound,
Crushing the cliffs, which, downward worn and rent
With his fierce footsteps, yield in chasms a fearful vent !   630

LXXI

To the broad column which rolls on, and shows
More like the fountain of an infant sea
Torn from the womb of mountains by the throes
Of a new world, than only thus to be
Parent of rivers, which flow gushingly,
With many windings, through the vale :—Look back !
Lo ! where it comes like an eternity,
As if to sweep down all things in its track,
Charming the eye with dread,—a matchless cataract,

LXXII

Horribly beautiful ! but on the verge,   640
From side to side, beneath the glittering morn
An Iris sits, amidst the infernal surge,
Like Hope upon a death-bed, and, unworn
Its steady dyes, while all around is torn
By the distracted waters, bears serene
Its brilliant hues with all their beams unshorn :
Resembling, 'mid the torture of the scene,
Love watching Madness with unalterable mien.

LXXIII

Once more upon the woody Apennine,
The infant Alps, which—had I not before   650
Gazed on their mightier parents, where the pine
Sits on more shaggy summits, and where roar
The thundering lauwine—might be worshipp'd more ;
But I have seen the soaring Jungfrau rear
Her never-trodden snow, and seen the hoar
Glaciers of bleak Mont Blanc both far and near,
And in Chimari heard the thunder-hills of fear,

LXXIV

Th' Acroceraunian mountains of old name ;
And on Parnassus seen the eagles fly
Like spirits of the spot, as 'twere for fame,   660
For still they soared unutterably high :
I've look'd on Ida with a Trojan's eye ;
Athos, Olympus, Aetna, Atlas, made
These hills seem things of lesser dignity,
All, save the lone Soracte's height, display'd
Not *now* in snow, which asks the lyric Roman's aid

LXXV

For our remembrance, and from out the plain
Heaves like a long-swept wave about to break,
And on the curl hangs pausing : not in vain
May he, who will, his recollections rake,   670
And quote in classic raptures, and awake
The hills with Latian echoes ; I abhorr'd
Too much, to conquer for the poet's sake,
The drill'd dull lesson, forced down word by word
In my repugnant youth, with pleasure to record

LXXVI

Aught that recalls the daily drug which turn'd
My sickening memory ; and, though Time hath taught
My mind to meditate what then it learn'd,
Yet such the fix'd inveteracy wrought
By the impatience of my early thought,   680
That, with the freshness wearing out before
My mind could relish what it might have sought,
If free to choose, I cannot now restore
Its health ; but what it then detested, still abhor.

LXXVII

Then farewell, Horace ; whom I hated so,
Not for thy faults, but mine ; it is a curse
To understand, not feel thy lyric flow,
To comprehend, but never love thy verse :
Although no deeper Moralist rehearse
Our little life, nor Bard prescribe his art,   690
Nor livelier Satirist the conscience pierce,
Awakening without wounding the touch'd heart,
Yet fare thee well—upon Soracte's ridge we part.

LXXVIII

Oh Rome ! my country ! city of the soul !
The orphans of the heart must turn to thee,
Lone mother of dead empires ! and control
In their shut breasts their petty misery.
What are our woes and sufferance ? Come and see
The cypress, hear the owl, and plod your way
O'er steps of broken thrones and temples, Ye !   700
Whose agonies are evils of a day—
A world is at our feet as fragile as our clay.

LXXIX

The Niobe of nations ! there she stands,
Childless and crownless, in her voiceless woe ;
An empty urn within her wither'd hands,
Whose holy dust was scatter'd long ago ;
The Scipios' tomb contains no ashes now ;
The very sepulchres lie tenantless
Of their heroic dwellers : dost thou flow,
Old Tiber ! through a marble wilderness ?   710
Rise, with thy yellow waves, and mantle her distress.

LXXX

The Goth, the Christian, Time, War, Flood, and Fire,
Have dealt upon the seven-hill'd city's pride;
She saw her glories star by star expire,
And up the steep barbarian monarchs ride,
Where the car climb'd the Capitol; far and wide
Temple and tower went down, nor left a site:—
Chaos of ruins! who shall trace the void,
O'er the dim fragments cast a lunar light,
And say, 'here was, or is,' where all is doubly night?   720

LXXXI

The double night of ages, and of her,
Night's daughter, Ignorance, hath wrapt and wrap
All round us: we but feel our way to err:
The ocean hath its chart, the stars their map,
And Knowledge spreads them on her ample lap;
But Rome is as the desert, where we steer
Stumbling o'er recollections; now we clap
Our hands, and cry 'Eureka!' it is clear—
When but some false mirage of ruin rises near.

LXXXII

Alas! the lofty city! and alas!   730
The trebly hundred triumphs! and the day
When Brutus made the dagger's edge surpass
The conqueror's sword in bearing fame away!
Alas, for Tully's voice, and Virgil's lay,
And Livy's pictured page!—but these shall be
Her resurrection; all beside—decay.
Alas, for Earth, for never shall we see
That brightness in her eye she bore when Rome was free!

LXXXIII

Oh thou, whose chariot roll'd on Fortune's wheel,
Triumphant Sylla! Thou, who didst subdue   740
Thy country's foes ere thou wouldst pause to feel
The wrath of thy own wrongs, or reap the due
Of hoarded vengeance till thine eagles flew
O'er prostrate Asia;—thou, who with thy frown
Annihilated senates—Roman, too,
With all thy vices, for thou didst lay down
With an atoning smile a more than earthly crown—

LXXXIV

The dictatorial wreath—couldst thou divine
To what would one day dwindle that which made
Thee more than mortal? and that so supine   750
By aught than Romans Rome should thus be laid?
She who was named Eternal, and array'd
Her warriors but to conquer—she who veil'd
Earth with her haughty shadow, and display'd,
Until the o'er-canopied horizon fail'd,
Her rushing wings—Oh! she who was Almighty hail'd!

LXXXV

Sylla was first of victors ; but our own,
The sagest of usurpers, Cromwell !—he
Too swept off senates while he hew'd the throne
Down to a block—immortal rebel ! See   760
What crimes it costs to be a moment free,
And famous through all ages ! but beneath
His fate the moral lurks of destiny ;
His day of double victory and death
Beheld him win two realms, and, happier, yield his breath.

LXXXVI

The third of the same moon whose former course
Had all but crown'd him, on the self-same day
Deposed him gently from his throne of force,
And laid him with the earth's preceding clay.
And show'd not Fortune thus how fame and sway,   770
And all we deem delightful, and consume
Our souls to compass through each arduous way,
Are in her eyes less happy than the tomb ?
Were they but so in man's, how different were his doom !

LXXXVII

And thou, dread statue ! yet existent in
The austerest form of naked majesty,
Thou who beheldest, 'mid the assassins' din,
At thy bathed base the bloody Caesar lie,
Folding his robe in dying dignity,
An offering to thine altar from the queen   780
Of gods and men, great Nemesis ! did he die,
And thou, too, perish, Pompey ? have ye been
Victors of countless kings, or puppets of a scene ?

LXXXVIII

And thou, the thunder-stricken nurse of Rome !
She-wolf ! whose brazen-imaged dugs impart
The milk of conquest yet within the dome
Where, as a monument of antique art,
Thou standest :—Mother of the mighty heart,
Which the great founder suck'd from thy wild teat,
Scorch'd by the Roman Jove's ethereal dart,   790
And thy limbs black with lightning—dost thou yet
Guard thine immortal cubs, nor thy fond charge forget ?

LXXXIX

Thou dost ; but all thy foster-babes are dead—
The men of iron : and the world hath rear'd
Cities from out their sepulchres : men bled
In imitation of the things they fear'd,
And fought and conquer'd, and the same course steer'd,
At apish distance ; but as yet none have,
Nor could, the same supremacy have near'd,
Save one vain man, who is not in the grave,   800
But, vanquish'd by himself, to his own slaves a slave—

XC

The fool of false dominion—and a kind
Of bastard Caesar, following him of old
With steps unequal; for the Roman's mind
Was modell'd in a less terrestrial mould,
With passions fiercer, yet a judgment cold,
And an immortal instinct which redeem'd
The frailties of a heart so soft, yet bold,
Alcides with the distaff now he seem'd
At Cleopatra's feet,—and now himself he beam'd,   810

XCI

And came—and saw—and conquer'd! But the man
Who would have tamed his eagles down to flee,
Like a train'd falcon, in the Gallic van,
Which he, in sooth, long led to victory,
With a deaf heart which never seem'd to be
A listener to itself, was strangely framed;
With but one weakest weakness—vanity,
Coquettish in ambition, still he aim'd—
At what? can he avouch, or answer what he claim'd?

XCII

And would be all or nothing—nor could wait   820
For the sure grave to level him; few years
Had fix'd him with the Caesars in his fate,
On whom we tread: For *this* the conqueror rears
The arch of triumph! and for this the tears
And blood of earth flow on as they have flow'd,
An universal deluge, which appears
Without an ark for wretched man's abode,
And ebbs but to reflow! Renew thy rainbow, God!

XCIII

What from this barren being do we reap?
Our senses narrow, and our reason frail,   830
Life short, and truth a gem which loves the deep,
And all things weigh'd in custom's falsest scale;
Opinion an omnipotence,—whose veil
Mantles the earth with darkness, until right
And wrong are accidents, and men grow pale
Lest their own judgments should become too bright,
And their free thoughts be crimes, and earth have too much light.

XCIV

And thus they plod in sluggish misery,
Rotting from sire to son, and age to age,
Proud of their trampled nature, and so die,   840
Bequeathing their hereditary rage
To the new race of inborn slaves, who wage
War for their chains, and rather than be free,
Bleed gladiator-like, and still engage
Within the same arena where they see
Their fellows fall before, like leaves of the same tree.

XCV

I speak not of men's creeds—they rest between
Man and his Maker—but of things allow'd,
Averr'd, and known, and daily, hourly seen—
The yoke that is upon us doubly bow'd,   850
And the intent of tyranny avow'd,
The edict of Earth's rulers, who are grown
The apes of him who humbled once the proud,
And shook them from their slumbers on the throne :
Too glorious, were this all his mighty arm had done.

XCVI

Can tyrants but by tyrants conquer'd be,
And Freedom find no champion and no child
Such as Columbia saw arise when she
Sprung forth a Pallas, arm'd and undefiled ?
Or must such minds be nourish'd in the wild,   860
Deep in the unpruned forest, 'midst the roar
Of cataracts, where nursing Nature smiled
On infant Washington ? Has Earth no more
Such seeds within her breast, or Europe no such shore ?

XCVII

But France got drunk with blood to vomit crime,
And fatal have her Saturnalia been
To Freedom's cause, in every age and clime ;
Because the deadly days which we have seen,
And vile Ambition, that built up between
Man and his hopes an adamantine wall,   870
And the base pageant last upon the scene,
Are grown the pretext for the eternal thrall
Which nips life's tree, and dooms man's worst—his second fall.

XCVIII

Yet, Freedom ! yet thy banner, torn, but flying,
Streams like the thunder-storm *against* the wind ;
Thy trumpet voice, though broken now and dying,
The loudest still the tempest leaves behind ;
Thy tree hath lost its blossoms, and the rind,
Chopp'd by the axe, looks rough and little worth,
But the sap lasts,—and still the seed we find   880
Sown deep, even in the bosom of the North ;
So shall a better spring less bitter fruit bring forth.

XCIX

There is a stern round tower of other days,
Firm as a fortress, with its fence of stone,
Such as an army's baffled strength delays,
Standing with half its battlements alone,
And with two thousand years of ivy grown,
The garland of eternity, where wave
The green leaves over all by time o'erthrown ;—
What was this tower of strength ? within its cave   890
What treasure lay so lock'd, so hid ?—A woman's grave.

C

But who was she, the lady of the dead,
Tomb'd in a palace ? Was she chaste and fair ?
Worthy a king's, or more—a Roman's bed ?
What race of chiefs and heroes did she bear ?
What daughter of her beauties was the heir ?
How lived, how loved, how died she ? Was she not
So honoured—and conspicuously there,
Where meaner relics must not dare to rot,
Placed to commemorate a more than mortal lot ?   900

CI

Was she as those who love their lords, or they
Who love the lords of others ? such have been
Even in the olden time, Rome's annals say.
Was she a matron of Cornelia's mien,
Or the light air of Egypt's graceful queen,
Profuse of joy—or 'gainst it did she war
Inveterate in virtue ? Did she lean
To the soft side of the heart, or wisely bar
Love from amongst her griefs ?—for such the affections are.

CII

Perchance she died in youth : it may be, bow'd   910
With woes far heavier than the ponderous tomb
That weigh'd upon her gentle dust, a cloud
Might gather o'er her beauty, and a gloom
In her dark eye, prophetic of the doom
Heaven gives its favourites—early death ; yet shed
A sunset charm around her, and illume
With hectic light, the Hesperus of the dead,
Of her consuming cheek the autumnal leaf-like red.

CIII

Perchance she died in age—surviving all,
Charms, kindred, children—with the silver gray   920
On her long tresses, which might yet recall,
It may be, still a something of the day
When they were braided, and her proud array
And lovely form were envied, praised, and eyed
By Rome—But whither would Conjecture stray ?
Thus much alone we know—Metella died,
The wealthiest Roman's wife : Behold his love or pride !

CIV

I know not why—but standing thus by thee
It seems as if I had thine inmate known,
Thou Tomb ! and other days come back on me   930
With recollected music, though the tone
Is changed and solemn, like the cloudy groan
Of dying thunder on the distant wind ;
Yet could I seat me by this ivied stone
Till I had bodied forth the heated mind
Forms from the floating wreck which Ruin leaves behind ;

CV

And from the planks, far shatter'd o'er the rocks,
Built me a little bark of hope, once more
To battle with the ocean and the shocks
Of the loud breakers, and the ceaseless roar   940
Which rushes on the solitary shore
Where all lies founder'd that was ever dear :
But could I gather from the wave-worn store
 Enough for my rude boat, where should I steer ?
There woos no home, nor hope, nor life, save what is here.

CVI

Then let the winds howl on ! their harmony
Shall henceforth be my music, and the night
The sound shall temper with the owlets' cry,
As I now hear them, in the fading light
Dim o'er the bird of darkness' native site,   950
Answering each other on the Palatine,
With their large eyes, all glistening gray and bright,
 And sailing pinions.—Upon such a shrine
What are our petty griefs ?—let me not number mine.

CVII

Cypress and ivy, weed and wallflower grown
Matted and mass'd together, hillocks heap'd
On what were chambers, arch crush'd, column strown
In fragments, choked up vaults, and frescos steep'd
In subterranean damps, where the owl peep'd,
Deeming it midnight :—Temples, baths, or halls ?   960
Pronounce who can ; for all that Learning reap'd
 From her research hath been, that these are walls—
Behold the Imperial Mount ! 'tis thus the mighty falls.

CVIII

There is the moral of all human tales ;
'Tis but the same rehearsal of the past,
First Freedom, and then Glory—when that fails,
Wealth, vice, corruption,—barbarism at last.
And History, with all her volumes vast,
Hath but *one* page,—'tis better written here
Where gorgeous Tyranny hath thus amass'd   970
All treasures, all delights, that eye or ear,
Heart, soul could seek, tongue ask—Away with words! draw near,

CIX

Admire, exult, despise, laugh, weep,—for here
There is such matter for all feeling :—Man !
Thou pendulum betwixt a smile and tear,
Ages and realms are crowded in this span,
This mountain, whose obliterated plan
The pyramid of empires pinnacled,
Of Glory's gewgaws shining in the van
Till the sun's rays with added flame were fill'd !   980
Where are its golden roofs ? where those who dared to build ?

CX

Tully was not so eloquent as thou,
Thou nameless column with the buried base
What are the laurels of the Caesar's brow ?
Crown me with ivy from his dwelling-place.
Whose arch or pillar meets me in the face,
Titus or Trajan's ? No—'tis that of Time :
Triumph, arch, pillar, all he doth displace
Scoffing ; and apostolic statues climb
To crush the imperial urn, whose ashes slept sublime,   990

CXI

Buried in air, the deep blue sky of Rome,
And looking to the stars : they had contain'd
A spirit which with these would find a home,
The last of those who o'er the whole earth reign'd,
The Roman globe, for after none sustain'd,
But yielded back his conquests :—he was more
Than a mere Alexander, and, unstain'd
With household blood and wine, serenely wore
His sovereign virtues—still we Trajan's name adore.

CXII

Where is the rock of Triumph, the high place   1000
Where Rome embraced her heroes ? where the steep
Tarpeian ? fittest goal of Treason's race,
The promontory whence the Traitor's Leap
Cured all ambition. Did the conquerors heap
Their spoils here ? Yes ; and in yon field below,
A thousand years of silenced factions sleep—
The Forum, where the immortal accents glow,
And still the eloquent air breathes—burns with Cicero !

CXIII

The field of freedom, faction, fame, and blood :
Here a proud people's passions were exhaled,   1010
From the first hour of empire in the bud
To that when further worlds to conquer fail'd :
But long before had Freedom's face been veil'd,
And Anarchy assumed her attributes ;
Till every lawless soldier who assail'd
Trod on the trembling senate's slavish mutes,
Or raised the venal voice of baser prostitutes.

CXIV

Then turn we to her latest tribune's name,
From her ten thousand tyrants turn to thee,
Redeemer of dark centuries of shame—   1020
The friend of Petrarch—hope of Italy—
Rienzi ! last of Romans ! While the tree
Of freedom's wither'd trunk puts forth a leaf
Even for thy tomb a garland let it be—
The forum's champion, and the people's chief—
Her new-born Numa thou—with reign, alas ! too brief.

CXV

Egeria! sweet creation of some heart
Which found no mortal resting-place so fair
As thine ideal breast; whate'er thou art
Or wert,—a young Aurora of the air,   1030
The nympholepsy of some fond despair;
Or, it might be, a beauty of the earth,
Who found a more than common votary there
Too much adoring; whatsoe'er thy birth,
Thou wert a beautiful thought, and softly bodied forth.

CXVI

The mosses of thy fountain still are sprinkled
With thine Elysian water-drops; the face
Of thy cave-guarded spring, with years unwrinkled,
Reflects the meek-eyed genius of the place,
Whose green, wild margin now no more erase   1040
Art's works; nor must the delicate waters sleep,
Prison'd in marble, bubbling from the base
Of the cleft statue, with a gentle leap
The rill runs o'er, and round fern, flowers, and ivy creep,

CXVII

Fantastically tangled: the green hills
Are clothed with early blossoms, through the grass
The quick-eyed lizard rustles, and the bills
Of summer-birds sing welcome as ye pass;
Flowers fresh in hue, and many in their class,
Implore the pausing step, and with their dyes,   1050
Dance in the soft breeze in a fairy mass;
The sweetness of the violet's deep blue eyes,
Kiss'd by the breath of heaven seems colour'd by its skies.

CXVIII

Here didst thou dwell, in this enchanted cover,
Egeria! thy all heavenly bosom beating
For the far footsteps of thy mortal lover;
The purple Midnight veil'd that mystic meeting
With her most starry canopy, and seating
Thyself by thine adorer, what befell?
This cave was surely shaped out for the greeting   1060
Of an enamour'd Goddess, and the cell
Haunted by holy Love—the earliest oracle!

CXIX

And didst thou not, thy breast to his replying,
Blend a celestial with a human heart;
And Love, which dies as it was born, in sighing,
Share with immortal transports? could thine art
Make them indeed immortal, and impart
The purity of heaven to earthly joys,
Expel the venom and not blunt the dart—
The dull satiety which all destroys—   1070
And root from out the soul the deadly weed which cloys?

CXX

Alas! our young affections run to waste,
Or water but the desert; whence arise
But weeds of dark luxuriance, tares of haste,
Rank at the core, though tempting to the eyes,
Flowers whose wild odours breathe but agonies,
And trees whose gums are poisons; such the plants
Which spring beneath her steps as Passion flies
O'er the world's wilderness, and vainly pants
For some celestial fruit forbidden to our wants.   1080

CXXI

Oh Love! no habitant of earth thou art—
An unseen seraph, we believe in thee,—
A faith whose martyrs are the broken heart,—
But never yet hath seen, nor e'er shall see
The naked eye, thy form, as it should be;
The mind hath made thee, as it peopled heaven,
Even with its own desiring phantasy,
And to a thought such shape and image given,
As haunts the unquench'd soul—parch'd, wearied, wrung, and riven.

CXXII

Of its own beauty is the mind diseased,   1090
And fevers into false creation:—where,
Where are the forms the sculptor's soul hath seiz'd?
In him alone. Can Nature show so fair?
Where are the charms and virtues which we dare
Conceive in boyhood and pursue as men,
The unreach'd Paradise of our despair,
Which o'er-informs the pencil and the pen,
And overpowers the page where it would bloom again?

CXXIII

Who loves, raves—'tis youth's frenzy—but the cure
Is bitterer still, as charm by charm unwinds   1100
Which robed our idols, and we see too sure
Nor worth nor beauty dwells from out the mind's
Ideal shape of such; yet still it binds
The fatal spell, and still it draws us on,
Reaping the whirlwind from the oft-sown winds;
The stubborn heart, its alchemy begun,
Seems ever near the prize—wealthiest when most undone.

CXXIV

We wither from our youth, we gasp away—
Sick—sick; unfound the boon, unslaked the thirst,
Though to the last, in verge of our decay,   1110
Some phantom lures, such as we sought at first—
But all too late,—so are we doubly curst.
Love, fame, ambition, avarice—'tis the same,
Each idle, and all ill, and none the worst—
For all are meteors with a different name,
And Death the sable smoke where vanishes the flame.

CXXV

Few—none—find what they love or could have loved,
Though accident, blind contact, and the strong
Necessity of loving, have removed
Antipathies—but to recur, ere long,   1120
Envenom'd with irrevocable wrong;
And Circumstance, that unspiritual god
And miscreator, makes and helps along
Our coming evils with a crutch-like rod,
Whose touch turns Hope to dust,—the dust we all have trod.

CXXVI

Our life is a false nature : 'tis not in
The harmony of things,—this hard decree,
This uneradicable taint of sin,
This boundless upas, this all-blasting tree,
Whose root is earth, whose leaves and branches be   1130
The skies which rain their plagues on men like dew—
Disease, death, bondage—all the woes we see,
And worse, the woes we see not—which throb through
The immedicable soul, with heart-aches ever new.

CXXVII

Yet let us ponder boldly—'tis a base
Abandonment of reason to resign
Our right of thought—our last and only place
Of refuge ; this, at least, shall still be mine :
Though from our birth the faculty divine
Is chain'd and tortured—cabin'd, cribb'd, confined,   1140
And bred in darkness, lest the truth should shine
Too brightly on the unprepared mind,
The beam pours in, for time and skill will couch the blind.

CXXVIII

Arches on arches ! as it were that Rome,
Collecting the chief trophies of her line,
Would build up all her triumphs in one dome,
Her Coliseum stands ; the moonbeams shine
As 'twere its natural torches, for divine
Should be the light which streams here to illume
This long-explored but still exhaustless mine   1150
Of contemplation ; and the azure gloom
Of an Italian night, where the deep skies assume

CXXIX

Hues which have words, and speak to ye of heaven,
Floats o'er this vast and wondrous monument,
And shadows forth its glory. There is given
Unto the things of earth, which Time hath bent,
A spirit's feeling, and where he hath leant
His hand, but broke his scythe, there is a power
And magic in the ruin'd battlement,
For which the palace of the present hour   1160
Must yield its pomp, and wait till ages are its dower.

CXXX

Oh Time ! the beautifier of the dead,
Adorner of the ruin, comforter
And only healer when the heart hath bled ;
Time ! the corrector where our judgments err,
The test of truth, love,—sole philosopher,
For all beside are sophists—from thy thrift,
Which never loses though it doth defer—
Time, the avenger ! unto thee I lift
My hands, and eyes, and heart, and crave of thee a gift : 1170

CXXXI

Amidst this wreck, where thou hast made a shrine
And temple more divinely desolate,
Among thy mightier offerings here are mine,
Ruins of years, though few, yet full of fate :—
If thou hast ever seen me too elate,
Hear me not ; but if calmly I have borne
Good, and reserved my pride against the hate
Which shall not whelm me, let me not have worn
This iron in my soul in vain—shall *they* not mourn ?

CXXXII

And thou, who never yet of human wrong   1180
Left the unbalanced scale, great Nemesis !
Here, where the ancient paid thee homage long—
Thou who didst call the Furies from the abyss,
And round Orestes bade them howl and hiss
For that unnatural retribution—just,
Had it but been from hands less near—in this
Thy former realm, I call thee from the dust !
Dost thou not hear my heart ?—Awake ! thou shalt, and must.

CXXXIII

It is not that I may not have incurr'd
For my ancestral faults or mine the wound   1190
I bleed withal, and, had it been conferr'd
With a just weapon, it had flow'd unbound ;
But now my blood shall not sink in the ground ;
To thee I do devote it—*thou* shalt take
The vengeance, which shall yet be sought and found,
Which if *I* have not taken for the sake——
But let that pass—I sleep, but thou shalt yet awake.

CXXXIV

And if my voice break forth, 'tis not that now
I shrink from what is suffer'd : let him speak
Who hath beheld decline upon my brow,   1200
Or seen my mind's convulsion leave it weak ;
But in this page a record will I seek.
Not in the air shall these my words disperse,
Though I be ashes ; a far hour shall wreak
The deep prophetic fulness of this verse,
And pile on human heads the mountain of my curse !

CXXXV

That curse shall be Forgiveness.—Have I not—
Hear me, my mother Earth! behold it, Heaven!—
Have I not had to wrestle with my lot?
Have I not suffer'd things to be forgiven?   1210
Have I not had my brain sear'd, my heart riven,
Hopes sapp'd, name blighted, Life's life lied away?
And only not to desperation driven,
Because not altogether of such clay
As rots into the souls of those whom I survey.

CXXXVI

From mighty wrongs to petty perfidy
Have I not seen what human things could do?
From the loud roar of foaming calumny
To the small whisper of the as paltry few,
And subtler venom of the reptile crew,   1220
The Janus glance of whose significant eye,
Learning to lie with silence, would *seem* true,
And without utterance, save the shrug or sigh,
Deal round to happy fools its speechless obloquy.

CXXXVII

But I have lived, and have not lived in vain:
My mind may lose its force, my blood its fire,
And my frame perish even in conquering pain;
But there is that within me which shall tire
Torture and Time, and breathe when I expire;
Something unearthly, which they deem not of,   1230
Like the remember'd tone of a mute lyre,
Shall on their soften'd spirits sink, and move
In hearts all rocky now the late remorse of love.

CXXXVIII

The seal is set.—Now welcome, thou dread power!
Nameless, yet thus omnipotent, which here
Walk'st in the shadow of the midnight hour
With a deep awe, yet all distinct from fear;
Thy haunts are ever where the dead walls rear
Their ivy mantles, and the solemn scene
Derives from thee a sense so deep and clear   1240
That we become a part of what has been,
And grow unto the spot, all-seeing but unseen.

CXXXIX

And here the buzz of eager nations ran,
In murmur'd pity, or loud-roar'd applause,
As man was slaughter'd by his fellow-man.
And wherefore slaughter'd? wherefore, but because
Such were the bloody Circus' genial laws,
And the imperial pleasure.—Wherefore not?
What matters where we fall to fill the maws
Of worms—on battle-plains or listed spot?   1250
Both are but theatres where the chief actors rot.

CXL

I see before me the Gladiator lie :
He leans upon his hand—his manly brow
Consents to death, but conquers agony,
And his droop'd head sinks gradually low—
And through his side the last drops, ebbing slow
From the red gash, fall heavy, one by one,
Like the first of a thunder-shower ; and now
The arena swims around him—he is gone,
Ere ceased the inhuman shout which hail'd the wretch who won.

CXLI

He heard it, but he heeded not—his eyes   1261
Were with his heart, and that was far away ;
He reck'd not of the life he lost nor prize,
But where his rude hut by the Danube lay,
There were his young barbarians all at play,
There was their Dacian mother—he, their sire,
Butcher'd to make a Roman holiday—
All this rush'd with his blood—Shall he expire
And unavenged ? Arise ! ye Goths, and glut your ire !

CXLII

But here, where Murder breathed her bloody steam ;   1270
And here, where buzzing nations choked the ways,
And roar'd or murmur'd like a mountain stream
Dashing or winding as its torrent strays ;
Here, where the Roman million's blame or praise
Was death or life, the playthings of a crowd,
My voice sounds much—and fall the stars' faint rays
On the arena void—seats crush'd—walls bow'd—
And galleries, where my steps seem echoes strangely loud.

CXLIII

A ruin—yet what ruin ! from its mass
Walls, palaces, half-cities, have been rear'd ;   1280
Yet oft the enormous skeleton ye pass,
And marvel where the spoil could have appear'd.
Hath it indeed been plunder'd, or but clear'd ?
Alas ! developed, opens the decay,
When the colossal fabric's form is near'd :
It will not bear the brightness of the day,
Which streams too much on all years, man, have reft away

CXLIV

But when the rising moon begins to climb
Its topmost arch, and gently pauses there ;
When the stars twinkle through the loops of time,   1290
And the low night-breeze waves along the air
The garland-forest, which the gray walls wear,
Like laurels on the bald first Caesar's head ;
When the light shines serene but doth not glare,
Then in this magic circle raise the dead :
Heroes have trod this spot—'tis on their dust ye tread.

CXLV

'While stands the Coliseum, Rome shall stand;
When falls the Coliseum, Rome shall fall;
And when Rome falls—the World.' From our own land
Thus spake the pilgrims o'er this mighty wall   1300
In Saxon times, which we are wont to call
Ancient; and these three mortal things are still
On their foundations, and unalter'd all;
Rome and her Ruin past Redemption's skill,
The World, the same wide den—of thieves, or what ye will.

CXLVI

Simple, erect, severe, austere, sublime—
Shrine of all saints and temple of all gods,
From Jove to Jesus—spared and blest by time;
Looking tranquillity, while falls or nods
Arch, empire, each thing round thee, and man plods   1310
His way through thorns to ashes—glorious dome!
Shalt thou not last? Time's scythe and tyrants' rods
Shiver upon thee—sanctuary and home
Of art and piety—Pantheon!—pride of Rome!

CXLVII

Relic of nobler days, and noblest arts!
Despoil'd yet perfect, with thy circle spreads
A holiness appealing to all hearts—
To art a model; and to him who treads
Rome for the sake of ages, Glory sheds
Her light through thy sole aperture; to those   1320
Who worship, here are altars for their beads;
And they who feel for genius may repose
Their eyes on honour'd forms, whose busts around them close.

CXLVIII

There is a dungeon, in whose dim drear light
What do I gaze on? Nothing: Look again!
Two forms are slowly shadow'd on my sight—
Two insulated phantoms of the brain:
It is not so; I see them full and plain—
An old man, and a female young and fair,
Fresh as a nursing mother, in whose vein   1330
The blood is nectar:—but what doth she there,
With her unmantled neck, and bosom white and bare?

CXLIX

Full swells the deep pure fountain of young life,
Where *on* the heart and *from* the heart we took
Our first and sweetest nurture, when the wife,
Blest into mother, in the innocent look,
Or even the piping cry of lips that brook
No pain and small suspense, a joy perceives
Man knows not, when from out its cradled nook
She sees her little bud put forth its leaves—   1340
What may the fruit be yet? I know not—Cain was Eve's.

CL

But here youth offers to old age the food,
The milk of his own gift : it is her sire
To whom she renders back the debt of blood
Born with her birth. No ; he shall not expire
While in those warm and lovely veins the fire
Of health and holy feeling can provide
Great Nature's Nile, whose deep stream rises higher
Than Egypt's river : from that gentle side
Drink, drink and live, old man ! Heaven's realm holds no
    such tide.   1350

CLI

The starry fable of the milky way
Has not thy story's purity ; it is
A constellation of a sweeter ray,
And sacred Nature triumphs more in this
Reverse of her decree, than in the abyss
Where sparkle distant worlds :—Oh, holiest nurse !
No drop of that clear stream its way shall miss
To thy sire's heart, replenishing its source
With life, as our freed souls rejoin the universe.

CLII

Turn to the mole which Hadrian rear'd on high,   1360
Imperial mimic of old Egypt's piles,
Colossal copyist of deformity
Whose travell'd phantasy from the far Nile's
Enormous model, doom'd the artist's toils
To build for giants, and for his vain earth,
His shrunken ashes, raise this dome : How smiles
The gazer's eye with philosophic mirth,
To view the huge design which sprung from such a birth !

CLIII

But lo ! the dome—the vast and wondrous dome,
To which Diana's marvel was a cell—   1370
Christ's mighty shrine above his martyr's tomb !
I have beheld the Ephesian's miracle ;—
Its columns strew the wilderness, and dwell
The hyaena and the jackal in their shade ;
I have beheld Sophia's bright roofs swell
Their glittering mass i' the sun, and have survey'd
Its sanctuary the while the usurping Moslem pray'd ;

CLIV

But thou, of temples old, or altars new,
Standest alone, with nothing like to thee—
Worthiest of God, the holy and the true.   1380
Since Zion's desolation, when that He
Forsook his former city, what could be,
Of earthly structures, in his honour piled,
Of a sublimer aspect ? Majesty,
Power, Glory, Strength, and Beauty all are aisled
In this eternal ark of worship undefiled.

CLV

Enter: its grandeur overwhelms thee not;
And why? It is not lessen'd; but thy mind,
Expanded by the genius of the spot,
Has grown colossal, and can only find   1390
A fit abode wherein appear enshrined
Thy hopes of immortality; and thou
Shalt one day, if found worthy, so defined,
See thy God face to face, as thou dost now
His Holy of Holies, nor be blasted by his brow.

CLVI

Thou movest, but increasing with the advance,
Like climbing some great Alp, which still doth rise,
Deceived by its gigantic elegance;
Vastness which grows, but grows to harmonize—
All musical in its immensities;   1400
Rich marbles, richer painting—shrines where flame
The lamps of gold—and haughty dome which vies
In air with Earth's chief structures, though their frame
Sits on the firm-set ground, and this the clouds must claim.

CLVII

Thou seest not all; but piecemeal thou must break,
To separate contemplation, the great whole;
And as the ocean many bays will make
That ask the eye—so here condense thy soul
To more immediate objects, and control
Thy thoughts until thy mind hath got by heart   1410
Its eloquent proportions, and unroll
In mighty graduations, part by part,
The glory which at once upon thee did not dart,

CLVIII

Not by its fault—but thine: Our outward sense
Is but of gradual grasp—and as it is
That what we have of feeling most intense
Outstrips our faint expression; even so this
Outshining and o'erwhelming edifice
Fools our fond gaze, and greatest of the great
Defies at first our Nature's littleness,   1420
Till, growing with its growth, we thus dilate
Our spirits to the size of that they contemplate.

CLIX

Then pause, and be enlighten'd; there is more
In such a survey than the sating gaze
Of wonder pleased, or awe which would adore
The worship of the place, or the mere praise
Of art and its great masters, who could raise
What former time, nor skill, nor thought could plan;
The fountain of sublimity displays
Its depth, and thence may draw the mind of man   1430
Its golden sands, and learn what great conceptions can.

CLX

Or, turning to the Vatican, go see
Laocoön's torture dignifying pain—
A father's love and mortal's agony
With an immortal's patience blending : Vain
The struggle ; vain, against the coiling strain
And gripe, and deepening of the dragon's grasp,
The old man's clench ; the long envenom'd chain
Rivets the living links,—the enormous asp
Enforces pang on pang, and stifles gasp on gasp.   1440

CLXI

Or view the Lord of the unerring bow,
The God of life, and poesy, and light—
The Sun in human limbs array'd, and brow
All radiant from his triumph in the fight ;
The shaft hath just been shot—the arrow bright
With an immortal's vengeance ; in his eye
And nostril beautiful disdain, and might
And majesty, flash their full lightnings by,
Developing in that one glance the Deity.

CLXII

But in his delicate form—a dream of Love,   1450
Shaped by some solitary nymph, whose breast
Long'd for a deathless lover from above,
And madden'd in that vision—are exprest
All that ideal beauty ever bless'd
The mind with in its most unearthly mood,
When each conception was a heavenly guest—
A ray of immortality—and stood
Starlike, around, until they gather'd to a god !

CLXIII

And if it be Prometheus stole from Heaven
The fire which we endure, it was repaid   1460
By him to whom the energy was given
Which this poetic marble hath array'd
With an eternal glory—which, if made
By human hands, is not of human thought ;
And Time himself hath hallow'd it, nor laid
One ringlet in the dust—nor hath it caught
A tinge of years, but breathes the flame with which 'twas v. rought.

CLXIV

But where is he, the Pilgrim of my song,
The being who upheld it through the past ?
Methinks he cometh late and tarries long.   1470
He is no more—these breathings are his last ;
His wanderings done, his visions ebbing fast,
And he himself as nothing :—if he was
Aught but a phantasy, and could be class'd
With forms which live and suffer—let that pass—
His shadow fades away into Destruction's mass.

CLXV

Which gathers shadow, substance, life, and all
That we inherit in its mortal shroud,
And spreads the dim and universal pall
Through which all things grow phantoms ; and the cloud
Between us sinks and all which ever glow'd,   1481
Till Glory's self is twilight, and displays
A melancholy halo scarce allow'd
To hover on the verge of darkness ; rays
Sadder than saddest night, for they distract the gaze,

CLXVI

And send us prying into the abyss,
To gather what we shall be when the frame
Shall be resolved to something less than this
Its wretched essence ; and to dream of fame,
And wipe the dust from off the idle name   1490
We never more shall hear,—but never more,
Oh, happier thought ! can we be made the same :
It is enough in sooth that *once* we bore
These fardels of the heart—the heart whose sweat was gore.

CLXVII

Hark ! forth from the abyss a voice proceeds,
A long low distant murmur of dread sound,
Such as arises when a nation bleeds
With some deep and immedicable wound ;
Through storm and darkness yawns the rending ground,
The gulf is thick with phantoms, but the chief   1500
Seems royal still, though with her head discrown'd,
And pale, but lovely, with maternal grief
She clasps a babe, to whom her breast yields no relief.

CLXVIII

Scion of chiefs and monarchs, where art thou ?
Fond hope of many nations, art thou dead ?
Could not the grave forget thee, and lay low
Some less majestic, less beloved head ?
In the sad midnight, while thy heart still bled,
The mother of a moment, o'er thy boy,
Death hush'd that pang for ever : with thee fled   1510
The present happiness and promised joy
Which fill'd the imperial isles so full it seem'd to cloy.

CLXIX

Peasants bring forth in safety.—Can it be,
Oh thou that wert so happy, so adored !
Those who weep not for kings shall weep for thee,
And Freedom's heart, grown heavy, cease to hoard
Her many griefs for ONE ; for she had pour'd
Her orisons for thee, and o'er thy head
Beheld her Iris.—Thou, too, lonely lord,
And desolate consort—vainly wert thou wed !   1520
The husband of a year ! the father of the dead !

CLXX

Of sackcloth was thy wedding garment made ;
Thy bridal's fruit is ashes : in the dust
The fair-hair'd Daughter of the Isles is laid,
The love of millions ! How we did intrust
Futurity to her ! and, though it must
Darken above our bones, yet fondly deem'd
Our children should obey her child, and bless'd
Her and her hoped-for seed, whose promise seem'd
Like stars to shepherd's eyes :—'twas but a meteor beam'd.

CLXXI

Woe unto us, not her ; for she sleeps well :   1531
The fickle reek of popular breath, the tongue
Of hollow counsel, the false oracle,
Which from the birth of monarchy hath rung
Its knell in princely ears, till the o'erstung
Nations have arm'd in madness, the strange fate
Which tumbles mightiest sovereigns, and hath flung
Against their blind omnipotence a weight
Within the opposing scale, which crushes soon or late,—

CLXXII

These might have been her destiny ; but no,   1540
Our hearts deny it : and so young, so fair,
Good without effort, great without a foe ;
But now a bride and mother—and now *there* !
How many ties did that stern moment tear !
From thy Sire's to his humblest subject's breast
Is link'd the electric chain of that despair,
Whose shock was as an earthquake's, and opprest
The land which loved thee so that none could love thee best.

CLXXIII

Lo, Nemi ! navell'd in the woody hills
So far, that the uprooting wind which tears   1550
The oak from his foundation, and which spills
The ocean o'er its boundary, and bears
Its form against the skies, reluctant spares
The oval mirror of thy glassy lake ;
And calm as cherish'd hate, its surface wears
A deep cold settled aspect nought can shake,
All coil'd into itself and round, as sleeps the snake.

CLXXIV

And near, Albano's scarce divided waves
Shine from a sister valley ;—and afar
The Tiber winds, and the broad ocean laves   1560
The Latian coast where sprung the Epic war,
' Arms and the man,' whose re-ascending star
Rose o'er an empire :—but beneath thy right
Tully reposed from Rome ;—and where yon bar
Of girdling mountains intercepts the sight
The Sabine farm was till'd, the weary bard's delight.

CLXXV

But I forget.—My Pilgrim's shrine is won,
And he and I must part,—so let it be,—
His task and mine alike are nearly done ;
Yet once more let us look upon the sea ;　　　1570
The midland ocean breaks on him and me,
And from the Alban Mount we now behold
Our friend of youth, that Ocean, which when we
Beheld it last by Calpe's rock unfold
Those waves, we follow'd on till the dark Euxine roll'd

CLXXVI

Upon the blue Symplegades : long years—
Long, though not very many—since have done
Their work on both ; some suffering and some tears
Have left us nearly where we had begun :
Yet not in vain our mortal race hath run ;　　　1580
We have had our reward, and it is here,—
That we can yet feel gladden'd by the sun,
And reap from earth, sea, joy almost as dear
As if there were no man to trouble what is clear.

CLXXVII

Oh ! that the Desert were my dwelling-place,
With one fair Spirit for my minister,
That I might all forget the human race,
And, hating no one, love but only her !
Ye elements !—in whose ennobling stir
I feel myself exalted—Can ye not　　　1590
Accord me such a being ? Do I err
In deeming such inhabit many a spot ?
Though with them to converse can rarely be our lot.

CLXXVIII

There is a pleasure in the pathless woods,
There is a rapture on the lonely shore,
There is society, where none intrudes,
By the deep Sea, and music in its roar :
I love not Man the less, but Nature more,
From these our interviews, in which I steal
From all I may be, or have been before,　　　1600
To mingle with the Universe, and feel
What I can ne'er express, yet cannot all conceal.

CLXXIX

Roll on, thou deep and dark blue Ocean—roll !
Ten thousand fleets sweep over thee in vain ;
Man marks the earth with ruin—his control
Stops with the shore ; upon the watery plain
The wrecks are all thy deed, nor doth remain
A shadow of man's ravage, save his own,
When, for a moment, like a drop of rain,
He sinks into thy depths with bubbling groan,　　　1610
Without a grave, unknell'd, uncoffin'd, and unknown.

CLXXX

His steps are not upon thy paths,—thy fields
Are not a spoil for him,—thou dost arise
And shake him from thee; the vile strength he wields
For earth's destruction thou dost all despise,
Spurning him from thy bosom to the skies,
And send'st him, shivering in thy playful spray
And howling, to his Gods, where haply lies
His petty hope in some near port or bay,
And dashest him again to earth:—there let him lay.   1620

CLXXXI

The armaments which thunderstrike the walls
Of rock-built cities, bidding nations quake,
And monarchs tremble in their capitals,
The oak leviathans, whose huge ribs make
Their clay creator the vain title take
Of lord of thee, and arbiter of war—
These are thy toys, and, as the snowy flake,
They melt into thy yeast of waves, which mar
Alike the Armada's pride or spoils of Trafalgar.

CLXXXII

Thy shores are empires, changed in all save thee—   1630
Assyria, Greece, Rome, Carthage, what are they ?
Thy waters wash'd them power while they were free,
And many a tyrant since; their shores obey
The stranger, slave, or savage; their decay
Has dried up realms to deserts:—not so thou ;—
Unchangeable, save to thy wild waves' play,
Time writes no wrinkle on thine azure brow :
Such as creation's dawn beheld, thou rollest now.

CLXXXIII

Thou glorious mirror, where the Almighty's form
Glasses itself in tempests; in all time,—   1640
Calm or convulsed, in breeze, or gale, or storm,
Icing the pole, or in the torrid clime
Dark-heaving—boundless, endless, and sublime,
The image of eternity, the throne
Of the Invisible; even from out thy slime
The monsters of the deep are made; each zone
Obeys thee; thou goest forth, dread, fathomless, alone.

CLXXXIV

And I have loved thee, Ocean ! and my joy
Of youthful sports was on thy breast to be
Borne, like thy bubbles, onward: from a boy   1650
I wanton'd with thy breakers—they to me
Were a delight; and if the freshening sea
Made them a terror—'twas a pleasing fear,
For I was as it were a child of thee,
And trusted to thy billows far and near,
And laid my hand upon thy mane—as I do here.

CLXXXV

My task is done, my song hath ceased, my theme
Has died into an echo; it is fit
The spell should break of this protracted dream.
The torch shall be extinguish'd which hath lit   1660
My midnight lamp—and what is writ, is writ;
Would it were worthier! but I am not now
That which I have been—and my visions flit
Less palpably before me—and the glow
Which in my spirit dwelt is fluttering, faint, and low.

CLXXXVI

Farewell! a word that must be, and hath been—
A sound which makes us linger;—yet—farewell!
Ye! who have traced the Pilgrim to the scene
Which is his last, if in your memories dwell
A thought which once was his, if on ye swell   1670
A single recollection, not in vain
He wore his sandal-shoon and scallop-shell;
Farewell! with *him* alone may rest the pain,
If such there were—with *you*, the moral of his strain.

THE PRISONER OF CHILLON

I

My hair is grey, but not with years,
   Nor grew it white
   In a single night,
As men's have grown from sudden fears:
My limbs are bow'd, though not with toil,
  But rusted with a vile repose,
For they have been a dungeon's spoil,
  And mine has been the fate of those
To whom the goodly earth and air
Are bann'd, and barr'd—forbidden fare: 10
But this was for my father's faith
I suffer'd chains and courted death;
That father perish'd at the stake
For tenets he would not forsake;
And for the same his lineal race
In darkness found a dwelling-place;
We were seven—who now are one,
  Six in youth, and one in age,
Finish'd as they had begun,
  Proud of Persecution's rage;   20
One in fire, and two in field,
Their belief with blood have seal'd,

Dying as their father died,
For the God their foes denied;
Three were in a dungeon cast,
Of whom this wreck is left the last.

II

There are seven pillars of Gothic mould,
In Chillon's dungeons deep and old,
There are seven columns, massy and grey,
Dim with a dull imprison'd ray,   30
A sunbeam which hath lost its way,
And through the crevice and the cleft
Of the thick wall is fallen and left;
Creeping o'er the floor so damp,
Like a marsh's meteor lamp:
And in each pillar there is a ring,
  And in each ring there is a chain;
That iron is a cankering thing,
  For in these limbs its teeth remain,
With marks that will not wear away,   40
Till I have done with this new day,
Which now is painful to these eyes,
Which have not seen the sun so rise
For years—I cannot count them o'er,
I lost their long and heavy score,
When my last brother droop'd and died,
And I lay living by his side.

III

They chain'd us each to a column stone,
And we were three—yet, each alone;
We could not move a single pace,   50
We could not see each other's face,
But with that pale and livid light
That made us strangers in our sight:
And thus together—yet apart,
Fetter'd in hand, but join'd in heart,
'Twas still some solace, in the dearth
Of the pure elements of earth,
To hearken to each other's speech,
And each turn comforter to each
With some new hope, or legend old,   60
Or song heroically bold;
But even these at length grew cold.
Our voices took a dreary tone,
An echo of the dungeon stone,
  A grating sound, not full and free,
  As they of yore were wont to be:
  It might be fancy, but to me
They never sounded like our own.

IV

I was the eldest of the three,
  And to uphold and cheer the rest   70
  I ought to do—and did my best—
And each did well in his degree.
  The youngest, whom my father loved,
Because our mother's brow was given
To him, with eyes as blue as heaven—
  For him my soul was sorely moved ;
And truly might it be distress'd
To see such bird in such a nest :
For he was beautiful as day—
  (When day was beautiful to me   80
  As to young eagles, being free)—
  A polar day, which will not see
A sunset till its summer 's gone,
  Its sleepless summer of long light,
The snow-clad offspring of the sun :
  And thus he was as pure and bright,
And in his natural spirit gay,
With tears for nought but others' ills,
And then they flow'd like mountain rills,
Unless he could assuage the woe   90
  Which he abhorr'd to view below.

V

The other was as pure of mind,
But form'd to combat with his kind ;
Strong in his frame, and of a mood
Which 'gainst the world in war had stood,
And perish'd in the foremost rank
  With joy :—but not in chains to pine :
His spirit wither'd with their clank,
  I saw it silently decline—
  And so perchance in sooth did mine :   100
But yet I forced it on to cheer
Those relics of a home so dear.
He was a hunter of the hills,
  Had follow'd there the deer and wolf ;
  To him his dungeon was a gulf,
And fetter'd feet the worst of ills.

VI

  Lake Leman lies by Chillon's walls :
A thousand feet in depth below
Its massy waters meet and flow ;
Thus much the fathom-line was sent   110
From Chillon's snow-white battlement,
  Which round about the wave inthrals :
A double dungeon wall and wave
Have made—and like a living grave.

Below the surface of the lake
The dark vault lies wherein we lay,
We heard it ripple night and day ;
   Sounding o'er our heads it knock'd ;
And I have felt the winter's spray
Wash through the bars when winds were high   120
And wanton in the happy sky ;
   And then the very rock hath rock'd,
   And I have felt it shake, unshock'd,
Because I could have smiled to see
The death that would have set me free.

VII

I said my nearer brother pined,
I said his mighty heart declined,
He loathed and put away his food ;
It was not that 'twas coarse and rude,
For we were used to hunter's fare,   130
And for the like had little care :
The milk drawn from the mountain goat
Was changed for water from the moat,
Our bread was such as captives' tears
Have moisten'd many a thousand years,
Since man first pent his fellow men
Like brutes within an iron den ;
But what were these to us or him ?
These wasted not his heart or limb ;
My brother's soul was of that mould   140
Which in a palace had grown cold,
Had his free breathing been denied
The range of the steep mountain's side ;
But why delay the truth ?—he died.
I saw, and could not hold his head,
Nor reach his dying hand—nor dead,—
Though hard I strove, but strove in vain,
To rend and gnash my bonds in twain.
He died, and they unlock'd his chain,
And scoop'd for him a shallow grave   150
Even from the cold earth of our cave.
I begg'd them as a boon to lay
His corse in dust whereon the day
Might shine—it was a foolish thought,
But then within my brain it wrought,
That even in death his freeborn breast
In such a dungeon could not rest.
I might have spared my idle prayer—
They coldly laugh'd, and laid him there :
The flat and turfless earth above   160
The being we so much did love ;
His empty chain above it leant,
Such murder's fitting monument !

VIII

But he, the favourite and the flower,
Most cherish'd since his natal hour,
His mother's image in fair face,
The infant love of all his race,
His martyr'd father's dearest thought,
My latest care, for whom I sought
To hoard my life, that his might be   170
Less wretched now, and one day free;
He, too, who yet had held untired
A spirit natural or inspired—
He, too, was struck, and day by day
Was wither'd on the stalk away.
Oh, God! it is a fearful thing
To see the human soul take wing
In any shape, in any mood:
I've seen it rushing forth in blood,
I've seen it on the breaking ocean   180
Strive with a swoln convulsive motion,
I've seen the sick and ghastly bed
Of Sin delirious with its dread;
But these were horrors—this was woe
Unmix'd with such—but sure and slow:
He faded, and so calm and meek,
So softly worn, so sweetly weak,
So tearless, yet so tender, kind,
And grieved for those he left behind;
With all the while a cheek whose bloom   190
Was as a mockery of the tomb,
Whose tints as gently sunk away
As a departing rainbow's ray;
An eye of most transparent light,
That almost made the dungeon bright,
And not a word of murmur, not
A groan o'er his untimely lot,—
A little talk of better days,
A little hope my own to raise,
For I was sunk in silence—lost   200
In this last loss, of all the most;
And then the sighs he would suppress
Of fainting nature's feebleness,
More slowly drawn, grew less and less
I listen'd, but I could not hear;
I call'd, for I was wild with fear;
I knew 'twas hopeless, but my dread
Would not be thus admonished;
I call'd, and thought I heard a sound
I burst my chain with one strong bound,   210
And rush'd to him:—I found him not,
I only stirr'd in this black spot,

I only lived, *I* only drew
The accursed breath of dungeon-dew ;
The last, the sole, the dearest link
Between me and the eternal brink,
Which bound me to my failing race,
Was broken in this fatal place.
One on the earth, and one beneath—
My brothers—both had ceased to breathe :   220
I took that hand which lay so still,
Alas ! my own was full as chill :
I had not strength to stir, or strive,
But felt that I was still alive—
A frantic feeling, when we know
That what we love shall ne'er be so.
    I know not why
    I could not die,
I had no earthly hope but faith,
And that forbade a selfish death.   230

IX

What next befell me then and there
    I know not well—I never knew—
First came the loss of light, and air,
    And then of darkness too :
I had no thought, no feeling—none—
Among the stones I stood a stone,
And was, scarce conscious what I wist,
As shrubless crags within the mist ;
For all was blank, and bleak, and grey ;
It was not night, it was not day ;   240
It was not even the dungeon-light,
So hateful to my heavy sight,
But vacancy absorbing space,
And fixedness without a place ;
There were no stars, no earth, no time,
No check, no change, no good, no crime,
But silence, and a stirless breath
Which neither was of life nor death ;
A sea of stagnant idleness,
Blind, boundless, mute, and motionless !   250

X

A light broke in upon my brain,—
    It was the carol of a bird ;
It ceased, and then it came again,
    The sweetest song ear ever heard,
And mine was thankful till my eyes
Ran over with the glad surprise,
And they that moment could not see
I was the mate of misery ;
But then by dull degrees came back
My senses to their wonted track ;   260

I saw the dungeon walls and floor
Close slowly round me as before,
I saw the glimmer of the sun
Creeping as it before had done,
But through the crevice where it came
That bird was perch'd, as fond and tame,
   And tamer than upon the tree;
A lovely bird, with azure wings,
And song that said a thousand things,
   And seem'd to say them all for me!   270
I never saw its like before,
I ne'er shall see its likeness more:
It seem'd like me to want a mate,
But was not half so desolate,
And it was come to love me when
None lived to love me so again,
And cheering from my dungeon's brink,
Had brought me back to feel and think.
I know not if it late were free,
   Or broke its cage to perch on mine,   280
But knowing well captivity,
   Sweet bird! I could not wish for thine!
Or if it were, in winged guise,
A visitant from Paradise;
For—Heaven forgive that thought! the while
Which made me both to weep and smile—
I sometimes deem'd that it might be
My brother's soul come down to me;
But then at last away it flew,
And then 'twas mortal well I knew,   290
For he would never thus have flown,
And left me twice so doubly lone,
Lone as the corse within its shroud,
Lone as a solitary cloud,—
   A single cloud on a sunny day,
While all the rest of heaven is clear,
A frown upon the atmosphere,
That hath no business to appear
   When skies are blue, and earth is gay.

XI

A kind of change came in my fate,   300
My keepers grew compassionate;
I know not what had made them so,
They were inured to sights of woe,
But so it was:—my broken chain
With links unfasten'd did remain,
And it was liberty to stride
Along my cell from side to side,
And up and down, and then athwart,
And tread it over every part;

And round the pillars one by one,   310
Returning where my walk begun,
Avoiding only, as I trod,
My brothers' graves without a sod ;
For if I thought with heedless tread
My step profaned their lowly bed,
My breath came gaspingly and thick,
And my crush'd heart fell blind and sick.

XII

I made a footing in the wall,
   It was not therefrom to escape,
For I had buried one and all   320
   Who loved me in a human shape ;
And the whole earth would henceforth be
A wider prison unto me :
No child, no sire, no kin had I,
No partner in my misery ;
I thought of this, and I was glad,
For thought of them had made me mad ;
But I was curious to ascend
To my barr'd windows, and to bend
Once more, upon the mountains high,   330
The quiet of a loving eye.

XIII

I saw them, and they were the same,
They were not changed like me in frame ;
I saw their thousand years of snow
On high—their wide long lake below,
And the blue Rhone in fullest flow ;
I heard the torrents leap and gush
O'er channell'd rock and broken bush ;
I saw the white-wall'd distant town,
And whiter sails go skimming down ;   340
And then there was a little isle,
Which in my very face did smile,
      The only one in view ;
A small green isle, it seem'd no more,
Scarce broader than my dungeon floor,
But in it there were three tall trees,
And o'er it blew the mountain breeze,
And by it there were waters flowing,
And on it there were young flowers growing,
      Of gentle breath and hue.   350
The fish swam by the castle wall,
And they seem'd joyous each and all ;
The eagle rode the rising blast,
Methought he never flew so fast
As then to me he seem'd to fly ;
And then new tears came in my eye,

And I felt troubled—and would fain
I had not left my recent chain;
And when I did descend again,
The darkness of my dim abode   360
Fell on me as a heavy load;
It was as is a new-dug grave,
Closing o'er one we sought to save,—
And yet my glance, too much opprest,
Had almost need of such a rest.

XIV

It might be months, or years, or days,
   I kept no count, I took no note,
I had no hope my eyes to raise,
   And clear them of their dreary mote;
At last men came to set me free;   370
   I ask'd not why, and reck'd not where;
It was at length the same to me,
Fetter'd or fetterless to be,
   I learn'd to love despair.
And thus when they appear'd at last,
And all my bonds aside were cast,
These heavy walls to me had grown
A hermitage—and all my own!
And half I felt as they were come
To tear me from a second home: 380
With spiders I had friendship made,
And watch'd them in their sullen trade,
Had seen the mice by moonlight play,
And why should I feel less than they?
We were all inmates of one place,
And I, the monarch of each race,
Had power to kill—yet, strange to tell!
In quiet we had learn'd to dwell;
My very chains and I grew friends,
So much a long communion tends   390
To make us what we are:—even I
Regain'd my freedom with a sigh.

THE VISION OF JUDGEMENT

'A Daniel come to judgement! yea, a Daniel!
I thank thee, Jew, for teaching me that word.'

I

SAINT PETER sat by the celestial gate:
  His keys were rusty, and the lock was dull,
So little trouble had been given of late;
  Not that the place by any means was full,
But since the Gallic era 'eighty-eight'
  The devils had ta'en a longer, stronger pull,
And 'a pull altogether,' as they say
At sea—which drew most souls another way.

II

The angels all were singing out of tune,
  And hoarse with having little else to do,
Excepting to wind up the sun and moon,
  Or curb a runaway young star or two,
Or wild colt of a comet, which too soon
  Broke out of bounds o'er th' ethereal blue,
Splitting some planet with its playful tail,
As boats are sometimes by a wanton whale.

III

The guardian seraphs had retired on high,
  Finding their charges past all care below;
Terrestrial business fill'd nought in the sky
  Save the recording angel's black bureau;
Who found, indeed, the facts to multiply
  With such rapidity of vice and woe,
That he had stripp'd off both his wings in quills,
And yet was in arrear of human ills.

IV

His business so augmented of late years,
  That he was forced, against his will no doubt,
(Just like those cherubs, earthly ministers,)
  For some resource to turn himself about,
And claim the help of his celestial peers,
  To aid him ere he should be quite worn out
By the increased demand for his remarks:
Six angels and twelve saints were named his clerks.

V

This was a handsome board—at least for heaven ;
　And yet they had even then enough to do,
So many conquerors' cars were daily driven,
　So many kingdoms fitted up anew ;
Each day too slew its thousands six or seven,
　Till at the crowning carnage, Waterloo,
They threw their pens down in divine disgust—
The page was so besmear'd with blood and dust. 　　40

VI

This by the way ; 'tis not mine to record
　What angels shrink from : even the very devil
On this occasion his own work abhorr'd,
　So surfeited with the infernal revel :
Though he himself had sharpen'd every sword,
　It almost quench'd his innate thirst of evil.
(Here Satan's sole good work deserves insertion—
'Tis, that he has both generals in reversion.)

VII

Let's skip a few short years of hollow peace,
　Which peopled earth no better, hell as wont, 　　50
And heaven none—they form the tyrant's lease,
　With nothing but new names subscribed upon 't ;
'Twill one day finish : meantime they increase,
　' With seven heads and ten horns,' and all in front,
Like Saint John's foretold beast ; but ours are born
Less formidable in the head than horn.

VIII

In the first year of freedom's second dawn
　Died George the Third ; although no tyrant, one
Who shielded tyrants, till each sense withdrawn
　Left him nor mental nor external sun : 　　60
A better farmer ne'er brush'd dew from lawn,
　A worse king never left a realm undone !
He died—but left his subjects still behind,
One half as mad—and t'other no less blind.

IX

He died ! his death made no great stir on earth :
　His burial made some pomp ; there was profusion
Of velvet, gilding, brass, and no great dearth
　Of aught but tears—save those shed by collusion ;
For these things may be bought at their true worth.
　Of elegy there was the due infusion— 　　70
Bought also ; and the torches, cloaks, and banners,
Heralds, and relics of old Gothic manners,

X

Form'd a sepulchral melodrame. Of all
　　The fools who flock'd to swell or see the show,
Who cared about the corpse? The funeral
　　Made the attraction, and the black the woe.
There throbb'd not there a thought which pierced the pall;
　　And when the gorgeous coffin was laid low,
It seem'd the mockery of hell to fold
The rottenness of eighty years in gold.　　　　　　80

XI

So mix his body with the dust! It might
　　Return to what it *must* far sooner, were
The natural compound left alone to fight
　　Its way back into earth, and fire, and air;
But the unnatural balsams merely blight
　　What nature made him at his birth, as bare
As the mere million's base unmummied clay—
Yet all his spices but prolong decay.

XII

He's dead—and upper earth with him has done;　　90
　　He's buried; save the undertaker's bill,
Or lapidary scrawl, the world is gone
　　For him, unless he left a German will:
But where's the proctor who will ask his son?
　　In whom his qualities are reigning still,
Except that household virtue, most uncommon,
Of constancy to a bad, ugly woman.

XIII

'God save the king!' It is a large economy
　　In God to save the like; but if he will
Be saving, all the better; for not one am I　　100
　　Of those who think damnation better still:
I hardly know too if not quite alone am I
　　In this small hope of bettering future ill
By circumscribing, with some slight restriction,
The eternity of hell's hot jurisdiction.

XIV

I know this is unpopular; I know
　　'Tis blasphemous; I know one may be damn'd
For hoping no one else may e'er be so;
　　I know my catechism; I know we're cramm'd
With the best doctrines till we quite o'erflow;
　　I know that all save England's church have shamm'd, 110
And that the other twice two hundred churches
And synagogues have made a *damn'd* bad purchase.

XV

God help us all! God help me too! I am,
　　God knows, as helpless as the devil can wish,
And not a whit more difficult to damn,
　　Than is to bring to land a late-hook'd fish,
Or to the butcher to purvey the lamb;
　　Not that I'm fit for such a noble dish,
As one day will be that immortal fry
Of almost everybody born to die.   120

XVI

Saint Peter sat by the celestial gate,
　　And nodded o'er his keys; when, lo! there came
A wondrous noise he had not heard of late—
　　A rushing sound of wind, and stream, and flame;
In short, a roar of things extremely great,
　　Which would have made aught save a saint exclaim;
But he, with first a start and then a wink,
Said, 'There's another star gone out, I think!'

XVII

But ere he could return to his repose,
　　A cherub flapp'd his right wing o'er his eyes—   130
At which St. Peter yawn'd, and rubb'd his nose:
　　'Saint porter,' said the angel, 'prithee rise!'
Waving a goodly wing, which glow'd, as glows
　　An earthly peacock's tail, with heavenly dyes:
To which the saint replied, 'Well, what's the matter?
Is Lucifer come back with all this clatter?'

XVIII

'No,' quoth the cherub; 'George the Third is dead.'
　　'And who is George the Third?' replied the apostle:
'What George? what Third?' 'The king of England,' said
　　The angel. 'Well! he won't find kings to jostle   140
Him on his way; but does he wear his head?
　　Because the last we saw here had a tustle,
And ne'er would have got into heaven's good graces,
Had he not flung his head in all our faces.

XIX

'He was, if I remember, king of France;
　　That head of his, which could not keep a crown
On earth, yet ventured in my face to advance
　　A claim to those of martyrs—like my own:
If I had had my sword, as I had once
　　When I cut ears off, I had cut him down;   150
But having but my keys, and not my brand,
I only knock'd his head from out his hand.

XX

' And then he set up such a headless howl,
   That all the saints came out and took him in ;
And there he sits by St. Paul, cheek by jowl ;
   That fellow Paul—the parvenù ! The skin
Of St. Bartholomew, which makes his cowl
   In heaven, and upon earth redeem'd his sin,
So as to make a martyr, never sped
Better than did this weak and wooden head.   160

XXI

' But had it come up here upon its shoulders,
   There would have been a different tale to tell :
The fellow-feeling in the saints beholders
   Seems to have acted on them like a spell,
And so this very foolish head heaven solders
   Back on its trunk : it may be very well,
And seems the custom here to overthrow
Whatever has been wisely done below.'

XXII

The angel answer'd, ' Peter ! do not pout :
   The king who comes has head and all entire,   170
And never knew much what it was about—
   He did as doth the puppet—by its wire,
And will be judged like all the rest, no doubt :
   My business and your own is not to inquire
Into such matters, but to mind our cue—
Which is to act as we are bid to do.'

XXIII

While thus they spake, the angelic caravan,
   Arriving like a rush of mighty wind,
Cleaving the fields of space, as doth the swan
   Some silver stream (say Ganges, Nile, or Inde.   180
Or Thames, or Tweed), and 'midst them an old man
   With an old soul, and both extremely blind,
Halted before the gate, and in his shroud
Seated their fellow traveller on a cloud.

XXIV

But bringing up the rear of this bright host
   A Spirit of a different aspect waved
His wings, like thunder-clouds above some coast
   Whose barren beach with frequent wrecks is paved ;
His brow was like the deep when tempest-toss'd ;
   Fierce and unfathomable thoughts engraved   190
Eternal wrath on his immortal face,
And *where* he gazed a gloom pervaded space.

XXV

As he drew near, he gazed upon the gate
  Ne'er to be enter'd more by him or Sin,
With such a glance of supernatural hate,
  As made Saint Peter wish himself within;
He patter'd with his keys at a great rate,
  And sweated through his apostolic skin:
Of course his perspiration was but ichor,
Or some such other spiritual liquor.   200

XXVI

The very cherubs huddled all together,
  Like birds when soars the falcon; and they felt
A tingling to the tip of every feather,
  And form'd a circle like Orion's belt
Around their poor old charge; who scarce knew whither
  His guards had led him, though they gently dealt
With royal manes (for by many stories,
And true, we learn the angels all are Tories).

XXVII

As things were in this posture, the gate flew
  Asunder, and the flashing of its hinges   210
Flung over space an universal hue
  Of many-colour'd flame, until its tinges
Reach'd even our speck of earth, and made a new
  Aurora borealis spread its fringes
O'er the North Pole; the same seen, when ice-bound,
By Captain Parry's crew, in 'Melville's Sound.'

XXVIII

And from the gate thrown open issued beaming
  A beautiful and mighty Thing of Light,
Radiant with glory, like a banner streaming
  Victorious from some world-o'erthrowing fight: 220
My poor comparisons must needs be teeming
  With earthly likenesses, for here the night
Of clay obscures our best conceptions, saving
Johanna Southcote, or Bob Southey raving.

XXIX

'Twas the archangel Michael; all men know
  The make of angels and archangels, since
There's scarce a scribbler has not one to show,
  From the fiends' leader to the angels' prince;
There also are some altar-pieces, though
  I really can't say that they much evince   230
One's inner notions of immortal spirits;
But let the connoisseurs explain *their* merits.

xxx

Michael flew forth in glory and in good ;
   A good'y work of him from whom all glory
And good arise ; the portal past—he stood ;
   Before him the young cherubs and saints hoary—
(I say *young,* begging to be understood
   By looks, not years ; and should be very sorry
To state, they were not older than St. Peter,
But merely that they seem'd a little sweeter).   240

xxxi

The cherubs and the saints bow'd down before
   That arch-angelic hierarch, the first
Of essences angelical, who wore
   The aspect of a god ; but this ne'er nursed
Pride in his heavenly bosom, in whose core
   No thought, save for his Master's service, durst
Intrude, however glorified and high ;
He knew him but the viceroy of the sky.

xxxii

He and the sombre, silent Spirit met—
   They knew each other both for good and ill ;   250
Such was their power, that neither could forget
   His former friend and future foe ; but still
There was a high, immortal, proud regret
   In either's eye, as if 'twere less their will
Than destiny to make the eternal years
Their date of war, and their ' champ clos ' the spheres.

xxxiii

But here they were in neutral space : we know
   From Job, that Satan hath the power to pay
A heavenly visit thrice a year or so ;
   And that the ' sons of God,' like those of clay,   260
Must keep him company ; and we might show
   From the same book, in how polite a way
The dialogue is held between the Powers
Of Good and Evil—but 'twould take up hours.

xxxiv

And this is not a theologic tract,
   To prove with Hebrew and with Arabic,
If Job be allegory or a fact,
   But a true narrative ; and thus I pick
From out the whole but such and such an act
   As sets aside the slightest thought of trick.   270
'Tis every tittle true, beyond suspicion,
And accurate as any other vision.

XXXV

The spirits were in neutral space, before
  The gate of heaven ; like eastern thresholds is
The place where Death's grand cause is argued o'er,
  And souls despatch'd to that world or to this ;
And therefore Michael and the other wore
  A civil aspect : though they did not kiss,
Yet still between his Darkness and his Brightness
There pass'd a mutual glance of great politeness.   280

XXXVI

The Archangel bow'd, not like a modern beau,
  But with a graceful Oriental bend,
Pressing one radiant arm just where below
  The heart in good men is supposed to tend ;
He turn'd as to an equal, not too low,
  But kindly ; Satan met his ancient friend
With more hauteur, as might an old Castilian
Poor noble meet a mushroom rich civilian.

XXXVII

He merely bent his diabolic brow
  An instant ; and then raising it, he stood   290
In act to assert his right or wrong, and show
  Cause why King George by no means could or should
Make out a case to be exempt from woe
  Eternal, more than other kings, endued
With better sense and hearts, whom history mentions,
Who long have ' paved hell with their good intentions.'

XXXVIII

Michael began : ' What wouldst thou with this man,
  Now dead, and brought before the Lord ? What ill
Hath he wrought since his mortal race began,
  That thou canst claim him ? Speak ! and do thy will, 300
If it be just : if in this earthly span
  He hath been greatly failing to fulfil
His duties as a king and mortal, say,
And he is thine ; if not, let him have way.'

XXXIX

' Michael ! ' replied the Prince of Air, ' even here,
  Before the Gate of him thou servest, must
I claim my subject ; and will make appear
  That as he was my worshipper in dust,
So shall he be in spirit, although dear
  To thee and thine, because nor wine nor lust   310
Were of his weaknesses ; yet on the throne
He reign'd o'er millions to serve me alone.

XL

'Look to *our* earth, or rather *mine ;* it was,
 Once, more thy master's : but I triumph not
In this poor planet's conquest ; nor, alas !
 Need he thou servest envy me my lot :
With all the myriads of bright worlds which pass
 In worship round him, he may have forgot
Yon weak creation of such paltry things :
I think few worth damnation save their kings,—   320

XLI

'And these but as a kind of quit-rent, to
 Assert my right as lord : and even had
I such an inclination, 'twere (as you
 Well know) superfluous ; they are grown so bad,
That hell has nothing better left to do
 Than leave them to themselves : so much more mad
And evil by their own internal curse,
Heaven cannot make them better, nor I worse.

XLII

'Look to the earth, I said, and say again :
 When this old, blind, mad, helpless, weak, poor worm 330
Began in youth's first bloom and flush to reign,
 The world and he both wore a different form,
And much of earth and all the watery plain
 Of ocean call'd him king : through many a storm
His isles had floated on the abyss of time ;
For the rough virtues chose them for their clime.

XLIII

'He came to his sceptre young ; he leaves it old :
 Look to the state in which he found his realm,
And left it ; and his annals too behold,
 How to a minion first he gave the helm ;   340
How grew upon his heart a thirst for gold,
 The beggar's vice, which can but overwhelm
The meanest hearts ; and for the rest, but glance
Thine eye along America and France.

XLIV

' 'Tis true, he was a tool from first to last
 (I have the workmen safe) ; but as a tool
So let him be consumed. From out the past
 Of ages, since mankind have known the rule
Of monarchs—from the bloody rolls amass'd
 Of sin and slaughter—from the Caesar's school,   350
Take the worst pupil ; and produce a reign
More drench'd with gore, more cumber'd with the slain.

XLV

' He ever warr'd with freedom and the free :
    Nations as men, home subjects, foreign foes,
So that they utter'd the word " Liberty ! "
    Found George the Third their first opponent. Whose
History was ever stain'd as his will be
    With national and individual woes ?
I grant his household abstinence ; I grant
His neutral virtues, which most monarchs want ;   360

XLVI

' I know he was a constant consort ; own
    He was a decent sire, and middling lord.
All this is much, and most upon a throne ;
    As temperance, if at Apicius' board,
Is more than at an anchorite's supper shown.
    I grant him all the kindest can accord ;
And this was well for him, but not for those
Millions who found him what oppression chose.

XLVII

' The New World shook him off ; the Old yet groans
    Beneath what he and his prepared, if not   370
Completed : he leaves heirs on many thrones
    To all his vices, without what begot
Compassion for him—his tame virtues ; drones
    Who sleep, or despots who have now forgot
A lesson which shall be re-taught them, wake
Upon the thrones of earth ; but let them quake !

XLVIII

' Five millions of the primitive, who hold
    The faith which makes ye great on earth, implored
A *part* of that vast *all* they held of old,—
    Freedom to worship—not alone your Lord,   380
Michael, but you, and you, Saint Peter ! Cold
    Must be your souls, if you have not abhorr'd
The foe to Catholic participation
In all the license of a Christian nation.

XLIX

' True ! he allow'd them to pray God ; but as
    A consequence of prayer, refused the law
Which would have placed them upon the same base
    With those who did not hold the saints in awe.'
But here Saint Peter started from his place,
    And cried, ' You may the prisoner withdraw :   390
Ere heaven shall ope her portals to this Guelph,
While I am guard, may I be damn'd myself !

L

'Sooner will I with Cerberus exchange
    My office (and *his* is no sinecure)
Than see this royal Bedlam bigot range
    The azure fields of heaven, of that be sure!'
'Saint!' replied Satan, 'you do well to avenge
    The wrongs he made your satellites endure;
And if to this exchange you should be given,
I'll try to coax *our* Cerberus up to heaven!'   400

LI

Here Michael interposed: 'Good saint! and devil!
    Pray, not so fast; you both outrun discretion.
Saint Peter! you were wont to be more civil!
    Satan! excuse this warmth of his expression,
And condescension to the vulgar's level:
    Even saints sometimes forget themselves in session.
Have you got more to say?'—'No.'—'If you please,
I'll trouble you to call your witnesses.'

LII

Then Satan turn'd and waved his swarthy hand,
    Which stirr'd with its electric qualities   410
Clouds farther off than we can understand,
    Although we find him sometimes in our skies;
Infernal thunder shook both sea and land
    In all the planets, and hell's batteries
Let off the artillery, which Milton mentions
As one of Satan's most sublime inventions.

LIII

This was a signal unto such damn'd souls
    As have the privilege of their damnation
Extended far beyond the mere controls
    Of worlds past, present, or to come; no station   420
Is theirs particularly in the rolls
    Of hell assign'd; but where their inclination
Or business carries them in search of game,
They may range freely—being damn'd the same.

LIV

They're proud of this—as very well they may,
    It being a sort of knighthood, or gilt key
Stuck in their loins; or like to an 'entré'
    Up the back stairs, or such free-masonry.
I borrow my comparisons from clay,
    Being clay myself. Let not those spirits be   430
Offended with such base low likenesses;
We know their posts are nobler far than these.

LV

When the great signal ran from heaven to hell—
  About ten million times the distance reckon'd
From our sun to its earth, as we can tell
  How much time it takes up, even to a second,
For every ray that travels to dispel
  The fogs of London, through which, dimly beacon'd,
The weathercocks are gilt some thrice a year,
If that the *summer* is not too severe: 440

LVI

I say that I can tell—'twas half a minute;
  I know the solar beams take up more time
Ere, pack'd up for their journey, they begin it;
  But then their telegraph is less sublime,
And if they ran a race, they would not win it
  'Gainst Satan's couriers bound for their own clime.
The sun takes up some years for every ray
To reach its goal—the devil not half a day.

LVII

Upon the verge of space, about the size
  Of half-a-crown, a little speck appear'd   450
(I've seen a something like it in the skies
  In the Ægean, ere a squall); it near'd,
And, growing bigger, took another guise;
  Like an aërial ship it tack'd, and steer'd,
Or *was* steer'd (I am doubtful of the grammar
Of the last phrase, which makes the stanza stammer;—

LVIII

But take your choice): and then it grew a cloud;
  And so it was—a cloud of witnesses.
But such a cloud! No land e'er saw a crowd
  Of locusts numerous as the heavens saw these;   460
They shadow'd with their myriads space; their loud
  And varied cries were like those of wild geese
(If nations may be liken'd to a goose),
And realised the phrase of 'hell broke loose.'

LIX

Here crash'd a sturdy oath of stout John Bull,
  Who damn'd away his eyes as heretofore:
There Paddy brogued 'By Jasus!'—'What's your wull?'
  The temperate Scot exclaim'd: the French ghost swore
In certain terms I shan't translate in full,
  As the first coachman will; and 'midst the war,   470
The voice of Jonathan was heard to express,
'*Our* president is going to war, I guess.'

LX

Besides there were the Spaniard, Dutch, and Dane;
    In short, an universal shoal of shades,
From Otaheite's isle to Salisbury Plain,
    Of all climes and professions, years and trades,
Ready to swear against the good king's reign,
    Bitter as clubs in cards are against spades:
All summon'd by this grand 'subpoena,' to
Try if kings mayn't be damn'd like me or you.   480

LXI

When Michael saw this host, he first grew pale,
    As angels can; next, like Italian twilight,
He turn'd all colours—as a peacock's tail,
    Or sunset streaming through a Gothic skylight
In some old abbey, or a trout not stale,
    Or distant lightning on the horizon *by* night,
Or a fresh rainbow, or a grand review
Of thirty regiments in red, green, and blue.

LXII

Then he address'd himself to Satan: 'Why—
    My good old friend, for such I deem you, though   490
Our different parties make us fight so shy,
    I ne'er mistake you for a *personal* foe;
Our difference is *political*, and I
    Trust that, whatever may occur below,
You know my great respect for you: and this
Makes me regret whate'er you do amiss—

LXIII

'Why, my dear Lucifer, would you abuse
    My call for witnesses? I did not mean
That you should half of earth and hell produce;
    'Tis even superfluous, since two honest, clean,   500
True testimonies are enough: we lose
    Our time, nay, our eternity, between
The accusation and defence: if we
Hear both, 'twill stretch our immortality.

LXIV

Satan replied, 'To me the matter is
    Indifferent, in a personal point of view:
I can have fifty better souls than this
    With far less trouble than we have gone through
Already; and I merely argued his
    Late majesty of Britain's case with you   510
Upon a point of form: you may dispose
Of him; I've kings enough below, God knows!'

LXV

Thus spoke the Demon (late call'd ' multifaced '
  By multo-scribbling Southey). ' Then we'll call
One or two persons of the myriads placed
  Around our congress, and dispense with all
The rest,' quoth Michael : ' Who may be so graced
  As to speak first ? there 's choice enough—who shall
It be ? ' Then Satan answer'd, ' There are many ;
But you may choose Jack Wilkes as well as any.'   520

LXVI

A merry, cock-eyed, curious-looking sprite
  Upon the instant started from the throng,
Dress'd in a fashion now forgotten quite ;
  For all the fashions of the flesh stick long
By people in the next world ; where unite
  All the costumes since Adam's, right or wrong,
From Eve's fig-leaf down to the petticoat,
Almost as scanty, of days less remote.

LXVII

The spirit look'd around upon the crowds
  Assembled, and exclaim'd, ' My friends of all   530
The spheres, we shall catch cold amongst these clouds ;
  So let 's to business : why this general call ?
If those are freeholders I see in shrouds,
  And 'tis for an election that they bawl,
Behold a candidate with unturn'd coat !
Saint Peter, may I count upon your vote ? '

LXVIII

' Sir,' replied Michael, ' you mistake ; these things
  Are of a former life, and what we do
Above is more august ; to judge of kings
  Is the tribunal met : so now you know.'   540
' Then I presume those gentlemen with wings,'
  Said Wilkes, ' are cherubs ; and that soul below
Looks much like George the Third, but to my mind
A good deal older—Bless me ! is he blind ? '

LXIX

' He is what you behold him, and his doom
  Depends upon his deeds,' the Angel said ;
' If you have aught to arraign in him, the tomb
  Gives license to the humblest beggar's head
To lift itself against the loftiest.'—' Some,'
  Said Wilkes, ' don't wait to see them laid in lead,   550
For such a liberty—and I, for one,
Have told them what I thought beneath the sun.'

LXX

'*Above* the sun repeat, then, what thou hast
 To urge against him,' said the Archangel. 'Why,'
Replied the spirit, 'since old scores are past,
 Must I turn evidence? In faith, not I.
Besides, I beat him hollow at the last,
 With all his Lords and Commons: in the sky
I don't like ripping up old stories, since
His conduct was but natural in a prince.   560

LXXI

'Foolish, no doubt, and wicked, to oppress
 A poor unlucky devil without a shilling;
But then I blame the man himself much less
 Than Bute and Grafton, and shall be unwilling
To see him punish'd here for their excess,
 Since they were both damn'd long ago, and still in
Their place below: for me, I have forgiven,
And vote his "habeas corpus" into heaven.'

LXXII

'Wilkes,' said the Devil, 'I understand all this;
 You turn'd to half a courtier ere you died, 570
And seem to think it would not be amiss
 To grow a whole one on the other side
Of Charon's ferry; you forget that *his*
 Reign is concluded; whatsoe'er betide,
He won't be sovereign more: you've lost your labour,
For at the best he will but be your neighbour.

LXXIII

'However, I knew what to think of it,
 When I beheld you in your jesting way,
Flitting and whispering round about the spit
 Where Belial, upon duty for the day, 580
With Fox's lard was basting William Pitt,
 His pupil; I knew what to think, I say:
That fellow even in hell breeds farther ills;
I'll have him *gagg'd*—'twas one of his own bills.

LXXIV

'Call Junius!' From the crowd a shadow stalk'd,
 And at the name there was a general squeeze,
So that the very ghosts no longer walk'd
 In comfort, at their own aërial ease,
But were all ramm'd, and jamm'd (but to be balk'd,
 As we shall see), and jostled hands and knees, 590
Like wind compress'd and pent within a bladder,
Or like a human colic, which is sadder.

LXXV

The shadow came—a tall, thin, grey-hair'd figure,
  That look'd as it had been a shade on earth ;
Quick in its motions, with an air of vigour,
  But nought to mark its breeding or its birth ;
Now it wax'd little, then again grew bigger,
  With now an air of gloom, or savage mirth ;
But as you gazed upon its features, they
Changed every instant—to *what*, none could say.   600

LXXVI

The more intently the ghosts gazed, the less
  Could they distinguish whose the features were ;
The Devil himself seem'd puzzled even to guess;
  They varied like a dream—now here, now there ;
And several people swore from out the press,
  They knew him perfectly ; and one could swear
He was his father : upon which another
Was sure he was his mother's cousin's brother :

LXXVII

Another, that he was a duke, or knight,
  An orator, a lawyer, or a priest,   610
A nabob, a man-midwife ; but the wight
  Mysterious changed his countenance at least
As oft as they their minds ; though in full sight
  He stood, the puzzle only was increased ;
The man was a phantasmagoria in
Himself—he was so volatile and thin.

LXXVIII

The moment that you had pronounced him *one*,
  Presto ! his face changed, and he was another ;
And when that change was hardly well put on,
  It varied, till I don't think his own mother   620
(If that he had a mother) would her son
  Have known, he shifted so from one to t'other ;
Till guessing from a pleasure grew a task,
At this epistolary 'Iron Mask.'

LXXIX

For sometimes he like Cerberus would seem—
  ' Three gentlemen at once ' (as sagely says
Good Mrs. Malaprop) ; then you might deem
  That he was not even *one ;* now many rays
Were flashing round him ; and now a thick steam
  Hid him from sight—like fogs on London days :   630
Now Burke, now Tooke, he grew to people's fancies,
And certes often like Sir Philip Francis.

LXXX

I've an hypothesis—'tis quite my own;
   I never let it out till now, for fear
Of doing people harm about the throne,
   And injuring some minister or peer,
On whom the stigma might perhaps be blown;
   It is—my gentle public, lend thine ear!
'Tis, that what Junius we are wont to call
Was *really*, *truly*, nobody at all.   640

LXXXI

I don't see wherefore letters should not be
   Written without hands, since we daily view
Them written without heads; and books, we see,
   Are filled as well without the latter too:
And really till we fix on somebody
   For certain sure to claim them as his due,
Their author, like the Niger's mouth, will bother
The world to say if *there* be mouth or author.

LXXXII

'And who and what art thou?' the Archangel said.
   'For *that* you may consult my title-page,'   650
Replied this mighty shadow of a shade:
   'If I have kept my secret half an age,
I scarce shall tell it now.'—'Canst thou upbraid,'
   Continued Michael, 'George Rex, or allege
Aught further?' Junius answer'd, 'You had better
First ask him for *his* answer to my letter:

LXXXIII

'My charges upon record will outlast
   The brass of both his epitaph and tomb.'
'Repent'st thou not,' said Michael, 'of some past
   Exaggeration? something which may doom   660
Thyself if false, as him if true? Thou wast
   Too bitter—is it not so?—in thy gloom
Of passion?'—'Passion!' cried the phantom dim,
'I loved my country, and I hated him.'

LXXXIV

'What I have written, I have written: let
   The rest be on his head or mine!' So spoke
Old 'Nominis Umbra;' and while speaking yet,
   Away he melted in celestial smoke.
Then Satan said to Michael, 'Don't forget
   To call George Washington, and John Horne Tooke, 670
And Franklin;'—but at this time there was heard
A cry for room, though not a phantom stirr'd.

LXXXV

At length with jostling, elbowing, and the aid
  Of cherubim appointed to that post,
The devil Asmodeus to the circle made
  His way, and look'd as if his journey cost
Some trouble. When his burden down he laid,
  'What 's this ? ' cried Michael ; ' why, 'tis not a ghost ? '
' I know it,' quoth the incubus ; ' but he
Shall be one, if you leave the affair to me.   680

LXXXVI

' Confound the renegado ! I have sprain'd
  My left wing, he 's so heavy ; one would think
Some of his works about his neck were chain'd.
  But to the point ; while hovering o'er the brink
Of Skiddaw (where as usual it still rain'd),
  I saw a taper, far below me, wink,
And stooping, caught this fellow at a libel—
No less on history than the Holy Bible.

LXXXVII

' The former is the devil's scripture, and
  The latter yours, good Michael : so the affair   690
Belongs to all of us, you understand.
  I snatch'd him up just as you see him there,
And brought him off for sentence out of hand :
  I 've scarcely been ten minutes in the air—
At least a quarter it can hardly be :
I dare say that his wife is still at tea.'

LXXXVIII

Here Satan said, ' I know this man of old,
  And have expected him for some time here ;
A sillier fellow you will scarce behold,
  Or more conceited in his petty sphere :   700
But surely it was not worth while to fold
  Such trash below your wing, Asmodeus dear :
We had the poor wretch safe (without being bored
With carriage) coming of his own accord.

LXXXIX

' But since he 's here, let 's see what he has done.'
  ' Done ! ' cried Asmodeus, ' he anticipates
The very business you are now upon,
  And scribbles as if head clerk to the Fates.
Who knows to what his ribaldry may run,
  When such an ass as this, like Balaam's, prates ? ' 710
' Let 's hear,' quoth Michael, ' what he has to say :
You know we're bound to that in every way.'

XC

Now the bard, glad to get an audience, which
  By no means often was his case below,
Began to cough, and hawk, and hem, and pitch
  His voice into that awful note of woe
To all unhappy hearers within reach
  Of poets when the tide of rhyme 's in flow ;
But stuck fast with his first hexameter,
Not one of all whose gouty feet would stir.   720

XCI

But ere the spavin'd dactyls could be spurr'd
  Into recitative, in great dismay
Both cherubim and seraphim were heard
  To murmur loudly through their long array ;
And Michael rose ere he could get a word
  Of all his founder'd verses under way,
And cried, ' For God's sake stop, my friend ! 'twere best—
Non Di, non homines—you know the rest.'

XCII

A general bustle spread throughout the throng,
  Which seem'd to hold all verse in detestation ;   730
The angels had of course enough of song
  When upon service ; and the generation
Of ghosts had heard too much in life, not long
  Before, to profit by a new occasion :
The monarch, mute till then, exclaim'd, ' What ! what !
Pye come again ? No more—no more of that ! '

XCIII

The tumult grew ; an universal cough
  Convulsed the skies, as during a debate,
When Castlereagh has been up long enough
  (Before he was first minister of state,   740
I mean—the *slaves hear now*) ; some cried ' Off, off ! '
  As at a farce ; till, grown quite desperate,
The bard Saint Peter pray'd to interpose
(Himself an author) only for his prose.

XCIV

The varlet was not an ill-favour'd knave ;
  A good deal like a vulture in the face,
With a hook nose and a hawk's eye, which gave
  A smart and sharper-looking sort of grace
To his whole aspect, which, though rather grave,
  Was by no means so ugly as his case ;   750
But that, indeed, was hopeless as can be,
Quite a poetic felony ' *de se*.'

Then Michael blew his trump, and still'd the noise
   With one still greater, as is yet the mode
On earth besides ; except some grumbling voice,
   Which now and then will make a slight inroad
Upon decorous silence, few will twice
   Lift up their lungs when fairly overcrow'd ;
And now the bard could plead his own bad cause,
With all the attitudes of self-applause.   760

XCVI

He said—(I only give the heads)—he said,
   He meant no harm in scribbling ; 'twas his way
Upon all topics ; 'twas, besides, his bread,
   Of which he butter'd both sides ; 'twould delay
Too long the assembly (he was pleased to dread),
   And take up rather more time than a day,
To name his works—he would but cite a few—
' Wat Tyler '—' Rhymes on Blenheim '—' Waterloo.'

XCVII

He had written praises of a regicide ;
   He had written praises of all kings whatever ;   770
He had written for republics far and wide,
   And then against them bitterer than ever ;
For pantisocracy he once had cried
   Aloud, a scheme less moral than 'twas clever ;
Then grew a hearty anti-jacobin—
Had turn'd his coat—and would have turn'd his skin.

XCVIII

He had sung against all battles, and again
   In their high praise and glory ; he had call'd
Reviewing ' the ungentle craft,' and then
   Become as base a critic as e'er crawl'd—   780
Fed, paid, and pamper'd by the very men
   By whom his muse and morals had been maul'd :
He had written much blank verse, and blanker prose,
And more of both than anybody knows.

XCIX

He had written Wesley's life :—here turning round
   To Satan, ' Sir, I'm ready to write yours,
In two octavo volumes, nicely bound,
   With notes and preface, all that most allures
The pious purchaser ; and there 's no ground
   For fear, for I can choose my own reviewers :   790
So let me have the proper documents,
   That I may add you to my other saints.'

C

Satan bow'd, and was silent. 'Well, if you,
  With amiable modesty, decline
My offer, what says Michael ? There are few
  Whose memoirs could be render'd more divine.
Mine is a pen of all work ; not so new
  As it was once, but I would make you shine
Like your own trumpet. By the way, my own
Has more of brass in it, and is as well blown.   800

CI

'But talking about trumpets, here 's my Vision !
  Now you shall judge, all people ; yes, you shall
Judge with my judgement, and by my decision
  Be guided who shall enter heaven or fall.
I settle all these things by intuition,
  Times present, past, to come, heaven, hell, and all,
Like King Alfonso. When I thus see double,
I save the Deity some worlds of trouble.'

CII

He ceased, and drew forth an MS. ; and no
  Persuasion on the part of devils, saints,   810
Or angels, now could stop the torrent ; so
  He read the first three lines of the contents ;
But at the fourth, the whole spiritual show
  Had vanish'd, with variety of scents,
Ambrosial and sulphureous, as they sprang,
Like lightning, off from his ' melodious twang.'

CIII

Those grand heroics acted as a spell :
  The angels stopp'd their ears and plied their pinions ;
The devils ran howling, deafen'd, down to hell ;
  The ghosts fled, gibbering, for their own dominions— 820
(For 'tis not yet decided where they dwell,
  And I leave every man to his opinions) ;
Michael took refuge in his trump—but, lo !
His teeth were set on edge, he could not blow !

CIV

Saint Peter, who has hitherto been known
  For an impetuous saint, upraised his keys,
And at the fifth line knock'd the poet down ;
  Who fell like Phaeton, but more at ease,
Into his lake, for there he did not drown ;
  A different web being by the Destinies   830
Woven for the Laureate's final wreath, whene'er
Reform shall happen either here or there.

CV

He first sank to the bottom—like his works,
　　But soon rose to the surface—like himself;
For all corrupted things are buoy'd like corks,
　　By their own rottenness, light as an elf,
Or wisp that flits o'er a morass: he lurks,
　　It may be, still, like dull books on a shelf,
In his own den, to scrawl some 'Life' or 'Vision,'
As Welborn says—'the devil turn'd precisian.'　　　　840

CVI

As for the rest, to come to the conclusion
　　Of this true dream, the telescope is gone
Which kept my optics free from all delusion,
　　And show'd me what I in my turn have shown;
All I saw farther, in the last confusion,
　　Was, that King George slipp'd into heaven for one;
And when the tumult dwindled to a calm,
I left him practising the hundredth psalm.

PERCY BYSSHE SHELLEY

ALASTOR

OR, THE SPIRIT OF SOLITUDE

PREFACE

THE poem entitled *Alastor* may be considered as allegorical of one of the most interesting situations of the human mind. It represents a youth of uncorrupted feelings and adventurous genius, led forth by an imagination inflamed and purified through familiarity with all that is excellent and majestic, to the contemplation of the universe. He drinks deep of the fountains of knowledge, and is still insatiate. The magnificence and beauty of the external world sinks profoundly into the frame of his conceptions, and affords to their modifications a variety not to be exhausted. So long as it is possible for his desires to point towards objects thus infinite and unmeasured, he is joyous, and tranquil, and self-possessed. But the period arrives when these objects cease to suffice. His mind is at length suddenly awakened and thirsts for intercourse with an intelligence similar to itself. He images to himself the Being whom he loves. Conversant with speculations of the sublimest and most perfect natures, the vision in which he embodies his own imaginations unites all of wonderful, or wise, or beautiful, which the poet, the philosopher, or the lover could depicture. The intellectual faculties, the imagination, the functions of sense, have their respective requisitions on the sympathy of corresponding powers in other human beings. The Poet is represented as uniting these requisitions, and attaching them to a single image. He seeks in vain for a prototype of his conception. Blasted by his disappointment, he descends to an untimely grave.

The picture is not barren of instruction to actual men. The Poet's self-centred seclusion was avenged by the furies of an irresistible passion pursuing him to speedy ruin. But that Power which strikes the luminaries of the world with sudden darkness and extinction, by awakening them to too exquisite a perception of its influences, dooms to a slow and poisonous decay those meaner spirits that dare to abjure its dominion. Their destiny is more abject and inglorious as their delinquency is more contemptible and pernicious. They who, deluded by no generous error, instigated by no sacred thirst of doubtful knowledge, duped by no illustrious superstition, loving nothing on this earth, and cherishing no hopes beyond, yet keep aloof from sympathies with their kind, rejoicing neither in human joy nor mourning with human grief; these, and such as they, have their apportioned curse. They languish, because none feel with them their common nature. They are morally dead. They are neither friends, nor lovers, nor fathers, nor citizens of the world, nor benefactors of their country. Among those who attempt to exist without human sympathy, the pure and tender-hearted perish through the intensity and passion of their search after its communities, when the vacancy of their spirit suddenly makes itself felt. All else, selfish, blind, and torpid, are those unforeseeing multitudes who constitute, together with their own, the lasting misery and loneliness of the world. Those who love not their fellow-beings live unfruitful lives, and prepare for their old age a miserable grave.

> ' The good die first,
> And those whose hearts are dry as summer dust,
> Burn to the socket ! '

December 14, 1815.

> Nondum amabam, et amare amabam, quaerebam quid
> amarem, amans amare.—*Confess. St. August.*

EARTH, ocean, air, beloved brotherhood !
If our great Mother has imbued my soul
With aught of natural piety to feel
Your love, and recompense the boon with mine :
If dewy morn, and odorous noon, and even,
With sunset and its gorgeous ministers,
And solemn midnight's tingling silentness ;
If autumn's hollow sighs in the sere wood,
And winter robing with pure snow and crowns
Of starry ice the grey grass and bare boughs ;   10
If spring's voluptuous pantings when she breathes
Her first sweet kisses, have been dear to me ;
If no bright bird, insect, or gentle beast
I consciously have injured, but still loved
And cherished these my kindred ; then forgive
This boast, belovèd brethren, and withdraw
No portion of your wonted favour now !

Mother of this unfathomable world !
Favour my solemn song, for I have loved
Thee ever, and thee only ; I have watched   20
Thy shadow, and the darkness of thy steps,
And my heart ever gazes on the depth
Of thy deep mysteries. I have made my bed
In charnels and on coffins, where black death
Keeps record of the trophies won from thee,
Hoping to still these obstinate questionings
Of thee and thine, by forcing some lone ghost
Thy messenger, to render up the tale
Of what we are. In lone and silent hours,
When night makes a weird sound of its own stillness, 30
Like an inspired and desperate alchymist
Staking his very life on some dark hope,
Have I mixed awful talk and asking looks
With my most innocent love, until strange tears
Uniting with those breathless kisses, made
Such magic as compels the charmèd night
To render up thy charge : . . . and, though ne'er yet

Thou hast unveiled thy inmost sanctuary,
Enough from incommunicable dream,
And twilight phantasms, and deep noon-day thought,   40
Has shone within me, that serenely now
And moveless, as a long-forgotten lyre
Suspended in the solitary dome
Of some mysterious and deserted fane,
I wait thy breath, Great Parent, that my strain
May modulate with murmurs of the air,
And motions of the forests and the sea,
And voice of living beings, and woven hymns
Of night and day, and the deep heart of man.

  There was a Poet whose untimely tomb   50
No human hands with pious reverence reared,
But the charmed eddies of autumnal winds
Built o'er his mouldering bones a pyramid
Of mouldering leaves in the waste wilderness :—
A lovely youth,—no mourning maiden decked
With weeping flowers, or votive cypress wreath,
The lone couch of his everlasting sleep :—
Gentle, and brave, and generous,—no lorn bard
Breathed o'er his dark fate one melodious sigh :
He lived, he died, he sung, in solitude.   60
Strangers have wept to hear his passionate notes,
And virgins, as unknown he passed, have pined
And wasted for fond love of his wild eyes.
The fire of those soft orbs has ceased to burn,
And Silence, too enamoured of that voice,
Locks its mute music in her rugged cell.

  By solemn vision, and bright silver dream,
His infancy was nurtured. Every sight
And sound from the vast earth and ambient air,
Sent to his heart its choicest impulses.   70
The fountains of divine philosophy
Fled not his thirsting lips, and all of great,
Or good, or lovely, which the sacred past
In truth or fable consecrates, he felt
And knew. When early youth had passed, he left
His cold fireside and alienated home
To seek strange truths in undiscovered lands.
Many a wide waste and tangled wilderness
Has lured his fearless steps ; and he has bought
With his sweet voice and eyes, from savage men,   80
His rest and food. Nature's most secret steps
He like her shadow has pursued, where'er
The red volcano overcanopies
Its fields of snow and pinnacles of ice
With burning smoke, or where bitumen lakes
On black bare pointed islets ever beat

With sluggish surge, or where the secret caves
Rugged and dark, winding among the springs
Of fire and poison, inaccessible
To avarice or pride, their starry domes   90
Of diamond and of gold expand above
Numberless and immeasurable halls,
Frequent with crystal column, and clear shrines
Of pearl, and thrones radiant with chrysolite.
Nor had that scene of ampler majesty
Than gems or gold, the varying roof of heaven
And the green earth lost in his heart its claims
To love and wonder ; he would linger long
In lonesome vales, making the wild his home,
Until the doves and squirrels would partake   100
From his innocuous hand his bloodless food,
Lured by the gentle meaning of his looks,
And the wild antelope, that starts whene'er
The dry leaf rustles in the brake, suspend
Her timid steps to gaze upon a form   .
More graceful than her own.
                                        His wandering step
Obedient to high thoughts, has visited
The awful ruins of the days of old :
Athens, and Tyre, and Balbec, and the waste
Where stood Jerusalem, the fallen towers   110
Of Babylon, the eternal pyramids,
Memphis and Thebes, and whatsoe'er of strange
Sculptured on alabaster obelisk,
Or jasper tomb, or mutilated sphynx,
Dark Aethiopia in her desert hills
Conceals. Among the ruined temples there,
Stupendous columns, and wild images
Of more than man, where marble daemons watch
The Zodiac's brazen mystery, and dead men
Hang their mute thoughts on the mute walls around, 120
He lingered, poring on memorials
Of the world's youth, through the long burning day
Gazed on those speechless shapes, nor, when the moon
Filled the mysterious halls with floating shades
Suspended he that task, but ever gazed
And gazed, till meaning on his vacant mind
Flashed like strong inspiration, and he saw
The thrilling secrets of the birth of time.

Meanwhile an Arab maiden brought his food,
Her daily portion, from her father's tent,   130
And spread her matting for his couch, and stole
From duties and repose to tend his steps :—
Enamoured, yet not daring for deep awe
To speak her love :—and watched his nightly sleep,
Sleepless herself, to gaze upon his lips

Parted in slumber, whence the regular breath
Of innocent dreams arose : then, when red morn
Made paler the pale moon, to her cold home
Wildered, and wan, and panting, she returned.

The Poet wandering on, through Arabie   140
And Persia, and the wild Carmanian waste,
And o'er the aërial mountains which pour down
Indus and Oxus from their icy caves,
In joy and exultation held his way ;
Till in the vale of Cashmire, far within
Its loneliest dell, where odorous plants entwine
Beneath the hollow rocks a natural bower,
Beside a sparkling rivulet he stretched
His languid limbs. A vision on his sleep
There came, a dream of hopes that never yet   150
Had flushed his cheek. He dreamed a veilèd maid
Sate near him, talking in low solemn tones.
Her voice was like the voice of his own soul
Heard in the calm of thought ; its music long,
Like woven sounds of streams and breezes, held
His inmost sense suspended in its web
Of many-coloured woof and shifting hues.
Knowledge and truth and virtue were her theme,
And lofty hopes of divine liberty,
Thoughts the most dear to him, and poesy,   160
Herself a poet. Soon the solemn mood
Of her pure mind kindled through all her frame
A permeating fire : wild numbers then
She raised, with voice stifled in tremulous sobs
Subdued by its own pathos : her fair hands
Were bare alone, sweeping from some strange harp
Strange symphony, and in their branching veins
The eloquent blood told an ineffable tale.
The beating of her heart was heard to fill
The pauses of her music, and her breath   170
Tumultuously accorded with those fits
Of intermitted song. Sudden she rose,
As if her heart impatiently endured
Its bursting burthen : at the sound he turned,
And saw by the warm light of their own life
Her glowing limbs beneath the sinuous veil
Of woven wind, her outspread arms now bare,
Her dark locks floating in the breath of night,
Her beamy bending eyes, her parted lips
Outstretched, and pale, and quivering eagerly.   180
His strong heart sunk and sickened with excess
Of love. He reared his shuddering limbs and quelled
His gasping breath, and spread his arms to meet
Her panting bosom : . . . she drew back a while,
Then, yielding to the irresistible joy,

With frantic gesture and short breathless cry
Folded his frame in her dissolving arms.
Now blackness veiled his dizzy eyes, and night
Involved and swallowed up the vision ; sleep,
Like a dark flood suspended in its course,　　　　190
Rolled back its impulse on his vacant brain.

　　Roused by the shock he started from his trance—
The cold white light of morning, the blue moon
Low in the west, the clear and garish hills,
The distinct valley and the vacant woods,
Spread round him where he stood. Whither have fled
The hues of heaven that canopied his bower
Of yesternight ? The sounds that soothed his sleep,
The mystery and the majesty of Earth,
The joy, the exultation ? His wan eyes　　　　200
Gaze on the empty scene as vacantly
As ocean's moon looks on the moon in heaven.
The spirit of sweet human love has sent
A vision to the sleep of him who spurned
Her choicest gifts. He eagerly pursues
Beyond the realms of dream that fleeting shade ;
He overleaps the bounds. Alas ! Alas !
Were limbs, and breath, and being intertwined
Thus treacherously ? Lost, lost, for ever lost,
In the wide pathless desert of dim sleep,　　　　210
That beautiful shape ! Does the dark gate of death
Conduct to thy mysterious paradise,
O Sleep ? Does the bright arch of rainbow clouds,
And pendent mountains seen in the calm lake,
Lead only to a black and watery depth,
While death's blue vault, with loathliest vapours hung,
Where every shade which the foul grave exhales
Hides its dead eye from the detested day,
Conducts, O Sleep, to thy delightful realms ?
This doubt with sudden tide flowed on his heart,　　　　220
The insatiate hope which it awakened, stung
His brain even like despair.

　　　　　　　　　　While daylight held
The sky, the Poet kept mute conference
With his still soul. At night the passion came,
Like the fierce fiend of a distempered dream,
And shook him from his rest, and led him forth
Into the darkness.—As an eagle grasped
In folds of the green serpent, feels her breast
Burn with the poison, and precipitates
Through night and day, tempest, and calm, and cloud,　230
Frantic with dizzying anguish, her blind flight
O'er the wide aëry wilderness : thus driven
By the bright shadow of that lovely dream,
Beneath the cold glare of the desolate night,

Through tangled swamps and deep precipitous dells,
Startling with careless step the moonlight snake,
He fled. Red morning dawned upon his flight,
Shedding the mockery of its vital hues
Upon his cheek of death. He wandered on
Till vast Aornos seen from Petra's steep   240
Hung o'er the low horizon like a cloud ;
Through Balk, and where the desolated tombs
Of Parthian kings scatter to every wind
Their wasting dust, wildly he wandered on,
Day after day a weary waste of hours,
Bearing within his life the brooding care
That ever fed on its decaying flame.
And now his limbs were lean ; his scattered hair
Sered by the autumn of strange suffering
Sung dirges in the wind ; his listless hand   250
Hung like dead bone within its withered skin ;
Life, and the lustre that consumed it, shone
As in a furnace burning secretly
From his dark eyes alone. The cottagers,
Who ministered with human charity
His human wants, beheld with wondering awe
Their fleeting visitant. The mountaineer,
Encountering on some dizzy precipice
That spectral form, deemed that the Spirit of wind
With lightning eyes, and eager breath, and feet   260
Disturbing not the drifted snow, had paused
In its career : the infant would conceal
His troubled visage in his mother's robe
In terror at the glare of those wild eyes,
To remember their strange light in many a dream
Of after-times ; but youthful maidens, taught
By nature, would interpret half the woe
That wasted him, would call him with false names
Brother, and friend, would press his pallid hand
At parting, and watch, dim through tears, the path 270
Of his departure from their father's door.

At length upon the lone Chorasmian shore
He paused, a wide and melancholy waste
Of putrid marshes. A strong impulse urged
His steps to the sea-shore. A swan was there,
Beside a sluggish stream among the reeds.
It rose as he approached, and with strong wings
Scaling the upward sky, bent its bright course
High over the immeasurable main.
His eyes pursued its flight.—' Thou hast a home,   280
Beautiful bird ; thou voyagest to thine home,
Where thy sweet mate will twine her downy neck
With thine, and welcome thy return with eyes
Bright in the lustre of their own fond joy.

And what am I that I should linger here,
With voice far sweeter than thy dying notes,
Spirit more vast than thine, frame more attuned
To beauty, wasting these surpassing powers
In the deaf air, to the blind earth, and heaven
That echoes not my thoughts ? ' A gloomy smile   290
Of desperate hope wrinkled his quivering lips.
For sleep, he knew, kept most relentlessly
Its precious charge, and silent death exposed,
Faithless perhaps as sleep, a shadowy lure,
With doubtful smile mocking its own strange charms.

  Startled by his own thoughts he looked around.
There was no fair fiend near him, not a sight
Or sound of awe but in his own deep mind.
A little shallop floating near the shore
Caught the impatient wandering of his gaze.   300
It had been long abandoned, for its sides
Gaped wide with many a rift, and its frail joints
Swayed with the undulations of the tide.
A restless impulse urged him to embark
And meet lone Death on the drear ocean's waste ;
For well he knew that mighty Shadow loves
The slimy caverns of the populous deep.

  The day was fair and sunny: sea and sky
Drank its inspiring radiance, and the wind
Swept strongly from the shore, blackening the waves. 310
Following his eager soul, the wanderer
Leaped in the boat, he spread his cloak aloft
On the bare mast, and took his lonely seat,
And felt the boat speed o'er the tranquil sea
Like a torn cloud before the hurricane.

  As one that in a silver vision floats
Obedient to the sweep of odorous winds
Upon resplendent clouds, so rapidly
Along the dark and ruffled waters fled
The straining boat.—A whirlwind swept it on,   320
With fierce gusts and precipitating force,
Through the white ridges of the chafèd sea.
The waves arose. Higher and higher still
Their fierce necks writhed beneath the tempest's scourge
Like serpents struggling in a vulture's grasp.
Calm and rejoicing in the fearful war
Of wave ruining on wave, and blast on blast
Descending, and black flood on whirlpool driven
With dark obliterating course, he sate :
As if their genii were the ministers   330
Appointed to conduct him to the light
Of those belovèd eyes, the Poet sate

Holding the steady helm. Evening came on,
The beams of sunset hung their rainbow hues
High 'mid the shifting domes of sheeted spray
That canopied his path o'er the waste deep ;
Twilight, ascending slowly from the east,
Entwined in duskier wreaths her braided locks
O'er the fair front and radiant eyes of day ;
Night followed, clad with stars. On every side   340
More horribly the multitudinous streams
Of ocean's mountainous waste to mutual war
Rushed in dark tumult thundering, as to mock
The calm and spangled sky. The little boat
Still fled before the storm ; still fled, like foam
Down the steep cataract of a wintry river ;
Now pausing on the edge of the riven wave ;
Now leaving far behind the bursting mass
That fell, convulsing ocean : safely fled—
As if that frail and wasted human form,   350
Had been an elemental god.

                   At midnight
The moon arose : and lo ! the ethereal cliffs
Of Caucasus, whose icy summits shone
Among the stars like sunlight, and around
Whose caverned base the whirlpools and the waves
Bursting and eddying irresistibly
Rage and resound for ever.—Who shall save ?—
The boat fled on,—the boiling torrent drove,—
The crags closed round with black and jagged arms,
The shattered mountain overhung the sea,   360
And faster still, beyond all human speed,
Suspended on the sweep of the smooth wave,
The little boat was driven. A cavern there
Yawned, and amid its slant and winding depths
Ingulfed the rushing sea. The boat fled on
With unrelaxing speed.—' Vision and Love ! '
The Poet cried aloud, ' I have beheld
The path of thy departure. Sleep and death
Shall not divide us long ! '

                  The boat pursued
The windings of the cavern. Daylight shone   370
At length upon that gloomy river's flow ;
Now, where the fiercest war among the waves
Is calm, on the unfathomable stream
The boat moved slowly. Where the mountain, riven,
Exposed those black depths to the azure sky,
Ere yet the flood's enormous volume fell
Even to the base of Caucasus, with sound
That shook the everlasting rocks, the mass
Filled with one whirlpool all that ample chasm ;
Stair above stair the eddying waters rose,   380

Circling immeasurably fast, and laved
With alternating dash the gnarlèd roots
Of mighty trees, that stretched their giant arms
In darkness over it. I' the midst was left,
Reflecting, yet distorting every cloud,
A pool of treacherous and tremendous calm.
Seized by the sway of the ascending stream,
With dizzy swiftness, round, and round, and round,
Ridge after ridge the straining boat arose,
Till on the verge of the extremest curve,   390
Where, through an opening of the rocky bank,
The waters overflow, and a smooth spot
Of glassy quiet mid those battling tides
Is left, the boat paused shuddering.—Shall it sink
Down the abyss ? Shall the reverting stress
Of that resistless gulf embosom it ?
Now shall it fall ?—A wandering stream of wind,
Breathed from the west, has caught the expanded sail,
And, lo ! with gentle motion, between banks
Of mossy slope, and on a placid stream,   400
Beneath a woven grove it sails, and, hark !
The ghastly torrent mingles its far roar,
With the breeze murmuring in the musical woods.
Where the embowering trees recede, and leave
A little space of green expanse, the cove
Is closed by meeting banks, whose yellow flowers
For ever gaze on their own drooping eyes,
Reflected in the crystal calm. The wave
Of the boat's motion marred their pensive task,
Which nought but vagrant bird, or wanton wind,   410
Or falling spear-grass, or their own decay
Had e'er disturbed before. The Poet longed
To deck with their bright hues his withered hair,
But on his heart its solitude returned,
And he forbore. Not the strong impulse hid
In those flushed cheeks, bent eyes, and shadowy frame
Had yet performed its ministry : it hung
Upon his life, as lightning in a cloud
Gleams, hovering ere it vanish, ere the floods
Of night close over it.

           The noonday sun   420
Now shone upon the forest, one vast mass
Of mingling shade, whose brown magnificence
A narrow vale embosoms. There, huge caves,
Scooped in the dark base of their aëry rocks
Mocking its moans, respond and roar for ever.
The meeting boughs and implicated leaves
Wove twilight o'er the Poet's path, as led
By love, or dream, or god, or mightier Death,
He sought in Nature's dearest haunt, some bank,
Her cradle, and his sepulchre. More dark   430

And dark the shades accumulate. The oak,
Expanding its immense and knotty arms,
Embraces the light beech. The pyramids
Of the tall cedar overarching, frame
Most solemn domes within, and far below,
Like clouds suspended in an emerald sky,
The ash and the acacia floating hang
Tremulous and pale. Like restless serpents, clothed
In rainbow and in fire, the parasites,
Starred with ten thousand blossoms, flow around   440
The grey trunks, and, as gamesome infants' eyes,
With gentle meanings, and most innocent wiles,
Fold their beams round the hearts of those that love,
These twine their tendrils with the wedded boughs
Uniting their close union ; the woven leaves
Make net-work of the dark blue light of day,
And the night's noontide clearness, mutable
As shapes in the weird clouds. Soft mossy lawns
Beneath these canopies extend their swells,
Fragrant with perfumed herbs, and eyed with blooms 450
Minute yet beautiful. One darkest glen
Sends from its woods of musk-rose, twined with jasmine,
A soul-dissolving odour, to invite
To some more lovely mystery. Through the dell,
Silence and Twilight here, twin-sisters, keep
Their noonday watch, and sail among the shades,
Like vaporous shapes half seen ; beyond, a well,
Dark, gleaming, and of most translucent wave,
Images all the woven boughs above,
And each depending leaf, and every speck   460
Of azure sky, darting between their chasms ;
Nor aught else in the liquid mirror laves
Its portraiture, but some inconstant star
Between one foliaged lattice twinkling fair,
Or painted bird, sleeping beneath the moon,
Or gorgeous insect floating motionless,
Unconscious of the day, ere yet his wings
Have spread their glories to the gaze of noon.

Hither the Poet came. His eyes beheld
Their own wan light through the reflected lines   470
Of his thin hair, distinct in the dark depth
Of that still fountain ; as the human heart,
Gazing in dreams over the gloomy grave,
Sees its own treacherous likeness there. He heard
The motion of the leaves, the grass that sprung
Startled and glanced and trembled even to feel
An unaccustomed presence, and the sound
Of the sweet brook that from the secret springs
Of that dark fountain rose. A Spirit seemed
To stand beside him—clothed in no bright robes   480

Of shadowy silver or enshrining light,
Borrowed from aught the visible world affords
Of grace, or majesty, or mystery ;—
But, undulating woods, and silent well,
And leaping rivulet, and evening gloom
Now deepening the dark shades, for speech assuming,
Held commune with him, as if he and it
Were all that was,—only . . . when his regard
Was raised by intense pensiveness, . . . two eyes,
Two starry eyes, hung in the gloom of thought,   490
And seemed with their serene and azure smiles
To beckon him.

            Obedient to the light
That shone within his soul, he went, pursuing
The windings of the dell.—The rivulet
Wanton and wild, through many a green ravine
Beneath the forest flowed. Sometimes it fell
Among the moss with hollow harmony
Dark and profound. Now on the polished stones
It danced ; like childhood laughing as it went :
Then, through the plain in tranquil wanderings crept, 500
Reflecting every herb and drooping bud
That overhung its quietness.—' O stream !
Whose source is inaccessibly profound,
Whither do thy mysterious waters tend ?
Thou imagest my life. Thy darksome stillness,
Thy dazzling waves, thy loud and hollow gulfs,
Thy searchless fountain, and invisible course
Have each their type in me : and the wide sky,
And measureless ocean may declare as soon
What oozy cavern or what wandering cloud   510
Contains thy waters, as the universe
Tell where these living thoughts reside, when stretched
Upon thy flowers my bloodless limbs shall waste
I' the passing wind ! '

            Beside the grassy shore
Of the small stream he went ; he did impress
On the green moss his tremulous step, that caught
Strong shuddering from his burning limbs. As one
Roused by some joyous madness from the couch
Of fever, he did move ; yet, not like him,
Forgetful of the grave, where, when the flame   520
Of his frail exultation shall be spent,
He must descend. With rapid steps he went
Beneath the shade of trees, beside the flow
Of the wild babbling rivulet ; and now
The forest's solemn canopies were changed
For the uniform and lightsome evening sky.
Grey rocks did peep from the spare moss, and stemmed

The struggling brook : tall spires of windlestrae
Threw their thin shadows down the rugged slope,
And nought but gnarled roots of ancient pines   530
Branchless and blasted, clenched with grasping roots
The unwilling soil. A gradual change was here,
Yet ghastly. For, as fast years flow away,
The smooth brow gathers, and the hair grows thin
And white, and where irradiate dewy eyes.
Had shone, gleam stony orbs :—so from his steps
Bright flowers departed, and the beautiful shade
Of the green groves, with all their odorous winds
And musical motions. Calm, he still pursued
The stream, that with a larger volume now   540
Rolled through the labyrinthine dell ; and there
Fretted a path through its descending curves
With its wintry speed. On every side now rose
Rocks, which, in unimaginable forms,
Lifted their black and barren pinnacles
In the light of evening, and, its precipice
Obscuring the ravine, disclosed above,
Mid toppling stones, black gulfs and yawning caves,
Whose windings gave ten thousand various tongues
To the loud stream. Lo ! where the pass expands   550
Its stony jaws, the abrupt mountain breaks,
And seems, with its accumulated crags,
To overhang the world : for wide expand
Beneath the wan stars and descending moon
Islanded seas, blue mountains, mighty streams,
Dim tracts and vast, robed in the lustrous gloom
Of leaden-coloured even, and fiery hills
Mingling their flames with twilight, on the verge
Of the remote horizon. The near scene,
In naked and severe simplicity,   560
Made contrast with the universe. A pine,
Rock-rooted, stretched athwart the vacancy
Its swinging boughs, to each inconstant blast
Yielding one only response, at each pause
In most familiar cadence, with the howl
The thunder and the hiss of homeless streams
Mingling its solemn song, whilst the broad river,
Foaming and hurrying o'er its rugged path,
Fell into that immeasurable void
Scattering its waters to the passing winds.   570

Yet the grey precipice and solemn pine
And torrent, were not all ;—one silent nook
Was there. Even on the edge of that vast mountain,
Upheld by knotty roots and fallen rocks,
It overlooked in its serenity
The dark earth, and the bending vault of stars.
It was a tranquil spot, that seemed to smile
Even in the lap of horror. Ivy clasped

The fissured stones with its entwining arms,
And did embower with leaves for ever green,   580
And berries dark, the smooth and even space
Of its inviolated floor, and here
The children of the autumnal whirlwind bore,
In wanton sport, those bright leaves, whose decay,
Red, yellow, or ethereally pale,
Rivals the pride of summer. 'Tis the haunt
Of every gentle wind, whose breath can teach
The wilds to love tranquillity. One step,
One human step alone, has ever broken
The stillness of its solitude :—one voice   590
Alone inspired its echoes ;—even that voice
Which hither came, floating among the winds,
And led the loveliest among human forms
To make their wild haunts the depository
Of all the grace and beauty that endued
Its motions, render up its majesty,
Scatter its music on the unfeeling storm,
And to the damp leaves and blue cavern mould,
Nurses of rainbow flowers and branching moss,
Commit the colours of that varying cheek,   600
That snowy breast, those dark and drooping eyes.

The dim and hornèd moon hung low, and poured
A sea of lustre on the horizon's verge
That overflowed its mountains. Yellow mist
Filled the unbounded atmosphere, and drank
Wan moonlight even to fulness : not a star
Shone, not a sound was heard ; the very winds,
Danger's grim playmates, on that precipice
Slept, clasped in his embrace.—O, storm of death !
Whose sightless speed divides this sullen night :   610
And thou, colossal Skeleton, that, still
Guiding its irresistible career
In thy devastating omnipotence,
Art king of this frail world, from the red field
Of slaughter, from the reeking hospital,
The patriot's sacred couch, the snowy bed
Of innocence, the scaffold and the throne,
A mighty voice invokes thee. Ruin calls
His brother Death. A rare and regal prey
He hath prepared, prowling around the world ;   620
Glutted with which thou mayst repose, and men
Go to their graves like flowers or creeping worms,
Nor ever more offer at thy dark shrine
The unheeded tribute of a broken heart.

When on the threshold of the green recess
The wanderer's footsteps fell, he knew that death
Was on him. Yet a little, ere it fled,
Did he resign his high and holy soul

To images of the majestic past,
That paused within his passive being now,   630
Like winds that bear sweet music, when they breathe
Through some dim latticed chamber. He did place
His pale lean hand upon the rugged trunk
Of the old pine. Upon an ivied stone
Reclined his languid head, his limbs did rest,
Diffused and motionless, on the smooth brink
Of that obscurest chasm ;—and thus he lay,
Surrendering to their final impulses
The hovering powers of life. Hope and despair,
The torturers, slept ; no mortal pain or fear   640
Marred his repose, the influxes of sense,
And his own being unalloyed by pain,
Yet feebler and more feeble, calmly fed
The stream of thought, till he lay breathing there
At peace, and faintly smiling :—his last sight
Was the great moon, which o'er the western line
Of the wide world her mighty horn suspended,
With whose dun beams inwoven darkness seemed
To mingle. Now upon the jaggèd hills
It rests, and still as the divided frame   650
Of the vast meteor sunk, the Poet's blood,
That ever beat in mystic sympathy
With nature's ebb and flow, grew feebler still :
And when two lessening points of light alone
Gleamed through the darkness, the alternate gasp
Of his faint respiration scarce did stir
The stagnate night :—till the minutest ray
Was quenched, the pulse yet lingered in his heart.
It paused—it fluttered. But when heaven remained
Utterly black, the murky shades involved   660
An image, silent, cold, and motionless,
As their own voiceless earth and vacant air.
Even as a vapour fed with golden beams
That ministered on sunlight, ere the west
Eclipses it, was now that wondrous frame—
No sense, no motion, no divinity—
A fragile lute, on whose harmonious strings
The breath of heaven did wander—a bright stream
Once fed with many-voicèd waves—a dream
Of youth, which night and time have quenched for ever,
Still, dark, and dry, and unremembered now.   671

O, for Medea's wondrous alchemy,
Which wheresoe'er it fell made the earth gleam
With bright flowers, and the wintry boughs exhale
From vernal blooms fresh fragrance ! O, that God,
Profuse of poisons, would concede the chalice
Which but one living man has drained, who now,
Vessel of deathless wrath, a slave that feels

No proud exemption in the blighting curse
He bears, over the world wanders for ever,   680
Lone as incarnate death ! O, that the dream
Of dark magician in his visioned cave,
Raking the cinders of a crucible
For life and power, even when his feeble hand
Shakes in its last decay, were the true law
Of this so lovely world ! But thou art fled
Like some frail exhalation, which the dawn
Robes in its golden beams,—ah ! thou hast fled !
The brave, the gentle, and the beautiful,
The child of grace and genius. Heartless things   690
Are done and said i' the world, and many worms
And beasts and men live on, and mighty Earth
From sea and mountain, city and wilderness,
In vesper low or joyous orison,
Lifts still its solemn voice :—but thou art fled—
Thou canst no longer know or love the shapes
Of this phantasmal scene, who have to thee
Been purest ministers, who are, alas !
Now thou art not. Upon those pallid lips
So sweet even in their silence, on those eyes   700
That image sleep in death, upon that form
Yet safe from the worm's outrage, let no tear
Be shed—not even in thought. Nor, when those hues
Are gone, and those divinest lineaments,
Worn by the senseless wind, shall live alone
In the frail pauses of this simple strain,
Let not high verse, mourning the memory
Of that which is no more, or painting's woe
Or sculpture, speak in feeble imagery
Their own cold powers. Art and eloquence,   710
And all the shows o' the world are frail and vain
To weep a loss that turns their lights to shade.
It is a woe ' too deep for tears ', when all
Is reft at once, when some surpassing Spirit,
Whose light adorned the world around it, leaves
Those who remain behind, not sobs or groans,
The passionate tumult of a clinging hope ;
But pale despair and cold tranquillity,
Nature's vast frame, the web of human things,
Birth and the grave, that are not as they were.   720

ADONAIS

AN ELEGY ON THE DEATH OF JOHN KEATS, AUTHOR OF ENDYMION, HYPERION, ETC.

Ἀστὴρ πρὶν μὲν ἔλαμπες ἐνὶ ζωοῖσιν Ἑῷος·
νῦν δὲ θανὼν λάμπεις Ἕσπερος ἐν φθιμένοις.—PLATO.

PREFACE

Φάρμακον ἦλθε, Βίων, ποτὶ σὸν στόμα, φάρμακον εἶδες.
πῶς τευ τοῖς χείλεσσι ποτέδραμε, κοὐκ ἐγλυκάνθη ;
τίς δὲ βροτὸς τοσσοῦτον ἀνάμερος, ἢ κεράσαι τοι,
ἢ δοῦναι λαλέοντι τὸ φάρμακον ; ἔκφυγεν ᾠδάν.
—MOSCHUS, *Epitaph. Bion.*

IT is my intention to subjoin to the London edition of this poem a criticism upon the claims of its lamented object to be classed among the writers of the highest genius who have adorned our age. My known repugnance to the narrow principles of taste on which several of his earlier compositions were modelled prove at least that I am an impartial judge. I consider the fragment of *Hyperion* as second to nothing that was ever produced by a writer of the same years.

John Keats died at Rome of a consumption, in his twenty-fourth year, on the —— of —— 1821 ; and was buried in the romantic and lonely cemetery of the Protestants in that city, under the pyramid which is the tomb of Cestius, and the massy walls and towers, now mouldering and desolate, which formed the circuit of ancient Rome. The cemetery is an open space among the ruins, covered in winter with violets and daisies. It might make one in love with death, to think that one should be buried in so sweet a place.

The genius of the lamented person to whose memory I have dedicated these unworthy verses was not less delicate and fragile than it was beautiful ; and where cankerworms abound, what wonder if its young flower was blighted in the bud ? The savage criticism on his *Endymion*, which appeared in the *Quarterly Review*, produced the most violent effect on his susceptible mind ; the agitation thus originated ended in the rupture of a blood-vessel in the lungs ; a rapid consumption ensued, and the succeeding acknowledgements from more candid critics of the true greatness of his powers were ineffectual to heal the wound thus wantonly inflicted.

It may be well said that these wretched men know not what they do. They scatter their insults and their slanders without heed as to whether the poisoned shaft lights on a heart made callous by many blows or one like Keats's composed of more penetrable stuff. One of their associates is, to my knowledge, a most base and unprincipled calumniator. As to *Endymion*, was it a poem, whatever might be its defects, to be treated contemptuously by those who had celebrated, with various degrees of complacency and panegyric, *Paris*, and *Woman*, and a *Syrian Tale*, and Mrs. Lefanu, and Mr. Barrett, and Mr. Howard Payne, and a long list of the illustrious obscure ? Are these the men who in their venal good nature presumed to draw a parallel between the Rev. Mr. Milman and Lord Byron ? What gnat did they strain at here, after having swallowed all those camels ? Against what woman taken in adultery dares the foremost of these literary prostitutes to cast his opprobrious stone ? Miserable man ! you, one of the meanest, have wantonly defaced one of the noblest specimens of the workmanship of God. Nor shall it be your excuse, that, murderer as you are, you have spoken daggers, but used none.

The circumstances of the closing scene of poor Keats's life were not made known to me until the *Elegy* was ready for the press. I am given to understand that the wound which his sensitive spirit had received from the criticism of *Endymion* was exasperated by the bitter sense of unrequited benefits ; the poor fellow seems to have been hooted from the stage of life, no less by those on whom he had wasted the promise of his genius, than those on whom he had lavished his fortune and his care. He was accompanied to Rome, and attended in his last illness by Mr. Severn, a young artist of the highest promise, who, I have been informed, ' almost risked his own life, and sacrificed every prospect to unwearied attendance upon his dying friend.' Had I known these circumstances before the completion of my poem, I should have been tempted to add my feeble tribute of applause to the more solid recompense which the virtuous man finds in the recollection of his own motives. Mr. Severn can dispense with a reward from ' such stuff as dreams are made of.' His conduct is a golden augury of the success of his future career—may the unextinguished Spirit of his illustrious friend animate the creations of his pencil, and plead against Oblivion for his name !

ADONAIS

I

I WEEP for Adonais—he is dead !
O, weep for Adonais ! though our tears
Thaw not the frost which binds so dear a head !
And thou, sad Hour, selected from all years
To mourn our loss, rouse thy obscure compeers,
And teach them thine own sorrow; say : ' With me
Died Adonais ; till the Future dares
Forget the Past, his fate and fame shall be
An echo and a light unto eternity ! '

II

Where wert thou, mighty Mother, when he lay,   10
When thy Son lay, pierced by the shaft which flies
In darkness ? where was lorn Urania
When Adonais died ? With veilèd eyes,
'Mid listening Echoes, in her Paradise
She sate, while one, with soft enamoured breath,
Rekindled all the fading melodies,
With which, like flowers that mock the corse beneath,
He had adorned and hid the coming bulk of Death.

III

Oh, weep for Adonais—he is dead!
Wake, melancholy Mother, wake and weep!   20
Yet wherefore? Quench within their burning bed
Thy fiery tears, and let thy loud heart keep,
Like his, a mute and uncomplaining sleep;
For he is gone, where all things wise and fair
Descend;—oh, dream not that the amorous Deep
Will yet restore him to the vital air;
Death feeds on his mute voice, and laughs at our despair.

IV

Most musical of mourners, weep again!
Lament anew, Urania!—He died,
Who was the Sire of an immortal strain,   30
Blind, old, and lonely, when his country's pride,
The priest, the slave, and the liberticide,
Trampled and mocked with many a loathèd rite
Of lust and blood; he went, unterrified,
Into the gulf of death; but his clear Sprite
Yet reigns o'er earth; the third among the sons of light.

V

Most musical of mourners, weep anew!
Not all to that bright station dared to climb;
And happier they their happiness who knew,
Whose tapers yet burn through that night of time   40
In which suns perished; others more sublime,
Struck by the envious wrath of man or god,
Have sunk, extinct in their refulgent prime;
And some yet live, treading the thorny road,
Which leads, through toil and hate, to Fame's serene abode.

VI

But now, thy youngest, dearest one, has perished—
The nursling of thy widowhood, who grew,
Like a pale flower by some sad maiden cherished,
And fed with true-love tears, instead of dew;
Most musical of mourners, weep anew!   50
Thy extreme hope, the loveliest and the last,
The bloom, whose petals nipped before they blew
Died on the promise of the fruit, is waste;
The broken lily lies—the storm is overpast.

VII

To that high Capital, where kingly Death
Keeps his pale court in beauty and decay,
He came; and bought, with price of purest breath,
A grave among the eternal.—Come away!
Haste, while the vault of blue Italian day
Is yet his fitting charnel-roof! while still   60
He lies, as if in dewy sleep he lay;
Awake him not! surely he takes his fill
Of deep and liquid rest, forgetful of all ill.

VIII

He will awake no more, oh, never more!—
Within the twilight chamber spreads apace
The shadow of white Death, and at the door
Invisible Corruption waits to trace
His extreme way to her dim dwelling-place;
The eternal Hunger sits, but pity and awe
Soothe her pale rage, nor dares she to deface   70
So fair a prey, till darkness, and the law
Of change, shall o'er his sleep the mortal curtain draw.

IX

Oh, weep for Adonais!—The quick Dreams,
The passion-wingèd Ministers of thought,
Who were his flocks, whom near the living streams
Of his young spirit he fed, and whom he taught
The love which was its music, wander not,—
Wander no more, from kindling brain to brain,
But droop there, whence they sprung; and mourn their lot
Round the cold heart, where, after their sweet pain,   80
They ne'er will gather strength, or find a home again.

X

And one with trembling hands clasps his cold head,
And fans him with her moonlight wings, and cries;
' Our love, our hope, our sorrow, is not dead;
See, on the silken fringe of his faint eyes,
Like dew upon a sleeping flower, there lies
A tear some Dream has loosened from his brain.'
Lost Angel of a ruined Paradise!
She knew not 'twas her own; as with no stain
She faded, like a cloud which had outwept its rain.   90

XI

One from a lucid urn of starry dew
Washed his light limbs as if embalming them;
Another clipped her profuse locks, and threw
The wreath upon him, like an anadem,
Which frozen tears instead of pearls begem;
Another in her wilful grief would break
Her bow and wingèd reeds, as if to stem
A greater loss with one which was more weak;
And dull the barbèd fire against his frozen cheek.

XII

Another Splendour on his mouth alit,   100
That mouth, whence it was wont to draw the breath
Which gave it strength to pierce the guarded wit,
And pass into the panting heart beneath
With lightning and with music: the damp death
Quenched its caress upon his icy lips;
And, as a dying meteor stains a wreath
Of moonlight vapour, which the cold night clips,
It flushed through his pale limbs, and passed to its eclipse.

XIII

And others came . . . Desires and Adorations,
Wingèd Persuasions and veiled Destinies,   110
Splendours, and Glooms, and glimmering Incarnations
Of hopes and fears, and twilight Phantasies ;
And Sorrow, with her family of Sighs,
And Pleasure, blind with tears, led by the gleam
Of her own dying smile instead of eyes,
   Came in slow pomp ;—the moving pomp might seem
Like pageantry of mist on an autumnal stream.

XIV

All he had loved, and moulded into thought,
From shape, and hue, and odour, and sweet sound,
Lamented Adonais.   Morning sought   120
Her eastern watch-tower, and her hair unbound,
Wet with the tears which should adorn the ground,
Dimmed the aëreal eyes that kindle day ;
Afar the melancholy thunder moaned,
   Pale Ocean in unquiet slumber lay,
And the wild Winds flew round, sobbing in ·their dismay.

XV

Lost Echo sits amid the voiceless mountains,
And feeds her grief with his remembered lay,
And will no more reply to winds or fountains,
Or amorous birds perched on the young green spray,   130
Or herdsman's horn, or bell at closing day ;
Since she can mimic not his lips, more dear
Than those for whose disdain she pined away
   Into a shadow of all sounds :—a drear
Murmur, between their songs, is all the woodmen hear.

XVI

Grief made the young Spring wild, and she threw down
Her kindling buds, as if she Autumn were,
Or they dead leaves ; since her delight is flown,
For whom should she have waked the sullen year ?
To Phoebus was not Hyacinth so dear   140
Nor to himself Narcissus, as to both
Thou, Adonais : wan they stand and sere
   Amid the faint companions of their youth,
With dew all turned to tears ; odour, to sighing ruth.

XVII

Thy spirit's sister, the lorn nightingale
Mourns not her mate with such melodious pain ;
Not so the eagle, who like thee could scale
Heaven, and could nourish in the sun's domain
Her mighty youth with morning, doth complain,
Soaring and screaming round her empty nest,   150
As Albion wails for thee : the curse of Cain
   Light on his head who pierced thy innocent breast,
And scared the angel soul that was its earthly guest !

XVIII

Ah, woe is me ! Winter is come and gone,
But grief returns with the revolving year ;
The airs and streams renew their joyous tone ;
The ants, the bees, the swallows reappear ;
Fresh leaves and flowers deck the dead Seasons' bier ;
The amorous birds now pair in every brake,
And build their mossy homes in field and brere ;   160
And the green lizard, and the golden snake,
Like unimprisoned flames, out of their trance awake.

XIX

Through wood and stream and field and hill and Ocean
A quickening life from the Earth's heart has burst
As it has ever done, with change and motion,
From the great morning of the world when first
God dawned on Chaos ; in its stream immersed,
The lamps of Heaven flash with a softer light ;
All baser things pant with life's sacred thirst ;
Diffuse themselves ; and spend in love's delight,   170
The beauty and the joy of their renewèd might.

XX

The leprous corpse, touched by this spirit tender,
Exhales itself in flowers of gentle breath ;
Like incarnations of the stars, when splendour
Is changed to fragrance, they illumine death
And mock the merry worm that wakes beneath ;
Nought we know, dies. Shall that alone which knows
Be as a sword consumed before the sheath
By sightless lightning ?—the intense atom glows
A moment, then is quenched in a most cold repose.   180

XXI

Alas ! that all we loved of him should be,
But for our grief, as if it had not been,
And grief itself be mortal ! Woe is me !
Whence are we, and why are we ? of what scene
The actors or spectators ? Great and mean
Meet massed in death, who lends what life must borrow.
As long as skies are blue, and fields are green,
Evening must usher night, night urge the morrow,
Month follow month with woe, and year wake year to sorrow.

XXII

He will awake no more, oh, never more !   190
' Wake thou,' cried Misery, ' childless Mother, rise
Out of thy sleep, and slake, in thy heart's core,
A wound more fierce than his, with tears and sighs.'
And all the Dreams that watched Urania's eyes,
And all the Echoes whom their sister's song
Had held in holy silence, cried : ' Arise ! '
Swift as a Thought by the snake Memory stung,
From her ambrosial rest the fading Splendour sprung.

XXIII

She rose like an autumnal Night, that springs
Out of the East, and follows wild and drear 200
The golden Day, which, on eternal wings,
Even as a ghost abandoning a bier,
Had left the Earth a corpse. Sorrow and fear
So struck, so roused, so rapt Urania ;
So saddened round her like an atmosphere
Of stormy mist ; so swept her on her way
Even to the mournful place where Adonais lay.

XXIV

Out of her secret Paradise she sped,
Through camps and cities rough with stone, and steel,
And human hearts, which to her aëry tread 210
Yielding not, wounded the invisible
Palms of her tender feet where'er they fell :
And barbèd tongues, and thoughts more sharp than they,
Rent the soft Form they never could repel,
Whose sacred blood, like the young tears of May,
Paved with eternal flowers that undeserving way.

XXV

In the death-chamber for a moment Death,
Shamed by the presence of that living Might,
Blushed to annihilation, and the breath
Revisited those lips, and Life's pale light 220
Flashed through those limbs, so late her dear delight.
' Leave me not wild and drear and comfortless,
As silent lightning leaves the starless night !
Leave me not ! ' cried Urania : her distress
Roused Death : Death rose and smiled, and met her vain caress.

XXVI

' Stay yet awhile ! speak to me once again ;
Kiss me, so long but as a kiss may live ;
And in my heartless breast and burning brain
That word, that kiss, shall all thoughts else survive,
With food of saddest memory kept alive, 230
Now thou art dead, as if it were a part
Of thee, my Adonais ! I would give
All that I am to be as thou now art !
But I am chained to Time, and cannot thence depart !

XXVII

' O gentle child, beautiful as thou wert,
Why didst thou leave the trodden paths of men
Too soon, and with weak hands though mighty heart
Dare the unpastured dragon in his den ?
Defenceless as thou wert, oh, where was then
Wisdom the mirrored shield, or scorn the spear ? 240
Or hadst thou waited the full cycle, when
Thy spirit should have filled its crescent sphere,
The monsters of life's waste had fled from thee like deer.

XXVIII

'The herded wolves, bold only to pursue;
The obscene ravens, clamorous o'er the dead;
The vultures to the conqueror's banner true,
Who feed where Desolation first has fed,
And whose wings rain contagion;—how they fled,
When, like Apollo, from his golden bow
The Pythian of the age one arrow sped   250
And smiled!—The spoilers tempt no second blow,
They fawn on the proud feet that spurn them lying low.

XXIX

'The sun comes forth, and many reptiles spawn;
He sets, and each ephemeral insect then
Is gathered into death without a dawn,
And the immortal stars awake again;
So is it in the world of living men:
A godlike mind soars forth, in its delight
Making earth bare and veiling heaven, and when
It sinks, the swarms that dimmed or shared its light 260
Leave to its kindred lamps the spirit's awful night.'

XXX

Thus ceased she: and the mountain shepherds came,
Their garlands sere, their magic mantles rent;
The Pilgrim of Eternity, whose fame
Over his living head like Heaven is bent,
An early but enduring monument,
Came, veiling all the lightnings of his song
In sorrow; from her wilds Ierne sent
The sweetest lyrist of her saddest wrong,
And Love taught Grief to fall like music from his tongue. 270

XXXI

Midst others of less note, came one frail Form,
A phantom among men; companionless
As the last cloud of an expiring storm
Whose thunder is its knell; he, as I guess,
Had gazed on Nature's naked loveliness,
Actaeon-like, and now he fled astray
With feeble steps o'er the world's wilderness,
And his own thoughts, along that rugged way,
Pursued, like raging hounds, their father and their prey.

XXXII

A pardlike Spirit beautiful and swift—   280
A Love in desolation masked;—a Power
Girt round with weakness;—it can scarce uplift
The weight of the superincumbent hour;
It is a dying lamp, a falling shower,
A breaking billow;—even whilst we speak
Is it not broken? On the withering flower
The killing sun smiles brightly: on a cheek
The life can burn in blood, even while the heart may break.

XXXIII

His head was bound with pansies overblown,
And faded violets, white, and pied, and blue ;   290
And a light spear topped with a cypress cone,
Round whose rude shaft dark ivy-tresses grew
Yet dripping with the forest's noonday dew,
Vibrated, as the ever-beating heart
Shook the weak hand that grasped it ; of that crew
He came the last, neglected and apart ;
A herd-abandoned deer struck by the hunter's dart.

XXXIV

All stood aloof, and at his partial moan
Smiled through their tears ; well knew that gentle band
Who in another's fate now wept his own,   300
As in the accents of an unknown land
He sung new sorrow ; sad Urania scanned
The Stranger's mien, and murmured : ' Who art thou ? '
He answered not, but with a sudden hand
Made bare his branded and ensanguined brow,
Which was like Cain's or Christ's—oh ! that it should be so ;

XXXV

What softer voice is hushed over the dead ?
Athwart what brow is that dark mantle thrown ?
What form leans sadly o'er the white death-bed,
In mockery of monumental stone,   310
The heavy heart heaving without a moan ?
If it be He, who, gentlest of the wise,
Taught, soothed, loved, honoured the departed one,
Let me not vex, with inharmonious sighs,
The silence of that heart's accepted sacrifice.

XXXVI

Our Adonais has drunk poison—oh !
What deaf and viperous murderer could crown
Life's early cup with such a draught of woe ?
The nameless worm would now itself disown :
It felt, yet could escape, the magic tone   320
Whose prelude held all envy, hate, and wrong,
But what was howling in one breast alone,
Silent with expectation of the song,
Whose master's hand is cold, whose silver lyre unstrung.

XXXVII

Live thou, whose infamy is not thy fame !
Live ! fear no heavier chastisement from me,
Thou noteless blot on a remembered name !
But be thyself, and know thyself to be !
And ever at thy season be thou free
To spill the venom when thy fangs o'erflow :   330
Remorse and Self-contempt shall cling to thee ;
Hot Shame shall burn upon thy secret brow,
And like a beaten hound tremble thou shalt—as now.

PARNASSUS   R

XXXVIII

Nor let us weep that our delight is fled
Far from these carrion kites that scream below;
He wakes or sleeps with the enduring dead;
Thou canst not soar where he is sitting now—
Dust to the dust! but the pure spirit shall flow
Back to the burning fountain whence it came,
A portion of the Eternal, which must glow   340
Through time and change, unquenchably the same,
Whilst thy cold embers choke the sordid hearth of shame.

XXXIX

Peace, peace! he is not dead, he doth not sleep—
He hath awakened from the dream of life—
'Tis we, who, lost in stormy visions, keep
With phantoms an unprofitable strife,
And in mad trance strike with our spirit's knife
Invulnerable nothings.—*We* decay
Like corpses in a charnel; fear and grief
Convulse us and consume us day by day,   350
And cold hopes swarm like worms within our living clay.

XL

He has outsoared the shadow of our night;
Envy and calumny and hate and pain,
And that unrest which men miscall delight,
Can touch him not and torture not again;
From the contagion of the world's slow stain
He is secure, and now can never mourn
A heart grown cold, a head grown gray in vain;
Nor, when the spirit's self has ceased to burn,
With sparkless ashes load an unlamented urn.   360

XLI

He lives, he wakes—'tis Death is dead, not he;
Mourn not for Adonais.—Thou young Dawn,
Turn all thy dew to splendour, for from thee
The spirit thou lamentest is not gone;
Ye caverns and ye forests, cease to moan!
Cease, ye faint flowers and fountains, and thou Air,
Which like a mourning veil thy scarf hadst thrown
O'er the abandoned Earth, now leave it bare
Even to the joyous stars which smile on its despair!

XLII

He is made one with Nature: there is heard   370
His voice in all her music, from the moan
Of thunder, to the song of night's sweet bird;
He is a presence to be felt and known
In darkness and in light, from herb and stone,
Spreading itself where'er that Power may move
Which has withdrawn his being to its own;
Which wields the world with never-wearied love,
Sustains it from beneath, and kindles it above.

XLIII

He is a portion of the loveliness
Which once he made more lovely : he doth bear   380
His part, while the one Spirit's plastic stress
Sweeps through the dull dense world, compelling there
All new successions to the forms they wear ;
Torturing th' unwilling dross that checks its flight
To its own likeness, as each mass may bear ;
And bursting in its beauty and its might
From trees and beasts and men into the Heavens' light.

XLIV

The splendours of the firmament of time
May be eclipsed, but are extinguished not ;
Like stars to their appointed height they climb,   390
And death is a low mist which cannot blot
The brightness it may veil. When lofty thought
Lifts a young heart above its mortal lair,
And love and life contend in it, for what
Shall be its earthly doom, the dead live there
And move like winds of light on dark and stormy air.

XLV

The inheritors of unfulfilled renown
Rose from their thrones, built beyond mortal thought,
Far in the Unapparent. Chatterton
Rose pale,—his solemn agony had not   400
Yet faded from him ; Sidney, as he fought
And as he fell and as he lived and loved
Sublimely mild, a Spirit without spot,
Arose ; and Lucan, by his death approved :
Oblivion as they rose shrank like a thing reproved.

XLVI

And many more, whose names on Earth are dark,
But whose transmitted effluence cannot die
So long as fire outlives the parent spark,
Rose, robed in dazzling immortality.
' Thou art become as one of us,' they cry,   410
' It was for thee yon kingless sphere has long
Swung blind in unascended majesty,
Silent alone amid an Heaven of Song.
Assume thy wingèd throne, thou Vesper of our throng ! '

XLVII

Who mourns for Adonais ? Oh, come forth,
Fond wretch ! and know thyself and him aright.
Clasp with thy panting soul the pendulous Earth ;
As from a centre, dart thy spirit's light
Beyond all worlds, until its spacious might
Satiate the void circumference : then shrink   420
Even to a point within our day and night ;
And keep thy heart light lest it make thee sink
When hope has kindled hope, and lured thee to the brink.

XLVIII

Or go to Rome, which is the sepulchre,
Oh, not of him, but of our joy : 'tis nought
That ages, empires, and religions there
Lie buried in the ravage they have wrought ;
For such as he can lend,—they borrow not
Glory from those who made the world their prey ;
And he is gathered to the kings of thought   430
Who waged contention with their time's decay,
And of the past are all that cannot pass away.

XLIX

Go thou to Rome,—at once the Paradise,
The grave, the city, and the wilderness ;
And where its wrecks like shattered mountains rise,
And flowering weeds, and fragrant copses dress
The bones of Desolation's nakedness
Pass, till the spirit of the spot shall lead
Thy footsteps to a slope of green access
Where, like an infant's smile, over the dead   440
A light of laughing flowers along the grass is spread ;

L

And gray walls moulder round, on which dull Time
Feeds, like slow fire upon a hoary brand ;
And one keen pyramid with wedge sublime,
Pavilioning the dust of him who planned
This refuge for his memory, doth stand
Like flame transformed to marble ; and beneath,
A field is spread, on which a newer band
Have pitched in Heaven's smile their camp of death,
Welcoming him we lose with scarce extinguished breath. 450

LI

Here pause : these graves are all too young as yet
To have outgrown the sorrow which consigned
Its charge to each ; and if the seal is set,
Here, on one fountain of a mourning mind,
Break it not thou ! too surely shalt thou find
Thine own well full, if thou returnest home,
Of tears and gall.   From the world's bitter wind
Seek shelter in the shadow of the tomb.
What Adonais is, why fear we to become ?

LII

The One remains, the many change and pass ;   460
Heaven's light forever shines, Earth's shadows fly ;
Life, like a dome of many-coloured glass,
Stains the white radiance of Eternity,
Until Death tramples it to fragments.—Die,
If thou wouldst be with that which thou dost seek !
Follow where all is fled !—Rome's azure sky,
Flowers, ruins, statues, music, words, are weak
The glory they transfuse with fitting truth to speak.

LIII

Why linger, why turn back, why shrink, my Heart?
Thy hopes are gone before: from all things here   470
They have departed; thou shouldst now depart!
A light is passed from the revolving year,
And man, and woman; and what still is dear
Attracts to crush, repels to make thee wither.
The soft sky smiles,—the low wind whispers near:
'Tis Adonais calls! oh, hasten thither,
No more let Life divide what Death can join together.

LIV

That Light whose smile kindles the Universe,
That Beauty in which all things work and move,
That Benediction which the eclipsing Curse   480
Of birth can quench not, that sustaining Love
Which through the web of being blindly wove
By man and beast and earth and air and sea,
Burns bright or dim, as each are mirrors of
The fire for which all thirst; now beams on me,
Consuming the last clouds of cold mortality.

LV

The breath whose might I have invoked in song
Descends on me; my spirit's bark is driven,
Far from the shore, far from the trembling throng
Whose sails were never to the tempest given;   490
The massy earth and spherèd skies are riven!
I am borne darkly, fearfully, afar;
Whilst, burning through the inmost veil of Heaven,
The soul of Adonais, like a star,
Beacons from the abode where the Eternal are.

JOHN KEATS

ISABELLA;

OR, THE POT OF BASIL

A Story from Boccaccio

I

Fair Isabel, poor simple Isabel!
  Lorenzo, a young palmer in Love's eye!
They could not in the self-same mansion dwell
  Without some stir of heart, some malady;
They could not sit at meals but feel how well
  It soothed each to be the other by;
They could not, sure, beneath the same roof sleep
But to each other dream, and nightly weep.

II

With every morn their love grew tenderer,
  With every eve deeper and tenderer still;   10
He might not in house, field, or garden stir,
  But her full shape would all his seeing fill;
And his continual voice was pleasanter
  To her, than noise of trees or hidden rill;
Her lute-string gave an echo of his name,
She spoilt her half-done broidery with the same.

III

He knew whose gentle hand was at the latch,
  Before the door had given her to his eyes;
And from her chamber-window he would catch
  Her beauty farther than the falcon spies;   20
And constant as her vespers would he watch,
  Because her face was turn'd to the same skies;
And with sick longing all the night outwear,
To hear her morning-step upon the stair.

IV

A whole long month of May in this sad plight
  Made their cheeks paler by the break of June:
'To-morrow will I bow to my delight,
  To-morrow will I ask my lady's boon.'—
'O may I never see another night,
  Lorenzo, if thy lips breathe not love's tune.'—   30
So spake they to their pillows; but, alas,
Honeyless days and days did he let pass;

V

Until sweet Isabella's untouch'd cheek
    Fell sick within the rose's just domain,
Fell thin as a young mother's, who doth seek
    By every lull to cool her infant's pain:
' How ill she is,' said he, ' I may not speak,
    And yet I will, and tell my love all plain:
If looks speak love-laws, I will drink her tears,
And at the least 'twill startle off her cares.'   40

VI

So said he one fair morning, and all day
    His heart beat awfully against his side;
And to his heart he inwardly did pray
    For power to speak; but still the ruddy tide
Stifled his voice, and puls'd resolve away—
    Fever'd his high conceit of such a bride,
Yet brought him to the meekness of a child:
Alas! when passion is both meek and wild!

VII

So once more he had wak'd and anguished
    A dreary night of love and misery,   50
If Isabel's quick eye had not been wed
    To every symbol on his forehead high;
She saw it waxing very pale and dead,
    And straight all flush'd; so, lisped tenderly,
' Lorenzo!'—here she ceas'd her timid quest,
But in her tone and look he read the rest.

VIII

' O Isabella, I can half perceive
    That I may speak my grief into thine ear;
If thou didst ever anything believe,
    Believe how I love thee, believe how near   60
My soul is to its doom: I would not grieve
    Thy hand by unwelcome pressing, would not fear
Thine eyes by gazing; but I cannot live
Another night, and not my passion shrive.

IX

' Love! thou art leading me from wintry cold,
    Lady! thou leadest me to summer clime,
And I must taste the blossoms that unfold
    In its ripe warmth this gracious morning time.
So said, his erewhile timid lips grew bold,
    And poesied with hers in dewy rhyme: 70
Great bliss was with them, and great happiness
Grew, like a lusty flower in June's caress.

X

Parting they seem'd to tread upon the air,
   Twin roses by the zephyr blown apart
Only to meet again more close, and share
   The inward fragrance of each other's heart.
She, to her chamber gone, a ditty fair
   Sang, of delicious love and honey'd dart;
He with light steps went up a western hill,
And bade the sun farewell, and joy'd his fill.   80

XI

All close they met again, before the dusk
   Had taken from the stars its pleasant veil,
All close they met, all eves, before the dusk
   Had taken from the stars its pleasant veil,
Close in a bower of hyacinth and musk,
   Unknown of any, free from whispering tale.
Ah! better had it been for ever so,
Than idle ears should pleasure in their woe.

XII

Were they unhappy then?—It cannot be—
   Too many tears for lovers have been shed,   90
Too many sighs give we to them in fee,
   Too much of pity after they are dead,
Too many doleful stories do we see,
   Whose matter in bright gold were best be read;
Except in such a page where Theseus' spouse
Over the pathless waves towards him bows.

XIII

But, for the general award of love,
   The little sweet doth kill much bitterness;
Though Dido silent is in under-grove,
   And Isabella's was a great distress,   100
Though young Lorenzo in warm Indian clove
   Was not embalm'd, this truth is not the less—
Even bees, the little almsmen of spring-bowers,
Know there is richest juice in poison-flowers.

XIV

With her two brothers this fair lady dwelt,
   Enriched from ancestral merchandize,
And for them many a weary hand did swelt
   In torched mines and noisy factories,
And many once proud-quiver'd loins did melt
   In blood from stinging whip;—with hollow eyes   110
Many all day in dazzling river stood,
To take the rich-ored driftings of the flood.

XV

For them the Ceylon diver held his breath,
   And went all naked to the hungry shark;
For them his ears gush'd blood; for them in death
   The seal on the cold ice with piteous bark
Lay full of darts; for them alone did seethe
   A thousand men in troubles wide and dark:
Half-ignorant, they turn'd an easy wheel,
That set sharp racks at work, to pinch and peel.   120

XVI

Why were they proud?   Because their marble founts
   Gush'd with more pride than do a wretch's tears?—
Why were they proud?   Because fair orange-mounts
   Were of more soft ascent than lazar stairs?—
Why were they proud?   Because red-lin'd accounts
   Were richer than the songs of Grecian years?—
Why were they proud? again we ask aloud,
Why in the name of Glory were they proud?

XVII

Yet were these Florentines as self-retired
   In hungry pride and gainful cowardice,   130
As two close Hebrews in that land inspired,
   Paled in and vineyarded from beggar-spies;
The hawks of ship-mast forests—the untired
   And pannier'd mules for ducats and old lies—
Quick cat's-paws on the generous stray-away,—
Great wits in Spanish, Tuscan, and Malay.

XVIII

How was it these same ledger-men could spy
   Fair Isabella in her downy nest?
How could they find out in Lorenzo's eye
   A straying from his toil?   Hot Egypt's pest   140
Into their vision covetous and sly!
   How could these money-bags see east and west?—
Yet so they did—and every dealer fair
Must see behind, as doth the hunted hare.

XIX

O eloquent and famed Boccaccio!
   Of thee we now should ask forgiving boon,
And of thy spicy myrtles as they blow,
   And of thy roses amorous of the moon,
And of thy lilies, that do paler grow
   Now they can no more hear thy ghitter's tune,   150
For venturing syllables that ill beseem
The quiet glooms of such a piteous theme.

XX

Grant thou a pardon here, and then the tale
   Shall move on soberly, as it is meet;
There is no other crime, no mad assail
   To make old prose in modern rhyme more sweet:
But it is done—succeed the verse or fail—
   To honour thee, and thy gone spirit greet;
To stead thee as a verse in English tongue,
An echo of thee in the north-wind sung.   160

XXI

These brethren having found by many signs
   What love Lorenzo for their sister had,
And how she lov'd him too, each unconfines
   His bitter thoughts to other, well nigh mad
That he, the servant of their trade designs,
   Should in their sister's love be blithe and glad,
When 'twas their plan to coax her by degrees
To some high noble and his olive-trees.

XXII

And many a jealous conference had they,
   And many times they bit their lips alone,   170
Before they fix'd upon a surest way
   To make the youngster for his crime atone;
And at the last, these men of cruel clay
   Cut Mercy with a sharp knife to the bone;
For they resolved in some forest dim
To kill Lorenzo, and there bury him.

XXIII

So on a pleasant morning, as he leant
   Into the sun-rise, o'er the balustrade
Of the garden-terrace, towards him they bent
   Their footing through the dews; and to him said, 180
'You seem there in the quiet of content,
   Lorenzo, and we are most loth to invade
Calm speculation; but if you are wise,
Bestride your steed while cold is in the skies.

XXIV

'To-day we purpose, aye, this hour we mount
   To spur three leagues towards the Apennine;
Come down, we pray thee, ere the hot sun count
   His dewy rosary on the eglantine.'
Lorenzo, courteously as he was wont,
   Bow'd a fair greeting to these serpents' whine;   190
And went in haste, to get in readiness,
With belt, and spur, and bracing huntsman's dress.

XXV

And as he to the court-yard pass'd along,
  Each third step did he pause, and listen'd oft
If he could hear his lady's matin-song,
  Or the light whisper of her footstep soft ;
And as he thus over his passion hung,
  He heard a laugh full musical aloft ;
When, looking up, he saw her features bright
Smile through an in-door lattice, all delight.   200

XXVI

'Love, Isabel !' said he, 'I was in pain
  Lest I should miss to bid thee a good morrow :
Ah ! what if I should lose thee, when so fain
  I am to stifle all the heavy sorrow
Of a poor three hours' absence ? but we'll gain
  Out of the amorous dark what day doth borrow.
Good bye ! I'll soon be back.'—'Good bye !' said she :—
And as he went she chanted merrily.

XXVII

So the two brothers and their murder'd man
  Rode past fair Florence, to where Arno's stream   210
Gurgles through straiten'd banks, and still doth fan
  Itself with dancing bulrush, and the bream
Keeps head against the freshets. Sick and wan
  The brothers' faces in the ford did seem,
Lorenzo's flush with love.—They pass'd the water
Into a forest quiet for the slaughter.

XXVIII

There was Lorenzo slain and buried in,
  There in that forest did his great love cease ;
Ah ! when a soul doth thus its freedom win,
  It aches in loneliness—is ill at peace   220
As the break-covert blood-hounds of such sin :
  They dipp'd their swords in the water, and did tease
Their horses homeward, with convulsed spur,
Each richer by his being a murderer.

XXIX

They told their sister how, with sudden speed,
  Lorenzo had ta'en ship for foreign lands,
Because of some great urgency and need
  In their affairs, requiring trusty hands.
Poor Girl ! put on thy stifling widow's weed,
  And 'scape at once from Hope's accursed bands ;   230
To-day thou wilt not see him, nor to-morrow,
And the next day will be a day of sorrow.

XXX

She weeps alone for pleasures not to be ;
　Sorely she wept until the night came on,
And then, instead of love, O misery !
　She brooded o'er the luxury alone :
His image in the dusk she seem'd to see,
　And to the silence made a gentle moan,
Spreading her perfect arms upon the air,
And on her couch low murmuring ' Where ? O where ? ' 240

XXXI

But Selfishness, Love's cousin, held not long
　Its fiery vigil in her single breast ;
She fretted for the golden hour, and hung
　Upon the time with feverish unrest—
Not long—for soon into her heart a throng
　Of higher occupants, a richer zest,
Came tragic ; passion not to be subdued,
And sorrow for her love in travels rude.

XXXII

In the mid days of autumn, on their eves,
　The breath of Winter comes from far away,　　　　250
And the sick west continually bereaves
　Of some gold tinge, and plays a roundelay
Of death among the bushes and the leaves,
　To make all bare before he dares to stray
From his north cavern. So sweet Isabel
By gradual decay from beauty fell,

XXXIII

Because Lorenzo came not. Oftentimes
　She ask'd her brothers, with an eye all pale,
Striving to be itself, what dungeon climes
　Could keep him off so long ? They spake a tale　　260
Time after time, to quiet her. Their crimes
　Came on them, like a smoke from Hinnom's vale ;
And every night in dreams they groan'd aloud,
To see their sister in her snowy shroud.

XXXIV

And she had died in drowsy ignorance,
　But for a thing more deadly dark than all ;
It came like a fierce potion, drunk by chance,
　Which saves a sick man from the feather'd pall
For some few gasping moments ; like a lance,
　Waking an Indian from his cloudy hall　　　　270
With cruel pierce, and bringing him again
Sense of the gnawing fire at heart and brain.

XXXV

It was a vision.—In the drowsy gloom,
  The dull of midnight, at her couch's foot
Lorenzo stood, and wept : the forest tomb
  Had marr'd his glossy hair which once could shoot
Lustre into the sun, and put cold doom
  Upon his lips, and taken the soft lute
From his lorn voice, and past his loamed ears
Had made a miry channel for his tears.   280

XXXVI

Strange sound it was, when the pale shadow spake ;
  For there was striving, in its piteous tongue,
To speak as when on earth it was awake,
  And Isabella on its music hung :
Languor there was in it, and tremulous shake,
  As in a palsied Druid's harp unstrung ;
And through it moan'd a ghostly under-song,
Like hoarse night-gusts sepulchral briars among.

XXXVII

Its eyes, though wild, were still all dewy bright
  With love, and kept all phantom fear aloof   290
From the poor girl by magic of their light,
  The while it did unthread the horrid woof
Of the late darken'd time,—the murderous spite
  Of pride and avarice,—the dark pine roof
In the forest,—and the sodden turfed dell,
Where, without any word, from stabs he fell.

XXXVIII

Saying moreover, 'Isabel, my sweet !
  Red whortle-berries droop above my head,
And a large flint-stone weighs upon my feet ;
  Around me beeches and high chestnuts shed   300
Their leaves and prickly nuts ; a sheep-fold bleat
  Comes from beyond the river to my bed :
Go, shed one tear upon my heather-bloom,
And it shall comfort me within the tomb.

XXXIX

' I am a shadow now, alas ! alas !
  Upon the skirts of human-nature dwelling
Alone : I chant alone the holy mass,
  While little sounds of life are round me knelling,
And glossy bees at noon do fieldward pass,
  And many a chapel bell the hour is telling,   310
Paining me through : those sounds grow strange to me,
And thou art distant in Humanity.

XL

'I know what was, I feel full well what is,
    And I should rage, if spirits could go mad;
Though I forget the taste of earthly bliss,
    That paleness warms my grave, as though I had
A Seraph chosen from the bright abyss
    To be my spouse: thy paleness makes me glad;
Thy beauty grows upon me, and I feel
A greater love through all my essence steal.'   320

XLI

The Spirit mourn'd 'Adieu!'—dissolv'd and left
    The atom darkness in a slow turmoil;
As when of healthful midnight sleep bereft,
    Thinking on rugged hours and fruitless toil,
We put our eyes into a pillowy cleft,
    And see the spangly gloom froth up and boil:
It made sad Isabella's eyelids ache,
And in the dawn she started up awake;

XLII

'Ha! ha!' said she, 'I knew not this hard life,
    I thought the worst was simple misery;   330
I thought some Fate with pleasure or with strife
    Portion'd us—happy days, or else to die;
But there is crime—a brother's bloody knife!
    Sweet Spirit, thou hast school'd my infancy:
I'll visit thee for this, and kiss thine eyes,
And greet thee morn and even in the skies.'

XLIII

When the full morning came, she had devised
    How she might secret to the forest hie;
How she might find the clay, so dearly prized,
    And sing to it one latest lullaby;   340
How her short absence might be unsurmised,
    While she the inmost of the dream would try.
Resolv'd, she took with her an aged nurse,
And went into that dismal forest-hearse.

XLIV

See, as they creep along the river side,
    How she doth whisper to that aged Dame,
And, after looking round the champaign wide,
    Shows her a knife.—'What feverous hectic flame
Burns in thee, child?—What good can thee betide,
    That thou should'st smile again?'—The evening came,
And they had found Lorenzo's earthy bed;   351
The flint was there, the berries at his head.

XLV

Who hath not loiter'd in a green church-yard,
    And let his spirit, like a demon-mole,
Work through the clayey soil and gravel hard,
    To see skull, coffin'd bones, and funeral stole;
Pitying each form that hungry Death hath marr'd,
    And filling it once more with human soul?
Ah! this is holiday to what was felt
When Isabella by Lorenzo knelt.   360

XLVI

She gaz'd into the fresh-thrown mould, as though
    One glance did fully all its secrets tell;
Clearly she saw, as other eyes would know
    Pale limbs at bottom of a crystal well;
Upon the murderous spot she seem'd to grow,
    Like to a native lily of the dell:
Then with her knife, all sudden, she began
To dig more fervently than misers can.

XLVII

Soon she turn'd up a soiled glove, whereon
    Her silk had play'd in purple phantasies,   370
She kiss'd it with a lip more chill than stone,
    And put it in her bosom, where it dries
And freezes utterly unto the bone
    Those dainties made to still an infant's cries:
Then 'gan she work again; nor stay'd her care,
But to throw back at times her veiling hair.

XLVIII

That old nurse stood beside her wondering,
    Until her heart felt pity to the core
At sight of such a dismal labouring,
    And so she kneeled, with her locks all hoar,   380
And put her lean hands to the horrid thing:
    Three hours they labour'd at this travail sore;
At last they felt the kernel of the grave,
And Isabella did not stamp and rave.

XLIX

Ah! wherefore all this wormy circumstance?
    Why linger at the yawning tomb so long?
O for the gentleness of old Romance,
    The simple plaining of a minstrel's song!
Fair reader, at the old tale take a glance,
    For here, in truth, it doth not well belong   390
To speak:—O turn thee to the very tale,
And taste the music of that vision pale.

L

With duller steel than the Perséan sword
   They cut away no formless monster's head,
But one, whose gentleness did well accord
   With death, as life. The ancient harps have said,
Love never dies, but lives, immortal Lord:
   If Love impersonate was ever dead,
Pale Isabella kiss'd it, and low moan'd.
'Twas love; cold,—dead indeed, but not dethroned. 400

LI

In anxious secrecy they took it home,
   And then the prize was all for Isabel:
She calm'd its wild hair with a golden comb,
   And all around each eye's sepulchral cell
Pointed each fringed lash; the smeared loam
   With tears, as chilly as a dripping well,
She drench'd away:—and still she comb'd, and kept
Sighing all day—and still she kiss'd, and wept.

LII

Then in a silken scarf,—sweet with the dews
   Of precious flowers pluck'd in Araby,   410
And divine liquids come with odorous ooze
   Through the cold serpent-pipe refreshfully,—
She wrapp'd it up; and for its tomb did choose
   A garden-pot, wherein she laid it by,
And cover'd it with mould, and o'er it set
Sweet Basil, which her tears kept ever wet.

LIII

And she forgot the stars, the moon, and sun,
   And she forgot the blue above the trees,
And she forgot the dells where waters run,
   And she forgot the chilly autumn breeze;   420
She had no knowledge when the day was done,
   And the new morn she saw not: but in peace
Hung over her sweet Basil evermore,
And moisten'd it with tears unto the core.

LIV

And so she ever fed it with thin tears,
   Whence thick, and green, and beautiful it grew,
So that it smelt more balmy than its peers
   Of Basil-tufts in Florence; for it drew
Nurture besides, and life, from human fears,
   From the fast mouldering head there shut from view:
So that the jewel, safely casketed,   431
Came forth and in perfumed leafits spread.

LV

O Melancholy, linger here awhile !
  O Music, Music, breathe despondingly !
O Echo, Echo, from some sombre isle,
  Unknown, Lethean, sigh to us—O sigh !
Spirits in grief, lift up your heads, and smile ;
  Lift up your heads, sweet Spirits, heavily,
And make a pale light in your cypress glooms,
Tinting with silver wan your marble tombs.   440

LVI

Moan hither, all ye syllables of woe,
  From the deep throat of sad Melpomene !
Through bronzed lyre in tragic order go,
  And touch the strings into a mystery ;
Sound mournfully upon the winds and low ;
  For simple Isabel is soon to be
Among the dead : She withers, like a palm
Cut by an Indian for its juicy balm.

LVII

O leave the palm to wither by itself ;
  Let not quick Winter chill its dying hour !—   450
It may not be—those Baälites of pelf,
  Her brethren, noted the continual shower
From her dead eyes ; and many a curious elf,
  Among her kindred, wonder'd that such dower
Of youth and beauty should be thrown aside
By one mark'd out to be a noble's bride.

LVIII

And, furthermore, her brethren wonder'd much
  Why she sat drooping by the Basil green,
And why it flourish'd, as by magic touch ;
  Greatly they wonder'd what the thing might mean : 460
They could not surely give belief, that such
  A very nothing would have power to wean
Her from her own fair youth, and pleasures gay,
And even remembrance of her love's delay.

LIX

Therefore they watch'd a time when they might sift
  This hidden whim ; and long they watch'd in vain ;
For seldom did she go to chapel-shrift,
  And seldom felt she any hunger-pain ;
And when she left, she hurried back, as swift
  As bird on wing to breast its eggs again ;   470
And, patient as a hen-bird, sat her there
Beside her Basil, weeping through her hair.

LX

Yet they contriv'd to steal the Basil-pot,
    And to examine it in secret place;
The thing was vile with green and livid spot,
    And yet they knew it was Lorenzo's face:
The guerdon of their murder they had got,
    And so left Florence in a moment's space,
Never to turn again.—Away they went,
With blood upon their heads, to banishment.   480

LXI

O Melancholy, turn thine eyes away!
    O Music, Music, breathe despondingly!
O Echo, Echo, on some other day,
    From isles Lethean, sigh to us—O sigh!
Spirits of grief, sing not your 'Well-a-way!'
    For Isabel, sweet Isabel, will die;
Will die a death too lone and incomplete,
Now they have ta'en away her Basil sweet.

LXII

Piteous she look'd on dead and senseless things,
    Asking for her lost Basil amorously;   490
And with melodious chuckle in the strings
    Of her lorn voice, she oftentimes would cry
After the Pilgrim in his wanderings,
    To ask him where her Basil was; and why
'Twas hid from her: 'For cruel 'tis,' said she,
'To steal my Basil-pot away from me.'

LXIII

And so she pined, and so she died forlorn,
    Imploring for her Basil to the last.
No heart was there in Florence but did mourn
    In pity of her love, so overcast.   500
And a sad ditty of this story born
    From mouth to mouth through all the country pass'd:
Still is the burthen sung—'O cruelty,
To steal my Basil-pot away from me!'

THE EVE OF ST. AGNES

I

St. Agnes' Eve—Ah, bitter chill it was!
The owl, for all his feathers, was a-cold;
The hare limp'd trembling through the frozen grass,
And silent was the flock in woolly fold:
Numb were the Beadsman's fingers, while he told
His rosary, and while his frosted breath,
Like pious incense from a censer old,
Seem'd taking flight for heaven, without a death,
Past the sweet Virgin's picture, while his prayer he saith.

II

His prayer he saith, this patient, holy man;   10
Then takes his lamp, and riseth from his knees,
And back returneth, meagre, barefoot, wan,
Along the chapel aisle by slow degrees:
The sculptur'd dead, on each side, seem to freeze,
Emprison'd in black, purgatorial rails:
Knights, ladies, praying in dumb orat'ries,
He passeth by; and his weak spirit fails
To think how they may ache in icy hoods and mails.

III

Northward he turneth through a little door,
And scarce three steps, ere Music's golden tongue   20
Flatter'd to tears this aged man and poor;
But no—already had his deathbell rung:
The joys of all his life were said and sung:
His was harsh penance on St. Agnes' Eve:
Another way he went, and soon among
Rough ashes sat he for his soul's reprieve,
And all night kept awake, for sinners' sake to grieve.

IV

That ancient Beadsman heard the prelude soft;
And so it chanc'd, for many a door was wide,
From hurry to and fro. Soon, up aloft,   30
The silver, snarling trumpets 'gan to chide:
The level chambers, ready with their pride,
Were glowing to receive a thousand guests:
The carved angels, ever eager-eyed,
Star'd, where upon their heads the cornice rests,
With hair blown back, and wings put cross-wise on their
    breasts.

V

At length burst in the argent revelry,
With plume, tiara, and all rich array,
Numerous as shadows haunting faerily
The brain, new stuff'd, in youth, with triumphs gay   40
Of old romance.   These let us wish away,
And turn, sole-thoughted, to one Lady there,
Whose heart had brooded, all that wintry day,
On love, and wing'd St. Agnes' saintly care,
As she had heard old dames full many times declare.

VI

They told her how, upon St. Agnes' Eve,
Young virgins might have visions of delight,
And soft adorings from their loves receive
Upon the honey'd middle of the night,
If ceremonies due they did aright;   50
As, supperless to bed they must retire,
And couch supine their beauties, lily white;
Nor look behind, nor sideways, but require
Of Heaven with upward eyes for all that they desire.

VII

Full of this whim was thoughtful Madeline:
The music, yearning like a God in pain,
She scarcely heard: her maiden eyes divine,
Fix'd on the floor, saw many a sweeping train
Pass by—she heeded not at all: in vain
Came many a tiptoe, amorous cavalier,   60
And back retir'd; not cool'd by high disdain,
But she saw not: her heart was otherwhere:
She sigh'd for Agnes' dreams, the sweetest of the year.

VIII

She danc'd along with vague, regardless eyes,
Anxious her lips, her breathing quick and short:
The hallow'd hour was near at hand: she sighs
Amid the timbrels, and the throng'd resort
Of whisperers in anger, or in sport;
'Mid looks of love, defiance, hate, and scorn,
Hoodwink'd with faery fancy; all amort,   70
Save to St. Agnes and her lambs unshorn,
And all the bliss to be before to-morrow morn.

IX

So, purposing each moment to retire,
She linger'd still. Meantime, across the moors,
Had come young Porphyro, with heart on fire
For Madeline. Beside the portal doors,
Buttress'd from moonlight, stands he, and implores
All saints to give him sight of Madeline,
But for one moment in the tedious hours,
That he might gaze and worship all unseen;   80
Perchance speak, kneel, touch, kiss—in sooth such things have been.

X

He ventures in : let no buzz'd whisper tell :
All eyes be muffled, or a hundred swords
Will storm his heart, Love's fev'rous citadel :
For him, those chambers held barbarian hordes,
Hyena foemen, and hot-blooded lords,
Whose very dogs would execrations howl
Against his lineage : not one breast affords
Him any mercy, in that mansion foul,
Save one old beldame, weak in body and in soul.   90

XI

Ah, happy chance ! the aged creature came,
Shuffling along with ivory-headed wand,
To where he stood, hid from the torch's flame,
Behind a broad hall-pillar, far beyond
The sound of merriment and chorus bland :
He startled her ; but soon she knew his face,
And grasp'd his fingers in her palsied hand,
Saying, ' Mercy, Porphyro ! hie thee from this place :
They are all here to-night, the whole blood-thirsty race !

XII

' Get hence ! get hence ! there 's dwarfish Hildebrand ; 100
He had a fever late, and in the fit
He cursed thee and thine, both house and land :
Then there 's that old Lord Maurice, not a whit
More tame for his gray hairs—Alas me ! flit !
Flit like a ghost away.'—' Ah, Gossip dear,
We're safe enough ; here in this arm-chair sit,
And tell me how '—' Good Saints ! not here, not here ;
Follow me, child, or else these stones will be thy bier.'

XIII

He follow'd through a lowly arched way,
Brushing the cobwebs with his lofty plume,   110
And as she mutter'd ' Well-a—well-a-day ! '
He found him in a little moonlight room,
Pale, lattic'd, chill, and silent as a tomb.
' Now tell me where is Madeline,' said he,
' O tell me, Angela, by the holy loom
Which none but secret sisterhood may see,
When they St. Agnes' wool are weaving piously.'

XIV

' St. Agnes ! Ah ! it is St. Agnes' Eve—
Yet men will murder upon holy days :
Thou must hold water in a witch's sieve,   120
And be liege-lord of all the Elves and Fays,
To venture so : it fills me with amaze
To see thee, Porphyro !—St. Agnes' Eve !
God's help ! my lady fair the conjuror plays
This very night : good angels her deceive !
But let me laugh awhile, I've mickle time to grieve.'

XV

Feebly she laugheth in the languid moon,
While Porphyro upon her face doth look,
Like puzzled urchin on an aged crone
Who keepeth clos'd a wond'rous riddle-book,   130
As spectacled she sits in chimney nook.
But soon his eyes grew brilliant, when she told
His lady's purpose; and he scarce could brook
Tears, at the thought of those enchantments cold,
And Madeline asleep in lap of legends old.

XVI

Sudden a thought came like a full-blown rose,
Flushing his brow, and in his pained heart
Made purple riot: then doth he propose
A stratagem, that makes the beldame start: 140
'A cruel man and impious thou art:
Sweet lady, let her pray, and sleep, and dream
Alone with her good angels, far apart
From wicked men like thee. Go, go!—I deem
Thou canst not surely be the same that thou didst seem.'

XVII

'I will not harm her, by all saints I swear,'
Quoth Porphyro: 'O may I ne'er find grace
When my weak voice shall whisper its last prayer,
If one of her soft ringlets I displace,
Or look with ruffian passion in her face:
Good Angela, believe me by these tears;   150
Or I will, even in a moment's space,
Awake, with horrid shout, my foemen's ears,
And beard them, though they be more fang'd than wolves and bears.'

XVIII

'Ah! why wilt thou affright a feeble soul?
A poor, weak, palsy-stricken, churchyard thing,
Whose passing-bell may ere the midnight toll;
Whose prayers for thee, each morn and evening,
Were never miss'd.'—Thus plaining, doth she bring
A gentler speech from burning Porphyro;
So woful, and of such deep sorrowing,   160
That Angela gives promise she will do
Whatever he shall wish, betide her weal or woe.

XIX

Which was, to lead him, in close secrecy,
Even to Madeline's chamber, and there hide
Him in a closet, of such privacy
That he might see her beauty unespied,
And win perhaps that night a peerless bride,
While legion'd faeries pac'd the coverlet,
And pale enchantment held her sleepy-eyed.
Never on such a night have lovers met,   170
Since Merlin paid his Demon all the monstrous debt.

XX

'It shall be as thou wishest,' said the Dame:
'All cates and dainties shall be stored there
Quickly on this feast-night: by the tambour frame
Her own lute thou wilt see: no time to spare,
For I am slow and feeble, and scarce dare
On such a catering trust my dizzy head.
Wait here, my child, with patience; kneel in prayer
The while: Ah! thou must needs the lady wed,
Or may I never leave my grave among the dead.'   180

XXI

So saying, she hobbled off with busy fear.
The lover's endless minutes slowly pass'd;
The dame return'd, and whispered in his ear
To follow her; with aged eyes aghast
From fright of dim espial. Safe at last,
Through many a dusky gallery, they gain
The maiden's chamber, silken, hush'd, and chaste;
Where Porphyro took covert, pleas'd amain.
His poor guide hurried back with agues in her brain.

XXII

Her falt'ring hand upon the balustrade,   190
Old Angela was feeling for the stair,
When Madeline, St. Agnes' charmed maid,
Rose, like a mission'd spirit, unaware:
With silver taper's light, and pious care,
She turn'd, and down the aged gossip led
To a safe level matting. Now prepare,
Young Porphyro, for gazing on that bed;
She comes, she comes again, like ring-dove fray'd and fled.

XXIII

Out went the taper as she hurried in;
Its little smoke, in pallid moonshine, died: 200
She clos'd the door, she panted, all akin
To spirits of the air, and visions wide:
No uttered syllable, or, woe betide!
But to her heart, her heart was voluble,
Paining with eloquence her balmy side;
As though a tongueless nightingale should swell
Her throat in vain, and die, heart-stifled, in her dell.

XXIV

A casement high and triple-arch'd there was,
All garlanded with carven imag'ries
Of fruits, and flowers, and bunches of knot-grass,   210
And diamonded with panes of quaint device,
Innumerable of stains and splendid dyes,
As are the tiger-moth's deep-damask'd wings;
And in the midst, 'mong thousand heraldries,
And twilight saints, and dim emblazonings,
A shielded scutcheon blush'd with blood of queens and kings.

XXV

Full on this casement shone the wintry moon,
And threw warm gules on Madeline's fair breast,
As down she knelt for heaven's grace and boon;
Rose-bloom fell on her hands, together prest, 220
And on her silver cross soft amethyst,
And on her hair a glory, like a saint:
She seem'd a splendid angel, newly drest,
 Save wings, for heaven:—Porphyro grew faint:
She knelt, so pure a thing, so free from mortal taint.

XXVI

Anon his heart revives: her vespers done,
Of all its wreathed pearls her hair she frees;
Unclasps her warmed jewels one by one;
Loosens her fragrant boddice; by degrees
Her rich attire creeps rustling to her knees: 230
Half-hidden, like a mermaid in sea-weed,
Pensive awhile she dreams awake, and sees,
 In fancy, fair St. Agnes in her bed,
But dares not look behind, or all the charm is fled.

XXVII

Soon, trembling in her soft and chilly nest,
In sort of wakeful swoon, perplex'd she lay,
Until the poppied warmth of sleep oppress'd
Her soothed limbs, and soul fatigued away;
Flown, like a thought, until the morrow-day;
Blissfully haven'd both from joy and pain; 240
Clasp'd like a missal where swart Paynims pray;
 Blinded alike from sunshine and from rain,
As though a rose should shut, and be a bud again.

XXVIII

Stol'n to this paradise, and so entranced,
Porphyro gazed upon her empty dress,
And listen'd to her breathing, if it chanced
To wake into a slumberous tenderness;
Which when he heard, that minute did he bless,
And breath'd himself: then from the closet crept,
Noiseless as fear in a wide wilderness, 250
 And over the hush'd carpet, silent, stept,
And 'tween the curtains peep'd, where, lo!—how fast she slept.

XXIX

Then by the bed-side, where the faded moon
Made a dim, silver twilight, soft he set
A table, and, half anguish'd, threw thereon
A cloth of woven crimson, gold, and jet:—
O for some drowsy Morphean amulet!
The boisterous, midnight, festive clarion,
The kettle-drum, and far-heard clarinet,
 Affray his ears, though but in dying tone:— 260
The hall door shuts again, and all the noise is gone.

XXX

And still she slept an azure-lidded sleep,
In blanched linen, smooth, and lavender'd,
While he from forth the closet brought a heap
Of candied apple, quince, and plum, and gourd ;
With jellies soother than the creamy curd,
And lucent syrops, tinct with cinnamon ;
Manna and dates, in argosy transferr'd
From Fez ; and spiced dainties, every one,
From silken Samarcand to cedar'd Lebanon.   270

XXXI

These delicates he heap'd with glowing hand
On golden dishes and in baskets bright
Of wreathed silver : sumptuous they stand
In the retired quiet of the night,
Filling the chilly room with perfume light.—
'And now, my love, my seraph fair, awake !
Thou art my heaven, and I thine eremite :
Open thine eyes, for meek St. Agnes' sake,
Or I shall drowse beside thee, so my soul doth ache.'

XXXII

Thus whispering, his warm, unnerved arm   280
Sank in her pillow. Shaded was her dream
By the dusk curtains :—'twas a midnight charm
Impossible to melt as iced stream :
The lustrous salvers in the moonlight gleam ;
Broad golden fringe upon the carpet lies :
It seem'd he never, never could redeem
From such a stedfast spell his lady's eyes ;
So mus'd awhile, entoil'd in woofed phantasies.

XXXIII

Awakening up, he took her hollow lute,—
Tumultuous,—and, in chords that tenderest be,   290
He play'd an ancient ditty, long since mute,
In Provence call'd, ' La belle dame sans mercy : '
Close to her ear touching the melody ;—
Wherewith disturb'd, she utter'd a soft moan :
He ceased—she panted quick—and suddenly
Her blue affrayed eyes wide open shone :
Upon his knees he sank, pale as smooth-sculptured stone.

XXXIV

Her eyes were open, but she still beheld,
Now wide awake, the vision of her sleep :
There was a painful change, that nigh expell'd   300
The blisses of her dream so pure and deep,
At which fair Madeline began to weep,
And moan forth witless words with many a sigh ;
While still her gaze on Porphyro would keep ;
Who knelt, with joined hands and piteous eye,
Fearing to move or speak, she look'd so dreamingly.

XXXV

' Ah, Porphyro ! ' said she, ' but even now
Thy voice was at sweet tremble in mine ear,
Made tuneable with every sweetest vow ;
And those sad eyes were spiritual and clear :   310
How chang'd thou art ! how pallid, chill, and drear !
Give me that voice again, my Porphyro,
Those looks immortal, those complainings dear !
Oh leave me not in this eternal woe,
For if thou diest, my Love, I know not where to go.'

XXXVI

Beyond a mortal man impassion'd far
At these voluptuous accents, he arose,
Ethereal, flush'd, and like a throbbing star
Seen mid the sapphire heaven's deep repose ;
Into her dream he melted, as the rose   320
Blendeth its odour with the violet,—
Solution sweet : meantime the frost-wind blows
Like Love's alarum pattering the sharp sleet
Against the window-panes ; St. Agnes' moon hath set.

XXXVII

'Tis dark : quick pattereth the flaw-blown sleet :
' This is no dream, my bride, my Madeline ! '
'Tis dark : the iced gusts still rave and beat :
' No dream, alas ! alas ! and woe is mine !
Porphyro will leave me here to fade and pine.—
Cruel ! what traitor could thee hither bring ?   330
I curse not, for my heart is lost in thine,
Though thou forsakest a deceived thing ;—
A dove forlorn and lost with sick unpruned wing.'

XXXVIII

' My Madeline ! sweet dreamer ! lovely bride !
Say, may I be for aye thy vassal blest ?
Thy beauty's shield, heart-shap'd and vermeil dyed ?
Ah, silver shrine, here will I take my rest
After so many hours of toil and quest,
A famish'd pilgrim,—sav'd by miracle.
Though I have found, I will not rob thy nest   340
Saving of thy sweet self ; if thou think'st well
To trust, fair Madeline, to no rude infidel.

XXXIX

' Hark ! 'tis an elfin-storm from faery land,
Of haggard seeming, but a boon indeed :
Arise—arise ! the morning is at hand ;—
The bloated wassaillers will never heed :—
Let us away, my love, with happy speed ;
There are no ears to hear, or eyes to see,—
Drown'd all in Rhenish and the sleepy mead :
Awake ! arise ! my love, and fearless be,   350
For o'er the southern moors I have a home for thee.'

XL

She hurried at his words, beset with fears,
For there were sleeping dragons all around,
At glaring watch, perhaps, with ready spears—
Down the wide stairs a darkling way they found.—
In all the house was heard no human sound.
A chain-droop'd lamp was flickering by each door;
The arras, rich with horseman, hawk, and hound,
Flutter'd in the besieging wind's uproar;
And the long carpets rose along the gusty floor.   360

XLI

They glide, like phantoms, into the wide hall;
Like phantoms, to the iron porch, they glide;
Where lay the Porter, in uneasy sprawl,
With a huge empty flaggon by his side:
The wakeful bloodhound rose, and shook his hide,
But his sagacious eye an inmate owns:
By one, and one, the bolts full easy slide:—
The chains lie silent on the footworn stones;—
The key turns, and the door upon its hinges groans.

XLII

And they are gone: aye, ages long ago   370
These lovers fled away into the storm.
That night the Baron dreamt of many a woe,
And all his warrior-guests, with shade and form
Of witch, and demon, and large coffin-worm,
Were long be-nightmar'd. Angela the old
Died palsy-twitch'd, with meagre face deform;
The Beadsman, after thousand aves told,
For aye unsought for slept among his ashes cold.

HYPERION

A FRAGMENT

BOOK I

DEEP in the shady sadness of a vale
Far sunken from the healthy breath of morn,
Far from the fiery noon, and eve's one star,
Sat gray-hair'd Saturn, quiet as a stone,
Still as the silence round about his lair;
Forest on forest hung about his head
Like cloud on cloud. No stir of air was there,
Not so much life as on a summer's day
Robs not one light seed from the feather'd grass,
But where the dead leaf fell, there did it rest.   10
A stream went voiceless by, still deadened more
By reason of his fallen divinity
Spreading a shade: the Naiad 'mid her reeds
Press'd her cold finger closer to her lips.

Along the margin-sand large foot-marks went,
No further than to where his feet had stray'd,
And slept there since.　Upon the sodden ground
His old right hand lay nerveless, listless, dead,
Unsceptred ;　and his realmless eyes were closed ;
While his bow'd head seem'd list'ning to the Earth,　20
His ancient mother, for some comfort yet.

It seem'd no force could wake him from his place ;
But there came one, who with a kindred hand
Touch'd his wide shoulders, after bending low
With reverence, though to one who knew it not.
She was a Goddess of the infant world ;
By her in stature the tall Amazon
Had stood a pigmy's height : she would have ta'en
Achilles by the hair and bent his neck ;
Or with a finger stay'd Ixion's wheel.　　　　30
Her face was large as that of Memphian sphinx,
Pedestal'd haply in a palace court,
When sages look'd to Egypt for their lore.
But oh ! how unlike marble was that face :
How beautiful, if sorrow had not made
Sorrow more beautiful than Beauty's self.
There was a listening fear in her regard,
As if calamity had but begun ;
As if the vanward clouds of evil days
Had spent their malice, and the sullen rear　　40
Was with its stored thunder labouring up.
One hand she press'd upon that aching spot
Where beats the human heart, as if just there,
Though an immortal, she felt cruel pain :
The other upon Saturn's bended neck
She laid, and to the level of his ear
Leaning with parted lips, some words she spake
In solemn tenour and deep organ tone :
Some mourning words, which in our feeble tongue
Would come in these like accents ;　O how frail　50
To that large utterance of the early Gods !
'Saturn, look up !—though wherefore, poor old King ?
I have no comfort for thee, no not one :
I cannot say, " O wherefore sleepest thou ? "
For heaven is parted from thee, and the earth
Knows thee not, thus afflicted, for a God ;
And ocean too, with all its solemn noise,
Has from thy sceptre pass'd ;　and all the air
Is emptied of thine hoary majesty.
Thy thunder, conscious of the new command,　　60
Rumbles reluctant o'er our fallen house ;
And thy sharp lightning in unpractis'd hands
Scorches and burns our once serene domain.
O aching time ! O moments big as years !

All as ye pass swell out the monstrous truth,
And press it so upon our weary griefs
That unbelief has not a space to breathe.
Saturn, sleep on :—O thoughtless, why did I
Thus violate thy slumbrous solitude ?
Why should I ope thy melancholy eyes ?   70
Saturn, sleep on ! while at thy feet I weep.'

   As when, upon a tranced summer-night,
Those green-rob'd senators of mighty woods,
Tall oaks, branch-charmed by the earnest stars,
Dream, and so dream all night without a stir,
Save from one gradual solitary gust
Which comes upon the silence, and dies off,
As if the ebbing air had but one wave ;
So came these words and went; the while in tears
She touch'd her fair large forehead to the ground,   80
Just where her falling hair might be outspread
A soft and silken mat for Saturn's feet.
One moon, with alteration slow, had shed
Her silver seasons four upon the night,
And still these two were postured motionless,
Like natural sculpture in cathedral cavern ;
The frozen God still couchant on the earth,
And the sad Goddess weeping at his feet :
Until at length old Saturn lifted up
His faded eyes, and saw his kingdom gone,   90
And all the gloom and sorrow of the place,
And that fair kneeling Goddess ; and then spake,
As with a palsied tongue, and while his beard
Shook horrid with such aspen-malady :
' O tender spouse of gold Hyperion,
Thea, I feel thee ere I see thy face ;
Look up, and let me see our doom in it ;
Look up, and tell me if this feeble shape
Is Saturn's ; tell me, if thou hear'st the voice
Of Saturn ; tell me, if this wrinkling brow,   100
Naked and bare of its great diadem,
Peers like the front of Saturn. Who had power
To make me desolate ? whence came the strength ?
How was it nurtur'd to such bursting forth,
While Fate seem'd strangled in my nervous grasp ?
But it is so ; and I am smother'd up,
And buried from all godlike exercise
Of influence benign on planets pale,
Of admonitions to the winds and seas,
Of peaceful sway above man's harvesting,   110
And all those acts which Deity supreme
Doth ease its heart of love in.—I am gone
Away from my own bosom : I have left
My strong identity, my real self,

Somewhere between the throne, and where I sit
Here on this spot of earth. Search, Thea, search!
Open thine eyes eterne, and sphere them round
Upon all space : space starr'd, and lorn of light ;
Space region'd with life-air ; and barren void ;
Spaces of fire, and all the yawn of hell.—   120
Search, Thea, search! and tell me, if thou seest
A certain shape or shadow, making way
With wings or chariot fierce to repossess
A heaven he lost erewhile : it must—it must
Be of ripe progress—Saturn must be King.
Yes, there must be a golden victory ;
There must be Gods thrown down, and trumpets blown
Of triumph calm, and hymns of festival
Upon the gold clouds metropolitan,
Voices of soft proclaim, and silver stir   130
Of strings in hollow shells ; and there shall be
Beautiful things made new, for the surprise
Of the sky-children ; I will give command :
Thea! Thea! Thea! where is Saturn?'

This passion lifted him upon his feet,
And made his hands to struggle in the air,
His Druid locks to shake and ooze with sweat,
His eyes to fever out, his voice to cease.
He stood, and heard not Thea's sobbing deep ;
A little time, and then again he snatch'd   140
Utterance thus.—'But cannot I create ?
'Cannot I form ? Cannot I fashion forth
Another world, another universe,
To overbear and crumble this to naught ?
Where is another chaos ? Where ?'—That word
Found way unto Olympus, and made quake
The rebel three.—Thea was startled up,
And in her bearing was a sort of hope,
As thus she quick-voic'd spake, yet full of awe.
'This cheers our fallen house : come to our friends,   150
O Saturn! come away, and give them heart ;
I know the covert, for thence came I hither.'
Thus brief ; then with beseeching eyes she went
With backward footing through the shade a space :
He follow'd, and she turn'd to lead the way
Through aged boughs, that yielded like the mist
Which eagles cleave upmounting from their nest.

Meanwhile in other realms big tears were shed,
More sorrow like to this, and such like woe,
Too huge for mortal tongue or pen of scribe :   160
The Titans fierce, self-hid, or prison-bound,
Groan'd for the old allegiance once more,
And listen'd in sharp pain for Saturn's voice.
But one of the whole mammoth-brood still kept

His sov'reignty, and rule, and majesty ;—
Blazing Hyperion on his orbed fire
Still sat, still snuff'd the incense, teeming up
From man to the sun's God ; yet unsecure :
For as among us mortals omens drear
Fright and perplex, so also shuddered he— 170
Not at dog's howl, or gloom-bird's hated screech,
Or the familiar visiting of one
Upon the first toll of his passing-bell,
Or prophesyings of the midnight lamp ;
But horrors, portion'd to a giant nerve,
Oft made Hyperion ache. His palace bright
Bastion'd with pyramids of glowing gold,
And touch'd with shade of bronzed obelisks,
Glar'd a blood-red through all its thousand courts,
Arches, and domes, and fiery galleries ; 180
And all its curtains of Aurorian clouds
Flush'd angerly : while sometimes eagle's wings,
Unseen before by Gods or wondering men,
Darken'd the place ; and neighing steeds were heard,
Not heard before by Gods or wondering men.
Also, when he would taste the spicy wreaths
Of incense, breath'd aloft from sacred hills,
Instead of sweets, his ample palate took
Savour of poisonous brass and metal sick :
And so, when harbour'd in the sleepy west, 190
After the full completion of fair day,—
For rest divine upon exalted couch
And slumber in the arms of melody,
He pac'd away the pleasant hours of ease
With stride colossal, on from hall to hall ;
While far within each aisle and deep recess,
His wingèd minions in close clusters stood,
Amaz'd and full of fear ; like anxious men
Who on wide plains gather in panting troops,
When earthquakes jar their battlements and towers. 200
Even now, while Saturn, rous'd from icy trance,
Went step for step with Thea through the woods,
Hyperion, leaving twilight in the rear,
Came slope upon the threshold of the west ;
Then, as was wont, his palace-door flew ope
In smoothest silence, save what solemn tubes,
Blown by the serious Zephyrs, gave of sweet
And wandering sounds, slow-breathed melodies ;
And like a rose in vermeil tint and shape,
In fragrance soft, and coolness to the eye, 210
That inlet to severe magnificence
Stood full blown, for the God to enter in.

He enter'd, but he enter'd full of wrath ;
His flaming robes stream'd out beyond his heels,

And gave a roar, as if of earthly fire,
That scar'd away the meek ethereal Hours
And made their dove-wings tremble. On he flared,
From stately nave to nave, from vault to vault,
Through bowers of fragrant and enwreathed light,
And diamond-paved lustrous long arcades,   220
Until he reach'd the great main cupola ;
There standing fierce beneath, he stamped his foot,
And from the basements deep to the high towers
Jarr'd his own golden region ; and before
The quavering thunder thereupon had ceas'd,
His voice leapt out, despite of godlike curb,
To this result : ' O dreams of day and night !
O monstrous forms ! O effigies of pain !
O spectres busy in a cold, cold gloom !
O lank-ear'd Phantoms of black-weeded pools !   230
Why do I know ye ? why have I seen ye ? why
Is my eternal essence thus distraught
To see and to behold these horrors new ?
Saturn is fallen, am I too to fall ?
Am I to leave this haven of my rest,
This cradle of my glory, this soft clime,
This calm luxuriance of blissful light,
These crystalline pavilions, and pure fanes,
Of all my lucent empire ? It is left
Deserted, void, nor any haunt of mine.   240
The blaze, the splendor, and the symmetry,
I cannot see—but darkness, death and darkness.
Even here, into my centre of repose,
The shady visions come to domineer,
Insult, and blind, and stifle up my pomp.—
Fall !—No, by Tellus and her briny robes !
Over the fiery frontier of my realms
I will advance a terrible right arm
Shall scare that infant thunderer, rebel Jove,
And bid old Saturn take his throne again.'—   250
He spake, and ceas'd, the while a heavier threat
Held struggle with his throat but came not forth ;
For as in theatres of crowded men
Hubbub increases more they call out ' Hush ! '
So at Hyperion's words the Phantoms pale
Bestirr'd themselves, thrice horrible and cold ;
And from the mirror'd level where he stood
A mist arose, as from a scummy marsh.
At this, through all his bulk an agony
Crept gradual, from the feet unto the crown,   260
Like a lithe serpent vast and muscular
Making slow way, with head and neck convuls'd
From over-strained might. Releas'd, he fled
To the eastern gates, and full six dewy hours
Before the dawn in season due should blush,

He breath'd fierce breath against the sleepy portals,
Clear'd them of heavy vapours, burst them wide
Suddenly on the ocean's chilly streams.
The planet orb of fire, whereon he rode
Each day from east to west the heavens through,   270
Spun round in sable curtaining of clouds ;
Not therefore veiled quite, blindfold, and hid,
But ever and anon the glancing spheres,
Circles, and arcs, and broad-belting colure,
Glow'd through, and wrought upon the muffling dark
Sweet-shaped lightnings from the nadir deep
Up to the zenith,—hieroglyphics old
Which sages and keen-eyed astrologers
Then living on the earth, with labouring thought
Won from the gaze of many centuries :   280
Now lost, save what we find on remnants huge
Of stone, or marble swart ; their import gone,
Their wisdom long since fled.—Two wings this orb
Possess'd for glory, two fair argent wings,
Ever exalted at the God's approach :
And now, from forth the gloom their plumes immense
Rose, one by one, till all outspreaded were ;
While still the dazzling globe maintain'd eclipse,
Awaiting for Hyperion's command.
Fain would he have commanded, fain took throne   290
And bid the day begin, if but for change.
He might not :—No, though a primeval God :
The sacred seasons might not be disturb'd.
Therefore the operations of the dawn
Stay'd in their birth, even as here 'tis told.
Those silver wings expanded sisterly,
Eager to sail their orb ; the porches wide
Open'd upon the dusk demesnes of night ;
And the bright Titan, phrenzied with new woes,
Unus'd to bend, by hard compulsion bent   300
His spirit to the sorrow of the time ;
And all along a dismal rack of clouds,
Upon the boundaries of day and night,
He stretch'd himself in grief and radiance faint.
There as he lay, the Heaven with its stars
Look'd down on him with pity, and the voice
Of Coelus, from the universal space,
Thus whisper'd low and solemn in his ear.
' O brightest of my children dear, earth-born
And sky-engendered, Son of Mysteries   310
All unrevealed even to the powers
Which met at thy creating ; at whose joys
And palpitations sweet, and pleasures soft,
I, Coelus, wonder, how they came and whence ;
And at the fruits thereof what shapes they be,
Distinct, and visible ; symbols divine,

Manifestations of that beauteous life
Diffus'd unseen throughout eternal space:
Of these new-form'd art thou, oh brightest child!
Of these, thy brethren and the Goddesses!   320
There is sad feud among ye, and rebellion
Of son against his sire. I saw him fall,
I saw my first-born tumbled from his throne!
To me his arms were spread, to me his voice
Found way from forth the thunders round his head!
Pale wox I, and in vapours hid my face.
Art thou, too, near such doom? vague fear there is:
For I have seen my sons most unlike Gods.
Divine ye were created, and divine
In sad demeanour, solemn, undisturb'd,   330
Unruffled, like high Gods, ye liv'd and ruled:
Now I behold in you fear, hope, and wrath;
Actions of rage and passion; even as
I see them, on the mortal world beneath,
In men who die.—This is the grief, O Son!
Sad sign of ruin, sudden dismay, and fall!
Yet do thou strive; as thou art capable,
As thou canst move about, an evident God;
And canst oppose to each malignant hour
Ethereal presence:—I am but a voice;   340
My life is but the life of winds and tides,
No more than winds and tides can I avail:—
But thou canst.—Be thou therefore in the van
Of circumstance; yea, seize the arrow's barb
Before the tense string murmur.—To the earth!
For there thou wilt find Saturn, and his woes.
Meantime I will keep watch on thy bright sun,
And of thy seasons be a careful nurse.'—
Ere half this region-whisper had come down,
Hyperion arose, and on the stars   350
Lifted his curved lids, and kept them wide
Until it ceas'd; and still he kept them wide:
And still they were the same bright, patient stars.
Then with a slow incline of his broad breast,
Like to a diver in the pearly seas,
Forward he stoop'd over the airy shore,
And plung'd all noiseless into the deep night.

BOOK II

JUST at the self-same beat of Time's wide wings
Hyperion slid into the rustled air,
And Saturn gain'd with Thea that sad place
Where Cybele and the bruised Titans mourn'd.
It was a den where no insulting light
Could glimmer on their tears; where their own groans

They felt, but heard not, for the solid roar
Of thunderous waterfalls and torrents hoarse,
Pouring a constant bulk, uncertain where.
Crag jutting forth to crag, and rocks that seem'd   10
Ever as if just rising from a sleep,
Forehead to forehead held their monstrous horns ;
And thus in thousand hugest phantasies
Made a fit roofing to this nest of woe.
Instead of thrones, hard flint they sat upon,
Couches of rugged stone, and slaty ridge
Stubborn'd with iron.   All were not assembled :
Some chain'd in torture, and some wandering.
Coeus, and Gyges, and Briareüs,
Typhon, and Dolor, and Porphyrion,   20
With many more, the brawniest in assault,
Were pent in regions of laborious breath ;
Dungeon'd in opaque element, to keep
Their clenched teeth still clench'd, and all their limbs
Lock'd up like veins of metal, crampt and screw'd ;
Without a motion, save of their big hearts
Heaving in pain, and horribly convuls'd
With sanguine feverous boiling gurge of pulse.
Mnemosyne was straying in the world ;
Far from her moon had Phoebe wandered ;   30
And many else were free to roam abroad,
But for the main, here found they covert drear.
Scarce images of life, one here, one there,
Lay vast and edgeways ; like a dismal cirque
Of Druid stones, upon a forlorn moor,
When the chill rain begins at shut of eve,
In dull November, and their chancel vault,
The Heaven itself, is blinded throughout night.
Each one kept shroud, nor to his neighbour gave
Or word, or look, or action of despair.   40
Creüs was one ; his ponderous iron mace
Lay by him, and a shatter'd rib of rock
Told of his rage, ere he thus sank and pined.
Iäpetus another ; in his grasp,
A serpent's plashy neck ; its barbed tongue
Squeez'd from the gorge, and all its uncurl'd length
Dead ; and because the creature could not spit
Its poison in the eyes of conquering Jove.
Next Cottus : prone he lay, chin uppermost,
As though in pain ; for still upon the flint   50
He ground severe his skull, with open mouth
And eyes at horrid working.   Nearest him
Asia, born of most enormous Caf,
Who cost her mother Tellus keener pangs,
Though feminine, than any of her sons :
More thought than woe was in her dusky face,
For she was prophesying of her glory ;

And in her wide imagination stood
Palm-shaded temples, and high rival fanes,
By Oxus or in Ganges' sacred isles.   60
Even as Hope upon her anchor leans,
So leant she, not so fair, upon a tusk
Shed from the broadest of her elephants.
Above her, on a crag's uneasy shelve,
Upon his elbow rais'd, all prostrate else,
Shadow'd Enceladus ; once tame and mild
As grazing ox unworried in the meads ;
Now tiger-passion'd, lion-thoughted, wroth,
He meditated, plotted, and even now
Was hurling mountains in that second war,   70
Not long delay'd, that scar'd the younger Gods
To hide themselves in forms of beast and bird.
Not far hence Atlas ; and beside him prone
Phorcus, the sire of Gorgons. Neighbour'd close
Oceanus, and Tethys, in whose lap
Sobb'd Clymene among her tangled hair.
In midst of all lay Themis, at the feet
Of Ops the queen all clouded round from sight ;
No shape distinguishable, more than when
Thick night confounds the pine-tops with the clouds : 80
And many else whose names may not be told.
For when the Muse's wings are air-ward spread,
Who shall delay her flight ? And she must chaunt
Of Saturn, and his guide, who now had climb'd
With damp and slippery footing from a depth
More horrid still. Above a sombre cliff
Their heads appear'd, and up their stature grew
Till on the level height their steps found ease :
Then Thea spread abroad her trembling arms
Upon the precincts of this nest of pain,   90
And sidelong fix'd her eye on Saturn's face :
There saw she direst strife ; the supreme God
At war with all the frailty of grief,
Of rage, of fear, anxiety, revenge,
Remorse, spleen, hope, but most of all despair.
Against these plagues he strove in vain ; for Fate
Had pour'd a mortal oil upon his head,
A disanointing poison : so that Thea,
Affrighted, kept her still, and let him pass
First onwards in, among the fallen tribe.   100

    As with us mortal men, the laden heart
Is persecuted more, and fever'd more,
When it is nighing to the mournful house
Where other hearts are sick of the same bruise ;
So Saturn, as he walk'd into the midst,
Felt faint, and would have sunk among the rest,
But that he met Enceladus's eye,
Whose mightiness, and awe of him, at once

Came like an inspiration ; and he shouted,
' Titans, behold your God ! ' at which some groan'd ;   110
Some started on their feet ; some also shouted ;
Some wept, some wail'd, all bow'd with reverence ;
And Ops, uplifting her black folded veil,
Show'd her pale cheeks, and all her forehead wan,
Her eye-brows thin and jet, and hollow eyes.
There is a roaring in the bleak-grown pines
When Winter lifts his voice ; there is a noise
Among immortals when a God gives sign,
With hushing finger, how he means to load
His tongue with the full weight of utterless thought,   120
With thunder, and with music, and with pomp :
Such noise is like the roar of bleak-grown pines :
Which, when it ceases in this mountain'd world,
No other sound succeeds ; but ceasing here,
Among these fallen, Saturn's voice therefrom
Grew up like organ, that begins anew
Its strain, when other harmonies, stopt short,
Leave the dinn'd air vibrating silverly.
Thus grew it up—' Not in my own sad breast,
Which is its own great judge and searcher out,   130
Can I find reason why ye should be thus :
Not in the legends of the first of days,
Studied from that old spirit-leaved book
Which starry Uranus with finger bright
Sav'd from the shores of darkness, when the waves
Low-ebb'd still hid it up in shallow gloom ;—
And the which book ye know I ever kept
For my firm-based footstool :—Ah, infirm !
Not there, nor in sign, symbol, or portent
Of element, earth, water, air, and fire,—   140
At war, at peace, or inter-quarreling
One against one, or two, or three, or all
Each several one against the other three,
As fire with air loud warring when rain-floods
Drown both, and press them both against earth's face,
Where, finding sulphur, a quadruple wrath
Unhinges the poor world ;—not in that strife,
Wherefrom I take strange lore, and read it deep,
Can I find reason why ye should be thus :
No, no-where can unriddle, though I search,   150
And pore on Nature's universal scroll
Even to swooning, why ye, Divinities,
The first-born of all shap'd and palpable Gods,
Should cower beneath what, in comparison,
Is untremendous might. Yet ye are here,
O'erwhelm'd, and spurn'd, and batter'd, ye are here !
O Titans, shall I say, " Arise ! "—Ye groan :
Shall I say " Crouch ! "—Ye groan. What can I then ?
O Heaven wide ! O unseen parent dear !

What can I ? Tell me, all ye brethren Gods,   160
How we can war, how engine our great wrath !
O speak your counsel now, for Saturn's ear
Is all a-hunger'd. Thou, Oceanus,
Ponderest high and deep ; and in thy face
I see, astonied, that severe content
Which comes of thought and musing : give us help ! '

    So ended Saturn ; and the God of the Sea,
Sophist and sage, from no Athenian grove,
But cogitation in his watery shades,
Arose, with locks not oozy, and began,   170
In murmurs, which his first-endeavouring tongue
Caught infant-like from the far-foamed sands.
' O ye, whom wrath consumes ! who, passion-stung,
Writhe at defeat, and nurse your agonies !
Shut up your senses, stifle up your ears,
My voice is not a bellows unto ire.
Yet listen, ye who will, whilst I bring proof
How ye, perforce, must be content to stoop :
And in the proof much comfort will I give,
If ye will take that comfort in its truth.   180
We fall by course of Nature's law, not force
Of thunder, or of Jove. Great Saturn, thou
Hast sifted well the atom-universe ;
But for this reason, that thou art the King,
And only blind from sheer supremacy,
One avenue was shaded from thine eyes,
Through which I wandered to eternal truth.
And first, as thou wast not the first of powers,
So art thou not the last ; it cannot be :
Thou art not the beginning nor the end.   190
From chaos and parental darkness came
Light, the first fruits of that intestine broil,
That sullen ferment, which for wondrous ends
Was ripening in itself. The ripe hour came,
And with it light, and light, engendering
Upon its own producer, forthwith touch'd
The whole enormous matter into life.
Upon that very hour, our parentage,
The Heavens and the Earth, were manifest :
Then thou first born, and we the giant race,   200
Found ourselves ruling new and beauteous realms.
Now comes the pain of truth, to whom 'tis pain ;
O folly ! for to bear all naked truths,
And to envisage circumstance, all calm,
That is the top of sovereignty. Mark well !
As Heaven and Earth are fairer, fairer far
Than Chaos and blank Darkness, though once chiefs ;
And as we show beyond that Heaven and Earth
In form and shape compact and beautiful,

In will, in action free, companionship,   210
And thousand other signs of purer life;
So on our heels a fresh perfection treads,
A power more strong in beauty, born of us
And fated to excel us, as we pass
In glory that old Darkness: nor are we
Thereby more conquer'd, than by us the rule
Of shapeless Chaos. Say, doth the dull soil
Quarrel with the proud forests it hath fed,
And feedeth still, more comely than itself?
Can it deny the chiefdom of green groves?   220
Or shall the tree be envious of the dove
Because it cooeth, and hath snowy wings
To wander wherewithal and find its joys?
We are such forest-trees, and our fair boughs
Have bred forth, not pale solitary doves,
But eagles golden-feather'd, who do tower
Above us in their beauty, and must reign
In right thereof; for 'tis the eternal law
That first in beauty should be first in might:
Yea, by that law, another race may drive   230
Our conquerors to mourn as we do now.
Have ye beheld the young God of the Seas,
My dispossessor? Have ye seen his face?
Have ye beheld his chariot, foam'd along
By noble winged creatures he hath made?
I saw him on the calmed waters scud,
With such a glow of beauty in his eyes,
That it enforc'd me to bid sad farewell
To all my empire: farewell sad I took,
And hither came, to see how dolorous fate   240
Had wrought upon ye; and how I might best
Give consolation in this woe extreme.
Receive the truth, and let it be your balm.'

Whether through poz'd conviction, or disdain,
They guarded silence, when Oceanus
Left murmuring, what deepest thought can tell?
But so it was, none answer'd for a space,
Save one whom none regarded, Clymene;
And yet she answer'd not, only complain'd,
With hectic lips, and eyes up-looking mild,   250
Thus wording timidly among the fierce:
'O Father, I am here the simplest voice,
And all my knowledge is that joy is gone,
And this thing woe crept in among our hearts,
There to remain for ever, as I fear:
I would not bode of evil, if I thought
So weak a creature could turn off the help
Which by just right should come of mighty Gods;
Yet let me tell my sorrow, let me tell

Of what I heard, and how it made we weep,   260
And know that we had parted from all hope.
I stood upon a shore, a pleasant shore,
Where a sweet clime was breathed from a land
Of fragrance, quietness, and trees, and flowers.
Full of calm joy it was, as I of grief;
Too full of joy and soft delicious warmth;
So that I felt a movement in my heart
To chide, and to reproach that solitude
With songs of misery, music of our woes;
And sat me down, and took a mouthed shell   270
And murmur'd into it, and made melody—
O melody no more! for while I sang,
And with poor skill let pass into the breeze
The dull shell's echo, from a bowery strand
Just opposite, an island of the sea,
There came enchantment with the shifting wind,
That did both drown and keep alive my ears.
I threw my shell away upon the sand,
And a wave fill'd it, as my sense was fill'd
With that new blissful golden melody.   280
A living death was in each gush of sounds,
Each family of rapturous hurried notes,
That fell, one after one, yet all at once,
Like pearl beads dropping sudden from their string:
And then another, then another strain,
Each like a dove leaving its olive perch,
With music wing'd instead of silent plumes,
To hover round my head, and make me sick
Of joy and grief at once. Grief overcame,
And I was stopping up my frantic ears,   290
When, past all hindrance of my trembling hands,
A voice came sweeter, sweeter than all tune,
And still it cried, "Apollo! young Apollo!
The morning-bright Apollo! young Apollo!"
I fled, it follow'd me, and cried "Apollo!"
O Father, and O Brethren, had ye felt
Those pains of mine; O Saturn, hadst thou felt,
Ye would not call this too indulged tongue
Presumptuous, in thus venturing to be heard.'

    So far her voice flow'd on, like timorous brook   300
That, lingering along a pebbled coast,
Doth fear to meet the sea: but sea it met,
And shudder'd; for the overwhelming voice
Of huge Enceladus swallow'd it in wrath:
The ponderous syllables, like sullen waves
In the half-glutted hollows of reef-rocks,
Came booming thus, while still upon his arm
He lean'd; not rising, from supreme contempt.
' Or shall we listen to the over-wise,

Or to the over-foolish, Giant-Gods?   310
Not thunderbolt on thunderbolt, till all
That rebel Jove's whole armoury were spent,
Not world on world upon these shoulders piled,
Could agonize me more than baby-words
In midst of this dethronement horrible.
Speak! roar! shout! yell! ye sleepy Titans all.
Do ye forget the blows, the buffets vile?
Are ye not smitten by a youngling arm?
Dost thou forget, sham Monarch of the Waves,
Thy scalding in the seas? What, have I rous'd   320
Your spleens with so few simple words as these?
O joy! for now I see ye are not lost:
O joy! for now I see a thousand eyes
Wide-glaring for revenge!'—As this he said,
He lifted up his stature vast, and stood,
Still without intermission speaking thus:
'Now ye are flames, I'll tell you how to burn,
And purge the ether of our enemies;
How to feed fierce the crooked stings of fire,
And singe away the swollen clouds of Jove,   330
Stifling that puny essence in its tent.
O let him feel the evil he hath done;
For though I scorn Oceanus's lore,
Much pain have I for more than loss of realms:
The days of peace and slumberous calm are fled;
Those days, all innocent of scathing war,
When all the fair Existences of heaven
Came open-eyed to guess what we would speak:—
That was before our brows were taught to frown,
Before our lips knew else but solemn sounds;   340
That was before we knew the winged thing,
Victory, might be lost, or might be won.
And be ye mindful that Hyperion,
Our brightest brother, still is undisgraced—
Hyperion, lo! his radiance is here!'

    All eyes were on Enceladus's face,
And they beheld, while still Hyperion's name
Flew from his lips up to the vaulted rocks,
A pallid gleam across his features stern:
Not savage, for he saw full many a God   350
Wroth as himself. He look'd upon them all,
And in each face he saw a gleam of light,
But splendider in Saturn's, whose hoar locks
Shone like the bubbling foam about a keel
When the prow sweeps into a midnight cove.
In pale and silver silence they remain'd,
Till suddenly a splendour, like the morn,
Pervaded all the beetling gloomy steeps,
All the sad spaces of oblivion,

And every gulf, and every chasm old,   360
And every height, and every sullen depth,
Voiceless, or hoarse with loud tormented streams :
And all the everlasting cataracts,
And all the headlong torrents far and near,
Mantled before in darkness and huge shade,
Now saw the light and made it terrible.
It was Hyperion :—a granite peak
His bright feet touch'd, and there he stay'd to view
The misery his brilliance had betray'd
To the most hateful seeing of itself.   370
Golden his hair of short Numidian curl,
Regal his shape majestic, a vast shade
In midst of his own brightness, like the bulk
Of Memnon's image at the set of sun
To one who travels from the dusking East :
Sighs, too, as mournful as that Memnon's harp
He utter'd, while his hands contemplative
He press'd together, and in silence stood.
Despondence seiz'd again the fallen Gods
At sight of the dejected King of Day,   380
And many hid their faces from the light :
But fierce Enceladus sent forth his eyes
Among the brotherhood ; and, at their glare,
Uprose Iäpetus, and Creüs too,
And Phorcus, sea-born, and together strode
To where he towered on his eminence.
There those four shouted forth old Saturn's name ;
Hyperion from the peak loud answered, ' Saturn ! '
Saturn sat near the Mother of the Gods,
In whose face was no joy, though all the Gods   390
Gave from their hollow throats the name of ' Saturn ! '

BOOK III

THUS in alternate uproar and sad peace,
Amazed were those Titans utterly.
O leave them, Muse ! O leave them to their woes ;
For thou art weak to sing such tumults dire :
A solitary sorrow best befits
Thy lips, and antheming a lonely grief.
Leave them, O Muse ! for thou anon wilt find
Many a fallen old Divinity
Wandering in vain about bewildered shores.
Meantime touch piously the Delphic harp,   10
And not a wind of heaven but will breathe
In aid soft warble from the Dorian flute ;
For lo ! 'tis for the Father of all verse.
Flush every thing that hath a vermeil hue,
Let the rose glow intense and warm the air,

And let the clouds of even and of morn
Float in voluptuous fleeces o'er the hills ;
Let the red wine within the goblet boil,
Cold as a bubbling well ; let faint-lipp'd shells,
On sands, or in great deeps, vermilion turn   20
Through all their labyrinths ; and let the maid
Blush keenly, as with some warm kiss surpris'd.
Chief isle of the embowered Cyclades,
Rejoice, O Delos, with thine olives green,
And poplars, and lawn-shading palms, and beech,
In which the Zephyr breathes the loudest song,
And hazels thick, dark-stemm'd beneath the shade :
Apollo is once more the golden theme !
Where was he, when the Giant of the Sun
Stood bright, amid the sorrow of his peers ?   30
Together had he left his mother fair
And his twin-sister sleeping in their bower,
And in the morning twilight wandered forth
Beside the osiers of a rivulet,
Full ankle-deep in lilies of the vale.
The nightingale had ceas'd, and a few stars
Were lingering in the heavens, while the thrush
Began calm-throated. Throughout all the isle
There was no covert, no retired cave
Unhaunted by the murmurous noise of waves,   40
Though scarcely heard in many a green recess.
He listen'd, and he wept, and his bright tears
Went trickling down the golden bow he held.
Thus with half-shut suffused eyes he stood,
While from beneath some cumbrous boughs hard by
With solemn step an awful Goddess came,
And there was purport in her looks for him,
Which he with eager guess began to read
Perplex'd, the while melodiously he said :
' How cam'st thou over the unfooted sea ?   50
Or hath that antique mien and robed form
Mov'd in these vales invisible till now ?
Sure I have heard those vestments sweeping o'er
The fallen leaves, when I have sat alone
In cool mid-forest. Surely I have traced
The rustle of those ample skirts about
These grassy solitudes, and seen the flowers
Lift up their heads, as still the whisper pass'd.
Goddess ! I have beheld those eyes before,
And their eternal calm, and all that face,   60
Or I have dream'd.'—' Yes,' said the supreme shape,
' Thou hast dream'd of me ; and awaking up
Didst find a lyre all golden by thy side,
Whose strings touch'd by thy fingers, all the vast
Unwearied ear of the whole universe
Listen'd in pain and pleasure at the birth

Of such new tuneful wonder. Is't not strange
That thou shouldst weep, so gifted ? Tell me, youth,
What sorrow thou canst feel ; for I am sad
When thou dost shed a tear : explain thy griefs   70
To one who in this lonely isle hath been
The watcher of thy sleep and hours of life,
From the young day when first thy infant hand
Pluck'd witless the weak flowers, till thine arm
Could bend that bow heroic to all times.
Show thy heart's secret to an ancient Power
Who hath forsaken old and sacred thrones
For prophecies of thee, and for the sake
Of loveliness new born.'—Apollo then,
With sudden scrutiny and gloomless eyes,   80
Thus answer'd, while his white melodious throat
Throbb'd with the syllables.—' Mnemosyne !
Thy name is on my tongue, I know not how ;
Why should I tell thee what thou so well seest ?
Why should I strive to show what from thy lips
Would come no mystery ? For me, dark, dark,
And painful vile oblivion seals my eyes :
I strive to search wherefore I am so sad,
Until a melancholy numbs my limbs ;
And then upon the grass I sit, and moan,   90
Like one who once had wings.—O why should I
Feel curs'd and thwarted, when the liegeless air
Yields to my step aspirant ? why should I
Spurn the green turf as hateful to my feet ?
Goddess benign, point forth some unknown thing :
Are there not other regions than this isle ?
What are the stars ? There is the sun, the sun !
And the most patient brilliance of the moon !
And stars by thousands ! Point me out the way
To any one particular beauteous star,   100
And I will flit into it with my lyre,
And make its silvery splendour pant with bliss.
I have heard the cloudy thunder : Where is power ?
Whose hand, whose essence, what divinity
Makes this alarum in the elements,
While I here idle listen on the shores
In fearless yet in aching ignorance ?
O tell me, lonely Goddess, by thy harp,
That waileth every morn and eventide,
Tell me why thus I rave, about these groves !   110
Mute thou remainest—mute ! yet I can read
A wondrous lesson in thy silent face :
Knowledge enormous makes a God of me.
Names, deeds, grey legends, dire events, rebellions,
Majesties, sovran voices, agonies,
Creations and destroyings, all at once
Pour into the wide hollows of my brain,

And deify **me**, as if some blithe wine
Or bright elixir peerless I had drunk,
And so become immortal.'—Thus the God,   120
While his enkindled eyes, with level glance
Beneath his white soft temples, stedfast kept
Trembling with light upon Mnemosyne.
Soon wild commotions shook him, and made flush
All the immortal fairness of his limbs ;
Most like the struggle at the gate of death ;
Or liker still to one who should take leave
Of pale immortal death, and with a pang
As hot as death's is chill, with fierce convulse
Die into life : so young Apollo anguish'd :   130
His very hair, his golden tresses famed
Kept undulation round his eager neck.
During the pain Mnemosyne upheld
Her arms as one who prophesied.—At length
Apollo shriek'd ;—and lo ! from all his limbs
Celestial .   .   .   .
    .

THE EVE OF ST. MARK

Upon a Sabbath-day it fell ;
Twice holy was the Sabbath-bell,
That call'd the folk to evening prayer ;
The city streets were clean and fair
From wholesome drench of April rains ;
And, on the western window panes,
The chilly sunset faintly told
Of unmatur'd green vallies cold,
Of the green thorny bloomless hedge,
Of rivers new with spring-tide sedge,   10
Of primroses by shelter'd rills,
And daisies on the aguish hills.
Twice holy was the Sabbath-bell :
The silent streets were crowded well
With staid and pious companies,
Warm from their fire-side orat'ries ;
And moving, with demurest air,
To even-song, and vesper prayer.
Each arched porch, and entry low,
Was fill'd with patient folk and slow,   20
With whispers hush, and shuffling feet,
While play'd the organ loud and sweet.

The bells had ceas'd, the prayers begun,
And Bertha had not yet half done

A curious volume, patch'd and torn,
That all day long, from earliest morn,
Had taken captive her two eyes,
Among its golden broideries ;
Perplex'd her with a thousand things,—
The stars of Heaven, and angels' wings,   30
Martyrs in a fiery blaze,
Azure saints in silver rays,
Moses' breastplate, and the seven
Candlesticks John saw in Heaven,
The winged Lion of Saint Mark,
And the Covenantal Ark,
With its many mysteries,
Cherubim and golden mice.

Bertha was a maiden fair,
Dwelling in the old Minster-square ;   40
From her fire-side she could see,
Sidelong, its rich antiquity,
Far as the Bishop's garden-wall ;
Where sycamores and elm-trees tall,
Full-leav'd, the forest had outstript,
By no sharp north-wind ever nipt,
So shelter'd by the mighty pile.
Bertha arose, and read awhile,
With forehead 'gainst the window-pane.
Again she try'd, and then again,   50
Until the dusk eve left her dark
Upon the legend of St. Mark.
From plaited lawn-frill, fine and thin,
She lifted up her soft warm chin,
With aching neck and swimming eyes,
And daz'd with saintly imageries.

All was gloom, and silent all,
Save now and then the still foot-fall
Of one returning homewards late,
Past the echoing minster-gate.   60

The clamorous daws, that all the day
Above tree-tops and towers play,
Pair by pair had gone to rest,
Each in its ancient belfry-nest,
Where asleep they fall betimes,
To music of the drowsy chimes.

All was silent, all was gloom,
Abroad and in the homely room :
Down she sat, poor cheated soul !
And struck a lamp from the dismal coal ;   70
Lean'd forward, with bright drooping hair
And slant book, full against the glare.

Her shadow, in uneasy guise,
Hover'd about, a giant size,
On ceiling-beam and old oak chair,
The parrot's cage, and panel square;
And the warm angled winter screen,
On which were many monsters seen,
Call'd doves of Siam, Lima mice,
And legless birds of Paradise,   80
Macaw, and tender Avadavat,
And silken-furr'd Angora cat.
Untir'd she read, her shadow still
Glower'd about, as it would fill
The room with wildest forms and shades,
As though some ghostly queen of spades
Had come to mock behind her back,
And dance, and ruffle her garments black.
Untir'd she read the legend page,
Of holy Mark, from youth to age,   90
On land, on sea, in pagan chains,
Rejoicing for his many pains.
Sometimes the learned eremite,
With golden star, or dagger bright,
Referr'd to pious poesies
Written in smallest crow-quill size
Beneath the text; and thus the rhyme
Was parcell'd out from time to time:
——'Als writith he of swevenis,
Men han beforne they wake in bliss,   100
Whanne that hir friendes thinke hem bound
In crimped shroude farre under grounde;
And how a litling child mote be
A saint er its nativitie,
Gif that the modre (God her blesse!)
Kepen in solitarinesse,
And kissen devoute the holy croce.
Of Goddes love, and Sathan's force,—
He writith; and thinges many mo:
Of swiche thinges I may not show.   110
Bot I must tellen verilie
Somdel of Saintè Cicilie,
And chieflie what he auctorethe
Of Saintè Markis life and dethe:'

At length her constant eyelids come
Upon the fervent martyrdom;
Then lastly to his holy shrine,
Exalt amid the tapers' shine
At Venice,—

LORD TENNYSON

THE LADY OF SHALOTT

PART I

On either side the river lie
Long fields of barley and of rye,
That clothe the wold and meet the sky;
And thro' the field the road runs by
     To many-tower'd Camelot;
And up and down the people go,
Gazing where the lilies blow
Round an island there below,
     The island of Shalott.

Willows whiten, aspens quiver,   **10**
Little breezes dusk and shiver
Thro' the wave that runs for ever
By the island in the river
     Flowing down to Camelot.
Four grey walls, and four grey towers,
Overlook a space of flowers,
And the silent isle embowers
     The Lady of Shalott.

By the margin, willow-veil'd,
Slide the heavy barges trail'd   **20**
By slow horses; and unhail'd
The shallop flitteth silken-sail'd
     Skimming down to Camelot:
But who hath seen her wave her hand?
Or at the casement seen her stand?
Or is she known in all the land,
     The Lady of Shalott?

Only reapers, reaping early
In among the bearded barley,
Hear a song that echoes cheerly   **30**
From the river winding clearly,
     Down to tower'd Camelot:
And by the moon the reaper weary,
Piling sheaves in uplands airy,
Listening, whispers ' 'Tis the fairy
     Lady of Shalott.'

Part II

There she weaves by night and day
A magic web with colours gay.
She has heard a whisper say,
A curse is on her if she stay   40
    To look down to Camelot.
She knows not what the curse may be,
And so she weaveth steadily,
And little other care hath she,
    The Lady of Shalott.

And moving thro' a mirror clear
That hangs before her all the year,
Shadows of the world appear.
There she sees the highway near
    Winding down to Camelot: 50
There the river eddy whirls,
And there the surly village-churls,
And the red cloaks of market girls,
    Pass onward from Shalott.

Sometimes a troop of damsels glad,
An abbot on an ambling pad,
Sometimes a curly shepherd-lad,
Or long-hair'd page in crimson clad,
    Goes by to tower'd Camelot;
And sometimes thro' the mirror blue   60
The knights come riding two and two:
She hath no loyal knight and true,
    The Lady of Shalott.

But in her web she still delights
To weave the mirror's magic sights,
For often thro' the silent nights
A funeral, with plumes and lights,
    And music, went to Camelot:
Or when the moon was overhead,
Came two young lovers lately wed;   70
'I am half sick of shadows,' said
    The Lady of Shalott.

Part III

A bow-shot from her bower-eaves,
He rode between the barley-sheaves,
The sun came dazzling thro' the leaves,
And flamed upon the brazen greaves
    Of bold Sir Lancelot.
A red-cross knight for ever kneel'd
To a lady in his shield,
That sparkled on the yellow field,   80
    Beside remote Shalott.

The gemmy bridle glitter'd free,
Like to some branch of stars we see
Hung in the golden Galaxy. *milky way*
The bridle bells rang merrily
   As he rode down to Camelot:
And from his blazon'd baldric slung
A mighty silver bugle hung,
And as he rode his armour rung,
   Beside remote Shalott.   90

All in the blue unclouded weather
Thick-jewell'd shone the saddle-leather,
The helmet and the helmet-feather
Burn'd like one burning flame together,
   As he rode down to Camelot.
As often thro' the purple night,
Below the starry clusters bright,
Some bearded meteor, trailing light,
   Moves over still Shalott.

His broad clear brow in sunlight glow'd; 100
On burnish'd hooves his war-horse trode;
From underneath his helmet flow'd
His coal-black curls as on he rode,
   As he rode down to Camelot.
From the bank and from the river
He flash'd into the crystal mirror,
' Tirra lirra,' by the river
   Sang Sir Lancelot.

She left the web, she left the loom,
She made three paces thro' the room, 110
She saw the water-lily bloom,
She saw the helmet and the plume,
   She look'd down to Camelot.
Out flew the web and floated wide;
The mirror cracked from side to side;
' The curse is come upon me,' cried
   The Lady of Shalott.

Part IV

In the stormy east-wind straining,
The pale yellow woods were waning,
The broad stream in his banks complaining, 120
Heavily the low sky raining
   Over tower'd Camelot;
Down she came and found a boat
Beneath a willow left afloat,
And round about the prow she wrote
   The Lady of Shalott.

And down the river's dim expanse—
Like some bold seër in a trance,
Seeing all his own mischance—
With a glassy countenance   130
   Did she look to Camelot.
And at the closing of the day
She loosed the chain, and down she lay;
The broad stream bore her far away,
   The Lady of Shalott.

Lying, robed in snowy white
That loosely flew to left and right—
The leaves upon her falling light—
Thro' the noises of the night
   She floated down to Camelot: 140
And as the boat-head wound along
The willowy hills and fields among,
They heard her singing her last song,
   The Lady of Shalott.

Heard a carol, mournful, holy,
Chanted loudly, chanted lowly,
Till her blood was frozen slowly,
And her eyes were darken'd wholly,
   Turn'd to tower'd Camelot;
For ere she reach'd upon the tide   150
The first house by the water-side,
Singing in her song she died,
   The Lady of Shalott.

Under tower and balcony,
By garden-wall and gallery,
A gleaming shape she floated by,
Dead-pale between the houses high,
   Silent into Camelot.
Out upon the wharfs they came,
Knight and burgher, lord and dame,   160
And round the prow they read her name,
   The Lady of Shalott.

Who is this? and what is here?
And in the lighted palace near
Died the sound of royal cheer;
And they cross'd themselves for fear,
   All the knights at Camelot:
But Lancelot mused a little space;
He said, ' She has a lovely face;
God in his mercy lend her grace,   170
   The Lady of Shalott.'

THE LOTOS-EATERS *Conscious Artists*

V. 1-3

'Courage!' he said, and pointed toward the land;
'This mounting wave will roll us shoreward soon.'
In the afternoon they came unto a land,
In which it seemed always afternoon.
All round the coast the languid air did swoon,
Breathing like one that hath a weary dream.
Full-faced above the valley stood the moon ;
And like a downward smoke, the slender stream
Along the cliff to fall and pause and fall did seem.

A land of streams ! some, like a downward smoke,   10
Slow-dropping veils of thinnest lawn, did go ;
And some thro' wavering lights and shadows broke,
Rolling a slumbrous sheet of foam below.
They saw the gleaming river seaward flow
From the inner land : far off, three mountain-tops,
Three silent pinnacles of aged snow,
Stood sunset-flush'd : and, dew'd with showery drops,
Up-clomb the shadowy pine above the woven copse.

The charmed sunset linger'd low adown
In the red West : thro' mountain clefts the dale   20
Was seen far inland, and the yellow down
Border'd with palm, and many a winding vale
And meadow, set with slender galingale ;
A land where all things always seem'd the same !
And round about the keel with faces pale,
Dark faces pale against that rosy flame,
The mild-eyed melancholy Lotos-eaters came.

Branches they bore of that enchanted stem,   *poetic diction*
Laden with flower and fruit, whereof they gave
To each, but whoso did receive of them,   *P.d.*   30
And taste, to him the gushing of the wave
Far far away did seem to mourn and rave
On alien shores ; and if his fellow spake,
His voice was thin, as voices from the grave ;
And deep-asleep he seem'd, yet all awake,
And music in his ears his beating heart did make.

They sat them down upon the yellow sand,
Between the sun and moon upon the shore ;
And sweet it was to dream of Father-land,
Of child, and wife, and slave ; but evermore   40
Most weary seem'd the sea, weary the oar,
Weary the wandering fields of barren foam.
Then some one said, 'We will return no more' ;
And all at once they sang, 'Our island home
Is far beyond the wave ; we will no longer roam.'

CHORIC SONG

I

There is sweet music here that softer falls
Than petals from blown roses on the grass,
Or night-dews on still waters between walls
Of shadowy granite, in a gleaming pass ;
Music that gentlier on the spirit lies,   50
Than tir'd eyelids upon tir'd eyes ;
Music that brings sweet sleep down from the blissful skies.
Here are cool mosses deep,
And thro' the moss the ivies creep,
And in the stream the long-leaved flowers weep,
And from the craggy ledge the poppy hangs in sleep.

II

Why are we weigh'd upon with heaviness,
And utterly consumed with sharp distress,
While all things else have rest from weariness ?
All things have rest : why should we toil alone,   60
We only toil, who are the first of things,
And make perpetual moan,
Still from one sorrow to another thrown :
Nor ever fold our wings,
And cease from wanderings,
Nor steep our brows in slumber's holy balm ;
Nor harken what the inner spirit sings,
' There is no joy but calm ! '
Why should we only toil, the roof and crown of things ?

III

Lo ! in the middle of the wood,   70
The folded leaf is woo'd from out the bud
With winds upon the branch, and there
Grows green and broad, and takes no care,
Sun-steep'd at noon, and in the moon
Nightly dew-fed ; and turning yellow
Falls, and floats adown the air.
Lo ! sweeten'd with the summer light,
The full-juiced apple, waxing over-mellow,
Drops in a silent autumn night.
All its allotted length of days,   80
The flower ripens in its place,
Ripens and fades, and falls, and hath no toil,
Fast-rooted in the fruitful soil.

IV

Hateful is the dark-blue sky,
Vaulted o'er the dark-blue sea.
Death is the end of life ; ah, why
Should life all labour be ?

Let us alone. Time driveth onward fast,
And in a little while our lips are dumb.
Let us alone. What is it that will last ?   90
All things are taken from us, and become
Portions and parcels of the dreadful Past.
Let us alone. What pleasure can we have
To war with evil ? Is there any peace
In ever climbing up the climbing wave ?
All things have rest, and ripen toward the grave
In silence ; ripen, fall and cease :
Give us long rest or death, dark death, or dreamful ease.

V

How sweet it were, hearing the downward stream,
With half-shut eyes ever to seem   100
Falling asleep in a half-dream !
To dream and dream, like yonder amber light,
Which will not leave the myrrh-bush on the height ;
To hear each other's whisper'd speech ;
Eating the Lotos day by day,
To watch the crisping ripples on the beach,
And tender curving lines of creamy spray ;
To lend our hearts and spirits wholly
To the influence of mild-minded melancholy ;
To muse and brood and live again in memory,   110
With those old faces of our infancy
Heap'd over with a mound of grass,
Two handfuls of white dust, shut in an urn of brass !

VI

Dear is the memory of our wedded lives,
And dear the last embraces of our wives
And their warm tears : but all hath suffer'd change ;
For surely now our household hearths are cold :
Our sons inherit us : our looks are strange :
And we should come like ghosts to trouble joy.
Or else the island princes over-bold   120
Have eat our substance, and the minstrel sings
Before them of the ten-years' war in Troy,
And our great deeds, as half-forgotten things.
Is there confusion in the little isle ?
Let what is broken so remain.
The Gods are hard to reconcile :
'Tis hard to settle order once again.
There *is* confusion worse than death,
Trouble on trouble, pain on pain,
Long labour unto aged breath,   130
Sore task to hearts worn out with many wars
And eyes grown dim with gazing on the pilot-stars.

VII

But, propt on beds of amaranth and moly,
How sweet (while warm airs lull us, blowing lowly)
With half-dropt eyelids still,
Beneath a heaven dark and holy
To watch the long bright river drawing slowly
His waters from the purple hill—
To hear the dewy echoes calling
From cave to cave thro' the thick-twined vine—   140
To watch the emerald-colour'd water falling
Thro' many a wov'n acanthus-wreath divine !
Only to hear and see the far-off sparkling brine,
Only to hear were sweet, stretch'd out beneath the pine.

VIII

The Lotos blooms below the barren peak :
The Lotos blows by every winding creek :
All day the wind breathes low with mellower tone :
Thro' every hollow cave and alley lone
Round and round the spicy downs the yellow Lotos-dust is
     blown.
We have had enough of action, and of motion we,   150
Roll'd to starboard, roll'd to larboard, when the surge was
     seething free,
Where the wallowing monster spouted his foam-fountains in
     the sea.
Let us swear an oath, and keep it with an equal mind,
In the hollow Lotos-land to live and lie reclined
On the hills like Gods together, careless of mankind.
For they lie beside their nectar, and the bolts are hurl'd
Far below them in the valleys, and the clouds are lightly curl'd
Round their golden houses, girdled with the gleaming world :
Where they smile in secret, looking over wasted lands,
Blight and famine, plague and earthquake, roaring deeps
     and fiery sands,   160
Clanging fights, and flaming towns, and sinking ships, and
     praying hands.
But they smile, they find a music centred in a doleful song
Steaming up, a lamentation and an ancient tale of wrong,
Like a tale of little meaning tho' the words are strong ;
Chanted from an ill-used race of men that cleave the soil,
Sow the seed, and reap the harvest with enduring toil,
Storing yearly little dues of wheat, and wine and oil ;
Till they perish and they suffer—some, 'tis whisper'd—down
     in hell
Suffer endless anguish, others in Elysian valleys dwell,
Resting weary limbs at last on beds of asphodel.   170
Surely, surely, slumber is more sweet than toil, the shore
Than labour in the deep mid-ocean, wind and wave and oar ;
Oh rest ye, brother mariners, we will not wander more.

ŒNONE

THERE lies a vale in Ida, lovelier
Than all the valleys of Ionian hills.
The swimming vapour slopes athwart the glen,
Puts forth an arm, and creeps from pine to pine,
And loiters, slowly drawn. On either hand
The lawns and meadow-ledges midway down
Hang rich in flowers, and far below them roars
The long brook falling thro' the clov'n ravine
In cataract after cataract to the sea.
Behind the valley topmost Gargarus   10
Stands up and takes the morning: but in front
The gorges, opening wide apart, reveal
Troas and Ilion's column'd citadel,
The crown of Troas.
             Hither came at noon
Mournful Œnone, wandering forlorn
Of Paris, once her playmate on the hills.
Her cheek had lost the rose, and round her neck
Floated her hair or seem'd to float in rest.
She, leaning on a fragment twined with vine,
Sang to the stillness, till the mountain-shade   20
Sloped downward to her seat from the upper cliff.

' O mother Ida, many-fountain'd Ida,
Dear mother Ida, harken ere I die.
For now the noonday quiet holds the hill:
The grasshopper is silent in the grass:
The lizard, with his shadow on the stone,
Rests like a shadow, and the cicala sleeps.
The purple flowers droop: the golden bee
Is lily-cradled: I alone awake.
My eyes are full of tears, my heart of love,   30
My heart is breaking, and my eyes are dim,
And I am all aweary of my life.

' O mother Ida, many-fountain'd Ida,
Dear mother Ida, harken ere I die.
Hear me O Earth, hear me O Hills, O Caves
That house the cold crown'd snake! O mountain brooks,
I am the daughter of a River-God,
Hear me, for I will speak, and build up all
My sorrow with my song, as yonder walls
Rose slowly to a music slowly breathed,   40
A cloud that gather'd shape: for it may be
That, while I speak of it, a little while
My heart may wander from its deeper woe.

'O mother Ida, many-fountain'd Ida,
Dear mother Ida, harken ere I die.
I waited underneath the dawning hills,
Aloft the mountain lawn was dewy-dark,
And dewy-dark aloft the mountain pine:
Beautiful Paris, evil-hearted Paris,
Leading a jet-black goat white-horn'd, white-hooved,   50
Came up from reedy Simois all alone.

'O mother Ida, harken ere I die.
Far-off the torrent call'd me from the cleft:
Far up the solitary morning smote
The streaks of virgin snow.   With down-dropt eyes
I sat alone: white-breasted like a star
Fronting the dawn he moved; a leopard-skin
Droop'd from his shoulder, but his sunny hair
Cluster'd about his temples like a God's;
And his cheek brighten'd as the foam-bow brightens   60
When the wind blows the foam, and all my heart
Went forth to embrace him coming ere he came.

'Dear mother Ida, harken ere I die.
He smiled, and opening out his milk-white palm
Disclosed a fruit of pure Hesperian gold,
That smelt ambrosially, and while I look'd
And listen'd, the full-flowing river of speech
Came down upon my heart.

                            '"My own Œnone,
Beautiful-brow'd Œnone, my own soul,
Behold this fruit, whose gleaming rind engrav'n   70
'For the most fair,' would seem to award it thine,
As lovelier than whatever Oread haunt
The knolls of Ida, loveliest in all grace
Of movement, and the charm of married brows."

'Dear mother Ida, harken ere I die.
He prest the blossom of his lips to mine
And added "This was cast upon the board,
When all the full-faced presence of the Gods
Ranged in the halls of Peleus; whereupon
Rose feud, with question unto whom 'twere due: 80
But light-foot Iris brought it yester-eve,
Delivering, that to me, by common voice
Elected umpire, Herè comes to-day,
Pallas and Aphrodite, claiming each
This meed of fairest.   Thou, within the cave
Behind yon whispering tuft of oldest pine,
Mayst well behold them unbeheld, unheard
Hear all, and see thy Paris judge of Gods."

'Dear mother Ida, harken ere I die.
It was the deep midnoon·: one silvery cloud　　90
Had lost his way between the piney sides
Of this long glen.　Then to the bower they came,
Naked they came to that smooth-swarded bower,
And at their feet the crocus brake like fire,
Violet, amaracus, and asphodel,
Lotos and lilies : and a wind arose,
And overhead the wandering ivy and vine,
This way and that, in many a wild festoon
Ran riot, garlanding the gnarled boughs
With bunch and berry and flower thro' and thro'.　　100

'O mother Ida, harken ere I die.
On the tree-tops a crested peacock lit,
And o'er him flow'd a golden cloud, and lean'd
Upon him, slowly dropping fragrant dew.
Then first I heard the voice of her, to whom
Coming thro' Heaven, like a light that grows
Larger and clearer, with one mind the Gods
Rise up for reverence.　She to Paris made
Proffer of royal power, ample rule
Unquestion'd, overflowing revenue　　110
Wherewith to embellish state, "from many a vale
And river-sunder'd champaign clothed with corn,
Or labour'd mines undrainable of ore.
Honour," she said, "and homage, tax and toll,
From many an inland town and haven large,
Mast-throng'd beneath her shadowing citadel
In glassy bays among her tallest towers."

'O mother Ida, harken ere I die.
Still she spake on and still she spake of power,
"Which in all action is the end of all ;　　120
Power fitted to the season ; wisdom-bred
And throned of wisdom—from all neighbour crowns
Alliance and allegiance, till thy hand
Fail from the sceptre-staff.　Such boon from me,
From me, Heaven's Queen, Paris, to thee king-born,
A shepherd all thy life but yet king-born,
Should come most welcome, seeing men, in power
Only, are likest Gods, who have attain'd
Rest in a happy place and quiet seats
Above the thunder, with undying bliss　　130
In knowledge of their own supremacy."

'Dear mother Ida, harken ere I die.
She ceased, and Paris held the costly fruit
Out at arm's-length, so much the thought of power
Flatter'd his spirit ; but Pallas where she stood
Somewhat apart, her clear and bared limbs

O'erthwarted with the brazen-headed spear
Upon her pearly shoulder leaning cold,
The while, above, her full and earnest eye
Over her snow-cold breast and angry cheek 140
Kept watch, waiting decision, made reply.

'"Self-reverence, self-knowledge, self-control,
These three alone lead life to sovereign power.
Yet not for power (power of herself
Would come uncall'd for), but to live by law,
Acting the law we live by without fear;
And, because right is right, to follow right
Were wisdom in the scorn of consequence."

'Dear mother Ida, harken ere I die.
Again she said: "I woo thee not with gifts. 150
Sequel of guerdon could not alter me
To fairer. Judge thou me by what I am,
So shalt thou find me fairest.
                              Yet, indeed,
If gazing on divinity disrobed
Thy mortal eyes are frail to judge of fair,
Unbiass'd by self-profit, oh! rest thee sure
That I shall love thee well and cleave to thee,
So that my vigour, wedded to thy blood,
Shall strike within thy pulses, like a God's,
To push thee forward thro' a life of shocks, 160
Dangers, and deeds, until endurance grow
Sinew'd with action, and the full-grown will,
Circled thro' all experiences, pure law,
Commeasure perfect freedom."
                            'Here she ceased,
And Paris ponder'd, and I cried, "O Paris,
Give it to Pallas!" but he heard me not,
Or hearing would not hear me, woe is me!

'O mother Ida, many-fountain'd Ida,
Dear mother Ida, harken ere I die.
Idalian Aphrodite beautiful, 170
Fresh as the foam, new-bathed in Paphian wells,
With rosy slender fingers backward drew
From her warm brows and bosom her deep hair
Ambrosial, golden round her lucid throat
And shoulder: from the violets her light foot
Shone rosy-white, and o'er her rounded form
Between the shadows of the vine-bunches
Floated the glowing sunlights, as she moved.

'Dear mother Ida, harken ere I die.
She with a subtle smile in her mild eyes, 180
The herald of her triumph, drawing nigh
Half-whisper'd in his ear, "I promise thee
The fairest and most loving wife in Greece."

She spoke and laugh'd: I shut my sight for fear:
But when I look'd, Paris had raised his arm,
And I beheld great Herè's angry eyes,
As she withdrew into the golden cloud,
And I was left alone within the bower;
And from that time to this I am alone,
And I shall be alone until I die.   190

  'Yet, mother Ida, harken ere I die.
Fairest—why fairest wife? am I not fair?
My love hath told me so a thousand times.
Methinks I must be fair, for yesterday,
When I past by, a wild and wanton pard,
Eyed like the evening star, with playful tail
Crouch'd fawning in the weed.   Most loving is she?
Ah me, my mountain shepherd, that my arms
Were wound about thee, and my hot lips prest
Close, close to thine in that quick-falling dew   200
Of fruitful kisses, thick as Autumn rains
Flash in the pools of whirling Simois.

  'O mother, hear me yet before I die.
They came, they cut away my tallest pines,
My dark tall pines, that plumed the craggy ledge
High over the blue gorge, and all between
The snowy peak and snow-white cataract
Foster'd the callow eaglet—from beneath
Whose thick mysterious boughs in the dark morn
The panther's roar came muffled, while I sat   210
Low in the valley.   Never, never more
Shall lone Œnone see the morning mist
Sweep thro' them; never see them overlaid
With narrow moon-lit slips of silver cloud,
Between the loud stream and the trembling stars.

  'O mother, hear me yet before I die.
I wish that somewhere in the ruin'd folds,
Among the fragments tumbled from the glens,
Or the dry thickets, I could meet with her,
The Abominable, that uninvited came   220
Into the fair Peleïan banquet-hall,
And cast the golden fruit upon the board,
And bred this change; that I might speak my mind,
And tell her to her face how much I hate
Her presence, hated both of Gods and men.

  'O mother, hear me yet before I die.
Hath he not sworn his love a thousand times,
In this green valley, under this green hill,
Ev'n on this hand, and sitting on this stone?
Seal'd it with kisses? water'd it with tears?   230
O happy tears, and how unlike to these!

O happy Heaven, how canst thou see my face ?
O happy earth, how canst thou bear my weight ?
O death, death, death, thou ever-floating cloud,
There are enough unhappy on this earth,
Pass by the happy souls, that love to live :
I pray thee, pass before my light of life,
And shadow all my soul, that I may die.
Thou weighest heavy on the heart within,
Weigh heavy on my eyelids : let me die.   240

' O mother, hear me yet before I die.
I will not die alone, for fiery thoughts
Do shape themselves within me, more and more,
Whereof I catch the issue, as I hear
Dead sounds at night come from the inmost hills,
Like footsteps upon wool. I dimly see
My far-off doubtful purpose, as a mother
Conjectures of the features of her child
Ere it is born : her child !—a shudder comes
Across me : never child be born of me,   250
Unblest, to vex me with his father's eyes !

' O mother, hear me yet before I die.
Hear me, O earth. I will not die alone,
Lest their shrill happy laughter come to me
Walking the cold and starless road of Death
Uncomforted, leaving my ancient love
With the Greek woman. I will rise and go
Down into Troy, and ere the stars come forth
Talk with the wild Cassandra, for she says
A fire dances before her, and a sound   260
Rings ever in her ears of armed men.
What this may be I know not, but I know
That, wheresoe'er I am by night and day,
All earth and air seem only burning fire.'

MORTE D'ARTHUR

From Idylls of the King

So all day long the noise of battle roll'd
Among the mountains by the winter sea ;
Until King Arthur's table, man by man,
Had fall'n in Lyonness about their Lord,
King Arthur : then, because his wound was deep,
The bold Sir Bedivere uplifted him,
Sir Bedivere, the last of all his knights,
And bore him to a chapel nigh the field,
A broken chancel with a broken cross,
That stood on a dark strait of barren land.   10
On one side lay the Ocean, and on one
Lay a great water, and the moon was full.

Then spake King Arthur to Sir Bedivere:
' The sequel of to-day unsolders all
The goodliest fellowship of famous knights
Whereof this world holds record.　Such a sleep
They sleep—the men I loved.　I think that we
Shall never more, at any future time,
Delight our souls with talk of knightly deeds,
Walking about the gardens and the halls　　　　　　20
Of Camelot, as in the days that were.
I perish by this people which I made,—
Tho' Merlin sware that I should come again
To rule once more—but let what will be, be,
I am so deeply smitten thro' the helm
That without help I cannot last till morn.
Thou therefore take my brand Excalibur,
Which was my pride : for thou rememberest how
In those old days, one summer noon, an arm
Rose up from out the bosom of the lake,　　　　　　30
Clothed in white samite, mystic, wonderful,
Holding the sword—and how I row'd across
And took it, and have worn it, like a king :
And, wheresoever I am sung or told
In aftertime, this also shall be known :
But now delay not : take Excalibur,
And fling him far into the middle mere :
Watch what thou seëst, and lightly bring me word.'
　To him replied the bold Sir Bedivere :
' It is not meet, Sir King, to leave thee thus,　　　　40
Aidless, alone, and smitten thro' the helm.
A little thing may harm a wounded man.
Yet I thy hest will all perform at full,
Watch what I see, and lightly bring thee word.'
　So saying, from the ruin'd shrine he stept
And in the moon athwart the place of tombs,
Where lay the mighty bones of ancient men,
Old knights, and over them the sea-wind sang
Shrill, chill, with flakes of foam.　He, stepping down
By zig-zag paths, and juts of pointed rock,　　　　　50
Came on the shining levels of the lake.
　There drew he forth the brand Excalibur,
And o'er him, drawing it, the winter moon,
Brightening the skirts of a long cloud, ran forth
And sparkled keen with frost against the hilt :
For all the haft twinkled with diamond sparks,
Myriads of topaz-lights, and jacinth-work
Of subtlest jewellery.　He gazed so long
That both his eyes were dazzled, as he stood,
This way and that dividing the swift mind,　　　　　60
In act to throw : but at the last it seem'd
Better to leave Excalibur conceal'd
There in the many-knotted waterflags,

That whistled stiff and dry about the marge.
So strode he back slow to the wounded king.
  Then spake King Arthur to Sir Bedivere:
' Hast thou perform'd my mission which I gave ?
What is it thou hast seen ? or what hast heard ?'
  And answer made the bold Sir Bedivere:
' I heard the ripple washing in the reeds,   70
And the wild water lapping on the crag.'
  To whom replied King Arthur, faint and pale:
' Thou hast betray'd thy nature and thy name,
Not rendering true answer, as beseem'd
Thy fëalty, nor like a noble knight:
For surer sign had follow'd, either hand,
Or voice, or else a motion of the mere.
This is a shameful thing for men to lie.
Yet now, I charge thee, quickly go again
As thou art lief and dear, and do the thing   80
I bad thee, watch, and lightly bring me word.'
  Then went Sir Bedivere the second time
Across the ridge, and paced beside the mere,
Counting the dewy pebbles, fix'd in thought ;
But when he saw the wonder of the hilt,
How curiously and strangely chased, he smote
His palms together, and he cried aloud.
   ' And if indeed I cast the brand away,
Surely a precious thing, one worthy note,
Should thus be lost for ever from the earth,   90
Which might have pleased the eyes of many men.
What good should follow this, if this were done ?
What harm, undone ? deep harm to disobey,
Seeing obedience is the bond of rule.
Were it well to obey then, if a king demand
An act unprofitable, against himself ?
The King is sick, and knows not what he does.
What record, or what relic of my lord
Should be to aftertime, but empty breath
And rumours of a doubt ? but were this kept,   100
Stored in some treasure-house of mighty kings,
Some one might show it at a joust of arms,
Saying, " King Arthur's sword, Excalibur,
Wrought by the lonely maiden of the Lake.
Nine years she wrought it, sitting in the deeps
Upon the hidden bases of the hills."
So might some old man speak in the aftertime
To all the people, winning reverence.
But now much honour and much fame were lost.'
  So spake he, clouded with his own conceit,   110
And hid Excalibur the second time,
And so strode back slow to the wounded King.
  Then spake King Arthur, breathing heavily:
' What is it thou hast seen ? or what hast heard ?'

And answer made the bold Sir Bedivere:
'I heard the water lapping on the crag,
And the long ripple washing in the reeds.'
　To whom replied King Arthur, much in wrath:
'Ah, miserable and unkind, untrue,
Unknightly, traitor-hearted! Woe is me!　　　　120
Authority forgets a dying king,
Laid widow'd of the power in his eye
That bow'd the will. I see thee what thou art,
For thou, the latest-left of all my knights,
In whom should meet the offices of all,
Thou wouldst betray me for the precious hilt;
Either from lust of gold, or like a girl
Valuing the giddy pleasure of the eyes.
Yet, for a man may fail in duty twice,
And the third time may prosper, get thee hence:　130
But, if thou spare to fling Excalibur,
I will arise and slay thee with my hands.'
　Then quickly rose Sir Bedivere, and ran,
And, leaping down the ridges lightly, plunged
Among the bulrush-beds, and clutch'd the sword,
And strongly wheel'd and threw it. The great brand
Made lightnings in the splendour of the moon,
And flashing round and round, and whirl'd in an arch,
Shot like a streamer of the northern morn,
Seen where the moving isles of winter shock　　140
By night, with noises of the northern sea.
So flash'd and fell the brand Excalibur:
But ere he dipt the surface, rose an arm
Clothed in white samite, mystic, wonderful,
And caught him by the hilt, and brandish'd him
Three times, and drew him under in the mere.
And lightly went the other to the King.
　Then spoke King Arthur, drawing thicker breath:
'Now see I by thine eyes that this is done.
Speak out: what is it thou hast heard, or seen?'　150
　And answer made the bold Sir Bedivere:
'Sir King, I closed mine eyelids, lest the gems
Should blind my purpose, for I never saw,
Nor shall see, here or elsewhere, till I die,
Not tho' I live three lives of mortal men,
So great a miracle as yonder hilt.
Then with both hands I flung him, wheeling him;
But when I look'd again, behold an arm,
Clothed in white samite, mystic, wonderful,
That caught him by the hilt, and brandish'd him　160
Three times, and drew him under in the mere.'
　And answer made King Arthur, breathing hard:
'My end draws nigh; 'tis time that I were gone.
Make broad thy shoulders to receive my weight,
And bear me to the margin; yet I fear

My wound hath taken cold, and I shall die.'
  So saying, from the pavement he half rose,
Slowly, with pain, reclining on his arm,
And looking wistfully with wide blue eyes
As in a picture. Him Sir Bedivere   170
Remorsefully regarded thro' his tears,
And would have spoken, but he found not words,
Then took with care, and kneeling on one knee,
O'er both his shoulders drew the languid hands,
And rising bore him thro' the place of tombs.
  But, as he walk'd, King Arthur panted hard,
Like one that feels a nightmare on his bed
When all the house is mute. So sigh'd the King,
Muttering and murmuring at his ear, 'Quick, quick !
I fear it is too late, and I shall die.'   180
But the other swiftly strode from ridge to ridge,
Clothed with his breath, and looking, as he walk'd,
Larger than human on the frozen hills.
He heard the deep behind him, and a cry
Before. His own thought drove him like a goad.
Dry clash'd his harness in the icy caves
And barren chasms, and all to left and right
The bare black cliff clang'd round him, as he based
His feet on juts of slippery crag that rang
Sharp-smitten with the dint of armed heels—   190
And on a sudden, lo ! the level lake,
And the long glories of the winter moon.
  Then saw they how there hove a dusky barge,
Dark as a funeral scarf from stem to stern,
Beneath them ; and descending they were ware
That all the decks were dense with stately forms
Black-stoled, black-hooded, like a dream—by these
Three Queens with crowns of gold—and from them rose
A cry that shiver'd to the tingling stars,
And, as it were one voice, an agony   200
Of lamentation, like a wind, that shrills
All night in a waste land, where no one comes,
Or hath come, since the making of the world.
  Then murmur'd Arthur, 'Place me in the barge,'
And to the barge they came. There those three Queens
Put forth their hands, and took the King, and wept.
But she, that rose the tallest of them all
And fairest, laid his head upon her lap,
And loosed the shatter'd casque, and chafed his hands,
And call'd him by his name, complaining loud,   210
And dropping bitter tears against his brow
Striped with dark blood : for all his face was white
And colourless, and like the wither'd moon
Smote by the fresh beam of the springing east ;
And all his greaves and cuisses dash'd with drops
Of onset ; and the light and lustrous curls—

That made his forehead like a rising sun
High from the daïs-throne—were parch'd with dust;
Or, clotted into points and hanging loose,
Mix'd with the knightly growth that fringed his lips. 220
So like a shatter'd column lay the King;
Not like that Arthur who, with lance in rest,
From spur to plume a star of tournament,
Shot thro' the lists at Camelot, and charged
Before the eyes of ladies and of kings.

  Then loudly cried the bold Sir Bedivere,
'Ah! my Lord Arthur, whither shall I go?
Where shall I hide my forehead and my eyes?
For now I see the true old times are dead,
When every morning brought a noble chance,   230
And every chance brought out a noble knight.
Such times have been not since the light that led
The holy Elders with the gift of myrrh.
But now the whole ROUND TABLE is dissolved
Which was an image of the mighty world;
And I, the last, go forth companionless,
And the days darken round me, and the years,
Among new men, strange faces, other minds.'

  And slowly answer'd Arthur from the barge:
'The old order changeth, yielding place to new,   240
And God fulfils Himself in many ways,
Lest one good custom should corrupt the world.
Comfort thyself: what comfort is in me?
I have lived my life, and that which I have done
May He within Himself make pure! but thou,
If thou shouldst never see my face again,
Pray for my soul. More things are wrought by prayer
Than this world dreams of. Wherefore, let thy voice
Rise like a fountain for me night and day.
For what are men better than sheep or goats   250
That nourish a blind life within the brain,
If, knowing God, they lift not hands of prayer
Both for themselves and those who call them friend?
For so the whole round earth is every way
Bound by gold chains about the feet of God.
But now farewell. I am going a long way
With these thou seëst—if indeed I go—
(For all my mind is clouded with a doubt)
To the island-valley of Avilion;
Where falls not hail, or rain, or any snow,   260
Nor ever wind blows loudly; but it lies
Deep-meadow'd, happy, fair with orchard-lawns
And bowery hollows crown'd with summer sea,
Where I will heal me of my grievous wound.'

  So said he, and the barge with oar and sail
Moved from the brink, like some full-breasted swan
That, fluting a wild carol ere her death,

Ruffles her pure cold plume, and takes the flood
With swarthy webs. Long stood Sir Bedivere
Revolving many memories, till the hull   270
Look'd one black dot against the verge of dawn,
And on the mere the wailing died away.

IN MEMORIAM A. H. H.

OBIIT MDCCCXXXIII

STRONG Son of God, immortal Love,
    Whom we, that have not seen thy face,
    By faith, and faith alone, embrace,
Believing where we cannot prove ;

Thine are these orbs of light and shade ;
    Thou madest Life in man and brute ;
    Thou madest Death ; and lo, thy foot
Is on the skull which thou hast made.

Thou wilt not leave us in the dust:
    Thou madest man, he knows not why ;   10
    He thinks he was not made to die ;
And thou hast made him : thou art just.

Thou seemest human and divine,
    The highest, holiest manhood, thou :
    Our wills are ours, we know not how ;
Our wills are ours, to make them thine.

Our little systems have their day ;
    They have their day and cease to be :
    They are but broken lights of thee,
And thou, O Lord, art more than they.   20

We have but faith : we cannot know ;
    For knowledge is of things we see ;
    And yet we trust it comes from thee,
A beam in darkness : let it grow.

Let knowledge grow from more to more,
    But more of reverence in us dwell ;
    That mind and soul, according well,
May make one music as before,

But vaster. We are fools and slight ;
    We mock thee when we do not fear :   30
    But help thy foolish ones to bear ;
Help thy vain worlds to bear thy light.

Forgive what seem'd my sin in me ;
    What seem'd my worth since I began ;
    For merit lives from man to man,
And not from man, O Lord, to thee.

Forgive my grief for one removed,
 Thy creature, whom I found so fair.
 I trust he lives in thee, and there
I find him worthier to be loved.   40

Forgive these wild and wandering cries,
 Confusions of a wasted youth ;
 Forgive them where they fail in truth,
And in thy wisdom make me wise.
 1849.

I

I HELD it truth, with him who sings
 To one clear harp in divers tones,
 That men may rise on stepping-stones
Of their dead selves to higher things.

But who shall so forecast the years
 And find in loss a gain to match ?
 Or reach a hand thro' time to catch
The far-off interest of tears ?

Let Love clasp Grief lest both be drown'd,
 Let darkness keep her raven gloss :   10
 Ah, sweeter to be drunk with loss,
To dance with death, to beat the ground,

Than that the victor Hours should scorn
 The long result of love, and boast,
 ' Behold the man that loved and lost,
But all he was is overworn.'

II

Old Yew, which graspest at the stones
 That name the under-lying dead,
 Thy fibres net the dreamless head,
Thy roots are wrapt about the bones.   20

The seasons bring the flower again,
 And bring the firstling to the flock ;
 And in the dusk of thee, the clock
Beats out the little lives of men.

O not for thee the glow, the bloom,
 Who changest not in any gale,
 Nor branding summer suns avail
To touch thy thousand years of gloom :

And gazing on thee, sullen tree,
 Sick for thy stubborn hardihood,   30
 I seem to fail from out my blood
And grow incorporate into thee.

III

O Sorrow, cruel fellowship,
    O Priestess in the vaults of Death,
    O sweet and bitter in a breath,
What whispers from thy lying lip ?

' The stars,' she whispers, ' blindly run ;
    A web is wov'n across the sky ;
    From out waste places comes a cry,
And murmurs from the dying sun :   40

' And all the phantom, Nature, stands—
    With all the music in her tone,
    A hollow echo of my own,—
A hollow form with empty hands.'

And shall I take a thing so blind,
    Embrace her as my natural good ;
    Or crush her, like a vice of blood,
Upon the threshold of the mind ?

IV

To Sleep I give my powers away ;
    My will is bondsman to the dark ;   50
    I sit within a helmless bark,
And with my heart I muse and say :

O heart, how fares it with thee now,
    That thou shouldst fail from thy desire,
    Who scarcely darest to inquire,
'What is it makes me beat so low ? '

Something it is which thou hast lost,
    Some pleasure from thine early years.
    Break, thou deep vase of chilling tears,
That grief hath shaken into frost !   60

Such clouds of nameless trouble cross
    All night below the darken'd eyes ;
    With morning wakes the will, and cries,
' Thou shalt not be the fool of loss.'

V

I sometimes hold it half a sin
    To put in words the grief I feel ;
    For words, like Nature, half reveal
And half conceal the Soul within.

But, for the unquiet heart and brain,
    A use in measured language lies ;   70
    The sad mechanic exercise,
Like dull narcotics, numbing pain.

In words, like weeds, I'll wrap me o'er,
    Like coarsest clothes against the cold ;
    But that large grief which these enfold
Is given in outline and no more.

VI

One writes, that ' Other friends remain,'
    That ' Loss is common to the race '—
    And common is the commonplace,
And vacant chaff well meant for grain.   80

That loss is common would not make
    My own less bitter, rather more :
    Too common ! Never morning wore
To evening, but some heart did break.

O father, wheresoe'er thou be,
    Who pledgest now thy gallant son ;
    A shot, ere half thy draught be done,
Hath still'd the life that beat from thee.

O mother, praying God will save
    Thy sailor,—while thy head is bow'd,   90
    His heavy-shotted hammock-shroud
Drops in his vast and wandering grave.

Ye know no more than I who wrought
    At that last hour to please him well ;
    Who mused on all I had to tell,
And something written, something thought

Expecting still his advent home ;
    And ever met him on his way
    With wishes, thinking, ' here to-day,'
Or ' here to-morrow will he come.'   100

O somewhere, meek unconscious dove,
    That sittest ranging golden hair ;
    And glad to find thyself so fair,
Poor child, that waitest for thy love !

For now her father's chimney glows
    In expectation of a guest ;
    And thinking ' this will please him best,'
She takes a riband or a rose ;

For he will see them on to-night ;
    And with the thought her colour burns ;   110
    And, having left the glass, she turns
Once more to set a ringlet right ;

And, even when she turn'd, the curse
    Had fallen, and her future Lord
    Was drown'd in passing thro' the ford,
Or kill'd in falling from his horse.

O what to her shall be the end ?
    And what to me remains of good ?
    To her, perpetual maidenhood,
And unto me no second friend.   120

VII

Dark house, by which once more I stand
    Here in the long unlovely street,
    Doors, where my heart was used to beat
So quickly, waiting for a hand,

A hand that can be clasp'd no more—
    Behold me, for I cannot sleep,
    And like a guilty thing I creep
At earliest morning to the door.

He is not here ; but far away
    The noise of life begins again,   130
    And ghastly thro' the drizzling rain
On the bald street breaks the blank day.

VIII

A happy lover who has come
    To look on her that loves him well,
    Who 'lights and rings the gateway bell,
And learns her gone and far from home ;

He saddens, all the magic light
    Dies off at once from bower and hall,
    And all the place is dark, and all
The chambers emptied of delight :   140

So find I every pleasant spot
    In which we two were wont to meet,
    The field, the chamber and the street,
For all is dark where thou art not.

Yet as that other, wandering there
    In those deserted walks, may find
    A flower beat with rain and wind,
Which once she foster'd up with care ;

So seems it in my deep regret,
    O my forsaken heart, with thee   150
    And this poor flower of poesy
Which little cared for fades not yet.

But since it pleased a vanish'd eye,
    I go to plant it on his tomb,
    That if it can it there may bloom,
Or dying, there at least may die.

IX

Fair ship, that from the Italian shore
    Sailest the placid ocean-plains
    With my lost Arthur's loved remains,
Spread thy full wings, and waft him o'er.   160

So draw him home to those that mourn
    In vain; a favourable speed
    Ruffle thy mirror'd mast, and lead
Thro' prosperous floods his holy urn.

All night no ruder air perplex
    Thy sliding keel, till Phosphor, bright
    As our pure love, thro' early light
Shall glimmer on the dewy decks.

Sphere all your lights around, above;
    Sleep, gentle heavens, before the prow;   170
    Sleep, gentle winds, as he sleeps now,
My friend, the brother of my love;

My Arthur, whom I shall not see
    Till all my widow'd race be run;
    Dear as the mother to the son,
More than my brothers are to me.

X

I hear the noise about thy keel;
    I hear the bell struck in the night;
    I see the cabin-window bright;
I see the sailor at the wheel.   180

Thou bring'st the sailor to his wife,
    And travell'd men from foreign lands;
    And letters unto trembling hands;
And, thy dark freight, a vanish'd life.

So bring him: we have idle dreams:
    This look of quiet flatters thus
    Our home-bred fancies: O to us,
The fools of habit, sweeter seems

To rest beneath the clover sod,
    That takes the sunshine and the rains,   190
    Or where the kneeling hamlet drains
The chalice of the grapes of God;

Than if with thee the roaring wells
    Should gulf him fathom-deep in brine;
    And hands so often clasp'd in mine,
Should toss with tangle and with shells.

XI

Calm is the morn without a sound,
　　Calm as to suit a calmer grief,
　　And only thro' the faded leaf
The chestnut pattering to the ground :　　　200

Calm and deep peace on this high wold,
　　And on these dews that drench the furze,
　　And all the silvery gossamers
That twinkle into green and gold :

Calm and still light on yon great plain
　　That sweeps with all its autumn bowers,
　　And crowded farms and lessening towers,
To mingle with the bounding main :

Calm and deep peace in this wide air,
　　These leaves that redden to the fall ;　　　210
　　And in my heart, if calm at all,
If any calm, a calm despair :

Calm on the seas, and silver sleep,
　　And waves that sway themselves in rest,
　　And dead calm in that noble breast
Which heaves but with the heaving deep.

XII

Lo, as a dove when up she springs
　　To bear thro' Heaven a tale of woe,
　　Some dolorous message knit below
The wild pulsation of her wings ;　　　220

Like her I go ; I cannot stay ;
　　I leave this mortal ark behind,
　　A weight of nerves without a mind,
And leave the cliffs, and haste away

O'er ocean-mirrors rounded large,
　　And reach the glow of southern skies,
　　And see the sails at distance rise,
And linger weeping on the marge,

And saying : ' Comes he thus, my friend ?
　　Is this the end of all my care ? '　　　230
　　And circle moaning in the air :
　Is this the end ?　Is this the end ? '

And forward dart again, and play
　　About the prow, and back return
　　To where the body sits, and learn,
That I have been an hour away.

XIII

Tears of the widower, when he sees
    A late-lost form that sleep reveals,
    And moves his doubtful arms, and feels
Her place is empty, fall like these;   240

Which weep a loss for ever new,
    A void where heart on heart reposed;
    And, where warm hands have prest and closed,
Silence, till I be silent too.

Which weep the comrade of my choice,
    An awful thought, a life removed,
    The human-hearted man I loved,
A Spirit, not a breathing voice.

Come Time, and teach me, many years,
    I do not suffer in a dream;   250
    For now so strange do these things seem,
Mine eyes have leisure for their tears;

My fancies time to rise on wing,
    And glance about the approaching sails,
    As tho' they brought but merchants' bales,
And not the burthen that they bring.

XIV

If one should bring me this report,
    That thou hadst touch'd the land to-day,
    And I went down unto the quay,
And found thee lying in the port;   260

And standing, muffled round with woe,
    Should see thy passengers in rank
    Come stepping lightly down the plank,
And beckoning unto those they know;

And if along with these should come
    The man I held as half-divine;
    Should strike a sudden hand in mine,
And ask a thousand things of home;

And I should tell him all my pain,
    And how my life had droop'd of late,   270
    And he should sorrow o'er my state
And marvel what possess'd my brain;

And I perceived no touch of change,
    No hint of death in all his frame,
    But found him all in all the same,
I should not feel it to be strange.

XV

To-night the winds begin to rise
    And roar from yonder dropping day :
    The last red leaf is whirl'd away,
The rooks are blown about the skies ;   280

The forest crack'd, the waters curl'd,
    The cattle huddled on the lea ;
    And wildly dash'd on tower and tree
The sunbeam strikes along the world :

And but for fancies, which aver
    That all thy motions gently pass
    Athwart a plane of molten glass,
I scarce could brook the strain and stir

That makes the barren branches loud ;
    And but for fear it is not so,   290
    The wild unrest that lives in woe
Would dote and pore on yonder cloud

That rises upward always higher,
    And onward drags a labouring breast,
    And topples round the dreary west,
A looming bastion fringed with fire.

XVI

What words are these have fall'n from me ?
    Can calm despair and wild unrest
    Be tenants of a single breast,
Or sorrow such a changeling be ?   300

Or doth she only seem to take
    The touch of change in calm or storm ;
    But knows no more of transient form
In her deep self, than some dead lake

That holds the shadow of a lark
    Hung in the shadow of a heaven ?
    Or has the shock, so harshly given,
Confused me like the unhappy bark

That strikes by night a craggy shelf,
    And staggers blindly ere she sink ?   310
    And stunn'd me from my power to think
And all my knowledge of myself ;

And made me that delirious man
    Whose fancy fuses old and new,
    And flashes into false and true,
And mingles all without a plan ?

XVII

Thou comest, much wept for : such a breeze
    Compell'd thy canvas, and my prayer
    Was as the whisper of an air
To breathe thee over lonely seas.   320

For I in spirit saw thee move
    Thro' circles of the bounding sky,
    Week after week : the days go by :
Come quick, thou bringest all I love.

Henceforth, wherever thou may'st roam,
    My blessing, like a line of light,
    Is on the waters day and night,
And like a beacon guards thee home.

So may whatever tempest mars
    Mid-ocean, spare thee, sacred bark ;   330
    And balmy drops in summer dark
Slide from the bosom of the stars.

So kind an office hath been done,
    Such precious relics brought by thee ;
    The dust of him I shall not see
Till all my widow'd race be run.

XVIII

'Tis well ; 'tis something ; we may stand
    Where he in English earth is laid,
    And from his ashes may be made
The violet of his native land.   340

'Tis little ; but it looks in truth
    As if the quiet bones were blest
    Among familiar names to rest
And in the places of his youth.

Come then, pure hands, and bear the head
    That sleeps or wears the mask of sleep,
    And come, whatever loves to weep,
And hear the ritual of the dead.

Ah yet, ev'n yet, if this might be,
    I, falling on his faithful heart,   350
    Would breathing thro' his lips impart
The life that almost dies in me ;

That dies not, but endures with pain,
    And slowly forms the firmer mind,
    Treasuring the look it cannot find,
The words that are not heard again.

XIX

The Danube to the Severn gave
 The darken'd heart that beat no more ;
 They laid him by the pleasant shore,
And in the hearing of the wave.   360

There twice a day the Severn fills ;
 The salt sea-water passes by,
 And hushes half the babbling Wye,
And makes a silence in the hills.

The Wye is hush'd nor moved along,
 And hush'd my deepest grief of all,
 When fill'd with tears that cannot fall,
I brim with sorrow drowning song.

The tide flows down, the wave again
 Is vocal in its wooded walls ;   370
 My deeper anguish also falls,
And I can speak a little then.

XX

The lesser griefs that may be said,
 That breathe a thousand tender vows,
 Are but as servants in a house
Where lies the master newly dead ;

Who speak their feeling as it is,
 And weep the fullness from the mind :
 ' It will be hard,' they say, ' to find
Another service such as this.'   380

My lighter moods are like to these,
 That out of words a comfort win ;
 But there are other griefs within,
And tears that at their fountain freeze ;

For by the hearth the children sit
 Cold in that atmosphere of Death,
 And scarce endure to draw the breath,
Or like to noiseless phantoms flit :

But open converse is there none,
 So much the vital spirits sink   390
 To see the vacant chair, and think,
' How good ! how kind ! and he is gone.'

XXI

I sing to him that rests below,
 And, since the grasses round me wave,
 I take the grasses of the grave,
And make them pipes whereon to blow.

The traveller hears me now and then,
    And sometimes harshly will he speak :
    'This fellow would make weakness weak,
And melt the waxen hearts of men.'   400

Another answers, ' Let him be,
    He loves to make parade of pain,
    That with his piping he may gain
The praise that comes to constancy.'

A third is wroth, ' Is this an hour
    For private sorrow's barren song,
    When more and more the people throng
The chairs and thrones of civil power ?

' A time to sicken and to swoon,
    When Science reaches forth her arms   410
    To feel from world to world, and charms
Her secret from the latest moon ? '

Behold, ye speak an idle thing :
    Ye never knew the sacred dust :
    I do but sing because I must,
And pipe but as the linnets sing :

And one is glad ; her note is gay,
    For now her little ones have ranged ;
    And one is sad ; her note is changed,
Because her brood is stol'n away.   420

XXII

The path by which we twain did go,
    Which led by tracts that pleased us well,
    Thro' four sweet years arose and fell,
From flower to flower, from snow to snow :

And we with singing cheer'd the way,
    And crown'd with all the season lent,
    From April on to April went,
And glad at heart from May to May :

But where the path we walk'd began
    To slant the fifth autumnal slope,   430
    As we descended following Hope,
There sat the Shadow fear'd of man :

Who broke our fair companionship,
    And spread his mantle dark and cold,
    And wrapt thee formless in the fold,
And dull'd the murmur on thy lip,

And bore thee where I could not see
    Nor follow, tho' I walk in haste,
    And think, that somewhere in the waste
The Shadow sits and waits for me.   440

XXIII

Now, sometimes in my sorrow shut,
 Or breaking into song by fits,
 Alone, alone, to where he sits,
The Shadow cloak'd from head to foot,

Who keeps the keys of all the creeds,
 I wander, often falling lame,
 And looking back to whence I came,
Or on to where the pathway leads;

And crying, 'How changed from where it ran
 Thro' lands where not a leaf was dumb; 450
 But all the lavish hills would hum
The murmur of a happy Pan:

'When each by turns was guide to each,
 And Fancy light from Fancy caught,
 And Thought leapt out to wed with Thought,
Ere Thought could wed itself with Speech;

'And all we met was fair and good,
 And all was good that Time could bring,
 And all the secret of the Spring
Moved in the chambers of the blood; 460

'And many an old philosophy
 On Argive heights divinely sang,
 And round us all the thicket rang
To many a flute of Arcady.'

XXIV

And was the day of my delight
 As pure and perfect as I say?
 The very source and fount of Day
Is dash'd with wandering isles of night.

If all was good and fair we met,
 This earth had been the Paradise 470
 It never look'd to human eyes
Since Adam left his garden yet.

And is it that the haze of grief
 Makes former gladness loom so great?
 The lowness of the present state,
That sets the past in this relief?

Or that the past will always win
 A glory from its being far;
 And orb into the perfect star
We saw not, when we moved therein? 480

XXV

I know that this was Life,—the track
 Whereon with equal feet we fared ;
 And then, as now, the day prepared
The daily burden for the back.

But this it was that made me move
 As light as carrier-birds in air ;
 I loved the weight I had to bear,
Because it needed help of Love :

Nor could I weary, heart or limb,
 When mighty Love would cleave in twain   490
 The lading of a single pain,
And part it, giving half to him.

XXVI

Still onward winds the dreary way ;
 I with it ; for I long to prove
 No lapse of moons can canker Love,
Whatever fickle tongues may say.

And if that eye which watches guilt
 And goodness, and hath power to see
 Within the green the moulder'd tree,
And towers fall'n as soon as built—   500

Oh, if indeed that eye foresee
 Or see (in Him is no before)
 In more of life true life no more,
And Love the indifference to be,

Then might I find, ere yet the morn
 Breaks hither over Indian seas,
 That Shadow waiting with the keys,
To shroud me from my proper scorn.

XXVII

I envy not in any moods
 The captive void of noble rage,   510
 The linnet born within the cage,
That never knew the summer woods :

I envy not the beast that takes
 His licence in the field of time,
 Unfetter'd by the sense of crime,
To whom a conscience never wakes ;

Nor, what may count itself as blest,
 The heart that never plighted troth
 But stagnates in the weeds of sloth ;
Nor any want-begotten rest.   520

I hold it true, whate'er befall ;
  I feel it, when I sorrow most ;
  'Tis better to have loved and lost
Than never to have loved at all.

XXVIII

The time draws near the birth of Christ :
  The moon is hid ; the night is still ;
  The Christmas bells from hill to hill
Answer each other in the mist.

Four voices of four hamlets round,
  From far and near, on mead and moor,   530
  Swell out and fail, as if a door
Were shut between me and the sound :

Each voice four changes on the wind,
  That now dilate, and now decrease,
  Peace and goodwill, goodwill and peace,
Peace and goodwill, to all mankind.

This year I slept and woke with pain,
  I almost wish'd no more to wake,
  And that my hold on life would break
Before I heard those bells again :   540

But they my troubled spirit rule,
  For they controll'd me when a boy ;
  They bring me sorrow touch'd with joy,
The merry merry bells of Yule.

XXIX

With such compelling cause to grieve
  As daily vexes household peace,
  And chains regret to his decease,
How dare we keep our Christmas-eve ;

Which brings no more a welcome guest
  To enrich the threshold of the night   550
  With shower'd largess of delight,
In dance and song and game and jest ?

Yet go, and while the holly boughs
  Entwine the cold baptismal font,
  Make one wreath more for Use and Wont,
That guard the portals of the house ;

Old sisters of a day gone by,
  Grey nurses, loving nothing new ;
  Why should they miss their yearly due
Before their time ? They too will die.   560

XXX

With trembling fingers did we weave
    The holly round the Christmas hearth ;
    A rainy cloud possess'd the earth,
And sadly fell our Christmas-eve.

At our old pastimes in the hall
    We gambol'd, making vain pretence
    Of gladness, with an awful sense
Of one mute Shadow watching all.

We paused : the winds were in the beech :
    We heard them sweep the winter land ;   570
    And in a circle hand-in-hand
Sat silent, looking each at each.

Then echo-like our voices rang ;
    We sung, tho' every eye was dim,
    A merry song we sang with him
Last year : impetuously we sang :

We ceased : a gentler feeling crept
    Upon us : surely rest is meet :
    'They rest,' we said, 'their sleep is sweet,'
And silence follow'd, and we wept.   580

Our voices took a higher range ;
    Once more we sang : 'They do not die
    Nor lose their mortal sympathy,
Nor change to us, although they change ;

'Rapt from the fickle and the frail
    With gather'd power, yet the same,
    Pierces the keen seraphic flame
From orb to orb, from veil to veil.'

Rise, happy morn, rise, holy morn,
    Draw forth the cheerful day from night :   590
    O Father, touch the east, and light
The light that shone when Hope was born.

XXXI

When Lazarus left his charnel-cave,
    And home to Mary's house return'd,
    Was this demanded—if he yearn'd
To hear her weeping by his grave ?

'Where wert thou, brother, those four days ? '
    There lives no record of reply,
    Which telling what it is to die
Had surely added praise to praise.   600

From every house the neighbours met,
   The streets were fill'd with joyful sound,
   A solemn gladness even crown'd
The purple brows of Olivet.

Behold a man raised up by Christ !
   The rest remaineth unreveal'd ;
   He told it not ; or something seal'd
The lips of that Evangelist.

XXXII

Her eyes are homes of silent prayer,
   Nor other thought her mind admits
   But, he was dead, and there he sits,
And he that brought him back is there.

Then one deep love doth supersede
   All other, when her ardent gaze
   Roves from the living brother's face,
And rests upon the Life indeed.

All subtle thought, all curious fears,
   Borne down by gladness so complete,
   She bows, she bathes the Saviour's feet
With costly spikenard and with tears.

Thrice blest whose lives are faithful prayers,
   Whose loves in higher love endure ;
   What souls possess themselves so pure,
Or is there blessedness like theirs ?

XXXIII

O thou that after toil and storm
   Mayst seem to have reach'd a purer air,
   Whose faith has centre everywhere,
Nor cares to fix itself to form,

Leave thou thy sister when she prays,
   Her early Heaven, her happy views ;
   Nor thou with shadow'd hint confuse
A life that leads melodious days.

Her faith thro' form is pure as thine,
   Her hands are quicker unto good :
   Oh, sacred be the flesh and blood
To which she links a truth divine !

See thou, that countest reason ripe
   In holding by the law within,
   Thou fail not in a world of sin,
And ev'n for want of such a type.

XXXIV

My own dim life should teach me this,
    That life shall live for evermore,
    Else earth is darkness at the core,
And dust and ashes all that is;

This round of green, this orb of flame,
    Fantastic beauty; such as lurks
    In some wild Poet, when he works
Without a conscience or an aim.

What then were God to such as I?
    'Twere hardly worth my while to choose   650
    Of things all mortal, or to use
A little patience ere I die;

'Twere best at once to sink to peace,
    Like birds the charming serpent draws,
    To drop head-foremost in the jaws
Of vacant darkness and to cease.

XXXV

Yet if some voice that man could trust
    Should murmur from the narrow house,
    'The cheeks drop in; the body bows;
Man dies: nor is there hope in dust:'   660

Might I not say: 'Yet even here,
    But for one hour, O Love, I strive
    To keep so sweet a thing alive'?
But I should turn mine ears and hear

The moanings of the homeless sea,
    The sound of streams that swift or slow
    Draw down Aeonian hills, and sow
The dust of continents to be;

And Love would answer with a sigh,
    '.The sound of that forgetful shore   670
    Will change my sweetness more and more,
Half-dead to know that I shall die.'

O me, what profits it to put
    An idle case? If Death were seen
    At first as Death, Love had not been,
Or been in narrowest working shut,

Mere fellowship of sluggish moods,
    Or in his coarsest Satyr-shape
    Had bruised the herb and crush'd the grape,
And bask'd and batten'd in the woods.   680

XXXVI

Tho' truths in manhood darkly join,
    Deep-seated in our mystic frame,
    We yield all blessing to the name
Of Him that made them current coin ;

For Wisdom dealt with mortal powers,
    Where truth in closest words shall fail,
    When truth embodied in a tale
Shall enter in at lowly doors.

And so the Word had breath, and wrought
    With human hands the creed of creeds   690
    In loveliness of perfect deeds,
More strong than all poetic thought ;

Which he may read that binds the sheaf,
    Or builds the house, or digs the grave,
    And those wild eyes that watch the wave
In roarings round the coral reef.

XXXVII

Urania speaks with darken'd brow :
    ' Thou pratest here where thou art least ;
    This faith has many a purer priest,
And many an abler voice than thou.   700

' Go down beside thy native rill,
    On thy Parnassus set thy feet,
    And hear thy laurel whisper sweet
About the ledges of the hill.'

And my Melpomene replies,
    A touch of shame upon her cheek :
    ' I am not worthy ev'n to speak
Of thy prevailing mysteries ;

' For I am but an earthly Muse,
    And owning but a little art   710
    To lull with song an aching heart,
And render human love his dues ;

' But brooding on the dear one dead,
    And all he said of things divine,
    (And dear to me as sacred wine
To dying lips is all he said),

' I murmur'd, as I came along,
    Of comfort clasp'd in truth reveal'd ;
    And loiter'd in the master's field,
And darken'd sanctities with song.'   720

XXXVIII

With weary steps I loiter on,
 Tho' always under alter'd skies
 The purple from the distance dies,
My prospect and horizon gone.

No joy the blowing season gives,
 The herald melodies of spring,
 But in the songs I love to sing
A doubtful gleam of solace lives.

If any care for what is here
 Survive in spirits render'd free,   730
 Then are these songs I sing of thee
Not all ungrateful to thine ear.

XXXIX

Could we forget the widow'd hour
 And look on Spirits breathed away,
 As on a maiden in the day
When first she wears her orange-flower!

When crown'd with blessing she doth rise
 To take her latest leave of home,
 And hopes and light regrets that come
Make April of her tender eyes;   740

And doubtful joys the father move,
 And tears are on the mother's face,
 As parting with a long embrace
She enters other realms of love;

Her office there to rear, to teach,
 Becoming as is meet and fit
 A link among the days, to knit
The generations each with each;

And, doubtless, unto thee is given
 A life that bears immortal fruit   750
 In such great offices as suit
The full-grown energies of heaven.

Ay me, the difference I discern!
 How often shall her old fireside
 Be cheer'd with tidings of the bride,
How often she herself return,

And tell them all they would have told,
 And bring her babe, and make her boast,
 Till even those that miss'd her most,
Shall count new things as dear as old: 760

But thou and I have shaken hands,
 Till growing winters lay me low;
 My paths are in the fields I know,
And thine in undiscover'd lands.

XL

Thy spirit ere our fatal loss
  Did ever rise from high to higher ;
  As mounts the heavenward altar-fire,
As flies the lighter thro' the gross.

But thou art turn'd to something strange,
  And I have lost the links that bound   770
  Thy changes ; here upon the ground,
No more partaker of thy change.

Deep folly ! yet that this could be—
  That I could wing my will with might
  To leap the grades of life and light,
And flash at once, my friend, to thee :

For tho' my nature rarely yields
  To that vague fear implied in death ;
  Nor shudders at the gulfs beneath,
The howlings from forgotten fields ;   780

Yet oft when sundown skirts the moor
  An inner trouble I behold,
  A spectral doubt which makes me cold,
That I shall be thy mate no more,

Tho' following with an upward mind
  The wonders that have come to thee,
  Thro' all the secular to-be,
But evermore a life behind.

XLI

I vex my heart with fancies dim :
  He still outstript me in the race ;   790
  It was but unity of place
That made me dream I rank'd with him.

And so may Place retain us still,
  And he the much-beloved again,
  A lord of large experience, train
To riper growth the mind and will :

And what delights can equal those
  That stir the spirit's inner deeps,
  When one that loves but knows not, reaps
A truth from one that loves and knows ?   800

XLII

If Sleep and Death be truly one,
  And every spirit's folded bloom
  Thro' all its intervital gloom
In some long trance should slumber on ;

Unconscious of the sliding hour,
    Bare of the body, might it last,
    And silent traces of the past
Be all the colour of the flower:

So then were nothing lost to man;
    So that still garden of the souls   810
    In many a figured leaf enrolls
The total world since life began;

And love will last as pure and whole
    As when he loved me here in Time,
    And at the spiritual prime
Rewaken with the dawning soul.

XLIII

How fares it with the happy dead?
    For here the man is more and more:
    But he forgets the days before
God shut the doorways of his head.   820

The days have vanish'd, tone and tint,
    And yet perhaps the hoarding sense
    Gives out at times (he knows not whence)
A little flash, a mystic hint;

And in the long harmonious years
    (If Death so taste Lethean springs)
    May some dim touch of earthly things
Surprise thee ranging with thy peers.

If such a dreamy touch should fall,
    O turn thee round, resolve the doubt;   830
    My guardian angel will speak out
In that high place, and tell thee all.

XLIV

The baby new to earth and sky,
    What time his tender palm is prest
    Against the circle of the breast,
Has never thought that ' this is I: '

But as he grows he gathers much,
    And learns the use of ' I,' and ' me,'
    And finds ' I am not what I see,
And other than the things I touch.'   840

So rounds he to a separate mind
    From whence clear memory may begin,
    As thro' the frame that binds him in
His isolation grows defined.

This use may lie in blood and breath,
    Which else were fruitless of their due,
    Had man to learn himself anew
Beyond the second birth of Death.

XLV

We ranging down this lower track,
    The path we came by, thorn and flower,   850
    Is shadow'd by the growing hour,
Lest life should fail in looking back.

So be it: there no shade can last
    In that deep dawn behind the tomb,
    But clear from marge to marge shall bloom
The eternal landscape of the past;

A lifelong tract of time reveal'd;
    The fruitful hours of still increase;
    Days order'd in a wealthy peace,
And those five years its richest field.   830

O Love, thy province were not large,
    A bounded field, nor stretching far;
    Look also, Love, a brooding star,
A rosy warmth from marge to marge.

XLVI

That each, who seems a separate whole,
    Should move his rounds, and fusing all
    The skirts of self again, should fall
Remerging in the general Soul,

Is faith as vague as all unsweet:
    Eternal form shall still divide   870
    The eternal soul from all beside;
And I shall know him when we meet:

And we shall sit at endless feast,
    Enjoying each the other's good:
    What vaster dream can hit the mood
Of Love on earth? He seeks at least

Upon the last and sharpest height,
    Before the spirits fade away,
    Some landing-place, to clasp and say,
'Farewell! We lose ourselves in light.'   880

XLVII

If these brief lays, of Sorrow born,
    Were taken to be such as closed
    Grave doubts and answers here proposed,
Then these were such as men might scorn:

Her care is not to part and prove;
    She takes, when harsher moods remit,
    What slender shade of doubt may flit,
And makes it vassal unto love:

And hence, indeed, she sports with words,
    But better serves a wholesome law,   890
    And holds it sin and shame to draw
The deepest measure from the chords :

Nor dare she trust a larger lay,
    But rather loosens from the lip
    Short swallow-flights of song, that dip
Their wings in tears, and skim away.

XLVIII

From art, from nature, from the schools,
    Let random influences glance,
    Like light in many a shiver'd lance
That breaks about the dappled pools :   900

The lightest wave of thought shall lisp,
    The fancy's tenderest eddy wreathe,
    The slightest air of song shall breathe
To make the sullen surface crisp.

And look thy look, and go thy way,
    But blame not thou the winds that make
    The seeming-wanton ripple break,
The tender-pencil'd shadow play.

Beneath all fancied hopes and fears
    Ay me, the sorrow deepens down,   910
    Whose muffled motions blindly drown
The bases of my life in tears.

XLIX

Be near me when my light is low,
    When the blood creeps, and the nerves prick
    And tingle ; and the heart is sick,
And all the wheels of Being slow.

Be near me when the sensuous frame
    Is rack'd with pangs that conquer trust ;
    And Time, a maniac scattering dust,
And Life, a Fury slinging flame.   920

Be near me when my faith is dry,
    And men the flies of latter spring,
    That lay their eggs, and sting and sing,
And weave their petty cells and die.

Be near me when I fade away,
    To point the term of human strife,
    And on the low dark verge of life
The twilight of eternal day.

L

Do we indeed desire the dead
 Should still be near us at our side ?
 Is there no baseness we would hide ?
No inner vileness that we dread ?

Shall he for whose applause I strove,
 I had such reverence for his blame,
 See with clear eye some hidden shame
And I be lessen'd in his love ?

I wrong the grave with fears untrue :
 Shall love be blamed for want of faith ?
 There must be wisdom with great Death :
The dead shall look me thro' and thro'.

Be near us when we climb or fall :
 Ye watch, like God, the rolling hours
 With larger other eyes than ours,
To make allowance for us all.

LI

I cannot love thee as I ought,
 For love reflects the thing beloved ;
 My words are only words, and moved
Upon the topmost froth of thought.

' Yet blame not thou thy plaintive song,'
 The Spirit of true love replied ;
 ' Thou canst not move me from thy side,
Nor human frailty do me wrong.

' What keeps a spirit wholly true
 To that ideal which he bears ?
 What record ? not the sinless years
That breathed beneath the Syrian blue :

' So fret not, like an idle girl,
 That life is dash'd with flecks of sin.
 Abide : thy wealth is gather'd in,
When Time hath sunder'd shell from pearl.'

LII

How many a father have I seen,
 A sober man, among his boys,
 Whose youth was full of foolish noise,
Who wears his manhood hale and green :

And dare we to this fancy give,
 That had the wild oat not been sown,
 The soil, left barren, scarce had grown
The grain by which a man may live ?

Or, if we held the doctrine sound
    For life outliving heats of youth,   970
    Yet who would preach it as a truth
To those that eddy round and round ?

Hold thou the good : define it well :
    For fear divine Philosophy
    Should push beyond her mark, and be
Procuress to the Lords of Hell.

LIII

Oh yet we trust that somehow good
    Will be the final goal of ill,
    To pangs of nature, sins of will,
Defects of doubt, and taints of blood ;   980

That nothing walks with aimless feet ;
    That not one life shall be destroy'd,
    Or cast as rubbish to the void,
When God hath made the pile complete ;

That not a worm is cloven in vain ;
    That not a moth with vain desire
    Is shrivel'd in a fruitless fire,
Or but subserves another's gain.

Behold, we know not anything ;
    I can but trust that good shall fall   990
    At last—far off—at last, to all,
And every winter change to spring.

So runs my dream : but what am I ?
    An infant crying in the night :
    An infant crying for the light :
And with no language but a cry.

LIV

The wish, that of the living whole
    No life may fail beyond the grave,
    Derives it not from what we have
The likest God within the soul ?   1000

Are God and Nature then at strife,
    That Nature lends such evil dreams ?
    So careful of the type she seems,
So careless of the single life ;

That I, considering everywhere
    Her secret meaning in her deeds,
    And finding that of fifty seeds
She often brings but one to bear,

I falter where I firmly trod,
    And falling with my weight of cares 1010
    Upon the great world's altar-stairs
That slope thro' darkness up to God,

I stretch lame hands of faith, and grope,
    And gather dust and chaff, and call
    To what I feel is Lord of all,
And faintly trust the larger hope.

LV

' So careful of the type ? ' but no.
    From scarped cliff and quarried stone
    She cries ' A thousand types are gone :
I care for nothing, all shall go. 1020

' Thou makest thine appeal to me :
    I bring to life, I bring to death :
    The spirit does but mean the breath :
I know no more.' And he, shall he,

Man, her last work, who seem'd so fair,
    Such splendid purpose in his eyes,
    Who roll'd the psalm to wintry skies,
Who built him fanes of fruitless prayer,

Who trusted God was love indeed
    And love Creation's final law— 1030
    Tho' Nature, red in tooth and claw
With ravine, shriek'd against his creed—

Who loved, who suffer'd countless ills,
    Who battled for the True, the Just,
    Be blown about the desert dust,
Or seal'd within the iron hills ?

No more ? A monster then, a dream,
    A discord. Dragons of the prime,
    That tare each other in their slime,
Were mellow music match'd with him. 1040

O life as futile, then, as frail !
    O for thy voice to soothe and bless !
    What hope of answer, or redress ?
Behind the veil, behind the veil.

LVI

Peace ; come away : the song of woe
    Is after all an earthly song :
    Peace ; come away : we do him wrong
To sing so wildly : let us go.

Come; let us go: your cheeks are pale;
    But half my life I leave behind:
      Methinks my friend is richly shrined;
But I shall pass; my work will fail.   1050

Yet in these ears, till hearing dies,
    One set slow bell will seem to toll
      The passing of the sweetest soul
That ever look'd with human eyes.

I hear it now, and o'er and o'er,
    Eternal greetings to the dead;
      And 'Ave, Ave, Ave,' said,
'Adieu, adieu,' for evermore.   1060

LVII

In those sad words I took farewell:
    Like echoes in sepulchral halls,
      As drop by drop the water falls
In vaults and catacombs, they fell;

And, falling, idly broke the peace
    Of hearts that beat from day to day,
      Half-conscious of their dying clay,
And those cold crypts where they shall cease.

The high Muse answer'd: 'Wherefore grieve
    Thy brethren with a fruitless tear?   1070
      Abide a little longer here,
And thou shalt take a nobler leave.'

LVIII

O Sorrow, wilt thou live with me
    No casual mistress, but a wife,
      My bosom-friend and half of life;
As I confess it needs must be;

O Sorrow, wilt thou rule my blood,
    Be sometimes lovely like a bride,
      And put thy harsher moods aside,
If thou wilt have me wise and good.   1080

My centred passion cannot move,
    Nor will it lessen from to-day;
      But I'll have leave at times to play
As with the creature of my love;

And set thee forth, for thou art mine,
    With so much hope for years to come,
      That, howsoe'er I know thee, some
Could hardly tell what name were thine.

LIX

He past ; a soul of nobler tone :
    My spirit loved and loves him yet,   1090
    Like some poor girl whose heart is set
On one whose rank exceeds her own.

He mixing with his proper sphere,
    She finds the baseness of her lot,
    Half jealous of she knows not what,
And envying all that meet him there.

The little village looks forlorn ;
    She sighs amid her narrow days,
    Moving about the household ways,
In that dark house where she was born.   1100

The foolish neighbours come and go,
    And tease her till the day draws by :
    At night she weeps, ' How vain am I !
How should he love a thing so low ? '

LX

If, in thy second state sublime,
    Thy ransom'd reason change replies
    With all the circle of the wise,
The perfect flower of human time ;

And if thou cast thine eyes below,
    How dimly character'd and slight,   1110
    How dwarf'd a growth of cold and night,
How blanch'd with darkness must I grow !

Yet turn thee to the doubtful shore,
    Where thy first form was made a man ;
    I loved thee, Spirit, and love, nor can
The soul of Shakespeare love thee more.

LXI

Tho' if an eye that 's downward cast
    Could make thee somewhat blench or fail,
    Then be my love an idle tale,
And fading legend of the past ;   1120

And thou, as one that once declined,
    When he was little more than boy,
    On some unworthy heart with joy,
But lives to wed an equal mind ;

And breathes a novel world, the while
    His other passion wholly dies,
    Or in the light of deeper eyes
Is matter for a flying smile.

LXII

Yet pity for a horse o'er-driven,
    And love in which my hound has part,   1130
    Can hang no weight upon my heart
In its assumptions up to heaven ;

And I am so much more than these,
    As thou, perchance, art more than I,
    And yet I spare them sympathy,
And I would set their pains at ease.

So may'st thou watch me where I weep,
    As, unto vaster motions bound,
    The circuits of thine orbit round
A higher height, a deeper deep.   1140

LXIII

Dost thou look back on what hath been,
    As some divinely gifted man,
    Whose life in low estate began
And on a simple village green ;

Who breaks his birth's invidious bar,
    And grasps the skirts of happy chance,
    And breasts the blows of circumstance,
And grapples with his evil star ;

Who makes by force his merit known
    And lives to clutch the golden keys,   1150
    To mould a mighty state's decrees,
And shape the whisper of the throne ;

And moving up from high to higher,
    Becomes on Fortune's crowning slope
    The pillar of a people's hope,
The centre of a world's desire ;

Yet feels, as in a pensive dream,
    When all his active powers are still,
    A distant dearness in the hill,
A secret sweetness in the stream,   1160

The limit of his narrower fate,
    While yet beside its vocal springs
    He play'd at counsellors and kings,
With one that was his earliest mate ;

Who ploughs with pain his native lea
    And reaps the labour of his hands,
    Or in the furrow musing stands :
Does my old friend remember me ? '

LXIV

Sweet soul, do with me as thou wilt;
    I lull a fancy trouble-tost   **1170**
    With 'Love's too precious to be lost,
A little grain shall not be spilt.'

And in that solace can I sing,
    Till out of painful phases wrought
    There flutters up a happy thought,
Self-balanced on a lightsome wing:

Since we deserved the name of friends,
    And thine effect so lives in me,
    A part of mine may live in thee,
And move thee on to noble ends.   **1180**

LXV

You thought my heart too far diseased;
    You wonder when my fancies play
    To find me gay among the gay,
Like one with any trifle pleased.

The shade by which my life was crost,
    Which makes a desert in the mind,
    Has made me kindly with my kind,
And like to him whose sight is lost;

Whose feet are guided thro' the land,
    Whose jest among his friends is free,   **1190**
    Who takes the children on his knee,
And winds their curls about his hand:

He plays with threads, he beats his chair
    For pastime, dreaming of the sky;
    His inner day can never die,
His night of loss is always there.

LXVI

When on my bed the moonlight falls,
    I know that in thy place of rest
    By that broad water of the west,
There comes a glory on the walls: **1200**

Thy marble bright in dark appears,
    As slowly steals a silver flame
    Along the letters of thy name,
And o'er the number of thy years.

The mystic glory swims away;
    From off my bed the moonlight dies:
    And closing eaves of wearied eyes
I sleep till dusk is dipt in grey:

And then I know the mist is drawn
 A lucid veil from coast to coast,   1210
 And in the dark church like a ghost
Thy tablet glimmers to the dawn.

LXVII

When in the down I sink my head,
 Sleep, Death's twin-brother, times my breath;
 Sleep, Death's twin-brother, knows not Death,
Nor can I dream of thee as dead:

I walk as ere I walk'd forlorn,
 When all our path was fresh with dew,
 And all the bugle breezes blew
Reveillée to the breaking morn.   1220

But what is this? I turn about,
 I find a trouble in thine eye,
 Which makes me sad I know not why,
Nor can my dream resolve the doubt:

But ere the lark hath left the lea
 I wake, and I discern the truth;
 It is the trouble of my youth
That foolish sleep transfers to thee.

LXVIII

I dream'd there would be Spring no more,
 That Nature's ancient power was lost: 1230
 The streets were black with smoke and frost,
They chatter'd trifles at the door:

I wander'd from the noisy town,
 I found a wood with thorny boughs:
 I took the thorns to bind my brows,
I wore them like a civic crown:

I met with scoffs, I met with scorns
 From youth and babe and hoary hairs:
 They call'd me in the public squares
The fool that wears a crown of thorns: 1240

They call'd me fool, they call'd me child:
 I found an angel of the night;
 The voice was low, the look was bright;
He look'd upon my crown and smiled:

He reach'd the glory of a hand,
 That seem'd to touch it into leaf:
 The voice was not the voice of grief;
The words were hard to understand.

LXIX

I cannot see the features right,
    When on the gloom I strive to paint   1250
    The face I know; the hues are faint
And mix with hollow masks of night;

Cloud-towers by ghostly masons wrought,
    A gulf that ever shuts and gapes,
    A hand that points, and palled shapes
In shadowy thoroughfares of thought;

And crowds that stream from yawning doors,
    And shoals of pucker'd faces drive;
    Dark bulks that tumble half alive,
And lazy lengths on boundless shores;   1260

Till all at once beyond the will
    I hear a wizard music roll,
    And thro' a lattice on the soul
Looks thy fair face and makes it still.

LXX

Sleep, kinsman thou to death and trance
    And madness, thou hast forged at last
    A night-long Present of the Past
In which we went thro' summer France.

Hadst thou such credit with the soul?   1270
    Then bring an opiate trebly strong,
    Drug down the blindfold sense of wrong
That so my pleasure may be whole;

While now we talk as once we talk'd
    Of men and minds, the dust of change,
    The days that grow to something strange,
In walking as of old we walk'd

Beside the river's wooded reach,
    The fortress, and the mountain ridge,
    The cataract flashing from the bridge,
The breaker breaking on the beach.   1280

LXXI

Risest thou thus, dim dawn, again,
    And howlest, issuing out of night,
    With blasts that blow the poplar white,
And lash with storm the streaming pane?

Day, when my crown'd estate begun
    To pine in that reverse of doom,
    Which sicken'd every living bloom,
And blurr'd the splendour of the sun;

Who usherest in the dolorous hour
 With thy quick tears that make the rose 1290
 Pull sideways, and the daisy close
Her crimson fringes to the shower;

Who might'st have heaved a windless flame
 Up the deep East, or, whispering, play'd
 A chequer-work of beam and shade
Along the hills, yet look'd the same,

As wan, as chill, as wild as now;
 Day, mark'd as with some hideous crime,
 When the dark hand struck down thro' time,
And cancell'd nature's best: but thou, 1300

Lift as thou may'st thy burthen'd brows
 Thro' clouds that drench the morning star,
 And whirl the ungarner'd sheaf afar,
And sow the sky with flying boughs,

And up thy vault with roaring sound
 Climb thy thick noon, disastrous day;
 Touch thy dull goal of joyless grey,
And hide thy shame beneath the ground.

LXXII

So many worlds, so much to do,
 So little done, such things to be, 1310
 How know I what had need of thee,
For thou wert strong as thou wert true?

The fame is quench'd that I foresaw,
 The head hath miss'd an earthly wreath:
 I curse not nature, no, nor death;
For nothing is that errs from law.

We pass; the path that each man trod
 Is dim, or will be dim, with weeds:
 What fame is left for human deeds
In endless age? It rests with God. 1320

O hollow wraith of dying fame,
 Fade wholly, while the soul exults,
 And self-infolds the large results
Of force that would have forged a name.

LXXIII

As sometimes in a dead man's face,
 To those that watch it more and more,
 A likeness, hardly seen before,
Comes out—to some one of his race:

So, dearest, now thy brows are cold,
    I see thee what thou art, and know   1330
    Thy likeness to the wise below,
Thy kindred with the great of old.

But there is more than I can see,
    And what I see I leave unsaid,
    Nor speak it, knowing Death has made
His darkness beautiful with thee.

LXXIV

I leave thy praises unexpress'd
    In verse that brings myself relief,
    And by the measure of my grief
I leave thy greatness to be guess'd;   1340

What practice howsoe'er expert
    In fitting aptest words to things,
    Or voice the richest-toned that sings,
Hath power to give thee as thou wert?

I care not in these fading days
    To raise a cry that lasts not long,
    And round thee with the breeze of song
To stir a little dust of praise.

Thy leaf has perish'd in the green,
    And, while we breathe beneath the sun,   1350
    The world which credits what is done
Is cold to all that might have been.

So here shall silence guard thy fame;
    But somewhere, out of human view,
    Whate'er thy hands are set to do
Is wrought with tumult of acclaim.

LXXV

Take wings of fancy, and ascend,
    And in a moment set thy face
    Where all the starry heavens of space
Are sharpen'd to a needle's end;   1360

Take wings of foresight; lighten thro'
    The secular abyss to come,
    And lo, thy deepest lays are dumb
Before the mouldering of a yew;

And if the matin songs, that woke
    The darkness of our planet, last,
    Thine own shall wither in the vast,
Ere half the lifetime of an oak.

Ere these have clothed their branchy bowers
   With fifty Mays, thy songs are vain ;   1370
   And what are they when these remain
The ruin'd shells of hollow towers ?

LXXVI

What hope is here for modern rhyme
   To him, who turns a musing eye
   On songs, and deeds, and lives, that lie
Foreshorten'd in the tract of time ?

These mortal lullabies of pain
   May bind a book, may line a box,
   May serve to curl a maiden's locks ;
Or when a thousand moons shall wane   1380

A man upon a stall may find,
   And, passing, turn the page that tells
   A grief, then changed to something else,
Sung by a long-forgotten mind.

But what of that ? My darken'd ways
   Shall ring with music all the same ;
   To breathe my loss is more than fame,
To utter love more sweet than praise.

LXXVII

Again at Christmas did we weave
   The holly round the Christmas hearth ;   1390
   The silent snow possess'd the earth,
And calmly fell our Christmas-eve :

The yule-clog sparkled keen with frost,
   No wing of wind the region swept,
   But over all things brooding slept
The quiet sense of something lost.

As in the winters left behind,
   Again our ancient games had place,
   The mimic picture's breathing grace,
And dance and song and hoodman-blind.   1400

Who show'd a token of distress ?
   No single tear, no mark of pain :
   O sorrow, then can sorrow wane ?
O grief, can grief be changed to less ?

O last regret, regret can die !
   No—mixt with all this mystic frame,
   Her deep relations are the same,
But with long use her tears are dry.

LXXVIII

'More than my brothers are to me'—
    Let this not vex thee, noble heart!   1410
    I know thee of what force thou art
To hold the costliest love in fee.

But thou and I are one in kind,
    As moulded like in nature's mint;
    And hill and wood and field did print
The same sweet forms in either mind.

For us the same cold streamlet curl'd
    Thro' all his eddying coves; the same
    All winds that roam the twilight came
In whispers of the beauteous world.   1420

At one dear knee we proffer'd vows,
    One lesson from one book we learn'd,
    Ere childhood's flaxen ringlet turn'd
To black and brown on kindred brows.

And so my wealth resembles thine,
    But he was rich where I was poor,
    And he supplied my want the more
As his unlikeness fitted mine.

LXXIX

If any vague desire should rise,
    That holy Death ere Arthur died   1430
    Had moved me kindly from his side,
And dropt the dust on tearless eyes;

Then fancy shapes, as fancy can,
    The grief my loss in him had wrought,
    A grief as deep as life or thought,
But stay'd in peace with God and man.

I make a picture in the brain;
    I hear the sentence that he speaks;
    He bears the burthen of the weeks,
But turns his burthen into gain.   1440

His credit thus shall set me free;
    And, influence-rich to soothe and save,
    Unused example from the grave
Reach out dead hands to comfort me.

LXXX

Could I have said while he was here,
    'My love shall now no further range;
    There cannot come a mellower change,
For now is love mature in ear.'

Love, then, had hope of richer store :
    What end is here to my complaint ?   1450
    This haunting whisper makes me faint,
' More years had made me love thee more.'

But Death returns an answer sweet :
    ' My sudden frost was sudden gain,
    And gave all ripeness to the grain,
It might have drawn from after-heat.'

LXXXI

I wage not any feud with Death
    For changes wrought on form and face ;
    No lower life that earth's embrace
May breed with him, can fright my faith.   1460

Eternal process moving on,
    From state to state the spirit walks ;
    And these are but the shatter'd stalks,
Or ruin'd chrysalis of one.

Nor blame I Death, because he bare
    The use of virtue out of earth :
    I know transplanted human worth
Will bloom to profit, otherwhere.

For this alone on Death I wreak
    The wrath that garners in my heart ;   1470
    He put our lives so far apart
We cannot hear each other speak.

LXXXII

Dip down upon the northern shore,
    O sweet new-year delaying long ;
    Thou doest expectant nature wrong ;
Delaying long, delay no more.

What stays thee from the clouded noons,
    Thy sweetness from its proper place ?
    Can trouble live with April days,
Or sadness in the summer moons ?   1480

Bring orchis, bring the foxglove spire,
    The little speedwell's darling blue,
    Deep tulips dash'd with fiery dew,
Laburnums, dropping-wells of fire.

O thou, new-year, delaying long,
    Delayest the sorrow in my blood,
    That longs to burst a frozen bud,
And flood a fresher throat with song.

LXXXIII

When I contemplate all alone
    The life that had been thine below,   1490
    And fix my thoughts on all the glow
To which thy crescent would have grown ;

I see thee sitting crown'd with good,
    A central warmth diffusing bliss
    In glance and smile, and clasp and kiss,
On all the branches of thy blood ;

Thy blood, my friend, and partly mine ;
    For now the day was drawing on,
    When thou should'st link thy life with one
Of mine own house, and boys of thine   1500

Had babbled ' Uncle ' on my knee ;
    But that remorseless iron hour
    Made cypress of her orange flower,
Despair of Hope, and earth of thee.

I seem to meet their least desire,
    To clap their cheeks, to call them mine.
    I see their unborn faces shine
Beside the never-lighted fire.

I see myself an honour'd guest,
    Thy partner in the flowery walk   **1510**
    Of letters, genial table-talk,
Or deep dispute, and graceful jest ;

While now thy prosperous labour fills
    The lips of men with honest praise,
    And sun by sun the happy days
Descend below the golden hills

With promise of a morn as fair ;
    And all the train of bounteous hours
    Conduct by paths of growing powers,
To reverence and the silver hair ;   1520

Till slowly worn her earthly robe,
    Her lavish mission richly wrought,
    Leaving great legacies of thought,
Thy spirit should fail from off the globe ;

What time mine own might also flee,
    As link'd with thine in love and fate,
    And, hovering o'er the dolorous strait
To the other shore, involved in thee,

Arrive at last the blessed goal,
    And He that died in Holy Land   1530
    Would reach us out the shining hand,
And take us as a single soul.

What reed was that on which I leant ?
　　Ah, backward fancy, wherefore wake
　　The old bitterness again, and break
The low beginnings of content.

LXXXIV

This truth came borne with bier and pall.
　　I felt it, when I sorrow'd most,
　　'Tis better to have loved and lost,
Than never to have loved at all——　　　　　　1540

O true in word, and tried in deed,
　　Demanding, so to bring relief
　　To this which is our common grief,
What kind of life is that I lead ;

And whether trust in things above
　　Be dimm'd of sorrow, or sustain'd ;
　　And whether love for him have drain'd
My capabilities of love ;

Your words have virtue such as draws
　　A faithful answer from the breast,　　　　　　1550
　　Thro' light reproaches, half exprest,
And loyal unto kindly laws.

My blood an even tenor kept,
　　Till on mine ear this message falls,
　　That in Vienna's fatal walls
God's finger touch'd him, and he slept.

The great Intelligences fair
　　That range above our mortal state,
　　In circle round the blessed gate,
Received and gave him welcome there ;　　　　　　1560

And led him thro' the blissful climes,
　　And show'd him in the fountain fresh
　　All knowledge that the sons of flesh
Shall gather in the cycled times.

But I remain'd, whose hopes were dim,
　　Whose life, whose thoughts were little worth,
　　To wander on a darken'd earth,
Where all things round me breathed of him.

O friendship, equal-poised control,
　　O heart, with kindliest motion warm,　　　　　　1570
　　O sacred essence, other form,
O solemn ghost, O crowned soul !

Yet none could better know than I,
　　How much of act at human hands
　　The sense of human will demands,
By which we dare to live or die.

Whatever way my days decline,
    I felt and feel, tho' left alone,
    His being working in mine own,
The footsteps of his life in mine ;   1580

A life that all the Muses deck'd
    With gifts of grace, that might express
    All comprehensive tenderness,
All-subtilizing intellect :

And so my passion hath not swerved
    To works of weakness, but I find
    An image comforting the mind,
And in my grief a strength reserved.

Likewise the imaginative woe,
    That loved to handle spiritual strife,   1590
    Diffused the shock thro' all my life,
But in the present broke the blow.

My pulses therefore beat again
    For other friends that once I met ;
    Nor can it suit me to forget
The mighty hopes that make us men.

I woo your love : I count it crime
    To mourn for any overmuch ;
    I, the divided half of such
A friendship as had master'd Time ;   1600

Which masters Time indeed, and is
    Eternal, separate from fears :
    The all-assuming months and years
Can take no part away from this :

But Summer on the steaming floods,
    And Spring that swells the narrow brooks,
    And Autumn, with a noise of rooks,
That gather in the waning woods,

And every pulse of wind and wave
    Recalls, in change of light or gloom,   1610
    My old affection of the tomb,
And my prime passion in the grave :

My old affection of the tomb,
    A part of stillness, yearns to speak :
    ' Arise, and get thee forth and seek
A friendship for the years to come.

' I watch thee from the quiet shore ;
    Thy spirit up to mine can reach ;
    But in dear words of human speech
We two communicate no more.'   1620

And I, ' Can clouds of nature stain
    The starry clearness of the free ?
    How is it ? Canst thou feel for me
Some painless sympathy with pain ? '

And lightly does the whisper fall:
   ' 'Tis hard for thee to fathom this;
   I triumph in conclusive bliss,
And that serene result of all.'

So hold I commerce with the dead;
   Or so methinks the dead would say;   1630
   Or so shall grief with symbols play,
And pining life be fancy-fed.

Now looking to some settled end,
   That these things pass, and I shall prove
   A meeting somewhere, love with love,
I crave your pardon, O my friend;

If not so fresh, with love as true,
   I, clasping brother-hands, aver
   I could not, if I would, transfer
The whole I felt for him to you.   1640

For which be they that hold apart
   The promise of the golden hours?
   First love, first friendship, equal powers,
That marry with the virgin heart.

Still mine, that cannot but deplore,
   That beats within a lonely place,
   That yet remembers his embrace,
But at his footstep leaps no more,

My heart, tho' widow'd, may not rest
   Quite in the love of what is gone,   1650
   But seeks to beat in time with one
That warms another living breast.

Ah, take the imperfect gift I bring,
   Knowing the primrose yet is dear,
   The primrose of the later year,
As not unlike to that of Spring.

LXXXV

Sweet after showers, ambrosial air,
   That rollest from the gorgeous gloom
   Of evening over brake and bloom
And meadow, slowly breathing bare   1660

The round of space, and rapt below
   Thro' all the dewy-tassell'd wood,
   And shadowing down the horned flood
In ripples, fan my brows and blow

The fever from my cheek, and sigh
   The full new life that feeds thy breath
   Throughout my frame, till Doubt and Death,
Ill brethren, let the fancy fly

From belt to belt of crimson seas
    On leagues of odour streaming far,   1670
    To where in yonder orient star
A hundred spirits whisper ' Peace.'

LXXXVI

I past beside the reverend walls
    In which of old I wore the gown ;
    I roved at random thro' the town,
And saw the tumult of the halls ;

And heard once more in college fanes
    The storm their high-built organs make,
    And thunder-music, rolling, shake
The prophets blazon'd on the panes ;   1680

And caught once more the distant shout,
    The measured pulse of racing oars
    Among the willows ; paced the shores
And many a bridge, and all about

The same grey flats again, and felt
    The same, but not the same ; and last
    Up that long walk of limes I past
To see the rooms in which he dwelt.

Another name was on the door :
    I linger'd ; all within was noise   1690
    Of songs, and clapping hands, and boys
That crash'd the glass and beat the floor ;

Where once we held debate, a band
    Of youthful friends, on mind and art,
    And labour, and the changing mart,
And all the framework of the land ;

When one would aim an arrow fair,
    But send it slackly from the string ;
    And one would pierce an outer ring,
And one an inner, here and there ;   1700

And last the master-bowman, he,
    Would cleave the mark. A willing ear
    We lent him. Who, but hung to hear
The rapt oration flowing free

From point to point, with power and grace
    And music in the bounds of law,
    To those conclusions when we saw
The God within him light his face,

And seem to lift the form, and glow
    In azure orbits heavenly-wise ;   1710
    And over those ethereal eyes
The bar of Michael Angelo.

LXXXVII

Wild bird, whose warble, liquid sweet,
    Rings Eden thro' the budded quicks,
      O tell me where the senses mix,
O tell me where the passions meet,

Whence radiate : fierce extremes employ
    Thy spirits in the darkening leaf,
      And in the midmost heart of grief
Thy passion clasps a secret joy :   1720

And I—my harp would prelude woe—
    I cannot all command the strings ;
      The glory of the sum of things
Will flash along the chords and go.

LXXXVIII

Witch-elms that counterchange the floor
    Of this flat lawn with dusk and bright ;
      And thou, with all thy breadth and height
Of foliage, towering sycamore ;

How often, hither wandering down,
    My Arthur found your shadows fair,   1730
      And shook to all the liberal air
The dust and din and steam of town :

He brought an eye for all he saw ;
    He mixt in all our simple sports ;
      They pleased him, fresh from brawling courts
And dusty purlieus of the law.

O joy to him in this retreat,
    Immantled in ambrosial dark,
      To drink the cooler air, and mark
The landscape winking thro' the heat :   1740

O sound to rout the brood of cares,
    The sweep of scythe in morning dew,
      The gust that round the garden flew,
And tumbled half the mellowing pears !

O bliss, when all in circle drawn
    About him, heart and ear were fed
      To hear him, as he lay and read
The Tuscan poets on the lawn :

Or in the all-golden afternoon
    A guest, or happy sister, sung,   1750
      Or here she brought the harp and flung
A ballad to the brightening moon :

Nor less it pleased in livelier moods,
　　Beyond the bounding hill to stray,
　　And break the livelong summer day
With banquet in the distant woods;

Whereat we glanced from theme to theme,
　　Discuss'd the books to love or hate,
　　Or touch'd the changes of the state,
Or threaded some Socratic dream;　　　　　**1760**

But if I praised the busy town,
　　He loved to rail against it still,
　　For 'ground in yonder social mill
We rub each other's angles down,

And merge,' he said, 'in form and gloss
　　The picturesque of man and man.'
　　We talk'd: the stream beneath us ran,
The wine-flask lying couch'd in moss,

Or cool'd within the glooming wave;
　　And last, returning from afar,　　　　　**1770**
　　Before the crimson-circled star
Had fail'n into her father's grave,

And brushing ankle-deep in flowers,
　　We heard behind the woodbine veil
　　The milk that bubbled in the pail,
And buzzings of the honied hours.

LXXXIX

He tasted love with half his mind,
　　Nor ever drank the inviolate spring
　　Where nighest heaven, who first could fling
This bitter seed among mankind;　　　　　**1780**

That could the dead, whose dying eyes
　　Were closed with wail, resume their life,
　　They would but find in child and wife
An iron welcome when they rise:

'Twas well, indeed, when warm with wine,
　　To pledge them with a kindly tear,
　　To talk them o'er, to wish them here,
To count their memories half divine;

But if they came who past away,　　　　　**1790**
　　Behold their brides in other hands;
　　The hard heir strides about their lands,
And will not yield them for a day.

Yea, tho' their sons were none of these,
　　Not less the yet-loved sire would make
　　Confusion worse than death, and shake
The pillars of domestic peace.

Ah dear, but come thou back to me:
  Whatever change the years have wrought,
  I find not yet one lonely thought
That cries against my wish for thee.   1800

XC

When rosy plumelets tuft the larch,
  And rarely pipes the mounted thrush;
  Or underneath the barren bush
Flits by the sea-blue bird of March;

Come, wear the form by which I know
  Thy spirit in time among thy peers;
  The hope of unaccomplish'd years
Be large and lucid round thy brow.

When summer's hourly-mellowing change
  May breathe, with many roses sweet,   1810
  Upon the thousand waves of wheat,
That ripple round the lonely grange;

Come: not in watches of the night,
  But where the sunbeam broodeth warm,
  Come, beauteous in thine after form,
And like a finer light in light.

XCI

If any vision should reveal
  Thy likeness, I might count it vain
  As but the canker of the brain;
Yea, tho' it spake and made appeal   1820

To chances where our lots were cast
  Together in the days behind,
  I might but say, I hear a wind
Of memory murmuring the past.

Yea, tho' it spake and bared to view
  A fact within the coming year;
  And tho' the months, revolving near,
Should prove the phantom-warning true.

They might not seem thy prophecies,
  But spiritual presentiments,   1830
  And such refraction of events
As often rises ere they rise.

XCII

I shall not see thee. Dare I say
  No spirit ever brake the band
  That stays him from the native land,
Where first he walk'd when claspt in clay?

No visual shade of some one lost,
    But he, the Spirit himself, may come
    When all the nerve of sense is numb ;
Spirit to Spirit, Ghost to Ghost.   1840

O, therefore from thy sightless range
    With gods in unconjectured bliss,
    O, from the distance of the abyss
Of tenfold-complicated change,

Descend, and touch, and enter ; hear
    The wish too strong for words to name ;
    That in this blindness of the frame
My Ghost may feel that thine is near.

XCIII

How pure at heart and sound in head,
    With what divine affections bold   1850
    Should be the man whose thought would hold
An hour's communion with the dead.

In vain shalt thou, or any, call
    The spirits from their golden day,
    Except, like them, thou too canst say,
My spirit is at peace with all.

They haunt the silence of the breast,
    Imaginations calm and fair,
    The memory like a cloudless air,
The conscience as a sea at rest :   1860

But when the heart is full of din,
    And doubt beside the portal waits,
    They can but listen at the gates,
And hear the household jar within.

XCIV

By night we linger'd on the lawn,
    For underfoot the herb was dry ;
    And genial warmth ; and o'er the sky
The silvery haze of summer drawn ;

And calm that let the tapers burn
    Unwavering : not a cricket chirr'd :   1870
    The brook alone far-off was heard,
And on the board the fluttering urn :

And bats went round in fragrant skies,
    And wheel'd or lit the filmy shapes
    That haunt the dusk, with ermine capes
And woolly breasts and beaded eyes ;

While now we sang old songs that peal'd
    From knoll to knoll, where, couch'd at ease,
    The white kine glimmer'd, and the trees
Laid their dark arms about the field.   1880

But when those others, one by one,
    Withdrew themselves from me and night,
    And in the house light after light
Went out, and I was all alone,

A hunger seized my heart; I read
    Of that glad year which once had been,
    In those fall'n leaves which kept their green,
The noble letters of the dead :

And strangely on the silence broke
    The silent-speaking words, and strange   1890
    Was love's dumb cry defying change
To test his worth ; and strangely spoke

The faith, the vigour, bold to dwell
    On doubts that drive the coward back,
    And keen thro' wordy snares to track
Suggestion to her inmost cell.

So word by word, and line by line,
    The dead man touch'd me from the past,
    And all at once it seem'd at last
His living soul was flash'd on mine,   1900

And mine in his was wound, and whirl'd
    About empyreal heights of thought,
    And came on that which is, and caught
The deep pulsations of the world,

Aeonian music measuring out
    The steps of Time—the shocks of Chance—
    The blows of Death. At length my trance
Was cancell'd, stricken thro' with doubt.

Vague words ! but ah how hard to frame
    In matter-moulded forms of speech,   1910
    Or ev'n for intellect to reach
Thro' memory that which I became :

Till now the doubtful dusk reveal'd
    The knolls once more where, couch'd at ease,
    The white kine glimmer'd, and the trees
Laid their dark arms about the field :

And suck'd from out the distant gloom
    A breeze began to tremble o'er
    The large leaves of the sycamore,
And fluctuate all the still perfume,   1920

And gathering freshlier overhead,
    Rock'd the full-foliaged elms, and swung
    The heavy-folded rose, and flung
The lilies to and fro, and said

'The dawn, the dawn,' and died away;
　　And East and West, without a breath,
　　Mixt their dim lights, like life and death,
To broaden into boundless day.

XCV

You say, but with no touch of scorn,
　　Sweet-hearted, you, whose light-blue eyes   1930
　　Are tender over drowning flies,
You tell me, doubt is Devil-born.

I know not: one indeed I knew
　　In many a subtle question versed,
　　Who touch'd a jarring lyre at first,
But ever strove to make it true:

Perplext in faith, but pure in deeds,
　　At last he beat his music out.
　　There lives more faith in honest doubt,
Believe me, than in half the creeds.   1940

He fought his doubts and gather'd strength,
　　He would not make his judgement blind,
　　He faced the spectres of the mind
And laid them: thus he came at length

To find a stronger faith his own;
　　And Power was with him in the night,
　　Which makes the darkness and the light,
And dwells not in the light alone,

But in the darkness and the cloud,
　　As over Sinaï's peaks of old,   1950
　　While Israel made their gods of gold,
Altho' the trumpet blew so loud.

XCVI

My love has talk'd with rocks and trees;
　　He finds on misty mountain-ground
　　His own vast shadow glory-crown'd;
He sees himself in all he sees.

Two partners of a married life—
　　I look'd on these and thought of thee
　　In vastness and in mystery,
And of my spirit as of a wife.   1960

These two—they dwelt with eye on eye,
　　Their hearts of old have beat in tune,
　　Their meetings made December June,
Their every parting was to die.

Their love has never past away;
   The days she never can forget
   Are earnest that he loves her yet,
Whate'er the faithless people say.

Her life is lone, he sits apart,
   He loves her yet, she will not weep,   1970
   Tho' rapt in matters dark and deep
He seems to slight her simple heart.

He thrids the labyrinth of the mind,
   He reads the secret of the star,
   He seems so near and yet so far,
He looks so cold: she thinks him kind,

She keeps the gift of years before,
   A wither'd violet is her bliss;
   She knows not what his greatness is;
For that, for all, she loves him more.   1980

For him she plays, to him she sings
   Of early faith and plighted vows;
   She knows but matters of the house,
And he, he knows a thousand things.

Her faith is fixt and cannot move,
   She darkly feels him great and wise,
   She dwells on him with faithful eyes,
'I cannot understand: I love.'

XCVII

You leave us: you will see the Rhine,
   And those fair hills I sail'd below,
   When I was there with him; and go   1990
By summer belts of wheat and vine

To where he breathed his latest breath,
   That City. All her splendour seems
   No livelier than the wisp that gleams
On Lethe in the eyes of Death.

Let her great Danube rolling fair
   Enwind her isles, unmark'd of me:
   I have not seen, I will not see
Vienna; rather dream that there,   2000

A treble darkness, Evil haunts
   The birth, the bridal; friend from friend
   Is oftener parted, fathers bend
Above more graves, a thousand wants

Gnarr at the heels of men, and prey
   By each cold hearth, and sadness flings
   Her shadow on the blaze of kings:
And yet myself have heard him say,

That not in any mother town
 With statelier progress to and fro   2010
 The double tides of chariots flow
By park and suburb under brown

Of lustier leaves ; nor more content,
 He told me, lives in any crowd,
 When all is gay with lamps, and loud
With sport and song, in booth and tent,

Imperial halls, or open plain ;
 And wheels the circled dance, and breaks
 The rocket molten into flakes
Of crimson or in emerald rain.   2020

XCVIII

Risest thou thus, dim dawn, again,
 So loud with voices of the birds,
 So thick with lowings of the herds,
Day, when I lost the flower of men ;

Who tremblest thro' thy darkling red
 On yon swoll'n brook that bubbles fast
 By meadows breathing of the past,
And woodlands holy to the dead ;

Who murmurest in the foliaged eaves
 A song that slights the coming care,   2030
 And Autumn laying here and there
A fiery finger on the leaves ;

Who wakenest with thy balmy breath
 To myriads on the genial earth,
 Memories of bridal, or of birth,
And unto myriads more, of death.

O, wheresoever those may be,
 Betwixt the slumber of the poles,
 To-day they count as kindred souls ;
They know me not, but mourn with me.   2040

XCIX

I climb the hill : from end to end
 Of all the landscape underneath,
 I find no place that does not breathe
Some gracious memory of my friend ;

No grey old grange, or lonely fold,
 Or low morass and whispering reed,
 Or simple stile from mead to mead,
Or sheepwalk up the windy wold ;

Nor hoary knoll of ash and haw
 That hears the latest linnet trill,   2050
 Nor quarry trench'd along the hill,
And haunted by the wrangling daw ;

Nor runlet tinkling from the rock ;
 Nor pastoral rivulet that swerves
 To left and right thro' meadowy curves,
That feed the mothers of the flock ;

But each has pleased a kindred eye,
 And each reflects a kindlier day ;
 And, leaving these, to pass away,
I think once more he seems to die.   2060

C

Unwatch'd, the garden bough shall sway,
 The tender blossom flutter down ;
 Unloved, that beech will gather brown,
This maple burn itself away ;

Unloved, the sunflower, shining fair,
 Ray round with flames her disk of seed,
 And many a rose-carnation feed
With summer spice the humming air ;

Unloved, by many a sandy bar,
 The brook shall babble down the plain, 2070
 At noon or when the lesser wain
Is twisting round the polar star ;

Uncared for, gird the windy grove,
 And flood the haunts of hern and crake ;
 Or into silver arrows break
The sailing moon in creek and cove ;

Till from the garden and the wild
 A fresh association blow,
 And year by year the landscape grow
Familiar to the stranger's child ;   2080

As year by year the labourer tills
 His wonted glebe, or lops the glades ;
 And year by year our memory fades
From all the circle of the hills.

CI

We leave the well-beloved place
 Where first we gazed upon the sky ;
 The roofs, that heard our earliest cry,
Will shelter one of stranger race.

We go, but ere we go from home,
 As down the garden-walks I move,   2090
  Two spirits of a diverse love
Contend for loving masterdom.

One whispers, ' Here thy boyhood sung
 Long since its matin song, and heard
  The low love-language of the bird
In native hazels tassel-hung.'

The other answers, ' Yea, but here
 Thy feet have stray'd in after hours
  With thy lost friend among the bowers,
And this hath made them trebly dear.'   2100

These two have striven half the day,
 And each prefers his separate claim,
  Poor rivals in a losing game,
That will not yield each other way.

I turn to go : my feet are set
 To leave the pleasant fields and farms ;
  They mix in one another's arms
To one pure image of regret.

CII

On that last night before we went
 From out the doors where I was bred,   2110
  I dream'd a vision of the dead,
Which left my after-morn content.

Methought I dwelt within a hall,
 And maidens with me : distant hills
  From hidden summits fed with rills
A river sliding by the wall.

The hall with harp and carol rang.
 They sang of what is wise and good
  And graceful.   In the centre stood
A statue veil'd, to which they sang ;   2120

And which, tho' veil'd, was known to me,
 The shape of him I loved, and love
  For ever : then flew in a dove
And brought a summons from the sea :

And when they learnt that I must go
 They wept and wail'd, but led the way
  To where a little shallop lay
At anchor in the flood below ;

And on by many a level mead,
 And shadowing bluff that made the banks,   2130
  We glided winding under ranks
Of iris, and the golden reed ;

And still as vaster grew the shore,
    And roll'd the floods in grander space,
    The maidens gather'd strength and grace
And presence, lordlier than before ;

And I myself, who sat apart
    And watch'd them, wax'd in every limb ;
    I felt the thews of Anakim,
The pulses of a Titan's heart ;   2140

As one would sing the death of war,
    And one would chant the history
    Of that great race, which is to be,
And one the shaping of a star ;

Until the forward-creeping tides
    Began to foam, and we to draw
    From deep to deep, to where we saw
A great ship lift her shining sides.

The man we loved was there on deck,
    But thrice as large as man he bent   2150
    To greet us. Up the side I went,
And fell in silence on his neck :

Whereat those maidens with one mind
    Bewail'd their lot ; I did them wrong :
    ' We served thee here,' they said, ' so long,
And wilt thou leave us now behind ? '

So rapt I was, they could not win
    An answer from my lips, but he
    Replying, ' Enter likewise ye
And go with us : ' they enter'd in.   2160

And while the wind began to sweep
    A music out of sheet and shroud,
    We steer'd her toward a crimson cloud
That landlike slept along the deep.

CIII

The time draws near the birth of Christ ;
    The moon is hid, the night is still ;
    A single church below the hill
Is pealing, folded in the mist.

A single peal of bells below,
    That wakens at this hour of rest   2170
    A single murmur in the breast,
That these are not the bells I know.

Like strangers' voices here they sound,
    In lands where not a memory strays,
    Nor landmark breathes of other days,
But all is new unhallow'd ground.

CIV

This holly by the cottage-eave,
  To-night, ungather'd, shall it stand:
  We live within the stranger's land,
And strangely falls our Christmas eve. 2180

Our father's dust is left alone
  And silent under other snows:
  There in due time the woodbine blows,
The violet comes, but we are gone.

No more shall wayward grief abuse
  The genial hour with mask and mime;
  For change of place, like growth of time,
Has broke the bond of dying use.

Let cares that petty shadows cast,
  By which our lives are chiefly proved, 2190
  A little spare the night I loved,
And hold it solemn to the past.

But let no footstep beat the floor,
  Nor bowl of wassail mantle warm;
  For who would keep an ancient form
Thro' which the spirit breathes no more?

Be neither song, nor game, nor feast;
  Nor harp be touch'd, nor flute be blown;
  No dance, no motion, save alone
What lightens in the lucid east 2200

Of rising worlds by yonder wood.
  Long sleeps the summer in the seed;
  Run out your measured arcs, and lead
The closing cycle rich in good.

CV

Ring out, wild bells, to the wild sky,
  The flying cloud, the frosty light:
  The year is dying in the night;
Ring out, wild bells, and let him die.

Ring out the old, ring in the new,
  Ring, happy bells, across the snow: 2210
  The year is going, let him go;
Ring out the false, ring in the true.

Ring out the grief that saps the mind,
  For those that here we see no more;
  Ring out the feud of rich and poor,
Ring in redress to all mankind.

Ring out a slowly dying cause,
 And ancient forms of party strife;
 Ring in the nobler modes of life,
With sweeter manners, purer laws.   2220

Ring out the want, the care, the sin,
 The faithless coldness of the times;
 Ring out, ring out my mournful rhymes,
But ring the fuller minstrel in.

Ring out false pride in place and blood,
 The civic slander and the spite;
 Ring in the love of truth and right,
Ring in the common love of good.

Ring out old shapes of foul disease;
 Ring out the narrowing lust of gold;   2230
 Ring out the thousand wars of old,
Ring in the thousand years of peace.

Ring in the valiant man and free,
 The larger heart, the kindlier hand;
 Ring out the darkness of the land,
Ring in the Christ that is to be.

CVI

It is the day when he was born,
 A bitter day that early sank
 Behind a purple-frosty bank
Of vapour, leaving night forlorn.   2240

The time admits not flowers or leaves
 To deck the banquet. Fiercely flies
 The blast of North and East, and ice
Makes daggers at the sharpen'd eaves,

And bristles all the brakes and thorns
 To yon hard crescent, as she hangs
 Above the wood which grides and clangs
Its leafless ribs and iron horns

Together, in the drifts that pass
 To darken on the rolling brine   2250
 That breaks the coast. But fetch the wine,
Arrange the board and brim the glass;

Bring in great logs and let them lie,
 To make a solid core of heat;
 Be cheerful-minded, talk and treat
Of all things ev'n as he were by;

We keep the day. With festal cheer,
 With books and music, surely we
 Will drink to him whate'er he be,
And sing the songs he loved to hear.   2260

CVII

I will not shut me from my kind,
    And, lest I stiffen into stone,
    I will not eat my heart alone,
Nor feed with sighs a passing wind:

What profit lies in barren faith,
    And vacant yearning, tho' with might
    To scale the heaven's highest height,
Or dive below the wells of Death?

What find I in the highest place,
    But mine own phantom chanting hymns?   2270
    And on the depths of death there swims
The reflex of a human face.

I'll rather take what fruit may be
    Of sorrow under human skies:
    'Tis held that sorrow makes us wise,
Whatever wisdom sleep with thee.

CVIII

Heart-affluence in discursive talk
    From household fountains never dry;
    The critic clearness of an eye,
That saw thro' all the Muses' walk;   2280

Seraphic intellect and force
    To seize and throw the doubts of man;
    Impassion'd logic, which outran
The hearer in its fiery course;

High nature amorous of the good,
    But touch'd with no ascetic gloom;
    And passion pure in snowy bloom
Thro' all the years of April blood;

A love of freedom rarely felt,
    Of freedom in her regal seat   2290
    Of England; not the schoolboy heat,
The blind hysterics of the Celt;

And manhood fused with female grace
    In such a sort, the child would twine
    A trustful hand, unask'd, in thine,
And find his comfort in thy face;

All these have been, and thee mine eyes
    Have look'd on: if they look'd in vain,
    My shame is greater who remain,
Nor let thy wisdom make me wise.   2300

CIX

Thy converse drew us with delight,
　　The men of rathe and riper years:
　　The feeble soul, a haunt of fears,
Forgot his weakness in thy sight.

On thee the loyal-hearted hung,
　　The proud was half disarm'd of pride,
　　Nor cared the serpent at thy side
To flicker with his double tongue.

The stern were mild when thou wert by,
　　The flippant put himself to school
　　And heard thee, and the brazen fool 　　　　2310
Was soften'd, and he knew not why;

While I, thy dearest, sat apart,
　　And felt thy triumph was as mine;
　　And loved them more, that they were thine,
The graceful tact, the Christian art;

Not mine the sweetness or the skill,
　　But mine the love that will not tire,
　　And, born of love, the vague desire
That spurs an imitative will. 　　　　2320

CX

The churl in spirit, up or down
　　Along the scale of ranks, thro' all,
　　To him who grasps a golden ball,
By blood a king, at heart a clown;

The churl in spirit, howe'er he veil
　　His want in forms for fashion's sake,
　　Will let his coltish nature break
At seasons thro' the gilded pale:

For who can always act? but he,
　　To whom a thousand memories call, 　　　　2330
　　Not being less but more than all
The gentleness he seem'd to be,

Best seem'd the thing he was, and join'd
　　Each office of the social hour
　　To noble manners, as the flower
And native growth of noble mind;

Nor ever narrowness or spite,
　　Or villain fancy fleeting by,
　　Drew in the expression of an eye,
Where God and Nature met in light; 　　　　· 2340

And thus he bore without abuse
　　The grand old name of gentleman,
　　Defamed by every charlatan,
And soil'd with all ignoble use.

CXI

High wisdom holds my wisdom less,
 That I, who gaze with temperate eyes
 On glorious insufficiencies,
Set light by narrower perfectness.

But thou, that fillest all the room
 Of all my love, art reason why   2350
 I seem to cast a careless eye
On souls, the lesser lords of doom.

For what wert thou ? some novel power
 Sprang up for ever at a touch,
 And hope could never hope too much,
In watching thee from hour to hour,

Large elements in order brought,
 And tracts of calm from tempest made,
 And world-wide fluctuation sway'd
In vassal tides that follow'd thought.   2360

CXII

'Tis held that sorrow makes us wise ;
 Yet how much wisdom sleeps with thee
 Which not alone had guided me,
But served the seasons that may rise ;

For can I doubt who knew thee keen
 In intellect, with force and skill
 To strive, to fashion, to fulfil—
I doubt not what thou wouldst have been:

A life in civic action warm,
 A soul on highest mission sent,   2370
 A potent voice of Parliament,
A pillar steadfast in the storm,

Should licensed boldness gather force,
 Becoming, when the time has birth,
 A lever to uplift the earth
And roll it in another course,

With thousand shocks that come and go,
 With agonies, with energies,
 With overthrowings, and with cries,
And undulations to and fro.   2380

CXIII

Who loves not Knowledge ? Who shall rail
 Against her beauty ? May she mix
 With men and prosper ! Who shall fix
Her pillars ? Let her work prevail.

But on her forehead sits a fire :
    She sets her forward countenance
    And leaps into the future chance,
Submitting all things to desire.

Half-grown as yet, a child, and vain—
    She cannot fight the fear of death.   2390
    What is she, cut from love and faith,
But some wild Pallas from the brain

Of Demons ? fiery-hot to burst
    All barriers in her onward race
    For power. Let her know her place ;
She is the second, not the first.

A higher hand must make her mild,
    If all be not in vain ; and guide
    Her footsteps, moving side by side
With wisdom, like the younger child :   2400

For she is earthly of the mind,
    But Wisdom heavenly of the soul.
    O, friend, who camest to thy goal
So early, leaving me behind,

I would the great world grew like thee,
    Who grewest not alone in power
    And knowledge, but by year and hour
In reverence and in charity.

CXIV

Now fades the last long streak of snow,
    Now burgeons every maze of quick   2410
    About the flowering squares, and thick
By ashen roots the violets blow.

Now rings the woodland loud and long,
    The distance takes a lovelier hue,
    And drown'd in yonder living blue
The lark becomes a sightless song.

Now dance the lights on lawn and lea,
    The flocks are whiter down the vale,
    And milkier every milky sail
On winding stream or distant sea ;   2420

Where now the seamew pipes, or dives
    In yonder greening gleam, and fly
    The happy birds, that change their sky
To build and brood ; that live their lives

From land to land ; and in my breast
    Spring wakens too ; and my regret
    Becomes an April violet,
And buds and blossoms like the rest.

CXV

Is it, then, regret for buried time
    That keenlier in sweet April wakes,   2430
    And meets the year, and gives and takes
The colours of the crescent prime ?

Not all : the songs, the stirring air,
    The life re-orient out of dust,
    Cry thro' the sense to hearten trust
In that which made the world so fair.

Not all regret : the face will shine
    Upon me, while I muse alone ;
    And that dear voice, I once have known,
Still speak to me of me and mine :   2440

Yet less of sorrow lives in me
    For days of happy commune dead ;
    Less yearning for the friendship fled,
Than some strong bond which is to be.

CXVI

O days and hours, your work is this,
    To hold me from my proper place,
    A little while from his embrace,
For fuller gain of after bliss :

That out of distance might ensue
    Desire of nearness doubly sweet ;   2450
    And unto meeting, when we meet,
Delight a hundredfold accrue

For every grain of sand that runs,
    And every span of shade that steals,
    And every kiss of toothed wheels,
And all the courses of the suns.

CXVII

Contemplate all this work of Time,
    The giant labouring in his youth ;
    Nor dream of human love and truth,
As dying Nature's earth and lime ;   2460

But trust that those we call the dead
    Are breathers of an ampler day
    For ever nobler ends. They say,
The solid earth whereon we tread

In tracts of fluent heat began,
    And grew to seeming-random forms,
    The seeming prey of cyclic storms,
Till at the last arose the man ;

Who throve and branch'd from clime to clime,
    The herald of a higher race,   2470
    And of himself in higher place,
If so he type this work of time

Within himself, from more to more ;
    Or, crown'd with attributes of woe
    Like glories, move his course, and show
That life is not as idle ore,

But iron dug from central gloom,
    And heated hot with burning fears,
    And dipt in baths of hissing tears,
And batter'd with the shocks of doom   2480

To shape and use. Arise and fly
    The reeling Faun, the sensual feast ;
    Move upward, working out the beast,
And let the ape and tiger die.

CXVIII

Doors, where my heart was used to beat
    So quickly, not as one that weeps
    I come once more ; the city sleeps ;
I smell the meadow in the street ;

I hear a chirp of birds ; I see
    Betwixt the black fronts long-withdrawn   2490
    A light-blue lane of early dawn,
And think of early days and thee,

And bless thee, for thy lips are bland,
    And bright the friendship of thine eye ;
    And in my thoughts with scarce a sigh
I take the pressure of thine hand.

CXIX

I trust I have not wasted breath :
    I think we are not wholly brain,
    Magnetic mockeries ; not in vain,
Like Paul with beasts, I fought with Death ;   2500

Not only cunning casts in clay :
    Let Science prove we are, and then
    What matters Science unto men,
At least to me ? I would not stay.

Let him, the wiser man who springs
    Hereafter, up from childhood shape
    His action like the greater ape,
But I was *born* to other things.

CXX

Sad Hesper o'er the buried sun
    And ready, thou, to die with him,
    Thou watchest all things ever dim
And dimmer, and a glory done:

The team is loosen'd from the wain,
    The boat is drawn upon the shore;
    Thou listenest to the closing door.
And life is darken'd in the brain.

Bright Phosphor, fresher for the night,
    By thee the world's great work is heard
    Beginning, and the wakeful bird;
Behind thee comes the greater light:

The market boat is on the stream,
    And voices hail it from the brink;
    Thou hear'st the village hammer clink,
And see'st the moving of the team.

Sweet Hesper-Phosphor, double name
    For what is one, the first, the last,
    Thou, like my present and my past,
Thy place is changed; thou art the same.

CXXI

Oh, wast thou with me, dearest, then,
    While I rose up against my doom,
    And yearn'd to burst the folded gloom,
To bare the eternal Heavens again,

To feel once more, in placid awe,
    The strong imagination roll
    A sphere of stars about my soul,
In all her motion one with law;

If thou wert with me, and the grave
    Divide us not, be with me now,
    And enter in at breast and brow,
Till all my blood, a fuller wave,

Be quicken'd with a livelier breath,
    And like an inconsiderate boy,
    As in the former flash of joy,
I slip the thoughts of life and death;

And all the breeze of Fancy blows,
    And every dewdrop paints a bow,
    The wizard lightnings deeply glow,
And every thought breaks out a rose.

2510

2520

2530

2540

CXXII

There rolls the deep where grew the tree.
　　O earth, what changes hast thou seen !　　2550
　　There where the long street roars, hath been
The stillness of the central sea.

The hills are shadows, and they flow
　　From form to form, and nothing stands ;
　　They melt like mist, the solid lands,
Like clouds they shape themselves and go.

But in my spirit will I dwell,
　　And dream my dream, and hold it true ;
　　For tho' my lips may breathe adieu,
I cannot think the thing farewell.　　2560

CXXIII

That which we dare invoke to bless ;
　　Our dearest faith ;　our ghastliest doubt ;
　　He, They, One, All ;　within, without :
The Power in darkness whom we guess ;

I found Him not in world or sun,
　　Or eagle's wing, or insect's eye ;
　　Nor thro' the questions men may try,
The petty cobwebs we have spun :

If e'er when faith had fall'n asleep,
　　I heard a voice ' believe no more,'　　2570
　　And heard an ever-breaking shore
That tumbled in the Godless deep ;

A warmth within the breast would melt
　　The freezing reason's colder part,
　　And like a man in wrath the heart
Stood up and answer'd ' I have felt.'

No, like a child in doubt and fear :
　　But that blind clamour made me wise ;
　　Then was I as a child that cries,
But, crying, knows his father near ;　　2580

And what I am beheld again
　　What is, and no man understands ;
　　And out of darkness came the hands
That reach thro' nature, moulding men.

CXXIV

Whatever I have said or sung,
　　Some bitter notes my harp would give,
　　Yea, tho' there often seem'd to live
A contradiction on the tongue,

2581.　am] seem 1850.

Yet Hope had never lost her youth;
 She did but look through dimmer eyes; 2590
 Or Love but play'd with gracious lies,
Because he felt so fix'd in truth:

And if the song were full of care,
 He breathed the spirit of the song;
 And if the words were sweet and strong
He set his royal signet there;

Abiding with me till I sail
 To seek thee on the mystic deeps,
 And this electric force, that keeps
A thousand pulses dancing, fail. 2600

CXXV

Love is and was my Lord and King,
 And in his presence I attend
 To hear the tidings of my friend,
Which every hour his couriers bring.

Love is and was my King and Lord,
 And will be, tho' as yet I keep
 Within his court on earth, and sleep
Encompass'd by his faithful guard,

And hear at times a sentinel
 Who moves about from place to place, 2610
 And whispers to the worlds of space,
In the deep night, that all is well.

CXXVI

And all is well, tho' faith and form
 Be sunder'd in the night of fear;
 Well roars the storm to those that hear
A deeper voice across the storm,

Proclaiming social truth shall spread,
 And justice, ev'n tho' thrice again
 The red fool-fury of the Seine
Should pile her barricades with dead. 2620

But ill for him that wears a crown,
 And him, the lazar, in his rags:
 They tremble, the sustaining crags;
The spires of ice are toppled down,

And molten up, and roar in flood;
 The fortress crashes from on high,
 The brute earth lightens to the sky,
And the great Æon sinks in blood,

And compass'd by the fires of Hell;
   While thou, dear spirit, happy star,   2630
   O'erlook'st the tumult from afar,
And smilest, knowing all is well.

CXXVII

The love that rose on stronger wings,
   Unpalsied when he met with Death,
   Is comrade of the lesser faith
That sees the course of human things.

No doubt vast eddies in the flood
   Of onward time shall yet be made,
   And throned races may degrade;
Yet O ye mysteries of good,   2640

Wild Hours that fly with Hope and Fear,
   If all your office had to do
   With old results that look like new;
If this were all your mission here,

To draw, to sheathe a useless sword,
   To fool the crowd with glorious lies,
   To cleave a creed in sects and cries,
To change the bearing of a word,

To shift an arbitrary power,
   To cramp the student at his desk,   2650
   To make old bareness picturesque
And tuft with grass a feudal tower;

Why then my scorn might well descend
   On you and yours. I see in part
   That all, as in some piece of art,
Is toil cöoperant to an end.

CXXVIII

Dear friend, far off, my lost desire,
   So far, so near in woe and weal;
   O loved the most, when most I feel
There is a lower and a higher;   2660

Known and unknown; human, divine;
   Sweet human hand and lips and eye;
   Dear heavenly friend that canst not die,
Mine, mine, for ever, ever mine;

Strange friend, past, present, and to be;
   Loved deeplier, darklier understood;
   Behold, I dream a dream of good,
And mingle all the world with thee.

CXXIX

Thy voice is on the rolling air ;
    I hear thee where the waters run ;
    Thou standest in the rising sun,
And in the setting thou art fair.

2670

What art thou then ? I cannot guess ;
    But tho' I seem in star and flower
    To feel thee some diffusive power,
I do not therefore love thee less :

My love involves the love before ;
    My love is vaster passion now ;
    Tho' mix'd with God and Nature thou,
I seem to love thee more and more.

2680

Far off thou art, but ever nigh ;
    I have thee still, and I rejoice ;
    I prosper, circled with thy voice ;
I shall not lose thee tho' I die.

CXXX

O living will that shalt endure
    When all that seems shall suffer shock,
    Rise in the spiritual rock,
Flow thro' our deeds and make them pure,

That we may lift from out of dust
    A voice as unto him that hears,
    A cry above the conquer'd years
To one that with us works, and trust,

2690

With faith that comes of self-control,
    The truths that never can be proved
    Until we close with all we loved,
And all we flow from, soul in soul.

O TRUE and tried, so well and long,
    Demand not thou a marriage lay ;
    In that it is thy marriage day
Is music more than any song.

2700

Nor have I felt so much of bliss
    Since first he told me that he loved
    A daughter of our house ; nor proved
Since that dark day a day like this ;

Tho' I since then have number'd o'er
    Some thrice three years : they went and came,
    Remade the blood and changed the frame,
And yet is love not less, but more ;

No longer caring to embalm
  In dying songs a dead regret,   2710
  But like a statue solid-set,
And moulded in colossal calm.

Regret is dead, but love is more
  Than in the summers that are flown,
  For I myself with these have grown
To something greater than before ;

Which makes appear the songs I made
  As echoes out of weaker times,
  As half but idle brawling rhymes,
The sport of random sun and shade.   2720

But where is she, the bridal flower
  That must be made a wife ere noon ?
  She enters, glowing like the moon
Of Eden on its bridal bower :

On me she bends her blissful eyes
  And then on thee ; they meet thy look
  And brighten like the star that shook
Betwixt the palms of paradise.

O when her life was yet in bud,
  He too foretold the perfect rose.   2730
  For thee she grew, for thee she grows
For ever, and as fair as good.

And thou art worthy ; full of power ;
  As gentle ; liberal-minded, great,
  Consistent ; wearing all that weight
Of learning lightly like a flower.

But now set out : the noon is near,
  And I must give away the bride ;
  She fears not, or with thee beside
And me behind her, will not fear :   2740

For I that danced her on my knee,
  That watch'd her on her nurse's arm,
  That shielded all her life from harm,
At last must part with her to thee ;

Now waiting to be made a wife,
  Her feet, my darling, on the dead ;
  Their pensive tablets round her head,
And the most living words of life

Breathed in her ear. The ring is on,
  The ' wilt thou ' answer'd, and again   2750
  The ' wilt thou ' ask'd, till out of twain
Her sweet ' I will ' has made ye one.

Now sign your names, which shall be read,
  Mute symbols of a joyful morn,
  By village eyes as yet unborn ;
The names are sign'd, and overhead

Begins the clash and clang that tells
    The joy to every wandering breeze ;
    The blind wall rocks, and on the trees
The dead leaf trembles to the bells.   2760

O happy hour, and happier hours
    Await them. Many a merry face
    Salutes them—maidens of the place,
That pelt us in the porch with flowers.

O happy hour, behold the bride
    With him to whom her hand I gave.
    They leave the porch, they pass the grave
That has to-day its sunny side.

To-day the grave is bright for me,   2770
    For them the light of life increased,
    Who stay to share the morning feast,
Who rest to-night beside the sea.

Let all my genial spirits advance
    To meet and greet a whiter sun ;
    My drooping memory will not shun
The foaming grape of eastern France.

It circles round, and fancy plays,
    And hearts are warm'd and faces bloom,
    As drinking health to bride and groom
We wish them store of happy days.   2780

Nor count me all to blame if I
    Conjecture of a stiller guest,
    Perchance, perchance, among the rest,
And, tho' in silence, wishing joy.

But they must go, the time draws on,
    And those white-favour'd horses wait ;
    They rise, but linger ; it is late ;
Farewell, we kiss, and they are gone.

A shade falls on us like the dark
    From little cloudlets on the grass,   2790
    But sweeps away as out we pass
To range the woods, to roam the park,

Discussing how their courtship grew,
    And talk of others that are wed,
    And how she look'd, and what he said,
And back we come at fall of dew.

Again the feast, the speech, the glee,
    The shade of passing thought, the wealth
    Of words and wit, the double health,
The crowning cup, the three-times-three,   2800

And last the dance ;—till I retire :
    Dumb is that tower which spake so loud,
    And high in heaven the streaming cloud,
And on the downs a rising fire :

And rise, O moon, from yonder down,
   Till over down and over dale
   All night the shining vapour sail
And pass the silent-lighted town,

The white-faced halls, the glancing rills,
   And catch at every mountain head,   2810
   And o'er the friths that branch and spread
Their sleeping silver thro' the hills;

And touch with shade the bridal doors,
   With tender gloom the roof, the wall;
   And breaking let the splendour fall
To spangle all the happy shores

By which they rest, and ocean sounds,
   And, star and system rolling past,
   A soul shall draw from out the vast
And strike his being into bounds,   2820

And, moved thro' life of lower phase,
   Result in man, be born and think,
   And act and love, a closer link
Betwixt us and the crowning race

Of those that, eye to eye, shall look
   On knowledge; under whose command
   Is Earth and Earth's, and in their hand
Is Nature like an open book;

No longer half-akin to brute,
   For all we thought and loved and did,   2830
   And hoped, and suffer'd, is but seed
Of what in them is flower and fruit;

Whereof the man, that with me trod
   This planet, was a noble type
   Appearing ere the times were ripe,
That friend of mine who lives in God,

That God, which ever lives and loves,
   One God, one law, one element,
   And one far-off divine event,
To which the whole creation moves.   2840

COME DOWN, O MAID

COME down, O maid, from yonder mountain height:
What pleasure lives in height (the shepherd sang),
In height and cold, the splendour of the hills?
But cease to move so near the Heavens, and cease
To glide a sunbeam by the blasted Pine,
To sit a star upon the sparkling spire;
And come, for Love is of the valley, come,
For Love is of the valley, come thou down

And find him; by the happy threshold, he,
Or hand in hand with Plenty in the maize,   10
Or red with spirted purple of the vats,
Or foxlike in the vine; nor cares to walk
With Death and Morning on the silver horns,
Nor wilt thou snare him in the white ravine,
Nor find him dropt upon the firths of ice,
That huddling slant in furrow-cloven falls
To roll the torrent out of dusky doors:
But follow; let the torrent dance thee down
To find him in the valley; let the wild   20
Lean-headed Eagles yelp alone, and leave
The monstrous ledges there to slope, and spill
Their thousand wreaths of dangling water-smoke,
That like a broken purpose waste in air:
So waste not thou; but come; for all the vales
Await thee; azure pillars of the hearth
Arise to thee; the children call, and I
Thy shepherd pipe, and sweet is every sound,
Sweeter thy voice, but every sound is sweet;
Myriads of rivulets hurrying thro' the lawn,
The moan of doves in immemorial elms,   30
And murmuring of innumerable bees.

ODE ON THE DEATH OF THE DUKE OF WELLINGTON

Funeral Ode.   *irregular*   *VI & VII most important*

I

BURY the Great Duke
  With an empire's lamentation,
Let us bury the Great Duke
  To the noise of the mourning of a mighty nation.
Mourning when their leaders fall,
Warriors carry the warrior's pall,
And sorrow darkens hamlet and hall.

II

Where shall we lay the man whom we deplore?
Here, in streaming London's central roar.
Let the sound of those he wrought for,   10
And the feet of those he fought for,
Echo round his bones for evermore.

III

Lead out the pageant: sad and slow,
As fits an universal woe,
Let the long long procession go,
And let the sorrowing crowd about it grow
And let the mournful martial music blow;
The last great Englishman is low.

IV

Mourn, for to us he seems the last,
Remembering all his greatness in the Past.   20
No more in soldier fashion will he greet
With lifted hand the gazer in the street.
O friends, our chief state-oracle is mute: *not true*
Mourn for the man of long-enduring blood,
The statesman-warrior, moderate, resolute,
Whole in himself, a common good.
Mourn for the man of amplest influence,
Yet clearest of ambitious crime,
Our greatest yet with least pretence,
Great in council and great in war, *no*   30
Foremost captain of his time,
Rich in saving common-sense,
And, as the greatest only are,
In his simplicity sublime.
O good grey head which all men knew,
O voice from which their omens all men drew, *axe & dd earn*
O iron nerve to true occasion true,
O fall'n at length that tower of strength
Which stood four-square to all the winds that blew !
Such was he whom we deplore.   40
The long self-sacrifice of life is o'er.
The great World-victor's victor will be seen no more.

V

All is over and done
Render thanks to the Giver,
England, for thy son.
Let the bell be toll'd.
Render thanks to the Giver,
And render him to the mould.
Under the cross of gold *St Paul's Dame.*
That shines over city and river.   50
There he shall rest for ever
Among the wise and the bold.
Let the bell be toll'd:
And a reverent people behold
The towering car, the sable steeds :
Bright let it be with its blazon'd deeds,
Dark in its funeral fold.
Let the bell be toll'd:
And a deeper knell in the heart be knoll'd ;
And the sound of the sorrowing anthem roll'd   60
Thro' the dome of the golden cross ;
And the volleying cannon thunder his loss ;
He knew their voices of old.
For many a time in many a clime

His captain's-ear has heard them boom
Bellowing victory, bellowing doom;
When he with those deep voices wrought,
Guarding realms and kings from shame;
With those deep voices our dead captain taught
The tyrant, and asserts his claim   70
In that dread sound to the great name,
Which he has worn so pure of blame,
In praise and in dispraise the same,
A man of well attemper'd frame.
O civic muse, to such a name,
To such a name for ages long,
To such a name,
Preserve a broad approach of fame,
And ever-ringing avenues of song.

Here nelson is supposed. t be VI *talking*

Who is he that cometh, like an honour'd guest,   80
With banner and with music, with soldier and with priest,
With a nation weeping, and breaking on my rest?
Mighty seaman, this is he
Was great by land as thou by sea.
Thine island loves thee well, thou famous man,
The greatest sailor since our world began.
Now, to the roll of muffled drums,
To thee the greatest soldier comes;
For this is he
Was great by land as thou by sea;   90
His foes were thine; he kept us free;
O give him welcome, this is he,
Worthy of our gorgeous rites,
And worthy to be laid by thee;
For this is England's greatest son,
He that gain'd a hundred fights,
Nor ever lost an English gun;
This is he that far away
Against the myriads of Assaye   *Defeated mahrates.*
Clash'd with his fiery few and won;   100
And underneath another sun,
Warring on a later day,
Round affrighted Lisbon drew
The treble works, the vast designs
Of his labour'd rampart-lines,
Where he greatly stood at bay,
Whence he issued forth anew,
And ever great and greater grew,
Beating from the wasted vines
Back to France her banded swarms,   110
Back to France with countless blows,
Till o'er the hills her eagles flew
Past the Pyrenean pines,

Follow'd up in valley and glen
With blare of bugle, clamour of men,
Roll of cannon and clash of arms,
And England pouring on her foes.
Such a war had such a close.
Again their ravening eagle rose
In anger, wheel'd on Europe-shadowing wings,　　　120
And barking for the thrones of kings;
Till one that sought but Duty's iron crown
On that loud sabbath shook the spoiler down; *Waterloo*
A day of onsets of despair!
Dash'd on every rocky square *squares (broken troops)*
Their surging charges foam'd themselves away;
Last, the Prussian trumpet blew;
Thro' the long-tormented air
Heaven flash'd a sudden jubilant ray,
And down we swept and charged and overthrew.　　　130
So great a soldier taught us there,
What long-enduring hearts could do
In that world's-earthquake, Waterloo!
Mighty seaman, tender and true,
And pure as he from taint of craven guile,
O saviour of the silver-coasted isle,
O shaker of the Baltic and the Nile,
If aught of things that here befall
Touch a spirit among things divine,
If love of country move thee there at all,　　　140
Be glad, because his bones are laid by thine!
And thro' the centuries let a people's voice
In full acclaim,
A people's voice,
The proof and echo of all human fame,
A people's voice, when they rejoice
At civic revel and pomp and game,
Attest their great commander's claim
With honour, honour, honour, honour to him,
Eternal honour to his name.　　　150

very important.

VII

A people's voice! we are a people yet.
Tho' all men else their nobler dreams forget,
Confused by brainless mobs and lawless Powers;
Thank Him who isled us here, and roughly set
His Saxon in blown seas and storming showers,
We have a voice, with which to pay the debt
Of boundless love and reverence and regret
To those great men who fought, and kept it ours.
And keep it ours, O God, from brute control;
O Statesmen, guard us, guard the eye, the soul　　　160
Of Europe, keep our noble England whole

And save the one true seed of freedom sown
Betwixt a people and their ancient throne,
That sober freedom out of which there springs
Our loyal passion for our temperate kings;
For, saving that, ye help to save mankind
Till public wrong be crumbled into dust,
And drill the raw world for the march of mind,
Till crowds at length be sane and crowns be just.
But wink no more in slothful overtrust.   170
Remember him who led your hosts;
He bad you guard the sacred coasts.
Your cannons moulder on the seaward wall;
His voice is silent in your council-hall
For ever; and whatever tempests lour
For ever silent; even if they broke
In thunder, silent; yet remember all
He spoke among you, and the Man who spoke;
Who never sold the truth to serve the hour,
Nor palter'd with Eternal God for power;   180
Who let the turbid streams of rumour flow
Thro' either babbling world of high and low;
Whose life was work, whose language rife
With rugged maxims hewn from life;
Who never spoke against a foe;
Whose eighty winters freeze with one rebuke
All great self-seekers trampling on the right:
Truth-teller was our England's Alfred named;
Truth-lover was our English Duke;
Whatever record leap to light   190
He never shall be shamed.

VIII

Lo, the leader in these glorious wars
Now to glorious burial slowly borne,
Follow'd by the brave of other lands,
He, on whom from both her open hands
Lavish Honour shower'd all her stars,
And affluent Fortune emptied all her horn.
Yea, let all good things await
Him who cares not to be great,
But as he saves or serves the state.   200
Not once or twice in our rough island-story,
The path of duty was the way to glory:
He that walks it, only thirsting
For the right, and learns to deaden
Love of self, before his journey closes,
He shall find the stubborn thistle bursting
Into glossy purples, which outredden
All voluptuous garden-roses.
Not once or twice in our fair island-story,
The path of duty was the way to glory: 210

He, that ever following her commands,
On with toil of heart and knees and hands,
Thro' the long gorge to the far light has won
His path upward, and prevail'd,
Shall find the toppling crags of Duty scaled
Are close upon the shining table-lands
To which our God Himself is moon and sun.
Such was he: his work is done.
But while the races of mankind endure,
Let his great example stand   220
Colossal, seen of every land,
And keep the soldier firm, the statesman pure;
Till in all lands and thro' all human story
The path of duty be the way to glory:
And let the land whose hearths he saved from shame
For many and many an age proclaim
At civic revel and pomp and game,
And when the long-illumined cities flame,
Their ever-loyal iron leader's fame,
With honour, honour, honour, honour to him,   230
Eternal honour to his name.

IX

Peace, his triumph will be sung
By some yet unmoulded tongue
Far on in summers that we shall not see:
Peace, it is a day of pain
For one about whose patriarchal knee
Late the little children clung:
O peace, it is a day of pain
For one, upon whose hand and heart and brain
Once the weight and fate of Europe hung.   240
Ours the pain, be his the gain!
More than is of man's degree
Must be with us, watching here
At this, our great solemnity.
Whom we see not we revere.
We revere, and we refrain
From talk of battles loud and vain,
And brawling memories all too free
For such a wise humility
As befits a solemn fane: *I temple*   250
We revere, and while we hear
The tides of Music's golden sea
Setting toward eternity,
Uplifted high in heart and hope are we,
Until we doubt not that for one so true
There must be other nobler work to do
Than when he fought at Waterloo,
And Victor he must ever be.
For tho' the Giant Ages heave the hill

And break the shore, and evermore   260
Make and break, and work their will ;
Tho' world on world in myriad myriads roll
Round us, each with different powers,
And other forms of life than ours,
What know we greater than the soul ?
On God and Godlike men we build our trust.
Hush, the Dead March wails in the people's ears :
The dark crowd moves, and there are sobs and tears :
The black earth yawns : the mortal disappears ;
Ashes to ashes, dust to dust ;   270
He is gone who seem'd so great.—
Gone ; but nothing can bereave him
Of the force he made his own
Being here, and we believe him
Something far advanced in State,
And that he wears a truer crown
Than any wreath that man can weave him.
But speak no more of his renown,
Lay your earthly fancies down,
And in the vast cathedral leave him.   280
God accept him, Christ receive him.

1852.

MILTON

Alcaics

O MIGHTY-MOUTH'D inventor of harmonies,
O skill'd to sing of Time or Eternity,
    God-gifted organ-voice of England,
        Milton, a name to resound for ages ;
Whose Titan angels, Gabriel, Abdiel,
Starr'd from Jehovah's gorgeous armouries,
    Tower, as the deep-domed empyrëan
        Rings to the roar of an angel onset—
Me rather all that bowery loneliness,
The brooks of Eden mazily murmuring,   10
    And bloom profuse and cedar arches
        Charm, as a wanderer out in ocean,
Where some refulgent sunset of India
Streams o'er a rich ambrosial ocean isle,
    And crimson-hued the stately palmwoods
        Whisper in odorous heights of even.

Dramatic lyric monologue ## ULYSSES

It little profits that an idle king,
By this still hearth, among these barren crags,
Match'd with an aged wife, I mete and dole
Unequal laws unto a savage race,
That hoard, and sleep, and feed, and know not me.
I cannot rest from travel: I will drink
Life to the lees: all times I have enjoy'd
Greatly, have suffer'd greatly, both with those
That loved me, and alone; on shore, and when
Thro' scudding drifts the rainy Hyades　　　　　　10
Vext the dim sea: I am become a name;
For always roaming with a hungry heart
Much have I seen and known; cities of men
And manners, climates, councils, governments,
Myself not least, but honour'd of them all;
And drunk delight of battle with my peers,
Far on the ringing plains of windy Troy.
I am a part of all that I have met;
Yet all experience is an arch wherethro'
Gleams that untravell'd world, whose margin fades　　20
For ever and for ever when I move.
How dull it is to pause, to make an end,
To rust unburnish'd, not to shine in use!
As tho' to breathe were life. Life piled on life
Were all too little, and of one to me
Little remains: but every hour is saved
From that eternal silence, something more,
A bringer of new things; and vile it were
For some three suns to store and hoard myself,
And this grey spirit yearning in desire　　　　　30
To follow knowledge, like a sinking star,
Beyond the utmost bound of human thought.
　This is my son, mine own Telemachus,
To whom I leave the sceptre and the isle—
Well-loved of me, discerning to fulfil
This labour, by slow prudence to make mild
A rugged people, and thro' soft degrees
Subdue them to the useful and the good.
Most blameless is he, centred in the sphere
Of common duties, decent not to fail　　　　　40
In offices of tenderness, and pay
Meet adoration to my household gods,
When I am gone. He works his work, I mine.
　There lies the port: the vessel puffs her sail:
There gloom the dark broad seas. My mariners,
Souls that have toil'd, and wrought, and thought with me—
That ever with a frolic welcome took

The thunder and the sunshine, and opposed
Free hearts, free foreheads—you and I are old ;
Old age hath yet his honour and his toil ;   50
Death closes all : but something ere the end,
Some work of noble note, may yet be done,
Not unbecoming men that strove with Gods.
The lights begin to twinkle from the rocks :
The long day wanes : the slow moon climbs : the deep
Moans round with many voices. Come, my friends,
'Tis not too late to seek a newer world.
Push off, and sitting well in order smite
The sounding furrows ; for my purpose holds
To sail beyond the sunset, and the baths   60
Of all the western stars, until I die.
It may be that the gulfs will wash us down :
It may be we shall touch the Happy Isles,
And see the great Achilles, whom we knew.
Tho' much is taken, much abides ; and tho'
We are not now that strength which in old days
Moved earth and heaven ; that which we are, we are ;
One equal temper of heroic hearts,
Made weak by time and fate, but strong in will
To strive, to seek, to find, and not to yield.   70

ROBERT BROWNING

MY LAST DUCHESS

FERRARA

THAT 's my last Duchess painted on the wall,
Looking as if she were alive ; I call
That piece a wonder, now : Frà Pandolf's hands
Worked busily a day, and there she stands.
Will 't please you sit and look at her ? I said
'Frà Pandolf' by design, for never read
Strangers like you that pictured countenance,
The depth and passion of its earnest glance,
But to myself they turned (since none puts by
The curtain I have drawn for you, but I)   10
And seemed as they would ask me, if they durst,
How such a glance came there ; so, not the first
Are you to turn and ask thus. Sir, 't was not
Her husband's presence only, called that spot
Of joy into the Duchess' cheek : perhaps
Frà Pandolf chanced to say 'Her mantle laps
Over my Lady's wrist too much,' or 'Paint
Must never hope to reproduce the faint
Half-flush that dies along her throat ;' such stuff
Was courtesy, she thought, and cause enough   20
For calling up that spot of joy. She had
A heart . . . how shall I say ? . . . too soon made glad,
Too easily impressed ; she liked whate'er
She looked on, and her looks went everywhere.
Sir, 't was all one ! My favour at her breast,
The dropping of the daylight in the West,
The bough of cherries some officious fool
Broke in the orchard for her, the white mule
She rode with round the terrace—all and each
Would draw from her alike the approving speech,   30
Or blush, at least. She thanked men,—good ; but thanked
Somehow . . . I know not how . . . as if she ranked
My gift of a nine-hundred-years-old name
With anybody's gift. Who'd stoop to blame
This sort of trifling ? Even had you skill
In speech—(which I have not)—to make your will
Quite clear to such an one, and say 'Just this
Or that in you disgusts me ; here you miss,
Or there exceed the mark '—and if she let
Herself be lessoned so, nor plainly set   40

Her wits to yours, forsooth, and made excuse,
—E'en then would be some stooping, and I chuse
Never to stoop. Oh, Sir, she smiled, no doubt,
Whene'er I passed her; but who passed without
Much the same smile? This grew; I gave commands;
Then all smiles stopped together. There she stands
As if alive. Will 't please you rise? We'll meet
The company below, then. I repeat,
The Count your Master's known munificence
Is ample warrant that no just pretence   50
Of mine for dowry will be disallowed;
Though his fair daughter's self, as I avowed
At starting, is my object. Nay, we'll go
Together down, Sir! Notice Neptune, though,
Taming a sea-horse, thought a rarity,
Which Claus of Innsbruck cast in bronze for me.

PICTOR IGNOTUS

FLORENCE, 15—

I COULD have painted pictures like that youth's
   Ye praise so. How my soul springs up! No bar
Stayed me—ah, thought which saddens while it soothes!
   —Never did fate forbid me, star by star,
To outburst on your night with all my gift
   Of fires from God: nor would my flesh have shrunk
From seconding my soul, with eyes uplift
   And wide to heaven, or, straight like thunder, sunk
To the centre, of an instant; or around
   Turned calmly and inquisitive, to scan   10
The licence and the limit, space and bound,
   Allowed to Truth made visible in Man.
And, like that youth ye praise so, all I saw,
   Over the canvas could my hand have flung,
Each face obedient to its passion's law,
   Each passion clear proclaimed without a tongue;
Whether Hope rose at once in all the blood,
   A-tiptoe for the blessing of embrace,
Or Rapture drooped the eyes, as when her brood
   Pull down the nesting dove's heart to its place;   20
Or Confidence lit swift the forehead up,
   And locked the mouth fast, like a castle braved,—
O human faces, hath it spilt, my cup?
   What did ye give me that I have not saved?
Nor will I say I have not dreamed (how well!)
   Of going—I, in each new picture,—forth,
As, making new hearts beat and bosoms swell,
   To Pope or Kaiser, East, West, South or North,

Bound for the calmly satisfied great State,
  Or glad aspiring little burgh, it went,   30
Flowers cast upon the car which bore the freight,
  Through old streets named afresh from its event,
Till it reached home, where learned Age should greet
  My face, and Youth, the star not yet distinct
Above his hair, lie learning at my feet!—
  Oh, thus to live, I and my picture, linked
With love about, and praise, till life should end,
  And then not go to heaven, but linger here,
Here on my earth, earth's every man my friend,—
  The thought grew frightful, 'twas so wildly dear!   40
But a voice changed it! Glimpses of such sights
  Have scared me, like the revels through a door
Of some strange House of Idols at its rites;
  This world seemed not the world it was before:
Mixed with my loving trusting ones there trooped
  . . . Who summoned those cold faces that begun
To press on me and judge me? Though I stooped
  Shrinking, as from the soldiery a nun,
They drew me forth, and spite of me . . . enough!
  These buy and sell our pictures, take and give,   50
Count them for garniture and household-stuff,
  And where they live our pictures needs must live
And see their faces, listen to their prate,
  Partakers of their daily pettiness,
Discussed of,—'This I love, or this I hate,
  This likes me more, and this affects me less!'
Wherefore I chose my portion. If at whiles
  My heart sinks, as monotonous I paint
These endless cloisters and eternal aisles
  With the same series, Virgin, Babe and Saint,   60
With the same cold, calm, beautiful regard,
  At least no merchant traffics in my heart;
The sanctuary's gloom at least shall ward
  Vain tongues from where my pictures stand apart:
Only prayer breaks the silence of the shrine
  While, blackening in the daily candle-smoke,
They moulder on the damp wall's travertine,
  'Mid echoes the light footstep never woke.
So die, my pictures; surely, gently die!
  Oh, youth, men praise so,—holds their praise its worth? 70
Blown harshly, keeps the trump its golden cry?
  Tastes sweet the water with such specks of earth?

THE BISHOP ORDERS HIS TOMB AT SAINT PRAXED'S CHURCH

ROME, 15— *Dramatic monologue.*
Italian Renaissance.

VANITY, saith the preacher, vanity!
Draw round my bed: is Anselm keeping back?
Nephews—sons mine . . . ah God, I know not! Well—
She, men would have to be your mother once,
Old Gandolf envied me, so fair she was!
What 's done is done, and she is dead beside,
Dead long ago, and I am Bishop since,
And as she died so must we die ourselves,
And thence ye may perceive the world 's a dream.
Life, how and what is it? As here I lie   10
In this state-chamber, dying by degrees,
Hours and long hours in the dead night, I ask
' Do I live, am I dead?' Peace, peace seems all.
Saint Praxed's ever was the church for peace;
And so, about this tomb of mine. I fought
With tooth and nail to save my niche, ye know:
—Old Gandolf cozened me, despite my care;
Shrewd was that snatch from out the corner South
He graced his carrion with, God curse the same!
Yet still my niche is not so cramped but thence   20
One sees the pulpit o' the epistle-side,
And somewhat of the choir, those silent seats,
And up into the aery dome where live
The angels, and a sunbeam 's sure to lurk:
And I shall fill my slab of basalt there,
And 'neath my tabernacle take my rest,
With those nine columns round me, two and two,
The odd one at my feet where Anselm stands:
Peach-blossom marble all, the rare, the ripe
As fresh-poured red wine of a mighty pulse   30
—Old Gandolf with his paltry onion-stone,
Put me where I may look at him! True peach,
Rosy and flawless: how I earned the prize!
Draw close: that conflagration of my church
—What then? So much was saved if aught were missed!
My sons, ye would not be my death? Go dig
The white-grape vineyard where the oil-press stood,
Drop water gently till the surface sinks,
And if ye find . . . Ah, God, I know not, I! . . .
Bedded in store of rotten figleaves soft,   40
And corded up in a tight olive-frail,
Some lump, ah God, of *lapis lazuli*,
Big as a Jew's head cut off at the nape,
Blue as a vein o'er the Madonna's breast . . .

Sons, all have I bequeathed you, villas, all,
That brave Frascati villa with its bath,
So, let the blue lump poise between my knees,
Like God the Father's globe on both His hands
Ye worship in the Jesu Church so gay,
For Gandolf shall not choose but see and burst!　　50
Swift as a weaver's shuttle fleet our years :
Man goeth to the grave, and where is he ?
Did I say basalt for my slab, sons ? Black—
'Twas ever antique-black I meant ! How else
Shall ye contrast my frieze to come beneath ?
The bas-relief in bronze ye promised me,
Those Pans and Nymphs ye wot of, and perchance
Some tripod, thyrsus, with a vase or so,
The Saviour at his sermon on the mount,
Saint Praxed in a glory, and one Pan　　60
Ready to twitch the Nymph's last garment off,
And Moses with the tables . . . but I know
Ye mark me not ! What do they whisper thee,
Child of my bowels, Anselm ? Ah, ye hope
To revel down my villas while I gasp
Bricked o'er with beggar's mouldy travertine
Which Gandolf from his tomb-top chuckles at !
Nay, boys, ye love me—all of jasper, then !
'Tis jasper ye stand pledged to, lest I grieve
My bath must needs be left behind, alas !　　70
One block, pure green as a pistachio-nut,
There 's plenty jasper somewhere in the world—
And have I not Saint Praxed's ear to pray
Horses for ye, and brown Greek manuscripts,
And mistresses with great smooth marbly limbs ?
—That 's if ye carve my epitaph aright,
Choice Latin, picked phrase, Tully's every word, *every*
No gaudy ware like Gandolf's second line—
Tully, my masters ? Ulpian serves his need ! *done out*
And then how I shall lie through centuries,　　80
And hear the blessed mutter of the mass,
And see God made and eaten all day long,
And feel the steady candle-flame, and taste
Good strong thick stupefying incense-smoke !
For as I lie here, hours of the dead night,
Dying in state and by such slow degrees,
I fold my arms as if they clasped a crook,
And stretch my feet forth straight as stone can point,
And let the bedclothes for a mortcloth drop
Into great laps and folds of sculptor's-work :　　90
And as yon tapers dwindle, and strange thoughts
Grow, with a certain humming in my ears,
About the life before I lived this life,
And this life too, Popes, Cardinals and Priests,
Saint Praxed at his sermon on the mount,

Your tall pale mother with her talking eyes,
And new-found agate urns as fresh as day,
And marble's language, Latin pure, discreet,
—Aha, ELUCESCEBAT quoth our friend ?
No Tully, said I, Ulpian at the best!   100
Evil and brief hath been my pilgrimage.
All *lapis*, all, sons! Else I give the Pope
My villas : will ye ever eat my heart ?
Ever your eyes were as a lizard's quick,
They glitter like your mother's for my soul,
Or ye would heighten my impoverished frieze,
Piece out its starved design, and fill my vase
With grapes, and add a vizor and a Term,
And to the tripod ye would tie a lynx
That in his struggle throws the thyrsus down,   110
To comfort me on my entablature
Whereon I am to lie till I must ask
' Do I live, am I dead ? ' There, leave me, there!
For ye have stabbed me with ingratitude
To death—ye wish it—God, ye wish it! Stone—
Gritstone, a-crumble! Clammy squares which sweat
As if the corpse they keep were oozing through—
And no more *lapis* to delight the world!
Well, go! I bless ye. Fewer tapers there,
But in a row : and, going, turn your backs   120
—Ay, like departing altar-ministrants,
And leave me in my church, the church for peace,
That I may watch at leisure if he leers—
Old Gandolf, at me, from his onion-stone,
As still he envied me, so fair she was!

UP AT A VILLA—DOWN IN THE CITY

(As Distinguished by an Italian Person of Quality)

I

HAD I but plenty of money, money enough and to spare,
The house for me, no doubt, were a house in the city-square ;
Ah, such a life, such a life, as one leads at the window there!

II

Something to see, by Bacchus, something to hear, at least!
There, the whole day long, one's life is a perfect feast ;
While up at a villa one lives, I maintain it, no more than
        a beast.

III

Well now, look at our villa! stuck like the horn of a bull
Just on a mountain's edge as bare as the creature's skull,
Save a mere shag of a bush with hardly a leaf to pull!
—I scratch my own, sometimes, to see if the hair 's turned
        wool.   10

IV

But the city, oh the city—the square with the houses! Why?
They are stone-faced, white as a curd, there's something to
    take the eye!
Houses in four straight lines, not a single front awry!
You watch who crosses and gossips, who saunters, who hurries
    by;
Green blinds, as a matter of course, to draw when the sun gets
    high;
And the shops with fanciful signs which are painted properly.

V

What of a villa? Though winter be over in March by rights,
'Tis May perhaps ere the snow shall have wither'd well off the
    heights:
You've the brown ploughed land before, where the oxen
    steam and wheeze,
And the hills over-smoked behind by the faint grey olive-
    trees.   20

VI

Is it better in May, I ask you? you've summer all at once;
In a day he leaps complete with a few strong April suns!
'Mid the sharp short emerald wheat, scarce risen three fingers
    well,
The wild tulip, at end of its tube, blows out its great red bell
Like a thin clear bubble of blood, for the children to pick
    and sell.

VII

Is it ever hot in the square? There's a fountain to spout and
    splash!
In the shade it sings and springs; in the shine such foam-
    bows flash
On the horses with curling fish-tails, that prance and paddle
    and pash
Round the lady atop in the conch—fifty gazers do not abash,
Though all that she wears is some weeds round her waist in
    a sort of sash!   30

VIII

All the year long at the villa, nothing's to see though you
    linger,
Except yon cypress that points like Death's lean lifted fore-
    finger.
Some think fireflies pretty, when they mix in the corn and
    mingle,
Or thrid the stinking hemp till the stalks of it seem a-tingle.
Late August or early September, the stunning cicala is shrill,
And the bees keep their tiresome whine round the resinous
    firs on the hill.
Enough of the seasons,—I spare you the months of the fever
    and chill.

IX

Ere opening your eyes in the city, the blessed church-bells begin :

No sooner the bells leave off, than the diligence rattles in :

You get the pick of the news, and it costs you never a pin. 40

By and by there 's the travelling doctor gives pills, lets blood, draws teeth ;

Or the Pulcinello-trumpet breaks up the market beneath.

At the post-office such a scene-picture—the new play, piping hot !

And a notice how, only this morning, three liberal thieves were shot.

Above it, behold the archbishop's most fatherly of rebukes,

And beneath, with his crown and his lion, some little new law of the Duke's !

Or a sonnet with flowery marge, to the Reverend Don So-and-so

Who is Dante, Boccaccio, Petrarca, Saint Jerome, and Cicero,

' And moreover,' (the sonnet goes rhyming,) ' the skirts of Saint Paul has reached,

Having preached us those six Lent lectures more unctuous than ever he preached.'   50

Noon strikes,—here sweeps the procession ! our Lady borne smiling and smart

With a pink gauze gown all spangles, and seven swords stuck in her heart !

Bang, whang, whang goes the drum, *tootle-te-tootle* the fife ;

No keeping one's haunches still : it 's the greatest pleasure in life.

X

But bless you, it 's dear—it 's dear ! fowls, wine, at double the rate.

They have clapped a new tax upon salt, and what oil pays passing the gate

It 's a horror to think of.   And so, the villa for me, not the city !

Beggars can scarcely be choosers : but still—ah, the pity, the pity !

Look, two and two go the priests, then the monks with cowls and sandals,

And the penitents dressed in white shirts, a-holding the yellow candles ;   60

One, he carries a flag up straight, and another a cross with handles,

And the Duke's guard brings up the rear, for the better prevention of scandals :

Bang, whang, whang goes the drum, *tootle-te-tootle* the fife.

Oh, a day in the city-square, there is no such pleasure in life !

FRA LIPPO LIPPI

I AM poor brother Lippo, by your leave!
You need not clap your torches to my face.
Zooks, what's to blame? you think you see a monk!
What, it's past midnight, and you go the rounds,
And here you catch me at an alley's end
Where sportive ladies leave their doors ajar?
The Carmine's my cloister: hunt it up,
Do,—harry out, if you must show your zeal,
Whatever rat, there, haps on his wrong hole,
And nip each softling of a wee white mouse,   10
Weke, weke, that's crept to keep him company!
Aha, you know your betters? Then, you'll take
Your hand away that's fiddling on my throat,
And please to know me likewise. Who am I?
Why, one, sir, who is lodging with a friend
Three streets off—he's a certain . . . how d' ye call?
Master—a . . . Cosimo of the Medici,
In the house that caps the corner. Boh! you were best!
Remember and tell me, the day you're hanged,
How you affected such a gullet's gripe!   20
But you, sir, it concerns you that your knaves
Pick up a manner nor discredit you.
Zooks, are we pilchards, that they sweep the streets
And count fair prize what comes into their net?
He's Judas to a tittle, that man is!
Just such a face! why, sir, you make amends.
Lord, I'm not angry! Bid your hangdogs go
Drink out this quarter-florin to the health
Of the munificent House that harbours me
(And many more beside, lads! more beside!)   30
And all's come square again. I'd like his face—
His, elbowing on his comrade in the door
With the pike and lantern,—for the slave that holds
John Baptist's head a-dangle by the hair
With one hand ('look you, now,' as who should say)
And his weapon in the other, yet unwiped!
It's not your chance to have a bit of chalk,
A wood-coal or the like? or you should see!
Yes, I'm the painter, since you style me so.
What, brother Lippo's doings, up and down,   40
You know them and they take you? like enough!
I saw the proper twinkle in your eye—
'Tell you, I liked your looks at very first.
Let's sit and set things straight now, hip to haunch.
Here's spring come, and the nights one makes up bands
To roam the town and sing out carnival,

And I've been three weeks shut within my mew,
A-painting for the great man, saints and saints
And saints again. I could not paint all night—
Ouf! I leaned out of window for fresh air.   50
There came a hurry of feet and little feet,
A sweep of lute-strings, laughs, and whiffs of song,
Flower o' the broom,
Take away love, and our earth is a tomb!
Flower o' the quince,
I let Lisa go, and what good's in life since?
Flower o' the thyme—and so on. Round they went.
Scarce had they turned the corner when a titter
Like the skipping of rabbits by moonlight,—three slim
      shapes—
And a face that looked up . . . zooks, sir, flesh and blood, 60
That's all I'm made of! Into shreds it went,
Curtain and counterpane and coverlet,
All the bed-furniture—a dozen knots,
There was a ladder! down I let myself,
Hands and feet, scrambling somehow, and so dropped,
And after them. I came up with the fun
Hard by Saint Laurence, hail fellow, well met,—
Flower o' the rose,
If I've been merry, what matter who knows?
And so as I was stealing back again   70
To get to bed and have a bit of sleep
Ere I rise up to-morrow and go work
On Jerome knocking at his poor old breast
With his great round stone to subdue the flesh,
You snap me of the sudden. Ah, I see!
Though your eye twinkles still, you shake your head—
Mine's shaved,—a monk, you say—the sting's in that!
If Master Cosimo announced himself,
Mum's the word naturally; but a monk!
Come, what am I a beast for? tell us, now!   80
I was a baby when my mother died
And father died and left me in the street.
I starved there, God knows how, a year or two
On fig skins, melon-parings, rinds and shucks.
Refuse and rubbish. One fine frosty day
My stomach being empty as your hat,
The wind doubled me up and down I went.
Old Aunt Lapaccia trussed me with one hand,
(Its fellow was a stinger as I knew)
And so along the wall, over the bridge,   90
By the straight cut to the convent. Six words, there,
While I stood munching my first bread that month:
'So, boy, you're minded,' quoth the good fat father
Wiping his own mouth, 'twas refection-time,—
'To quit this very miserable world?
Will you renounce' . . . The mouthful of bread? thought I;

By no means! Brief, they made a monk of me;
I did renounce the world, its pride and greed,
Palace, farm, villa, shop and banking-house,
Trash, such as these poor devils of Medici   100
Have given their hearts to—all at eight years old.
Well, sir, I found in time, you may be sure,
'Twas not for nothing—the good bellyful,
The warm serge and the rope that goes all round,
And day-long blessed idleness beside!
'Let's see what the urchin's fit for'—that came next.
Not overmuch their way, I must confess.
Such a to-do! they tried me with their books.
Lord, they'd have taught me Latin in pure waste!
Flower o' the clove,   110
All the Latin I construe is, 'amo' I love!
But, mind you, when a boy starves in the streets
Eight years together, as my fortune was,
Watching folk's faces to know who will fling
The bit of half-stripped grape-bunch he desires,
And who will curse or kick him for his pains—
Which gentleman processional and fine,
Holding a candle to the Sacrament
Will wink and let him lift a plate and catch
The droppings of the wax to sell again,   120
Or holla for the Eight and have him whipped,—
How say I?—nay, which dog bites, which lets drop
His bone from the heap of offal in the street,—
Why, soul and sense of him grow sharp alike,
He learns the look of things, and none the less
For admonitions from the hunger-pinch.
I had a store of such remarks, be sure,
Which, after I found leisure, turned to use:
I drew men's faces on my copy-books,
Scrawled them within the antiphonary's marge,   130
Joined legs and arms to the long music-notes,
Found nose and eyes and chin for A.s and B.s,
And made a string of pictures of the world
Betwixt the ins and outs of verb and noun,
On the wall, the bench, the door. The monks looked black.
'Nay,' quoth the Prior, 'turn him out, d' ye say?
In no wise. Lose a crow and catch a lark.
What if at last we get our man of parts,
We Carmelites, like those Camaldolese
And Preaching Friars, to do our church up fine   140
And put the front on it that ought to be!'
And hereupon they bade me daub away.
Thank you! my head being crammed, their walls a blank,
Never was such prompt disemburdening.
First, every sort of monk, the black and white,
I drew them, fat and lean: then, folks at church,
From good old gossips waiting to confess

Their cribs of barrel-droppings, candle-ends,—
To the breathless fellow at the altar-foot,
Fresh from his murder, safe and sitting there   150
With the little children round him in a row
Of admiration, half for his beard and half
For that white anger of his victim's son
Shaking a fist at him with one fierce arm,
Signing himself with the other because of Christ
(Whose sad face on the cross sees only this
After the passion of a thousand years)
Till some poor girl, her apron o'er her head
Which the intense eyes looked through, came at eve
On tip-toe, said a word, dropped in a loaf,   160
Her pair of earrings and a bunch of flowers
The brute took growling, prayed, and then was gone.
I painted all, then cried ''tis ask and have—
Choose, for more 's ready!'—laid the ladder flat,
And showed my covered bit of cloister-wall.
The monks closed in a circle and praised loud
Till checked,—taught what to see and not to see,
Being simple bodies,—' that 's the very man!
Look at the boy who stoops to pat the dog!
That woman 's like the Prior's niece who comes   170
To care about his asthma: it 's the life!'
But there my triumph 's straw-fire flared and funked—
Their betters took their turn to see and say:
The Prior and the learned pulled a face
And stopped all that in no time. ' How? what 's here?
Quite from the mark of painting, bless us all!
Faces, arms, legs and bodies like the true
As much as pea and pea! it 's devil's-game!
Your business is not to catch men with show,
With homage to the perishable clay,   180
But lift them over it, ignore it all,
Make them forget there 's such a thing as flesh.
Your business is to paint the souls of men—
Man's soul, and it 's a fire, smoke . . . no it 's not . . .
It 's vapour done up like a new-born babe—
(In that shape when you die it leaves your mouth)
It 's . . . well, what matters talking, it 's the soul!
Give us no more of body than shows soul!
Here 's Giotto, with his Saint a-praising God,
That sets you praising,—why not stop with him?   190
Why put all thoughts of praise out of our heads
With wonder at lines, colours, and what not?
Paint the soul, never mind the legs and arms!
Rub all out, try at it a second time.
Oh, that white smallish female with the breasts,
She 's just my niece . . . Herodias, I would say,—
Who went and danced and got men's heads cut off—
Have it all out!' Now, is this sense, I ask?

A fine way to paint soul, by painting body
So ill, the eye can't stop there, must go further   200
And can't fare worse! Thus, yellow does for white
When what you put for yellow 's simply black,
And any sort of meaning looks intense
When all beside itself means and looks nought.
Why can't a painter lift each foot in turn,
Left foot and right foot, go a double step,
Make his flesh liker and his soul more like,
Both in their order? Take the prettiest face,
The Prior's niece . . . patron-saint—is it so pretty
You can't discover if it means hope, fear,   210
Sorrow or joy? won't beauty go with these?
Suppose I've made her eyes all right and blue,
Can't I take breath and try to add life's flash,
And then add soul and heighten them threefold?
Or say there 's beauty with no soul at all—
(I never saw it—put the case the same—)
If you get simple beauty and nought else,
You get about the best thing God invents,—
That 's somewhat. And you'll find the soul you have missed,
Within yourself when you return Him thanks,   220
' Rub all out!' Well, well, there 's my life, in short.
And so the thing has gone on ever since.
I'm grown a man no doubt, I've broken bounds—
You should not take a fellow eight years old
And make him swear to never kiss the girls.
I'm my own master, paint now as I please—
Having a friend, you see, in the Corner-house!
Lord, it 's fast holding by the rings in front—
Those great rings serve more purposes than just
To plant a flag in, or tie up a horse!   230
And yet the old schooling sticks, the old grave eyes
Are peeping o'er my shoulder as I work,
The heads shake still—' It 's Art's decline, my son!
You're not of the true painters, great and old;
Brother Angelico 's the man, you'll find;
Brother Lorenzo stands his single peer:
Fag on at flesh, you'll never make the third!'
Flower o' the pine,
You keep your mistr . . . manners, and I'll stick to mine!
I'm not the third, then: bless us, they must know!   240
Don't you think they're the likeliest to know,
They with their Latin? so, I swallow my rage,
Clench my teeth, suck my lips in tight, and paint
To please them—sometimes do, and sometimes don't,
For, doing most, there 's pretty sure to come
A turn, some warm eve finds me at my saints—
A laugh, a cry, the business of the world—
(Flower o' the peach,
Death for us all, and his own life for each!)

And my whole soul revolves, the cup runs over,   250
The world and life's too big to pass for a dream,
And I do these wild things in sheer despite,
And play the fooleries you catch me at,
In pure rage! the old mill-horse, out at grass
After hard years, throws up his stiff heels so,
Although the miller does not preach to him
The only good of grass is to make chaff.
What would men have? Do they like grass or no—
May they or mayn't they? all I want 's the thing
Settled for ever one way: as it is,   260
You tell too many lies and hurt yourself.
You don't like what you only like too much,
You do like what, if given you at your word,
You find abundantly detestable.
For me, I think I speak as I was taught—
I always see the Garden and God there
A-making man's wife—and, my lesson learned,
The value and significance of flesh,
I can't unlearn ten minutes afterwards.

You understand me: I'm a beast, I know.   270
But see, now—why, I see as certainly
As that the morning-star 's about to shine,
What will hap some day. We've a youngster here
Comes to our convent, studies what I do,
Slouches and stares and lets no atom drop—
His name is Guidi—he'll not mind the monks—
They call him Hulking Tom, he lets them talk—
He picks my practice up—he'll paint apace,
I hope so—though I never live so long,
I know what 's sure to follow. You be judge!   280
You speak no Latin more than I, belike—
However, you're my man, you've seen the world
—The beauty and the wonder and the power,
The shapes of things, their colours, lights and shades,
Changes, surprises,—and God made it all!
—For what? do you feel thankful, ay or no,
For this fair town's face, yonder river's line,
The mountain round it and the sky above,
Much more the figures of man, woman, child,
These are the frame to? What 's it all about?   290
To be passed over, despised? or dwelt upon,
Wondered at? oh, this last of course!—you say.
But why not do as well as say,—paint these
Just as they are, careless what comes of it?
God's works,—paint anyone, and count it crime
To let a truth slip. Don't object, 'His works
Are here already—nature is complete:
Suppose you reproduce her—(which you can't)
There 's no advantage! you must beat her, then.'

For, don't you mark, we're made so that we love   300
First when we see them painted, things we have passed
Perhaps a hundred times nor cared to see;
And so they are better, painted—better to us,
Which is the same thing. Art was given for that—
God uses us to help each other so,
Lending our minds out. Have you noticed, now,
Your cullion's hanging face ? A bit of chalk,
And trust me but you should, though ! How much more,
If I drew higher things with the same truth !
That were to take the Prior's pulpit-place,   310
Interpret God to all of you ! oh, oh,
It makes me mad to see what men shall do
And we in our graves ! This world 's no blot for us,
Nor blank—it means intensely, and means good :
To find its meaning is my meat and drink.
' Ay, but you don't so instigate to prayer ! '
Strikes in the Prior : ' when your meaning 's plain
It does not say to folks—remember matins,
Or, mind you fast next Friday.' Why, for this
What need of art at all ? A skull and bones,   320
Two bits of stick nailed cross-wise, or, what 's best,
A bell to chime the hour with, does as well.
I painted a Saint Laurence six months since
At Prato, splashed the fresco in fine style :
' How looks my painting, now the scaffold 's down ? '
I ask a brother : ' Hugely,' he returns—
' Already not one phiz of your three slaves
That turn the Deacon off his toasted side,
But 's scratched and prodded to our heart's content,
The pious people have so eased their own   330
When coming to say prayers there in a rage :
We get on fast to see the bricks beneath.
Expect another job this time next year,
For pity and religion grow i' the crowd—
Your painting serves its purpose ! ' Hang the fools !

—That is—you'll not mistake an idle word
Spoke in a huff by a poor monk, God wot,
Tasting the air this spicy night which turns
The unaccustomed head like Chianti wine !
Oh, the church knows ! don't misreport me, now !   340
It 's natural a poor monk out of bounds
Should have his apt word to excuse himself :
And hearken how I plot to make amends.
I have bethought me : I shall paint a piece
. . . There 's for you ! Give me six months, then go, see
Something in Sant' Ambrogio's ! Bless the nuns !
They want a cast of my office. I shall paint
God in the midst, Madonna and her babe,
Ringed by a bowery, flowery angel-brood,

Lilies and vestments and white faces, sweet 350
As puff on puff of grated orris-root
When ladies crowd to church at midsummer.
And then in the front, of course a saint or two—
Saint John, because he saves the Florentines,
Saint Ambrose, who puts down in black and white
The convent's friends and gives them a long day,
And Job, I must have him there past mistake,
The man of Uz, (and Us without the z,
Painters who need his patience.) Well, all these
Secured at their devotions, up shall come 360
Out of a corner when you least expect,
As one by a dark stair into a great light,
Music and talking, who but Lippo! I!—
Mazed, motionless and moon-struck—I'm the man!
Back I shrink—what is this I see and hear?
I, caught up with my monk's things by mistake,
My old serge gown and rope that goes all round,
I, in this presence, this pure company!
Where's a hole, where's a corner for escape?
Then steps a sweet angelic slip of a thing 370
Forward, puts out a soft palm—' Not so fast!'
—Addresses the celestial presence, ' nay—
He made you and devised you, after all,
Though he's none of you! Could Saint John there, draw—
His camel-hair make up a painting-brush?
We come to brother Lippo for all that,
Iste perfecit opus! ' So, all smile—
I shuffle sideways with my blushing face
Under the cover of a hundred wings
Thrown like a spread of kirtles when you're gay 380
And play hot cockles, all the doors being shut,
Till, wholly unexpected, in there pops
The hothead husband! Thus I scuttle off
To some safe bench behind, not letting go
The palm of her, the little lily thing
That spoke the good word for me in the nick,
Like the Prior's niece . . . Saint Lucy, I would say.
And so all's saved for me, and for the church
A pretty picture gained. Go, six months hence!
Your hand, sir, and good-bye: no lights, no lights! 390
The street's hushed, and I know my own way back,
Don't fear me! There's the grey beginning. Zooks!

A TOCCATA OF GALUPPI'S

I

OH, Galuppi, Baldassaro, this is very sad to find !
I can hardly misconceive you ; it would prove me deaf and
   blind ;
But although I take your meaning, 'tis with such a heavy
   mind !

II

Here you come with your old music, and here 's all the good
   it brings.
What, they lived once thus at Venice where the merchants
   were the kings,
Where St. Mark's is, where the Doges used to wed the sea
   with rings ?

III

Ay, because the sea 's the street there ; and 'tis arched by . . .
   what you call
. . . Shylock's bridge with houses on it, where they kept the
   carnival :
I was never out of England—it 's as if I saw it all !

IV

Did young people take their pleasure when the sea was warm
   in May ?   10
Balls and masks begun at midnight, burning ever to mid-day
When they made up fresh adventures for the morrow, do
   you say ?

V

Was a lady such a lady, cheeks so round and lips so red,—
On her neck the small face buoyant, like a bell-flower on its
   bed,
O'er the breast's superb abundance where a man might base
   his head ?

VI

Well, (and it was graceful of them) they'd break talk off and
   afford
—She, to bite her mask's black velvet, he, to finger on his
   sword,
While you sat and played Toccatas, stately at the clavichord ?

VII

What ? Those lesser thirds so plaintive, sixths diminished,
   sigh on sigh,
Told them something ? Those suspensions, those solutions—
   ' Must we die ? '   20
Those commiserating sevenths—' Life might last ! we can
   but try ! '

VIII

' Were you happy ? '—' Yes.'—' And are you still as happy ? '
    —' Yes.   And you ? '
—' Then, more kisses ! '—' Did *I* stop them, when a million
    seemed so few ? '
Hark ! the dominant's persistence, till it must be answered to !

IX

So an octave struck the answer. Oh, they praised you,
    I dare say !
' Brave Galuppi ! that was music ! good alike at grave
    and gay !
I can always leave off talking, when I hear a master play.'

X

Then they left you for their pleasure : till in due time, one
    by one,
Some with lives that came to nothing, some with deeds as
    well undone,
Death came tacitly and took them where they never see the
    sun.   30

XI

But when I sit down to reason, think to take my stand nor
    swerve,
While I triumph o'er a secret wrung from nature's close reserve,
In you come with your cold music, till I creep thro' every nerve.

XII

Yes, you, like a ghostly cricket, creaking where a house was
    burned—
' Dust and ashes, dead and done with, Venice spent what
    Venice earned !
The soul, doubtless, is immortal—where a soul can be discerned.

XIII

Yours for instance, you know physics, something of geology,
Mathematics are your pastime ; souls shall rise in their degree ;
Butterflies may dread extinction,—you'll not die, it cannot be !

XIV

As for Venice and its people, merely born to bloom and drop,   40
Here on earth they bore their fruitage, mirth and folly were
    the crop :
What of soul was left, I wonder, when the kissing had to stop ?

XV

' Dust and ashes ! ' So you creak it, and I want the heart
    to scold.
Dear dead women, with such hair, too—what 's become of
    all the gold
Used to hang and brush their bosoms ? I feel chilly and
    grown old.

BISHOP BLOUGRAM'S APOLOGY

No more wine ? then we'll push back chairs and talk.
A final glass for me, though : cool, i' faith !
We ought to have our Abbey back, you see.
It 's different, preaching in basilicas,
And doing duty in some masterpiece
Like this of brother Pugin's, bless his heart !
I doubt if they're half baked, those chalk rosettes,
Ciphers and stucco-twiddlings everywhere ;
It 's just like breathing in a lime-kiln : eh ?
These hot long ceremonies of our church   10
Cost us a little—oh, they pay the price,
You take me—amply pay it ! Now, we'll talk.

So, you despise me, Mr. Gigadibs.
No deprecation,—nay, I beg you, sir !
Beside 'tis our engagement : don't you know,
I promised, if you'd watch a dinner out,
We'd see truth dawn together ?—truth that peeps
Over the glass's edge when dinner 's done,
And body gets its sop and hold its noise
And leaves soul free a little. Now 's the time—   20
'Tis break of day ! You do despise me then.
And if I say, ' despise me,'—never fear—
I know you do not in a certain sense—
Not in my arm-chair for example : here,
I well imagine you respect my place
(Status, *entourage*, worldly circumstance)
Quite to its value—very much indeed
—Are up to the protesting eyes of you
In pride at being seated here for once—
You'll turn it to such capital account !   30
When somebody, through years and years to come,
Hints of the bishop,—names me—that 's enough—
' Blougram ? I knew him '—(into it you slide)
' Dined with him once, a Corpus Christi Day,
All alone, we two—he 's a clever man—
And after dinner,—why, the wine you know,—
Oh, there was wine, and good !—what with the wine . . .
'Faith, we began upon all sorts of talk !
He 's no bad fellow, Blougram—he had seen
Something of mine he relished—some review—   40
He 's quite above their humbug in his heart,
Half-said as much, indeed—the thing 's his trade—
I warrant, Blougram 's sceptical at times—
How otherwise ? I liked him, I confess ! '
Che che, my dear sir, as we say at Rome,
Don't you protest now ! It 's fair give and take :

You have had your turn and spoken your home-truths:
The hand 's mine now, and here you follow suit.

   Thus much conceded, still the first fact stays—
You do despise me ; your ideal of life   50
Is not the bishop's—you would not be I—
You would like better to be Goethe, now,
Or Buonaparte—or, bless me, lower still,
Count D'Orsay,—so you did what you preferred,
Spoke as you thought, and, as you cannot help,
Believed or disbelieved, no matter what,
So long as on that point, whate'er it was,
You loosed your mind, were whole and sole yourself.
—That, my ideal never can include,
Upon that element of truth and worth   60
Never be based ! for say they make me Pope
(They can't—suppose it for our argument)
Why, there I'm at my tether's end—I've reached
My height, and not a height which pleases you.
An unbelieving Pope won't do, you say.
It 's like those eerie stories nurses tell,
Of how some actor played Death on a stage
With pasteboard crown, sham orb and tinselled dart,
And called himself the monarch of the world,
Then, going in the tire-room afterward   70
Because the play was done, to shift himself,
Got touched upon the sleeve familiarly
The moment he had shut the closet door
By Death himself. Thus God might touch a Pope
At unawares, ask what his baubles mean,
And whose part he presumed to play just now ?
Best be yourself, imperial, plain and true !

So, drawing comfortable breath again,
You weigh and find whatever more or less
I boast of my ideal realized   80
Is nothing in the balance when opposed
To your ideal, your grand simple life,
Of which you will not realize one jot.
I am much, you are nothing ; you would be all,
I would be merely much—you beat me there.

No, friend, you do not beat me,—hearken why.
The common problem, yours, mine, every one's,
Is not to fancy what were fair in life
Provided it could be,—but, finding first
What may be, then find how to make it fair   90
Up to our means—a very different thing !
No abstract intellectual plan of life
Quite irrespective of life's plainest laws,
But one, a man, who is man and nothing more,

May lead within a world which (by your leave)
Is Rome or London—not Fool's-paradise.
Embellish Rome, idealize away,
Make Paradise of London if you can,
You're welcome, nay, you're wise.

                           A simile !
We mortals cross the ocean of this world   100
Each in his average cabin of a life—
The best's not big, the worst yields elbow-room.
Now for our six months' voyage—how prepare ?
You come on shipboard with a landsman's list
Of things he calls convenient—so they are !
An India screen is pretty furniture,
A piano-forte is a fine resource,
All Balzac's novels occupy one shelf,
The new edition fifty volumes long ;
And little Greek books, with the funny type   110
They get up well at Leipsic, fill the next—
Go on ! slabbed marble, what a bath it makes !
And Parma's pride, the Jerome, let us add !
'Twere pleasant could Correggio's fleeting glow
Hang full in face of one where'er one roams,
Since he more than the others brings with him
Italy's self,—the marvellous Modenese !
Yet 'twas not on your list before, perhaps.
—Alas ! friend, here's the agent . . . is't the name ?
The captain, or whoever's master here—   120
You see him screw his face up ; what's his cry
Ere you set foot on shipboard ? ' Six feet square ! '
If you won't understand what six feet mean,
Compute and purchase stores accordingly—
And if in pique because he overhauls
Your Jerome, piano and bath, you come on board
Bare—why, you cut a figure at the first
While sympathetic landsmen see you off ;
Not afterwards, when, long ere half seas over,
You peep up from your utterly naked boards   130
Into some snug and well-appointed berth,
Like mine, for instance (try the cooler jug—
Put back the other, but don't jog the ice)
And mortified you mutter ' Well and good—
He sits enjoying his sea-furniture—
'Tis stout and proper, and there's store of it,
Though I've the better notion, all agree,
Of fitting rooms up ! hang the carpenter,
Neat ship-shape fixings and contrivances—
I would have brought my Jerome, frame and all ! ' 140
And meantime you bring nothing : never mind—
You've proved your artist-nature : what you don't,
You might bring, so despise me, as I say.

Now come, let's backward to the starting-place.
See my way: we're two college friends, suppose—
Prepare together for our voyage, then,
Each note and check the other in his work,—
Here's mine, a bishop's outfit; criticize!
What's wrong? why won't you be a bishop too?

Why, first, you don't believe, you don't and can't, 150
(Not statedly, that is, and fixedly
And absolutely and exclusively)
In any revelation called divine.
No dogmas nail your faith—and what remains
But say so, like the honest man you are?
First, therefore, overhaul theology!
Nay, I too, not a fool, you please to think,
Must find believing every whit as hard,
And if I do not frankly say as much,
The ugly consequence is clear enough. 160

Now, wait, my friend: well, I do not believe—
If you'll accept no faith that is not fixed,
Absolute and exclusive, as you say.
(You're wrong—I mean to prove it in due time.)
Meanwhile, I know where difficulties lie
I could not, cannot solve, nor ever shall,
So give up hope accordingly to solve—
(To you, and over the wine). Our dogmas then
With both of us, though in unlike degree,
Missing full credence—overboard with them! 170
I mean to meet you on your own premise—
Good, there go mine in company with yours!

And now what are we? unbelievers both,
Calm and complete, determinately fixed
To-day, to-morrow, and for ever, pray?
You'll guarantee me that? Not so, I think!
In no-wise! all we've gained is, that belief,
As unbelief before, shakes us by fits,
Confounds us like its predecessor. Where's
The gain? how can we guard our unbelief, 180
Make it bear fruit to us?—the problem here.
Just when we are safest, there's a sunset-touch,
A fancy from a flower-bell, some one's death,
A chorus-ending from Euripides,—
And that's enough for fifty hopes and fears
As old and new at once as Nature's self,
To rap and knock and enter in our soul,
Take hands and dance there, a fantastic ring,
Round the ancient idol, on his base again,—
The grand Perhaps! we look on helplessly,— 190
There the old misgivings, crooked questions are—
This good God,—what He could do, if He would,

Would, if He could—then must have done long since:
If so, when, where, and how ? some way must be,—
Once feel about, and soon or late you hit
Some sense, in which it might be, after all.
Why not, ' The Way, the Truth, the Life ? '

　　　　　　　　　　　　　　　　　—That way
Over the mountain, which who stands upon
Is apt to doubt if it be indeed a road ;
While if he views it from the waste itself,　　　　　200
Up goes the line there, plain from base to brow,
Not vague, mistakeable ! what 's a break or two
Seen from the unbroken desert either side ?
And then (to bring in fresh philosophy)
What if the breaks themselves should prove at last
The most consummate of contrivances
To train a man's eye, teach him what is faith ?
And so we stumble at truth's very test !
All we have gained then by our unbelief
Is a life of doubt diversified by faith,　　　　　210
For one of faith diversified by doubt :
We called the chess-board white,—we call it black.

　' Well,' you rejoin, ' the end 's no worse, at least ;
We've reason for both colours on the board :
Why not confess, then, where I drop the faith
And you the doubt, that I'm as right as you ? '

Because, friend, in the next place, this being so,
And both things even,—faith and unbelief
Left to a man's choice,—we'll proceed a step,
Returning to our image, which I like.　　　　　220

　A man's choice, yes—but a cabin-passenger's—
The man made for the special life of the world—
Do you forget him ? I remember though !
Consult our ship's conditions and you find
One and but one choice suitable to all,
The choice, that you unluckily prefer,
Turning things topsy-turvy—they or it
Going to the ground. Belief or unbelief
Bears upon life, determines its whole course,
Begins at its beginning. See the world　　　　　230
Such as it is,—you made it not, nor I ;
I mean to take it as it is,—and you
Not so you'll take it,—though you get nought else.
I know the special kind of life I like,
What suits the most my idiosyncrasy,
Brings out the best of me and bears me fruit
In power, peace, pleasantness and length of days.
I find that positive belief does this
For me, and unbelief, no whit of this.
—For you, it does, however ?—that we'll try !　　　　　240

'Tis clear, I cannot lead my life, at least,
Induce the world to let me peaceably,
Without declaring at the outset, ' Friends,
I absolutely and peremptorily
Believe ! '—I say, faith is my waking life.
One sleeps, indeed, and dreams at intervals,
We know, but waking 's the main point with us,
And my provision 's for life's waking part.
Accordingly, I use heart, head and hands
All day, I build, scheme, study and make friends ;   250
And when night overtakes me, down I lie,
Sleep, dream a little, and get done with it,
The sooner the better, to begin afresh.
What 's midnight's doubt before the dayspring's faith ?
You, the philosopher, that disbelieve,
That recognize the night, give dreams their weight—
To be consistent you should keep your bed,
Abstain from healthy acts that prove you a man,
For fear you drowse perhaps at unawares !
And certainly at night you'll sleep and dream,   260
Live through the day and bustle as you please.
And so you live to sleep as I to wake,
To unbelieve as I to still believe ?
Well, and the common sense of the world calls you
Bed-ridden,—and its good things come to me.
Its estimation, which is half the fight,
That 's the first cabin-comfort I secure—
The next . . . but you perceive with half an eye !
Come, come, it 's best believing, if we may—
You can't but own that !

                         Next, concede again—   270
If once we choose belief, on all accounts
We can't be too decisive in our faith,
Conclusive and exclusive in its terms,
To suit the world which gives us the good things.
In every man's career are certain points
Whereon he dares not be indifferent ;
The world detects him clearly, if he dares,
As baffled at the game, and losing life.
He may care little or he may care much
For riches, honour, pleasure, work, repose,   280
Since various theories of life and life's
Success are extant which might easily
Comport with either estimate of these ;
And whoso chooses wealth or poverty,
Labour or quiet, is not judged a fool
Because his fellows would choose otherwise :
We let him choose upon his own account
So long as he 's consistent with his choice.
But certain points, left wholly to himself,
When once a man has arbitrated on,   290

We say he must succeed there or go hang.
Thus, he should wed the woman he loves most
Or needs most, whatsoe'er the love or need—
For he can't wed twice. Then, he must avouch
Or follow, at the least, sufficiently,
The form of faith his conscience holds the best,
Whate'er the process of conviction was :
For nothing can compensate his mistake
On such a point, the man himself being judge—
He cannot wed twice, nor twice lose his soul.   300

Well now, there 's one great form of Christian faith
I happened to be born in—which to teach
Was given me as I grew up, on all hands,
As best and readiest means of living by ;
The same on examination being proved
The most pronounced moreover, fixed, precise
And absolute form of faith in the whole world—
Accordingly, most potent of all forms
For working on the world. Observe, my friend,
Such as you know me, I am free to say,   310
In these hard latter days which hamper one,
Myself, by no immoderate exercise
Of intellect and learning, and the tact
To let external forces work for me,
—Bid the street's stones be bread and they are bread,
Bid Peter's creed, or, rather, Hildebrand's,
Exalt me o'er my fellows in the world
And make my life an ease and joy and pride;
It does so,—which for me 's a great point gained,
Who have a soul and body that exact   320
A comfortable care in many ways.
There 's power in me and will to dominate
Which I must exercise, they hurt me else :
In many ways I need mankind's respect,
Obedience, and the love that 's born of fear :
While at the same time, there 's a taste I have,
A toy of soul, a titillating thing,
Refuses to digest these dainties crude.
The naked life is gross till clothed upon :
I must take what men offer, with a grace   330
As though I would not, could I help it, take !
An uniform I wear though over-rich—
Something imposed on me, no choice of mine ;
No fancy-dress worn for pure fancy's sake
And despicable therefore ! now men kneel
And kiss my hand—of course the Church's hand.
Thus I am made, thus life is best for me,
And thus that it should be I have procured ;
And thus it could not be another way,
I venture to imagine.

You'll reply—   340

So far my choice, no doubt, is a success;
But were I made of better elements,
With nobler instincts, purer tastes, like you,
I hardly would account the thing success
Though it did all for me I say.

But, friend,

We speak of what is—not of what might be,
And how 'twere better if 'twere otherwise.
I am the man you see here plain enough—
Grant I'm a beast, why, beasts must lead beasts' lives!
Suppose I own at once to tail and claws—   350
The tailless man exceeds me; but being tailed
I'll lash out lion-fashion, and leave apes
To dock their stump and dress their haunches up.
My business is not to remake myself,
But make the absolute best of what God made.
Or—our first simile—though you proved me doomed
To a viler berth still, to the steerage-hole,
The sheep-pen or the pig-stye, I should strive
To make what use of each were possible;
And as this cabin gets upholstery,   360
That hutch should rustle with sufficient straw.

But, friend, I don't acknowledge quite so fast
I fail of all your manhood's lofty tastes
Enumerated so complacently,
On the mere ground that you forsooth can find
In this particular life I choose to lead
No fit provision for them. Can you not?
Say you, my fault is I address myself
To grosser estimators than I need?
And that's no way of holding up the soul—   370
Which, nobler, needs men's praise perhaps, yet knows
One wise man's verdict outweighs all the fools',—
Would like the two, but, forced to choose, takes that?
I pine among my million imbeciles
(You think) aware some dozen men of sense
Eye me and know me, whether I believe
In the last winking Virgin, as I vow,
And am a fool, or disbelieve in her
And am a knave,—approve in neither case,
Withhold their voices though I look their way: 380
Like Verdi when, at his worst opera's end
(The thing they gave at Florence,— what's its name?)
While the mad houseful's plaudits near out-bang
His orchestra of salt-box, tongs and bones,
He looks through all the roaring and the wreaths
Where sits Rossini patient in his stall.

Nay, friend, I meet you with an answer here—

That even your prime men who appraise their kind
Are men still, catch a wheel within a wheel,
See more in a truth than the truth's simple self,   390
Confuse themselves. You see lads walk the street
Sixty the minute; what's to note in that?
You see one lad o'erstride a chimney-stack;
Him you must watch—he's sure to fall, yet stands!
Our interest's on the dangerous edge of things.
The honest thief, the tender murderer,
The superstitious atheist, demireps
That love and save their souls in new French books—
We watch while these in equilibrium keep
The giddy line midway: one step aside,   400
They're classed and done with. I, then, keep the line
Before your sages,—just the men to shrink
From the gross weights, coarse scales, and labels broad
You offer their refinement. Fool or knave?
Why needs a bishop be a fool or knave
When there's a thousand diamond weights between?
So I enlist them. Your picked Twelve, you'll find,
Profess themselves indignant, scandalized
At thus being held unable to explain
How a superior man who disbelieves   410
May not believe as well: that's Schelling's way!
It's through my coming in the tail of time,
Nicking the minute with a happy tact.
Had I been born three hundred years ago
They'd say, 'What's strange? Blougram of course
   believes;'
And, seventy years since, 'disbelieves of course.'
But now, 'He may believe; and yet, and yet
How can he?'—All eyes turn with interest.
Whereas, step off the line on either side—
You, for example, clever to a fault,   420
The rough and ready man that write apace,
Read somewhat seldomer, think perhaps even less—
You disbelieve! Who wonders and who cares?
Lord So-and-so—his coat bedropt with wax,
All Peter's chains about his waist, his back
Brave with the needlework of Noodledom,
Believes! Again, who wonders and who cares?
But I, the man of sense and learning too,
The able to think yet act, the this, the that,
I, to believe at this late time of day!   430
Enough; you see, I need not fear contempt.

   —Except it's yours! admire me as these may,
You don't. But whom at least do you admire?
Present your own perfections, your ideal,
Your pattern man for a minute—oh, make haste?
Is it Napoleon you would have us grow?

Concede the means ; allow his head and hand,
(A large concession, clever as you are)
Good !—In our common primal element
Of unbelief (we can't believe, you know—   440
We're still at that admission, recollect)
Where do you find—apart from, towering o'er
The secondary temporary aims
Which satisfy the gross tastes you despise—
Where do you find his star ?—his crazy trust
God knows through what or in what ? it 's alive
And shines and leads him and that 's all we want.
Have we aught in our sober night shall point
Such ends as his were, and direct the means
Of working out our purpose straight as his,   450
Nor bring a moment's trouble on success
With after-care to justify the same ?
—Be a Napoleon and yet disbelieve !
Why, the man 's mad, friend, take his light away.
What 's the vague good of the world for which you'd dare
With comfort to yourself blow millions up ?
We neither of us see it ! we do see
The blown-up millions—spatter of their brains
And writhing of their bowels and so forth,
In that bewildering entanglement   460
Of horrible eventualities
Past calculation to the end of time !
Can I mistake for some clear word of God
(Which were my ample warrant for it all)
His puff of hazy instincts, idle talk,
' The State, that 's I,' quack-nonsense about crowns,
And (when one beats the man to his last hold)
A vague idea of setting things to rights,
Policing people efficaciously,
More to their profit, most of all to his own ;   470
The whole to end that dismallest of ends
By an Austrian marriage, cant to us the Church,
And resurrection of the old *régime* ?
Would I, who hope to live a dozen years,
Fight Austerlitz for reasons such and such ?
No : for, concede me but the merest chance
Doubt may be wrong—there 's judgement, life to come !
With just that chance, I dare not. Doubt proves right ?
This present life is all ?—you offer me
Its dozen noisy years without a chance   480
That wedding an Arch-Duchess, wearing lace,
And getting called by divers new-coined names,
Will drive off ugly thoughts and let me dine,
Sleep, read and chat in quiet as I like !
Therefore, I will not.

                    Take another case ;
Fit up the cabin yet another way.

What say you to the poet's ? shall we write
Hamlets, Othellos—make the world our own,
Without a risk to run of either sort ?
I can't !—to put the strongest reason first.   490
' But try,' you urge, ' the trying shall suffice ;
The aim, if reached or not, makes great the life :
Try to be Shakespeare, leave the rest to fate ! '
Spare my self-knowledge—there 's no fooling me !
If I prefer remaining my poor self,
I say so not in self-dispraise but praise.
If I'm a Shakespeare, let the well alone—
Why should I try to be what now I am ?
If I'm no Shakespeare, as too probable,—
His power and consciousness and self-delight   500
And all we want in common, shall I find—
Trying for ever ? while on points of taste
Wherewith, to speak it humbly, he and I
Are dowered alike—I'll ask you, I or he,
Which in our two lives realizes most ?
Much, he imagined—somewhat, I possess.
He had the imagination ; stick to that !
Let him say ' In the face of my soul's works
Your world is worthless and I touch it not
Lest I should wrong them '—I'll withdraw my plea.   510
But does he say so ? look upon his life !
Himself, who only can, gives judgement there.
He leaves his towers and gorgeous palaces
To build the trimmest house in Stratford town ;
Saves money, spends it, owns the worth of things,
Giulio Romano's pictures, Dowland's lute ;
Enjoys a show, respects the puppets, too,
And none more, had he seen its entry once,
Than ' Pandulph, of fair Milan cardinal.'
Why then should I who play that personage,   520
The very Pandulph Shakespeare's fancy made,
Be told that had the poet chanced to start
From where I stand now (some degree like mine
Being just the goal he ran his race to reach)
He would have run the whole race back, forsooth,
And left being Pandulph, to begin write plays ?
Ah, the earth's best can be but the earth's best !
Did Shakespeare live, he could but sit at home
And get himself in dreams the Vatican,
Greek busts, Venetian paintings, Roman walls,   530
And English books, none equal to his own,
Which I read, bound in gold, (he never did).
—Terni and Naples' bay and Gothard's top—
Eh, friend ? I could not fancy one of these—
But, as I pour this claret, there they are—
I've gained them—crossed St. Gothard last July
With ten mules to the carriage and a bed

Slung inside ; is my hap the worse for that ?
We want the same things, Shakespeare and myself,
And what I want, I have : he, gifted more,   540
Could fancy he too had it when he liked,
But not so thoroughly that if fate allowed
He would not have it also in my sense.
We play one game. I send the ball aloft
No less adroitly that of fifty strokes
Scarce five go o'er the wall so wide and high
Which sends them back to me : I wish and get.
He struck balls higher and with better skill,
But at a poor fence level with his head,
And hit—his Stratford house, a coat of arms,   550
Successful dealings in his grain and wool,—
While I receive Heaven's incense in my nose
And style myself the cousin of Queen Bess.
Ask him, if this life 's all, who wins the game ?

Believe—and our whole argument breaks up.
Enthusiasm 's the best thing, I repeat ;
Only, we can't command it ; fire and life
Are all, dead matter 's nothing, we agree :
And be it a mad dream or God's very breath,
The fact 's the same,—belief's fire once in us,   560
Makes of all else mere stuff to show itself :
We penetrate our life with such a glow
As fire lends wood and iron—this turns steel,
That burns to ash—all 's one, fire proves its power
For good or ill, since men call flare success.
But paint a fire, it will not therefore burn.
Light one in me, I'll find it food enough !
Why, to be Luther—that 's a life to lead,
Incomparably better than my own.
He comes, reclaims God's earth for God, he says,   570
Sets up God's rule again by simple means,
Re-opens a shut book, and all is done.
He flared out in the flaring of mankind ;
Such Luther's luck was—how shall such be mine ?
If he succeeded, nothing 's left to do :
And if he did not altogether—well,
Strauss is the next advance. All Strauss should be
I might be also. But to what result ?
He looks upon no Future : Luther did.
What can I gain on the denying side ?   580
Ice makes no conflagration. State the facts,
Read the text right, emancipate the world—
The emancipated world enjoys itself
With scarce a thank-you—Blougram told it first
It could not owe a farthing,—not to him
More than Saint Paul ! 'twould press its pay, you think ?
Then add there 's still that plaguy hundredth chance

Strauss may be wrong. And so a risk is run—
For what gain ? not for Luther's, who secured
A real Heaven in his heart throughout his life,   590
Supposing death a little altered things.

'Ay, but since really you lack faith,' you cry,
'You run the same risk really on all sides,
In cool indifference as bold unbelief.
As well be Strauss as swing 'twixt Paul and him.
It's not worth having, such imperfect faith,
Nor more available to do faith's work
Than unbelief like mine. Whole faith, or none ! '

Softly, my friend ! I must dispute that point.
Once own the use of faith, I'll find you faith.   600
We're back on Christian ground. You call for faith :
I show you doubt, to prove that faith exists.
The more of doubt, the stronger faith, I say,
If faith o'ercomes doubt. How I know it does ?
By life and man's free will, God gave for that !
To mould life as we choose it, shows our choice :
That's our one act, the previous work's His own.
You criticize the soil ? it reared this tree—
This broad life and whatever fruit it bears !
What matter though I doubt at every pore,   610
Head-doubts, heart-doubts, doubts at my fingers' ends,
Doubts in the trivial work of every day,
Doubts at the very bases of my soul
In the grand moments when she probes herself—
If finally I have a life to show,
The thing I did, brought out in evidence
Against the thing done to me underground
By Hell and all its brood, for aught I know ?
I say, whence sprang this ? shows it faith or doubt ?
All's doubt in me; where's break of faith in this ?   620
It is the idea, the feeling and the love,
God means mankind should strive for and show forth,
Whatever be the process to that end,—
And not historic knowledge, logic sound,
And metaphysical acumen, sure !
' What think ye of Christ,' friend ? when all's done and said,
Like you this Christianity or not ?
It may be false, but will you wish it true ?
Has it your vote to be so if it can ?
Trust you an instinct silenced long ago   630
That will break silence and enjoin you love
What mortified philosophy is hoarse,
And all in vain, with bidding you despise ?
If you desire faith—then you've faith enough :
What else seeks God—nay, what else seek ourselves ?
You form a notion of me, we'll suppose,

On hearsay; it's a favourable one:
'But still,' (you add) 'there was no such good man,
Because of contradictions in the facts.
One proves, for instance, he was born in Rome,   640
This Blougram—yet throughout the tales of him
I see he figures as an Englishman.'
Well, the two things are reconcileable.
But would I rather you discovered that,
Subjoining—'Still, what matter though they be?
Blougram concerns me nought, born here or there.'

Pure faith indeed—you know not what you ask!
Naked belief in God the Omnipotent,
Omniscient, Omnipresent, sears too much
The sense of conscious creatures to be borne.   650
It were the seeing Him, no flesh shall dare.
Some think, Creation's meant to show Him forth:
I say, it's meant to hide Him all it can,
And that's what all the blessed Evil's for.
Its use in Time is to environ us,
Our breath, our drop of dew, with shield enough
Against that sight till we can bear its stress.
Under a vertical sun, the exposed brain
And lidless eye and disemprisoned heart
Less certainly would wither up at once   660
Than mind, confronted with the truth of Him.
But time and earth case-harden us to live;
The feeblest sense is trusted most; the child
Feels God a moment, ichors o'er the place,
Plays on and grows to be a man like us.
With me, faith means perpetual unbelief
Kept quiet like the snake 'neath Michael's foot
Who stands calm just because he feels it writhe.
Or, if that's too ambitious,—here's my box—
I need the excitation of a pinch   670
Threatening the torpor of the inside-nose
Nigh on the imminent sneeze that never comes.
'Leave it in peace' advise the simple folk—
Make it aware of peace by itching-fits,
Say I—let doubt occasion still more faith!

You'll say, once all believed, man, woman, child,
In that dear middle-age these noodles praise.
How you'd exult if I could put you back
Six hundred years, blot out cosmogony,
Geology, ethnology, what not,   680
(Greek endings with the little passing-bell
That signifies some faith's about to die
And set you square with Genesis again,
When such a traveller told you his last news,
He saw the ark a-top of Ararat

But did not climb there since 'twas getting dusk
And robber-bands infest the mountain's foot!
How should you feel, I ask, in such an age,
How act? As other people felt and did;
With soul more blank than this decanter's knob,   690
Believe—and yet lie, kill, rob, fornicate
Full in belief's face, like the beast you'd be!

No, when the fight begins within himself,
A man's worth something. God stoops o'er his head,
Satan looks up between his feet—both tug—
He's left, himself, in the middle: the soul wakes
And grows. Prolong that battle through his life!
Never leave growing till the life to come!
Here, we've got callous to the Virgin's winks
That used to puzzle people wholesomely—   700
Men have outgrown the shame of being fools.
What are the laws of Nature, not to bend
If the Church bid them?—brother Newman asks.
Up with the Immaculate Conception, then—
On to the rack with faith!—is my advice.
Will not that hurry us upon our knees,
Knocking our breasts, 'It can't be—yet it shall!
Who am I, the worm, to argue with my Pope?
Low things confound the high things!' and so forth.
That's better than acquitting God with grace   710
As some folks do. He's tried—no case is proved,
Philosophy is lenient—He may go!

You'll say—the old system's not so obsolete
But men believe still: ay, but who and where?
King Bomba's lazzaroni foster yet
The sacred flame, so Antonelli writes;
But even of these, what ragamuffin-saint
Believes God watches him continually,
As he believes in fire that it will burn,
Or rain that it will drench him? Break fire's law,   720
Sin against rain, although the penalty
Be just a singe or soaking? 'No,' he smiles;
'Those laws are laws that can enforce themselves.'

The sum of all is—yes, my doubt is great,
My faith's still greater—then my faith's enough.
I have read much, thought much, experienced much,
Yet would die rather than avow my fear
The Naples' liquefaction may be false,
When set to happen by the palace-clock
According to the clouds or dinner-time.   730
I hear you recommend, I might at least
Eliminate, decrassify my faith
Since I adopt it; keeping what I must
And leaving what I can—such points as this!

I won't—that is, I can't throw one away.
Supposing there's no truth in what I said
About the need of trials to man's faith,
Still, when you bid me purify the same,
To such a process I discern no end,
Clearing off one excrescence to see two ; 740
There's ever a next in size, now grown as big,
That meets the knife—I cut and cut again !
First cut the Liquefaction, what comes last
But Fichte's clever cut at God Himself ?
Experimentalize on sacred things !
I trust nor hand nor eye nor heart nor brain
To stop betimes : they all get drunk alike.
The first step, I am master not to take.

You'd find the cutting-process to your taste
As much as leaving growths of lies unpruned, 750
Nor see more danger in it, you retort.
Your taste's worth mine ; but my taste proves more wise
When we consider that the steadfast hold
On the extreme end of the chain of faith
Gives all the advantage, makes the difference,
With the rough purblind mass we seek to rule.
We are their lords, or they are free of us
Just as we tighten or relax that hold.
So, other matters equal, we'll revert
To the first problem—which, if solved my way 760
And thrown into the balance, turns the scale—
How we may lead a comfortable life,
How suit our luggage to the cabin's size.

Of course you are remarking all this time
How narrowly and grossly I view life,
Respect the creature-comforts, care to rule
The masses, and regard complacently
' The cabin,' in our old phrase ! Well, I do.
I act for, talk for, live for this world now,
As this world calls for action, life and talk— 770
No prejudice to what next world may prove,
Whose new laws and requirements, my best pledge
To observe then, is that I observe these now,
Shall do hereafter what I do meanwhile.
Let us concede (gratuitously though)
Next life relieves the soul of body, yields
Pure spiritual enjoyments : well, my friend,
Why lose this life in the meantime, since its use
May be to make the next life more intense ?

Do you know, I have often had a dream 780
(Work it up in your next month's article)
Of man's poor spirit in its progress still
Losing true life for ever and a day

Through ever trying to be and ever being
In the evolution of successive spheres,
Before its actual sphere and place of life,
Halfway into the next, which having reached,
It shoots with corresponding foolery
Halfway into the next still, on and off!
As when a traveller, bound from North to South,   790
Scouts fur in Russia—what's its use in France?
In France spurns flannel—where's its need in Spain?
In Spain drops cloth—too cumbrous for Algiers!
Linen goes next, and last the skin itself,
A superfluity at Timbuctoo.
When, through his journey, was the fool at ease?
I'm at ease now, friend—worldly in this world
I take and like its way of life; I think
My brothers who administer the means
Live better for my comfort—that's good too;   800
And God, if He pronounce upon it all,
Approves my service, which is better still.
If He keep silence,—why, for you or me
Or that brute-beast pulled-up in to-day's 'Times,'
What odds is 't, save to ourselves, what life we lead?

    You meet me at this issue—you declare,
All special-pleading done with, truth is truth,
And justifies itself by undreamed ways.
You don't fear but it 's better, if we doubt,
To say so, acting up to our truth perceived   810
However feebly. Do then,—act away!
'Tis there I'm on the watch for you! How one acts
Is, both of us agree, our chief concern:
And how you'll act is what I fain would see
If, like the candid person you appear,
You dare to make the most of your life's scheme
As I of mine, live up to its full law
Since there 's no higher law that counterchecks.
Put natural religion to the test
You've just demolished the revealed with—quick,   820
Down to the root of all that checks your will,
All prohibition to lie, kill and thieve
Or even to be an atheistic priest!
Suppose a pricking to incontinence—
Philosophers deduce you chastity
Or shame, from just the fact that at the first
Whoso embraced a woman in the plain,
Threw club down, and forewent his brains beside,
So stood a ready victim in the reach
Of any brother-savage club in hand—   830
Hence saw the use of going out of sight
In wood or cave to prosecute his loves—
I read this in a French book t' other day.

Does law so analysed coerce you much ?
Oh, men spin clouds of fuzz where matters end,
But you who reach where the first thread begins,
You'll soon cut that !—which means you can, but won't
Through certain instincts, blind, unreasoned-out,
You dare not set aside, you can't tell why,
But there they are, and so you let them rule.   840
Then, friend, you seem as much a slave as I,
A liar, conscious coward and hypocrite,
Without the good the slave expects to get,
Suppose he has a master after all !
You own your instincts—why, what else do I,
Who want, am made for, and must have a God
Ere I can be aught, do aught ?—no mere name
Want, but the true thing with what proves its truth,
To wit, a relation from that thing to me,
Touching from head to foot—which touch I feel,   850
And with it take the rest, this life of ours !
I live my life here ; yours you dare not live.

  —Not as I state it, who (you please subjoin)
Disfigure such a life and call it names,
While, in your mind, remains another way
For simple men : knowledge and power have rights,
But ignorance and weakness have rights too.
There needs no crucial effort to find truth
If here or there or anywhere about—
We ought to turn each side, try hard and see,   860
And if we can't, be glad we've earned at least
The right, by one laborious proof the more,
To graze in peace earth's pleasant pasturage.
Men are not angels, neither are they brutes.
Something we may see, all we cannot see—
What need of lying ? I say, I see all,
And swear to each detail the most minute
In what I think a Pan's face—you, mere cloud :
I swear I hear him speak and see him wink,
For fear, if once I drop the emphasis,   870
Mankind may doubt there's any cloud at all.
You take the simpler life—ready to see,
Willing to see—for no cloud's worth a face—
And leaving quiet what no strength can move,
And which, who bids you move ? who has the right ?
I bid you ; but you are God's sheep, not mine—
' Pastor est tui Dominus.' You find
In these the pleasant pastures of this life
Much you may eat without the least offence,
Much you don't eat because your maw objects,   880
Much you would eat but that your fellow-flock
Open great eyes at you and even butt,
And thereupon you like your mates so well

You cannot please yourself, offending them—
Though when they seem exorbitantly sheep,
You weigh your pleasure with their butts and bleats
And strike the balance. Sometimes certain fears
Restrain you—real checks since you find them so—
Sometimes you please yourself and nothing checks ;
And thus you graze through life with not one lie,   890
And like it best.

                But do you, in truth's name ?
If so, you beat—which means, you are not I—
Who needs must make earth mine and feed my fill
Not simply unbutted at, unbickered with,
But motioned to the velvet of the sward
By those obsequious wethers' very selves.
Look at me, sir ; my age is double yours :
At yours, I knew beforehand, so enjoyed,
What now I should be—as, permit the word,
I pretty well imagine your whole range   900
And stretch of tether twenty years to come.
We both have minds and bodies much alike.
In truth's name, don't you want my bishopric,
My daily bread, my influence and my state ?
You're young, I'm old, you must be old one day ;
Will you find then, as I do hour by hour,
Women their lovers kneel to, that cut curls
From your fat lap-dog's ears to grace a brooch—
Dukes, that petition just to kiss your ring—
With much beside you know or may conceive ?   910
Suppose we die to-night : well, here am I,
Such were my gains, life bore this fruit to me,
While writing all the same my articles
On music, poetry, the fictile vase
Found at Albano, chess, or Anacreon's Greek.
But you—the highest honour in your life,
The thing you'll crown yourself with, all your days,
Is—dining here and drinking this last glass
I pour you out in sign of amity
Before we part for ever. Of your power   920
And social influence, worldly worth in short,
Judge what 's my estimation by the fact,
I do not condescend to enjoin, beseech,
Hint secrecy on one of all these words !
You're shrewd and know that should you publish one
The world would brand the lie—my enemies first,
Who'd sneer—' the bishop 's an arch-hypocrite,
And knave perhaps, but not so frank a fool.'
Whereas I should not dare for both my ears
Breathe one such syllable, smile one such smile,   930
Before my chaplain who reflects myself—
My shade 's so much more potent than your flesh.

What's your reward, self-abnegating friend ?
Stood you confessed of those exceptional
And privileged great natures that dwarf mine—
A zealot with a mad ideal in reach,
A poet just about to print his ode,
A statesman with a scheme to stop this war,
An artist whose religion is his art,
I should have nothing to object ! such men   940
Carry the fire, all things grow warm to them,
Their drugget's worth my purple, they beat me.
But you,—you're just as little those as I—
You, Gigadibs, who, thirty years of age,
Write statedly for Blackwood's Magazine,
Believe you see two points in Hamlet's soul
Unseized by the Germans yet—which view you'll print—
Meantime the best you have to show being still
That lively lightsome article we took
Almost for the true Dickens,—what's its name ?   950
'The Slum and Cellar—or Whitechapel life
Limned after dark !' it made me laugh, I know,
And pleased a month and brought you in ten pounds.
—Success I recognize and compliment,
And therefore give you, if you choose, three words
(The card and pencil-scratch is quite enough)
Which whether here, in Dublin or New York,
Will get you, prompt as at my eyebrow's wink,
Such terms as never you aspired to get
In all our own reviews and some not ours.   960
Go write your lively sketches—be the first
'Blougram, or The Eccentric Confidence'—
Or better simply say, 'The Outward-bound.'
Why, men as soon would throw it in my teeth
As copy and quote the infamy chalked broad
About me on the church-door opposite.
You will not wait for that experience though,
I fancy, howsoever you decide,
To discontinue—not detesting, not
Defaming, but at least—despising me !   970

    Over his wine so smiled and talked his hour
Sylvester Blougram, styled *in partibus*
Episcopus, nec non—(the deuce knows what
It's changed to by our novel hierarchy)
With Gigadibs the literary man,
Who played with spoons, explored his plate's design,
And ranged the olive-stones about its edge,
While the great bishop rolled him out his mind.

    For Blougram, he believed, say, half he spoke.
The other portion, as he shaped it thus   980
For argumentatory purposes,
He felt his foe was foolish to dispute.

Some arbitrary accidental thoughts
That crossed his mind, amusing because new,
He chose to represent as fixtures there,
Invariable convictions (such they seemed
Beside his interlocutor's loose cards
Flung daily down, and not the same way twice)
While certain Hell-deep instincts, man's weak tongue
Is never bold to utter in their truth   990
Because styled Hell-deep ('tis an old mistake
To place Hell at the bottom of the earth)
He ignored these,—not having in readiness
Their nomenclature and philosophy:
He said true things, but called them by wrong names.
'On the whole,' he thought, 'I justify myself
On every point where cavillers like this
Oppugn my life: he tries one kind of fence—
I close—he's worsted, that's enough for him;
He's on the ground! if the ground should break away
I take my stand on, there's a firmer yet   1001
Beneath it, both of us may sink and reach.
His ground was over mine and broke the first:
So let him sit with me this many a year!'

He did not sit five minutes. Just a week
Sufficed his sudden healthy vehemence.
(Something had struck him in the 'Outward-bound'
Another way than Blougram's purpose was)
And having bought, not cabin-furniture
But settler's-implements (enough for three)   1010
And started for Australia—there, I hope,
By this time he has tested his first plough,
And studied his last chapter of St. John.

CALIBAN UPON SETEBOS;

OR,

NATURAL THEOLOGY IN THE ISLAND

'THOU THOUGHTEST THAT I WAS ALTOGETHER SUCH AN ONE
AS THYSELF'

[WILL sprawl, now that the heat of day is best,
Flat on his belly in the pit's much mire,
With elbows wide, fists clenched to prop his chin;
And, while he kicks both feet in the cool slush,
And feels about his spine small eft-things course,
Run in and out each arm, and make him laugh;
And while above his head a pompion-plant,
Coating the cave-top as a brow its eye,
Creeps down to touch and tickle hair and beard,

And now a flower drops with a bee inside,   10
And now a fruit to snap at, catch and crunch :
He looks out o'er yon sea which sunbeams cross
And recross till they weave a spider-web
(Meshes of fire, some great fish breaks at times),
And talks to his own self, howe'er he please,
Touching that other, whom his dam called God.
Because to talk about Him, vexes—ha,
Could He but know ! and time to vex is now,
When talk is safer than in winter-time.
Moreover Prosper and Miranda sleep   20
In confidence he drudges at their task,
And it is good to cheat the pair, and gibe,
Letting the rank tongue blossom into speech.]

Setebos, Setebos, and Setebos !
'Thinketh, He dwelleth i' the cold o' the moon.
'Thinketh He made it, with the sun to match,
But not the stars ; the stars came otherwise ;
Only made clouds, winds, meteors, such as that :
Also this isle, what lives and grows thereon,
And snaky sea which rounds and ends the same.   30

'Thinketh, it came of being ill at ease :
He hated that He cannot change His cold,
Nor cure its ache. 'Hath spied an icy fish
That longed to 'scape the rock-stream where she lived,
And thaw herself within the lukewarm brine
O' the lazy sea her stream thrusts far amid,
A crystal spike 'twixt two warm walls of wave ;
Only she ever sickened, found repulse
At the other kind of water, not her life,
(Green-dense and dim-delicious, bred o' the sun)   40
Flounced back from bliss she was not born to breathe,
And in her old bounds buried her despair,
Hating and loving warmth alike : so He.

'Thinketh, He made thereat the sun, this isle,
Trees and the fowls here, beast and creeping thing.
Yon otter, sleek-wet, black, lithe as a leech ;
Yon auk, one fire-eye in a ball of foam,
That floats and feeds ; a certain badger brown
He hath watched hunt with that slant white-wedge eye
By moonlight ; and the pie with the long tongue   50
That pricks deep into oakwarts for a worm,
And says a plain word when she finds her prize,
But will not eat the ants ; the ants themselves
That build a wall of seeds and settled stalks
About their hole—He made all these and more,
Made all we see, and us, in spite : how else ?
He could not, Himself, make a second self
To be His mate ; as well have made Himself.

He would not make what He mislikes or slights,
An eyesore to Him, or not worth His pains :   60
But did, in envy, listlessness or sport,
Make what Himself would fain, in a manner, be—
Weaker in most points, stronger in a few,
Worthy, and yet mere playthings all the while,
Things He admires and mocks too,—that is it.
Because, so brave, so better though they be,
It nothing skills if He begin to plague.
Look now, I melt a gourd-fruit into mash,
Add honeycomb and pod, I have perceived,
Which bite like finches when they bill and kiss,—   70
Then, when froth rises bladdery, drink up all,
Quick, quick, till maggots scamper through my brain ;
And throw me on my back i' the seeded thyme,
And wanton, wishing I were born a bird.
Put case, unable to be what I wish,
I yet could make a live bird out of clay :
Would not I take clay, pinch my Caliban
Able to fly ?—for, there, see, he hath wings,
And great comb like the hoopoe's to admire,
And there, a sting to do his foes offence,   80
There, and I will that he begin to live,
Fly to yon rock-top, nip me off the horns
Of grigs high up that make the merry din,
Saucy through their veined wings, and mind me not.
In which feat, if his leg snapped, brittle clay,
And he lay stupid-like,—why, I should laugh ;
And if he, spying me, should fall to weep,
Beseech me to be good, repair his wrong,
Bid his poor leg smart less or grow again,—
Well, as the chance were, this might take or else   90
Not take my fancy : I might hear his cry,
And give the manikin three legs for his one,
Or pluck the other off, leave him like an egg,
And lessoned he was mine and merely clay.
Were this no pleasure, lying in the thyme,
Drinking the mash, with brain become alive,
Making and marring clay at will ? So He.

'Thinketh, such shows nor right nor wrong in Him,
Nor kind, nor cruel : He is strong and Lord.
'Am strong myself compared to yonder crabs   100
That march now from the mountain to the sea ;
'Let twenty pass, and stone the twenty-first,
Loving not, hating not, just choosing so.
'Say, the first straggler that boasts purple spots
Shall join the file, one pincer twisted off ;
'Say, this bruised fellow shall receive a worm,
And two worms he whose nippers end in red ;
As it likes me each time, I do : so He.

Well then, 'supposeth He is good i' the main,   110
Placable if His mind and ways were guessed,
But rougher than His handiwork, be sure!
Oh, He hath made things worthier than Himself,
And envieth that, so helped, such things do more
Than He who made them! What consoles but this?
That they, unless through Him, do nought at all,
And must submit: what other use in things?
'Hath cut a pipe of pithless elder-joint
That, blown through, gives exact the scream o' the jay
When from her wing you twitch the feathers blue:
Sound this, and little birds that hate the jay   120
Flock within stone's throw, glad their foe is hurt:
Put case such pipe could prattle and boast forsooth
'I catch the birds, I am the crafty thing,
I make the cry my maker cannot make
With his great round mouth; he must blow through mine!'
Would not I smash it with my foot? So He.

But wherefore rough, why cold and ill at ease?
Aha, that is a question! Ask, for that,
What knows,—the something over Setebos
That made Him, or He, may be, found and fought,   130
Worsted, drove off and did to nothing, perchance.
There may be something quiet o'er His head,
Out of His reach, that feels nor joy nor grief,
Since both derive from weakness in some way.
I joy because the quails come; would not joy
Could I bring quails here when I have a mind:
This Quiet, all it hath a mind to, doth.
'Esteemeth stars the outposts of its couch,
But never spends much thought nor care that way.
It may look up, work up,—the worse for those   140
It works on! 'Careth but for Setebos
The many-handed as a cuttle-fish,
Who, making Himself feared through what He does,
Looks up, first, and perceives He cannot soar
To what is quiet and hath happy life;
Next looks down here, and out of very spite
Makes this a bauble world to ape yon real,
These good things to match those as hips do grapes.
'Tis solace making baubles, ay, and sport.
Himself peeped late, eyed Prosper at his books   150
Careless and lofty, lord now of the isle:
Vexed, 'stitched a book of broad leaves, arrow-shaped,
Wrote thereon, he knows what, prodigious words;
Has peeled a wand and called it by a name;
Weareth at whiles for an enchanter's robe
The eyed skin of a supple oncelot;
And hath an ounce sleeker than youngling mole,
A four-legged serpent he makes cower and couch.

Now snarl, now hold its breath and mind his eye,
And saith she is Miranda and my wife: 160
'Keeps for his Ariel a tall pouch-bill crane
He bids go wade for fish and straight disgorge;
Also a sea-beast, lumpish, which he snared,
Blinded the eyes of, and brought somewhat tame,
And split its toe-webs, and now pens the drudge
In a hole o' the rock and calls him Caliban;
A bitter heart, that bides its time and bites.
'Plays thus at being Prosper in a way,
Taketh his mirth with make-believes: so He.

His dam held that the Quiet made all things 170
Which Setebos vexed only: 'holds not so.
Who made them weak, meant weakness He might vex.
Had He meant other, while His hand was in,
Why not make horny eyes no thorn could prick,
Or plate my scalp with bone against the snow,
Or overscale my flesh 'neath joint and joint,
Like an orc's armour? Ay,—so spoil His sport!
He is the One now: only He doth all.

'Saith, He may like, perchance, what profits Him.
Ay, himself loves what does him good; but why? 180
'Gets good no otherwise. This blinded beast
Loves whoso places flesh-meat on his nose,
But, had he eyes, would want no help, but hate
Or love, just as it liked him: He hath eyes.
Also it pleaseth Setebos to work,
Use all His hands, and exercise much craft,
By no means for the love of what is worked.
'Tasteth, himself, no finer good i' the world
When all goes right, in this safe summertime,
And he wants little, hungers, aches not much, 190
Than trying what to do with wit and strength.
'Falls to make something: 'piled yon pile of turfs,
And squared and stuck there squares of soft white chalk,
And, with a fish-tooth, scratched a moon on each,
And set up endwise certain spikes of tree,
And crowned the whole with a sloth's skull a-top,
Found dead i' the woods, too hard for one to kill.
No use at all i' the work, for work's sole sake;
'Shall some day knock it down again: so He.

'Saith He is terrible: watch His feats in proof! 200
One hurricane will spoil six good months' hope.
He hath a spite against me, that I know,
Just as He favours Prosper, who knows why?
So it is, all the same, as well I find.
'Wove wattles half the winter, fenced them firm
With stone and stake to stop she-tortoises
Crawling to lay their eggs here: well, one wave.

Feeling the foot of Him upon its neck,
Gaped as a snake does, lolled out its large tongue,
And licked the whole labour flat: so much for spite. 210
'Saw a ball flame down late (yonder it lies)
Where, half an hour before, I slept i' the shade:
Often they scatter sparkles: there is force!
'Dug up a newt He may have envied once
And turned to stone, shut up inside a stone.
Please Him and hinder this?—What Prosper does?
Aha, if He would tell me how! Not He!
There is the sport: discover how or die!
All need not die, for of the things o' the isle
Some flee afar, some dive, some run up trees; 220
Those at His mercy,—why, they please Him most
When . . when . . well, never try the same way twice!
Repeat what act has pleased, He may grow wroth.
You must not know his ways, and play Him off,
Sure of the issue. 'Doth the like himself:
'Spareth a squirrel that it nothing fears
But steals the nut from underneath my thumb,
And when I threat, bites stoutly in defence:
'Spareth an urchin that, contrariwise,
Curls up into a ball, pretending death 230
For fright at my approach: the two ways please.
But what would move my choler more than this,
That either creature counted on its life
To-morrow and next day and all days to come,
Saying forsooth in the inmost of its heart,
' Because he did so yesterday with me,
And otherwise with such another brute,
So must he do henceforth and always.'—Ay?
'Would teach the reasoning couple what ' must ' means!
'Doth as he likes, or wherefore Lord? So He. 240

'Conceiveth all things will continue thus,
And we shall have to live in fear of Him
So long as He lives, keeps His strength: no change,
If He have done His best, make no new world
To please Him more, so leave off watching this,—
If He surprise not even the Quiet's self
Some strange day,—or, suppose, grow into it
As grubs grow butterflies: else, here are we,
And there is He, and nowhere help at all.

'Believeth with the life, the pain shall stop. 250
His dam held different, that after death
He both plagued enemies and feasted friends:
Idly! He doth His worst in this our life,
Giving just respite lest we die through pain,
Saving last pain for worst,—with which, an end.
Meanwhile, the best way to escape His ire
Is, not to seem too happy. Sees, himself,

Yonder two flies, with purple films and pink,
Bask on the pompion-bell above : kills both.
'Sees two black painful beetles roll their ball   260
On head and tail as if to save their lives :
Moves them the stick away they strive to clear.

Even so, 'would have Him misconceive, suppose
This Caliban strives hard and ails no less,
And always, above all else, envies Him.
Wherefore he mainly dances on dark nights,
Moans in the sun, gets under holes to laugh,
And never speaks his mind save housed as now :
Outside, 'groans, curses. If He caught me here,
O'erheard this speech, and asked ' What chucklest at ? '   270
'Would, to appease Him, cut a finger off,
Or of my three kid yearlings burn the best,
Or let the toothsome apples rot on tree,
Or push my tame beast for the orc to taste :
While myself lit a fire, and made a song
And sung it, ' *What I hate, be consecrate*
To celebrate Thee and Thy state, no mate
For Thee ; what see for envy in poor me ? '
Hoping the while, since evils sometimes mend,
Warts rub away, and sores are cured with slime,   280
That some strange day, will either the Quiet catch
And conquer Setebos, or likelier He
Decrepit may doze, doze, as good as die.

[What, what ? A curtain o'er the world at once !
Crickets stop hissing ; not a bird—or, yes,
There scuds His raven that hath told Him all !
It was fool's play, this prattling ! Ha ! The wind
Shoulders the pillared dust, death's house o' the move,
And fast invading fires begin ! White blaze—
A tree's head snaps—and there, there, there, there, there,
His thunder follows ! Fool to gibe at Him !   291
Lo ! 'Lieth flat and loveth Setebos !
'Maketh his teeth meet through his upper lip,
Will let those quails fly, will not eat this month
One little mess of whelks, so he may 'scape !]

MATTHEW ARNOLD

THE SCHOLAR GIPSY

Go, for they call you, shepherd, from the hill;
　Go, shepherd, and untie the wattled cotes:
　　No longer leave thy wistful flock unfed,
　Nor let thy bawling fellows rack their throats,
　　Nor the cropp'd grasses shoot another head.
　　　But when the fields are still,
　And the tired men and dogs all gone to rest,
　　And only the white sheep are sometimes seen
　　Cross and recross the strips of moon-blanch'd green,
Come, shepherd, and again renew the quest.　　10

Here, where the reaper was at work of late,
　In this high field's dark corner, where he leaves
　　His coat, his basket, and his earthen cruise,
　And in the sun all morning binds the sheaves,
　　Then here, at noon, comes back his stores to use;
　　　Here will I sit and wait,
　While to my ear from uplands far away
　　The bleating of the folded flocks is borne,
　　With distant cries of reapers in the corn—
All the live murmur of a summer's day.　　20

Screen'd is this nook o'er the high, half-reap'd field,
　And here till sun-down, shepherd, will I be.
　　Through the thick corn the scarlet poppies peep,
　And round green roots and yellowing stalks I see
　　Pale blue convolvulus in tendrils creep:
　　　And air-swept lindens yield
　Their scent, and rustle down their perfum'd showers
　　Of bloom on the bent grass where I am laid,
　　And bower me from the August sun with shade;
And the eye travels down to Oxford's towers:　　30

And near me on the grass lies Glanvil's book—
　Come, let me read the oft-read tale again,
　　The story of that Oxford scholar poor
　Of pregnant parts and quick inventive brain,
　　Who, tir'd of knocking at preferment's door,
　　　One summer morn forsook
　His friends, and went to learn the gipsy lore,
　　And roam'd the world with that wild brotherhood,
　　And came, as most men deem'd, to little good,
But came to Oxford and his friends no more.　　40

But once, years after, in the country lanes,
  Two scholars whom at college erst he knew
    Met him, and of his way of life enquir'd.
Whereat he answer'd, that the gipsy crew,
  His mates, had arts to rule as they desir'd
    The workings of men's brains;
And they can bind them to what thoughts they will:
  'And I,' he said, 'the secret of their art,
  When fully learn'd, will to the world impart:
But it needs heaven-sent moments for this skill.'   50

This said, he left them, and return'd no more,
  But rumours hung about the country side
    That the lost Scholar long was seen to stray,
Seen by rare glimpses, pensive and tongue-tied,
  In hat of antique shape, and cloak of grey,
    The same the gipsies wore.
Shepherds had met him on the Hurst in spring:
  At some lone alehouse in the Berkshire moors,
  On the warm ingle bench, the smock-frock'd boors
Had found him seated at their entering,   60

But, mid their drink and clatter, he would fly:
  And I myself seem half to know thy looks,
    And put the shepherds, wanderer, on thy trace;
And boys who in lone wheatfields scare the rooks
  I ask if thou hast pass'd their quiet place;
    Or in my boat I lie
Moor'd to the cool bank in the summer heats,
  Mid wide grass meadows which the sunshine fills,
  And watch the warm green-muffled Cumner hills,
And wonder if thou haunt'st their shy retreats.   70

For most, I know, thou lov'st retired ground.
  Thee, at the ferry, Oxford riders blithe,
    Returning home on summer nights, have met
Crossing the stripling Thames at Bab-lock-hithe,
  Trailing in the cool stream thy fingers wet,
    As the slow punt swings round:
And leaning backwards in a pensive dream,
  And fostering in thy lap a heap of flowers
  Pluck'd in shy fields and distant Wychwood bowers,
And thine eyes resting on the moonlit stream.   80

And then they land, and thou art seen no more.
  Maidens who from the distant hamlets come
    To dance around the Fyfield elm in May,
Oft through the darkening fields have seen thee roam,
  Or cross a stile into the public way.
    Oft thou hast given them store
Of flowers—the frail-leaf'd, white anemone—
  Dark bluebells drench'd with dews of summer eves—
  And purple orchises with spotted leaves—
But none has words she can report of thee.   90

And, above Godstow bridge, when hay-time's here
  In June, and many a scythe in sunshine flames,
    Men who through those wide fields of breezy grass
  Where black-wing'd swallows haunt the glittering Thames,
    To bathe in the abandon'd lasher pass,
      Have often pass'd thee near
  Sitting upon the river bank o'ergrown:
    Mark'd thy outlandish garb, thy figure spare,
    Thy dark vague eyes, and soft abstracted air;
  But, when they came from bathing, thou wert gone. 100

At some lone homestead in the Cumner hills,
  Where at her open door the housewife darns,
    Thou hast been seen, or hanging on a gate
  To watch the threshers in the mossy barns.
    Children, who early range these slopes and late
      For cresses from the rills,
  Have known thee watching, all an April day,
    The springing pastures and the feeding kine;
    And mark'd thee, when the stars come out and shine,
  Through the long dewy grass move slow away. 110

In autumn, on the skirts of Bagley wood,
  Where most the gipsies by the turf-edg'd way
    Pitch their smok'd tents, and every bush you see
  With scarlet patches tagg'd and shreds of grey,
    Above the forest ground call'd Thessaly—
      The blackbird picking food
  Sees thee, nor stops his meal, nor fears at all;
    So often has he known thee past him stray
    Rapt, twirling in thy hand a wither'd spray,
  And waiting for the spark from Heaven to fall. 120

And once, in winter, on the causeway chill
  Where home through flooded fields foot-travellers go,
    Have I not pass'd thee on the wooden bridge
  Wrapt in thy cloak and battling with the snow,
    Thy face towards Hinksey and its wintry ridge?
      And thou hast climb'd the hill
  And gain'd the white brow of the Cumner range,
    Turn'd once to watch, while thick the snowflakes fall,
    The line of festal light in Christ-Church hall—
  Then sought thy straw in some sequester'd grange. 130

But what—I dream! Two hundred years are flown
  Since first thy story ran through Oxford halls,
    And the grave Glanvil did the tale inscribe
  That thou wert wander'd from the studious walls
    To learn strange arts, and join a gipsy tribe:
      And thou from earth art gone
  Long since, and in some quiet churchyard laid;
    Some country nook, where o'er thy unknown grave
    Tall grasses and white flowering nettles wave—
  Under a dark red-fruited yew-tree's shade. 140

––No, no, thou hast not felt the lapse of hours.
For what wears out the life of mortal men?
 'Tis that from change to change their being rolls:
'Tis that repeated shocks, again, again,
  Exhaust the energy of strongest souls
   And numb the elastic powers.
Till having us'd our nerves with bliss and teen,
  And tir'd upon a thousand schemes our wit,
  To the just-pausing Genius we remit
Our worn-out life, and are—what we have been. 150

Thou hast not liv'd, why should'st thou perish, so?
 Thou hadst *one* aim, *one* business, *one* desire:
  Else wert thou long since number'd with the dead—
Else hadst thou spent, like other men, thy fire.
  The generations of thy peers are fled,
   And we ourselves shall go;
But thou possessest an immortal lot,
  And we imagine thee exempt from age
  And living as thou liv'st on Glanvil's page,
Because thou hadst—what we, alas, have not! 160

For early didst thou leave the world, with powers
 Fresh, undiverted to the world without,
  Firm to their mark, not spent on other things;
Free from the sick fatigue, the languid doubt,
  Which much to have tried, in much been baffled, brings.
   O life unlike to ours!
Who fluctuate idly without term or scope,
  Of whom each strives, nor knows for what he strives,
  And each half lives a hundred different lives;
Who wait like thee, but not, like thee, in hope. 170

Thou waitest for the spark from Heaven: and we,
 Light half-believers of our casual creeds,
  Who never deeply felt, nor clearly will'd,
Whose insight never has borne fruit in deeds,
  Whose vague resolves never have been fulfill'd;
   For whom each year we see
Breeds new beginnings, disappointments new;
  Who hesitate and falter life away,
  And lose to-morrow the ground won to-day—
Ah, do not we, wanderer, await it too? 180

Yes, we await it, but it still delays,
 And then we suffer; and amongst us one,
  Who most has suffer'd, takes dejectedly
His seat upon the intellectual throne;
  And all his store of sad experience he
   Lays bare of wretched days;
Tells us his misery's birth and growth and signs,
  And how the dying spark of hope was fed,
  And how the breast was sooth'd, and how the head,
And all his hourly varied anodynes. 190

This for our wisest: and we others pine,
    And wish the long unhappy dream would end,
      And waive all claim to bliss, and try to bear
With close-lipp'd patience for our only friend,
      Sad patience, too near neighbour to despair:
        But none has hope like thine.
Thou through the fields and through the woods dost stray,
    Roaming the countryside, a truant boy,
    Nursing thy project in unclouded joy,
And every doubt long blown by time away.   200

O born in days when wits were fresh and clear,
    And life ran gaily as the sparkling Thames;
      Before this strange disease of modern life,
With its sick hurry, its divided aims,
      Its heads o'ertax'd, its palsied hearts, was rife—
        Fly hence, our contact fear!
Still fly, plunge deeper in the bowering wood!
    Averse, as Dido did with gesture stern
    From her false friend's approach in Hades turn,
Wave us away, and keep thy solitude.   210

Still nursing the unconquerable hope,
    Still clutching the inviolable shade,
      With a free onward impulse brushing through,
By night, the silver'd branches of the glade—
      Far on the forest skirts, where none pursue,
        On some mild pastoral slope
Emerge, and resting on the moonlit pales,
    Freshen thy flowers, as in former years,
    With dew, or listen with enchanted ears,
From the dark dingles, to the nightingales.   220

But fly our paths, our feverish contact fly!
    For strong the infection of our mental strife,
      Which, though it gives no bliss, yet spoils for rest;
And we should win thee from thy own fair life,
      Like us distracted, and like us unblest.
        Soon, soon thy cheer would die,
Thy hopes grow timorous, and unfix'd thy powers,
    And thy clear aims be cross and shifting made:
    And then thy glad perennial youth would fade,
Fade, and grow old at last, and die like ours.   230

Then fly our greetings, fly our speech and smiles!
    —As some grave Tyrian trader, from the sea,
      Descried at sunrise an emerging prow
Lifting the cool-haired creepers stealthily,
      The fringes of a southward-facing brow
        Among the Aegean isles:
And saw the merry Grecian coaster come,
    Freighted with amber grapes, and Chian wine,
    Green bursting figs, and tunnies steep'd in brine;
And knew the intruders on his ancient home,   240

The young light-hearted Masters of the waves ;
  And snatch'd his rudder, and shook out more sail,
    And day and night held on indignantly
  O'er the blue Midland waters with the gale,
    Betwixt the Syrtes and soft Sicily
      To where the Atlantic raves
  Outside the Western Straits, and unbent sails
    There, where down cloudy cliffs, through sheets of foam,
    Shy traffickers, the dark Iberians come ;
  And on the beach undid his corded bales.   250

THYRSIS

A MONODY, *to commemorate the author's friend*, ARTHUR
    HUGH CLOUGH, *who died at Florence*, 1861

How changed is here each spot man makes or fills !
  In the two Hinkseys nothing keeps the same ;
    The village-street its haunted mansion lacks
And from the sign is gone Sibylla's name,
    And from the roofs the twisted chimney-stacks.
      Are ye too changed, ye hills ?
See, 'tis no foot of unfamiliar men
    To-night from Oxford up your pathway strays !
    Here came I often, often, in old days ;
Thyrsis and I ; we still had Thyrsis then.   10

Runs it not here, the track by Childsworth farm,
  Up past the wood, to where the elm-tree crowns
    The hill behind whose ridge the sunset flames ?
The Signal-Elm, that looks on Ilsley Downs,
    The Vale, the three lone wears, the youthful Thames ?—
      This winter-eve is warm,
Humid the air ; leafless, yet soft as spring,
    The tender purple spray on copse and briers ;
    And that sweet city with her dreaming spires,
She needs not June for beauty's heightening,   20

Lovely all times she lies, lovely to-night !
  Only, methinks, some loss of habit's power
    Befalls me wandering through this upland dim.
Once pass'd I blindfold here, at any hour,
    Now seldom come I, since I came with him.
      That single elm-tree bright
Against the west—I miss it ! is it gone ?
    We prized it dearly ; while it stood, we said,
    Our friend, the Scholar-Gipsy, was not dead ;
While the tree lived, he in these fields lived on.   30

Too rare, too rare, grow now my visits here!
　But once I knew each field, each flower, each stick,
　　And with the country-folk acquaintance made
　By barn in threshing-time, by new-built rick.
　　Here, too, our shepherd-pipes we first assay'd.
　　　Ah me! this many a year
　My pipe is lost, my shepherd's-holiday.
　　Needs must I lose them, needs with heavy heart
　　Into the world and wave of men depart;
　But Thyrsis of his own will went away.　　　　　　40

It irk'd him to be here, he could not rest.
　He loved each simple joy the country yields,
　　He loved his mates; but yet he could not keep,
　For that a shadow lower'd on the fields,
　　Here with the shepherds and the silly sheep.
　　　Some life of men unblest
　He knew, which made him droop, and fill'd his head.
　　He went; his piping took a troubled sound
　　Of storms that rage outside our happy ground;
　He could not wait their passing, he is dead.　　　50

So, some temptuous morn in early June,
　When the year's primal burst of bloom is o'er,
　　Before the roses and the longest day—
　When garden-walks, and all the grassy floor,
　　With blossoms, red and white, of fallen May,
　　　And chestnut-flowers are strewn—
　So have I heard the cuckoo's parting cry,
　　From the wet field, through the vext garden-trees,
　　Come with the volleying rain and tossing breeze:
　The bloom is gone, and with the bloom go I.　　　60

Too quick despairer, wherefore wilt thou go?
　Soon will the high Midsummer pomps come on,
　　Soon will the musk carnations break and swell,
　Soon shall we have gold-dusted snapdragon,
　　Sweet-William with its homely cottage-smell,
　　　And stocks in fragrant blow;
　Roses that down the alleys shine afar,
　　And open, jasmine-muffled lattices,
　　And groups under the dreaming garden-trees,
　And the full moon, and the white evening-star.　　70

He hearkens not! light comer, he is gone!
　What matters it? next year he will return,
　　And we shall have him in the sweet spring-days,
　With whitening hedges, and uncrumpling fern,
　　And blue-bells trembling by the forest-ways,
　　　And scent of hay new-mown.
　But Thyrsis never more we swains shall see;
　　See him come back, and cut a smoother reed,
　　And blow a strain the world at last shall heed—
　For Time, not Corydon, hath conquer'd thee!　　　80

Alack, for Corydon no rival now!
  But when Sicilian shepherds lost a mate,
    Some good survivor with his flute would go,
  Piping a ditty sad for Bion's mate,
    And cross the unpermitted ferry's flow,
      And unbend Pluto's brow,
  And make leap up with joy the beauteous head
    Of Proserpine, among whose crowned hair
    Are flowers, first open'd on Sicilian air;
  And flute his friend, like Orpheus, from the dead.   90
O easy access to the hearer's grace,
  When Dorian shepherds sang to Proserpine!
    For she herself had trod Sicilian fields,
  She knew the Dorian water's gush divine,
    She knew each lily white which Enna yields,
      Each rose with blushing face;
  She loved the Dorian pipe, the Dorian strain.
    But ah, of our poor Thames she never heard!
    Her foot the Cumner cowslips never stirr'd;
  And we should tease her with our plaint in vain!   100
Well! wind-dispersed and vain the words will be,
  Yet, Thyrsis, let me give my grief its hour
    In the old haunt, and find our tree-topp'd hill!
  Who, if not I, for questing here hath power?
    I know the wood which hides the daffodil,
      I know the Fyfield tree,
  I know what white, what purple fritillaries
    The grassy harvest of the river-fields,
    Above by Ensham, down by Sandford, yields;
  And what sedged brooks are Thames's tributaries;   110
I know these slopes; who knows them if not I?—
  But many a dingle on the loved hill-side,
    With thorns once studded, old, white-blossom'd trees,
  Where thick the cowslips grew, and, far descried,
    High tower'd the spikes of purple orchises,
      Hath since our day put by
  The coronais of that forgotten time;
    Down each green bank hath gone the ploughboy's team,
    And only in the hidden brookside gleam
  Primroses, orphans of the flowery prime.   120
Where is the girl, who by the boatman's door,
  Above the locks, above the boating throng,
    Unmoor'd our skiff, when, through the Wytham flats,
  Red loosestrife and blond meadow-sweet among,
    And darting swallows, and light water-gnats,
      We track'd the shy Thames shore?
  Where are the mowers, who, as the tiny swell
    Of our boat passing heaved the river-grass,
    Stood with suspended scythe to see us pass?
  They all are gone, and thou art gone as well.   130

Yes, thou art gone! and round me too the night
  In ever-nearing circle waves her shade.
    I see her veil draw soft across the day,
  I feel her slowly chilling breath invade
    The cheek grown thin, the brown hair sprent with grey;
      I feel her finger light
  Laid pausefully upon life's headlong train;
    The foot less prompt to meet the morning dew,
    The heart less bounding at emotion new,
  And hope, once crush'd, less quick to spring again.   140

And long the way appears, which seem'd so short
  To the unpractised eye of sanguine youth;
    And high the mountain-tops, in cloudy air,
  The mountain-tops where is the throne of truth,
    Tops in life's morning-sun so bright and bare.
      Unbreachable the fort
  Of the long-batter'd world uplifts its wall;
    And strange and vain the earthly turmoil grows.
    And near and real the charm of thy repose,
  And night as welcome as a friend would fall.   150

But hush! the upland hath a sudden loss
  Of quiet;—Look! adown the dusk hill-side,
    A troop of Oxford hunters going home
  As in old days, jovial and talking, ride.
    From hunting with the Berkshire hounds they come.
      Quick! let me fly, and cross
  Into yon further field!—'Tis done; and see,
    Back'd by the sunset, which doth glorify
    The orange and pale violet evening-sky,
  Bare on its lonely ridge, the Tree! the Tree!   160

I take the omen! Eve lets down her veil,
  The white fog creeps from bush to bush about,
    The west unflushes, the high stars grow bright,
  And in the scatter'd farms the lights come out.
    I cannot reach the Signal-Tree to-night,
      Yet, happy omen, hail!
  Hear it from thy broad lucent Arno vale
    (For there thine earth-forgetting eyelids keep
    The morningless and unawakening sleep
  Under the flowery oleanders pale),   170

Hear it, O Thyrsis, still our Tree is there!—
  Ah, vain! These English fields, this upland dim,
    These brambles pale with mist engarlanded,
  That lone, sky-pointed Tree, are not for him.
    To a boon southern country he is fled,
      And now in happier air,
  Wandering with the great Mother's train divine
    (And purer or more subtle soul than thee,
    I trow, the mighty Mother doth not see!)
  Within a folding of the Apennine,   180

Thou hearest the immortal strains of old.
　Putting his sickle to the perilous grain,
　　In the hot cornfield of the Phrygian king,
　For thee the Lityerses song again
　　　Young Daphnis with his silver voice doth sing;
　　　Sings his Sicilian fold,
　His sheep, his hapless love, his blinded eyes;
　　And how a call celestial round him rang,
　　And heavenward from the fountain-brink he sprang,
And all the marvel of the golden skies.　　　190

There thou art gone, and me thou leavest here,
　Sole in these fields; yet will I not despair.
　　Despair I will not, while I yet descry
　Neath the soft canopy of English air
　　　That lonely Tree against the western sky.
　　　Still, still these slopes, 'tis clear,
　Our Gipsy-Scholar haunts, outliving thee!
　　Fields where the sheep from cages pull the hay,
　　Woods with anemones in flower till May,
Know him a wanderer still; then why not me?　　200

A fugitive and gracious light he seeks,
　Shy to illumine; and I seek it too.
　　This does not come with houses or with gold,
　With place, with honour, and a flattering crew;
　　　'Tis not in the world's market bought and sold.
　　　But the smooth-slipping weeks
　Drop by, and leave its seeker still untired.
　　Out of the heed of mortals is he gone,
　　He wends unfollow'd, he must house alone;
Yet on he fares, by his own heart inspired.　　210

Thou too, O Thyrsis, on like quest wert bound,
　Thou wanderedst with me for a little hour.
　　Men gave thee nothing; but this happy quest,
　If men esteem'd thee feeble, gave thee power,
　　If men procured thee trouble, gave thee rest.
　　　And this rude Cumner ground,
　Its fir-topped Hurst, its farms, its quiet fields,
　　Here cam'st thou in thy jocund youthful time,
　　Here was thine height of strength, thy golden prime;
And still the haunt beloved a virtue yields.　　220

What though the music of thy rustic flute
　Kept not for long its happy, country tone;
　　Lost it too soon, and learnt a stormy note
　Of men contention-tost, of men who groan,
　　　Which task'd thy pipe too sore, and tired thy throat—
　　　It fail'd, and thou wert mute.
　Yet hadst thou alway visions of our light,
　　And long with men of care thou couldst not stay,
　　And soon thy foot resumed its wandering way,
Left human haunt, and on alone till night.　　230

Too rare, too rare, grow now my visits here!
'Mid city-noise, not, as with thee of yore,
 Thyrsis, in reach of sheep-bells, is my home.
Then through the great town's harsh, heart-wearying roar,
 Let in thy voice a whisper often come,
  To chase fatigue and fear:
Why faintest thou? I wander'd till I died.
 Roam on; the light we sought is shining still.
 Dost thou ask proof? Our Tree yet crowns the hill,
Our Scholar travels yet the loved hill-side.   240

SOHRAB AND RUSTUM

AN EPISODE

AND the first grey of morning fill'd the east,
And the fog rose out of the Oxus stream.
But all the Tartar camp along the stream
Was hush'd, and still the men were plunged in sleep:
Sohrab alone, he slept not: all night long
He had lain wakeful, tossing on his bed;
But when the grey dawn stole into his tent,
He rose, and clad himself, and girt his sword,
And took his horseman's cloak, and left his tent,
And went abroad into the cold wet fog,   10
Through the dim camp to Peran-Wisa's tent.
 Through the black Tartar tents he pass'd, which stood
Clustering like bee-hives on the low flat strand
Of Oxus, where the summer floods o'erflow
When the sun melts the snows in high Pamere:
Through the black tents he pass'd, o'er that low strand,
And to a hillock came, a little back
From the stream's brink, the spot where first a boat,
Crossing the stream in summer, scrapes the land.
The men of former times had crown'd the top 20
With a clay fort: but that was fall'n; and now
The Tartars built there Peran-Wisa's tent,
A dome of laths, and o'er it felts were spread.
And Sohrab came there, and went in, and stood
Upon the thick-pil'd carpets in the tent,
And found the old man sleeping on his bed
Of rugs and felts, and near him lay his arms.
And Peran-Wisa heard him, though the step
Was dull'd; for he slept light, an old man's sleep;
And he rose quickly on one arm, and said:— 30
 'Who art thou? for it is not yet clear dawn.
Speak! is there news, or any night alarm?'
 But Sohrab came to the bedside, and said:—
'Thou know'st me, Peran-Wisa: it is I.
The sun is not yet risen, and the foe

Sleep ; but I sleep not ; all night long I lie
Tossing and wakeful, and I come to thee.
For so did King Afrasiab bid me seek
Thy counsel, and to heed thee as thy son,
In Samarcand, before the army march'd ;   40
And I will tell thee what my heart desires.
Thou knowest if, since from Ader-baijan first
I came among the Tartars, and bore arms,
I have still serv'd Afrasiab well, and shown,
At my boy's years, the courage of a man.
This too thou know'st, that, while I still bear on
The conquering Tartar ensigns through the world,
And beat the Persians back on every field,
I seek one man, one man, and one alone—
Rustum, my father ; who, I hop'd, should greet,   50
Should one day greet, upon some well-fought field
His not unworthy, not inglorious son.
So I long hop'd, but him I never find.
Come then, hear now, and grant me what I ask.
Let the two armies rest to-day : but I
Will challenge forth the bravest Persian lords
To meet me, man to man : if I prevail,
Rustum will surely hear it ; if I fall—
Old man, the dead need no one, claim no kin.
Dim is the rumour of a common fight,   60
Where host meets host, and many names are sunk :
But of a single combat fame speaks clear.'
   He spoke : and Peran-Wisa took the hand
Of the young man in his, and sigh'd, and said :—
   ' O Sohrab, an unquiet heart is thine !
Canst thou not rest among the Tartar chiefs,
And share the battle's common chance with us
Who love thee, but must press for ever first,
In single fight incurring single risk,
To find a father thou hast never seen ?   70
That were far best, my son, to stay with us
Unmurmuring ; in our tents, while it is war,
And when 'tis truce, then in Afrasiab's towns.
But, if this one desire indeed rules all,
To seek out Rustum—seek him not through fight :
Seek him in peace, and carry to his arms,
O Sohrab, carry an unwounded son !
But far hence seek him, for he is not here.
For now it is not as when I was young,
When Rustum was in front of every fray :   80
But now he keeps apart, and sits at home,
In Seistan, with Zal, his father old.
Whether that his own mighty strength at last
Feels the abhorr'd approaches of old age ;
Or in some quarrel with the Persian King.
There go :—Thou wilt not ? Yet my heart forebodes

Danger or death awaits thee on this field.
Fain would I know thee safe and well, though lost
To us : fain therefore send thee hence, in peace
To seek thy father, not seek single fights   90
In vain :—but who can keep the lion's cub
From ravening ? and who govern Rustum's son ?
Go : I will grant thee what thy heart desires.'
    So said he, and dropp'd Sohrab's hand, and left
His bed, and the warm rugs whereon he lay,
And o'er his chilly limbs his woollen coat
He pass'd, and tied his sandals on his feet,
And threw a white cloak round him, and he took
In his right hand a ruler's staff, no sword ;
And on his head he placed his sheep-skin cap,   100
Black, glossy, curl'd, the fleece of Kara-Kul ;
And raised the curtain of his tent, and call'd
His herald to his side, and went abroad.
    The sun, by this, had risen, and clear'd the fog
From the broad Oxus and the glittering sands :
And from their tents the Tartar horsemen fil'd
Into the open plain ; so Haman bade ;
Haman, who next to Peran-Wisa rul'd
The host, and still was in his lusty prime.
From their black tents, long files of horse, they stream'd :
As when, some grey November morn, the files,   111
In marching order spread, of long-neck'd cranes,
Stream over Casbin, and the southern slopes
Of Elburz, from the Aralian estuaries,
Or some frore Caspian reed-bed, southward bound
For the warm Persian sea-board : so they stream'd.
The Tartars of the Oxus, the King's guard,
First with black sheep-skin caps and with long spears ;
Large men, large steeds ; who from Bokhara come
And Khiva, and ferment the milk of mares.   120
Next the more temperate Toorkmuns of the south,
The Tukas, and the lances of Salore,
And those from Attruck and the Caspian sands ;
Light men, and on light steeds, who only drink
The acrid milk of camels, and their wells.
And then a swarm of wandering horse, who came
From far, and a more doubtful service own'd ;
The Tartars of Ferghana, from the banks
Of the Jaxartes, men with scanty beards
And close-set skull-caps ; and those wilder hordes 130
Who roam o'er Kipchak and the northern waste,
Kalmuks and unkemp'd Kuzzaks, tribes who stray
Nearest the Pole, and wandering Kirghizzes,
Who come on shaggy ponies from Pamere.
These all fil'd out from camp into the plain.
And on the other side the Persians form'd :
First a light cloud of horse, Tartars they seem'd,

The Ilyats of Khorassan : and behind,
The royal troops of Persia, horse and foot,
Marshall'd battalions bright in burnish'd steel.   140
But Peran-Wisa with his herald came
Threading the Tartar squadrons to the front,
And with his staff kept back the foremost ranks.
And when Ferood, who led the Persians, saw
That Peran-Wisa kept the Tartars back,
He took his spear, and to the front he came,
And check'd his ranks, and fix'd them where they stood.
And the old Tartar came upon the sand
Betwixt the silent hosts, and spake, and said :—
   'Ferood, and ye, Persians and Tartars, hear !   150
Let there be truce between the hosts to-day.
But choose a champion from the Persian lords
To fight our champion Sohrab, man to man.'
   As, in the country, on a morn in June,
When the dew glistens on the pearled ears,
A shiver runs through the deep corn for joy—
So, when they heard what Peran-Wisa said,
A thrill through all the Tartar squadrons ran
Of pride and hope for Sohrab, whom they lov'd.
   But as a troop of pedlars, from Cabool,   160
Cross underneath the Indian Caucasus,
That vast sky-neighbouring mountain of milk snow ;
Winding so high, that, as they mount, they pass
Long flocks of travelling birds dead on the snow,
Chok'd by the air, and scarce can they themselves
Slake their parch'd throats with sugar'd mulberries—
In single file they move, and stop their breath,
For fear they should dislodge the o'erhanging snows—
So the pale Persians held their breath with fear.
   And to Ferood his brother Chiefs came up   170
To counsel : Gudurz and Zoarrah came,
And Feraburz, who rul'd the Persian host
Second, and was the uncle of the King :
These came and counsell'd ; and then Gudurz said :
   'Ferood, shame bids us take their challenge up,
Yet champion have we none to match this youth.
He has the wild stag's foot, the lion's heart.
But Rustum came last night ; aloof he sits
And sullen, and has pitch'd his tents apart :
Him will I seek, and carry to his ear   180
The Tartar challenge, and this young man's name.
Haply he will forget his wrath, and fight.
Stand forth the while, and take their challenge up.'
   So spake he ; and Ferood stood forth and said :—
   'Old man, be it agreed as thou hast said.
Let Sohrab arm, and we will find a man.'
   He spoke ; and Peran-Wisa turn'd, and strode
Back through the opening squadrons to his tent.

But through the anxious Persians Gudurz ran,
And cross'd the camp which lay behind, and reach'd, 190
Out on the sands beyond it, Rustum's tents.
Of scarlet cloth they were, and glittering gay,
Just pitch'd : the high pavilion in the midst
Was Rustum's, and his men lay camp'd around.
And Gudurz enter'd Rustum's tent, and found
Rustum : his morning meal was done, but still
The table stood beside him, charg'd with food ;
A side of roasted sheep, and cakes of bread,
And dark green melons ; and there Rustum sate
Listless, and held a falcon on his wrist,   200
And play'd with it ; but Gudurz came and stood
Before him ; and he look'd, and saw him stand ;
And with a cry sprang up, and dropp'd the bird,
And greeted Gudurz with both hands, and said :—
  ' Welcome ! these eyes could see no better sight.
What news ? but sit down first, and eat and drink.'
  But Gudurz stood in the tent door, and said :—
' Not now : a time will come to eat and drink,
But not to-day : to-day has other needs.
The armies are drawn out, and stand at gaze :   210
For from the Tartars is a challenge brought
To pick a champion from the Persian lords
To fight their champion—and thou know'st his name—
Sohrab men call him, but his birth is hid.
O Rustum, like thy might is this young man's !
He has the wild stag's foot, the lion's heart.
And he is young and Iran's chiefs are old,
Or else too weak ; and all eyes turn to thee.
Come down and help us, Rustum, or we lose.'
  He spoke : but Rustum answer'd with a smile :—   220
' Go to ! if Iran's chiefs are old, then I
Am older : if the young are weak, the King
Errs strangely : for the King, for Kai Khosroo,
Himself is young, and honours younger men,
And lets the aged moulder to their graves.
Rustum he loves no more, but loves the young—
The young may rise at Sohrab's vaunts, not I.
For what care I, though all speak Sohrab's fame ?
For would that I myself had such a son,
And not that one slight helpless girl I have,   230
A son so fam'd, so brave, to send to war,
And I to tarry with the snow-hair'd Zal,
My father, whom the robber Afghans vex,
And clip his borders short, and drive his herds,
And he has none to guard his weak old age.
There would I go, and hang my armour up,
And with my great name fence that weak old man,
And spend the goodly treasures I have got,
And rest my age, and hear of Sohrab's fame,

And leave to death the hosts of thankless kings,   240
And with these slaughterous hands draw sword no more.'
  He spoke, and smil'd ; and Gudurz made reply :—
' What then, O Rustum, will men say to this,
When Sohrab dares our bravest forth, and seeks
Thee most of all, and thou, whom most he seeks,
Hidest thy face ? Take heed, lest men should say,
*Like some old miser, Rustum hoards his fame,
And shuns to peril it with younger men.*'
  And, greatly mov'd, then Rustum made reply :—
' O Gudurz, wherefore dost thou say such words ?   250
Thou knowest better words than this to say.
What is one more, one less, obscure or fam'd,
Valiant or craven, young or old, to me ?
Are not they mortal, am not I myself ?
But who for men of nought would do great deeds ?
Come, thou shalt see how Rustum hoards his fame.
But I will fight unknown, and in plain arms ;
Let not men say of Rustum, he was match'd
In single fight with any mortal man.'
  He spoke, and frown'd ; and Gudurz turn'd, and ran   260
Back quickly through the camp in fear and joy,
Fear at his wrath, but joy that Rustum came.
But Rustum strode to his tent door, and call'd
His followers in, and bade them bring his arms,
And clad himself in steel : the arms he chose
Were plain, and on his shield was no device,
Only his helm was rich, inlaid with gold,
And from the fluted spine atop a plume
Of horsehair wav'd, a scarlet horsehair plume.
So arm'd he issued forth ; and Ruksh, his horse,   270
Follow'd him, like a faithful hound, at heel,
Ruksh, whose renown was nois'd through all the earth,
The horse, whom Rustum on a foray once
Did in Bokhara by the river find
A colt beneath its dam, and drove him home,
And rear'd him ; a bright bay, with lofty crest ;
Dight with a saddle-cloth of broider'd green
Crusted with gold, and on the ground were work'd
All beasts of chase, all beasts which hunters know :
So follow'd, Rustum left his tents, and cross'd   280
The camp, and to the Persian host appear'd.
And all the Persians knew him, and with shouts
Hail'd ; but the Tartars knew not who he was.
And dear as the wet diver to the eyes
Of his pale wife who waits and weeps on shore,
By sandy Bahrein, in the Persian Gulf,
Plunging all day in the blue waves, at night,
Having made up his tale of precious pearls,
Rejoins her in their hut upon the sands—
So dear to the pale Persians Rustum came.   290

And Rustum to the Persian front advanc'd,
And Sohrab arm'd in Haman's tent, and came.
And as afield the reapers cut a swathe
Down through the middle of a rich man's corn,
And on each side are squares of standing corn,
And in the midst a stubble, short and bare ;
So on each side were squares of men, with spears
Bristling, and in the midst, the open sand.
And Rustum came upon the sand, and cast
His eyes towards the Tartar tents, and saw   300
Sohrab come forth, and ey'd him as he came.
  As some rich woman, on a winter's morn,
Eyes through her silken curtains the poor drudge
Who with numb blacken'd fingers makes her fire—
At cock-crow, on a starlit winter's morn,
When the frost flowers the whiten'd window panes—
And wonders how she lives, and what the thoughts
Of that poor drudge may be ; so Rustum ey'd
The unknown adventurous youth, who from afar
Came seeking Rustum, and defying forth   310
All the most valiant chiefs : long he perus'd
His spirited air, and wonder'd who he was.
For very young he seem'd, tenderly rear'd ;
Like some young cypress, tall, and dark, and straight,
Which in a queen's secluded garden throws
Its slight dark shadow on the moonlit turf,
By midnight, to a bubbling fountain's sound—
So slender Sohrab seem'd, so softly rear'd.
And a deep pity enter'd Rustum's soul
As he beheld him coming ; and he stood,   320
And beckon'd to him with his hand, and said :—
  ' O thou young man, the air of Heaven is soft,
And warm, and pleasant ; but the grave is cold.
Heaven's air is better than the cold dead grave.
Behold me : I am vast, and clad in iron,
And tried ; and I have stood on many a field
Of blood, and I have fought with many a foe :
Never was that field lost, or that foe sav'd.
O Sohrab, wherefore wilt thou rush on death ?
Be govern'd : quit the Tartar host, and come   330
To Iran, and be as my son to me,
And fight beneath my banner till I die.
There are no youths in Iran brave as thou.'
  So he spake, mildly : Sohrab heard his voice,
The mighty voice of Rustum ; and he saw
His giant figure planted on the sand,
Sole, like some single tower, which a chief
Has builded on the waste in former years
Against the robbers ; and he saw that head,
Streak'd with its first grey hairs : hope fill'd his soul ;   340
And he ran forwards and embrac'd his knees,

And clasp'd his hand within his own and said :—
  ' Oh, by thy father's head ! by thine own soul !
Art thou not Rustum ? Speak ! art thou not he ? '
  But Rustum ey'd askance the kneeling youth,
And turn'd away, and spoke to his own soul :—
  ' Ah me, I muse what this young fox may mean.
False, wily, boastful, are these Tartar boys.
For if I now confess this thing he asks,
And hide it not, but say—*Rustum is here*—   350
He will not yield indeed, nor quit our foes,
But he will find some pretext not to fight,
And praise my fame, and proffer courteous gifts,
A belt or sword perhaps, and go his way.
And on a feast-tide, in Afrasiab's hall,
In Samarcand, he will arise and cry—
" I challeng'd once, when the two armies camp'd
Beside the Oxus, all the Persian lords
To cope with me in single fight ; but they
Shrank ; only Rustum dar'd : then he and I   360
Chang'd gifts, and went on equal terms away."
So will he speak, perhaps, while men applaud.
Then were the chiefs of Iran sham'd through me.'
  And then he turn'd, and sternly spake aloud :—
' Rise ! wherefore dost thou vainly question thus
Of Rustum ? I am here, whom thou hast call'd
By challenge forth : make good thy vaunt, or yield.
Is it with Rustum only thou wouldst fight ?
Rash boy, men look on Rustum's face and flee.
For well I know, that did great Rustum stand   370
Before thy face this day, and were reveal'd,
There would be then no talk of fighting more.
But being what I am, I tell thee this ;
Do thou record it in thine inmost soul :
Either thou shalt renounce thy vaunt, and yield ;
Or else thy bones shall strew this sand, till winds
Bleach them, or Oxus with his summer floods,
Oxus in summer wash them all away.'
  He spoke : and Sohrab answer'd, on his feet :—
' Art thou so fierce ? Thou wilt not fright me so. 380
I am no girl, to be made pale by words.
Yet this thou hast said well, did Rustum stand
Here on this field, there were no fighting then.
But Rustum is far hence, and we stand here.
Begin : thou art more vast, more dread than I,
And thou art prov'd, I know, and I am young—
But yet Success sways with the breath of Heaven.
And though thou thinkest that thou knowest sure
Thy victory, yet thou canst not surely know.
For we are all, like swimmers in the sea,   390
Pois'd on the top of a huge wave of Fate,
Which hangs uncertain to which side to fall.

And whether it will heave us up to land,
Or whether it will roll us out to sea,
Back out to sea, to the deep waves of death,
We know not, and no search will make us know:
Only the event will teach us in its hour.'
   He spoke; and Rustum answer'd not, but hurl'd
His spear: down from the shoulder, down it came,
As on some partridge in the corn a hawk   400
That long has tower'd in the airy clouds
Drops like a plummet: Sohrab saw it come,
And sprang aside, quick as a flash: the spear
Hiss'd, and went quivering down into the sand,
Which it sent flying wide:—then Sohrab threw
In turn, and full struck Rustum's shield: sharp rang,
The iron plates rang sharp, but turn'd the spear.
And Rustum seiz'd his club, which none but he
Could wield: an unlopp'd trunk it was, and huge,
Still rough; like those which men in treeless plains   410
To build them boats fish from the flooded rivers,
Hyphasis or Hydaspes, when, high up
By their dark springs, the wind in winter-time
Has made in Himalayan forests wrack,
And strewn the channels with torn boughs; so huge
The club which Rustum lifted now, and struck
One stroke; but again Sohrab sprang aside
Lithe as the glancing snake, and the club came
Thundering to earth, and leapt from Rustum's hand.
And Rustum follow'd his own blow, and fell   420
To his knees, and with his fingers clutch'd the sand:
And now might Sohrab have unsheath'd his sword,
And pierc'd the mighty Rustum while he lay
Dizzy, and on his knees, and chok'd with sand:
But he look'd on, and smil'd, nor bar'd his sword,
But courteously drew back, and spoke, and said:—
   'Thou strik'st too hard: that club of thine will float
Upon the summer floods, and not my bones.
But rise, and be not wroth; not wroth am I:
No, when I see thee, wrath forsakes my soul.   430
Thou say'st, thou art not Rustum: be it so.
Who art thou then, that canst so touch my soul?
Boy as I am, I have seen battles too;
Have waded foremost in their bloody waves,
And heard their hollow roar of dying men;
But never was my heart thus touch'd before.
Are they from Heaven, these softenings of the heart?
O thou old warrior, let us yield to Heaven!
Come, plant we here in earth our angry spears,
And make a truce, and sit upon this sand,   440
And pledge each other in red wine, like friends,
And thou shalt talk to me of Rustum's deeds.
There are enough foes in the Persian host

Whom I may meet, and strike, and feel no pang ;
Champions enough Afrasiab has, whom thou
Mayst fight ; fight them, when they confront thy spear.
But oh, let there be peace 'twixt thee and me ! '
  He ceas'd : but while he spake, Rustum had risen,
And stood erect, trembling with rage : his club
He left to lie, but had regain'd his spear,   450
Whose fiery point now in his mail'd right-hand
Blaz'd bright and baleful, like that autumn Star,
The baleful sign of fevers : dust had soil'd
His stately crest, and dimm'd his glittering arms.
His breast heav'd ; his lips foam'd ; and twice his voice
Was chok'd with rage : at last these words broke way :—
  ' Girl ! nimble with thy feet, not with thy hands !
Curl'd minion, dancer, coiner of sweet words !
Fight ; let me hear thy hateful voice no more !
Thou art not in Afrasiab's gardens now   460
With Tartar girls, with whom thou art wont to dance ;
But on the Oxus sands, and in the dance
Of battle, and with me, who make no play
Of war : I fight it out, and hand to hand.
Speak not to me of truce, and pledge, and wine !
Remember all thy valour : try thy feints
And cunning : all the pity I had is gone :
Because thou hast sham'd me before both the hosts
With thy light skipping tricks, and thy girl's wiles.'
  He spoke ; and Sohrab kindled at his taunts,   470
And he too drew his sword : at once they rush'd
Together, as two eagles on one prey
Come rushing down together from the clouds,
One from the east, one from the west : their shields
Dash'd with a clang together, and a din
Rose, such as that the sinewy woodcutters
Make often in the forest's heart at morn,
Of hewing axes, crashing trees : such blows
Rustum and Sohrab on each other hail'd.
And you would say that sun and stars took part   480
In that unnatural conflict ; for a cloud
Grew suddenly in Heaven, and dark'd the sun
Over the fighters' head ; and a wind rose
Under their feet, and moaning swept the plain,
And in a sandy whirlwind wrapp'd the pair.
In gloom they twain were wrapp'd, and they alone ;
For both the on-looking hosts on either hand
Stood in broad daylight, and the sky was pure,
And the sun sparkled on the Oxus stream.
But in the gloom they fought, with bloodshot eyes   490
And labouring breath ; first Rustum struck the shield
Which Sohrab held stiff out : the steel-spik'd spear
Rent the tough plates, but fail'd to reach the skin,
And Rustum pluck'd it back with angry groan.

Then Sohrab with his sword smote Rustum's helm,
Nor clove its steel quite through ; but all the crest
He shore away, and that proud horsehair plume,
Never till now defil'd, sank to the dust ;
And Rustum bow'd his head ; but then the gloom
Grew blacker : thunder rumbled in the air,   500
And lightnings rent the cloud ; and Ruksh, the horse,
Who stood at hand, utter'd a dreadful cry :
No horse's cry was that, most like the roar
Of some pain'd desert lion, who all day
Has trail'd the hunter's javelin in his side,
And comes at night to die upon the sand :—
The two hosts heard that cry, and quak'd for fear,
And Oxus curdled as it cross'd his stream.
But Sohrab heard, and quail'd not, but rush'd on,
And struck again ; and again Rustum bow'd   510
His head ; but this time all the blade, like glass,
Sprang in a thousand shivers on the helm,
And in his hand the hilt remain'd alone.
Then Rustum rais'd his head : his dreadful eyes
Glar'd, and he shook on high his menacing spear,
And shouted, *Rustum !* Sohrab heard that shout,
And shrank amaz'd : back he recoil'd one step,
And scann'd with blinking eyes the advancing form :
And then he stood bewilder'd ; and he dropp'd
His covering shield, and the spear pierc'd his side.   520
He reel'd, and staggering back, sunk to the ground.
And then the gloom dispers'd, and the wind fell,
And the bright sun broke forth, and melted all
The cloud ; and the two armies saw the pair ;
Saw Rustum standing, safe upon his feet,
And Sohrab, wounded, on the bloody sand.
    Then, with a bitter smile, Rustum began :—
'Sohrab, thou thoughtest in thy mind to kill
A Persian lord this day, and strip his corpse,
And bear thy trophies to Afrasiab's tent.   530
Or else that the great Rustum would come down
Himself to fight, and that thy wiles would move
His heart to take a gift, and let thee go.
And then that all the Tartar host would praise
Thy courage or thy craft, and spread thy fame,
To glad thy father in his weak old age.
Fool ! thou art slain, and by an unknown man !
Dearer to the red jackals shalt thou be,
Than to thy friends, and to thy father old.'
    And with a fearless mien Sohrab replied :—   540
'Unknown thou art ; yet thy fierce vaunt is vain.
Thou dost not slay me, proud and boastful man !
No ! Rustum slays me, and this filial heart.
For were I match'd with ten such men as thou,
And I were he who till to-day I was,

They should be lying here, I standing there.
But that beloved name unnerv'd my arm—
That name, and something, I confess, in thee,
Which troubles all my heart, and made my shield
Fall; and thy spear transfix'd an unarm'd foe.   550
And now thou boastest and insult'st my fate.
But hear thou this, fierce man, tremble to hear!
The mighty Rustum shall avenge my death!
My father, whom I seek through all the world,
He shall avenge my death, and punish thee!'
    As when some hunter in the spring hath found
A breeding eagle sitting on her nest,
Upon the craggy isle of a hill lake,
And pierc'd her with an arrow as she rose,
And follow'd her to find out where she fell   560
Far off;—anon her mate comes winging back
From hunting, and a great way off descries
His huddling young left sole; at that, he checks
His pinion, and with short uneasy sweeps
Circles above his eyry, with loud screams
Chiding his mate back to her nest; but she
Lies dying, with the arrow in her side,
In some far stony gorge out of his ken,
A heap of fluttering feathers: never more
Shall the lake glass her, flying over it;   570
Never the black and dripping precipices
Echo her stormy scream as she sails by :—
As that poor bird flies home, nor knows his loss—
So Rustum knew not his own loss, but stood
Over his dying son, and knew him not.
    But with a cold, incredulous voice, he said :—
'What prate is this of fathers and revenge?
The mighty Rustum never had a son.'
    And, with a failing voice, Sohrab replied :—
'Ah yes, he had! and that lost son am I.   580
Surely the news will one day reach his ear,
Reach Rustum, where he sits, and tarries long,
Somewhere, I know not where, but far from here;
And pierce him like a stab, and make him leap
To arms, and cry for vengeance upon thee.
Fierce man, bethink thee, for an only son!
What will that grief, what will that vengeance be!
Oh, could I live, till I that grief had seen!
Yet him I pity not so much, but her,
My mother, who in Ader-baijan dwells   590
With that old king, her father, who grows grey
With age, and rules over the valiant Koords.
Her most I pity, who no more will see
Sohrab returning from the Tartar camp,
With spoils and honour, when the war is done.
But a dark rumour will be bruited up,

From tribe to tribe, until it reach her ear ;
And then will that defenceless woman learn
That Sohrab will rejoice her sight no more ;
But that in battle with a nameless foe,   600
By the far-distant Oxus, he is slain.'
   He spoke ; and as he ceas'd he wept aloud,
Thinking of her he left, and his own death.
He spoke ; but Rustum listen'd, plung'd in thought.
Nor did he yet believe it was his son
Who spoke, although he call'd back names he knew ;
For he had had sure tidings that the babe,
Which was in Ader-baijan born to him,
Had been a puny girl, no boy at all :
So that sad mother sent him word, for fear   610
Rustum should take the boy, to train in arms ;
And so he deem'd that either Sohrab took,
By a false boast, the style of Rustum's son ;
Or that men gave it him, to swell his fame.
So deem'd he ; yet he listen'd, plung'd in thought ;
And his soul set to grief, as the vast tide
Of the bright rocking Ocean sets to shore
At the full moon : tears gathered in his eyes ;
For he remembered his own early youth,
And all its bounding rapture ; as, at dawn,   620
The shepherd from his mountain lodge descries
A far bright city, smitten by the sun,
Through many rolling clouds ;—so Rustum saw
His youth ; saw Sohrab's mother, in her bloom ;
And that old king, her father, who lov'd well
His wandering guest, and gave him his fair child
With joy ; and all the pleasant life they led,
They three, in that long-distant summer-time—
The castle, and the dewy woods, and hunt
And hound, and morn on those delightful hills   630
In Ader-baijan. And he saw that Youth,
Of age and looks to be his own dear son,
Piteous and lovely, lying on the sand,
Like some rich hyacinth, which by the scythe
Of an unskilful gardener has been cut,
Mowing the garden grass-plots near its bed,
And lies, a fragrant tower of purple bloom,
On the mown, dying grass ;—so Sohrab lay,
Lovely in death, upon the common sand.
And Rustum gaz'd on him with grief, and said :—   640
  ' O Sohrab, thou indeed art such a son
Whom Rustum, wert thou his, might well have lov'd !
Yet here thou errest, Sohrab, or else men
Have told thee false ;—thou art not Rustum's son.
For Rustum had no son : one child he had—
But one—a girl : who with her mother now
Plies some light female task, nor dreams of us—

Of us she dreams not, nor of wounds, nor war.'
  But Sohrab answer'd him in wrath ; for now
The anguish of the deep-fix'd spear grew fierce,   650
And he desired to draw forth the steel,
And let the blood flow free, and so to die ;
But first he would convince his stubborn foe—
And, rising sternly on one arm, he said :—
  ' Man, who art thou who dost deny my words ?
Truth sits upon the lips of dying men,
And falsehood, while I liv'd, was far from mine.
I tell thee, prick'd upon this arm I bear
That seal which Rustum to my mother gave,
That she might prick it on the babe she bore.'   660
  He spoke : and all the blood left Rustum's cheeks ;
And his knees totter'd, and he smote his hand
Against his breast, his heavy mailed hand,
That the hard iron corslet clank'd aloud :
And to his heart he press'd the other hand,
And in a hollow voice he spake, and said :—
  ' Sohrab, that were a proof which could not lie.
If thou shew this, then art thou Rustum's son.'
  Then, with weak hasty fingers, Sohrab loos'd
His belt, and near the shoulder bar'd his arm,   670
And show'd a sign in faint vermilion points
Prick'd : as a cunning workman, in Pekin,
Pricks with vermilion some clear porcelain vase,
An emperor's gift—at early morn he paints,
And all day long, and, when night comes, the lamp
Lights up his studious forehead and thin hands :—
So delicately prick'd the sign appear'd
On Sohrab's arm, the sign of Rustum's seal.
It was that griffin, which of old rear'd Zal,
Rustum's great father, whom they left to die,   680
A helpless babe, among the mountain rocks.
Him that kind creature found, and rear'd, and lov'd—
Then Rustum took it for his glorious sign.
And Sohrab bar'd that figure on his arm,
And himself scann'd it long with mournful eyes,
And then he touched it with his hand and said :—
  ' How say'st thou ? Is that sign the proper sign
Of Rustum's son, or of some other man's ? '
  He spoke : but Rustum gaz'd, and gaz'd, and stood
Speechless ; and then he utter'd one sharp cry—   690
O boy—thy father !—and his voice choked there.
And then a dark cloud pass'd before his eyes,
And his head swam, and he sunk down to earth.
But Sohrab crawl'd to where he lay, and cast
His arms about his neck, and kiss'd his lips,
And with fond faltering fingers strok'd his cheeks,
Trying to call him back to life : and life
Came back to Rustum, and he op'd his eyes

And they stood wide with horror ; and he seiz'd
In both his hands the dust which lay around,   700
And threw it on his head, and smirch'd his hair,
His hair, and face, and beard, and glittering arms :
And strong convulsive groanings shook his breast,
And his sobs chok'd him ; and he clutch'd his sword,
To draw it, and for ever let life out.
But Sohrab saw his thought, and held his hands,
And with a soothing voice he spoke and said :—
  ' Father, forbear : for I but meet to-day
The doom that at my birth was written down
In Heaven, and thou art Heaven's unconscious hand.   710
Surely my heart cried out that it was thou,
When first I saw thee ; and thy heart spoke too,
I know it : but Fate trod those promptings down
Under its iron heel ; Fate, Fate engag'd
The strife and hurl'd me on my father's spear.
But let us speak no more of this : I find
My father ; let me feel that I have found.
Come, sit beside me on this sand, and take
My head betwixt thy hands, and kiss my cheeks,
And wash them with thy tears, and say, " My son ! " 720
Quick ! quick ! for number'd are my sands of life,
And swift ; for like the lightning to this field
I came, and like the wind I go away—
Sudden, and swift, and like a passing wind.
But it was writ in Heaven that this should be.'
  So said he : and his voice releas'd the heart
Of Rustum, and his tears broke forth ; he cast
His arms round his son's neck, and wept aloud,
And kiss'd him. And awe fell on both the hosts
When they saw Rustum's grief : and Ruksh, the horse, 730
With his head bowing to the ground, and mane
Sweeping the dust, came near, and in mute woe
First to the one then to the other mov'd
His head, as if enquiring what their grief
Might mean ; and from his dark, compassionate eyes,
The big warm tears roll'd down, and cak'd the sand.
But Rustum chid him with stern voice, and said :—
  ' Ruksh, now thou grievest ; but, O Ruksh, thy feet
Should then have rotted on their nimble joints,
When first they bore thy master to this field.'   740
  But Sohrab look'd upon the horse and said :—
' Is this then Ruksh ? How often, in past days,
My mother told me of thee, thou brave steed !
My terrible father's terrible horse ; and said,
That I should one day find thy lord and thee.
Come, let me lay my hand upon thy mane.
O Ruksh, thou art more fortunate than I ;
For thou hast gone where I shall never go,
And snuff'd the breezes of my father's home.

And thou hast trod the sands of Seistan,   750
And seen the river of Helmund, and the lake
Of Zirrah ; and the aged Zal himself
Has often strok'd thy neck, and given thee food,
Corn in a golden platter soak'd with wine,
And said—" O Ruksh ! bear Rustum well ! "—but I
Have never known my grandsire's furrow'd face,
Nor seen his lofty house in Seistan,
Nor slak'd my thirst at the clear Helmund stream :
But lodg'd among my father's foes, and seen
Afrasiab's cities only, Samarcand,   760
Bokhara, and lone Khiva in the waste,
And the black Toorkmun tents ; and only drunk
The desert rivers, Moorghab and Tejend,
Kohik, and where the Kalmuks feed their sheep,
The northern Sir ; and this great Oxus stream—
The yellow Oxus, by whose brink I die.'
    And, with a heavy groan, Rustum replied :—
' Oh that its waves were flowing over me !
Oh that I saw its grains of yellow silt
Roll tumbling in the current o'er my head ! '   770
    And, with a grave mild voice, Sohrab replied :—
' Desire not that, my father ; thou must live.
For some are born to do great deeds, and live,
As some are born to be obscur'd, and die.
Do thou the deeds I die too young to do,
And reap a second glory in thine age.
Thou art my father, and thy gain is mine.
But come : thou seest this great host of men
Which follow me ; I pray thee, slay not these :
Let me entreat for them : what have they done ?   780
They follow'd me, my hope, my fame, my star.
Let them all cross the Oxus back in peace.
But me thou must bear hence, not send with them,
But carry me with thee to Seistan,
And place me on a bed, and mourn for me,
Thou, and the snow-hair'd Zal, and all thy friends.
And thou must lay me in that lovely earth,
And heap a stately mound above my bones,
And plant a far-seen pillar over all :
That so the passing horseman on the waste   790
May see my tomb a great way off, and say—
*Sohrab, the mighty Rustum's son, lies there,
Whom his great father did in ignorance kill—*
And I be not forgotten in my grave.'
    And, with a mournful voice, Rustum replied :—
' Fear not ; as thou hast said, Sohrab, my son,
So shall it be : for I will burn my tents,
And quit the host, and bear thee hence with me,
And carry thee away to Seistan,
And place thee on a bed, and mourn for thee,   800

With the snow-headed Zal, and all my friends.
And I will lay thee in that lovely earth,
And heap a stately mound above thy bones,
And plant a far-seen pillar over all:
And men shall not forget thee in thy grave.
And I will spare thy host: yea, let them go:
Let them all cross the Oxus back in peace.
What should I do with slaying any more?
For would that all whom I have ever slain
Might be once more alive; my bitterest foes,   810
And they who were call'd champions in their time,
And through whose death I won that fame I have;
And I were nothing but a common man,
A poor, mean soldier, and without renown;
So thou mightest live too, my son, my son!
Or rather would that I, even I myself,
Might now be lying on this bloody sand,
Near death, and by an ignorant stroke of thine,
Not thou of mine; and I might die, not thou;
And I, not thou, be borne to Seistan;   820
And Zal might weep above my grave, not thine;
And say—*O son, I weep thee not too sore,*
For willingly, I know, thou met'st thine end.—
But now in blood and battles was my youth,
And full of blood and battles is my age;
And I shall never end this life of blood.'
    Then, at the point of death, Sohrab replied:—
' A life of blood indeed, thou dreadful man!
But thou shalt yet have peace; only not now;
Not yet: but thou shalt have it on that day,   830
When thou shalt sail in a high-masted ship,
Thou and the other peers of Kai-Khosroo,
Returning home over the salt blue sea,
From laying thy dear master in his grave.'
    And Rustum gaz'd on Sohrab's face, and said:—
' Soon be that day, my son, and deep that sea!
Till then, if fate so wills, let me endure.'
    He spoke; and Sohrab smil'd on him, and took
The spear, and drew it from his side, and eas'd
His wound's imperious anguish: but the blood   840
Came welling from the open gash, and life
Flow'd with the stream: all down his cold white side
The crimson torrent ran, dim now, and soil'd,
Like the soil'd tissue of white violets
Left, freshly gather'd, on their native bank,
By romping children, whom their nurses call
From the hot fields at noon: his head droop'd low,
His limbs grew slack; motionless, white, he lay—
White, with eyes clos'd; only when heavy gasps,
Deep, heavy gasps, quivering through all his frame,   850
Convuls'd him back to life, he open'd them,

And fix'd them feebly on his father's face:
Till now all strength was ebb'd, and from his limbs
Unwillingly the spirit fled away,
Regretting the warm mansion which it left,
And youth and bloom, and this delightful world.
  So, on the bloody sand, Sohrab lay dead.
And the great Rustum drew his horseman's cloak
Down o'er his face, and sate by his dead son.
As those black granite pillars, once high-rear'd   860
By Jemshid in Persepolis, to bear
His house, now, mid their broken flights of steps,
Lie prone, enormous, down the mountain side—
So in the sand lay Rustum by his son.
  And night came down over the solemn waste,
And the two gazing hosts, and that sole pair,
And darken'd all; and a cold fog, with night,
Crept from the Oxus. Soon a hum arose,
As of a great assembly loos'd, and fires
Began to twinkle through the fog: for now   870
Both armies mov'd to camp, and took their meal:
The Persians took it on the open sands
Southward; the Tartars by the river marge:
And Rustum and his son were left alone.
  But the majestic river floated on,
Out of the mist and hum of that low land,
Into the frosty starlight, and there mov'd,
Rejoicing, through the hush'd Chorasmian waste,
Under the solitary moon: he flow'd
Right for the polar star, past Orgunjè,   880
Brimming, and bright, and large: then sands begin
To hem his watery march, and dam his streams,
And split his currents; that for many a league
The shorn and parcell'd Oxus strains along
Through beds of sand and matted rushy isles—
Oxus, forgetting the bright speed he had
In his high mountain cradle in Pamere,
A foil'd circuitous wanderer:—till at last
The long'd-for dash of waves is heard, and wide
His luminous home of waters opens, bright   890
And tranquil, from whose floor the new-bath'd stars
Emerge, and shine upon the Aral Sea.

EDWARD FITZ GERALD

RUBAIYÁT OF OMAR KHAYYÁM OF NAISHÁPÚR

1

Awake! for Morning in the Bowl of Night
Has flung the Stone that puts the Stars to Flight:
  And Lo! the Hunter of the East has caught
The Sultán's Turret in a Noose of Light.

2

Dreaming when Dawn's Left Hand was in the Sky
I heard a Voice within the Tavern cry,
  'Awake, my Little ones, and fill the Cup
Before Life's Liquor in its Cup be dry.'

3

And, as the Cock crew, those who stood before
The Tavern shouted—'Open then the Door!
  'You know how little while we have to stay,
'And, once departed, may return no more.'

4

Now the New Year reviving old Desires,
The thoughtful Soul to Solitude retires,
  Where the WHITE HAND OF MOSES on the Bough
Puts out, and Jesus from the Ground suspires.

5

Irám indeed is gone with all its Rose,
And Jamshýd's Sev'n-ring'd Cup where no one knows;
  But still the Vine her ancient Ruby yields,
And still a Garden by the Water blows.

6

And David's Lips are lock't; but in divine
High-piping Pehleví, with 'Wine! Wine! Wine!
  '*Red* Wine!'—the Nightingale cries to the Rose
That yellow Cheek of her's to incarnadine.

7

Come, fill the Cup, and in the Fire of Spring
The Winter Garment of Repentance fling:
  The Bird of Time has but a little way
To fly—and Lo! the Bird is on the Wing.

8

And look—a thousand Blossoms with the Day
Woke—and a thousand scatter'd into Clay :   30
  And this first Summer Month that brings the Rose
Shall take Jamshýd and Kaikobád away.

9

But come with old Khayyám, and leave the Lot
Of Kaikobád and Kaikhosrú forgot :
  Let Rustum lay about him as he will,
Or Hátim Tai cry Supper—heed them not.

10

With me along some Strip of Herbage strown
That just divides the desert from the sown,
  Where name of Slave and Sultán scarce is known,
And pity Sultán Máhmúd on his Throne.   40

11

Here with a Loaf of Bread beneath the Bough,
A Flask of Wine, a Book of Verse—and Thou
  Beside me singing in the Wilderness—
And Wilderness is Paradise enow.

12

' How sweet is mortal Sovranty '—think some :
Others—' How blest the Paradise to come ! '
  Ah, take the Cash in hand and waive the Rest ;
Oh, the brave Music of a *distant* Drum !

13

Look to the Rose that blows about us—' Lo,
' Laughing,' she says, ' into the World I blow :   50
  ' At once the silken Tassel of my Purse
' Tear, and its Treasure on the Garden throw.'

14

The Worldly Hope men set their Hearts upon
Turns Ashes—or it prospers ; and anon,
  Like Snow upon the Desert's dusty Face
Lighting a little Hour or two—is gone.

15

And those who husbanded the Golden Grain,
And those who flung it to the Winds like Rain,
  Alike to no such aureate Earth are turn'd
As, buried once, Men want dug up again.   60

16

Think, in this batter'd Caravanserai
Whose Doorways are alternate Night and Day,
  How Sultán after Sultán with his Pomp
Abode his Hour or two, and went his way.

17

They say the Lion and the Lizard keep
The Courts where Jamshýd gloried and drank deep;
  And Bahrám, that great Hunter—the Wild Ass
Stamps o'er his Head, and he lies fast asleep.

18

I sometimes think that never blows so red
The Rose as where some buried Caesar bled;   70
  That every Hyacinth the Garden wears
Dropt in its Lap from some once lovely Head.

19

And this delightful Herb whose tender Green
Fledges the River's Lip on which we lean—
  Ah, lean upon it lightly! for who knows
From what once lovely Lip it springs unseen!

20

Ah, my Belovéd, fill the Cup that clears
To-DAY of past Regrets and future Fears—
  To-morrow ?—Why, To-morrow I may be
Myself with Yesterday's Sev'n Thousand Years.   80

21

Lo! some we loved, the loveliest and best
That Time and Fate of all their Vintage prest,
  Have drunk their Cup a Round or two before,
And one by one crept silently to Rest.

22

And we, that now make merry in the Room
They left, and Summer dresses in new Bloom,
  Ourselves must we beneath the Couch of Earth
Descend, ourselves to make a Couch—for whom ?

23

Ah, make the most of what we yet may spend,
Before we too into the Dust descend;   90
  Dust into Dust, and under Dust, to lie,
Sans Wine, sans Song, sans Singer, and—sans End!

24

Alike for those who for To-DAY prepare,
And those that after a To-MORROW stare,
  A Muezzín from the Tower of Darkness cries
'Fools! your Reward is neither Here nor There!'

25

Why, all the Saints and Sages who discuss'd
Of the Two Worlds so learnedly, are thrust
  Like foolish Prophets forth; their Words to Scorn
Are scatter'd, and their Mouths are stopt with Dust.   100

26

Oh, come with old Khayyám, and leave the Wise
To talk ; one thing is certain, that Life flies ;
　One thing is certain, and the Rest is Lies ;
The Flower that once has blown for ever dies.

27

Myself when young did eagerly frequent
Doctor and Saint, and heard great Argument
　About it and about : but evermore
Came out by the same Door as in I went.

28

With them the Seed of Wisdom did I sow,
And with my own hand labour'd it to grow :　　　　110
　And this was all the Harvest that I reap'd—
' I came like Water, and like Wind I go.'

29

Into this Universe, and *why* not knowing,
Nor *whence*, like Water willy-nilly flowing :
　And out of it, as Wind along the Waste,
I know not *whither*, willy-nilly blowing.

30

What, without asking, hither hurried *whence ?*
And, without asking, *whither* hurried hence !
　Another and another Cup to drown
The Memory of this Impertinence !　　　　120

31

Up from Earth's Centre through the Seventh Gate
I rose, and on the Throne of Saturn sate,
　And many Knots unravel'd by the Road ;
But not the Knot of Human Death and Fate.

32

There was a Door to which I found no Key :
There was a Veil past which I could not see :
　Some little Talk awhile of ME and THEE
There seem'd—and then no more of THEE and ME.

33

Then to the rolling Heav'n itself I cried,
Asking, ' What Lamp had Destiny to guide　　　　130
　' Her little Children stumbling in the Dark ? '
And—' A blind Understanding ! ' Heav'n replied.

34

Then to this earthen Bowl did I adjourn
My Lip the secret Well of Life to learn :
　And Lip to Lip it murmur'd—' While you live
' Drink !—for once dead you never shall return.'

35

I think the Vessel, that with fugitive
Articulation answer'd, once did live,
    And merry-make ; and the cold Lip I kiss'd
How many Kisses might it take—and give !   140

36

For in the Market-place, one Dusk of Day,
I watch'd the Potter thumping his wet Clay :
    And with its all obliterated Tongue
It murmur'd—' Gently, Brother, gently, pray ! '

37

Ah, fill the Cup :—what boots it to repeat
How Time is slipping underneath our Feet :
    Unborn TO-MORROW and dead YESTERDAY,
Why fret about them if TO-DAY be sweet !

38

One Moment in Annihilation's Waste,
One Moment, of the Well of Life to taste—   150
    The Stars are setting and the Caravan
Starts for the Dawn of Nothing—Oh, make haste !

39

How long, how long, in definite Pursuit
Of This and That endeavour and dispute ?
    Better be merry with the fruitful Grape
Than sadder after none, or bitter, Fruit.

40

You know, my Friends, how long since in my House
For a new Marriage I did make Carouse :
    Divorced old barren Reason from my Bed,
And took the Daughter of the Vine to Spouse.   160

41

For ' Is ' and ' IS-NOT ' though *with* Rule and Line,
And ' UP-AND-DOWN ' *without*, I could define,
    I yet in all I only cared to know,
Was never deep in anything but—Wine.

42

And lately, by the Tavern Door agape,
Came stealing through the Dusk an Angel Shape
    Bearing a Vessel on his Shoulder ; and
He bid me taste of it ; and 'twas—the Grape !

43

The Grape that can with Logic absolute
The Two-and-Seventy jarring Sects confute :   170
    The subtle Alchemist that in a Trice
Life's leaden Metal into Gold transmute.

44

The mighty Mahmúd, the victorious Lord,
That all the misbelieving and black Horde
  Of Fears and Sorrows that infest the Soul
Scatters and slays with his enchanted Sword.

45

But leave the Wise to wrangle, and with me
The Quarrel of the Universe let be:
  And, in some corner of the Hubbub coucht,
Make Game of that which makes as much of Thee.   180

46

For in and out, above, about, below,
'Tis nothing but a Magic Shadow-show,
  Play'd in a Box whose Candle is the Sun,
Round which we Phantom Figures come and go.

47

And if the Wine you drink, the Lip you press,
End in the Nothing all Things end in—Yes—
  Then fancy while Thou art, Thou art but what
Thou shalt be—Nothing—Thou shalt not be less.

48

While the Rose blows along the River Brink,
With old Khayyám the Ruby Vintage drink: 190
  And when the Angel with his darker Draught
Draws up to Thee—take that, and do not shrink.

49

'Tis all a Chequer-board of Nights and Days
Where Destiny with Men for Pieces plays:
  Hither and thither moves, and mates, and slays,
And one by one back in the Closet lays.

50

The Ball no Question makes of Ayes and Noes,
But Right or Left as strikes the Player goes;
  And He that toss'd Thee down into the Field,
He knows about it all—HE knows—HE knows!   200

51

The Moving Finger writes; and, having writ,
Moves on: nor all thy Piety nor Wit
  Shall lure it back to cancel half a Line,
Nor all thy Tears wash out a Word of it.

52

And that inverted Bowl we call The Sky,
Whereunder crawling coop't we live and die,
  Lift not thy hands to *It* for help—for It
Rolls impotently on as Thou or I.

53

With Earth's first Clay They did the last Man's knead,
And then of the Last Harvest sow'd the Seed :   210
    Yea, the first Morning of Creation wrote
What the Last Dawn of Reckoning shall read.

54

I tell Thee this—When, starting from the Goal,
Over the shoulders of the flaming Foal
    Of Heav'n Parwín and Mushtarí they flung,
In my predestin'd Plot of Dust and Soul

55

The Vine had struck a Fibre ; which about
If clings my Being—let the Súfi flout ;
    Of my Base Metal may be filed a Key,
That shall unlock the Door he howls without.   220

56

And this I know : whether the one True Light,
Kindle to Love, or Wrath consume me quite,
    One glimpse of It within the Tavern caught
Better than in the Temple lost outright.

57

Oh, Thou, who did'st with Pitfall and with Gin
Beset the Road I was to wander in,
    Thou wilt not with Predestination round
Enmesh me, and impute my Fall to Sin ?

58

Oh, Thou, who Man of baser Earth didst make,
And who with Eden didst devise the Snake ;   230
    For all the Sin wherewith the Face of Man
Is blacken'd, Man's Forgiveness give—and take !

. . . .

KÚZA—NÁMA

59

Listen again. One Evening at the Close
Of Ramazán, ere the better Moon arose,
    In that old Potter's Shop I stood alone
With the clay Population round in Rows.

60

And, strange to tell, among the Earthen Lot
Some could articulate, while others not :
    And suddenly one more impatient cried—
' Who *is* the Potter, pray, and who the Pot ? '   240

61

Then said another—' Surely not in vain
' My substance from the common Earth was ta'en,
  ' That He who subtly wrought me into Shape
' Should stamp me back to common Earth again.'

62

Another said—' Why, ne'er a peevish Boy,
' Would break the Bowl from which he drank in Joy ;
  ' Shall He that *made* the Vessel in pure Love
' And Fancy, in an after Rage destroy ! '

63

None answer'd this ; but after Silence spake
A Vessel of a more ungainly Make :   250
  ' They sneer at me for leaning all awry ;
' What ! did the Hand then of the Potter shake ? '

64

Said one—' Folks of a surly Tapster tell,
' And daub his Visage with the Smoke of Hell ;
  ' They talk of some strict Testing of us—Pish !
' He 's a Good Fellow, and 'twill all be well.'

65

Then said another with a long-drawn Sigh,
' My Clay with long oblivion is gone dry :
  ' But, fill me with the old familiar Juice,
' Methinks I might recover by and by ! '   260

66

So while the Vessels one by one were speaking,
One spied the little Crescent all were seeking :
  And then they jogg'd each other, ' Brother, Brother !
' Hark to the Porter's Shoulder-knot a-creaking ! '

    .   .   .   .

67

Ah, with the Grape my fading Life provide,
And wash my Body whence the Life has died,
  And in a Winding-sheet of Vine-leaf wrapt,
So bury me by some sweet Garden-side.

68

That ev'n my buried Ashes such a Snare
Of Perfume shall fling up into the Air,   270
  As not a True Believer passing by
But shall be overtaken unaware.

69

Indeed the Idols I have loved so long
Have done my Credit in Men's Eye much wrong :
  Have drown'd my Honour in a shallow Cup,
And sold my Reputation for a Song.

70

Indeed, indeed, Repentance oft before
I swore—but was I sober when I swore?
   And then and then came Spring, and Rose-in-hand
My thread-bare Penitence apieces tore.   289

71

And much as Wine has play'd the Infidel,
And robb'd me of my Robe of Honour—well,
   I often wonder what the Vintners buy
One half so precious as the Goods they sell.

72

Alas, that Spring should vanish with the Rose!
That Youth's sweet-scented Manuscript should close!
   The Nightingale that in the Branches sang,
Ah, whence, and whither flown again, who knows!

73

Ah Love! could thou and I with Fate conspire
To grasp this sorry Scheme of Things entire,   290
   Would not we shatter it to bits—and then
Re-mould it nearer to the Heart's Desire!

74

Ah, Moon of my Delight who know'st no wane,
The Moon of Heav'n is rising once again:
   How oft hereafter rising shall she look
Through this same Garden after me—in vain!

75

And when Thyself with shining Foot shall pass
Among the Guests Star-scatter'd on the Grass,
   And in thy joyous Errand reach the Spot
Where I made one—turn down an empty Glass!   300

TAMÁM SHUD.

NOTES

GEOFFREY CHAUCER (1340–1400)

THE CANTERBURY TALES

The Prologue to the *Canterbury Tales* is the first English poem which is at once a work of conscious and consummate art and completely national in subject and spirit. From Anglo-Saxon poetry we are separated by a chasm both of language and of character. The English language and the English people both emerged other than merely Saxon from that jostling and blending of races, tongues, and cultures which followed the Norman Conquest. The new national consciousness had begun before Chaucer to seek expression in literature, chiefly in political and satirical songs and poems. But these are rude and inartistic, and even the *Vision of Piers Plowman*, our first English picture of English society, is more interesting as a social, religious, and personal document than as a poem and a work of art. Its form, the long alliterative line, was incapable of any great artistic development. Art in English poetry begins with Chaucer; and before he wrote the *Prologue*, Chaucer's art had attained full maturity in style, verse, and picturesque, dramatic narrative. But for his themes Chaucer had hitherto gone exclusively, under French and Italian guidance, to that storehouse of mediaeval romance, allegory, and legend which was the common possession of Western Europe, and contains nothing distinctively national in character. Daunger and Bielaecoil, the Queen of Love and Daun Cupido, Ector and Troilus, Theseus and Palamon, belong to no country but the fantastic land of mediaeval romance in which so many incongruous elements are united. Nevertheless, through all Chaucer's romantic poems, except when in obedience to a mood or a behest he writes of Christian saints and Love's martyrs, one can trace the trend of his genius towards dramatic realism and satiric humour, whether in allegories like the *Parlement of Foules* and the *Hous of Fame*, or a love-romance like *Troylus and Criseyde*, the simple dramatic truthfulness of which shocked those who cultivated the ideal sentiment and ritual of the first part of the *Romance of the Rose*. It was a long time, however, before this dramatic bent in Chaucer found its natural outlet in the portrayal of real life. It may be, as Ten Brink thought, that his first essays in this direction were the prologue to the Wife of Bath's tale and such a story as *January and May*. It would be as natural that he should pass from romance to satirical *fabliau* as that later prose romancers should turn from chivalrous sentiment to picaresque story of thief and cheat. Realism always begins with low life and shady character. But be this as it may, the crown and flower of Chaucer's dramatic and humorous realism is the *Prologue* just because the picture is not confined to these, and the tone is not satirical only. In the same way, *Don Quixote* is greater than any picaresque romance because its canvas is so ample, its humanity so genial. In the *Prologue* to the *Canterbury Tales* the fantastic world of romance and allegory melts away, Troy and Thebes, palaces made of glass, and temples 'of brass y-founded stronge', allegorical gardens and marvellous fountains, and in their place we see the whole stream of English society in the fourteenth century, gentle and simple, clerical and lay, flowing along the white highway between green fields and hawthorn hedges, past Rochester and Boughton-under-Blee, bound on pious and merry pilgrimage to the shrine of St. Thomas, and beguiling the way with stories in all the forms and on all the themes that delighted the Middle Ages. 'Here is God's plenty.' We see their features, their horses, their quaint and variously coloured attire, and underneath that attire the English character as we know it to-day, 'for mankind is ever the same and nothing lost out of nature though everything is altered.' And nowhere is Chaucer's satire more all-pervasive, more elfin and elusive. We seem to detect it even in the solid, worthy, pious knight contrasted with his counterparts in chivalrous fiction, as well as in the squire who by night slept 'no more than doth a nightingale', and yet 'singing he was or floyting al the daye'. It is at its height in the picture of the men of religion accomplished in everything but what their calling demands. In the pictures of the middle and lower classes there is more than meets the eye at a first glance. The only quite seriously drawn figures are the parson and the ploughman; and they supply the necessary relief, give to the tones in the other, especially the clerical pictures, their full values.

Chaucer may have taken the suggestion for the framework of his tales from Boccaccio, but there is no significant resemblance between his pilgrims on the road and the elegant young gentlemen and ladies who amuse each other in the sumptuous gardens of the *Decameron*. It is more interesting to think that Chaucer caught the idea for the national setting he adopted from the 'faire felde ful of folk' of the first Vision of William, and to compare his merry pilgrims with the company that set out to seek the 'corseint that men call treuthe' under the guidance of Piers the Plowman. The social picture and satire of the two poets repay careful comparison. Of one class, the minstrels, on whom 'Langland' is very severe, Chaucer has nothing to say, though he parodies their art. Socially and artistically he was their superior, but he could not condemn their calling on moral and religious grounds without condemning himself. In the gloom of religious remorse he was capable even of that.

The Knightes Tale is a condensed and free rendering of Boccaccio's *Teseide* (1340), some stanzas of which Chaucer had already borrowed for his *Troylus and Criseyde, Anelida and Arcyte* and *Parlement of Foules.* The source of Boccaccio's story is unknown; possibly some lost Greek romance. The wars of Thebes are related in Statius' *Thebais*; whence the opening quotation and some of Chaucer's descriptive touches.

The fantastic world of mediaeval romance to which reference has been made in the previous note, as well as the realism and elusive humour of Chaucer's mature art can be studied to advantage in this delightful story. Boccaccio had written, as he believed, a classical epic stiff with detailed descriptions and pedantic mythology. Chaucer's skill as a story-teller relieved the romance of a good deal of this epic cumber; and indeed nothing can differ more profoundly in dress and spirit from classical epic than this quintessence of mediaeval romance. The trappings of the story are entirely romantic, or, if classical in origin—like the chariot in which Ligurge is carried, or the temples of Mars and Venus and Diana—are mediaevalized in the most fantastic manner. Mail-clad knights, cote armure' by which their rank is known to 'heraudes', lists and tourneys and chapels, 'haukes sitting on the perche above and houndes ligging on the floor below,' these things blend into a picture strangely different from that presented in the clear, sun-lit pages of Homer. But more striking still is the difference in spirit due to the mediaeval cult of chivalry and love. Pity and love and generosity in war govern the action in the story from beginning to end in a manner which Homer could not have understood. The motive which sent Theseus to the war with Thebes would have been as strange to him as the seven years' service of the lovers or the mutual assistance they render one another in arming. It was for Helen the Trojan War was fought, but how little we hear in Homer of the passion she inspired. 'Small blame is it that for such a woman Trojans and well-greav'd Achaeans should long time suffer hardships. Yet . . . let her go upon their ships and not stay to vex us and our children after.' Over Hector, who even in Homer is the first knight of romance, Helen laments that he and Priam alone have never spoken to her 'despiteful words'. Contrast the tone of such passages with that of Chaucer's poem, where every one is the unwearied servant of love ; and

> Beautee ne sleighte, strengthe, ne hardinesse,
> Ne may with Venus holde champartye ;
> For as hir list the world than may she gye.

Strange too is the fate that has befallen the classical deities, and very strange the religion of mediaeval romance. Homer's gods are not always divine ; and scholars tell us that they have already suffered some debasement ; but when they ride on the ridges of the battle, like stormy petrels on the angry waves, mingling in the combat, and inspiring panic or confidence, we feel still their beauty and their power. In mediaeval romance they have become entirely decorative. Two powers alone rule the life of man—Love, and behind Love, controlling even her, purveyance of God, or Fortune, the power which, whatever we may call it, raises men to power and casts them down again, brings lovers to 'pleyn felicitee' and exiles them, for no reason that we can descry or forecast :—

> We seken faste after felicitee
> But we gon wrong ful often trewely.

With the mediaeval ritual of love Chaucer has dealt in a more orthodox manner in this charming romance than in *Troylus and Criseyde*, that dramatic and realistic, powerful, but not altogether pleasant, tale of passionate and frail humanity. Yet even here it is difficult not to detect a subtle undercurrent of irony, not mordant but simply amused, in his story of the seven years' service of Palamon and Arcite. The sympathetic and serious current of the story is occasionally disturbed by a little bubble of laughter :—

> But this is yet the beste game of alle,
> That she, for whom they han this iolitee,
> Can hem ther-for as muche thank as me ;
> She woot namore of al this hote fare,
> By God, than woot a cokkow or an hare !

In unobserved ways Chaucer makes Boccaccio's characters more real and their romantic conduct thereby a trifle absurd. This was always Chaucer's tone, more or less evident, when he wrote of the ritual or service of love in tale or allegory. What love really is he showed in

Troylus and Criseyde, and shocked Queen Anne and the ladies of the Court. The spirit of mediaeval chivalry was moribund. Chaucer's irony reappears intensified in Berni and Ariosto. When a genuine note of chivalry to women revives in Sidney and Spenser and the early poems and prose of Milton, it is under the quickening influence of Platonism and of the finer spirit of the Reformation.

The Cock and the Fox. The beast fable or *Ysopet*, as it was called from its ultimate literary source, the fables of Æsop, was a great favourite in the Middle Ages. Of this particular story of the Cock and the Fox the oldest version extant is a short fable written by Marie de France, a French poetess of the twelfth century living in England, who herself declares she got her fables from King Alfred, that is, from a collection of early English fables attributed to Alfred. Marie's fable (which has been translated into verse by Professor Skeat in his *Chaucer*, vol. iii, p. 432) was expanded by one of the authors of the famous romance of Reynard the Fox which has come down to us in French, Latin, High and Low German (see Carlyle's essay on *German Literature of the Fourteenth and Fifteenth Centuries*). Here the incident of the dream was introduced, but when Pintain hears of it from her husband ' Li cos ' she does not scold and encourage him as in Chaucer's tale, but foretells his death. Chaucer makes several other little improvements in the story, but his chief addition is the philosophy which he puts into the mouths of Chauntecleer and Pertelote, and the embroidery of humorously inappropriate learning and allusion with which he has enriched the story. It was not the first time that Chaucer had made birds the mouthpiece of those philosophic reflections on life, half serious, half humorous, of which he was so fond. In the *Parlement of Foules* courtly ideals of love and fidelity are exposed to the matter-of-fact comment of the goose and the duck :—

> I seye, I rede him, though he were my brother
> But she wol love him, lat him love another.
>
> . . . .
> ' Ye, quek ! ' yit quod the doke, ful wel and faire,
> ' There been mo sterres, god wot, than a paire ! '

In the *Prologue* Chaucer's humour plays through a realistic picture of English society ; in the *Knightes Tale* it forms a just perceptible undercurrent to a chivalrous and pathetic romance ; here it is the staple of the whole. In all it is the same arch, sly, penetrating, and inventive humour, a humour of a kind that has never been surpassed in English literature.

THOMAS SACKVILLE (1536–1608)

The Mirrour for Magistrates was planned and commenced by some printers about 1553 as a continuation to *The Fall of Princes*, a version by John Lydgate of Boccaccio's *De Casibus Virorum Illustrium*. This was just such a series of tragedies as that with which the Monk in the *Canterbury Tales* oppressed his hearers :—

> ' Ho ! ' quod the knight, ' good sir, namore of this,
> That ye han seyd is right y-nough y-wis,
> And mochel more ; for litel hevinesse
> Is right y-nough to mochel folk, I gesse.'

The intention of the printers was to 'have the story contynued from whereas Bochas left unto this present time'.

Chaucer's knight would certainly have found the tragedies of 'such as fortune hath dalyed with here in this island' narrated by Baldwin the printer, Ferrers (about the worst of the group), Challoner, Churchyard, Segar, and their fellows 'right y-nough'. The three parts have more than a little of heaviness in every sense of the word. The 'precious jewel' in the head of this monster is the *Induction* written by Sackville when about 1560 he meditated taking over the scheme himself, and his *The Complaynt of Henry Duke of Buckingham*, especially the former, which is the first poem of high merit that had appeared in English since the publication of *Tottel's Miscellany* (1557), the most striking proof of poetic genius given in England between the *Canterbury Tales* and the *Shepheardes Kalender*.

Virgil, not Dante, is Sackville's model, both in the description of the lower world and of such details as the 'targe' of War. The lower world he describes is not Dante's *Inferno*, nor 'the blissful place of rest', to which Sorrow refers, the Christian Paradise. They are the place of punishments and the Elysian fields described in the sixth book of the *Aeneid*. In places Sackville follows Virgil closely, and some of his details have been traced to Gawain Douglas's version. But what is greatest in his sombre and eloquent poem Sackville owes to his own intense and vivid imagination. The opening landscape—which the student might compare with some of Douglas's winter scenes—has the intensity of Burns's painting of inclement skies :—

> When hailstanes drive wi' bitter skyte.

But the greatest thing in the poem are the personifications. These are suggested by Virgil's lines :—

> Just in the gate, and in the jaws of hell,
> Revengeful Cares and sullen Sorrows dwell ;
> And pale Diseases and repining Age ;
> Want, Fear, and Famine's unresisted rage.
> Here Toils, and Death, and Death's half-brother Sleep,
> Forms terrible to view, their sentry keep.

Sackville has omitted some of Virgil's figures and added a few of his own ; but in describing them he has expanded Virgil's single epithets (e.g. 'tristis Senectus') into detailed and elaborate pictures. Such personifications are common in Mediaeval poetry. Some of Sackville's may be compared with the figures painted on the outer wall of the Garden of Mirth in the *Romaunt of the Rose* (ll. 147–474) ; and the spirit of Sackville's description will recall the temple of Mars in the *Knightes Tale* (ll. 1117–1182). But in the whole range of English poetry there are no personifications with more of the peculiar quality of Dante's poetry,—clear, detailed description, every feature of which is intensely significant and impressive. Spenser's personifications are richer in Renaissance colouring, occasionally they are transfigured by a finer spirit of poetry, but as a rule they are weakest just in the quality of impressive significance. The student should examine carefully the attributes of the figures in the House of Holiness (*F. Q.* i. 10), the Masque of Cupid (iii. 12), and the Temple of Venus (v. 10). Milton's Death (*P. L.* ii. 661–673) is an example of sublimity secured by a method other than Dante's and Sackville's, by suggestion rather than minute description. It is of Dante's poetry, or still more of the art of Holbein's Dance of Death, and Albrecht Dürer's etchings, that one is reminded by Sackville's Old Age, 'crook-back'd, tooth-shaken, and blear-eyed', or his Famine and Death.

EDMUND SPENSER (1551 ?–1599)

Spenser's *Epithalamion* was published with his sonnets, the *Amoretti*, in 1595, having been written to celebrate his marriage in June of the previous year. The *Prothalamion* was composed the following year, when the poet was in London hoping vainly for some preferment which might deliver him from exile in Ireland. As in all that Spenser wrote, the influence of Italy and the Renaissance is obvious in the form and colour and music of Spenser's elaborate lyrics. The *canzone* of Dante, Petrarch, and later Italian poets has a more definite division of the stanza than any English poet adopted. The opening prelude, the *chiave* (or key line) which repeats the last rime of the prelude, and the concluding *fugue* give to the stanza the scheme of a dance with a momentary pause between two movements. This Spenser did not attempt to reproduce, but the main principle, of lines of varying length woven together by irregularly recurring rimes, he did, and with the result of at once enlarging the compass of English lyrical harmonies. The lyric of French origin which was popular in England until the new influence from Italy began to be felt is comparatively simple in theme and cadence. Even when, as in the 'balade' form used by Chaucer, the rime scheme is elaborate, the harmony remains simple, because each line is a unit, an equal length finished and tipped with its rime. There is a ripple of rime, but no ground-swell of varying cadence. But the lines of unequal length, and the rimes that the ear has to wait for, necessitate, and Spenser supplies, the larger harmony in which each line becomes a part of the whole movement. The Spenserian stanza, the 'enjambed' decasyllabic couplet, the blank verse paragraph, are all results of the Elizabethan demand for an enrichment of metrical harmony corresponding to the enrichment of thought, and feeling, and expression. In the naturalization of the *canzone* Spenser's most interesting immediate successor was Drummond; but the masterpiece in this harmony, depending on the use of lines of various lengths and freely interwoven rimes, is *Lycidas*. Thereafter the longer lyric tended, in the rhetorical Pindaric ode, towards lawless noise or studied artifice. The natural yet sonorous cadences of *Lycidas* find no echo in English poetry till we come to Keats's Odes.

The ardour and glow of the *Epithalamion* has given it the first place in critical estimate. One may accept this estimate and yet see in the *Prothalamion* a perfect expression of Spenser's most characteristic gifts, his delightful fancy, his rhythms which eddy and turn back and flow on again, his style logically diffuse but without a word which is poetically superfluous.

CHRISTOPHER MARLOWE (1563–1593)

As there is no English poet who more brilliantly represents the Renaissance fervour and passion than Marlowe, so there is no English poem which burns with so pure a flame of Renaissance feeling as *Hero and Leander*. Typical of that whole movement is the intense and recovered delight in the human body, in human beauty, which meets us here and blazes out with equal splendour in the description of Tamburlaine :—

> Of stature tall, and straightly fashioned,
> Like his desire, lift upwards and divine ;
> So large of limbs, his joints so strongly knit,
> Such breadth of shoulders as might mainly bear
> Old *Atlas'* burthen ; twixt his manly pitch,
> A pearl more worth than all the world is placed :
> Wherein, by curious soveraranty of Art,
> Are fixt his piercing instruments of sight :
> Whose fiery circles bear encompassed
> A heaven of heavenly bodies in their Spheres :
> That guides his steps and actions to the throne,
> Where honour sits invested royally :
> Pale of complexion : wrought in him with passion,
> Thirsting with soveraranty, with love of armes.
> His lofty browes in foldes do figure death,
> And in their smoothnesse amity and life :
> About them hangs a knot of amber hair,
> Wrapped in curles, as fierce *Achilles* was,
> On which the breath of heaven delights to play,
> Making it dance with wanton majestie :
> His armes and fingers long and sinewy,
> Betokening valour and excess of strength :
> In every part proportioned like the man,
> Should make the world subdued to *Tamburlaine.*

Of all our poets Marlowe was perhaps the most original. He was no man's debtor. Neither in the idea nor in the form of his drama was he a follower of tradition. He created our serious drama, not only giving it a fitting vestment of musical blank verse, but shifting the centre of interest from the moral sentences of Senecan tragedy, and the incident of popular plays, to the soul of man. Tamburlaine was the first living spirit that trod the English stage, and his influence was felt in Elizabethan tragedy till it closed in *Samson Agonistes.* Though surrounded by amorists, Marlowe produced no love lyrics full of sighs and tears and ingenious fancies. Though sonnets darkened the air, he dipped no pen to write them. In the age of pastoral he wrote but one, insolently superior to all its tribe. Thus disdainful of contemporary fashion as of authority, he stands in a higher degree even than Shakespeare for the new spirit, the spirit of freedom, daring ambition, innovation, exploration, conquest, which fired the century and the country of his birth.

BEN JONSON (1573–1637)

Jonson's complimentary epigrams and verses, though marred by harshness of diction and an ' incurable stiffness ' of versification, are among the very best that the seventeenth century produced. A robust champion of the classics, Jonson leaves to Donne and Francis Beaumont and their innumerable imitators the high *a priori*, metaphysical vein of compliment illustrated in the *Second Anniversary*, and writes inductively, with his eye on his subject. He can turn an elegantly conceited compliment to a noble lady, but the best of his eulogies are, as this to Shakespeare, reasoned though enthusiastic enumerations of the qualities Jonson admired in men and literature. What he says here of Shakespeare's natural genius was to be echoed by every critic of the next two hundred years: it was left to Coleridge and the Germans to justify and amplify Jonson's comment on Shakespeare's art.

Of all the 'Sons of Ben' none inherited so much of his classical inspiration as

ROBERT HERRICK (1591–1674)

(p. 147)

His *Hesperides*, published in 1647, is written in the same pagan spirit, and shows the same single-hearted devotion to classical poetry, as the French poetry of the *Pléiade* a hundred years earlier. It is as untouched by the religious temper of the seventeenth century as by the deeper spirit of 'reason' and the return to nature which underlay the admiration of the classics. Love, song, wine, the country and its superstitions are all to Herrick subjects for epicurean and exquisite verses. His treatment of each is equally light and charming. It is quite natural that to such a temperament the somewhat flimsy, but richly coloured and poetically attired, drama of Beaumont and Fletcher should seem the perfection of art. The deeper things of Shakespeare, as of life, left his spirit untroubled. His was by far the best of the eulogies prefixed to the 1647 collection of their plays.

JOHN DONNE (1573–1631)

OF THE PROGRESS OF THE SOULE, ETC.

THE SECOND ANNIVERSARY

Elizabeth Drury, daughter of Sir Robert Drury of Hanstead in Suffolk, and of Anne, sister to Sir Francis Bacon, died in 1610 at the age of fifteen. In 1611 was published *An Anatomie of the World. Wherein By occasion of the untimely death of Mistris Elizabeth Drury, the frailty and the decay of the whole World is represented.* This was followed in 1612 by *Of the Progresse of the Soule. Wherein, &c.* The title *An Anatomie, &c.,* has been extended by some editors to the two parts considered as one poem, but this is a mistake. The *Progresse* follows the *Anatomie*; from the consideration of this world, the poet passes to the next. It would be impossible to assign any source of this or any other of Donne's poems, but its idealizing treatment of Elizabeth Drury may be compared with the idealization of Beatrice in Dante's *Vita Nuova*, and its *meditatio mortis* with some of Donne's own sermons.

It would not be impossible to make Donne's great Elegy play the part of the drunken Helot in a poetical education, and by comparing its occasionally overstrained hyperboles and frigid conceits with the poetically handled conventions of *Lycidas*, the passionate imagery of *Adonais*, the luminous pictures and carefully woven, musical regrets of *In Memoriam*, to illustrate the difference between poetry that is born of the happy union of feeling and imagination, and poetry that is the offspring of a passionate imagination unequally yoked with wit and erudition. But if the reader can overcome his first distaste of 'metaphysical' or fantastic poetry he will find that Donne's elegy is certainly not more artificial than *Lycidas*; that it contains all the elements of great poetry —passion, imagination, and harmony ; and that it is the work of a mind of extraordinary vigour, insight, and learning. He may even come to feel that Donne's strikes the deepest note of elegiac poetry with greater power and resonance than either Milton or Tennyson. If no more than Milton or Shelley he has shaped for us a definite and moving image of the subject of his elegy, no one of the three poets mentioned has risen to so high a note of exultation in the soul's release by death. The pastoral and apocalyptic vision with which Milton closes is beautiful and soothing. Tennyson's hopes and beliefs are too wavering and in substance too earthly for comparison. Shelley rises in the last stanzas of *Adonais* to the same strain of ecstasy ; but the vision if larger is more indefinite ; the last note less triumphant, more troubled. Donne inherited from his Catholic upbringing an unshakable conviction of the immortality of that 'one precious thing' the soul, and his elegy is, not a lament for Mistress Drury, whom the poet never knew, but a paean, passionate, ecstatic, and metaphysical (as Dante's *Paradiso* is metaphysical) over the glory of the life that is unseen, the vanity and fleetingness of this world where no beauty or perfection may endure. Despite its faults, no poem in the language conveys so vivid a sense of a life which is not the life of sense, so transcendent a consciousness of that 'death of ecstasy and rapture' on which Donne expatiates in the noblest of his sermons.

JOHN MILTON (1608-1674)

No poet since the dawn of history ever wrote a more original style than Milton, yet it would be untrue to say that he owed nothing to his predecessors. He was learned in literature, an artist, and a humanist, and bent his learning to the service of the Muse. In his earliest verses he shows himself a student of Chaucerian and Spenserian measures, and already enamoured of classical fable. The Renaissance manner, which unhesitatingly placed Apollo and the Muses with Michael and Gabriel, which surrounded St. Peter, as in *Lycidas*, with Fauns and Nymphs, Hippotades and Amaryllis and Neaera—strange company for the Apostle—culminated in Milton and died with him. In the Nativity Ode and in *Lycidas* he displays a wide, easy, familiar acquaintance with a great range of mythology and legend, and lays the entire Pagan world under contribution to his purposes. The Miltonic diction, too, follows the ancient models. It is everywhere distinguished by extreme lucidity, by inexorable precision. Thought and expression are alike without hesitancy or mistiness, for Milton, like all classical artists, seeks form rather than atmosphere, finish rather than suggestion, finality rather than mystery ; the idea and the word rise together, sharp and clear. Of such art the Greek temple is at once the creation and the unfading symbol. It stands in every line revealed under a cloudless sky.

No reflection of the age or its controversies appears in Milton's poetry before *L'Allegro* and *Il Penseroso*. Even in these poems the cloud of coming controversy is hardly seen above the horizon, or, if seen, no bigger than a man's hand. These companion pictures are perhaps the most brilliant examples in our literature of the descriptive or objective, as distinguished from the subjective or passionate lyric. As with Shakespeare's or Scott's, the personality of the author is behind, not in them. The parallelism in these poems is singularly close—note the music, literature, scenery preferred in one and in the other—but *Il Penseroso* is the longer by twenty-four lines, and nothing in *L'Allegro* corresponds to the aspiration in its concluding passage. It may be that we have here a suggestion that the reflective temper is likely to outlive the mirthful and to supersede it as the years increase. The distinction which goes deepest, however, between the two moods here portrayed is that one is a social, the other a solitary mood, the one seems akin to that of the Cavalier, who finds much of his pleasure in the world of men, the other that of the Puritan, who seeks it within himself, in the life of the spirit. Other, though slight, indications of Milton's own preferences have been remarked. The bird that gives the note to *Il Penseroso* is the nightingale, his favourite bird, to whom one of his sonnets is addressed. The studies preferred are those to which the poet was himself most strongly drawn ; such music as he was known to love is three times mentioned in the poem; there is a reference to Spenser's world of romance, and Spenser, he told Dryden, he looked upon as his poetical father.

The choice of Melancholy as a companion in *Il Penseroso* foreshadows the tone of those early Romantics, the Wartons, who found Milton an ally, classic though he was, in their revolt against the Augustans and the conventions and restrictions of social life, with its routs and assemblies and tinsel glare, and who sought in solitary communion with the vast and mysterious in nature a refuge for the spirit, 'an ampler aether, a diviner air.'

In *Lycidas* the poet bids farewell to his college friend, drowned in the Irish Channel, but also to his own youth. It betrays in its political references that the great division in national feeling had come home to him and disturbed his poetic dreams. And it is eminently characteristic of Milton's self-centred mind that only in the political references, which are remote indeed from the proper subject of the elegy, the fire of passion bursts through the pastoral convention, and the prophet's warning voice is heard above the poet's. From this time forth Milton was no longer for himself ; he listens for the call of the trumpet.

Lycidas has been praised as the very touchstone of taste, as the most wonderful poem in the language. Yet it is artificial, not only in itself but in respect of its form, the most artificial of poetic forms, the Pastoral, and in Milton's day already out of date. It is an elegy which expresses no obvious sincerity of grief, reveals no intimate sense of loss, and exhibits a strangely incongruous group of personages. It is composed of conceptions the most heterogeneous that it is possible to heap together. Despite all this it achieves a consummate triumph, appealing through every nerve to the reader who has any acquaintance with classical literature. Milton, saturated with the old world's poetry, had absorbed the abstractions of its mythology into the very texture of his mind, and in *Lycidas* weaves a decorative pattern from the stuff of ancient story, the blue and purple and scarlet dyes of the Greek looms. The secret of the poem seems to lie in its amazing verbal and emotional suggestiveness, for it is suffused with memories, of Theocritus and his Sicily, of Greece and Greek romance. It is not so much an elegy, a song of grief, as a monument carved by a great Renaissance artist to the memory of a friend.

Metrically this poem may be regarded as a succession of irregular stanzas, varying in length and containing both rimed and unrimed lines. The rimes are extremely irregular, and the general movement, though prevailingly iambic pentameter, is diversified by the introduction of shorter lines. Each stanza or paragraph introduces and treats of a separate theme.

The epitaph on Shakespeare is distinguished by the splendour of the concluding verses. The poet conceives of Shakespeare's readers, that vast assembly, as transformed to marble, and forming a great sculptured group around his grave, so mighty and so impressive a monument ' that kings for such a tomb might wish to die.' The conceit is in the best manner of the so-called metaphysical poets.

ANDREW MARVELL (1621–1678)

Marvell, privileged to call Milton friend, and recommended by him as Assistant-Secretary to the Council of State, was, like Milton, controversialist as well as poet, but his pamphlets are forgotten and his satires no longer read. Like Milton, too, he was a scholar. Some of his best poems were originally composed in Latin, and afterwards rendered into English, and his *Ode on Cromwell* is rightly named Horatian, since it is still the best example in our language of the calculated and ordered beauty, the measured style of Horace. We see in it the transition to the restrained pedestrian manner of the eighteenth century. Though incomparably the greater poet, Milton is at once less generous and less spiritual than Marvell, witness the magnanimity of the reference to Charles I in the Cromwellian ode, and those lyrics, like *The Garden*, the first English poem in which Nature is sought as a companion for the soul. And it may be questioned whether there are any lines in the whole majestic expanse of Milton's territory that disturb the heart as these of Marvell's have power to disturb it—

> But at my back I always hear
> Time's wingèd chariot hurrying near,
> And yonder all before us lie
> Deserts of vast eternity.

JOHN DRYDEN (1631–1700)

It is usually conceded that Dryden's rank in the hierarchy of letters owes more to his historical importance than to his intrinsic merits as a poet. He is the true founder of the classical tradition, the lawgiver, the framer of the canon. To understand that tradition we must remember that the Augustan poets looked upon society and its institutions as a conquest slowly and laboriously achieved, a clearing in the savage forest, a province rescued from the wild uncultivated realm of nature. They desired to preserve the gains of civilization and to add to them, to impose order and beauty upon all their surroundings, to become still more humane, polite, lettered, artistic. For them city life represented what man had painfully achieved, its regulated streets and stately buildings were the outcome of his struggle with primaeval savagery, the dearly won fruits of his thought and labour. The town was the symbol of civilization ; outside the town lay the pathless unkempt places, not at all or only partially redeemed from wildness, difficult for travel, unfriendly to human intercourse, often dangerous to life. The very words ' urbanity ', ' politeness ', suggest the point of view. We may contrast the attitude of Cowper, who held that ' God made the country, man the town ', with the ineradicable conviction of the Augustans, like Pope and Johnson, that love of the country was the merest affectation or a symptom of mental degeneration. The dislike of the mediaeval or Gothic, so prominent in the thought of the seventeenth and eighteenth centuries, has the same root. It sprang from the instinctive sense that the mediaeval or Gothic was precisely what men had outgrown or escaped, the painful insecurity, the rude habits, the grotesque superstitions, the childish ignorance of a barbarous age. In the past of human history the Augustans concentrated their gaze upon the spaces illuminated by Greek and Roman genius, and found there and there alone what they desired for themselves—reason, law, philosophy, culture, the arts. Hence their enthusiasm for the ancient world revealed by the Renaissance, their passionate humanism, their determination to imitate only the qualities to be found in classical authors. Hence too their impatience of a preference for the romantic in literature, to them another name for the extravagant, fantastic, clownish, unintelligent. For Pope and Johnson a preference for the romantic was merely reactionary; it meant not only a return to barbarism but a sinful apostasy from the very idea of progress.

With Dryden poetry for the first time ranges itself consciously on the side of civilization and keeps in view practical concerns, the application of reason to life, the extension of the kingdom of law and order. With him poetry addresses the man of affairs, engaged in public business, and in addressing him naturally adopts the tone of the Senate house, the rhetorical and epigrammatic style of debate.

For more than a hundred years poetry, which with the Elizabethans had for its aim ecstasy, delight, allied itself with the intelligence, and proceeded to argue, inform, criticize, to inculcate reasonableness, moderation, to insist on the social and civic virtues. It asked men to remember what they owed to the community. And Dryden's place in literary history is due to the success with which he employed verse in satire, and satire as an instrument in social and political reform. The possibilities of the heroic couplet in didactic verse was his discovery, a discovery so brilliant that for the hundred and fifty years during which poetry placed itself in willing subjection to municipal interests it neither found nor feared a rival. So distinguished a servant of his country has well earned his title to remembrance :—

> Though never tender nor sublime,
> He wrestles with and conquers Time.

ALEXANDER POPE (1688–1744)

The Essay on Criticism. Published in 1711, the *Essay* was commented on by Addison in *The Spectator* of December 20 in that year. It became popular at once, and was repeatedly republished in the succeeding years. Pope's sources and models, from Horace's *De Arte Poetica* to the Earl of Mulgrave's *Essay upon Poetry* (1682) and the Earl of Roscommon's *Essay on Translated Verse* (1684), may be studied in Spingarn's *Critical Essays of the Seventeenth Century* and Saintsbury's *Loci Critici*.

The *Essay on Criticism* is the most brilliant statement in English of the doctrines of the classical school of poetry as formulated by the Italian critics of the Renaissance and their successors in Holland, France, and England. The two fundamental doctrines of the school, truth to nature and the imitation of the classics, are stated by Pope with distinctness and felicity :—

> First follow nature, &c.,

and

> Be Homer's works your study and delight, &c.

There is nothing new in Pope's poem. Every principle he enunciated had been formulated before by critics and poets from Aristotle and Horace to Dryden and Addison. Even the final perfection of phrasing which Pope gave them owes something to his gleanings from the poets of his youth, Dryden, Garth, and others, as well as older and at the time forgotten poets. Pope did not even understand very clearly or believe very strongly in all the principles he expounds. The *Essay on Criticism* is not such a convinced and consistent expression of the narrow classical ideals of the seventeenth century as Boileau's *L'Art Poétique* ; far less is it a dignified eulogium, in a poem which is itself a model of what it commends, on the finer qualities of classical art such as might perhaps have been written by Gray, or Landor, or Matthew Arnold. It is not a classical temple which Pope has erected in honour of the classics, but a Chinese pagoda bright with shining tiles and gilded pinnacles. For Pope was primarily a wit, the Donne of a new age and fashion, surpassing his contemporaries by the sustained brilliance of his phrasing in epigram, aphorism, and declamation. The *Essay* coruscates with memorable lines and phrases : it has neither connected argument nor harmonizing unity of spirit. And just as Donne could not always be witty and ingenious without becoming frigid and puerile, Pope could not be always condensed and epigrammatic without lapses into shallow aphorisms, forced and unnatural phrasing. His ellipses are often violent, his inversions unjustifiable, his grammar incorrect, his rimes unpleasing. No collection of these faults, however, should blind us to the perfection of Pope's style within its own well-defined limits, or to the brilliance with which he realized that ideal of ' correctness ' which he set before himself : the expression of thought in the language of actual conversation, achieved without concession to poetic licences and makeshifts—such as the use of the expletives ' do ' and ' did '—and the regular fall of the metrical beat on those syllables which usage and the logic and rhetoric of the sentence have stressed. It was a narrow ideal, and its rigorous pursuit deprived poetry for a time of much beauty and variety, both of phrase and rhythm, but it provided a discipline of which English poetic diction and versification stood in need at the end of the seventeenth century. Donne was not the only poet among Pope's predecessors who, in Jonson's words, ' for not keeping of accent deserved hanging.'

The *Essay on Criticism* has an interest beyond its brilliant phrasing of current critical doctrine as the first poem in which Pope appeared as a satirist. His sketch of Dennis as Appius was the first of the piquant portraits with which he edged and heightened his later satires, of which

the greatest, because the most finely shaded and proportioned, is that
of his first friend and critic, Addison :—

> Peace to all such, but were there one whose fires
> True genius kindles, and fair fame inspires ;
> Blest with each talent, and each art to please,
> And born to write, converse, and live with ease :
> Should such a man, too fond to rule alone,
> Bear, like the Turk, no brother near the throne,
> View him with scornful, yet with jealous eyes,
> And hate for arts that caused himself to rise ;
> Damn with faint praise, assent with civil leer,
> And without sneering teach the rest to sneer ;
> Willing to wound and yet afraid to strike,
> Just hint a fault and hesitate dislike ;
> Alike reserved to blame, or to commend,
> A timorous foe, and a suspicious friend ;
> Dreading e'en fools, by flatterers besieged,
> And so obliging that he ne'er obliged ;
> Like Cato give his little Senate laws
> And sit attentive to his own applause ;
> While Wits and Templars every sentence raise
> And wonder with a foolish face of praise—
> Who but must laugh if such a man there be ?
> Who would not weep if Atticus were he ?

The Rape of the Lock. Published anonymously, in the original form,
in *Lintot's Miscellany*, 1711, and separately in 1712 : the enlarged edition,
with the added Rosicrucian machinery, in 1714. Among works that may
have influenced Pope are Tassoni's *La Secchia Rapita* (1622), Boileau's
Le Lutrin (1674–1683), and the essays on fashions and the 'Fair Sex'
in the *Tatler* (1709–1711) and the *Spectator* (1711–1713). The game of
cards was suggested by the *Scacchia Ludus* (1527) of Marco Girolamo
Vida.

'The *Rape of the Lock* is,' Dr. Johnson says, ' the most airy, the most
ingenious, and the most delightful of all Pope's compositions.' It is
perhaps the only one we can read still with unalloyed delight, with no
necessity to adjust ourselves to a past fashion in wit and poetry. Here
Pope's theme is in perfect harmony with his genius, far more than when
he is expounding a philosophy of criticism or of life which he has never
made his own, but is merely rewording in pointed and shining phrases.
The concrete, fanciful, inventive treatment of the subject, too, gives the
poem a fresher charm than the later satires possess, condensed and pointed
as their art is, and brightened by the 'divine' compliments to his friends.
Not much is to be gained by a comparison of Pope's poem with earlier
mock-heroic poetry. It is not as a burlesque of the epic that it triumphs ;
the least pleasing part of the poem is the Homeric combat at the close.
The true parallel to the *Rape of the Lock* is the social and satirical essays
of the *Tatler* and the *Spectator* in which the fashions and foibles of the
reign of Queen Anne have been portrayed. What Addison and Steele did
in delightful, humorous prose, Pope has achieved in poetry, heightening
the wit, the sparkle, and the beauty of the picture by his pointed,
felicitous, incomparable style and the framework of his finished verse.
To the question whether Pope is a poet, able to throw on what he writes

of, thoughts or things, the 'light of beautiful words', it is enough to point to the description of Belinda's toilet, or her voyage down the Thames. Even the mock-heroic tone of the poem, it will be noticed, is just a heightening of the tone in which Addison always writes of the 'Fair Sex'. That the satire was not altogether pleasing to Miss Arabella Fermor is hardly surprising.

Eloisa to Abelard first appeared in the quarto of 1717 (which also contained the *Elegy*). A second edition with other poems on kindred subjects was issued in 1720. The poem was repeatedly reprinted in *Lintot's Miscellany*. Based on a translation by Hughes (1714) of a French translation (1693) of the Latin letters of Abelard and Héloisa, the poem is of the class of Ovid's *Heroides*, which had been already imitated in English in Drayton's *England's Heroicall Epistles* (1597), Donne's *Sappho to Philaenis*, and Wither's *Fidelia* (1615) (which Pope certainly knew), while a free translation of Ovid's Epistles by several hands had been issued in 1680 with a preface by Dryden.

Eloisa to Abelard and the *Elegy to the Memory of an Unfortunate Lady* stand alone among Pope's poems as poems not of sentiment, reflection, and satire, but of passion, the primal stuff of poetry. A careful study of these pieces of 'high-wrought eloquence' will show just what could be achieved in the rhetorical kind which Pope perfected, and what inevitable disadvantages there are in this oratorical treatment of such personal, intimate passions as love and grief.

Hazlitt has very justly compared *Eloisa to Abelard* with Dryden's *Tancred and Sigismunda*, and as the whole of that poem (a version of a tale from Boccaccio's *Decameron*) is not fitted for reproduction in such a selection as ours, we have thought it well to give here the speech which Sigismunda addressed to the heart of her lover sent to her in a golden casket by her angry father. It is worth while to compare Pope's vivid, coloured eloquence of contending emotions with the massive force of Dryden's oratory, still touched with the intellectual conceits of the seventeenth century:—

> Source of my life, and lord of my desires,
> In whom I lived, with whom my soul expires!
> Poor heart! no more the spring of vital heat:
> Cursed be the hands that tore thee from thy seat!
> The course is finished which thy fates decreed,
> And thou from thy corporeal prison freed:
> Soon hast thou reached the goal with mended pace;
> A world of woes dispatch'd in little space.
> Forced by thy worth, thy foe, in death become
> Thy friend, has lodged thee in a costly tomb.
> There yet remained thy funeral exequies,
> The weeping tribute of thy widow's eyes;
> And those indulgent heaven has found the way,
> That I, before my death, have leave to pay.
> My father even in cruelty is kind,
> Or heaven has turned the malice of his mind
> To better uses than his hate designed:
> And made th' insult which in his gift appears,
> The means to mourn thee with my pious tears;
> Which I will pay thee down before I go,
> And save myself the pains to weep below,

If souls can weep. Though once I meant to meet
My fate with face unmoved, and eyes unwet,
Yet, since I have thee here in narrow room,
My tears shall set thee first afloat within thy tomb;
Then (as I know thy spirit hovers nigh)
Under thy friendly conduct will I fly
To regions unexplored, secure to share
Thy state ; nor hell shall punishment appear;
And heaven is double heaven if thou art there.

SAMUEL JOHNSON (1709–1784)

THE VANITY OF HUMAN WISHES (1749)

The adaptation of an ancient writer's thought to modern conditions was a natural extension of the theory of translation current during the later seventeenth and early eighteenth century. Good translation, according to this view, set forth by Denham, Cowley, Dryden, Roscommon, and later by Johnson, is not a literal paraphrase but a free rendering of the author's spirit and intention in another language. It is thus Sir John Denham praises Sir Richard Fanshawe's translation of the *Pastor Fido* of Guarini :—

That servile way thou nobly dost decline
Of tracing word by word and line by line :
A new and nobler way thou dost pursue
To make translations and translators too :
They but preserve the ashes, thou the flame,
True to his sense, but truer to his fame.

From such translations as Cowley's of Pindar's *Odes*, where 'the customs and ceremonies of ancient Greece are still preserved ', it is but a step to a new poem modelled on the old, and retaining most of its sentiments, but applying them to modern customs and contemporary names. Oldham essayed it; and Dryden and Soame, in translating *L'Art Poétique* of Boileau, substituted English names for French. But the most famous of such adaptations were Pope's *Imitations of Horace* (1733–1738). It was by these that Johnson's first imitation of Juvenal was suggested. His *London, a Poem, in Imitation of the Third Satire of Juvenal*, was issued in the same year and on the same day as the last of Pope's series, and in it Johnson adopts the pose which Pope had maintained throughout as the champion of the Opposition and satirist of the Court. Johnson too mourns a degenerate age under a court that despises literature, and a government which has neglected the honour of England abroad and corrupted her statesmen at home. He praises the country, which he never loved, and denounces London, which was as dear to him as to Lamb. The sincerest lines are those on the evils of poverty :—

Has Heav'n reserv'd, in pity to the poor,
No pathless waste, or undiscovered shore ?
No secret island in the boundless main ?
No peaceful desert yet unclaim'd by Spain ?
Quick let us rise, the happy seats explore,
And bear Oppression's insolence no more.
This mournful truth is everywhere confess'd,
Slow rises Worth, by Poverty depressed.

It was in 1749, when he had published the *Life of Savage*, and was labouring at the Dictionary, that Johnson composed *The Vanity of Human Wishes*. The tenth satire of Juvenal awakened a sincerer echo in Johnson's heart than the third. His satire will not bear comparison with Pope's imitations in felicity and beauty of language. Johnson's eloquence is encumbered with adjectives, periphrases, and forced antitheses. Yet the *Vanity of Human Wishes* is better known than the *Epistle to Arbuthnot*, because it is less hampered with allusions which require notes to explain them, and because it strikes a deeper ethical note. The great defect of Pope's moral poetry is, that it is not moral but peevish and personal. Johnson's poem, with all its faults of rhetoric, utters with sincerity and gravity the noble stoicism of the greatest writers of the middle of the eighteenth century,—poets, novelists, essayists, and orators. Theirs was neither the shallow optimism of *An Essay on Man* nor the misanthropy of *A Voyage to the Houyhnhynms*. They recognized the evils of life without preferring an indictment against Providence; they knew the faults and follies of men without ceasing to love and respect their virtues.

OLIVER GOLDSMITH (1728–1774)

Goldsmith rescued the heroic couplet from the metallic monotony into which it had fallen with Pope and his imitators. He recovered for it something of the periodic structure and the flexibility with which Chaucer had endowed and Keats was later to restore to it. Of this old weapon of satire he made too an instrument of sympathy. While he carried on the didactic tradition in his choice of subject, with him poetry became again, as it should be, the utterance of the heart rather than the head. Yet he remained an artist: *Nullum quod tetigit non ornavit.* In his *Traveller* Goldsmith is following in the footsteps of Johnson, but in *The Deserted Village* (1770) he takes his own way. Goldsmith owed nothing, as did Gray and Collins, to foreign sources, whether classical or mediaeval, nothing of consequence to his forerunners or contemporaries: he reflects on matters which had come under his own observation—the political and social conditions of his own time—and the qualities of his mind and style are as unborrowed as they are distinguished. The gentlest spirit that ever wrote with pen, he strangely endears himself to his audience, since in the clear mirror of his verse are reflected the sweetness and magnanimity of an angelic nature. Even his irony is tender, and his humour a summer lightning. *Retaliation* is evidence that in satire Goldsmith might have rivalled the great, but the region of the affections of human-heartedness, as in *The Deserted Village*, is his natural home.

'It will be objected,' said the author of this poem, 'that the depopulation it deplores is nowhere to be seen, and the disorders it laments are only to be found in the poet's own imagination. To this I can scarcely make any other answer than that I sincerely believe what I have written: that I have taken all possible pains in my country excursions these four or five years past, to be certain of what I allege, and that all my views and inquiries have led me to believe those miseries real which I have attempted to display.' It is for political economy, not literary criticism, to determine these problems.

THOMAS GRAY (1716–1771

For the student the poetry of Gray is perhaps the most instructive in our language. His correspondence and recorded conversations prove how deeply he occupied himself with every side of the poetic art; the many problems of language, metre, and the proper subjects of poetry are immediately suggested by his work and methods; his lot was cast in that interesting period during which the classical ideals were slowly yielding to other fashions of thought and feeling, and he exhibits in his literary career almost every phase of the rise and progress of romanticism. Beginning, as was natural, in the didactic manner of his predecessors, as in his verses *On the Alliance of Education and Government*, he passed through the elegiac mood, the region of reflective melancholy, which, in the so-called 'grave-yard poetry' of the time, preceded the Romantic revival, and left an enduring monument of his passage in the famous *Elegy*. After a lengthy courtship, he espoused in his latest odes the Romantic Muse. It is true that Gray only partially freed himself from the artificialities and ingenuities of the preceding school of English poetry, but he was alive to its chief faults, awake to the first stirrings of interest in Northern saga, heroic lay, and the forgotten beauties of mediaeval art, and he was early initiated into the new brotherhood— the lovers of mountains and wild nature. He was, too, a gleaner in the fields of foreign literature, wrote admirable Latin verses, imitated Greek metres, translated from Tasso and Dante, and read Racine with enthusiastic appreciation. His mind was the most open and receptive in that age.

Gray describes *The Progress of Poetry* and *The Bard* (1757) as Pindaric odes. The Odes of Pindar were set to music which has been lost, and his English imitators, Ben Jonson, Cowley, Congreve, were imitators either simply of what they regarded as the metrical irregularity of Pindar or of his external form, that is of the divisions, strophe, antistrophe, epode, and the symmetrical grouping of his verses. This metrical arrangement, separated from the music which gave it meaning, was, as Gray indeed recognized, wholly artificial, possessed of no real significance in English, and incapable of delighting the ear. In Gray's odes the introduction of rime serves to bind the paragraphs together and to satisfy the musical sense, which receives no direct gratification from the epodic structure. In these poems the author aimed at the qualities which he found in the lyrics of Pindar. They are musical chants, in which the ringing splendour of phrases, the elaborated language, the carefully-planned allusions and echoes from heroic history, captivate and elevate the mind. Such poems make no bid for popularity, but in the *Elegy* (published 1751) probably the best known of English poems, Gray had already found acceptance.

As the palmary example in our literature of success in poetry attained by choice of subject, happy phrasing and the illustration of obvious reflections the *Elegy* has its established position and value. The very qualities which have earned for it unbounded admiration have also indeed provoked disdain. But intellectual superiority may be purchased at too high a price, and he must possess a sturdy confidence in his literary judgement who permits it to stand between himself and the pleasure to which so many minds have borne ardent and emphatic witness. Some stanzas, hardly if at all inferior to those included, were excluded by the author's fastidious taste from the printed version, e. g.

> There scatter'd oft, the earliest of the year,
>   By hands unseen are show'rs of violets found ;
> The red-breast loves to build and warble there,
>   And little footsteps lightly print the ground.

The stanza in which this poem was written, and its peculiar cadence, were probably suggested to Gray by Joseph Warton's *Ode to Evening.* Cf. the following stanza :—

> Hail, meek-eyed maiden, clad in sober grey,
>   Whose soft approach the weary woodman loves,
> As homeward bent to kiss his prattling babes
>   He jocund whistles to the twilight groves.

The measure had, however, been frequently employed, e. g. in Denham's *Gondibert* and Dryden's *Annus Mirabilis.*

WILLIAM COLLINS (1721–1759)

AN ODE ON THE POPULAR SUPERSTITIONS OF THE HIGHLANDS

Printed first in the *Transactions of the Royal Society of Edinburgh*, vol. i, 1788, from a MS. copy in which the poem was as given here. The interpolations of the editors have been omitted. It is regrettable not to have the whole poem, but it is pleasant to be able to omit a eulogy on ' Butcher ' Cumberland from a poem on the Highlands.

In 1749 John Home, the author of the once celebrated tragedy *Douglas* and one of the first Scotchmen to take an interest in the character, history, and traditions of the Celtic Highlanders (he served against the rebels in 1745, and in 1759 became Macpherson's first patron), visited England and made the acquaintance of William Collins in the house of a common friend at Winchester. It was doubtless from his conversations with Home that Collins derived the material which he wove into the long ode he addressed to him on his return to Scotland. The first stirrings of the romantic revival were in the air ; Collins and his school-friend, Joseph Warton, were in the vanguard of the movement ; and Home's account of Scottish scenes and superstitions fell on a sympathetic mind. In 1748 Thomson in *The Castle of Indolence* had written,—

> As when a shepherd of the Hebrid Isles
> Placed far amid the melancholy main,
> (Whether it be lone fancy him beguiles
> Or that aerial beings sometimes deign
> To stand embodied to our senses plain)
> Sees on the naked hill or valley low,
> The whilst in ocean Phoebus dips his wain,
> A vast assembly waving to and fro ;
>   Then all at once in air dissolves the wondrous show.

In the classical *Seasons* there are no more imaginative or romantic lines than these:

> Or, where the Northern Ocean in vast whirls
> Boils round the naked, melancholy isles
> Of farthest Thule, and the Atlantic surge
> Pours in among the stormy Hebrides.

Thus early, Scottish scenery and superstitions became a quickening factor in the imaginative revival of the century. Of the first phase of that revival there is no more complete document than Collins's ode. The sonnet structure of the stanza; the Spenserian Alexandrine at the close; the themes—the virtuous 'child of nature' on St. Kilda's Isle, the 'luckless swain' and his 'anxious wife' and babes ('the short and simple annals of the poor'); the romantic scenery, romantic ruins, and romantic superstitions; the literature of romance—ballads, and Shakespeare and Tasso—all are characteristic. Collins touches every note of the revival, and in a style which is redolent of Coleridge and Scott rather than of Warton and Gray. To Gray he is inferior in sustained constructive power and brilliance of phrasing, but he is a finer and purer lyric poet. His style is quite unmarred by the 'pseudo-poetic' diction which calls trundling a hoop and playing football—

> To chase the rolling circle's speed
> Or urge the flying ball.

His epithets are neither otiose nor rhetorical, but subdued in colouring, accurate, and imaginative—note 'with sheeny gold', 'in gleamy pageant' (Dr. Johnson would have made it 'gloomy'). As a delicate painter in silver and grey the poet of *Evening*, of 'How sleep the brave,' and of this Ode has no fellow till we come to Mr. Robert Bridges.

WILLIAM COWPER (1731–1800)

LINES ON THE RECEIPT OF MY MOTHER'S PICTURE

Cowper's mother died in 1737. It was in 1790 that the present of her picture evoked this expression of passionate and tender recollection. 'The world could not have furnished you with a present so acceptable to me as the picture which you have so kindly sent me. I received it the night before last, and viewed it with a trepidation of nerves and spirits somewhat akin to what I should have felt had the dear original presented herself to my embraces. I kissed it, and hung it where it is the last object that I see at night and . . . the first on which I open my eyes in the morning. She died when I had completed my sixth year, yet I remember her well, and am an ocular witness of the great fidelity of the copy. . . . There is in me, I believe, more of the Donne than the Cowper, and though I love all of both names, and have a thousand reasons to love those of my own name, yet I feel the bond of nature draw me vehemently to your side. I was thought in the days of my childhood much to resemble my mother. . . . Add to all this I deal much in poetry as did our venerable ancestor the Dean of St. Paul's, and I think I shall have proved myself a Donne at all points. The truth is that, whatever I am, I love you all.' (Cowper's *Letters*, February 27, 1790.)

It is a strange accident that links the most complex and daring of English poets with one of the simplest and gentlest. Yet there are more demonstrable connexions between them than that of blood. Both had, in different degrees, the 'melancholy' temperament which at one time plunges its possessor into the depths of despondence, at another makes him 'kindle squibs about' himself 'and fly into sportiveness'. Cowper's despondence was the deeper, for he is one of the strange group of eighteenth-century poets—Collins, Smart, Blake are the others—who found

escape from the tyranny of ' reason ' by that overbalance of the imaginative temperament which we call madness. ' They who are said to have
lost their wits have more than other people ' (Cowper's *Letters*, June 3,
1788). The poetry of Cowper and Donne, too, has the common tie of
sincerity of self-expression. The deepening of the personal note is
Cowper's principal contribution to the poetic movement which began
about 1740. His poetry is not romantic in theme or temper as Collins's
Ode is, or Gray's *Bard*, or Beattie's *Minstrel*. It is of the classical school
by its didactic intention and the politeness—the gentility and dignity—
even of its simplicity, its occasional ' pseudo-poetic diction '. But in its
treatment of nature, so much more intimate and personal than
Thomson's, approaching at moments—in the *Winter Walk at Noon*, for
instance—to Wordsworth's in its expression of the healing power of
nature, and in the frank simplicity of its self-revelation, Cowper's poetry
is of the age of Rousseau's *Confessions*, the herald of the *Prelude*, *Childe
Harold*, the lyrics of Shelley, and all that followed here and abroad—
Chateaubriand, Heine, Leopardi. To note the movement of English
poetry one has but to compare these lines with Pope's oratorical *Elegy
on an Unfortunate Lady*. To appreciate the richness of English poetry
one may compare and contrast them both with the classical *Lycidas*, the
passionate cry of *Adonais*, the intellectual and mystical ecstasy of the
Second Anniversary.

ROBERT BURNS (1759–1796)

Tam o' Shanter was written in 1791 and first printed in *The Antiquities
of Scotland* by Captain Francis Grose, at whose suggestion the story was
written. ' The poem,' says Lockhart, ' is said to have been the work of
one day, and Mrs. Burns well remembers the circumstances. He spent
most of the day on his favourite walk by the river, where in the afternoon
she joined him with some of her children. He was busily engaged
crooning to himsel ; and Mrs. Burns, perceiving that her presence was
an interruption, loitered behind with the little ones among the broom.
Her attention was presently attracted by the strange and wild gesticula-
tions of the bard, who, now at some distance, was agonized with an
ungovernable access of joy. He was reciting very loud, and with the
tears rolling down his cheeks, the lines

Now Tam ! O Tam ! had they been queans, &c.'

To the last Burns was of opinion that *Tam o' Shanter* was the best of
his poems. The present editors share that opinion so entirely as regards
his longer poems that they have found no question more difficult to
answer than what other of these should be included in this selection.
In an anthology of lyrics Burns must hold a first place. In a larger
selection than this it would be easy to include a great part of the
Kilmarnock volume, so rich is it in poetry descriptive, humorous, sentimental, and satirical. The difficulty is to select, and the purpose of
this volume is not to sample poets but to gather poems which are pre-
eminent. As a complete work of art *Tam o' Shanter* has no rivals among
the longer poems except *The Jolly Beggars*, for which the first place has
been claimed by Carlyle and Matthew Arnold. The more serious, fiercer,
and more philosophic note of that rollicking poem accounts for this
judgement, for technically the songs are not all of Burns's best:

> But the godly old chaplain left him in the lurch;
> The sword I forsook for the sake of the church.

That is not in the tone of the purest Scottish song. It has the inferior swaggering note of the tradition of Durfey's *Pills to Purge Melancholy*, Ramsay's *Tea-Table Miscellany*, and Gay's *Beggar's Opera*, and there is a little too much of this throughout the poem, though the tone is deepened by Burns's democratic ardour. *Tam o' Shanter* is purely humorous; but joy and fun are perhaps the sincerest emotions in Burns's poetry :—

> But why o' death begin a tale ?
> Just now we're living sound and hale;
> Then top and maintop crowd the sail,
> > Heave Care o'er-side !
> And large before Enjoyment's gale
> > Let 's tak' the tide.

It is this amazing *joie de vivre* which lends its unequalled animation and verve to *Tam o' Shanter*; while the narrative art of the poem is as great as Chaucer's, and between Chaucer and Burns comes no third. 'No poet,' says Sir Walter Scott, speaking of this poem, 'with the exception of Shakespeare, ever possessed the power of exciting the most varied and discordant emotions with such rapid transitions.' To Burns's descriptions we may apply what Dryden said of Shakespeare—when he describes anything you more than see it, you feel it too.

Of other poems we have chosen the *Address to the Deil* as a poem *sui generis* in English poetry. Here is the Scottish devil *par excellence*, the product of popular superstition blended with Calvinist theology; and both the 'sensibility' of the age, and Burns's own genial and splendid humanity, colour the surprising and effective change of tone in the closing stanza. In the epistles—a favourite form of Scottish poetry —the *joie de vivre* which glows in all Burns's best poetry burns with a purer and more ideal flame than elsewhere. Neither passion nor revelry is their theme, but love of country and love of song. In homely and vibrating phrase Burns preaches the same high doctrine of song the consoler as Gray's classic lines :—

> Man's feeble race what Ills await,
> Labour and Penury, the racks of Pain,
> Disease and Sorrow's weeping train,
> And Death sad refuge from the storms of Fate !
> The fond complaint, my Song, disprove,
> And justify the laws of Jove.
> > Say has he given in vain the heavenly Muse

The remainder of Gray's stanza might be fitly taken as a description of Burns's poetry when contrasted with the modern poetry of longing and melancholy, the poetry of 'Shadow-vested Misery' :

> Night, and all her sickly dews,
> Her Spectres wan, and birds of boding cry,
> He gives to range the dreary sky :
> Till down the eastern cliffs afar
> > Hyperion's march they spy and glittering shafts of war.

The inner core of Burns's genius was untouched by the sorrows of his life. 'Man was made to mourn' and similar poems are but the declamatory expression of his reflections, worthless as poetry. When a poet he knows only one sorrow, the sorrow of disappointed love, the shadow of life's keenest joy. Of his love poems even, the best sing of the joy of mutual love and blend humour and passion with unequalled felicity and force. The faults of Burns's are obvious enough; but no poet except Shakespeare has woven more splendid poetry from the warp and woof of ordinary men's everyday experiences. The joys of living—labour and love and revelry, nature and native land and song—simple emotions but raised to sublimity by the intensity with which they are felt and expressed—that is Burns's poetry. Wordsworth alone of the romantic poets has the same sense of joy; but the inspiration of Wordsworth's content was drawn from deeper and more mystical sources:

> He sang of love and quiet blending,
> Slow to begin and never ending;
> Of serious faith, and inward glee;
> That was the song,—the song for me.

GEORGE CRABBE (1754–1832)

To Edmund Burke was due the rescue of a poet from oblivion, perhaps from death by want, whose name is often associated with Cowper as standing midway between the school of Pope and the school of Wordsworth. Crabbe and Cowper introduce us to the modern world and the intellectual problems of the modern world. The thoughts with which they were occupied are also ours. Crabbe is our first realist in poetry. It is not a little remarkable that the vein of realism in Chaucer, so brilliantly exposed in the *Prologue*, failed to attract his successors; for more than three centuries he was classed as a pure romancist. After Chaucer English poetry occupied itself mainly with romantic matter or with political matter. Swift alone dared to substitute observation in the region of fact for imagination in the region of ideals. Crabbe turns resolutely away from romance, from pastoral fancy, he turns away with equal deliberation from the political and civic interests of Dryden and Pope, and attempts to recall poetry from these preoccupations to the hard realities of English provincial life. He chose to draw, with perfect and unmitigated faithfulness, life as he knew it in East Anglia, a life not of cultivated persons, who wrote or read poetry, but of toilers, men and women at the base of the social pyramid. Instead of the knights and ladies of mediaeval narrative, the nymphs and belles and gallants of the courtier poets, he drew the portraits of the peasant at work in the fields, or the fisherman battling with the storm for his daily bread. He told the story of the poor. Crabbe has been called 'a Pope in worsted stockings', and it is clear that in his handling of the heroic couplet he was the disciple, though not the equal of Pope. But his minute and finished pictures of sordid toil-embittered life, his scientific, deliberate exposure of its tragic elements, are of such power as to place him among the English classics. Crabbe's scenery suits the sombre character of his narratives—the low shore and yellow discoloured waves of the Suffolk coast, the stunted trees, the mud flats, the melancholy heaps of decaying seaweed. 'Nature's sternest painter, yet the best,' was Byron's verdict upon Crabbe. We need not take it literally, but we may allow to him the same faithfulness in his delineation of the scenery he knew, as of the human nature he knew. Truth rather than beauty was his aim, an aim which separates him by a great gulf from the romancists.

Crabbe and Cowper represent in our poetical literature what has been called, since Rousseau gave currency to the phrase, *the return to Nature*. It is not easy to define the precise significance of these famous words.

In the political doctrine of Rousseau the return to Nature meant the overthrow of the conventional and the artificial elements in the social system. Kings and aristocracies, the distinctions of rank which kept men apart, were to be swept away, and a nobler, freer type of society established, such as was supposed to have existed before men became the slaves of routine, meaningless custom, and artificial civilization. But the wider humanitarian ideals survived the political doctrines with which they were at first associated, and with Cowper, Crabbe, Blake, and Burns they entered into and renewed the youth of poetry. The return to Nature is connected in our literature with the progress of democratic ideas, with new interpretations of the phenomena of the physical world, and with the transference of intellectual interest to social from political problems.

WILLIAM WORDSWORTH (1770–1850)

While English poets were occupied with the attempt to recover all that the world had lost with the overthrow of the Roman empire by Goth and Vandal, while they were concerned with the political and religious problems which affected men as members of a civic society whose inner relations required adjustment, the spell of antiquity remained unbroken. When, however, the interest in these problems began to flag, when a working political and social scheme was agreed upon, when religious toleration was secured, when a firm foundation had been laid for the advance of science, and the place of the arts in human life was acknowledged, poetry unaccountably languished. What had been achieved ceased to command interest, the smooth and ordered arrangements of social life seemed tame and valueless, and civilization a mere bondage to convention. The emotions, no longer engaged, sought a fresh outlet, and found it in a neglected past, in a forgotten age. To war with the present seems the function of romance, to lay siege to the towers and defences of the city that is built. Opposed to it and always with us are the times and the places and the people that we know. We enter this familiar region in Chaucer's *Prologue* or Dryden's *Absalom and Achitophel*, which mirror our acquaintances and describe broad universal human features. We are there when we discuss political maxims with Bacon, or engage in social functions with Addison or laugh with Swift. For it is simply the world of human nature in its least variable aspects, as we learn it in personal experience and understand it in authentic and unchallenged history. We moralize over it with Horace as with Johnson, we are not beyond its limits in so ancient an author as Homer, nor out of sympathy with the pictures drawn of it by Juvenal. The tone in which literature renders this world is usually quiet and critical, subdued to the key of fact. But in every generation to which are presented this real and immediate world, and its concerns only, there lie hidden the smouldering ashes of revolt. An uneasy sense of its insufficiency arises, a sense of imprisonment. Such a generation becomes susceptible to disturbing influences, its equilibrium is easily shaken, even in its serenest hours, as the equilibrium of Browning's sceptical Bishop was shaken—

> Just when we're safest, there's a sunset touch,
> A fancy from a flower-bell, some one's death,
> A chorus-ending from Euripides,
> And that's enough for fifty hopes and fears,
> As old and new at once as Nature's self,
> To rap and knock and enter in our soul.

And mediaeval literature was full of such touches, strange musical airs which stirred the soul in some nameless fashion, and like the deep moaning round with many voices which called Ulysses and his fellow mariners once more to the quest, seemed to summon heart and mind to things unknown and mightier issues. It stirred to its depths the spirit of eighteenth-century Europe, half weary of its rationalism, and even of the triumphant victories it had achieved in the establishment of the principles of social and political order, of just and refined taste.

Crude indeed were the stimulants at first demanded and supplied. Anything in legend or story which was unfamiliar or exciting, which could minister to the 'longing for a shudder', the strong situations of the Northern sagas, the grotesque supernaturalism of the *Castle of Otranto*, the unnatural gloom of Macpherson's *Ossian*, were sufficient. But gradually above the horizon rose the full orb of the Feudal and Catholic world of the Middle Ages, and just as the old Greek and Roman world had charmed the spirit in its search for reason, knowledge, culture, so in its turn the new seemed rich and wonderful, and the despised centuries came to their own again. For it grew rapidly clear that no epoch of the past was so rich in imagination-stirring quality, so varied in emotional content, so capable of supplying the poet with moving subjects as the great Christian age, the age of faith that built the cathedrals, the age of chivalry and knightly ideals, of spiritual symbolism and passionate loyalties. And the spirit of poetry, pining for release from its city prison, turned eagerly to the world beyond its walls, the shining mediaeval world, a dim wonderland, as remote and shadowy and enchanted as any fairy vision. It was not indeed without visible monuments, as the ancient world had not been without them; it had its abbeys and castles, its manuscripts too, and its parchments, legal document and illuminated missal. But its spirit had vanished, its habits and manners were outgrown, its ideals extinguished. It was a forgotten age, as forgotten as the ancient civilization had been after the fall of Rome; its ways of life and thought were in large measure matters of speculation; yet it was somehow felt that in those long centuries, which Renaissance enthusiasm had derided as Gothic and dark and barbaric, there had flourished great men and great enterprises, a spirit of heroism had been abroad, and that in the days of the noble chivalric and Christian society of Europe, before France was France, or England England, a mighty system of idealism, still distinguishable in its architecture and its literature, had swayed and controlled the issues in the human drama.

For the generation to which Gray and Collins belonged the rediscovered mediaeval world offered an escape into immensity. The dark ages proved a night of stars, in which 'creation widened on man's view', the night which is more potent to stir the sense of the infinite, which arouses a deeper sense of wonder than the day, and though it seems to remove us from the actual world, which lies revealed in the sunlight of reason and common sense, permits us vision of a larger reality, no less actual, and spiritually far more impressive. This world, so strange and unexplored, developed an undreamt-of significance. History opened a majestic book, in which the records of Greece and Rome shrank to a page; literature, conceived as the fine flower of cultivated city life, grew to that infinitely greater thing, the art by which men had made beautiful in speech what in all ages they had felt and thought and known; the noble and the courtier gave unaccustomed precedence to man as man, to the toiler and maker and dreamer of dreams. And just as the poet was set free from such official duties as Prior and Steele and

Addison had performed, was dismissed, as it were, from the service of the state, the discovery of the mediaeval world dismissed the imagination from that service also, and sent it forth on spiritual quests. An unknown ocean called adventurous keels to set sail for the farthest shores of human history, to gather intellectual spoils from all lands and peoples. It was a liberation of the soul from certain narrow interests, civic and artistic and political, leaving it free to embrace larger ideals of liberty and justice, such as bore their part in the French Revolution, calling it to view men as citizens of the universe rather than of any one state or city, compelling a sense of brotherhood which dared not exclude peasant or ploughman, or rank him below the gentleman, dismissing artifice and fashion and convention to feel the divine depth and largeness of simplicity, whether in the use of language which disdained the devices of rhetoric, or in the unfolded mystery of childhood, or in the strange dumb hidden life of animals. The colour and pomp and pageantry of the Middle Ages, its picturesque features in dress and armour, its glittering splendours, had too their influence. They took captive the mind of Scott, they cast upon Chatterton, 'the marvellous boy,' and upon the youthful Keats a cunning spell, they have fascinated many a poet since. But the mediaeval revival held far deeper meanings. Its most precious things were its purely human things, the tender humanity which underlies like the calm of deep water the turbulent surface of mediaeval adventures and mediaeval passions. 'There is,' said Byron, speaking of the great spokesman of the Middle Ages, 'a gentleness in Dante beyond all gentleness'; 'Dante,' said Shelley, 'understood the deep things of love even more than Petrarch . . . the *Paradise* is a perpetual hymn of everlasting love.' This tenderness, this touch of nature, this piercing fellow-feeling was felt by all who did feel as the secret of the mysterious charm, the magic of the Middle Age; its pure humanity took captive the world. 'O for the gentleness of old Romance,' cried Keats in his *Isabella*, and again, in a letter, 'I looked over a book of prints taken from the church at Milan . . . full of romance and the most tender feeling.' Various aspects of mediaeval life and art attracted different minds, but at the root of their devotion lay a profound sense that here the affections had come to their own, that at no period of the world's history had literature been so steeped in feeling, that at no period had art so vividly presented human nature, touched by all the mortal accidents of time and place, none in which it had revealed itself so unconsciously, so naïvely, or so fully, for what it is and will ever be. And Wordsworth, since he stands first and last for the individual as against the state, for the heart and its affections, who held that 'the ploughshare of passion' it is which 'tears down to our primitive rock', Wordsworth, since unhesitatingly he rejects the exclusive authority of the reason, and stretches out a hand of trust for the guidance of instinct and affection, since he could declare, 'we live by admiration, hope, and love,' though he makes no use of mediaeval pomp and pageantry, is a true son of the romantic revival, truer even than Scott, who loved its dazzling shows and circumstance, for through every phase of his work its currents stream to their natural and untrammelled issues. Through the romance of the past as through a gateway he enters the measureless romance of the present. It is not that he was drawn in youth to romantic subjects, though he was so drawn; it is not that he can speak as one who has seen

the Lady of the Mere
Sole-sitting by the shores of old romance,

or that he can thus describe the poet of chivalry whom he loved—

> Sweet Spenser moving through his clouded heaven
> With the moon's beauty and the moon's soft pace.

It is that for him above all modern poets the world and life were charged with dreams, that at the thought of such sufferings and lonely fortitude as those of *Michael* and *The Leech-gatherer*, at the thought of childhood, touched with the glory of the imperial palace whence it came, at the thought of the history and powers of the human mind

> That feeds upon infinity, that broods
> Over the dark abyss, intent to hear
> Its voices,

at the sight of

> the immeasurable height
> Of woods decaying, never to be decayed,

of mountain peak or sounding cataract that ' haunted him like a passion ', he was rapt away into a region of immeasurable astonishment. To be capable of such astonishment is to be a romantic, for it is to be a visionary.

SAMUEL TAYLOR COLERIDGE (1772–1834)

It was in November, 1797, that Coleridge and the Wordsworths set out from Alfoxden on their famous walking-tour and that the *Ancient Mariner* was planned and begun. As well as contributing one or two lines, Wordsworth suggested the navigation of the ship by the dead and the slaying of the albatross—of which bird he had read in *Shelvocke's Voyages*, the source of some of his own most picturesque images. But the poem was Coleridge's creation. In it for once all the diverse currents of his reading and speculation—romantic German ballads, old travels, mystical and occult philosophies—flowed together to compose a poem of imagination and melody all compact ; a poem of a pure loveliness of words and description and music unknown in English since Milton and Marlowe and Chaucer. This is Coleridge's most distinctive contribution to English poetry in *The Ancient Mariner* and *Christabel*, more important than his treatment of the supernatural, beauty—beauty of word and image and melody. Wordsworth can write with a sheer force, ' an echoing detonation, an auroral light,' to borrow Professor Saintsbury's epithets, in which Coleridge is never his rival, and he can communicate to us a deeper thrill of wonder and awe than all the marvels of Coleridge's poems. But Wordsworth has no descriptions which give the pure delight of loveliness as do the descriptions and imagery of *The Ancient Mariner*, or, to name but one, the picture of the chamber to which Christabel led the Lady Geraldine ; nor has Wordsworth's verse ever quite the vowelled melody with which Coleridge's cadences fall upon the ear :—

> And now 'twas like all instruments,
> Now like a lonely flute.

Into the Palace of Art towards which Collins was struggling, Coleridge enters, and behind him follow Keats and Tennyson and Rossetti and Morris, and all who in one way or another have made beauty, beauty of description and image and cadence, their sole aim in poetry, at the cost sometimes it may be of fullness of life and truth.

On March 23, 1798, Dorothy Wordsworth records in her diary: ' Coleridge dined with us. He brought his ballad finished.' On April 20 she enters : ' William all the morning engaged in wearisome composition. The moon crescent. *Peter Bell* begun.' There is a little irony to us in these words, for *Peter Bell* is Wordsworth's counterpart to the *Ancient Mariner*, in which he was to show how the supernatural should be treated in poetry. But his method can be studied in other and more successful poems, as *Hartleap Well*. This question, how the supernatural might be introduced in fiction and poetry in an age of ' reason ', had been in the air since Horace Walpole wrote *The Castle of Otranto*. Burns's method in *Tam o' Shanter* and the *Address to the Deil* is thoroughly eighteenth-century. These things are old wives' tales and drunken farmers' adventures, fit subjects for a poetic *éclat de rire*. Sir Walter Scott's masterpiece in the kind, *Wandering Willie's Tale*, is woven of the same strands, the traditions and imaginings of the excited peasant mind ; but Scott has not so entirely subordinated the weird and awe-inspiring to the humorous. There is nothing in Burns's tale or Coleridge's poem finer than the Scottish peasant's vision of the great reckless men who had spilled the blood of the saints : ' There was the fierce Middleton and the dissolute Rothes, and the crafty Lauderdale ; and Dalzell, with his bald head and a beard to his girdle ; and Earlshall with Cameron's blude on his hand; and wild Bonshaw that tied blessed Mr. Cargill's limbs till the blude sprang ; and Dunbarton, the twice turned traitor baith to country and King. There was the bludy Advocate Mackenzie, who for his worldly wit and wisdom had been to the rest as a God. And there was Claverhouse as beautiful as when he lived, with his long dark curled locks streaming down over his laced buff-coat, and his left hand always on his right spule-blade to hide the wound that the silver bullet had made.' To Wordsworth also it seemed right that the supernatural must be presented through a temperament, through a disturbed and excited imagination, but he found the source of this disturbance in some violence done to the moral nature, to the elemental instincts and affections of the heart. That is the lesson of the poems mentioned above, as well as of *The Thorn* and *Harry Blake* and *Goody Gill*. It was the ground of Wordsworth's criticism of *The Ancient Mariner*, ' that the principal person has no distinct character, either in his profession of Mariner, or as a human being who having been long under the controul of supernatural impressions might be supposed himself to partake of something supernatural,' and ' that he does not act but is continually acted upon '. Wordsworth never succeeded in writing a poem which quite justifies his theory ; but it is the principle on which Shakespeare worked. It is just so that he presents the supernatural in *Macbeth*. The ' air-drawn dagger ' and the ghost of Banquo, though the one be an hallucination, the other an apparition, are both essentially the outer manifestation of the inner storm,—

> the blot upon the brain
> That *will* show itself without.

Peter Grimes is Crabbe's characteristically homespun rendering of the same theme.

Among Coleridge's many projects was ' an essay on the uses of the Supernatural in poetry and the principles that regulate its introduction '. What his practice proves is that a poet with imagination and music may do what he chooses. The *Ancient Mariner* affects us simply as a marvellously vivid and coherent dream. The deeper moral roots of the supernatural—'the fear that sits as guardian of the soul forcing it into wisdom'—are untouched by such a poem, whose moral is 'as superficial as that of the Arabian Nights' Tale of the merchant sitting down to eat dates by the side of a well and throwing the shells aside, and lo ! a genie starts up, and says he *must* kill the merchant, because one of the date shells had, it seems, put out the eye of the genie's son' (*Coleridge's Table Talk*, May 31, 1830).

The fragment of *Christabel* (which is full of lines evidently suggested by phrases of Dorothy Wordsworth's) promised a greater poem than the *Ancient Mariner*, just because into the witchery of its imagery and rimes the poet distils a subtle sense of spiritual evil, something of deeper significance than the 'miracles', as Lamb described them, of the Mariner's experiences in 'silent seas'. But *Christabel* is the merest fragment; and *Kubla Khan* if finished would have been pure dream and music. No poet's fame rests so securely on so slender an achievement—one complete poem, perhaps the most original in the language, two fragments, a ballad, and some melancholy strains of regret, the last red leaves on a tree that had promised a splendid fruitage.

LORD BYRON (1788–1824)

Byron had already achieved something of a reputation with his *English Bards and Scotch Reviewers* when, at twenty-one, he left England for the first time. It was on this journey that he began *Childe Harold*, the four cantos of which, written in the Spenserian stanza—a measure, he said, he 'could weave faster than a couplet'—deal generally with the author's travels in Spain, Greece, Switzerland, and Italy. The first two cantos made him famous. Byron's first intention was a poem in the manner of Ariosto, mingling the grave with the vivacious, but the few attempts made in the early cantos to introduce the jesting tone were not successful and soon abandoned. In this style *Don Juan* was a happier effort. The third canto of *Childe Harold* was not published until four years after the first and second, and the fourth not till six years after them. In the interval Byron made great progress as a poetical artist, published his Oriental tales, and rose to the zenith of his fame. Then came the separation from his wife, the quarrel with society, the public obloquy, and he left England never to return. The early cantos were hardly more than a poetical chronicle of his travel, in the later we have a wholly new and distinct poem, the quintessence of Byronism in the maturity of the author's genius. Although he retained the idea of the *Childe*, a pilgrim in exile, 'The wandering outlaw of his own dark mind,' he dropped the useless mask at first adopted of a character not his own, and stood forth confessed as his own hero. At the same time he abandoned the mediaeval words and colour at first introduced, and gave a frankly modern tone to the whole composition. Speaking in his own person, he exchanged the romance of the past for the romance of the present, and thus broke with the literary tradition which had sought for the authentic springs of poetic inspiration in some far-off age. The mediaevalism of Scott was driven out of the field by the passion and power of a newly discovered interest, the romantic gloom of a disillusioned spirit. In the place of the adventures of some knight of chivalry Byron offered the adventures of his own soul on a pilgrimage through the heroic history of Europe. His disillusionment, which found an echo in so many hearts, may be traced to the reaction from the revolutionary dreams from which his generation had awakened, to the spiritual void left by that reaction, to the sceptical rejection of the old religious creeds which accompanied it, and to the poet's own quarrel with society and his consequent estrangement from England and English ideals. The theme of the later cantos of *Childe Harold* may be briefly described as the mutability of all human things. As the melancholy traveller pondered on the ruins of empires once mighty, on the decay of religions, on the transience of human glory, as he pondered on the ignorance of man making his blind voyage across the uncharted waters, he found full justification for his own despair. At times he turns from his sombre reflections to Nature for consolation, Nature which fails not, which repairs the ruins of the past, remains though kingdoms pass, and preserves her loveliness though all human glories fade. It was no novel theme, but Byron's indictment of human life gained its power from the freshness and splendour of its setting, while a piquant flavour was added for contemporary readers by the personal references to the author's ostracism from society and his angry criticism of the value of its judgements.

In *The Prisoner of Chillon* (1816) Byron shows himself still somewhat under the influence of Scott, which predominates in the earlier romances, like *The Corsair* and *The Bride of Abydos*, but here is giving place to that of Shelley and Wordsworth (e. g. lines 329–31). It is improbable that in writing the poem he had in memory any historical facts. Bonnivard, to whom he refers in his only Sonnet, was imprisoned in Chillon, but there is no connexion between his story and that here related.

Byron's intellectual as distinguished from his social estrangement from his countrymen, begun in *Don Juan* and carried on in *Cain*, was finally completed in the *Vision of Judgement* (1822). He there directs his battery of derision against that last and most sacred tenet of English faith, the belief in the British Constitution and the holy office of kingship. The poem arose out of the author's quarrel with Southey, who in the capacity of Poet-Laureate wrote an absurd and indecent panegyric cn George III, entitled *A Vision of Judgement*, described by Byron as 'the apotheosis of George III'. The poem, ridiculous in itself, was prefixed by a violent attack upon Byron as the author of *Don Juan*. Byron's travesty was refused by his own publisher, Murray, and also by Longman, but eventually appeared in Leigh Hunt's journal *The Liberal*. It was accounted so scandalous that the publisher was prosecuted and fined. The *Vision* exhibits Byron's satirical powers in their full strength, and perhaps no poem in the language can compare with it as a sarcastic performance, for humour, irony, flashing scorn. The poet was here writing with absolute sincerity, but writing in a mood of personal irritation which gave edge to his satire.

With the instinct of genius Goethe saw in Byron something more than the accomplished aristocrat, more than the cynical satirist of social conventions. He saw in him the soul of the modern world attempting to free itself from the cramping limitations not only of certain outworn creeds and absurd restrictions, but of all limitations whatever; he saw in him the poet in revolt, the idealist attempting to outsoar time and space and human conditions. In the pride and passion of his youth Byron threw himself upon the world and life to master and enjoy them. They were to yield to him their treasures, they were to supply all the necessities, and these necessities were very many, of his heart and intellect. He was so far successful that he set the conventions at defiance, that he annihilated in the fire of his contempt a thousand abuses of reason, that he hunted down with royal success a legion of hypocrisies and pretences. In his campaign against society Byron held his own, but he suffered defeat at the hands of more powerful enemies. The world gave him less than he asked from it, neither his mind nor his heart achieved the looked-for harvest. He learnt in his own person the lesson that humanity is continuously studying, that the gods are stronger than men, that the soul is harboured in a body which cannot obey its imperial behests, and confined within an inexorable circle from which it can issue only in death. The spectacle of this tremendous struggle with the elemental conditions, of this titanic energy endeavouring to break a way for itself to a region where all desires are satisfied because all desires have been met, fascinated every nation in Europe. And however lawless had been the effort, however much of an outlaw the man who made it, when the word came that at Missolonghi the fiery spirit had put off mortality, it seemed as if human nature itself had suffered some great reverse, as if some conflict, in which all men were personally involved, had gone against the race. ' I thought,' said Tennyson* when the news of Byron's death reached England in 1824, ' I thought that everything was over and finished for every one—that nothing else mattered. I remember I walked out alone and carved " Byron is dead " into the sandstone.' And there was something of moral significance in the fact that at the moment of his death the Greeks who loved him, and thronged the streets to hear news of his state, read in the thunderstorm which then broke over the town the signal of his end, and cried to each other, ' The great man must be dead.'

* See also *Carlyle's Early Life*, by Froude, vol. i, pp. 220-1.

PERCY BYSSHE SHELLEY (1792–1822)

ALASTOR, 1816. ADONAIS, 1821

Alastor, Epipsychidion, and *Adonais* are the longest and most elaborate of Shelley's personal poems. In their larger compass and narrative measures—blank verse, riming couplet, and Spenserian stanza—Shelley utters his deepest and most personal feelings as lyrically as in the *Ode to the West Wind* or the *Lines written in Dejection at Naples.*

Alastor belongs to the years of quixotic, tragic adventure, of intellectual, imaginative ferment which preceded Shelley's final departure from England. It is the first poem that marks the subsidence of that fermentation, the clarifying of the wine of his poetry. The potent influence of Wordsworth, especially the *Excursion*, which had been published in 1814, is traceable in *Alastor*, but rather in the intellectual conception of the poem as stated in the preface than in its imaginative texture. That owes more to Southey than to Wordsworth. The scenery of Shelley's poem, so different from that of the *Excursion*, and the wanderings of the poet, are full of reflections, in Shelley's more poetical imagination and more harmonious verse, of the adventures of Thalaba by ' bitumen lakes ', in ' secret caves ', among ' the fallen towers of Babylon ', and on mysterious boats which sail without much guidance or propulsion by river and sea. The lawlessness of Southey's Oriental scenery, its suggestions of the weird and awe-inspiring, appealed more to Shelley's imagination than Wordsworth's quiet hills and dales ; and the impressions of river and forest scenery had been intensified by his own experience of voyaging by boat down the swift current of the Reuss and the Rhine (*History of a Six Weeks' Tour, &c.*, 1817) and his life ' on the borders of Windsor Forest '.

If the framework and scenery of *Alastor* owe something to Southey, the spirit of the poem is entirely Shelleyan. It is an expression of the two most ardent aspirations of Shelley's poetry, which is all one musical cry of longing and regret,

> O cease ! must hate and death return ?
> Cease ! must men kill and die ?

The one of these aspirations, and that which the preface specially emphasizes, is love, ' intercourse with an intelligence similar to itself,' that love of perfect sympathy and understanding, the passionate pursuit of which is the true history of Shelley's heart. The other is the desire, which his early dabbling in science first quickened into an inextinguishable thirst, to penetrate the secrets of Nature, to read the riddle of life and death. The first is said by Shelley to be the main theme and to contain the lesson of the poem, the lesson of the story of the Solitary in Wordsworth's *Excursion* taught in Shelley's own way; but in truth the second is the more insistent. *Epipsychidion* is the cry of Shelley's soul for perfect love, his *Vita Nuova*. When he wrote *Alastor*, Shelley believed himself to be dying, and it is, as much as the *Second Anniversary*, a *meditatio mortis*. The passionate question at the heart of the poem is, What is death ? Whither does it conduct ? Does it open the doorway to the ' mysterious paradise ' of sleep ? Or is it the ' brother of Ruin ', the end of all that is noble, and rare, and beautiful ? The closing lines are an agonized protest against the unspeakable waste involved,—

> When some surpassing Spirit
> Whose light adorned the world around it leaves
> Those who remain behind . . .
> But pale despair and cold tranquillity,
> Nature's vast frame, the web of human things,
> Birth and the grave that are not as they were.

Keats was such a surpassing spirit ; and the *Adonais* might be described as the *Alastor* rewritten for a different occasion, under other literary influence, and in a higher, clearer, nobler strain. Shelley's poem should be read with its immediate models, Bion's *Lament for Adonis*, and Moschus' *Lament for Bion*. *Adonais* is just a modification of Adonais intended to suggest that Keats was as dear to Urania, the Goddess of Heavenly Love and Muse of high poetry, poetry that quickens in men's souls the love of liberty (notice the poets with whom Shelley associates Keats,—Milton and Lucan, as well as Sidney and Chatterton), as Adonis was to Aphrodite. The poem abounds in borrowed phrases, elaborated sometimes (v. 15) into conceits, at others (v. 18) illumined with a new splendour of passion, and description, and cadence. But whatever Shelley may borrow for the vestment of his song, its spirit is his own, and its burden is essentially that of *Alastor*, a lament for the want of love among men, a passionate questioning of the tantalizing mystery of death, ' that contemplation of inexhaustible melancholy whose shadow eclipses the brightness of the world ' (*Fragment on a Future State*). The young poet dies because he cannot find on earth the love he has dreamed of : Keats is dead because his song evoked not love but

> Envy and calumny and hate ;

and his death is contemplated from the eighteenth to the twenty-first stanzas in the same mood of passionate horror in which *Alastor* closes. But at the end of *Adonais* there is a change. The pastoral dirge closed traditionally on a note of hope and consolation, and to this too Shelley attains in his own way. In the most rapt and intense stanzas he ever wrote Shelley seems to see Death and Life change places, and to discover a deeper source than he had yet suspected of his own discontent. Kings and priests;

> Envy and calumny and hate and pain
> And that unrest which men miscall delight;

are all but shadows of the one evil, finite life. That is 'the body of this death', the

> earthly load
> Of death called life; which us from life doth sever,

and death itself is the portal by which we return to

> That Benediction which the eclipsing curse
> Of birth can quench not.

In his beautiful essay on Shelley, the late Francis Thompson contrasts Milton's hope with Shelley's want of hope of personal immortality. But we are too ignorant of the relation between the individual and the whole, we know too little what we mean when we say we hope for personal immortality, to be quite sure that the antithesis is a sound one. To seek, as Shelley does, a life in God, 'the One,' 'the Eternal,' and to crave for a fuller personal life cannot in the long run be contradictory aspirations, for in God there can be no loss, in Him the meaning of our individual personality is hidden. But these things are only descried for moments in the dream consciousness of poetry.

JOHN KEATS (1795–1821)

No poet was ever more indisputably a child of the Muse than Keats; he was a singer born. But he was not ignorant that 'a good poet's made as well as born', and it is the more interesting to note under what masters he put himself to school and what were the doctrines he most eagerly imbibed. His letters tell us where for him, in his age, the deeper currents ran, to what books and scenes he naturally turned, whither in history and poetry he was chiefly drawn, and the stars by which he steered on his too brief voyage. We learn that it was his early creed that 'poetry should surprise by a fine excess', that he prayed for 'a life of sensations rather than of thoughts', that like the youthful Shakespeare, and most good poets since, he was intoxicated by verbal melody, the 'fine sounds' that 'were floating wild about the earth'. We learn that on a visit to Scotland he wrote, 'I know not how it is, the clouds, the sky, the houses all seem Anti-Grecian and Anti-Charlemagnish', thus placing, as of equal interest and inspiration, the Greek world with the Middle Ages. We know that poetry in those days was for Keats no earnest-eyed Muse of social reform or grave philosophy, that she was simply 'The singing maid with pictures in her eyes'. But we know too that he was soon, whether for better or for worse, concerned with a drastic revision of his literary creed. He talked of 'devoting himself to the ardours rather than the pleasures of song'. 'I find,' he wrote, 'there is no worthy pursuit but the doing of some good in the world. . . . I have been hovering some time between an exquisite sense of the luxurious and a love of philosophy,' and again, 'Some think I have lost that poetic fire and ardour they say I once had. The fact is I perhaps have, but instead of that I hope I shall substitute a more thoughtful and quiet power. I am more contented to read and think.' What would have come of these second thoughts we cannot tell, save that, had he lived, the poetry of his maturer life would have offered points of wide contrast to that which he has left us, and that, like Milton, he would have increased his fame without overshadowing his younger self.

In the three poems upon mediaeval subjects here given Keats displays his sympathy with three aspects of mediaeval life and feeling—in the *Eve of St. Mark*, with the beauty and spiritual symbolism of its church ritual; in the *Eve of St. Agnes*, with that external wealth of colour and picturesqueness which Scott found so fascinating: in *Isabella*, where there is no attempt to render these accessories or make decorative use of them, with the intensity of passion that triumphs over the natural human repugnance to death and all the physical horrors which come in its train, that extreme of devotion and loyalty which appears so often and so poignantly as an element in early Christian art. For though the 'wormy circumstance' of *Isabella*, as Keats himself describes it, recalls the naked terrors of the early Romancists, the poet has added the note of inextinguishable affection, partaking of infinity, which outlives and outlasts the mortal mansion, and is yet so far earthly that it cannot separate the beloved spirit from the beloved body it once inhabited. And in this mingled Christian and Pagan feeling, this fervour of devotion both to soul and flesh, this almost spiritual savagery, we are reminded of many a mediaeval picture, which dwells with strange constancy upon the physical wounds and sufferings of saint and lover and martyr, and with all its faith in the unseen and eternal world will not let go its hold upon the seen and temporal, loyal with a kind of unconquerable humanity to the ruins of a shattered but beloved and once noble fabric.

Hyperion, in which the youthful Atlas endeavoured to support the too vast orb of the Greek mythology, a task hardly indeed too great for him but for his years, was discontinued, yet the measure of his success disarmed criticism and astonished the poets themselves who best knew the magnitude of the undertaking. 'He contrived,' as Byron said, to talk about the gods 'much as they might have been supposed to speak'. Among the later poets who found high inspiration in the Middle Ages only Swinburne shared with Keats the same full sympathy with ancient art. Rossetti exhibited absolutely no interest in it, and Morris declared that he 'loathed all classical art and literature'. The breadth of Keats's genius may be partly judged by the breadth of his appreciations.

ALFRED TENNYSON (1809–1892)

When one turns to Tennyson from the rich luxuriance, the abundant and splendid but unequal poetry of Wordsworth and Coleridge and Shelley and Keats, the image that rises in the mind is that of a gardener—not a Popean gardener, caring only for neatness and uniformity, but a gardener who knows that the beauty of nature may be enhanced by art and arrangement, the massing of blooms, the varying of effects, the background of velvet lawn and grassy bank and ordered hedgerow; above all, by the enrichment of the soil, which adds a deeper crimson to the rose and blends with simpler flowers the splendours of the exotic. In his pictures of nature; his pastoral and classical idylls; his mediaeval studies, he continues the tradition of the earlier poets, but in his own way. His landscapes have a less manifold wealth of detail, a less purely sensuous intensity than Keats, and still less of Wordsworth's deep spiritual significance; but they are drawn and coloured with the conscious care of the pictorial artist who has studied them intently through half-closed eyes, noting the values of the colours, the balance and arrangement of the significant features. Consider the ordering of the opening picture in *Oenone*, the sense of colour-values in such lines :—

> Now droops the milkwhite peacock like a ghost,
> And like a ghost she glimmers on to me.

The earliest anticipation of the Pre-Raphaelite movement in English poetry may perhaps be traced in Collins's personifications; more clearly in Coleridge's picture of Christabel's room, and some of Keats's earliest sketches :—

> Lo! I must tell a tale of chivalry;
> For while I muse *the lance points slantingly
> Athwart the morning air*: some lady sweet
> Who cannot *feel for cold her tender feet*
> From the worn top of some old battlement
> Hails it with tears:

as well as in his *Eve of St. Mark*; but Tennyson's early poems, with their clear drawing and colouring, and the emotional significance of the details presented, are the immediate precursors of the movement.

This same conscious art distinguishes Tennyson's expression of the mood in which poems like the *Lady of Shalott*, the *Lotos-Eaters*, *Oenone*, *Tithonus*, and so many others, are conceived. An intensely realized dramatic mood is essential to Pre-Raphaelite poetry and painting. And the same conscious, studied effects are Tennyson's contribution to the new music which Coleridge and Shelley and Keats had brought back into English lyric measures and blank verse. There are finer qualities—a higher, rarer lyric note, more splendid and perfect cadences —in the best verse of all these than of Tennyson; but no poet has maintained a more equable perfection of measured movement and pure, flute-like melody in a surprising variety of metres.

As with Tennyson's art so is it with the thought and sentiment of his classical, romantic, and philosophical poems. Tennyson has not divined with such marvellous inspiration the spirit of Greek art and of the Greek worship of beauty as Keats in the *Ode on a Grecian Urn* or *Hyperion*; his classical idylls are not informed with the moral sublimity of *Laodamia* and *Dion*; but the soil on which *Oenone* and *Lucretius* and *Ulysses* are grown is fertilized with culture, with an intimate knowledge of the classical authors, and that knowledge is used to express moods of simple and enduring pathos and interest. Of the mediaeval spirit, in like manner, he had no profound apprehension; but of its literature he has a wider knowledge than Keats, of its picturesque aspects a more accurate appreciation; so much so that the description of the armed Sir Lancelot—

> All in the blue unclouded weather
> Thick jewell'd shone the saddle leather—

has been taken by Ruskin as a text for a disquisition on the beauty of mediaeval dress.

The burden of Tennyson's thought on politics and life may be studied entire in *In Memoriam* (1850), although certain moods are developed more fully in other poems, and some of them with a more troubled intensity in his last work. For though the death of Arthur Henry Hallam (1833) provided the occasion of the poem and the centre round which the thought moves, it reflects the whole conflict of a mind clinging to a religious and ideal conception of life with the naturalistic, Lucretian trend of thought in the mid-century. The development of biological science and historical criticism were altering the whole character of the conflict between faith and reason from what it had been in the first conflict between Christianity and Deism or between Christianity and Deism revived and animated with Revolutionary fervour in the work of Godwin and Shelley. Tennyson, who divined with wonderful sensitiveness the trend of thought—for he wrote before Darwin and Spencer had given distinctness to the theory of evolution—can accept entirely neither the mystical conservatism to which Wordsworth attained after years of hope and disappointment nor Shelley's belief in the regenerative power of political changes, while he had no sympathy with his antagonism to Christianity. He sought in the idea of evolution a reconciliation. The *In Memoriam* is a poetic vindication of what Kant calls the postulates of reason—God, Freedom, Immortality—with an appeal for their ultimate vindication to ' the far future '—

> The one, far-off, divine event
> To which the whole creation moves.

The poem shows the influence of Goethe, to whom the first verse refers, of Shakespeare's sonnets, but more especially of Dante and Petrarch. ' The Tuscan poets ' had been among the favourite studies of Hallam and Tennyson. He would seem to have thought of *In Memoriam* as his *Divina Commedia*, beginning in sorrow, ending in hope. Even the verse —which Tennyson adopted without knowing of its previous use by Ben Jonson and Lord Herbert of Cherbury—is probably an endeavour to secure without imitation the effect of the *terza rima*, of a stanza which may stand by itself or may link itself easily to that which follows.

It is to the beauty of its workmanship, the Virgilian tenderness of its humanity, that *In Memoriam* owes its value, and it is this intensely human note in Tennyson's poetry which limits its range in the region of religious ecstasy and vision. Judging *In Memoriam*, not by the tenor of its argument, but by the final impression it leaves on the imagination, one is constrained to say that the earth was still too sweet to Tennyson for him to divine a meaning in death. Life, despite one shattering blow, is yet so full of happy memories and glad anticipations that of another life he can think only in terms of this. His friend would have been a member of Parliament here had he lived ; he must be serving there ' In such great offices as suit the full-grown energies of heaven '. But as within the compass of this volume we may see in Donne and Milton and Shelley, it is when the poet feels intensely the limitations of this life, the worthlessness of its values, that he attains to the vision of another life which can be described only in myth and symbol :—

> O fond anxiety of mortal men !
> How vain and inconclusive arguments
> Are those which make thee beat thy wings below.

For statutes one, and one for aphorisms
Was hunting ; this the priesthood followed ; that
By force or sophistry aspired to rule ;
To rob another ; and another sought,
By civil business, wealth ; one moiling lay
Tangled in net of sensual delight ;
And one to listless indolence resign'd ;
What time from all these empty things escaped,
With Beatrice I thus gloriously
Was borne aloft, and made the guest of heaven.

ROBERT BROWNING (1812–1889)

A poet's surest title to coming fame is probably to be found, not in his acceptance by the public, which is generally wrong, or right too late, but by the poets of the generation immediately following his own. Jeffrey might declare on reading the *Excursion*, 'This will never do,' but Wordsworth was already shaping the poetry of Byron and Shelley and Keats ; and in like manner, while he was still *caviare* to the multitude, Browning, in some respects more than Tennyson, was inspiring Rossetti and Morris and Swinburne. And the poets were captivated by the poetry—not by the philosophy of *Paracelsus*, the religion of *Rabbi ben Ezra*, the apologetics of *Cleon* and *A Death in the Desert*; not, in short, by Browning's teaching, about which so much was to be heard later, when Browning was at last discovered, but by the poetic and dramatic art of his studies in mood and character.

The thought of Browning does not differ profoundly from that of Tennyson. It represents the same conflict between a religious, idealist temperament and the Lucretian trend of thought in an age of physical science and historical criticism : but Browning delights more than Tennyson in nimble dialectics, and his spirit is one of a more buoyant, at times facile, optimism. The general scope of Browning's art, too, is not so distinct from Tennyson's as it appeared to contemporaries. The dramatic lyric or idyll, the dramatic expression in a poem more or less lyrical in form of some mood, some phase of character, is the *forte* of both rather than the personal lyric of Wordsworth and Shelley or the dramatic presentation of character in action. The mood is often more intensely realized by Tennyson, and his expression of it more equably finished and musical. But Browning's range is wider, his insight subtler, his presentation more instinct with life and movement and humour.

One of the most felicitous appreciations of Browning's genius came from a poet of the generation preceding his own, the veteran Landor :—

There is delight in singing though none hear
Beside the singer ; and there is delight
In praising though the praiser sit alone
And see the praised far off him, far above.
Shakespeare is not our poet but the world's ;
Therefore of him no speech ! and brief for thee,
Browning ! Since Chaucer was alive and hale
No man hath walkt along our roads with step
So active, so inquiring eye, or tongue
So varied in discourse. But warmer climes

Give brighter plumage, stronger wing ; the breeze
Of Alpine heights thou playest with, borne on
Beyond Sorrento to Amalti, where
The Sirens wait thee singing song for song.

This comparison with Chaucer probably touches what is essential in Browning's genius more closely than any dissertation on his philosophy of life. The same genial dramatic curiosity and sympathy with which Chaucer portrays his Canterbury pilgrims, or humanizes the weakness of Criseyde and the knavery of Pandarus, inspires Browning's studies of problematical characters like Sordello and Paracelsus ; his brilliant miniatures of conscienceless Renaissance rascals like the duke in *My Last Duchess* or the bishop anxious to outshine his rival even after death ; his parleyings with and *apologiae* for all sorts and conditions of men. Of his artists, Fra Lippo Lippi is a type that suggests Chaucer himself. Pictor Ignotus would have been quite comprehensible to the poets of Hugh of Lincoln and other tender and edifying saints' legends. Andrea del Sarto would certainly have had his monologue cut short by the Host as too heavy and depressing. Browning's range is wider ; his analysis deeper ; his method more philosophic, less simply poetic and concrete ; his lyrical impulse stronger. He has the historic sense of which the Middle Ages knew nothing. Not only men of all ranks and professions but of all climes and times interested him, from David or St. John in the desert to an Italian patriot or a Cardinal Wiseman of to-day. But in both poets we find the same amused and sympathetic interest in all that smacks of human nature. The dominant note of Browning's sometimes fantastic music is ' the C major of this life '. He has not Donne's complexity of soul, though his love-poetry recalls that of the metaphysicals by its passionate yet intellectual evolution, and its realistic contempt for conventional imagery.

The most interesting difference between Chaucer and Browning emerges when one considers the serious intention which runs through the work of the latter. For Browning is a teacher, as Chaucer is in the main a satirist. In the work of both an intention can generally be divined. Neither the one nor the other has the almost superhuman creative indifference of Shakespeare. But in Chaucer the secular and the religious are separated from one another with the sharp dualism of the Middle Ages ; in Browning they constantly interpenetrate. Bold as Browning's art and humour sometimes are he could never have written in the detached, naughty vein of Chaucer in the *Wife of Bath's* prologue and some of his tales. For all his wide sympathies Browning remains at heart a Camberwell dissenter, moral in a definite, English sense of the word, very much ' hand in glove with them above ' (to borrow a phrase of Mr. Hardy's rustics), terribly sure that he knows why God did this or that, and ' what all the blessed Evil's for '. Chaucer has a certain sympathy with the common sense and Epicurean worldliness of the Monk (' And I seyde, his opinioun was good '), but he sets him in sharp opposition to his true Christian, the poor parson. It interests Browning to show us in Bishop Blougram a certain blend of the two, a man of the world who is at bottom ' a good man of religioun ' ; an intellectual sceptic whose will believes. His apology is one of the most brilliant of Browning's longer studies, because in Blougram there is so much of Browning himself, the man of the world, the Epicurean lover of all the good things of experience, the intellectual athlete, the ' hell-deep ' religious instincts which no love of this world or play of sceptical dialectics could invalidate. Among the seers of poetry Browning is not likely to take a place, despite his high aims and his philosophy. But English poetry would be vastly poorer without his tireless dramatic curiosity, his buoyant vitality, his deep and reverend sense of the worth of life and love.

Of the faults and obscurity of Browning's style much was said in his life-time. His earliest poems were frequently obscure, his later frequently diffuse. But the art of a poem like *My Last Duchess* is as faultless and inevitable as that of the most jewelled idyll Tennyson ever wrote. It can never be said of Browning's poems, as of Southey's, that they should have been written in prose. His work is rhythmical and poetic to the core ; and nowhere is the poet more obvious than in the similes. Swinburne declared that the finest lines in English literature are these from Sordello :—

> As the King-bird with ages in his plumes
> Travels to die in his ancestral glooms.

MATTHEW ARNOLD (1822–1888)

In the poetry of Matthew Arnold the elegiac note prevails. Of a spirit less buoyant than Browning, more critical than Tennyson, he found a certain bitterness, *amari aliquid*, in the wells of their inspiration. The meaning of life was less obvious to him, human ambitions less worthy, the sources of happiness less abundant, the grounds of hope less secure than to the poets of the previous generation. The tide of belief in revelation was ebbing fast from a desolate shore :—

> But now I only hear
> Its melancholy, long withdrawing roar,
> Retreating, to the breath
> Of the night-wind, down the vast edges drear
> And naked shingles of the world.

' What gain', as wrote one of his contemporaries, ' to watch for an hour the inscrutable pageant, to be summoned out of nothingness into illusion, and evolved but to aspire and to decay ?' Arnold was not sure of the values by which men were content to walk, and accepted life, it would seem, as a doubtful gift, in the spirit of passionless Stoic acquiescence rather than with eagerness and joyful desire of it. He knew himself to belong to an age of questions and hesitations rather than of answers and actions. For consolation amid moral and intellectual perplexities he turned to nature and to art, which supplied in some measure and degree the support more generally sought and obtained in religion, to nature and art, where the spirit of man can forget itself and the discords that vex it, and escape into wider regions of passionless and unbroken harmony. In *Thyrsis*, where he laments a poet who, like himself, was burdened by the uncertainty of human issues, and in *The Scholar Gipsy*, he touches the scenes and subjects,—English landscape, classical art and literature,— which were for him the best spiritual simples. In *Sohrab and Rustum* he attempts heroic narrative in the restrained, disinterested classical manner he never tired of praising, but it is difficult not to believe that at least in the concluding passage which describes Oxus as 'a foiled circuitous wanderer' the poet touches as in an allegory the history of his own disturbed and divided spirit.

EDWARD FITZGERALD (1809–1883)

The Bodleian MS. of the *Rubáiyát* of Omar Khayyám, a Persian astronomer and poet who lived in the eleventh century, was brought to Fitzgerald's notice by his friend Prof. Cowell. He found something of himself in the old poet, and his imagination was fired. But Fitzgerald's version is rather a new poem inspired by Omar's stanzas than an actual rendering. Poetry is untranslatable, but it has sometimes happened that the music of an earlier poet so charmed a later of another race and language that he re-wrote the score for a different instrument, it may be of finer quality and tone. It was so with Fitzgerald. The first edition, containing seventy-five stanzas, was printed by Quaritch, in 1859, as a shilling pamphlet, but in default of purchasers was relegated to a bookstall, where it was sold for a penny. There it was discovered by some friends of Rossetti's, and quickly attained celebrity in a narrow literary circle. The second edition, containing 110 stanzas, was published in 1868; the third in 1872, and the fourth in 1879, each containing 101 stanzas, were the last in the author's lifetime.

Omar's theme, the unconquered mystery of life and death, the flux, beyond arrest, of human things, the sorrowful and swift flight of beauty and joy, was a theme old as the world itself. But his philosophy, touched with all the sadness of an unwilling surrender to human destiny, enriched with Eastern imagery, and set to new and stately harmonies, ministered to the temper of a generation later than that which found rest in the philosophy of *In Memoriam* or *Christmas Eve and Easter Day*, a generation to which intellectual despair was very near, and Epicurean counsels seemed the only wisdom. Nor is it likely to lose its power, so subtly does it render the bitter-sweet of reflective existence, the thought of beauty that must be loved and yet must be relinquished, the uneasy fear, never wholly to be banished from the hearts of men, that their exile from the joys of conscious being will be without return, that the only affections they have known can never again be known. It may well remain, while the language lasts, its most finished expression of the spirit's darker broodings, its most searching music in the minor key.

GLOSSARY

This glossary, primarily of Chaucer's words, is intended for the general reader. The student will use his English and Middle English dictionaries and historical grammar. It makes no pretence to exhaust either the words which might be glossed or the meanings which those glossed might bear, but merely to explain such words as might trouble a general reader, and to give as accurately as possible the meanings which they bear in these texts. In the case of Burns's words we have made careful use of the glossary which he attached to the Edinburgh edition of his works.

Middle English (i.e. in this volume, Chaucer's) spelling is phonetic, and many words which appear strange to the eye will be found familiar when pronounced. Later English spelling became chaotic owing to changes of sound, the silencing of letters which are still printed, the influence of analogies and etymologies real or mistaken.

To give a full account of the changes in English pronunciation is impossible, but the following notes on a few sounds may be of service in reading Chaucer and Burns, and in appreciating some Elizabethan and later rimes :—

(1) *ā*. Chaucer's long *a* (e. g. in ' name ') had the broad sound heard in the modern interjection 'ah!' This sound was later what phonologists call ' fronted ' (*æ*), getting the sound of the *a* in ' can ', but long, which is probably its Elizabethan sound. This passed through the long sound of *e* in 'ken' (which is its general value in Scotch, in e. g. ' name ', 'face') to its modern sound—' eh ' in Northern, *e-i* in Southern English.

(2) *ē*. Long *e* had in Chaucer's English two sounds, the close sound heard in the modern ' they ' (e.g. ' he ', ' see '); the open sound heard in the modern ' there ' (e.g. sea). These are difficult to distinguish in Chaucer without some knowledge of their origin, but roughly, those which had the close sound are in later English spelt with *ee*, those with the open sound with *ea* (e.g. ' beech ' and ' sheath '). The close sound soon after the Middle English period changed to the *ee* sound it now has, and words such as ' be ', ' me ', ' decree ', were pronounced in Shakespeare's time as now. But the open *e* retained its sound for a considerable time, which explains such rimes as, e. g. p. 113 (Ben Jonson), ' sweat '—' heat ', ' were '—' appeare ', ' Hemisphere '—' there '. Later this open *e* became close *e* (eh !), and Pope rimes (p. 189), ' obey '—' tea '. Ultimately its pronunciation became that of *ee*, so that ' tea '—' see ' is now a correct rime.

(3) *ī*. Long *i* has in Chaucer the continental sound of long *i*—our *ee* in ' see '. This early became a diphthong *a-i*, and was identical with the then pronunciation of the old French diphthong *oi*. Dryden and Pope (e.g. p. 206, ll. 346–7) rime ' join—line ' (ja-in—la-in). Later the influence of the spelling gave ' join ' its present sound (jo-in), but in dialectal English and in Scotch the older sound remains—see Burns, p. 261, ll. 37–42, ' while—style—isle—boil '.

(4) *ō*. Long *o* in Chaucer had two sounds—*close* as heard in modern ' so ', *open* as in the Italian open *o*, somewhat as in ' soar '. These two are not as a rule rimed together. The former passed into *oo*—e. g. ' rote ' (p. 1) is our ' root '. The open *o* (' soar ') was the only

o sound in early Modern English (sixteenth and seventeenth centuries), and is very general in Scotch.

(5) *ū*. Long *u* (written under the influence of French orthography *ou*) had in Chaucer the continental value, i.e. *oo* in e.g. Modern English 'good'. This fairly early became, possibly influenced by the spelling, diphthongal *ou*, *ow*. In Scotch, however, this did not occur, and 'house', 'cow', &c., sound 'hoose', 'coo'.

(6) About the sound of *aw* (e.g. in 'awe', 'law'), and of *a* before *l* (e.g. all, call) in early Modern English (sixteenth and seventeenth centuries), there is some division of opinion among philologists. Sweet and others maintain that it had, as in Chaucer, a diphthongal sound, much, if not quite, as to-day. Viëtor, appealing to Ben Jonson and other grammarians, holds that it had simply the sound of a broad, open *a* (āh!). In Scotch it has generally this sound, e.g. 'lawfu'' (lah-fu'), and a final *l* is frequently dropped, e.g. p. 262, *a'*, i.e. 'all'.

(7) The diphthongs *ai*, *ei* (*or* 'ay', 'ey') are in Chaucer and in Early Modern English real diphthongs, and in Chaucer possibly distinct from one another. About the first part of the sixteenth century they were assimilated, and ultimately took their present sound of 'eh!' In Scotch the diphthong is frequently preserved, e.g. key (keh-ee).

(8) *ow* (sometimes *ou*) in Chaucer is a diphthong, as in modern 'how'. In early modern English it was, and in Scotch frequently is, a diphthong in words in which it has since lost this sound and become simply *ō*, (oh!) in Modern Northern English, e.g. 'though', 'grow', 'soule'. Shakespeare rimes 'growing—allowing'. In Southern English the sound seems still to be diphthongal.

(9) In Middle English, vowels that had been long in Old English were frequently shortened before dentals. This checked the normal development of the sound. Thus Old English or Anglo-Saxon 'rēad' and 'dēad' should have become 'reed' and 'deed' in sound (see Note 2). In Scotch it will be noticed this has happened, e.g. (p. 267) Burns rimes 'heed'—'speed'—'thread'—'dead'.

(10) In Chaucer's English *gh* had two sounds, that of German 'Ich' as in 'knight', 'night', and that of German 'Ach' as in 'broughte'. His *ch* was pronounced as in Modern English, e.g. 'chirche'. In Scotch both *ch* and *gh* have the sounds of Chaucer's *gh*, e.g. night, broght (or nicht, brocht).

(11) In Scotch *d* is often dropped after *l* and *n*, e.g. 'warl',' 'an',' 'frien'.' At p. 267, ll. 67–72, the final *d* of 'understand', &c., though written, was probably not sounded. Burns's spelling, it may be noted, though often, is not uniformly phonetic. He mingles Scotch and English freely. Only the English pronunciation of 'brows' (p. 267, l. 50), will rime with the Scotch 'howes' (l. 53). His riming is often very partial.

(12) The final *e* in Chaucer's words is, or may be if the metre requires, pronounced when the next word begins with a consonant. The preterite termination -ed is pronounced when written till about the end of the seventeenth century.

aboghte, atoned for, paid for.
abood (n.), delay.
abrayde, started, awoke.
abregge, to abridge.
accord, *acord*, agreement.
achat, purchase, thing bought.

achatour, buyer.
acorde, to agree.
adrad, *aferd*, *afered*, *affrayed*, afraid, terrified.
Aeonian (Tennyson), secular, lasting for ages.

affyle, to polish, smooth.

agaste him, was afraid.

agrief, take, take amiss.

agon, agoon, gone, past.

aiblins (Burns), perhaps.

airns (Burns), irons.

alaunts, a species of dog, used for hunting wild beasts as the bear or wolf: 'Three alans, wolf-greyhounds, that is' (Scott).

al be, although.

alderbest (see *aller*), best of all.

ale-stake, a horizontal stake projecting from an ale-house to support the sign,—a garland or bush.

algate, always.

aller, of all—*Our aller*, of all of us.

also, as.

amaranth (Tennyson), a celestial flower that never fades.

amblere, a nag, an easy-paced horse.

ambrosial (Shelley), celestial; (Tennyson), fragrant.

amort (Keats), half dead.

amorwe, on the morrow.

amounte, mean, indicate, denote.

anadem (Shelley), a chaplet, garland.

and = an, if.

anhanged, hung up.

anlas (or *anelace*), knife or dagger, usually worn at the girdle.

anon, anoon, anon, forthwith.

apalled, become pale or feeble.

apayd, appeased, satisfied.

ape (metaphorically), a fool.

apostem (Donne), a large deep-seated abscess, impostume.

apparailling, preparation.

apyked, trimmed, adorned.

arest, in, couched, levelled (of lances).

areste, seizure, custody.

areste, to stop (a horse).

aretted, accounted, imputed, deemed.

arm-greet, as thick as a man's arm.

armipotente, mighty in arms.

arrerage, arrears.

ars-metrik, arithmetic.

arwe, arrow.

aryve, arrival, or perhaps disem-

barkation (of troops). Best MSS. read *Armee*, i. e. an armed expedition, Armada.

aslake, to assuage, appease, slake.

as nouthe, as now, at present.

asseged, besieged.

assoiling, absolution, pardon.

astat, estate, rank.

asterte, to escape, start away.

astoned, astonished.

astored, stored.

asur, azure.

athamaunte, adamant, a fabulous rock or mineral of surpassing hardness. *Consult* N.E.D.

atrede, to surpass in counsel, wisdom.

atrenne, outrun.

atte, at the.

attempree, temperate.

avaunt, boast.

ava (Burns), of all, at all.

avadavat (Keats), love-bird.

avale (Sackville), descend, lower, degrade.

ave (Tennyson), farewell.

aventure, chance.

avisioun, vision.

avoy, fie!

avys, consideration, opinion.

ayeins, against.

ayel, grandfather, ancestor.

balled, bald.

bane, destruction, death.

bareyn, bareyne, bare, devoid of, unfruitful.

barmie (Burns), fermenting, working like barm.

barres, ornaments of a girdle.

basto (Pope), ace of clubs.

batailed, indented as a wall with battlements.

bauldricke (Spenser), see *bawdrik*.

bawdrik, a belt or girdle worn transversely across the chest.

bayne (Sackville), bathe.

bear (Burns), barley.

bedreynt (Sackville), drenched.

beer, did bear.

beggestere, beggar, *orig.* a beggar-woman, and perhaps so here.

bem, beem, beam, rafter.

bemes, trumpets, horns.

bent, hillside, slope, field.

bergamott (Marvell), a fine kind of pear.

besouth (Burns), south of.

bet, better.

bete, to beat, *p.p.* beaten, embroidered, ornamented.

bete, to supply with fuel, kindle.

bi-bled, covered over with blood.

bi-hote (*v.*), promise (*v.*).

bi-knewe, acknowledged, confessed.

bi-knowe, to acknowledge.

bile, bill, beak.

bill, doctor's (Pope), prescription.

bill (Burns), bull.

billies (Burns), fellows.

binne, bin, chest.

birk (Burns), birch.

bisette, to employ.

bismotered, stained—probably with rust.

bit, bids, commands.

biwreye, to make known, reveal, betray.

bizz (Burns), flurry.

blankmanger, a white coloured dish made of grated chicken, cream, and other ingredients.

blate (Burns), bashful.

blellum (Burns), babbler.

bleynte, blenched, started back.

blyve, quickly, forthwith.

bocher, butcher.

boddle (Burns), farthing.

bokeler, buckler, small round shield.

bokelinge, buckling.

boket, bucket.

boles, bulls.

bone, boone, prayer, petition.

boon, bone.

boor (*plu.* bores), boar.

boord (Burns), board.

boortrees (Burns), elders, 'planted much of old in hedges of barnyards, &c.' (Burns).

boras, borax.

bord, table.

bore (Burns), chink.

borwe, pledge, security.

bote, remedy.

boteler, butler.

bouk, body, belly.

bour, inner room, where the master and mistress slept,—distinguished from the 'halle' or public room (where, in N.P.T., the hens slept).

bracer, guard for the arm, where it is struck by the bowstring—of wood sometimes.

brast, burst.

braun, muscle.

brawlie (Burns), well.

braxie, 'a morkin sheep' (Burns), i. e. a sheep that has died, not been killed. 'Some sorry morkin that unbidden dies' (Hall's *Satires*, 1597).

brayde, started.

bream, bream (a fresh-water fish).

brede, breadth.

breef (Burns), spell.

breme, fiercely, furiously.

bren, bran, chaff.

brenne, *p.p. brend*, to burn.

brenningly, fiercely, ardently.

breres, briars.

bresten, to burst.

bretful, brimful.

bretherhed, brotherhood, fraternity.

briddes, birds.

brogue (Burns), trick.

brondes, firebrands, logs for burning.

brouke, to have the use of, enjoy.

broyded, braided, plaited.

browding, embroidery.

bugloss, the blue (Crabbe), *Lycopsis arvensis*, whose leaves are 'blue, bristly, lanceolate', and which grows in 'fields and wastes'. The name is applied to other flowers, e. g. *Echium vulgare*, which is pink.

bulte, sift.

burdies (Burns), maidens.

burdoun, a stif, a strong bass accompaniment.

burgeys, citizen, burgess.

burned, burnished.

buskin (Jonson), a kind of half boot or a high shoe worn by actors in tragedy among the ancients, in contradistinction to the *sock* worn by comedians.

but, unless.

but (*prep.*) (Burns), without.

by and by, side by side.

by-iaped, deceived, befooled.

byke (Burns), hive.

caird (Burns), tinker, gipsy, beggar.

caitif, wretched, a wretch.

can, know, knows ; acknowledge.

cannie (Burns), quiet, cautious.

cantel, corner, cantle.

cantraip (Burns), magic, sleight.

caravanserai (Omar). An Eastern inn where caravans put up.

careful, sorrowful.

careyne, carcase.

carl, churl.

carlin (Burns), beldam, gossip.

carol, a round dance accompanied by singing.

carpe, to talk, converse.

cas, quiver.

cast, device, plot.

caste, casten, to plan, devise, consider, suppose.

catapus, catapuce, lesser spurge, *Euphorbia Lathyris*.

catel, wealth, goods, stock, *opp. to* 'rente', income.

caytyves, pl. of caitif.

cedar, juice of (Herrick), a preservative.

ceint, cincture, girdle.

celle, a smaller religious house dependent on some larger one.

centaure, centaury, a plant whose properties were discovered by Chiron the Centaur; in N.P.T. the lesser centaury (*Erythraea Centaurium*), purging phlegm, and choler (see *humours*).

cerial, belonging to the species of oak called *Cerrus*, 'quercia ceriale' (Boccaccio).

ceruce, white lead.

cesternes (Marlowe), cisterns, *here* eyes.

champ clos (Byron), tilt-yard.

champartye, a partnership in power.

chanters (Burns), bagpipes, *strictly* the drone of a bagpipe.

chapman, a merchant (Burns), pedlar.

charlock (Crabbe), field-mustard (*Sinapis arvensis*).

char, car, chariot.

charge, burden, consideration.

charnel, a mortuary chapel, charnel-house.

chasteyn, a chestnut-tree.

chaunterie, chantrey, an endow-ment for the payment of a priest to sing mass for the soul of the founder, or as he might appoint.

chese, imper. chees, to choose.

chevisaunce, money-lending, usury.

chiel (Burns), young fellow.

chirking, shrieking, grating noise.

chivachye, an expedition or raid of mounted troops.

citole, a kind of musical instrument with strings.

claree, wine mixed with honey and spices.

clarioun, clarion, trumpet.

clash (Burns), talk.

cleekit (Burns), took hold.

clepen, to call, cry, name.

clerk, a scholar, a student at the University.

clos, enclosure, yard.

clothered, clotted.

clout (Burns), hoof.

clymacterick (Marvell), critical, dangerous.

coft (Burns), bought.

colere, choler, red or yellow bile.

col-fox, the brant-fox, 'distinguished by a greater admixture of black in its fur'. N.E.D.

colpons, see *culpons*.

colure (Keats), 'Each of two great circles which intersect each other at right angles at the poles, and divide the equinoctial and the ecliptic into four equal parts'. N.E.D.

compas, circle, circumference.

compassing, contrivance.

compeer, gossip, comrade.

compleccioun, temperament, constitution.

conne, know, be able, see *can*.

conscience, feeling, 'sensibility'.

contek, contest.

coost (Burns), cast.

cootie (Burns), a wooden kitchen-dish—used here (p. 263) like a scoop for bailing a boat.

cop, top of anything.

cope, a cloak, cape.

coppe, cup.

corage, heart, spirit, courage.

core (Burns), company.

coroune, crown, garland.

corrumpable, corruptible.
corrumpe, to corrupt.
corven, cut (*p.p.*).
cote, cottage.
cote armure, a garment worn over armour, upon which the heraldic ensigns of the wearer were emblazoned.
couched, laid, inlaid, embroidered.
countour, accountant.
cour (Burns), stoop, crouch.
courtepy, a cape or cloak of coarse material.
couthe, *p.p.*, well known.
covyne, privy and fraudulent agreement ; deceit.
coy, quiet, shy.
cracching, scratching.
creeshie (Burns), greasy.
croods (Burns), coos.
croppe, top, shoot.
croys, cross.
crulle, curly, curled.
crummock (Burns), 'staff with crooked head for leaning on', Jamieson.
cryke, creek.
cullion (Browning), rascal.
culpons, *colpons*, shreds, strips, bundles.
cure, care, anxiety.
curious, careful.
cut, lot.
cutty-sark (Burns), short shift.
cynosure (Milton). The constellation *Ursa Minor* containing the Polar star, a guiding star, a centre of attraction.

daliaunce, conversation, gossip.
dampned, condemned, doomed.
dan, *daun*, lord ; Benedictine monks are still called ' Dom '.
darkling (Johnson), in darkness.
darreyne, to decide by wager of battle.
daun, see *dan*.
daunger, power (*Lat.* dominiarium), danger.
dawen, to dawn.
daweninge, dawn.
dawtit (Burns), petted.
dear (Milton), heart-felt.
debonaire, kind, gracious.
deduyt, delight, diversion.

deel, *del*, a part, bit. ' Never a del', not a whit.
degree, step ; rank.
delivere, quick, active, nimble.
deliverly, quickly.
deme, to consider, judge.
demirep (Browning), woman of doubtful reputation.
departe, to part, separate.
departing, separation.
depeynted, painted, depicted.
dere, dear, dearly.
dere (*v.*), to hurt, injure.
despitous, stern, scornful.
despyt, malicious anger, scorn.
destreyneth, holds in its grasp, oppresses, afflicts.
devoir, duty.
devys, *at his*, by his decision, direction.
devyse, (1) to tell, relate, (2) to order, determine.
dewle (Sackville), lamentation.
deye, a dairymaid.
deys, dais, the high table, seat of honour.
diapason (Milton). A swelling sound as of a great burst of harmony involving a whole range of tones or notes.
diapred, variegated, diversely embroidered.
diched, diked.
dight, prepared, dressed.
digne, worthy ; haughty.
ding (Burns), beat.
dirl (Burns), ring (*v.*).
dischevele, with hair hanging loose.
discoloured (Donne), variegated.
disconfiture, *disconfitinge*, defeat, discomfiture.
disconforten, to dishearten, discomfort.
disioynt, a difficult situation, dilemma.
dispence, expenditure ; *personified*, lavish giving (for love's sake).
dispitously, angrily, scornfully.
disport, gaiety, diversion.
disposicioun, disposition, ordering, position.
divisioun, distinction, party, strife.
divyninge, guessing, conjecture.
divynistre, a diviner (N.E.D.), *or*

here perhaps rather a divine, theologian.

doghtren, daughters.

doke, a duck.

dokked, cut short.

dome, decision, judgement, opinion. See *deme*.

dong, dung.

douce (Burns), sedate.

dowves, doves.

drecched, troubled, tormented.

dredful, full of fear.

drenching, drowning.

drere (Sackville), sorrow.

dreynt, drowned.

drogges, drugs.

drouthy (Burns), thirsty.

drugge, to drudge, do laborious work.

dub (Burns), puddle.

duddies (Burns), rags.

duk, a leader, duke.

dwelle, to tarry.

dyke, to make dikes or ditches.

dys, dice.

echon, echoon, each one.

eek, also, moreover.

eft, again.

eir, air.

elde, age, old age.

eldritch (Burns), unearthly.

electrum (Donne), an alloy of silver and gold in use among the ancients. 'The ancient electrum had in it a fifth of silver to the gold' (Bacon).

ellebor, hellebore (a remedy for melancholy).

embrouded, embroidered.

emforth, according to.

empryse, an undertaking, enterprise.

empyreal (Tennyson), heavenly, transcendent.

encens, incense.

encombred, hampered, stuck fast; wearied, burdened.

endelong, lengthways, along.

endere, finisher.

endyte, to compose.

engyned, racked, tortured.

enhauncen, to raise.

enhorte, to encourage.

enoynt, anointed.

enthrilling (Sackville), piercing.

entuned, intoned.

envyned, stored with wine.

equinoxial, the celestial equator.

erchedeknes, archdeacon's.

ere, to plough.

Erse (Burns), Gaelic.

erst than, for *er than*, before that.

eschue, to avoid, shun.

esed, entertained.

estatlich, estatly, stately, dignified.

estres, the inward parts of a building.

ettle (Burns), aim.

even, with equanimity, with moderation.

everich, every.

everichon, every one.

ey, an egg.

eyen, eyes.

eyle, to ail.

fadme, fathoms.

falding, a sort of coarse cloth, frieze.

falwe, pale, yellow.

fantastyk celle. 'The brain . . . is divided in three celles or dens. . . . In the formost cell . . . imagination is conformed and made' *Batman on Bartholome*.

fare, proceeding, affair.

fare, faren (*pret.* ferde, *p.p.* fare), to go, to fare (well or ill).

farsed, stuffed.

fash (Burns), trouble about.

faste, quickly, eagerly, near, hard by.

feateously (Spenser), daintily.

feer, feere (Sackville), companion.

fel, cruel, fierce.

felle, see *fel*.

fellon (Milton), cruel.

ferde, *pret.* of fare, *which see.*

ferforthly, far forth.

ferly (Burns), *v.* to wonder; *n.* a marvel (somewhat contemptuously).

fermacie, a medicine, drug.

ferme, rent.

ferne, distant *or* ancient.

ferre, ferrer, farther.

ferthing, farthing, fourth part; a very small portion.

fet, fetched, brought.

fetis, neat, well-made.

fetisly, neatly, properly.

fey, good faith, honour.

fidge (Burns), fidget, tingle.

fil, fell.

filed (Byron), defiled (from *Macbeth*).

finde, provide, supply.

fit (Burns), foot.

fithele, fiddle.

flashy (Milton), void of meaning, trashy.

flatour, flatterer.

flaw-blown (Keats), blown by a gust of wind.

flete, to float, swim.

flex, flax.

fley, flew.

flikeringe, fluttering.

flinging (Burns), kicking.

flotery, wavy, flowing, *with idea of* unkempt.

flough, flew.

floytinge, 'playing on a flute'; *probably just* 'whistling' (cf. *Du.* fluiten).

foil (Milton), gold-leaf, tinsel.

for-blak, very black.

fordo, ruined, destroyed.

forfaynt (Sackville), fainted, overcome.

forn-cast, pre-ordained.

forneys, furnace.

for-old, very old.

for-pyned, wasted away, tormented.

fors, force. *Do no fors of* = make no account of.

forsleuthen, to lose through sloth.

forster, forester.

forthren, to further, aid.

forthy, therefore.

fortunen, to forecast, determine the fortune of.

forward, covenant, agreement.

forwityng, foreknowledge.

forwot, foreknows.

fother, a cart-load, a large quantity.

fou (Burns), drunk.

foundered, was lamed.

fowl, fowel, a bird.

foyne, to thrust.

frail (Browning), a basket made of rushes, used for packing figs, raisins, and here (p. 629), olives.

fraknes, freckles.

frere, a friar.

freten, to eat.

frounct (Milton), frizzled, curled.

fume, exhalation, effects of gluttony or drunkenness.

fumetere, fumitory, a plant of the genus *Fumaria*, a purge.

furbelow (Pope), pleated border of a petticoat.

fyke (Burns), fret, restless motion.

gab (Burns), mouth.

gabbe, to lie.

galingale (Chaucer), 'the aromatic root of certain East Indian plants of the genera *Alpinia* and *Kaempferia*, formerly much used in medicine and cookery'. N.E.D. (Tennyson), an English species of sedge (*Cyperus longus*).

gamed, verb impers., pleased.

gar (Burns), make, cause, compel.

gargat, the throat.

garleek, garlic.

gaste, to terrify. See *agaste*.

gate (Burns), road, way.

gattothed, having teeth far apart.

gauded with grene, furnished with green larger beads for the *Pater Nosters*.

gayler, a jailer.

gaytres beryis, 'Probably the berries of the buck-thorn, *Rhamnus catharticus*' (Skeat, whose note see, *Works of Chaucer*, V. 252), *a purge*.

gentil, noble.

gentilesse, gentleness, nobility.

gere, manner, habit.

gere, gear, all sorts of instruments, tools, utensils, armour, apparel, fashion.

gerful, changeable, capricious.

gerner, a garner.

gery, changeable.

gigginge, fitting (of shields) with straps for the arm.

ginglen, to jingle.

gipoun, the coat or tunic worn beneath the armour.

gipser, a pouch or purse suspended from a belt.

girles, young people of either sex.

girt, girded, girt.

girt, pierced.
gizz (Burns), ' a periwig ' (Burns).
gladere, one who makes glad.
glede, a live coal.
go, walk.
gobet, piece, morsel, fragment.
gnarr (Tennyson), snarl.
golden-eye, the clanging (Crabbe),
  Clangula glaucion. A bird of the
  goose and duck order (*Anseres*)
  whose ' rapidly beating wings produce a loud whistling sound '.
goldes, marigolds.
goliardeys, a buffoon, ribald.
gree, bure the (Burns), carried off
  the prize.
greet (Burns), weep.
greve, to grieve (*act.*), annoy.
greves (*plur.* of grove), groves, leafy
  boughs.
griffoun, a griffin.
grope, to try, test.
groyning, groaning, murmuring,
  discontent.
grucchen, to murmur, grumble.
gruf, grovelling, with face flat to
  the ground.
grys, a costly grey fur.
gules (Keats), red (in heraldry).
gye, to turn, direct, guide.
gyle, deceit.

haberdassher, a seller of small
  goods, ' including caps and probably hats '. N.E.D.
habergeoun, a hauberk, coat of mail.
hain (Burns), restrain, spare, save.
halwes, saints.
hardily, certainly.
hardiness, boldness.
haried, harried, driven, dragged.
harlot, fellow, rascal.
harn (Burns), coarse cloth.
harneised, equipped.
harneys, armour, mounting.
harre, a hinge.
harrow, cryden, raised the hue and
  cry.
hauberk, a coat of mail. See
  habergeoun.
haugh (Burns), hollow.
haunt, practice, skill.
hawkie (Burns), ' An affectionate
  name for a favourite cow '
  (Jamieson).

heed, on his, on pain of death.
hegge, a hedge.
heigh, high.
hele, health.
heled, hidden, kept secret.
henne, hence.
hente, henten, seize, take hold of,
  get.
heraud, a herald.
herbergage, herberwe, lodging, inn.
herde, a herd, shepherd.
herte-spoon, ' the depression at the
  end of the breast-bone '. N.E.D.
hete, to promise.
heugh (Burns), hollow.
hey, heye, heygh, heyh, high, highly.
hight, promised, was called.
highte, on highte = aloud.
hindreste, hindmost.
hirplin (Burns), limping.
hoastin (Burns), coughing.
hog-shouther (Burns), push.
holde, holden, beholden, esteemed,
  held.
holt, a wood, grove.
hooked chariot (Milton), ' currus
  falcatus ', chariot armed with
  scythes.
hool, hole, whole.
hoolie ! (Burns), softly !
hoolly, wholly.
hoppesteres, dancing. For Boccaccio's *bellatrici*, i. e. war-ships,
  Chaucer read *ballatrici*, dancing.
hostiler, innkeeper.
hotch'd (Burns), jogged the pipes
  or fidgeted, with impatience.
houped, whooped.
howes (Burns), hollows.
howkit (Burns), disinterred, dug up.
humours, the fluids of the body, depending on the elements. Earth,
  which is dry and cold, gives
  melancholy ; water, which is wet
  and cold, *phlegm* ; air, which is
  warm and wet, blood, or the *sanguine* humour ; and fire, warm
  and dry, *choler.* Health, according
  to Hippocrates, depends on their
  proper commingling. The pre-
  dominance of one or other determines a man's temperament.
hunte, a hunter.
hurdies (Burns), buttocks.
hurtle, to push, knock down.

hust, hushed.
hye, haste.
hyne, hind, servant.

ichors (*v.*) (Browning), formed from 'ichor', a discharge from wounds or sores, so 'forms a scab over'; but the poetical associations of the word as meaning the ethereal blood of the ever youthful Gods colours the use here.
ilke, same.
Incubus, evil spirit which oppresses in sleep.
infect, invalidated.
inned, lodged, entertained.
in principio, first words of St. John's Gospel, to which a magical value was attached.
intelligences (Tennyson), *intelligenze*, angels (in Dante and the Tuscan poets).
iyen (Sackville), eyes, see *eyen*.
jade, a poor horse.
iangle, to prate, talk idly.
ianglere, a prater, babbler.
iapes, tricks, jests.
iape, to befool, deceive.
ieet, jet.
iet, fashion, mode.
jinkin' (Burns), moving quickly and jerkily; eluding, dodging.
iolyf, joyful, pleasant.
jouk (Burns), duck (*v.*).
iournee, a day's journey.
joyntenants (Donne), joint tenants.
jundie (Burns), justle.
iuste, *iusten*, to joust, tilt, engage in a tournament.
iustes, a tournament.
iuwyse, judgement.

keep, care, attention, heed.
kempe heres, coarse hairs.
kempt, combed.
kepe, to guard, preserve.
kervere, a carver.
kerving, cutting, carving.
kirn (Burns), churn.
kittle (Burns), tickle.
knarre, a knotted, thick-set fellow.
knarry, full of knots, knotty.
knave, a boy, servant.
knobbe, a pimple.

kynd, *kynde*, nature; *by kynde* = by instinct, naturally.

lacerte, a muscle.
lafte, left, ceased.
lag, backward (Burns).
lallan (Burns), lowland.
large, *at his*, free.
las, a lace, cord; net, snare.
latoun, latten, an alloy of metal.
launde, glade or clearing in a wood, in crossing which the deer could be seen and shot at or coursed.
laurer, a laurel.
lauriol, spurge laurel (*a violent purgative*).
lauwine (Byron), avalanche (*Ger.* lawine).
layneres, straps (lanyards), lash.
lazar, a leper (*from the name* Lazarus) or otherwise diseased poor person.
leames (Sackville), brightness, gleams, rays.
leed, a cauldron, copper.
leef, a leaf.
leef (*comp.* lever), dear, beloved; pleasing, lief.
leet, let, left.
leme (*v.*), gleam, shine.
lene (*imper.* leen), to lend, give.
lene, lean, poor.
lepart, a leopard.
lere, to learn.
lese, to lose.
lesing, loss.
lesinges, leasing, lies.
lest, pleasure, delight, joy.
lest (*v. impers.*), pleased; pleases, Kentish rhyme-form for '*liste*' q. v.
lete, to leave.
lette, to hinder, prevent. *To letten of his wille* = forgo his will.
lette (*n.*), hindrance, delay.
letuaries, remedies, *strictly* drugs done up in some kind of syrup.
leve, to believe.
levere, rather (see *leef*).
lewed, *lewd*, ignorant, unlearned.
leyser, leisure.
liberticide (Shelley), assassin of liberty.
licentiat, one licensed by the Pope to hear confessions without leave

of the parson, and to absolve from weightier sins than he.

liche-wake, the vigil or wake held over the body of the dead.

lief, beloved.

ligging, lying.

like (*v. impers.*), to please.

limitour, a friar licensed to ask alms within a certain limit.

linde, lime-tree.

linkin (Burns), tripping.

lintwhite (Burns), linnet.

list, it pleases.

liste, it pleased.

litarge, white lead.

lith, a limb, any member of the body.

lodemenage, pilotage.

lodesterre, a loadstar, the pole-star.

loken, to see, look.

loken, locked, enclosed.

loonges, lungs.

looth, disagreeable, repugnant, loath.

lorn, lost. See *lese*.

los, loss.

losengeour, a flatterer (with intent to deceive).

louping (Burns), leaping.

lowin (Burns), flaming.

luce, a pike.

lug (Burns), ear.

lust, pleaseth. See *list*

lust, pleasure.

lustinesse, pleasure.

lyfly, in a lifelike way.

lyn (Sackville), to cease.

lyves, alive, living.

maat, *mat*, dejected, downcast (*as in* checkmate).

maistow, mayest thou.

maistrye, *for the*, surpassingly, above all others.

make, a companion, mate.

male, a bag, wallet.

mallow, the slimy (Crabbe), probably the marsh mallow, *Althaea officinalis*.

mantelet, a short mantle.

manifest (Dryden), convicted (*manifestus sceleris*).

manye, mania, madness.

martyreth, tortures.

mary-bones, marrow-bones.

mase, a wild fancy, maggot (of the brain).

mat, see *maat*.

matin-songs (Tennyson), 'writings of the great early Poets'.

maugree, in spite of.

maun (Burns), must.

maunciple, a servant who has the care of purchasing victuals for an Inn of Court or College ; purveyor.

medlee, parti-coloured.

meikle (Burns), big.

melder (Burns), taking of corn to be ground.

men, one.

mere, *meare* (Burns), a mare.

meschief, *at*, in distress, in his enemy's power.

mester, *mister*, occupation, craft, task. 'What mister men,' what kind of men.

mesurable, moderate.

met (*p.p.*), dreamed.

mete, *pret. mette*, to dream. *me mette* = I dreamed.

meth, mead, 'an alcoholic drink made by fermenting a mixture of honey and water' (N.E.D.), metheglin.

mewe, a cage or coop (originally for moulting birds, here apparently to keep birds ready for killing).

meynee, household, suite, domestics.

minister, an officer of justice.

mirk (Burns), dark.

misboden, insulted, injured.

mithridate (Donne), a universal antidote or preservative against poison and infectious diseases, made by the compounding together of many ingredients.

modish (Johnson), fashionable, modern.

moevere, the first, God, Fate, Jupiter.

moly (Tennyson), the plant given to Ulysses to protect him from Circe's enchantments.

mood, anger.

moot, may, must, ought.

mormal, 'an inflamed sore, especially on the leg'. N.E.D.

mortreux, a stew made of meat brayed in a mortar and mixed with milk, eggs, spices, &c., and coloured with saffron.

morwe, morweninge, morning, morrow.

mosel, muzzle, nose of an animal.

mot, may, must ; *mote, plu.* must. See *moot*.

mountaunce, amount, value.

mowe, are able.

muezzin (Omar), crier of the regular hours of prayer from the minaret or roof of a mosque.

murye, glad, merry.

mushtara (Omar), Jupiter (the planet).

muslin-kail (Burns), broth composed simply of water, shelled barley, and greens, with no stock.

mynour, a miner.

naig (Burns), horse.

nakers, kettle-drums.

namely, especially.

namo, no more.

nappy (Burns), ale.

nedely, nedes-cost, of necessity.

neer, nearer.

neet, neat, cattle.

nercotikes, narcotics.

never-singling (Marlowe), never driving apart, as a deer is singled from the herd to be pursued.

nieve (Burns), fist.

nightertale, the night-time.

noddle, head, brain.

nones, for the, expressly ; *but often a mere tag to secure a rhyme*.

nonne, a nun.

noot, not = ne + wot, know not, knows not. See *wost*.

norice, nurse.

norissing, norisshinge, nutriment, nurture.

nose-thirles, nostrils. See *thirle*.

notabilitee, a thing worthy to be known.

not-heed, a head with closely cropped hair.

nouthe, just now, at present.

nyce, foolish, fastidious, scrupulous.

offertorie, a sentence or sentences of Scripture sung while the alms are collected, therefore specially well sung by the pardoner.

ofte sythes, oftentimes.

oncelot (Browning), a small ounce, *Felis uncia*.

opie, opium.

orc (Browning), killer-whale.

ordres foure, Franciscans, Dominicans, Carmelites, and Augustinians.

orisoun, prayer, orison.

orlogge, a sun-dial, or other instrument for telling the time.

ounces, small portions.

outhees, outcry, alarm.

outrely, utterly, wholly.

over, upper; *overest*, uppermost.

overal, everywhere.

owher, anywhere.

oynement, ointment, unguent.

oynouns, onions.

pace, passe, to pass, go ; surpass.

paleys, palace.

palladium (Johnson), effigy of a tutelary deity (originally of Pallas).

pan, the skull, brain-pan.

pantisocracy (Byron), the communistic state planned by Coleridge and Southey in 1794.

paraments, ornamented robes of state.

paramour, as a lover.

paramours, with great affection, passionately.

parde, pardee = par Dieu, by God.

pardoner, an authorized (or unauthorized) seller of papal indulgences or of relics to which indulgences were attached.

parisshen, a parishioner.

parte, party, company.

party, partly.

partye, a part ; *be no partye*, take no side.

parvys, the portico (of St. Paul's) where lawyers interviewed their clients.

pas, a litel more than, at a little more than a foot-pace.

Pastor est tui Dominus, the Lord is thy shepherd. *Modified from* Psalm xxiii. 1.

pawkie (Burns), artful, sly.

payen, pagan.

pekke, to pick.

penoun, a pennant or ensign.

perrye, jewellery.

pers, blue.

persoun, a parson or parish-priest.

peyne, peynen, to take pains, endeavour ; *to dyen in the peyne*, to die by torture.

phraisin (Burns), flattering, coaxing, wheedling.

pighte, pitched.

piked, trimmed.

piled, pilde (Sackville), stripped of hair, bald.

piler, a pillar.

pilour, a plunderer.

pilwe-beer, a pillow-case.

pinche, to find fault (with).

pipe in an ivy-leaf, go whistle for.

pitaunce, ' a mess of victuals ' ; an alms (apparently in the friar's case of money).

plat, plain, flat.

pleyn, plain.

pleyn, full, fully, openly.

pleyne, pleynen, to complain.

pleynly, fully.

pocock, peacock.

point, in good, comfortable, in good condition, *French* embonpoint.

pollax, a halberd, pole-axe.

pomel, crown of the head.

pomely, marked with spots as big as an apple, dappled.

poplexye, apoplexy.

poraille, the poor.

pore, see *povre*.

port, carriage, behaviour.

portly (Spenser), dignified.

portreiture, a picture or set of pictures.

portreyour, a painter.

pose, to assume, put the question.

poudre-marchaunt, a kind of spice used for flavouring.

pouped, piped, blew.

poure, to pore over.

povre, poor.

poynaunt, pungent.

practisour, practitioner.

prest, ready.

preve, prief (Burns), proof.

pricasour, hard rider, ' or perhaps a huntsman'. N.E.D.

prike, to incite, quicken; spur, ride.

priking, riding.

prikke, a piercing stroke, thrust.

prow, advantage, profit.

pryme, the time from 6 to 9 a.m.

pulle, to pluck.

purchas, earnings, proceeds of begging.

purchasour, conveyancer.

purchasing, conveyancing.

pure, the, the very, even the.

purfiled, bordered, fringed.

purveiaunce, foresight, providence, provision.

pussie (Burns), the hare.

pyne, torment, pain, grief.

pyne, pynen, to torture, grieve.

qualm, disease.

quat (Burns), quit, leave.

quelle, to kill.

questio quid juris, the question is what section of the law applies to the case.

queynte (*pret.*), quenched, went out. *queynt* (*p.p.*), extinguished.

queynte, strange, quaint, uncouth.

quicks (Tennyson), sloes or hawthorns.

quitly, free, at liberty.

quook, trembled, quaked.

quyte, to free.

rage, to play, toy wantonly.

ragweed (Burns), ragwort.

rair (Burns), roar.

ram-stam (Burns), headlong, reckless.

rash-buss (Burns), clump of rushes.

rather, sooner ; *rathe* (Milton), early.

raughte, reached.

raunsoun, ransom.

reaming(Burns),foaming,creaming.

rebec (Milton), a three-stringed fiddle.

recche, rekke, to care, take heed to.

record, to remind, record.

rede, to advise, explain, interpret.

rede, to read.

redoutinge, reverence.

reduced (Sackville), brought back.
reed, plan. See *rede*.
reed, rede, red.
reed (*imp.* of *rede*), read.
reed, counsel; adviser.
reekit (Burns), steamed, smoked.
reestit (Burns), scorched, smoke-dried.
regne, kingdom.
reme, realm.
renges, ranks.
renne, to run.
rente, income as distinguished from 'catel', capital, and 'purchas', irregular profits; *perhaps* the 'ferme' or fixed sum paid by the friar to his house for right to beg over a certain area.
replicacioun, a reply.
rescous, rescue.
rese, to quake, shake.
resoune, to resound.
retchles (Sackville), reckless, indifferent.
rethor, a rhetorician.
rette, to ascribe, impute.
reule, rule.
reve, steward, bailiff.
rever (Sackville), robber.
rewe, to be sorry for, to have pity on.
rewe, a row, line.
rewthe, ruth, pity.
reyse, to make a military expedition.
rief (Burns), plunder.
rieve, take away, rob (Sackville).
rightes, rightly.
rigwoodie (Burns), *prob.* tough and wizened, *perh.* fit for the gallows.
rit, rides.
rivelled (Pope), shrivelled.
roghte, cared for. See *recche*.
ronnen (*plu.*), ran.
rote, a small harp, psaltery.
rouke, crouch, huddle together.
rouncy, a hackney.
roundel, a short poem constructed on two rhymes, with refrain.
route, a company, assembly.
rowth (Burns), plenty.
ruddock (Spenser), robin.
rudeliche, rudely.
ruggy, rugged, rough.

sad, sober, staid.
sadly, firmly.
sangwyn, red, rubicund.
sautrye, a psaltery.
save, the herb sage. *Lat.* salvia, 'from its supposed healing virtues' (Skeat).
sawceflem, pimpled.
say, saw. See *se*.
scalled, scabby, scurvy.
scarsly, parsimoniously.
scathe, that was, a misfortune, pity.
scaur (Burns), apt to be scared.
scawl (Burns), a scold.
sclendre, slender, slight.
scoleye, to attend school, to study.
sconner (Burns), sicken.
scrannel (Milton), harsh, grating (*stridens*).
screed (*n.*) (Burns), rent, tear.
secree, secret.
sege, a siege.
seigh, saw. See *se*.
seistow, sayest thou.
selde, seldom.
selle, to give.
sely, simple, poor.
semicope, a short cope.
sendal, a thin silk.
sentence, sense, meaning, judgement, matter of a story.
sentences (Pope), the collection by Peter Lombard (d. 1164) of sentences from St. Augustine and other fathers on points of doctrine, with objections and replies from authors of repute.
sergeant of lawe, a servant of the sovereign for his law business.
serye, train of argument.
seththen, since. See *sith*.
seurtee, security, surety.
sewed, followed.
sey, seyh, see *seigh*.
seyn (*p.p.*), seen.
seyn, to say.
seynd, singed, fried.
shamfastnesse, shyness.
shape, shapen, to plan, purpose, ordain.
shaply, fit, likely.
sheeldes, shields; French coins, *écus*, which the merchant exchanged at a profit to himself.

shend (Spenser), diminish (by out-shining).

shene, bright, beautiful.

shent, hurt, destroyed.

shepne, shed, *here apparently* stables or byre.

shere, shears, scissors.

sherte, a shirt.

shet, shut.

shirreve, sheriff.

sho, shoe.

shode, the temple (of the head).

shog (Burns), shake.

shrewe, to curse, beshrew.

shrighte, shryked, shryght (Sackville), shrieked.

shines, shins, legs.

shiveren, to be shattered, fly in splinters.

sidelins (Burns), sideways.

significavit, writ for the imprisonment of an excommunicated person.

siker, sure, certain.

sincerely (Dryden), purely, without alloy.

sinowie (Marlowe), strung with sinew.

sith, sithen, since, afterwards.

skellum (Burns), a good-for-nothing.

skelpit (Burns), spanked.

skirl (Burns), shriek, cry shrilly.

sklent, slant, inclination.

sklented (Burns), 'run or hit in an oblique direction' (Burns), shot askance.

slake, slow, slack.

slap (Burns), a gate, a breach in a fence.

slawe, slain.

slee, sleen, to slay.

sleere, a slayer.

sleight (Burns), see *sleighte*.

sleighte, contrivance, craft, device.

slepy, causing sleep.

slider, slippery.

slogardye, sloth.

slough, slow, slew.

slyly, prudently, discreetly, *Scot.* cannily.

smerte, smarting, painful.

smerte, to pain, hurt, displease.

smoking, full of the smoke (of incense).

smoor'd (Burns), smothered.

smoutie (Burns), smutty, obscene, ugly.

snewede, swarmed, abounded.

snibbe, to reprove, snub.

snick-drawing, cunning, crafty. A snick- (or sneck-) drawer is one who, by craft and experience, is able to succeed (in love or business) where others fail; 'an old hand'.

sock (Jonson). See *buskin*.

solempne, festive, important.

solempnely, pompously.

solempnitee, feast, festivity.

som-del, somewhat.

somnour, summoner of offenders to the church courts.

sond, sand.

sonnet (Burns), song.

soor, sore.

soote, sweet.

sooth, sothe, truth, true.

soother (Keats), softer—as K. uses it.

soothfastnesse, truth.

sophister (Marlowe), subtle arguer.

sort, destiny, chance.

sotil, finely-wrought, thin, skilful.

sough (Burns), moan. See *swough*.

soun, a sound.

souter (Burns), cobbler.

sowne, sound, came to sound.

sowninge, sowninge in, tending to, *or* resounding with, full of (Bentinck Smith).

spairges (Burns), splashes, dashes about.

sparre, bar, bolt.

sparth, a battleaxe or halberd.

spean (Burns), wean.

sped (Milton), provided for, have got their fat livings.

speel (Burns), to climb.

spercled (Sackville), sparkling, glittering, shining.

spill (Sackville), kill.

spronge (*p.p.*), become famous, sprung up.

spyced, sophisticated *or* scrupulous.

spycerye, spices.

starf, died. See *sterve*.

stemed, shone, glowed.

stent (Sackville), period.

stenten, to stop, cease ; cause to stop or cease.

stepe, bright, glittering.

sterre, star.

stert, at a, at a bound, in a moment.

sterte, to start, leap.

sterting, better *startlynge,* restive.

sterve, to die.

steven, stevene, voice, sound ; time appointed, season ; *at unset stevene,* at an unexpected moment.

stewe, fish-pond.

stint (imper. s.), stop.

stinte, to stop.

stith, an anvil, stithy.

stoke, to stab.

stongen, stung.

stoor, store, stock (of a farm).

stoor (Burns), harsh, hollow.

stope, advanced.

stot, a cob, undersized horse.

stounde, a moment, space of time.

stree, straw.

strepe, to strip.

streyne, to constrain.

streyt, narrow, strict, drawn (sword).

streyte (adv.), closely, tightly.

strike, a hank (of flax).

stubbes, stumps, roots.

surcote, an upper coat.

swats (Burns), new ale.

swelte, fainted, despaired.

swelth (Sackville), *apparently from swelgh,* a whirlpool or pit, *but here obviously* pitch or filth.

swevene, a dream.

swinge (Sackville and Milton), sway.

swink, labour, toil.

swinken, to labour, toil.

swinkere, a labourer.

swough, sough, whistling sound of wind through trees or a crevice.

swowne, to swoon.

swymbul, the moaning or sighing of the wind. *Rumbel,* a rumbling, rattling noise, is another reading.

syke, a sigh (Sackville).

sythe, sythes, times.

taas, see *tas.*

tabard, a herald's sleeveless coat, used as an inn-sign ; a labourer's sleeveless coat or smock.

taille, took by, took on account.

takel, shooting tackle, arrows.

talen, to tell tales.

tannen (Byron), *Ger.* fir-trees, ' A species peculiar to the Alps ' (Byron's note), *prob.* spruces.

tapets (Sackville), tapestry of leaves with which the trees are covered.

tapicer, an upholsterer.

tappestere, a tapster.

targe, a target or shield.

tas, a heap.

tawed (Sackville), tanned, hard, horny.

tead (Spenser), torch.

techen, direct, guide.

temper'd (Milton), modulated.

tene, vexation, annoyance.

tent (Burns), heed.

tentless (Burns), careless.

terciane, a fever ; a tertian fever, recurring every three days.

term (Browning), a figure having the head, or head and bust, of a god resting upon a plain block-like shaft. *The bishop wishes to have his frieze highly decorated with the ordinary subject-matter of Greco-Roman and Renaissance sculpture.* See *visor.*

testers, head-pieces, helmets.

thankes, his or *hir,* with his *or* their good-will.

thee, to thrive, prosper.

theffect, the upshot.

therto, besides.

thilke, that.

thikkeherd, thick-haired.

thinke, thynke, to seem.

thirled, pierced.

tho (1) then, (2) those.

thombe of gold, he hadde a, he was an honest miller ! No one could convict *him* of theft.

thral, slave, serf.

thrang, crowded on all sides.

thridde, third.

thrust (Donne), crowd.

thryes, thrice.

tide (Sackville), happen.

tint (Burns), lost.

tirlin' (Burns), uncovering.

to-, as a verbal prefix, in twain.

toccata (Browning), fantasia.

tollen, to take toll or payment.

tonne-greet, great as a tun.

torets, small holes made at intervals in the collar, or rings fitted into it.

touzie (Burns), shaggy.

trappures, trappings of a horse.

travertine (Browning), a whitish concretionary lime-stone.

trays, traces.

tretys, well-formed.

trompe, a trumpet.

tronchoun, short staff, *here perhaps* broken shaft of a spear.

trowe, to believe.

trussed up, packed up.

turneyinge, a tournament.

tustle, Byron's spelling of 'tussle.'

tweye, two, twain.

twinne, to depart.

tyde, time.

tyke (Burns), dog.

unco (Burns) (*adv.*), rarely, very ; (*adj.*), strange, prodigious.

undern, at or about 9 a.m.

undersong (Spenser). A subordinate song serving as accompaniment or burden to another.

undertake, to affirm.

unexpressive (Milton), inexpressible, not to be uttered. Rev. xiv. 3–4.

unkonning, ignorant.

unwist, unknown. See *wite*.

unyolden, not having yielded.

uphaf, lifted up. See *heve*.

up-yaf, gave up.

usquebae (Burns), whisky.

vare (Dryden), a wand or white staff (*Span.* vara).

vasselage, loyal service and prowess.

vauntie (Burns), proud.

vavasour, a feudal tenant below rank of baron, *here* a country squire.

venerye, hunting.

venim, poison, venom.

ventusyng, cupping, a surgical term.

vernicle, a copy in miniature of the picture of Christ, miraculously imprinted on the handkerchief of St. Veronica and preserved in St. Peter's, Rome ; thus the token of a pilgrimage to Rome.

vese, a rush of wind.

vizor (Browning), *metri causa for* mask, the architectural term for a 'representation of the front part of the head of man, beast, or fantastic creature' (Russell Sturgis, *Dictionary of Architecture and Building*). Here a grotesque face is probably contemplated.

voyden, to expel.

waar, see *war*.

wake-pleyes, waking or funeral games.

walie (Burns), choice, 'ample, large, jolly' (Burns).

wanhope, despair.

wanie, to wane.

war, aware, cautious, prudent.

war him, to beware.

warlock (Burns), wizard.

warly (Burns), worldly.

wastel-breed, a specially fine bread.

wawes, waves.

wayke, weak.

waymenting, waymentinge, a lamentation, wailing.

wealked (Sackville), withered, pale.

webbe, a weaver.

wedde, to, as security.

wede, clothing.

wele, happiness, prosperity.

wende, wenden, to go, pass away.

wene, pret. wende, think.

werd (Sackville), fate.

were, to defend, guard.

werken, to work.

werre, war.

werreye, werreyen, to make war against.

werte, a wart.

wessh (*pret.*), washed.

wexe, to increase, grow, become.

weymentinge, see *waymenting*.

whelkes, pimples, blotches.

wher, where, *also* whether.

whids (Burns), gambols.

whippeltre, the cornel-tree, dogwood.

whist (Milton), hushed, silent.

whortle-berries, red (Keats), cowberries, one of the genus *Vaccinium*, others of which are blaeberries and cranberries.

whunstane (Burns), whinstone.
whylom, formerly, once.
wight, any living creature.
wighte, weight.
wikke, malign, wicked.
wilne, to desire.
wimpel, a kind of head-dress, covering the neck also.
winnock-bunker (Burns), window-seat.
wirche, to work.
wis = ywis, certainly.
wisly, truly.
wite, witen, to know.
withholde, maintained, or secluded.
witing, knowledge.
wlatsome, loathsome, hateful.
wode, see *wood.*
wodebynde, woodbine.
wommanhede, womanly feeling.
wonder, wondrous, wonderful.
wone, custom, habit.
wone, to dwell.
woning, a dwelling, habitation.
wood, mad.
woodly, madly.
woodnesse, madness.
woot, know, knows. See *wite.*
wortes, herbs.
wost, knowest. See *wite.*
wreke, to avenge, wreak vengeance on.
wrighte, a carpenter.
wrooth, angry.
wun (Sackville), dwelling.
wykes, weeks.
wyte, wyten, know.

y-, a prefix used especially with the past participle, like *A.S.* ge-, *Ger.* ge-.
yaf, gave ; *hence,* cared.
yate, a gate.
y-chaped, capped, mounted.
y-cleped, y-clept, called.
ye, yea.
yë, eye.
yeddinges, songs.
yeldhalle, a guildhall.
yeldyng, yielding, return, produce.
yell (Burns), dry.
yelpe, to boast.
yeman, a yeoman, retainer.
yerd, yerde, rod, yard (length); enclosure.
yerde, slepy, virgam somniferam. Ovid, *Met.* i. 671–2, the sleep-bringing wand of Hermes.
yet now, just now.
yeve, to give.
yifte, gift.
yill (Burns), ale.
yive, yiven, to give.
y-lad, carried (in a cart).
y-meynd, mingled, mixed.
yolden, yielded.
yolle, to yell.
yon (Milton), there, yonder.
yore, agon, long ago.
youling, yelling.
y-spreyned, sprinkled, scattered.
y-stiked, pierced.
y-storve, dead.
y-wis, certainly, truly.
y-wrye, covered.

tomb of Petrarch, the Italian poet and lover of Laura.

Arvon's shore (Gray). The shores of Carnarvonshire opposite Anglesey.

Ashtaroth (Milton). A goddess of the Phoenicians, the Moon. Selden, a scholar of Milton's day, describes her as 'regina coeli' and 'mater deum', so 'Queen of Heaven'. *P. L.* i. 439.

Asmodeus (Byron). The devil in Le Sage's story, *Le Diable Boiteux* (1707).

Assaye (Tennyson). Where Wellington, then Sir Arthur Wellesley, defeated the Marathas and French in 1803.

Atalantis (Pope). Mrs. Manley's novel, *The New Atalantis* (1709).

Athens, the Etrurian (Byron). Florence on the Arno in Tuscany (Etruria).

Atthalante. Atalanta, who first wounded the Calydonian boar, and received the head from Meleager, who thereby wrought his own doom. See Swinburne's *Atalanta in Calydon*.

Attheon. Actaeon.

Attick boy (Milton). Cephalus, the lover and husband of Procris, but loved by Aurora, the Dawn. Ovid, *Met.* vii.

Austyn, Augustyn. St. Augustine of Hippo.

Austria, fair (Johnson). Maria Theresa (1717–80), who, on succeeding to her father Charles VI, was at once attacked by Charles Albert of Bavaria, supported by the French and others.

Averrois. Averroes, an Arabian physician.

Avicen. Avicenna, an Arabian physician.

Baalim or Baal (Milton). A God of the Moabites, Phoenicians, and nations bordering upon the Jews. Probably the host of heaven, the stars. The -im is a plural termination.

Bacon's Mansion (Johnson). House of Roger Bacon on the bridge at

Oxford, which it was said would fall when the bridge was crossed by one more learned than he.

Bahram (Omar). A Persian hero and warrior, who defeated the Turks, usurped the throne (A. D. 590), and was ultimately defeated by the Romans. He is the hero of many legends, and was nicknamed from his speed and strength 'the wild ass'.

Balaam. See Num. xxii–xxiii. Here the Earl of Huntingdon, one of the seventeen peers who petitioned Charles to consult Parliament in 1679.

Bard of Prose (Byron). Boccaccio (1313–75) whose *Decameron*, the first masterpiece of Italian prose, contained one hundred tales.

Barleycorn, John (Burns), a cant name for beer, derived from an old song which goes back to 1620 at least.

Barnaby, the bright (Spenser). Ecclesiastical tradition fixed the martyrdom of Barnabas, companion of St. Paul, as June 11, in the old reckoning the longest day of the year, as St. Lucy's Day, December 10, was the shortest.

Barzillai (Dryden). See 2 Sam. xvii. 27. Here James Butler, Duke of Ormond, a notable Royalist under Charles I and Charles II.

Bavarian, The bold (Johnson). Charles Albert, Elector of Bavaria, who claimed the Austrian domains devised by her father to Maria Theresa. Bavaria was overrun by an Austrian army of irregular Hungarian and Croatian troops.

Bellerus (Milton). A name for a legendary giant coined by Milton from Bellerium, i. e. Land's End.

Belmarie. Benmarin, a Moorish kingdom in North Africa.

Benet. Benedictus, founder of the Benedictine Order.

Berenice (Pope). Wife of Ptolemy III of Egypt, whose hair, dedicated for the safe return of her husband, was said to have become a constellation. Catullus, lxvi.

Bion's mate (Arnold). Moschus lamented Bion in a famous elegy.

Birds of calm (Milton). Halcyons. Ovid, *Met.* xi.

Blackmore (Pope). Sir Richard Blackmore, a Whig poet (d. 1729), author of various epic poems, frequently ridiculed by Pope.

Boar, the bristled (Gray). Richard III, who used the boar as his device.

Bodley's dome (Johnson). The Bodleian library, founded by Sir Thomas Bodley (1545–1613).

Boece. Anicius Manlius Severinus Boethius (470–524), author of *De Consolatione Philosophiae*, from which Chaucer borrows most of his philosophy. See Gibbon, *Decline and Fall*, chap. 39.

Boileau (Pope and Byron). French critic and poet of the seventeenth century, author of a poem *L'Art Poétique*, which Pope's to some extent follows.

Boloigne. Probably Boulogne.

Bomba's lazzaroni (Browning), loafers of Naples. Ferdinand II (1810–59), king of the Two Sicilies, was offensively styled Bomba (from his bombardment of Palermo in 1849). His name stank in the nostrils of all who wished for a United Italy.

Bradwardyn. Thomas Bradwardyn, Divinity Professor at Oxford after 1325 and Chancellor of St. Paul's; author of *De Causa Dei*.

Brunswick's fated chieftain (Byron). Frederick William, Duke of Brunswick-Oels, killed at Quatre-Bras. His father, blinded at the battle of Auerstädt, was driven from his duchy by Napoleon after Jena (1806), and died a few weeks later.

Brutus bust (Byron). At the funeral of Junia, Brutus's sister and wife of Cassius, Tiberius forbade their busts to be carried in the procession. 'Sed praefulgebant Cassius atque Brutus eo ipso quod effigies eorum non

visebantur.' Tacitus, *Annales,* iii. 76.

Bucentaur, the (Byron). The galley in which the Doge of Venice went out to wed the Adriatic with a ring. See Browning's *A Toccata,* &c.

Buckingham, Henry duke of (Sackville). Henry Stafford, second duke of B., accomplice of all Richard III's crimes, rebelled and was beheaded, 1483.

Cadme. Cadmus, founder of Thebes.

Cadwallo — Hoel — Llewellyn — Taliessin—Urien (Gray). Welsh bards, historical or traditional.

Caesar, bastard (Byron). Napoleon Bonaparte.

Caleb, 'a dog'. Here Lord Grey of Wark.

Caliban upon Setebos (Browning). See *Tempest,* esp. I. ii. 373, 'my dam's god, Setebos'.

Callistopee. Callisto, a companion of Artemis, whom Zeus loved. Changed after death into the Great Bear, which Chaucer here confounds with the Lesser Bear.

Calpe's rock (Byron). Gibraltar.

Camaldolese (Browning), a monastic order, founded 1027, whose monastery was built on the Campo Maldoni. *Brother Lorenzo, Monaco,* was their great painter,

Cambria (Gray). Wales. A variant of Cymry, the native name of the Welsh people.

Cambuscan — Camball — Algarsife—Canace (Milton). Characters in Chaucer's Squire's Tale in the *Canterbury Tales.*

Camelot (Tennyson). The seat of King Arthur and the knights of the Round Table.

Camilla (Pope). A Volscian woman warrior opposed to Aeneas, so swift of foot that Virgil says she *might have* sped over the corn-field. Dryden translates, she
  Flew o'er the field, nor hurt the bearded grain,
and Pope follows. *Aeneid,* vii. 803–17.

Camus (Milton). The river Cam, so Cambridge.

Candia (Byron). Crete, which the Venetians defended against the Turks for twenty-four years, 1645–69, fourteen years longer than the siege of Troy.

Canna's field (Sackville), *Cannae* (Byron). See *Hannibal*.

Canova (Byron). An Italian sculptor in the classical manner (1757–1822). His Helen ' is, without exception to my mind, the most perfectly beautiful of human conceptions, and far beyond my ideas of human execution '. Byron, *Letters*, iv. 14–15 (Prothero).

Capaneus. An Argive warrior, slain at the siege of Thebes by a thunderbolt, for contempt of Jove.

Capital, high (Shelley). Rome.

Caryl (Pope). Pope's friend and fellow Catholic at whose request the poem was written.

Catoun, Cato, the reputed author of certain moral distichs.

Cerberus (Byron). The three-headed dog that guarded Hades. Virgil, *Aen.* vi. 417 ff.

Ceres golden reign (Gray). Cornfields, Ceres or Demeter being goddess of the earth and its fertility.

Charles, Swedish (Johnson). Charles XII. He was defeated by the Russians at Pultowa (1709) and died while besieging the castle of Fredrikshald (1718).

Chatterton (Wordsworth). The young author of the Rowley Poems in pseudo-Middle English, who poisoned himself at the age of seventeen.

Chillon, Prisoner of (Byron). François Bonivard, reformer, patriot, and author, imprisoned in the castle of Chillon from 1530 to 1536 by Duke Charles III of Savoy.

Chimari (Byron). *Chimaera's alps* (*Childe Harold*, ii. 453). The Acroceraunian mountains in Greece.

Cipioun. Scipio Africanus the younger.

Circes, Circe the enchantress. Hom. *Od.* x ; Ovid, *Met.* xiv. 245–319. Chaucer uses the genitive form.

Citheroun. Mount Cithaeron in Boeotia, sacred to Zeus and the Muses, but in mediaeval literature made sacred to Venus from misunderstanding of her epithet ' Cytheraea ', from the island Cythera.

Clarens (Byron), a village on the Lake of Geneva, in which Rousseau laid the scene of *La Nouvelle Héloïse*, the sentimental novel on which Byron is here rhapsodizing.

Clerke, The Olde. Boethius, *De Cons. Phil.* lib. iii, met. 12 ' Quis legem det amantibus ? '

Clitumnus (Byron). A small river in Umbria, sacred to a god Clitumnus, (' a Temple '), flowing through beautiful scenery ; mentioned by Virgil in his enumeration of the glories of Italy (Virg. *Georg.* ii. 146). See also Carducci's *Alle Fonti del Clitumno*.

Coila (Burns). Kyle, one of the districts of Ayrshire, Burns's native county.

Coliseum (Byron). The great amphitheatre at Rome where games were held.

Conway's foaming flood (Gray). A river in North Wales.

Corah (Dryden). See Num. xvi. Here Titus Oates, the fabricator of the ' Popish Plot '.

Cordova, him of (Jonson). Lucius Annaeus Seneca, whose tragedies were the models for Renaissance tragedy.

Corpus Christi Day (Browning). The feast of the Blessed Sacrament or Body of Christ celebrated in the Roman Church on the Thursday after Trinity Sunday.

Correggio (Browning). Antonio Allegri da C. near Modena, 1494–1534, an artist whose chief work was done at Parma, where the *St. Jerome* is in the Ducal Academy.

Corydon (Arnold), herdsman and poet in Theocritus and Virgil, here perhaps Arnold himself.

Corydon and Thyrsis (Milton). Shepherds in Theocritus, *Eclog.* i, iv, and **v**, and Virgil, *Eclog.* ii, v, and vii.

Cosimo de' Medici (Browning), the first of the great Medici (1389–1464), grandfather of Lorenzo.

Count D'Orsay (Browning). A dilettante artist of distinction, and leader of fashion in London between 1829 and 1850.

Crab (Spenser). Cancer (June–July).

Creon. King of Thebes after the death of the sons of Oedipus. See 'Statius'.

Cristofre, brooch in form of St. Christopher bearing the Christ Child, worn for good luck.

Croesus (Chaucer and Sackville). King of Lydia, conquered by Cyrus. Herodotus I, and *The Monkes Tale.*

Cruscan quire (Byron). The Accademia della Crusca, founded at Florence in 1582, took up the cause of Ariosto in the controversy as to the relative merits of that poet and Tasso, which embittered Tasso's last days.

Cumberland (Goldsmith). Richard Cumberland (1732–1811), a noted dramatist.

Cybele (Byron). The wife of Saturn, goddess of the Earth, represented as crowned with towers.

Cyrus (Sackville), founder of the Persian empire, slain by Tomyris, the *Queene* of the Massagetae, 529 B.C. Herodotus, i. 214.

Dacian mother (Byron). Dacia, now Roumania, supplied many of the captives who were forced to fight in the amphitheatre.

Damoetas (Milton). Theocritus, *Eclog.* vi, and Virgil, *Eclog.* iii.

Dandolo (Byron). The Doge of Venice (1108–1205), who joined the Fourth Crusade, which captured Constantinople in 1204.

Dane. Daphne, d. of the Thessalian river-god Peneus; changed to a laurel. Ovid, *Met.* i. 452 ff.

Danube (Tennyson). Hallam died at Vienna, 1833, and was buried at Clevedon on the *Wye.*

Daphnis (Arnold), 'the ideal Sicilian shepherd of Greek pastoral poetry, was said to have followed into Phrygia his mistress Piplea, who had been carried off by robbers, and to have found her in the power of the king of Phrygia, Lityerses. L. used to make strangers try a contest with him in reaping corn, and to put them to death if he overcame them. Hercules arrived in time to save Daphnis, took upon himself the reaping contest with Lityerses, overcame him, and slew him. The Lityerses-song connected with this tradition . . . used to be sung by corn-reapers' (from Arnold's note).

Dardan Shepherd's prize, the (Byron). The apple awarded by Paris to Aphrodite (Venus).

Daun Burnel the asse. The hero of the *Speculum Stultorum*, a twelfth-century satire on society.

David (Dryden). Here Charles II.

Dean, the good (Goldsmith). Doctor Barnard, Dean of Derry (1769), to whom Dr. Johnson described the Irish as 'a fair people ; they never speak well of one another'.

Delphi (Gray). A small town in Phocis, famous as the seat of the temple and oracle of Apollo. The early name was Pytho, whence the Pythian oracles and Pythian games.

Democritus (Johnson), of Abdera. A Greek philosopher, who, according to tradition, laughed at human follies and vain pursuits.

Denham (Pope). Sir John Denham (1615–69), author of *Cooper's Hill.*

Dennis (Pope). John Dennis, a contemporary critic who censured Pope. He is the *Appius* of l. 585, so called from his play of *Appius and Virginia* (1709).

Deva (Milton). The Cheshire Dee.

Milton connects the word with *divus* 'divine', 'the wizard stream'.

Diana's marvel (Byron). The temple of Diana at Ephesus.

Dido (Arnold), see *Trojan*. The ref. here is to Virgil, *Aeneid*, vi. 450–76.

Diogenes (Byron). The Cynic philosopher, follower of Antisthenes, who taught complete independence of external goods, including the respect of one's fellow men.

Dionysius (Pope), of Halicarnassus. A Greek critic, author of a treatise on prose melody and rhythm, *De Compositione Verborum*, which contains many analyses of passages from Homer.

Dodd (Goldsmith). The Rev. Dr. Dodd was hanged for forgery in 1777. See Boswell's *Johnson* under that year.

Dome, the (Byron). The Church of St. Peter's.

Dome, Him of the western (Dryden), i. e. Dolben, Bishop of Rochester and Dean of Westminster.

Doria, Peter (Byron). A Genoese captain in the wars with Venice.

Doricke music (Marlowe). Apparently the music of shepherds' pipes in pastoral, love strains. The Dorian mood in music was severe and martial.

Douglas (Goldsmith). The Rev. John Douglas, afterwards Bishop of Salisbury, exposed the forgeries of Lauder, who had accused Milton of plagiarism.

Dowland's lute (Browning). John D. the lutanist, whose three *Books of Songs or Airs* were published in 1597, 1600, and 1603, his *Pilgrim's Solace* in 1612.

Drachenfels (Byron). A castle on one of the Siebengebirge opposite Bonn.

Drummond (Collins). William D. of Hawthornden (near Edinburgh), a Scottish poet who wrote in English and entertained Ben Jonson in 1619.

Duck (Crabbe). Stephen D., Wiltshire farm-labourer and poet (1705–56).

Duck-lane (Pope). Place where old and second-hand books were sold formerly, near Smithfield.

Durfey's Tales (Pope). The *Tales, Tragical and Comical* and *Tales, Moral and Comical* of Thomas Durfey, a minor dramatist and poet, serious and burlesque, of Dryden's day (1653–1723).

Ecclesiaste. Ecclesiasticus, xii. 10–11, 16.

Ector. Hector.

Edmund (Goldsmith). Burke, the great Whig orator and champion of America ('for a patriot too cool').

Egeria (Byron). See *Numa*.

Ehrenbreitstein (Byron). A strong fortress opposite Coblenz, destroyed by the French at the truce of Leoben (1797).

Eneidos. Virgil's *Aeneid*.

Erasmus (Pope). The Dutch scholar and critic of the Renaissance (1466–1536).

Epicurus. The Greek philosopher (307–270 b. c.) who taught that pleasure is the chief good.

Episcopus, in partibus (Browning). Before the establishment of the R.C. hierarchy in England bishops were given the titles of lost sees *in partibus infidelium* (in the lands of the infidel). E. g. Card. Wiseman, who is thought to be caricatured here, was Bp. of Melipotamus before being created Abp. of Westminster (1850).

Ethiop queen (Milton). Cassiope, wife of Cepheus, king of Ethiopia and brother of Andromeda.

Femenye, the regne of. The kingdom of women (*femina*), or Amazonia.

Ferguson (Burns). Robert Fergusson (1750–74), the young Edinburgh poet, whose *Rivers of Scotland* celebrates the Forth, Tweed, and Tay.

Ferney (Byron), near Geneva. The home of Voltaire.

Ferrara (Byron). Alphonso II, D'Este, Duke of Ferrara, was the chief patron of Tasso the poet. The latter was imprisoned as mad in 1579 and released in 1586. He died at Rome in 1595, when on the point of being crowned with laurel as Petrarch had been.

Fichte (1762–1814) and *Schelling* (1775–1854) (Browning). German philosophers who developed the transcendental, idealistic philosophy of Kant and prepared the way for Hegel, who is the chief source of the idealistic thought of the nineteenth century of which Coleridge had been the first sponsor in England.

Form, one frail (Shelley). Shelley himself.

Fra Lippo Lippi (Browning). Florentine painter (1412–69), placed at the age of eight in the Community of the Carmelite Friars of the Carmine in Florence. See Vasari, *Lives of the Painters*. ' Rejoicing in life, he loved to introduce its incidents even in the solemn often mystic scenes, he had to represent ' (National Gallery Catalogue).

Frà Pandolf and *Claus of Innsbruck* (Browning), imaginary artists.

Franklin (Byron). Benjamin Franklin (1701–90), American statesman and philosopher, champion of American independence in London and Paris.

Friar's Lanthorn (Milton). Ignis fatuus, Will-o'-the-wisp, Jack a' lantern, &c. Cf. Collins, *Superstitions*, st. vi.

Fungoso (Pope). A citizen's would-be fashionable son in Ben Jonson's *Every Man out of his Humour*. He is always a suit behind the courtier Fastidious Brisk.

Galgopheye. Gargaphia, where Actaeon was turned into a stag (Skeat).

Galice at Seint Jame. Shrine of St. James the Greater at Compostella in Galicia, Spain.

Galileo (Johnson). The Italian astronomer and physicist, imprisoned by the Inquisition; died blind and in great suffering (1642).

Galuppi (Browning). Baldassare G. (1706–85), a celebrated Italian composer, organist of St. Mark's, Venice. ' The main features of his operas are melodic elegance and lively and spirited comic forms ; but they are rather thin and weak in their execution.' Ritter, *Hist. of Music*.

Gargarus (Tennyson). Southern peak of Mt. Ida. Homer, *Il.* xiv. 292.

Garth (Pope). Sir Samuel Garth (1661–1719), a physician and poet, author of a mock-heroic poem, *The Dispensary*, 1699.

Gath (Dryden). Here the Land of Exile, especially Brussels.

Gaufred. Geoffrey de Vinsauf, whose poem on the death of Richard I is printed in Leyser's *Hist. Poet. Med. Aev.*, pp. 162–978.

Genilon. Ganelon, the traitor among Charlemagne's peers in the *Song of Roland*.

Genius (Spenser). The power which gives fruitfulness to man or to the earth. The word has other meanings as a man's protecting spirit or daimon.

Gentlest of the wise (Shelley). Leigh Hunt, poet and essayist, friend of Shelley and Keats.

Gernade. Granada.

Gilbertfield (Burns). William Hamilton of G., a minor Scottish poet who interchanged verse letters with Ramsay.

Gladiator, the (Byron). The statue in the Capitoline Museum of a dying warrior, now believed to be a Gaul not a gladiator.

Glanvil (Arnold). Joseph Glanvill (1636–80), scholar and divine, from whose *Vanity of Dogmatizing* (1661) was derived

the story of *The Scholar Gipsy.*
See Arnold's note.

Goddess, the (Byron, *C.H.* IV. xlix).
The Venus dei Medici.

Gothic (Johnson), Swedish. Charles
XII was officially styled King
of Sweden, of the Goths, and
of the Wends. The Goths (Old
Norse *Gautar*) were originally an
independent kingdom and their
name survives in the provinces
of Öster- and Västergötland.

Grafton (Byron). The third Duke
of Grafton, Whig Prime Minister
when the Wilkes affair began.

Greek books, little (Browning).
Probably the Teubner editions of
the classics issued at Leipzig
in Saxony.

Guidi (Browning). Tommaso
Guidi (1401–28), nicknamed
Masaccio (*Hulking Tom*). Fra
Lippo seems rather to have learnt
from than to have taught him,
as Browning implies.

Hammon or Amon (Milton). An
Egyptian god identified by
Greek and Roman colonists with
Zeus or Jupiter.

Hampton (Pope). Hampton
Court, a royal palace near
London on the Thames; built
originally by Wolsey.

Hannibal (Sackville). Carthaginian general in second Punic
War; defeated the Romans at
Trebia, 218 B.C., Lake *Trasi-
menus*, 217 B.C., and *Cannae*,
216 B.C., where the consul
Aemilius *Paulus* perished. Was
defeated by P. *Scipio* at *Zama*
' before Carthago gate ', 202 B.C.

Harley (Johnson). Robert, Earl
of Oxford, statesman of Queen
Anne's reign, friend of Swift and
Pope.

Harmodius (Byron). The assassin,
with Aristogeiton, of Hipparchus,
brother of Hippias the last of the
Pisistratid tyrants of Athens. In
the later republican Athens they
were regarded as heroes and
celebrated in song and sculpture.
Herodotus v. 55, &c.

Hasdrubal. Carthaginian General
when C. was burned by the
Romans, 146 B.C. See Orosius, iv.
13. 3.

Hátim Tai (Omar). A type of
Oriental generosity.

Hebrew priests (Dryden), i.e. Angli-
can clergy.

Hebron (Dryden). See 2 Sam. ii,
&c. Used for Holland (l. 59), and
later for Scotland.

Helicon's harmonious springs
(Gray). Helicon, a range of
mountains in Boeotia, sacred to
Apollo and the Muses, whence
flowed Aganippe and Hippocrene,
the fountains of the Muses.

Heroes. Erōs, Love.

Hesper-Phosphor (Tennyson). The
evening which is also the morning
star, Venus. Compare Donne,
l. 198.

Hickey (Goldsmith). A celebrated
Irish attorney.

Hildebrand (Browning). Gregory
VII, 1073–85, who asserted
the Papal power and humbled the
Emperor at Canossa.

Hinksey (Arnold), mentioned with
other places in the immediate
vicinity of Oxford.

Hinnom's vale (Keats). Where
Ahaz ' burnt his children in the
fire after the abominations of the
heathens ', 2 Chronicles xxviii. 3.

Hippolytus (Marlow). Son of Theseus. He despised love (hence
' wilde '), serving Diana, and was
loved and brought to his death
by his stepmother Phaedra.

Hippotades (Milton). Aeolus, the
god of winds.

Horace (Pope and Byron). Roman
lyric and satiric poet, author of
the *Ars Poetica.*

Howard (Byron), Major. Son of the
Earl of Carlisle, Byron's guardian,
satirized by him in *English
Bards and Scotch Reviewers.*

Hyacinth (Shelley). Beloved by
Apollo but accidentally slain by
him with a quoit. From his
blood sprang the flower so called :
et Ai Ai

Flos habet inscriptum.—Ovid,

Met. x. 163–219. Compare Milton, *Lycidas*, l. 106.

Hyades (Tennyson). A constellation whose rising simultaneously with the sun announces rain.

Hyde (Johnson), Edward, Earl of Clarendon. Historian of the Civil War, exiled by Charles II.

Hyperion (Keats). A Titan, father by Thea of Helios the Sun, Selene the Moon and Eos the Dawn. Keats, with other English poets, makes him god of the Sun before Apollo. The characters in the poem are (1) Titans, i. e. sons and daughters of Coelus (Heaven), and Tellus (Earth), viz. Saturn or Cronus and Cybele or Rhea, Oceanus and Tethys, with their daughter Clymene, Hyperion and Thea, Coeus and Phoebe, Themis, Mnemosyne and Iapetus; (2) Giants, as Enceladus, Briareus, Typhon, &c., who, according to Homer and Hesiod, took no part in the war of the Gods, the Gigantomachia being a later story.

Idalia (Gray), or Idalium in Cyprus where Venus (*Cytherea*) was worshipped, whence she is called Idalia. Virgil, *Aen.* i. 693–4.

Ierne (Shelley). Greek name of Ireland ; the reference is to Thomas Moore, author of *Irish Melodies*.

Ilissus (Gray and Burns). A small river in Attica.

Imperial Mount (Byron). The Palatine Hill on which stood the palace of the Emperors.

Ipolita. Hippolyta, Queen of the Amazons.

Iron Mask (Byron). A mysterious prisoner in the Bastille under Louis XIV, now identified with Count Ercole Antonio Mattioli, a minister of the Duke of Mantua.

Irus (Sackville). The ' common beggar ' who tried to expel Ulysses from his hall and was beaten by him (*Od.* xviii. 1 ff.). There was a proverb ' Iro pauperior '.

Ishbosheth (Dryden). See 2 Sam. iii and iv. Here Richard Cromwell.

Isis and *Orus* (Milton). Egyptian gods worshipped in animal forms, ' brutish ', and especially at *Memphis* the ancient capital of Egypt where little or no rain falls, so ' unshowr'd grasse '. *Orus* was the son of *Osiris* and *Isis*. Milton recalls Virgil's description of the monstrous Egyptian gods portrayed on Aeneas' shield :

Omnigenumque deum monstra et *latrator Anubis*

Contra Neptunum et Venerem contraque Minervam

Tela tenent.—*Aen.* viii. 698–700.

Issachar (Dryden). ' Issachar is a strong ass ' Gen. xlix. 14. Thomas Thynne, of Longleat Hall, a supporter of Monmouth.

Iulius. Julius Caesar, whose death, with those of Nero and Antony, is *prophetically* inscribed on the wall of the temple of Mars.

Ixion (Pope). King of the Lapithae, who for his attempt to win the love of Hera was bound by Zeus to a wheel which whirled perpetually in the lower world.

Ixions shaggy-footed race (Marlowe). The Centaurs.

Jakke Straw. A leader of the Peasants' Revolt of 1381

Jame. Santiago dé Compostella.

Jamshyd (Omar). An heroic monarch of Persian myth. His seven-ringed divining cup typified the seven heavens, planets, &c.

Jebusites (Dryden). See 2 Sam. v. Here the Roman Catholics.

Jonas (Dryden). Sir William Jones, the Attorney-General who conducted the prosecutions of those concerned in the Popish Plot.

Jordan's sand (Dryden), i.e. Dover strand. *Jordan's flood* (l. 821) is the Irish Channel.

Jotham (Dryden), 'the Lord is upright'. Here Sir George Saville, Marquis (at this time Viscount) Halifax (1633–95), whose eloquence persuaded the Lords to throw out the Exclusion Bill (1679).

Julia (Byron). A maiden reputed, on the strength of a forged inscription, to have died after trying to save her father.

Julie (Byron). See *Rousseau*.

Junius (Byron). The anonymous author of the famous Letters attacking George III and his ministers (1768–73). He has been identified with Sir Philip Francis the opponent in India of Warren Hastings—but this is uncertain.

Jura (Byron). The hills to the west of the Lake of Geneva, facing the Alps.

Kaikobad and Kaikhosru. Famous kings of the Kaianian dynasty in Persian tradition. Kaikhosru defeated the Turanian invader Afrasiyab, with whom Rustum had warred.

Kenelm. Succeeded Kenulph as king of Mercia in 821 and was murdered by his sister Quinride.

Kenrick (Goldsmith), William (d. 1779), a miscellaneous author who libelled every successful author of his day—Goldsmith, Fielding, Johnson, Coleman ; translated *La Nouvelle Héloïse.*

Kubla Khan (Coleridge), A. D. 1216–94. Founder of the Mongol dynasty of China, conquered China and a large part of Tartary, Tibet, Burma, and other countries ; a cultured and magnificent ruler whose court is described by Marco Polo. See Chaucer's *Squire's Tale*

Lake Leman (Byron). The Lake of Geneva, the Lacus Lemanus of the Romans. Caesar, *B.G.* i. 8.

La Mancha's Knight (Pope). Don Quixote the hero of Cervantes' famous novel. But this incident comes from a spurious second part.

Laocoon's torture (Byron). The statue of Laocoon and his sons in the Vatican. See Virgil, *Aen.* ii. 201–26, and Lessing's *Laokoon* (1766).

Laodamia, wife of Protesilaus who sacrificed himself before Troy to fulfil an oracle and ensure victory for the Greeks. Her prayer to converse with him again was granted by the Gods, Hermes bringing his shade from the lower world. When he returned, Laodamia too died. Wordsworth has given his own reading of the story morally and dramatically. Cf. Ovid, *Heroides,* xiii.

Lars and Lemures (Milton). Good and evil spirits of the dead, the former worshipped in the Roman family and state as protecting powers.

Latian coast (Byron). Coast of Latium on which commenced the war which is the theme of the last six books of the *Aeneid* (' Arms and the Man ').

Laud (Johnson). Archbishop of Canterbury, beheaded by the Long Parliament (1645). He was a benefactor of the University and of St. John's College, Oxford.

Lausanne (Byron). A town above the Lake of Geneva, where Gibbon composed most of the *Decline and Fall of the Roman Empire.* (1776–81, 1788.)

Leo (Pope). Giovanni de' Medici, who became Pope Leo X (1513–21), a great patron of art and learning.

Lepanto's fight! (Byron). The naval battle of Lepanto (1571), where Don John of Austria, aided by the Venetians, defeated the Turks.

Lethaean (Tennyson). Of Lethe, the river of oblivion in Hades. Milton, *P. L.* ii. 582–6.

Libyan Jove (Pope). Jupiter Ammon : see *Alexander.*

Lettow. Lithuania.

Levites (Dryden), i. e. Dissenting, esp. Presbyterian, clergy.

Ligurge. Lycurgus. Statius, *Theb.* iv. 386 ; Homer, *Iliad*, vi. 130.

Lisbon (Tennyson). The reference is to the lines of Torres Vedras which checked the French advance and led to their retreat from Portugal.

Lochiel (Byron). The Laird of Lochiel was the chief of the Highland clan of the Camerons. A Lochiel had been one of Prince Charles Edward's principal supporters, and was wounded at Culloden.

Longinus (Pope). Greek critic, author of a treatise on the sublime in style.

Lord of the unerring bow (Byron). The Belvedere statue of Apollo in the Vatican.

Lord of War (Byron). Mars or Ares whose amour with Venus is related by Homer, *Odyssey*, viii. 266 ff. See the picture by Botticelli (No. 915) in the National Gallery.

Loy. St. Eligius (588–659), Bishop of Noyon, who, like the later Quakers, scrupled to take an oath.

Lu (Pope). Usually *Loo*, a card game fashionable in the eighteenth century.

Lucan (Shelley). Roman poet, author of the *Pharsalia*, conspirator against Nero, turned informer, died by his own hand.

Lucyna (Spenser). Diana in her function as protectress of women in child-birth.

Lycidas (Milton). Here of course Edward King. The name is that of a shepherd in Theocritus, *Eclog.* vii, Bion, *Eclog.* ii, and Virgil, *Eclog.* ix.

Lyde. Lydia.

Lydian airs (Gray). The four Greek modes of music were the Lydian, Ionian, Phrygian, and Dorian. Socrates banishes from his Republic the Lydian as expressing sorrow, and the Ionian as ' soft or drinking harmonies '. Plato, *Republic*, 398 B–399 E.

Lydia's monarch (Johnson). Croesus, the last King of Lydia and Conqueror of the Greeks in Asia Minor, was warned by Solon to count no man happy till he died. He was defeated by Cyrus the Persian (546), who, after condemning him to be burnt, spared his life.

Lydiat (Johnson). Thomas Lydiat (1572–1646), a famous chronologer, who lived in extreme poverty.

Lyeys. The modern town of Ayas in Armenia. It was captured and burned (the citadel escaping) by Pierre de Lusignan in 1367.

Macedo (Sackville). Alexander the Great, King of Macedon, who defeated *Darius*, King of Persia, at the battle of Issus, 333 B. C.

Machiavelli (d. 1527). Italian writer on politics and history, author especially of *The Prince*, to which are ascribed political doctrines known as Machiavellian. See Lord Morley, *Machiavelli* (Romanes Lecture, 1897).

Macpherson (Goldsmith), James, the translator or author of Ossian's *Fingal*, *Temora*, and other poems.

Macrobeus. Macrobius, Proconsul of Africa, 410 A. D., wrote a long commentary on Cicero's *Somnium Scipionis*, in which he classifies dreams and their significance.

Maeander (Pope). The famous winding river of Asia Minor referred to by Ovid in connexion with the tradition of the swan's dying song. Ovid, *Heroides*, vii. 2.

Maeonian star (Pope). Homer, traditionally the son of Maeon, ' blind Maeonides '. Milton, *P. L.* iii.

Maevius (Pope). A malevolent poetaster who attacked Virgil and Horace. Virgil, *Eclogues*, iii. 90.

Malaprop, Mrs. (Byron). See Sheridan's comedy, *The Rivals*, IV. ii.

Mall, the (Pope). Pall Mall, a

fashionable promenade till the middle of the reign of George III.

Mantuan Muse (Pope). Virgil, born at Mantua.

Marceau (Byron). General Marceau, who helped to quell the rebellion of the Vendée, and was mortally wounded at Altenkirchen (1796), when the Austrians repelled the French under Jourdan.

Maro (Pope). Cognomen of Virgil.

Mars his Campe (Donne). The Planet Mars; but there seems to be a punning reference to the Campus Martius at Rome where the young men practised gymnastic and military exercises.

Matadore (Pope). The three best cards in the game of Ombre, viz. the ace of spades (*Spadillio*), the ace of clubs (*Basto*), and *Manilio*, i. e. two or seven of trumps according as the trump-suit was black or red.

Maudelayne, St. Mary Magdalene. Cf. pronunciation of names of Colleges dedicated to her at Oxford and Cambridge.

Maure, St., favourite pupil of St. Benedict, established the Benedictine Order in France (d. 584).

Medea's wondrous alchemy (Shelley): Medea restored to youth the father of her husband Jason. The magic broth she used gave new life to whatever it fell upon, dry wood or bare earth. Ovid, *Met.* vii. 179–293.

Melpomene (Tennyson). The Tragic Muse, here used of the Elegiac, as in Spenser, *Shepherd's Calendar*, xi. 53.

Memnon's sister (Milton). An imaginary sister of the black but beautiful Memnon, prince of the Ethiopians, who was slain by Achilles. Homer, *Odyssey*, xi. 522.

Mercenrike. Mercia.

Merlin (Keats). The great wizard of the Arthurian legend who paid the debt of his 'monstrous', i. e. unnatural existence (his father was a demon), when he

fell a victim to his own spells communicated to Vivien. See Tennyson's *Vivien* in *The Idylls of the King*.

Metella (Byron). Caecilia Metella, wife of M. Croesus. Her tomb is on the Appian Way two miles from Rome.

Middelburgh and Orewelle. Middel-burg, on the Dutch island of Walcheren, nearly opposite the mouth of the Orwell, on which stands Harwich. This reference dates *The Prologue*, since the wool staple was only established at Middelburg between 1384 and 1388.

Mighty seaman (Tennyson). Nelson, 'shaker of the Baltic and the Nile '.

Milbourn (Pope). Luke Milbourne (1649–1720), a translator of Virgil and subsequently a critic of Dryden's version.

Mincius(Milton). *Mincio*(Crabbe), a river near Mantua. Virgil, *Eclogues* vii. 12–13.

Minion, a (Byron). John Stuart, Earl of Bute, Prime Minister, 1762–3; was highly unpopular.

Mole, the (Byron). The Castle of St. Angelo, formerly the Mausoleum of Hadrian.

Moloch (Milton). ' Horrid King.' *P. L.* i. 391. A god of the Ammonites and Phoenicians generally, worshipped with human sacrifices, especially of children.

Morat (Byron). Where the Duke of Burgundy was defeated by the Swiss fighting in defence of their freedom, 1476.

Morpheus (Marlowe). God of dreams. Ovid, *Met.* xi, and Chaucer, *Boke of the Duchesse*, ll. 153 ff.

Mulla (Spenser). A river near Spenser's home, Kilcolman, in the south of Ireland. See *Faerie Queene*, VII vi. 40.

Musaeus . . . Orpheus (Milton and Wordsworth). Mythical Greek poets.

Musaeus (Marlowe). A grammarian whose Greek poem on

Hero and Leander Marlowe is freely translating.

Mushtari (Omar). Jupiter, the planet.

Nadab (Dryden). See Lev. x. 1, 2. Here Lord Howard of Escrick.

Namancos and Bayona's hold (Milton). Places in north of Spain, near Cape Finisterre, marked in an old map by a tower and a castle.

Naples' liquefaction (Browning). A miracle publicly performed at Naples on the feast of St. Januarius (September 19); a portion of the Saint's blood, normally coagulated, liquefies when brought into the presence of his head.

Narcisus. Narcissus fell in love with his own image and, pining away, was changed into a flower. Ovid, *Met.* iii. 341–510.

Nemi (Byron). Lakes Nemi and Albano are in craters of the Alban Hills which rise from the Campagna of Rome.

Nero. Fifth Roman Emperor, A. D. 54–68, popularly made responsible for the burning of Rome; slew himself when deserted by the Pretorian Guard. See *Monkes Tale*, ll. 473–560.

New Holland (Burns), Australia.

Niobe (Byron), whose twelve children were slain, because of her boasting, by Apollo and Artemis: so Rome is left desolate.

Nominis Umbra (Byron). ' Stat magni nominis umbra.' Lucan, *Pharsalia*, i. 135, used of Pompey. ' Stat nominis umbra ' was Junius's motto.

Numa (Byron). The second of the Roman kings renowned for wisdom and piety and esteemed the founder of the Roman religion. He was instructed by the nymph *Egeria* whose valley and fountain was near the southern gate of Rome. *Juvenal*, 3. 12.

Nurse of Rome (Byron). The bronze wolf of the Capitoline

Museum, perhaps that referred to by Cicero as struck by lightning, as there is a fissure in one leg. Cicero, *Catiline Or.* iii. 8.

Oenone (Tennyson). The wife of Paris and daughter of a river-god, deserted by Paris for Helen after the Judgement which the poem describes. Later she refused to help Paris mortally wounded, repented, and died on his funeral-pyre. See Tennyson, *Death of O.*

Olympia (Dryden). Properly Olympias, the wife of Philip of Macedon. The poet refers to the tradition that the real father of Alexander was Jupiter Ammon who visited Olympias in the form of a serpent or dragon. Plutarch, *Life of Alexander*, ii–iii.

Ossian (Wordsworth). The son of Finn or Fingal, and the poet of Celtic, Irish, and Scottish traditions, whose poems James Macpherson (1736–96) purported to have collected and translated. Wordsworth compares him with Orpheus and Musaeus, traditional Greek poets of whose work nothing is known.

One of the grettest auctours. Cicero, *De Divinationibus.*

Pacuvius (Jonson). A Roman tragedian who lived about 220 to 130 B. C. Some fragments of his work are extant.

Palatye. Palathia.

Palestine, twice battered god of (Milton). Dagon, a god of the Philistines, half human, half fish. 1 *Sam.* v. 1–9. *P. L.* i. 457–76.

Pallas from the brain (Tennyson). Pallas Athene (Minerva) sprang full-armed from the head of Zeus. Pindar, *Olymp.* iii. 35.

Pam (Pope). Knave of Clubs.

Pan (Tennyson). God of flocks and inventor of the shepherd's pipe, an especially Arcadian god.

Pandulph (Browning). See *King John*, III. i. 135 ff.

Panope (Milton). One of the Nereids or sea-nymphs invoked

by sailors in storms. Virgil, *Georg.* i. 437, and *Aen.* v. 820–6.

Pantheon (Byron). A temple ('very divine') in Rome to Mars, Venus, and the deified ancestors of the Julian gens, erected by M. Agrippa, friend of Augustus in 27 B.C. Its chief feature is a magnificent dome, a circular opening in which lights the building. The most perfectly preserved monument of antiquity. See Shelley's *Letters*, March 23, 1819.

Paraclete (Pope). The abbey dedicated to the Holy Ghost by Abelard, where he and Eloisa were buried.

Partridge (Pope). The famous maker of prophetic almanacs satirized by Swift and the wits.

Parwin (Omar), the Pleiades.

Paul with beasts (Tennyson). 'If after the manner of men I have fought with beasts at Ephesus, what advantageth it me, if the dead rise not? Let us eat and drink; for to-morrow we die.' 1 Cor. xv. 32.

Peer, a noble (Spenser). The Earl of Essex who had in 1596 stormed Cadiz (Cales) near Gibraltar ('Hercules two pillors').

Pehlevi (Omar). The heroic language of Persia, a later dialect of Zend.

Pelops shoulder (Marlowe). Made of ivory, Ovid, *Met.* vi. 404.

Peor (Milton) or 'Chemos, the obscene dread of Moab's sons', *P. L.* i. 406. See 1 Kings xi. 7, &c.

Perotheus, Pirithous, son of Ixion, king of the Lapithae, descended to Hades, accompanied by Theseus, to carry off Persephone, and was chained to a rock. Theseus was liberated by Hercules, not Pirithous. Chaucer follows the *Roman de la Rose*, ll. 8186 ff.

Persean sword (Keats). The sword of Perseus with which he cut off the head of Medusa.

Petronius (Pope). A companion of Nero, to whom is ascribed the

Satyricon, of which the best-known fragment is the *Cena Trimalchionis* which with much other matter includes criticism of style and of epic poetry.

Phaeton (Byron), who attempting to drive the chariot of his father, the sun, did so much mischief that Zeus hurled him down to earth. Ovid, *Met.* i. 751 to ii. 400.

Pharaoh (Dryden). Here the King of France.

Phillis (Milton). Phyllis, name of a shepherdess in Virgil, *Eclog.* iii. 78.

Phlegethon (Byron) The river of flame in Hades. Byron recalls Virgil's description of *Aeneid*, vi. 548–51.

Physiologus. Mediaeval accounts of the nature and properties of beasts, &c., used as allegorical and mystical illustrations of Christian dogma—recklessly attributed to Aristotle, 'the Physiologus'.

Pierian spring (Pope). Spring of the Pierides or Muses—learning.

Pierre (Byron). A character in Otway's *Venice Preserved.*

Pirrus. Pyrrhus, the son of *Achilles.* See *Hamlet*, II. 2. 481 ff.

Planter of the Lion (Byron). Venice, whose standard was the Lion of St. Mark. But the word Pantaloon to which Byron refers had nothing to do with a lion.

Plinlimmon (Gray). A mountain in Montgomeryshire.

Pluto (Arnold), the god of the underworld, carried off Proserpine, daughter of Demeter, from the valley of Enna in Sicily.

Pouke (Spenser). Puck.

Preaching Friars (Browning), Dominicans, so called by Innocent III.

Proculus (Pope) The senator to whom Romulus, after he was carried up to heaven by Mars, appeared and ordered that he should be worshipped as the guardian god of Rome.

Pruce. Prussia, home of the Teutonic knights who were fighting with the heathen in Russia (Ruce) and Lithuania (Lettow).

Puella and Rubeus. The names of two figures used in geomancy, a method of divination. See Skeat's note, *Chaucer*, v. 82–3.

Pugin (Browning). Augustus P. (1812–52), a Catholic architect of the Gothic revival.

Pulcinello (Browning), the Italian origin of our Punch.

Pye (Byron). Henry James Pye, a poetaster, made poet laureate 1790–1813, a constant butt for contemporary ridicule.

Pyramid of precious stones (Byron). The chapel in the Church of San Lorenzo where the tombs of the later Medici are collected.

Pyramid, one keen (Shelley). The tomb of Cestius above the Protestant cemetery in Rome.

Pythian of the age . . . Pilgrim of Eternity (Shelley). Byron as satirist, especially *English Bards and Scotch Reviewers* and author of *Childe Harold's Pilgrimage.*

Quintilian (Pope). The most celebrated Roman critic, author of the *De Institutione Oratoria*, a treatise on the education of the orator, A. D. 40–100.

Radcliffe (Byron). Mrs. Ann Radcliffe (1764–1823), the scene of whose romantic novel, *The Mysteries of Udolpho* (1794) is laid chiefly in and near Venice.

Ram, Aries (March 12–April 11).

Ramazan (Omar). The ninth month of the Mohammedan year during which all Moslems fast from sunrise to sunset; ' which makes the Mussulman unhealthy and unamiable ' (Fitzgerald).

Ramsay (Burns), Allan, the Scottish poet, author of *The Gentle Shepherd* and other poems.

Raphael (Pope) (1483–1520), the most famous Italian painter of the Roman school, who decorated the state apartments of the Vatican for Pope Julius II.

Ravenna . . . Fortress of falling empire (Byron). Ravenna was the refuge of the later Roman Emperors in the time of the barbarian invasions. Dante died and was buried at Ravenna (1321).

Reynolds (Goldsmith), Sir Joshua, the great painter.

Rialto, the (Byron). A covered bridge over the Grand Canal at Venice. See *Merchant of Venice*, I. iii. 107.

Richard (Goldsmith). Richard Burke, the statesman's brother.

Rienzi (Byron). Nicholas di Lorenzo who in 1347 attempted to restore the Roman Republic.

Romano, Giulio (Browning). G. Pippi, or rather de' Giannuzzi, called G. R. from his birthplace Rome ; the ablest of Raphael's pupils (1492–1546). His *Beatific Vision of the Magdalene* is in the National Gallery.

Rosamunda's lake (Pope). A small pond in St. James's Park, now filled up.

Roscommon (Pope). Wentworth Dillon, Earl of R. (1633 ?–1685), author of a poetical treatise, *Essay on Translated Verse* (1684), to which Dryden prefixed a glowing eulogy which Pope here follows.

Rossini (Browning). Gioacchino Antonio R., (1792–1868), the greatest Italian operatic composer of his day : *Il Barbiere di Seviglia, Guillaume Tell.*

Rouncivale. A hospital in London, near Charing Cross.

Rousseau (Byron). Jean Jacques, author of the *Contrat Social* which supplied the philosophy of the French Revolution and of *La Nouvelle Héloïse,* the first of the Romantic stories of passion. The heroine is Julia (lxxix), the scene of the story Clarens (xcix).

Rustum (Arnold and Omar), or Rustai, Prince of Sagestan, the Persian Hercules.

Sabbath, that loud (Tennyson). Waterloo, Sunday, June 18, 1815.

Sagan, the, of Jerusalem (Dryden), i. e. Compton, the Bishop of London.

Saint Agnes Eve (Keats). January 20th. See Burton's *Anatomy of Melancholy*, p. iii, sect. ii, mem. iii, subs. i.

Saint Lucy's Night (Donne). See *Barnaby*.

Saint Mark's Eve (Keats). April 24th.

Saint Praxed's Church (Browning), a church in Rome, dedicated to a *Virgin* saint of the second century.

Santa Croce (Byron). The Church of Santa Croce at Florence which Byron calls the Westminster Abbey of Italy. It contains the tombs of Machiavelli, Michael Angelo, Galileo, and Alfieri. Byron, *Letters*, iv. 114 (Prothero).

Satalye. Attalia, modern Adalia, on the coast of Asia Minor opposite Cyprus. Captured by Pierre de Lusignan in 1361.

Saul (Dryden). Here Oliver Cromwell.

Scariot. Judas Iscariot.

Schiller (Byron). The German dramatist, poet, &c., the scene of whose story *Der Geisterseher* was laid in Venice. An English version appeared in 1796.

Scion of chiefs (Byron). Princess Charlotte, the only daughter of George IV, and heir to the throne, died November 6, 1817.

Scipio (Byron). The elder Scipio Africanus. See *Hannibal.* He died in voluntary exile on the Campanian coast, 183 B. C.

Scotists and Thomists (Pope). Schoolmen, disciples of Duns Scotus and Thomas Aquinas respectively.

Scott, the southern (Byron). Ariosto (whom Byron thus compares to Sir Walter Scott) author of the *Orlando Furioso*.

Scylla . . . Nisus (Pope). Scylla, daughter of Nisus king of Megara, sacrificed her father and city to her love for Minos, by pulling out the purple hair on which her father's life depended. Minos rejected her love, whereupon, in attempting to follow him, she was changed into a bird. Ovid, *Metam.* viii. ll. 1–151.

Sea-blue bird of March (Tennyson). Kingfisher. Tennyson acknowledged his debt to the Greek poet Alcman's ἁλιπόρφυρος εἴαρος ὄρνις.

Sedley (Johnson). Catherine, Countess of Dorchester, mistress of James II.

See, the Grete. The Eastern Mediterranean.

Seint Julian, the patron saint of hospitality.

Seint Thomas, wateryng of, a brook two miles from Southwark on the road to Canterbury.

Shalott (Tennyson). Astolat (through Italian *Scalot*). The poem is a far-off echo of the story of Lancelot and the Maid of Astolat. See Malory's *Mort Darthur* and Tennyson's *Idylls of the King.*

Shimei (Dryden). See 2 Sam. xvi. Here Slingsby Bethel, one of the Sheriffs of London, a staunch republican and great miser.

Sicilian Muse (Milton). Pastoral Poetry.

Sidney (Shelley). Sir Philip Sidney, courtier, poet, and soldier, mortally wounded at battle of Zutphen (1586). See *Greville's Life of Sir P. S.*, c. xii (*Tudor and Stuart Library*).

Simois (Tennyson), flows, with Scamander, through the plain of Troy.

Sinon, persuaded the Trojans to admit the Wooden Horse. Virgil, *Aen.* ii. 57 ff.

Sire of an immortal strain (Shelley). Milton.

Socratic dream (Tennyson). Dream of a Utopian state such as is elaborated by Socrates in *The Republic* of Plato.

Sohrab and Rustum (Arnold). The story of the combat between father and son is derived from the *Shah-Nama*, the Persian epic.

Solon (Johnson) of Athens, one of the Seven Wise Men of Greece. See *Croesus*.

Solymaean rout (Dryden). Here the mob of London, properly of Jerusalem.

Sophia's bright roofs (Byron). The church of St. Sophia at Constantinople, now a Mahometan mosque.

Soracte (Byron). A mountain rising from the plain to the north of Rome. ' Vides ut alta stet nive candidum Soracte.' Horace, *Od.* i. 9. 1.

Southcote, Joanna (Byron). An impostor who issued doggerel prophecies, and in 1802 declared that she was to become the mother of the new Messiah.

Stace of Thebes, i.e. Statius' *Thebaid*, an epic poem on the strife between Eteocles and Polyneices and the subsequent history of Thebes to the death of Creon : the ultimate source of Chaucer's and Boccaccio's poems.

Stagirite (Pope). Aristotle, born at Stagira, author of the first great critical treatise, *The Poetics*.

Stratford atte Bowe, after the Scole of. Norman French, formerly courtly, but by this time old-fashioned.

Strauss (Browning), David Friedrich S. (1808–74), German theologian of the Tübingen School whose ' Life of Jesus ' was the first of the attempted rationalist reconstructions of the life of Christ, the most famous of which was by Renan.

Sufi (Omar). One of the sect of Mohammedan ascetics and mystics, who held Pantheistic views.

Swabian, the (Byron). Frederic Barbarossa, who made submission to Pope Alexander III in front of the church of St. Mark, 1177.

Swart star, the (Milton). Canicula, the dog-star. Horace, *Odes*, iii. 13. 9, ' te flagrantis atrox hora caniculae Nescit tangere '. See

also Arnold, *Sohrab and Rustum*, l. 452.

Sylla (Byron). Correctly Sulla, the Roman general who, when Marius and his rivals had seized power in Rome, would not return to defend his cause till he had defeated the great enemy of Rome, Mithridates of Pontus, 84 B. C. Made dictator. Later he resigned on completing his reforms.

Symplegades (Byron). Two small islands at the entrance of the Black Sea or Euxine.

Syracuse (Byron). Where the Athenians were defeated disastrously in 413. Of the captives some, tradition says, obtained freedom by reciting passages from Euripides. Plutarch, *Nicias*, c. 29.

Syrtes (Arnold), the two great gulfs in the east half of the north coast of Africa.

Tarpeian, the steep (Byron). The rock from which traitors were thrown down.

Tasso (Collins and Byron). The Italian poet (1544–95), whose *Gerusalemme Liberata* was translated by Edward Fairfax (1600). Stanzas from this poem were sung by the gondoliers of Venice.

Teeme, Venus silver (Spenser). *Teeme* here apparently means *chariot*, as still used dialectally for *cart*. Ovid, *Met.* x. 708 ; *Ars. Amat.* iii. 809.

Thais (Dryden). A courtesan of Athens, who accompanied Alexander in the East, and at whose instance he is said to have burned Persepolis.

Thamuz (Milton), a Syrian god whose killing by a boar and resurrection was celebrated by women. See Ezek. viii. 12–14, *P. L.* i. 446–57.

Theban eagle (Gray). Pindar (522– 442 B. C.), the greatest lyrical poet of Greece, a native of Thebes Gray is imitating the style and verse of his odes. Compare Horace, *Odes*, iv. 2.

Thestylis (Milton). A maiden in Theocritus, *Eclog.* ii.

Thracia's hills (Gray). Thrace was specially connected with the worship of Mars. See Chaucer's *Knightes Tale*, 1109 ff.

Timotheus (Dryden). A Boeotian musician and favourite of Alexander.

Tirynthian groome (Spenser). Hercules, child of Zeus and Alcmena of Thebes. He served Eurystheus at Tiryns.

Tithon's bed (Spenser). Tithonus husband of Aurora, the dawn. See Tennyson, *Tithonus*. Spenser echoes Virgil, *Georg.* i. 446, 'Tithoni croceum linquens Aurora cubile'.

Titus (Byron). Son and successor of Vespasian, the captor of Jerusalem, A. D. 70.

Tom the second . . . Tom the first (Dryden). Thomas Shadwell succeeded Dryden as Poet Laureate and Historiographer Royal (1688), and was succeeded in the first post by Nahum Tate (1692), in the second by Thomas Rymer (1692) 'a useful antiquary, a miserable critic and a worse poet' (Walter Scott). Dryden adapts satirically Shakespeare's *2 King Henry IV*, v. ii. 48–9.

Tooke (Byron). John Horne Tooke (1736–1812), a political writer of radical sympathies, and a pioneer in philology.

Towers of Julius (Gray). The Tower of London traditionally erected by Julius Caesar. See Shakespeare's *Richard III*, III. i. 68–78.

Townshend (Goldsmith). Thomas Townshend, M.P. for Whitchurch, afterwards Lord Sydney, from whom the town of Sydney is named.

Trajan (Byron). Successor to Nerva, A. D. 98, '*proverbially* the best of the Roman emperors' (Byron), i. e. the highest compliment which was paid to an emperor was 'felicior Augusto, melior Trajano'. His column now carries a statue of St. Peter.

Tramissene (Chaucer). Tremezen, a Moorish kingdom next to Benmarin.

Trasimene (Sackville). Where Hannibal defeated Flaminius, 217 B.C.

Trojan, the (Pope). Aeneas, who, having seduced, forsook Dido, Queen of Carthage, despite her tears and the petitions of her sister Anna. Virgil, *Aeneid*, iv. 361 f.

Tully, the friend of (Byron). Servius Sulpicius, whose letter to Cicero (*Ep. Fam.* iv. 5) on the death of the orator's daughter is here echoed by Byron. Compare *Tristram Shandy*, Bk. v, c. 3.

Turkeys, Turkish; *deux ars turquois* (*Roman de la Rose*, l. 913).

Turnus, king of the Rutuli, the chief opponent of Aeneas in the war recounted in the later books of the Aeneid; a fierce warrior.

Tuscan father, the. (Byron). Dante, *La Commedia Divina*.

Twins of Jove which deck the baldric of the Heavens bright (Spenser). Castor and Pollux, placed among the stars as Gemini in the Zodiac.

Two-and-Seventy jarring Sects (Omar). 'The Seventy-two Religions supposed to divide the World, *including* Islamism as some think: but others not' (Fitzgerald).

Tyrians (Dryden), i. e. the Dutch, so called from their position ('thy borders are in the midst of the seas', Ezek. xxvii. 4) and wealth. Byron calls Venice 'a new Tyre', *C. H.* IV. xiv.

Ulpian (Browning), a celebrated Roman jurist (d. 228), whose style was clear but not Ciceronian: ELUCESCEBAT ('he was celebrated') is not classical.

Ulysses (Pope) was given by Aeolus a bag of winds to take him home, but the bag was opened by his companions and his boat was blown back to the island of Aeolus who refused further aid. *Odyssey*, x. 1–75.

Urania (Shelley and Tennyson). The Muse of Astronomy, taken as of heavenly, divine, elevated poetry. Compare Milton, *P. L.* vii. 1–20.

Vane (Johnson). Anne Vane, mistress of Frederick, Prince of Wales ; died 1736.

Velino (Byron). The waterfall of Terni is formed by this river which flows into a tributary of the Tiber; 'worth all the cascades and torrents of Switzerland put together.' *Byron.*

Venite, God's great (Donne). See Matthew xxv. 34–6.

Verdi (Browning). Giuseppe Verdi (1813–1901), author of the popular operas *Il Trovatore, Aida*, and others.

Vida (Pope). Marco Girolamo, an Italian Bishop and critic of the Renaissance, author of a *Poetica.*

Villiers, George (Johnson), Duke of Buckingham, favourite of James I and Charles I; murdered by Felton.

Vitruvius (Dryden). Marcus Vitruvius Pollio, a Roman writer on architecture, from whom the Renaissance doctrine of the Orders (Doric, Ionic, &c.) was derived.

Waller (Pope). Edmund Waller (1606–87). Author of ' Go lovely rose ' and other elegant poems.

Walsh (Pope), William (1663–1708), a minor poet and critic who advised Pope to study ' correctness ' and to copy the ancients.

Welborn (Byron). A character in Massinger's *A New Way to Pay Old Debts*, i. 1.

Wentworth (Johnson), Sir Thomas, Earl of Strafford. Charles's favourite, attainted by Parliament and executed, 1641.

Wilkes, Jack (Byron). The demagogue and pamphleteer (edited *The North Briton*) whose conflict with George III and his ministers secured the full rights of the electors in their choice of a member. See Burke, *Thoughts on the Present Discontents.*

William (Goldsmith). William Burke, a relation of the statesman.

Winander (Wordsworth). Lake Windermere.

Xanadu (Coleridge). 'In Xanadu did Cublai Can build a stately palace.' *Purchas, his Pilgrimage*, IV, ch. xxii, 1621.

Xerxes (Sackville and Johnson). ' Persia's tyrant ' who invaded Greece where his fleet was destroyed at Salamis (480) and his army under Mardonius defeated at Plataea (479).

Ydelnesse, the portress of the garden in the *Romaunt of the Rose*, Chaucer's trans., ll. 531 ff.

Ypocras. Hippocrates (*c.* 460 B.C.), mentioned by Chaucer along with Aesculapius, ' the blameless physician ' of Homer and later god of the medical art, and Galen (A. D. 130–200) in a list of celebrated Greek, Arabian, and mediaeval writers on medicine.

Zadoc. See 2 Sam. xv. 24. Here Sancroft, Archbishop of Canterbury, a rigid High Churchman and later Non-juror.

Zal (Omar). The father of Rustum; their exploits are celebrated in the *Shah-nama.*

Zimri. See 1 Kings xvi. Here George Villiers, Duke of Buckingham (1627–87), son of James's favourite. See Pope's *Moral Essays*, iii. 299–314.

Zoilus (Pope). A fourth-century grammarian who severely criticized Homer. Ovid, *Rem. Amoris*, 366.